Ego Functions in Schizophrenics, Neurotics, and Normals: A Systematic Study of Conceptual, Diagnostic, and Therapeutic Aspects
by Leopold Bellak, Marvin Hurvich, and Helen A. Gediman

Innovative Treatment Methods in Psychopathology
edited by Karen S. Calhoun, Henry E. Adams, and Kevin M. Mitchell

The Changing School Scene: Challenge to Psychology
by Leah Gold Fein

Troubled Children: Their Families, Schools, and Treatments
by Leonore R. Love and Jaques W. Kaswan

Research Strategies in Psychotherapy
by Edward S. Bordin

The Volunteer Subject
by Robert Rosenthal and Ralph L. Rosnow

Innovations in Client-Centered Therapy
by David A. Wexler and Laura North Rice

The Rorschach: A Comprehensive System
by John E. Exner

Theory and Practice in Behavior Therapy
by Aubrey J. Yates

Principles of Psychotherapy
by Irving B. Weiner

Psychoactive Drugs and Social Judgment: Theory and Research
edited by Kenneth Hammond and C. R. B. Joyce

Clinical Methods in Psychology
edited by Irving B. Weiner

Human Resources for Troubled Children
by Werner I. Halpern and Stanley Kissel

Hyperactivity
by Dorothea M. Ross and Sheila A. Ross

Heroin Addiction: Theory, Research, and Treatment
by Jerome J. Platt and Christina Labate

Children's Rights and the Mental Health Profession
edited by Gerald P. Koocher

The Role of the Father in Child Development
edited by Michael E. Lamb

Handbook of Behavioral Assessment
edited by Anthony R. Ciminero, Karen S. Calhoun, and Henry E. Adams

HANDBOOK OF
BEHAVIORAL ASSESSMENT

HANDBOOK OF BEHAVIORAL ASSESSMENT

Edited by

ANTHONY R. CIMINERO

KAREN S. CALHOUN

HENRY E. ADAMS

University of Georgia
Athens

A WILEY-INTERSCIENCE PUBLICATION

JOHN WILEY & SONS, New York • London • Sydney • Toronto

Library of Congress Cataloging in Publication Data:

Main entry under title:
Handbook of behavioral assessment.

(Wiley series on personality processes)
"A Wiley-Interscience publication."
Includes bibliographies and indexes.
1. Psychodiagnostics. 2. Behavior therapy.

I. Ciminero, Anthony R. II. Calhoun, Karen S.
III. Adams, Henry E., 1931-

RC469.H36 616.8'914 76-54170
ISBN 0-471-15797-X

Printed in the United States of America

10 9 8 7 6 5 4 3 2 1

Contributors

HENRY E. ADAMS, Department of Psychology, University of Georgia

PETER N. ALEVIZOS, Camarillo-Neuropsychiatric Institute Research Program, University of California at Los Angeles

DAVID H. BARLOW, Section of Psychiatry and Human Behavior, Brown University and Butler Hospital

ALAN S. BELLACK, Department of Psychology, University of Pittsburgh

DOUGLAS A. BERNSTEIN, Department of Psychology, University of Illinois

THOMAS D. BORKOVEC, Department of Psychology, University of Iowa

KAREN S. CALHOUN, Department of Psychology, University of Georgia

EDWARD J. CALLAHAN, Camarillo-Neuropsychiatric Institute Research Program, University of California at Los Angeles

ANTHONY R. CIMINERO, Department of Psychology, University of Georgia

JOSEPH A. DOSTER, Department of Psychology, University of Georgia

IAN M. EVANS, Department of Psychology, University of Hawaii

MICHAEL FEUERSTEIN, Department of Psychology, University of Georgia

SHARON L. FOSTER, Department of Psychology, State University of New York at Stony Brook

MARVIN R. GOLDFRIED, Department of Psychology, State University of New York at Stony Brook

MICHEL HERSEN, Department of Psychiatry, Western Psychiatric Institute and Clinic, University of Pittsburgh School of Medicine

WILLIAM M. KALLMAN, Department of Psychology, Virginia Commonwealth University

RONALD N. KENT, Department of Psychology, State University of New York at Stony Brook

ANDRÉE LIDDELL, Department of Psychology, North East London Polytechnic

MARSHA M. LINEHAN, Department of Psychology, Catholic University of America

DAVID P. LIPINSKI, Henry Wiseman Kendall Center for the Developmentally Disabled, Greensboro, North Carolina

MAUREEN LYONS, Department of Psychological Medicine, Kings College Hospital

GAYLA MARGOLIN, Department of Psychology, University of Oregon

VICTOR MEYER, Academic Department of Psychiatry, Medical School, Middlesex Hospital

PETER M. MILLER, Department of Psychiatry and Human Behavior, University of Mississippi Medical Center

W. ROBERT NAY, Department of Psychology, University of Illinois

ROSEMERY O. NELSON, Department of Psychology, University of North Carolina at Greensboro

JOHN D. RUGH, Department of Psychology, Claremont Graduate School

ROBERT L. SCHWITZGEBEL, Department of Psychology, Claremont Graduate School

DONALD L. TASTO, Stanford Research Institute, Menlo Park, California

THEODORE C. WEERTS, Department of Psychology, University of Iowa

ROBERT L. WEISS, Department of Psychology, University of Oregon

Series Preface

This series of books is addressed to behavioral scientists interested in the nature of human personality. Its scope should prove pertinent to personality theorists and researchers as well as to clinicians concerned with applying an understanding of personality processes to the amelioration of emotional difficulties in living. To this end, the series provides a scholarly integration of theoretical formulations, empirical data, and practical recommendations.

Six major aspects of studying and learning about human personality can be designated: personality theory, personality structure and dynamics, personality development, personality assessment, personality change, and personality adjustment. In exploring these aspects of personality, the books in the series discuss a number of distinct but related subject areas: the nature and implications of various theories of personality; personality characteristics that account for consistencies and variations in human behavior; the emergence of personality processes in children and adolescents; the use of interviewing and testing procedures to evaluate individual differences in personality; efforts to modify personality styles through psychotherapy, counseling, behavior therapy, and other methods of influence; and patterns of abnormal personality functioning that impair individual competence.

IRVING B. WEINER

Case Western Reserve University
Cleveland, Ohio

Preface

Behavioral assessment is undoubtedly one of the most rapidly growing topics in the contemporary field of behavior therapy. Although several journal articles relating to various aspects of behavioral assessment have begun to accumulate over the past seven or eight years, at the time of this writing there was no one source that provided an in-depth coverage of behavioral assessment. It seemed clear to us that there was a distinct need for a book to cover this topic in a comprehensive fashion. This was the purpose of this handbook. We organized a large group of contributors from around the world to discuss topics ranging from general issues in assessment to the specific approaches used in behavioral assessment.

The book is divided into three main sections that provide a rather comprehensive review of behavioral assessment. General issues in assessment as well as critical issues relating specifically to behavioral assessment are discussed in the first section of the book. Included in this section are chapters on classification of behavior problems and the instrumentation available for assessment. The second part of the book devotes a separate chapter to each of six general approaches used in behavioral assessment. The methods described include behavioral interviews, self-report schedules and inventories, self-monitoring procedures, direct observation in both analogue and naturalistic settings, and psychophysiological techniques. The third section describes how these general methods are used to assess various behavior problems such as anxiety and social, sexual, addictive, and psychotic behaviors. Chapters on specific problems in children and marital dyads are also included in this section of the book.

Although the book was originally designed for use by behavior therapy practitioners, it soon became apparent that the content would be of equal utility to the researcher. As such, the *Handbook* is ideal as a text for those being trained for clinical and/or research endeavors. This includes graduate programs in clinical, counseling, and school psychology, psychiatry, social work as well as advanced undergraduate programs for behavioral technicians and paraprofessionals who will function in clinical or research settings.

Obviously, the book is most appropriate for specific courses in behavioral assessment. However, the book is quite valuable as a supplementary text for behavior therapy courses as well as traditional assessment courses.

We would like to thank the many individuals including faculty members and graduate students who have helped with various aspects of this project. Special thanks go to Lorna Farrow who helped with many of the more tedious aspects of editing this book, and Walter Maytham, our editor at John Wiley and Sons. We also thank the publishers and authors who granted us permission to reproduce copyrighted material in this book.

ANTHONY R. CIMINERO
KAREN S. CALHOUN
HENRY E. ADAMS

Athens, Georgia
October 1976

Contents

HANDBOOK OF
BEHAVIORAL ASSESSMENT

PART ONE

General Issues in Assessment

CHAPTER 1

Behavioral Assessment: An Overview

ANTHONY R. CIMINERO

Although behavior therapy has shown tremendous advances over the past fifteen years, behavioral assessment has lagged behind in its development. This delay may have been due to a negative reaction exhibited by many behavior therapists to the word *assessment.* Prior to the 1960s assessment was often associated with testing procedures [e.g., the Rorschach, TAT, and MMPI] that were frequently criticized for their lack of reliability, validity, and clinical utility (Kanfer & Phillips, 1970). Goldfried and Pomeranz (1968) suggested that the avoidance of assessment may have been due to additional factors such as the professional status of psychometricians, the dynamic or trait conceptualization of personaltiy that generally went along with traditional methods of assessment, and the lack of a systematic relationship between the assessment strategies and treatment. Fortunately many of us by this time have been desensitized to the word *assessment,* and preceding *assessment* with the word *behavioral* makes us feel even more relaxed. The legitimate concern with behavioral assessment over the past few years suggests that this topic has literally begun to flourish in the 1970s. This, of course, has been advocated for some time by many prominent investigators including Bandura (1969), Cautela (1968), Goldfried and his colleagues (Goldfried & D'Zurilla, 1969; Goldfried & Kent, 1972; Goldfried & Pomeranz, 1968; Goldfried & Sprafkin, 1974), Kanfer and Phillips (1970), Kanfer and Saslow (1969), Mischel (1968), and Stuart (1970).

The present chapter will introduce some of the major topics in behavioral assessment that will be discussed in detail throughout this volume. This chapter will summarize (1) differences between behavioral and traditional approaches to assessment, (2) various models of behavioral assessment and their functions in assessment, and (3) the general methods of assessment.

BEHAVIORAL AND TRADITIONAL ASSESSMENT

Although behavioral and traditional approaches to assessment share some of the same concerns in their desire to produce reliable, valid, and useful data, the methods vary considerably because of differing assumptions (see Table 1–1 for summary). Goldfried and Kent (1972) summarized three major differences in the assumptions of behavioral and traditional assessment. The first difference revolves around the general concept of personality held by the two orientations (see Mischel, 1968). Traditionally, both state (dynamic) and trait (psychometric) approaches have inferred some underlying constructs that account for the consistency in an individual's behavior. Assessment, in turn, has viewed behavior as a *sign* of these hypothetical constructs which are of central importance in predicting behavior. In contrast, the behavioral approach prefers to be less inferential in postulating underlying factors to account for overt behavior. As Michel (1968) has aptly stated, "In behavioral analyses the emphasis is on what a person *does* in situations rather than on inferences about what attributes he *has* more globally" (p. 10). Thus the behavioral approach is more likely to look at relationships between behavior and specific environmental factors.

This latter point relates to the second difference between behavioral and traditional approaches discussed by Goldfried and Kent. The selection of test items or situations differs for the two assessment procedures. Since the traditional approach assumes that behavior will be quite stable regardless

Table 1–1. A Comparison of Traditional and Behavioral Assessment Strategies

	Behavioral Assessment	Traditional Assessment
Assumptions		
1. Personality concept	Behavior (f) environment	Behavior (f) underlying causes
2. "Test" interpretation	Behavior as sample	Behavior as sign
3. Situations sampled	Varied and specific	Limited and ambiguous
Primary Functions	Description in behavioral-analytic terms	Description in psychodynamic terms
	Treatment selection	Diagnostic labeling
	Treatment evaluation	
Practical aspects		
1. Relation to treatment	Direct	Indirect
2. Time of assessment	Continuous with treatment	Prior to treatment

of the specific situational context, there is little concern for the *content* of test items. In certain cases (i.e., with projective techniques), there is an overt attempt to disguise the content by making the items ambiguous (Goldfried & Sprafkin, 1974). The behavioral approach is concerned with the relationship between behavior and specific environmental contexts and, therefore, makes an attempt to sample these situations adequately (Goldfried & D'Zurilla, 1969). This concern for adequate sampling of various situations has been interpreted as demonstrating the importance of content validity in behavioral assessment (Goldfried & Kent, 1972).

The final difference in assumptions relates to the *sign* versus *sample* interpretation of test responses and was summarized by Goldfried and Kent (1972) as follows:

"In discussing the assumptions underlying the interpretation of behavioral tests, we may note the basic distinction drawn by Goodenough (1949) between the 'sign' and the 'sample' approaches to the interpretation of test responses. The sign approach assumes that the response may best be construed as an indirect manifestation of some underlying personality characteristic. The sample approach, on the other hand, assumes that the test behavior constitutes a subset of the actual behaviors of interest. Whereas traditional personality tests have typically taken the sign approach to interpretation, behavioral procedures approach test interpretation with the sample orientation." (p. 413)

It can be seen how the general differences in the conception of personality affect the interpretation of assessment data with one approach being highly intuitive and the other striving to be more empirically oriented.

Another frequently noted difference between behavioral and traditional assessment is the relationship between assessment and treatment (e.g., Bandura, 1969; Goldfried & Pomeranz, 1968; Kanfer & Phillips, 1970; Peterson, 1968; Stuart, 1970). There appears to be little relationship between traditional assessment and treatment; the primary connection between these two activities is indirect in that assessment may lead to a diagnosis that in turn may lead to the recommendation of a particular treatment technique. However, Stuart (1970) has argued that diagnoses resulting from traditional methods of assessment do not accurately predict what treatment should be implemented.

In contrast to the traditional approach, two primary functions of behavioral assessment are the selection of a treatment technique and the subsequent evaluation of the effects of treatment. If behavioral assessment is successful in the selection and evaluation of treatment, the clinical utility certainly will have been demonstrated.

BEHAVIORAL-ANALYTIC MODELS AND FUNCTIONS OF ASSESSMENT

Before discussing some of the more popular models for behavioral assessment, the primary functions of assessment should be summarized since some of the models are more useful depending on the particular goal of assessment. There are three predominant purposes or functions of behavioral assessment: (1) *description* of the problem, (2) *selection* of a treatment strategy, and (3) *evaluation* of the treatment outcome.

Description

An accurate description of the problem requires the identification of the specific behaviors needing modification as well as the variables (both antecedents and consequences) controlling these behaviors. Probably the most comprehensive guide for describing behavior is offered by Kanfer and Saslow (1969). The simpler *S–R* model was expanded first by Lindsley (1964) to include stimulus (*S*), response (*R*), contingency (*K*), and consequence (*C*) (see Kanfer & Saslow, 1969, p. 426). The *S* refers to the antecedent events or discriminative stimuli, the *R* refers to the behaviors, the *K* represents various contingencies (e.g., the schedules of reinforcement), and the *C* refers to the consequences of the behavior (e.g., the presentation or removal of a positive or negative reinforcer). Kanfer and Saslow (also see Kanfer & Phillips, 1970) added *O*, the biological condition of the organism, to expand the model to a *S–O–R–K–C* sequence. A very similar approach is that of Goldfried and Sprafkin (1974) who described an *S–O–R–C* model for behavioral analysis. Each of these systems appears to give a rather complete description of the problem situation.

Evaluation

A behavioral-analytic approach that is useful in evaluating the effectiveness of treatment has been referred to as the *functional analysis of behavior*. Peterson (1968) summarized this procedure as follows:

"The central features of the method are (1) systematic observation of the problem behavior to obtain a response frequency baseline, (2) systematic observation of the stimulus conditions following and/or preceding the behavior, with special concern for antecedent discriminative cues and consequent reinforcers, (3) experimental manipulation of a condition which seems functionally, hence causally, related to the problem behavior, and (4) further observation to record any changes in behavior which may occur." (p. 114)

In essence a functional analysis is a simple *A–B* experimental single-case design where the *A* phase represents a baseline and the *B* phase represents some form of treatment. By observing whether or not appropriate changes occur in the target behavior, one can demonstrate whether a given treatment approach is effective. Stuart (1970) proposed similar idiographic methods of assessment that would help avoid iatrogenic effects (i.e., detrimental effects caused by a treatment procedure). It seems clear that single-case design methodology is a vital strategy in meeting the evaluation function of behavioral assessment. For a complete description of single-case methodology see Hersen and Barlow (1976), Leitenberg (1973), and Sidman (1960).

Selection of Treatment

The *S–O–R–C* and *S–O–R–K–C* models are useful in gaining a complete description of the problem behavior whereas the functional analysis seems to have its utility in evaluating the effects of treatment. However, there is no general model that helps in *selecting* an appropriate treatment strategy. Still, researchers have found some important relationships between assessment data and effective treatment strategies. At a simple level, some studies have shown that various behavioral deficits may interfere with certain treatment strategies. For example, DeMoor (1970) and Hain, Butcher, and Stevensen (1966) found that the effectiveness of systematic desensitization was limited if the subjects had difficulty with relaxation or visual imagery. Similarly, there are data that suggest systematic desensitization is most effective with individuals experiencing few rather than multiple phobias and with individuals with low levels of physiological arousal (Marks, Boulougouris, & Marset, 1971). These same authors also found that individuals with high levels of arousal responded well to flooding procedures.

At a more general level, it can be speculated that the most efficient and effective treatment technique depends on which response mode (i.e., overt-motor, physiological-emotional, or verbal-cognitive) is most affected. In line with some of Borkovec's (1973) suggestions, fear reduction techniques (e.g., systematic desensitization, flooding, or implosion) or direct modification by means of biofeedback may be most useful when disturbances are predominant in the physiological response system. However, if the problem is primarily a verbal-cognitive one, an approach such as Ellis's rational-emotive therapy may be quite useful. Finally, if it is the overt behaviors of the client that need modification, operant techniques may be most effective. Although these suggestions are basically speculations at this time, similar conceptualizations have been proposed for specific problem areas. For example, in treating sexual behavior (see Barlow, this volume) or social skills (see Hersen & Bellack, this volume), various problem behaviors may be due to anxiety associated with certain situations, or the problem may simply be due to specific behavioral deficits. Depending on how the problem is assessed, different treatment strategies would be selected.

The behavioral analytic models developed thus far seem to adequately meet the descriptive and evaluative functions of behavioral assessment. The problem of selecting appropriate treatment techniques is just beginning to make some progress. However, the continued striving for objective, reliable, and valid measures will improve the chances of choosing the correct intervention strategy for any given individual.

GENERAL METHODS OF BEHAVIORAL ASSESSMENT

Just as there are various approaches to traditional assessment (e.g., objective and projective tests) there is a variety of behavioral assessment methods, each having certain advantages and disadvantages. There are three general approaches to behavioral assessment: (1) self-report, (2) direct behavioral observations, and (3) physiological recordings. Self-report measures include data collected in behavioral interviews, on surveys and inventories, and through self-monitoring procedures. Direct behavioral observations are collected in naturalistic settings or in contrived analogue settings. Finally, a variety of physiological measures can be collected, although these are typically limited to clinical-laboratory settings. The purpose of this section is to introduce these methods, which will be discussed in detail in the second part of this book where individual chapters are devoted to each method of assessment.

Self-report Measures

Although information about all three response modes (i.e., overt-motor, physiological-emotional, verbal-cognitive) can be collected by means of self-report, these measures are used primarily to assess the verbal-cognitive response system. The first method of self-report, the behavioral interview, is probably the least structured assessment strategy. Although the content of behavioral interviews can differ considerably from that of a traditional clinical interview, the major overlap between traditional and behavioral approaches occurs at this point. For this reason, behavioral assessors should become familiar with research on traditional interviewing methods (Matarazzo, 1965).

Thus far, the major contribution to what should be covered in a behavioral interview is the work of Kanfer and Saslow (1969, pp. 430–437). An outline of their approach includes:

1. An initial analysis of the problem situation in which problematic behavioral excesses and deficits as well as nonproblematic behavioral assets are specified.

2. A clarification of the problem situation in which the individuals who object to the problem behavior and who may be affected by any behavior change made by the client are identified. The clarification should also help to specify the conditions in which the behavior occurs.

3. A motivational analysis in which reinforcers (both positive and negative) that may be maintaining the problem behavior or that may be useful in shaping more appropriate behaviors are specified.

4. A developmental analysis in which several questions are raised about the biological, sociological, and behavioral changes that may be pertinent to the problem behavior.

5. An analysis of the client's self-control in which the limitations, conditions, and methods of self-control are defined.

6. An analysis of social relationships in which significant others and their potential influence on the client are specified.

7. The analysis of the client's social-cultural-physical environment in which several questions are raised about cultural norms relating to the problem behavior, the similarity of norms in different settings, and various environmental restraints impinging on the client.

Kanfer and Saslow suggest that this guide should provide not only the initial information collected from the client but also data relevant to the formulation of a treatment plan. A similar model is presented by Meyer, Liddell, and Lyons (this volume).

The second major method for collecting self-report data is through some written behavioral survey or inventory. Aside from being more objective and standardized than an interview, there are several other advantages to surveys and inventories. Wolff and Merrens (1974) indicated that written surveys are quick, inexpensive, easy to administer, and can provide objective measures for various assessment purposes. Some of the more familiar behavioral surveys and inventories include the various Fear Survey Schedules (see Tasto, this volume), the Reinforcement Survey Schedule (Cautela & Kastenbaum, 1967), Assertiveness Scales (e.g., Rathus, 1973), and marital inventories (Stuart & Stuart, 1972).

Behavioral surveys and inventories must deal with the same issues and problems faced by traditional psychometric approaches. These issues include the problems of reliability, validity, norms, standardization, and statistical analysis of the data. Clearly, behavioral approaches will be evaluated on the basis of the same criteria by which traditional approaches have been judged. Therefore, behavioral assessors (especially those developing self-report surveys and inventories) cannot afford to ignore the developments and standards of traditional psychometric approaches (Cronbach, 1970).

The final method of self-report requires clients to monitor various aspects of their behavior in daily living situations. This method is frequently required if a private or covert behavior, which cannot be observed by anyone other than the client, is to be recorded. Since self-monitoring is generally conducted in naturalistic settings, this approach differs considerably from the other self-report methods employed in the clinic. Another major difference is that self-monitoring is often continued while the treatment program is in operation and therefore provides an ongoing evaluation of the effects of treatment. Two major problems associated with self-monitoring procedures are the unreliability and reactivity of the measures (see Ciminero, Nelson, & Lipinski, this volume).

Direct Behavioral Observation Measures

Direct recording of an individual's behavior by some independent observer is probably the hallmark of behavioral assessment. This method is used primarily in the assessment of the overt-motor response mode by having the client's behavior directly observed by trained recorders or other individuals (e.g., parents, spouses, etc.). Direct behavioral observations can be extremely useful in the specification of the target behavior and its controlling events as well as in the evaluation of a treatment program. Behavior can be observed in naturalistic settings (see Kent & Foster, this volume) or in contrived (analogue) settings in the clinic or laboratory (see Nay, this volume). Although both of these approaches have methodological advantages over the self-report procedures, there are still problems such as reactivity and observer bias that must be considered in using direct behavioral observations.

Physiological Measures

There are various physiological measures available for the assessment of the physiological-emotional response mode. Although there are several physiological outcome measures that are used as *indirect* indices of changes in behavior (e.g., urine analyses to measure drug usage, blood-alcohol levels to measure alcohol consumption, etc.), the emphasis seems to be more on *direct* measurement of psychophysiological response systems (e.g., cardiovascular responses). In spite of some criticism for using physiological measures in behavioral assessment (Wolff & Merrens, 1974), many investigators consider this form of assessment vital (see Barlow; Borkovec, Bernstein, & Weerts; Kallman & Feuerstein, all in this volume).

Psychophysiological assessment can be useful in meeting all three functions of assessment (i.e., gaining a complete description of the behavior problem, evaluating the effects of treatment, and selecting appropriate intervention strategies). Although considerable work is still needed to establish the reliability, validity, and utility of psychophysiological measures, the primary drawback to the widespread use of these methods is the cost. Relatively few facilities can afford the more elaborate equipment necessary to record psychophysiological responses.

Although the types of measures used in behavioral assessment are described as three separate approaches, each method is generally not used alone. It is much more common for behavioral assessors who are interested in more than one response mode (i.e., verbal-cognitive, overt-motor, and physiological-emotional) to collect data by using two or more response measures. Since the three types of response measures frequently are not correlated highly with each other, the ideal assessment would be multifaceted and would include each of these measures.

CONCLUSION

This brief overview suggests that in spite of the many differences between traditional and behavioral assessment, there are many problems and issues common to both approaches. Goldfried and Linehan (this volume) summarize these basic issues in relationship to the general topic of behavioral assessment. Several of the other contributors to this book deal similarly with these issues in regard to their specific topics.

Although behavioral assessment has made several advances in its brief history, this approach is still quite young, and the need for further development is obvious. At this time refinement of the relation between assessment and the selection of an appropriate therapeutic strategy is needed most. The clinical utility of the behavioral approach is a function of the same factors (e.g., reliability, validity, reactivity, standardization, and the establishment of norms) with which traditional approaches have been contending for years. Therefore, it appears that behavioral assessors can certainly benefit by attending to the successes and failures of the traditional approach to assessment. Even though the two approaches are quite different, ignoring what has been accomplished in the past can only delay the further development of behavioral assessment.

REFERENCES

Bandura, A. *Principles of behavior modification.* New York: Holt, Reinhart, & Winston, 1969.

Borkovec, T. D. The effects of instructional suggestion and physiological cues on analogue fear. *Behavior Therapy*, 1973, **4,** 185–192.

Cautela, J. R. Behavior therapy and the need for behavioral assessment. *Psychotherapy: Theory, Research, and Practice*, 1968, **4,** 175–179.

Cautela, J. R., & Kastenbaum, R. A. A reinforcement survey schedule for use in therapy, training and research. *Psychological Reports*, 1967, **20,** 1115–1130.

Cronbach, L. J. *Essentials of psychological testing* (3rd ed.). New York: Harper & Row, 1970.

DeMoor, W. Systematic desensitization versus prolonged high intensity stimulation (flooding). *Journal of Behavior Therapy and Experimental Psychiatry*, 1970, **1,** 45–52.

Goldfried, M. R., & D'Zurilla, T. J. A behavioral-analytic model for assessing competence. In C. D. Spielberger (Ed.), *Current topics in clinical and community psychology*. Vol. 1. New York: Academic, 1969.

Goldfried, M. R., & Kent, R. N. Traditional versus behavioral assessment: A comparison of methodological and theoretical assumptions. *Psychological Bulletin*, 1972, **77,** 409–420.

Goldfried, M. R., & Pomeranz, D. M. Role of assessment in behavior modification. *Psychological Reports*, 1968, **23,** 75–87.

Goldfried, M. R., & Sprafkin, J. N. *Behavioral personality assessment*. Morristown, N.J.: General Learning Press, 1974.

Goodenough, F. L. *Mental testing*. New York: Rinehart, 1949.

Hain, J. D., Butcher, H. G., & Stevenson, I. Systematic desensitization therapy: An analysis of results in 27 patients. *British Journal of Psychiatry*, 1966, **112** 295–307.

Hersen, M., & Barlow, D. H. *Single case experimental designs: Strategies for studying behavior change*. New York: Pergamon, 1976.

Kanfer, F. H., & Phillips, J. S. *Learning foundations of behavior therapy*. New York: Wiley, 1970.

Kanfer, F. H., & Saslow, G. Behavioral diagnosis. In C. M. Franks (Ed.), *Behavior therapy: Appraisal and status*. New York: McGraw-Hill, 1969.

Leitenberg, H. The use of single-case methodology in psychotherapy research. *Journal of Abnormal Psychology*, 1973, **82,** 87–101.

Lindsley, O. R. Direct measurement and prosthesis of retarded behavior. *Journal of Education*, 1964, **147,** 62–81.

Marks, I., Boulougouris, J., & Marset, P. Flooding versus desensitization in the treatment of phobic patients: A crossover study. *British Journal of Psychiatry*, 1971, **119,** 353–375.

Matarazzo, J. D. The interview. In B. B. Wolman (Ed.), *Handbook of clinical psychology*. New York: McGraw-Hill, 1965.

Mischel, W. *Personality and assessment*. New York: Wiley, 1968.

Peterson, D. R. *The clinical study of social behavior*. New York: Appleton-Century-Crofts, 1968.

Rathus, S. A. A 30-item schedule for assessing assertive behavior. *Behavior Therapy*, 1973, **4,** 398–406.

Sidman, M. *Tactics of scientific research*. New York: Basic Books, 1960.

Stuart, R. B. *Trick or treatment: How and when psychotherapy fails.* Champaign, Ill.: Research Press, 1970.

Stuart, R. B., & Stuart, F. *Marital Pre-counseling Inventory*. Champaign, Ill.: Research Press, 1972.

Wolff, W. T., & Merrens, M. R. Behavioral assessment: A review of clinical methods. *Journal of Personality Assessment*, 1974, **38,** 3–16.

CHAPTER 2

Basic Issues in Behavioral Assessment

MARVIN R. GOLDFRIED and MARSHA M. LINEHAN

The upsurge of interest in behavioral assessment within the past decade is unmistakable. That this is a growing trend is evidenced by this book, as well as other recent reviews of the field (Cone & Hawkins, in press; Goldfried, 1976; Goldfried & Sprafkin, 1974; Hersen & Bellack, 1976; McReynolds, 1975; Wiggins, 1973). All this is owing, no doubt, to the recognition that it is difficult, if not impossible, to carry out effective clinical behavior therapy without a thorough behavioral analysis, and that controlled outcome research on behavior therapy is only as good as its measures of behavior change.

Despite these clear trends, the area of behavioral assessment has yet to achieve the same level of methodological sophistication that is associated with many of our behavior therapy procedures. For example, in a review of behavioral assessment, Dickson (1975) concluded that "The FSS [Fear Survey Schedule] represents the most sophisticated assessment instrument in the conventional test format that has yet been developed within the behavioral model" (pp. 360–361). Although this conclusion may very well be warranted, it distressingly illustrates our current status.

The field of behavioral assessment appears to be at a point when the need for measures currently outstrips the available procedures. As a result, we are faced with the danger that poorly conceived assessment procedures may begin to fill the existing vacuum and may establish them-

Preparation of this chapter was facilitated in part by Grants MH24327 and MH27984 from the National Institute of Mental Health. The authors are grateful to Anita Powers Goldfried and Maurice Lorr for their helpful comments on an earlier version of this chapter. The publisher has changed the author's use of he/she and the like in this chapter. It should be understood that the use of the masculine pronoun refers to a person, male or female.

selves as "behavioral measures." There is a striking similarity here to the status of psychological assessment in the 1940s, when a hospitable *Zeitgeist* resulted in the proliferation of numerous projective techniques. Rabin (1968) has described this trend as follows:

"The sudden freedom from the shackles of the psychometric tradition that was experienced by some psychologists led to rather spurious trends in the field of projective techniques. Since projection and projective techniques were so broadly defined, any type of situation that was conducive to the elicitation of individual differences and 'uniqueness' or idiosyncracy in response could be nominated to membership in the new assessment armamentarium. Many issues of journals published 'still another projective technique,' mainly on the basis of novel stimuli of different modalities and some differentiation between normals and some psychopathological classifications. Little attention was paid to the theoretical underpinnings of these new methods or to the conceptualization of the response patterns within some theoretical framework of personality theory. Many of them were mere suggestions, prematurely published, and lacking in sufficient data of a validating nature. . . . " (p. 15)

History has an unfortunate way of repeating itself. Although there admittedly have been numerous conceptual and methodological advances over the past 30 years, behavioral assessment is not immune to many of the pitfalls that have been experienced in the past. Once any measure appears in the literature, it becomes capable of developing its own momentum. If the procedure is clearly specified and easily administered, researchers and clinicians are likely to use it. At that point it becomes a "frequently used" assessment procedure, thereby justifying its utility by assessors in the future. It then only requires a factor analysis—and perhaps a short form—to provide it with a completely independent life of its own.

If our analysis is a bit exaggerated—and we are not certain that it is—it is only to make our point: There are certain basic issues in current attempts to develop and validate behavioral assessment measures that need to be attended to in order to ensure that the field will progress in a methodologically sophisticated and clinically useful manner. The purpose of this chapter is to raise some of these issues.

APPLICATIONS OF BEHAVIORAL ASSESSMENT

One major use of behavioral assessment has been within the *clinical* setting, where the primary goal has been to determine those variables maintaining any particular maladaptive behavior pattern and any client characteristics having implications for both the selection and implementation of the most appropriate behavior therapy procedure. Although the application of behavioral assessment in the clinical context has been discussed elsewhere (Goldfried & Davison, 1976; Goldfried & Pomeranz, 1968; Linehan, in press), virtually no research has been carried out in this area.

A second potential use of behavioral assessment is for *selection* purposes. Although various psychological tests have frequently been employed for selection purposes within professional, educational, and industrial settings, behavioral assessment procedures have not yet extended into such spheres (Wiggins, 1973).

The third application of behavioral assessment has been within the *research* context. Since the pioneering outcome study by Paul (1966), there has been a marked upsurge in clinical outcome research. Such efforts have no doubt contributed significantly to the increased interest in behavioral assessment methods. The behavioral assessment strategy used in clinical research has typically focused on overt behavior, subjective report, and direct physiological measurement (Goldfried & Sprafkin, 1974; Lang, 1968). The behavioral observation may be conducted in naturalistic settings, may involve contrived situations that closely simulate real-life events (e.g., giving speeches before an audience), or may involve a more hypothetical task (e.g., using role playing to measure assertiveness). Subjective reports have similarly taken various forms, such as self-report estimates while the individual is in a naturalistic or contrived situation, or paper-and-pencil questionnaires that rely on the individual's recollection of behavior patterns or emotional reactions over a period of time. The physiological assessments frequently used in outcome research have employed such measures as GSR, muscle tension, heart rate, respiration rate, blood pressure, and specific indicators of sexual arousal.

THE ESSENCE OF BEHAVIORAL ASSESSMENT

The distinction between traditional and behavioral approaches to assessment has been discussed at length by Goldfried (1976), Goldfried and Kent (1972), Mischel (1968), and Wiggins (1973). Each of these writers has noted that behavioral assessment is characterized by relatively fewer inferential assumptions, remaining instead closer to observables. This holds true for the behavioral conceptualization of human functioning, as well as the interpretation of the person's response to situations within the assessment setting.

One of the earliest arguments for using operational terms in assessing and changing human behavior can be found in Johnson's *People in Quandaries* (1946):

"To say that Henry is mean implies that he has some sort of inherent trait, but it tells us nothing about what Henry has done. Consequently, it fails to suggest any specific means of improving Henry. If, on the other hand, it is said that Henry snatched Billy's cap and threw it in the bonfire, the situation is rendered somewhat more clear and actually more helpful. You might never eliminate 'meanness,' but there are fairly definite steps to be taken in order to remove Henry's incentives or opportunities for throwing caps in bonfires. . . .

What the psychiatrist has to do . . . is to get the person to tell him not what he *is* or what he *has,* but what he *does,* and the conditions under which he does it. When he stops talking about what *type* of person he *is,* what his outstanding *traits are,* and what type of disorder he *has*—when he stops making these subject-predicate statements, and begins to use actional terms to describe his behavior and its circumstances—both he and the psychiatrist begin to see what specifically may be done in order to change both the behavior and the circumstances." (p. 220)

Within the scope of contemporary behavioral assessment, "personality" is typically construed as an intervening variable that provides a summary of the individual's reactions to a wide variety of life situations. Stated in this way, however, the concept "personality" has little practical utility for behavioral assessment, in that it would be a near-impossible task to obtain systematic samples of all day-to-day situations. In actual practice behavioral assessment has instead focused on behavior patterns associated with a given class of performance capabilities, such as social skills or fearfulness.

The concept of behavioral capability refers to whether or not an individual has a given response available in his repertoire. The specific focus of assessment is on the determination of which capabilities a person has in any given class of situations. It should be clear that the specification of "capabilities" relates to maladaptive behavioral repertoires as well as to behavioral competencies. Thus it may be inferred that a person who is observed to berate others is capable of taking on an aggressive role or has aggressive capabilities.

A capabilities conceptualization of personality functioning, when viewed within the broad context of psychometric methodology, relates most directly to *content validity,* where careful item sampling becomes a most important issue. As described in the *Standards for Educational and Psychological Tests* (American Psychological Association, American Educational Research Association, and National Council on Measurement in Education, 1974), "Evidence of content validity is required when the test user wishes to estimate how an individual performs in the universe of situations the test is intended to represent" (p. 28). Although content validity has long been described as an important aspect of test construction, its relevance has typically been advocated for achievement tests, not personality assessment.

In their discussion of the behavioral-analytic approach to assessing competence, Goldfried and D'Zurilla (1969) have outlined a procedure for establishing the content validity of behavioral measures. The initial step consists of a *situational analysis,* involving a sampling of typical situations in which a given behavior of interest is likely to occur (e.g., aggressive behavior, heterosexual interaction). The next phase consists of a *response enumeration,* which entails a sampling of typical responses to each of the situations generated during the situational analysis. Both this phase and the previous one may be carried out by means of direct observations, that is, reports from individuals who have occasion to observe the behaviors within a naturalistic setting, as well as self-observations by those for whom the assessment is specifically designed. In the final phase of the criterion analysis, a *response evaluation* is conducted to judge each response with regard to capability level. In the measurement of competence, these judgments are carried out by significant others in the environment who typically label behavior patterns as being effective or maladaptive. In other instances, such as the assessment of empathic or fearful behavior, these judgments are made in light of how well they fit the definition of the behavioral capability of interest to the investigator. As illustrated diagrammatically in Figure 2-1, each situation may have associated with it an array of different responses, which can be grouped functionally according to their judged capability level. This three-stage criterion analysis may then be used to select the items in one's measuring instrument, and also to provide empirically derived criteria for scoring the measure.

It should be emphasized that the behavioral-analytic model for test construction focuses on only sampling and not on method issues. Once a criterion analysis is conducted, the assessor must consider the format for measuring the obtained situation-response interactions. Should he observe the individual in a naturalistic setting? Should he somehow contrive situations within the laboratory setting and then observe the person's response? Should the individual sit back and imagine the situation and then verbalize how he might react to it if it were actually occurring? Should the measuring procedure take the form of a structured interview? Should it involve a paper-and-pencil test? In deciding on which procedure to employ, various issues of method variance become relevant, such as the reactivity of the measuring procedure and the reliability of observers or scorers, as well as the comparative validities of the several assessment procedures.

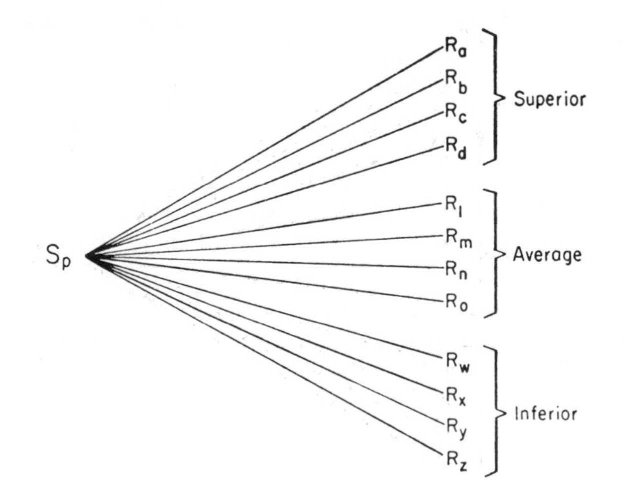

Figure 2–1. Diagramatic conception of a situation with varying ability levels (From M. R. Goldfried and T. J. D'Zurilla, A behavioral-analytic model for assessing competence. In C. D. Spielberger (Ed.) *Current topics in clinical and community psychology, Vol. I.* Copyright 1969 by Academic Press. Reproduced by permission.)

PSYCHOMETRIC ISSUES

Psychometric issues in behavioral assessment arise whenever observations are combined to give a person a numerical score on one or more attributes, when observations in test situations are used to make inferences about a person's behavior in nontest situations, and/or when observations are interrelated to make statements about functional relationships. Although the psychometric properties of more traditional assessment procedures have received a great deal of attention, the same cannot be said for behavioral assessment. As noted by Wiggins (1973):

> ". . . the fact that many social behaviorists rely heavily on clinical impressions gained from interviews, construct self-report 'surveys' of questionable psychometric properties, and generally operate without regard for decision-theoretic principles, seems to suggest that freedom from traditional models implies freedom from traditional psychometric principles as well." (p. 364)

In light of the increasing trend toward studying the validity and reliability of many behavioral assessment techniques, this may be somewhat overstated. The fact remains, however, that in contrast to the field of traditional assessment, few systematic research programs have been mounted to assess the psychometric properties of behavioral techniques.

Although the validity of behavioral assessment typically refers to whether or not the test behavior is a true reflection of behavior in natural settings, other types of validity are equally important. As noted previously, with the emphasis on the assessment of behavioral capabilities, content validity is of critical importance. Finally, to the extent that the assessor is interested in utilizing assessment data to make inferences about characteristics of the person, or to evaluate the effectiveness of a given therapeutic manipulation, construct validity becomes a relevant consideration. It is obvious, then, that we cannot speak of *the validity* of an assessment technique but must instead refer to types of validity. The type of validity one focuses on is in turn determined by the inferences one wishes to make.

Criterion-Related Validity

Criterion-related validity focuses on the extent to which assessment data can be used to estimate a person's behavior in certain concurrent or future nontest situations. One of the major problems in the field of behavioral assessment, however, is arriving at an acceptable criterion against which to validate the measure. If it is argued that the best assessment strategy is to directly sample behavior in criterion situations, then what other situations or behaviors can one turn to in validating the measure? Measurement of the same behaviors in similar situations at a later time will give an estimate of the temporal reliability of the assessment procedure, but this in itself is not evidence of validity.

The important issue here, as in all validity questions, is the nature of the inferences to be made from the assessment. In most cases the assessor is interested in inferring the degree of generalization from behavior in test situations to behavior in criterion situations. To the extent that the criterion situation and the test situation are one and the same, generalizability is not an issue, and questions of validity are thus by definition meaningless. The measurement issues involved in these instances are essentially the same as those encountered in the measurement of physical events (cf. Ebel, 1960). For example, when considering methods of measuring weight, one might be interested in the comparative reliability or accuracy of calibration of the scales. Questions of the validity of the scales as a measurement of weight, however, would not arise.

Validity, however, does become a question when a shorthand substitute replaces extensive measurements of actual criterion behavior. The shorthand methods most commonly used in behavioral assessment include self-report inventories, observation of behavior in semistructured situations, role-playing tests, and peer reports. In clinical practice the behavioral interview is perhaps the most commonly used assessment procedure. In the case of assessment involving contrived situations (e.g., speech giving in front of associates, role playing of social interaction, parent-child interactions observed through one-way mirrors) there seems to be a trend in the behavioral literature toward *assuming* that the procedure provides an adequate approximation of the criterion situations toward which predictions are to be made. Surprisingly little research has been done on the criterion-related validity of these procedures. Instead, one finds contrived situation procedures being compared to other shorthand procedures, such as direct observations of friendly behavior toward an associate while sitting in a waiting room being compared with peer reports of friendly behavior (Bem & Allen, 1974). No serious line of study has yet been undertaken to compare contrived situation tests directly with naturalistic observation, where the criterion behaviors and situations are the same as those in the testing procedure.

A major problem in selecting the criterion against which to validate a behavioral measure involves the degree of similarity needed between the test and criterion situations. For example, in assessing assertive behavior, if one's item pool includes refusal behavior in a supermarket situation, does one then have to go to a supermarket and observe subjects who have been assessed? And if one does go to the supermarket, does the situation have to be exactly the same with respect to the sex of other people in the situation, time of day, or number of people surrounding the subject? Even if one takes an extreme situationalist stand, the question of how to define a "similar" situation still exists. Data reported by Eisler, Hersen, Miller, and Blanchard (1975), for instance, indicate that in assertive role-playing situations, the degree of assertive behavior varies as a function of both the sex and the familiarity of the other person. Using a self-report inventory, Linehan and Glasser (Note 1) similarly found that the reported difficulty of behaving assertively depends on whether the other person is a friend or stranger. These studies suggest that, at least within the area of assertion assessment, sex and familiarity of persons are important parameters in selecting the appropriate criterion situation.

It is apparent, then, that estimates of criterion-related validity are directly related to the issue of cross-situational behavioral consistency. In the debate over this issue, the hallmark of the behavioral approach has been its emphasis on the situational specificity of behavior. Although impressive evidence has been marshaled to support this view (Mischel, 1968), several recent studies seem to indicate that, at least in some instances, behavior may be consistent across dissimilar situations. As Bem and Allen (1974) suggest, it would appear that one can predict some of the people some of the time. Bem and Allen's data specifically indicate that it is possible to identify on a priori grounds those individuals who will be cross-situationally consistent on specified behavioral attributes and those who will not. With respect to the behavioral attribute of friendliness, they found that individuals who report that they do not vary much from one situation to another display significantly less variability across situations than those who say they do vary.

Other findings that bear on the question suggest that behavioral consistency is related to deviance. Data reported by Jones, Reid and Patterson (1975) appear to confirm Wachtel's (1973) suggestion that differential consistency may be found within different types of populations. Specifically, Jones et al. found that when using Patterson's code for observing maladaptive behavior (Patterson, Ray, Shaw, & Cobb, 1969), 80 percent of the variance of the Total Deviant score, when applied to a sample of aggressive boys, was due to subject factors. When the same code was applied to a normal sample, virtually no subject consistency was found; approximately 81 percent of the variance was due instead to subject by situation interactions. Endler and Okada (1975) offer additional support for this viewpoint. Using a format based on the *S–R* Inventory of Anxiousness (Endler, Hunt, & Rosenstein, 1962), they sampled self-report anxiety responses in four general situations (interpersonal, physical danger, ambiguous, and innocuous). Their results indicate that as one goes from normal to neurotic to psychotic populations, individual differences account for more, and situational factors for less, of the variance.

If it can be established that a high degree of situational consistency exists within certain classes of behaviors or certain populations, then the task of establishing criterion situations will be much easier. The data of Bem and Allen suggest that the best predictor of generalization will be the interaction between the person and the behavior pattern in question. Much more empirical work, however, is needed to determine the parameters of this interaction effect. Until this research is done, the safer course is to have test situations closely parallel criterion situations.

Content Validity

As noted earlier, when the objective of assessment is to provide an estimate of the individual's capabilities or performance across a range of situations, a representative sampling of the situations in the domain of interest is essential. Unfortunately, this aspect of assessment has been largely neglected. There are, however, several exceptions.

Goldsmith and McFall (1975), in an analysis of interpersonal competency among male psychiatric patients, followed the behavioral-analytic model (Goldfried & D'Zurilla, 1969) and intensively interviewed patients to elicit a sample of problematic interpersonal situations. The interview protocols were condensed to a list of 55 common problem situations covering several general situational classes (e.g., dating, making friends, having job interviews, relating to authorities, etc.). Responses were then generated and evaluated for effectiveness by hospital staff. The resulting Interpersonal Situation Inventory and Interpersonal Behavior Role-Playing Test were used to evalute a skill-training program, where changes between pretesting and posttesting on both procedures were found to discriminate between the treated and the control group.

Freedman (1974) similarly used the behavioral-analytic model to collect and key items for assessing delinquent behavior among adolescent boys. Her data reveal that the responses in role-played situations significantly differentiated among three groups of adolescent boys who were independently determined to vary according to level of interpersonal competency.

Within the area of assertion MacDonald (1974) used the behavioral-analytic model to collect and key items for her College Women's Assertion Sample. In the development of their Conflict Resolution Inventory McFall and Lillesand (1971) also used an empirical sampling technique to obtain situations involving unreasonable requests that college students had difficulty in refusing.

Although many other instruments appear to be sampling a wide variety of situations, it is important to note that the appearance of validity (so-called face validity) is *not* evidence of content validity. For example, although items in the Fear Survey Schedule-II (Geer, 1965) were generated empirically, most other forms of the schedule have no such empirical base. Cautela and Kastenbaum's (1967) Reinforcement Survey Schedule also suffers from sampling problems and seems to contain items based on the idiosyncratic decisions of the authors. By contrast, MacPhillamy and Lewinsohn's (1972) Pleasant Events Schedule includes items that are generated from an actual situational analysis in a college population. In the area of assertion, where questionnaires are rapidly proliferating, sampling problems are particularly evident. Until recently, the most frequently used assessment inventory was the Wolpe and Lazarus Assertiveness Questionnaire (Wolpe & Lazarus, 1966), which is a compilation of intuitively generated items. A steady stream of inventories has since appeared in the literature, including the Rathus Assertiveness Scale (Rathus, 1973a), the College Self-Expression Scale (Galassi, DeLo, Galassi, & Bastien, 1974), the Adult Self-Expression Scale (Gay, Hollandsworth, & Galassi, 1975) and the Gambrill and Richey (1975) assertion inventory. For the most part these inventories were taken from previous questionnaires and supplemented by unsystematically collected reports from students or clients, hardly a procedure for satisfying sampling assumptions. In addition, each of these inventories suffers from problems in construct definition, an issue to be discussed later.

It is interesting to note that in almost all cases where content validity has been attended to, it has been for a college or institutionalized population, perhaps an indication of the difficulty of the process. As noted in a candid remark by Goldsmith and McFall (1975), the construction of their assessment procedures was far more time-consuming than the development of their treatment program. It is unfortunate that we are left with an array of instruments useful for research and clinical work with college and institutional populations but few instruments with sufficient content validity for use with the general population.

Questions of content validity may also be raised with respect to the widely used behavioral avoidance tests, which typically measure how close a person can approach a feared object in a laboratory setting. It is questionable whether this situational context adequately represents the domain of situations to which the approach behavior is to be generalized. In a series of studies on behavioral avoidance tests, Bernstein (1973) has demonstrated that approach behavior varies as a function of situational context. If it is impossible to administer behavioral avoidance tests in a representative sample of situations in which the feared object might be encountered, a possibility worth exploring might be to arrange "contrived" situations in the laboratory. This might involve the use of imagination, role playing, or other contextual aids as part of the behavioral avoidance test. In a similar vein, procedures that involve assessing fear of heights by having subjects climb ladders on roofs, or public-speaking anxiety by having subjects give a speech in front of a small group of associates may also be questioned as to content validity. Although these tests may be useful in the analogue research context, care must be taken in using them to assess performance in a wider performance domain.

Related to the issue of content validity is the extent to which certain behavior patterns are sampled over time. Unfortunately, relatively few behavioral assessors have addressed themselves to the question of whether the behavior sample is comprehensive. Inasmuch as classroom and home observations are often made during brief intervals over a relatively short period of time, the representativeness of such a sample becomes a most serious question. A notable instance in which this is not an issue is the case of the time-sample behavioral checklist developed by Paul for use with psychiatric patients (Mariotto & Paul, 1974; Paul, Tobias, & Holly, 1972). Such observations are carried out in the hospital setting, enabling the patient's behavior to be sampled during each of his waking hours for the entire day.

When it is feasible to observe behavior for only brief time periods, the behavioral assessor should seriously consider the possibility of utilizing the observations of individuals typically present in the subject's natural environment, such as relatives, teachers, nurses, and other significant individuals. This obviously represents a trade-off when one settles for less detailed and possibly less accurate observations but obtains behavior samples occurring over a longer period of time and in a wider range of situations. In addition, the reactivity problem, to be discussed later, becomes minimized.

Construct Validity

What is not frequently acknowledged by behavioral assessors is that a response capability conception of personality does, in fact, require the formulation of some sort of unobserved construct. This point will be elaborated on later. In talking about the construct validity of a behavioral measure, however, it should be noted that we are not necessarily dealing with any highly abstract theoretical formulations. Rather, the constructs employed within a behavioral framework are typically tied to observables having clear behavioral referents within appropriate situational contexts. In this sense, such inferences might be most appropriately construed as "intervening variables" (MacCorquodale & Meehl, 1948).

Specification of Behavioral Referents

There are several different ways that behavioral referents can be specified. One method, essentially the same as the response enumeration and evaluation phases in the behavioral-analytic method of test construction, is to elicit responses to situations relevant to the construct from a large number of persons. The responses can then be evaluated by "expert" judges, with the behaviors defining the construct being derived from the pooled evaluations. This procedure is best illustrated by MacDonald's (1974) definition of the "assertiveness" of college women, Goldsmith and McFall's (1975) work on "interpersonal skills" among psychiatric inpatients, and Freedman's (1974) research on "social-behavioral skills" in delinquent boys.

A second method has been to observe groups of individuals independently rated as differing in their performance level on a given dimension. This method has been used most frequently with the constructs "interpersonal skills" and "assertiveness." Arkowitz, Lichtenstein, McGovern, and Hines (1975), for example, investigated the behavioral referents of heterosexual social competence in males. Using taped role-plays, live interactions with female associates, and a contrived telephone task, they found relatively few behaviors that discriminated between persons independently rated as high or low daters. Their findings revealed that only a global rating of social skill, and number of silences, differentiated between the groups. In a related study Borkovec, Stone, O'Brien, and Kaloupek (1974) were interested in the behavioral referents of social anxiety. Using a modified version of Paul's timed behavioral checklist, they observed subjects independently differentiated on social anxiety in contrived interactional situations. As in the Arkowitz et al. study, the majority of specific overt behavioral measures did not differentiate the groups. Once again, global ratings did discriminate. In the area of assertiveness, however, the work of Eisler, Miller, and Hersen (1973) has been successful in isolating several behavioral components that discriminate among groups.

A third method that might be used to generate behavioral referents is based on a combined theoretical and empirical analysis of the construct. Libet and Lewinsohn (1973), for example, generated a list of behaviors associated with "social skills" which, in their framework, is defined as the ability to elicit positive reinforcement from the environment. Working from the theoretical premise that depressed individuals receive less social reinforcement from their environment than nondepressed individuals, they found that three behavior patterns (rate of behavior emitted, rate of positive reactions emitted, and action latency) reliably discriminated between independently assessed depressed and control groups.

Each of the methods described above focuses on behaviors in a given response system. Many of our constructs, however, such as "anxiety," have traditionally focused on referents from more than one response system, including the cognitive-verbal, instrumental-motor, and physiological. If one uses referents from more than one response system within the definition of the construct, then any measure of the construct must sample behaviors *across* these response systems. A good example of this is in the case of constructs that deal with emotions. Emotional responses have been defined by Lang (1971) as "Multiple system responses—verbal-cognitive, motor, and physiological events . . . [where] . . . a coincidence of activity in more than one system is what we most confidently refer to as an emotion, and a highly general response characterizes states of intense affect" (p. 108). As further noted by Lang, the partial independence of the systems makes it possible for cognitive aspects of emotionality to occur without accompanying motor behavior or physiological indicators. Aggressive behavior can occur without hostile cognitions, and avoidance behavior without fearful cognitions. Thus any construct definition must include a consideration of the particular response system measured. In the case of "anxiety," then, one might more appropriately use the constructs of "verbal-cognitive anxiety," "physiological anxiety," or "behavioral anxiety."

It is important here to keep in mind the distinction between methods of measurement or sampling and the response system being tapped. Thus one might measure aspects of the physiological system by a variety of methods (e.g., self-reports of palm sweating or GSR measurements of palm sweating). Similarly, one might choose to sample motor behavior by any of several methods including peer reports, self-monitoring, interviewing, or direct observation. As noted by Cone (in press), the confounding of method of assessment with system being measured in much of the validity research has led both to ambiguities in construct definition and problems in interpreting the generalizability of test behavior.

Since specification of behavioral referents for a given construct is ultimately a definitional problem, it is fruitless to argue about the "real" meaning of a construct. However, to the extent that different investigators define the same construct with different sets of behavioral referents, or refer to similar sets of referents with different labels, the overall process of construct validation is hampered.

Appropriateness of Situational Context

Another important issue in construct validity is the relevance of situational contexts to the construct in question. Situational relevance can be determined by either of two methods. The first involves a specification of the *functional relationship* of various situations defining the construct. This method can be carried out at either the idiographic or the nomothetic level and involves a simple enumeration of the situations in which the behavior of interest occurs. At an idiographic level, for example, if a child is observed behaving aggressively when other children take his toys, when a parent refuses a request, and at bedtime, these situations can be considered to be aggressive-related for the child. At the nomothetic level, situations in which the behavior of interest typically occurs across a large sample of individuals would be judged as being relevant to the construct. For example, since many people behave "socially" at parties and "assertively" when brought the wrong meal in a restaurant, these situations can be considered relevant to the constructs of "sociability" and "assertiveness," respectively. On the other hand, situations in which very few people respond in the predicted way would not be relevant; a crowded subway during rush hour is probably not the most relevant situation for measuring social skills.

A second method of determining situational relevance involves asking the individual in the case of idiographic assessment, or a representative sample in the case of nomothetic assessment, to generate a set of situations that are *perceived* as relevant to the construct. The advantage of this method is that it allows for a distinction to be made between response capability and the belief that a particular response would be appropriate. Presumably, at least in the area of behavioral skill assessment, an important criterion for situational relevance is whether the behaviors defining the construct are indeed perceived as being appropriate in the specified situation.

Methods of Determining Construct Validity

Two general points are important to keep in mind in considering the construct validity of a particular assessment procedure. First, the construct validity of any given measure cannot be determined on the basis of any one study. It is established incrementally over time and on the basis of a large number of studies using the measures. Second, the concept of construct validity refers to the validity of a particular assessment procedure as an appropriate operational definition of a specified construct and does not necessarily reflect the theoretical utility of the construct itself. This point is most relevant when one fails to establish construct validity for a particular measure. For example, if a particular measure of "anxiety" has little or no construct validity, that does not mean that "anxiety" is a useless construct. Other measurement procedures may have acceptable construct validity. On the other hand, the accumulation of evidence for construct validity of a particular measure increases one's confidence in the utility of the construct being measured.

Bearing these points in mind, several types of evidence can be used to establish construct validity. The construct validity of a behavioral measure may be reflected by its ability to change as a function of a given experimental manipulation. Thus one may assume that the decrement in observed disruptive behavior following the institution of a token reinforcement program in a school context offers evidence of construct validity for the observational code. Similarly, the increase in a certain characteristic, such as anxiety on a given measure, may offer evidence of construct validity for that measure if the increase follows threat of shock. Data indicating that a measure discriminates between groups known to differ on a particular characteristic can also be taken as evidence of construct validity.

Studies that offer evidence of convergent and discriminant validity (Campbell & Fiske, 1959) are especially important in establishing the construct validity of an assessment procedure. Although the multitrait-multimethod research strategy has been emphasized in traditional assessment, it is just beginning to be applied in the area of behavioral assessment. For example, the discriminant validities of verbal-cognitive measures of specific fears has recently been reported by Klorman, Weerts, Hastings, Melamed, and Lang (1974). Correlations between four tests of specific fears, the Snake Questionnaire, the Spider Questionnaire, the Mutilation Questionnaire (Lang, Melamed, & Hart, 1970; Hastings, 1971), and the Personal Report of Confidence as a Speaker (Paul, 1966) were found to be insignificant. In addition, none of the measures correlated highly with other tests of general anxiety. Additional data obtained by Hastings (1971), as reported by Klorman et al. (1974), indicate that subjects differentiated on the basis of their scores on the snake, spider, and mutilation questionnaires reported greater distress in the presence of fear-relevant than fear-irrelevant slides. There were no differences in response to neutral slides. Both of these studies offer evidence of the discriminant validity of the specific fear measures.

Discriminant validity is tied to the unidimensionality of a particular measurement instrument, which in turn is related to the conceptual clarity of the construct in question. A construct in the behavioral literature having a great deal of conceptual ambiguity is that of "assertion." Almost all definitions of assertion involve some reference to the ability to stand up for one's rights and resist unjust demands. However, in looking both at published definitions of assertion as well as content areas included in assertion inventories and role-playing procedures, it would appear that almost any positively valued interpersonal behavior might be labeled as assertive. The Rathus Assertiveness Inventory (Rathus, 1973a), for example, includes items representing a wide range of response categories. In a subsequent article, Rathus (1973b) refers to nine types of assertive behavior (e.g., feeling talk, greeting talk, disagreeing passively and actively, etc.). Interestingly, only *one* of the nine categories is labeled "assertive talk" and is defined as not being taken advantage of by others. On the other hand, McFall and his associates (McFall & Marston, 1970, McFall & Lillesand, 1971, McFall & Twentyman, 1973) have limited the construct of assertion to the ability to refuse unjust demands.

It seems that several constructs are typically included under the general heading of "assertion," such as the defense of one's rights and the rejection of unjust demands, social competency, independence, capacity to take control in various situations (typically called dominance), initiatory skills, communication of positive feelings, and personal expressiveness. The result of this conceptual ambiguity has been the development of assertion inventories that appear to be multi- rather than unidimensional in scope. For example, Gambrill and Richey (1975) found 11 factors in their assertion inventory, and Galassi and Galassi (Note 2) discovered nine factors in the College Self-Expression Inventory. Although Gambrill and Richey interpret these findings as evidence for the situation-specific nature of assertive skills, it is likely that the instruments are also measuring a variety of different response categories. For example, Gambrill and Richey found several factors that seem to be better conceptualized as different behavioral skills (e.g., initiating interactions and engaging in "happy talk") rather than as categories of situations in which assertive behavior might be called for (e.g., service situations, bothersome situations, interactions with friends, etc.).

Further work is needed in developing clear and parsimonious definitions of behavioral constructs. Once the definitions are clarified, there is a need for appropriate sampling of situation-response categories for inclusion in behavioral tests.

Method Variance

For the most part, behavioral assessors have tended to assume that having decided upon the behavior sample on which to focus, a valid measure is likely to be forthcoming. Only recently has the field become attuned to what Campbell and Fiske (1959) have described as method variance, referring to those sources of error attributable to the particular measurement procedure itself. Most of the work done to date on method variance associated with behavioral assessment has dealt with questions of observer reliability and the reactivity of the measurement procedure. Included among the other important issues that still need to be studied are the reliability of behavioral measures over time; basic considerations associated with the use of paper-and-pencil tests, such as social desirability, response style, and rating-scale format; and the importance of procedural parameters associated with situation tests, such as variations in the characteristics of associates used in role-playing assessment.

The need for more research on method variance can be graphically illustrated in the use of role playing as an outcome measure in assertion training. In such uses the researchers typically assume that method variance contributes relatively little to the data obtained and that the scores can unequivocably be used to assess behavior change. Inasmuch as most assertion training programs make use of role playing for purposes of behavior rehearsal, it is most surprising that no one has questioned the possibility that subjects in such studies are simply being taught to perform more adequately during the role-playing assessment. We hasten to add that we are not suggesting that this in fact is the case; we merely wish to illustrate the relative lack of attention to method variance in our assessment procedures.

Many of the basic issues associated with method variance are described in detail by Wiggins (1973) and will not be reviewed here. Instead, our discussion primarily focuses on what has already been most extensively studied in behavioral assessment, namely, observer reliability and the reactivity of the measures.

Observer Reliability

In most of the work on behavioral observation, the findings typically indicate that trained observers can reliably code various behavior patterns. Despite some of the cautions that observers' expectancies may provide a source of error variance (Rosenthal, 1966), clearly defined behavioral codes have apparently been able to override such potential bias. For example, Kent, O'Leary, Diament, and Dietz (1974) found that trained observers obtained accurate ratings of classroom behavior, despite the attempt to experimentally manipulate their expectations of what they were about to observe. Similarly, research on the use of a time-sample behavior checklist among psychiatric patients found that trained raters continue to make reliable observations, even when hospitalized patients manifested atypical behavior patterns (Redfield & Paul, 1976).

Despite the reports of good interobserver agreement, potential sources of scorer unreliability exist, nonetheless. Such unreliability was demonstrated by Reid (1970), who told trained observers that reliability checks were no longer being carried out on their observations. In comparison to a reliability coefficient of 0.76 when the observers knew that a reliability estimate was being made, interobserver agreement dropped to 0.51 when a surreptitious reliability check was made. These findings were confirmed by Romanczyk, Kent, Diament and O'Leary (1973), who additionally found that interobserver reliability could be made even greater if the raters knew who was monitoring their accuracy. Thus despite the concrete criteria involved in such behavioral rating codes, there nonetheless remains room for idiosyncratic interpretation, and observers can readily make shifts in the criteria they employ.

O'Leary and Kent (1973) have uncovered another potential source of observer reliability that might easily go unnoticed, which they call the "drift" problem. Behavioral observation is typically carried out by teams of observers, who frequently have the opportunity to compare and discuss their sources of unreliability after periods of observation. Although this affords them the opportunity to clarify any ambiguities in the use of the code, it also may result in any given team's developing its own idiosyncratic interpretations. Inasmuch as interobserver reliability checks are typically made *within* rating teams, such drifts in the use of the code may not be readily apparent. To avoid having observer pairs unwittingly use different behavioral codes, it is recommended that team members be periodically reassigned to minimize such drift (see Kent & Foster, this volume).

In developing a behavioral coding system that is likely to yield high interobserver reliability, care must be taken to deal with certain issues. Goldfried and Sprafkin (1974) have suggested that among the questions that need to be asked are the following:

"Can the observer reasonably keep in mind the number of different categories involved? Can each category be defined behaviorally? Are the distinctions among categories easy to make? Is sufficient opportunity provided for observers to code and record the behaviors they have observed? Have the observers all reached a common level of training that enables them to deal adequately with any ambiguities that may exist within the coding system? Is the total period of observation brief enough so as to prevent the observers from becoming fatigued or bored? Interobserver reliability will increase as each of these questions is answered in the affirmative." (p. 9)

Related to the issue of interobserver agreement in the use of behavioral codes is the reliability of self-recordings. Research by Lipinski and Nelson (1974) and Nelson, Lipinski, and Black (1975) indicates that although the reliability of a simple self-recording task (e.g., frequency of face touching) was typically in the 0.80s when subjects were aware that their accuracy was being monitored, it dropped to the 0.50s when surreptitious reliability checks were made. In addition to implementing random checks on self-monitoring as a means of maintaining high reliability (Taplin & Reid, 1973), reliability may also be kept at acceptable levels by reinforcing subjects for accurate self-observation (Bolstad & Johnson, 1972; Fixsen, Phillips, & Wolf, 1972; Flowers, 1972; Lipinski, Black, Nelson, & Ciminero, 1975; Risley & Hart, 1968). As in the case of interobserver reliability, accuracy of self-observation depends on motivational variables.

Reactivity

An important issue associated with any assessment procedure is the extent to which the measurement procedure itself alters the phenomenon that is being assessed. This reactivity issue has been investigated in conjunction with behavioral observations in naturalistic settings, contrived situational tests, and self-monitoring.

In an early study of the reactivity problem within *behavioral observation,* Purcell and Brady (1966) were interested in determining the extent to which the verbal behavior of adolescents would be affected by being monitored with a miniature wireless radio transmitter. Although the authors concluded that subjects began to behave more naturally after the first few days of monitoring, the criteria for drawing such a conclusion were indirect, being based on the amount of talking done, verbal references made about the transmitter, as well as the subjects' own impressionistic reports.

Moos (1968) studied the reactive effects of wearing a wireless transmitter with a group of psychiatric patients by comparing their behavior during periods when they were wearing the transmitter with times when the transmitter was not used. The observed reactivity was slight, appeared to occur among the more disturbed patients, and was also a function of the setting in which the observation took place. Johnson and Bolstad (1975) studied the effect of observers in the home on family interactions and found that tape recordings of family interactions did not differ when observers were present or absent. In interpreting both of these studies, however, it is important to keep in mind that the distinction between being observed and not being observed was not clear cut. Moos' subjects, even when not wearing the transmitter, knew they were being otherwise observed, and Johnson and Bolstad's families were undoubtedly aware of the tape recorder, even when the observers were absent.

Some support for the nonreactivity of behavioral observations comes from Hagen, Craighead, and Paul (1975), who found that the amount, rate, and nature of staff interactions with hospitalized patients was not affected by the presence or absence of an observer. The independent check on reactivity was carried out by means of a concealed microphone, continuously monitoring verbal interaction.

Johnson, Christensen, and Bellamy (1976) have developed an ingenious procedure that has the potential for dealing with the reactivity problem. With the focus being on observation of verbal interactions in the home setting, Johnson et al. have the child wear a radio transmitter that broadcasts interactions to a concealed tape recorder that can be activated at random intervals during the day. The child and other family members are aware that their interactions are being monitored but have no knowledge of the sampling procedure. Although it seems likely that after a period of adaptation the reactivity would be less of an issue under such circumstances, no research has been carried out to test this directly. In addition to having implications for the reactivity question, such a procedure also has the potential for dealing with many of the other methodological problems associated with behavioral observation, such as observer bias and inadequate samplings of interactions.

The reactivity problem, as it exists within *contrived* behavioral measures, presents more of a potential difficulty. With the behavioral avoidance test, there is evidence that the subject's perception of the demand characteristics can have an important effect. For example, Miller and Bernstein (1972) found that claustrophobic subjects would remain in a small dark chamber for varying lengths of time, depending on whether the emphasis was on feeling free to leave any time they felt uncomfortable or on remaining for a given period. Further research has shown that performance on behavioral avoidance tests assessing small animal phobias is similarly affected by the subject's perception of the task requirements (Bernstein & Nietzel, 1973; Smith, Diener, & Beaman, 1974).

In drawing any conclusion about the reactivity associated with a behavioral avoidance test, it is important to specify the response system that is likely to be influenced. Although the research evidence indicates that overt motor behavior varies as a function of demand characteristics, verbal reports and physiological reactions have typically been unaffected. Thus the differential experimental instructions given to claustrophobics in the Miller and Bernstein study had no impact on the anxiety reaction as measured by either verbal-cognitive or physiological measures. Smith et al. (1974), while demonstrating that demand characteristics significantly influenced subject's approach to caged rats, similarly found no differences on verbal-cognitive and physiological anxiety measures. Finally, Borkovec et al. (1974) found that instructions to behave "in a relaxed, nonanxious manner" did not influence subjects' performance in a situational test of heterosexual anxiety. Taken together, these findings suggest that the reactivity associated with situation tests probably depends on the degree to which the target behavior or response system being assessed is under the subject's voluntary control.

In instances where there is reason to believe that the subject has some voluntary control over the behavior that is being assessed, some decision must be made with regard to demand characteristics built into the situation test. If the purpose of the assessment is to eliminate all but the most phobic of individuals, then subjects should be encouraged as much as possible to approach the feared object. One should bear in mind, however, that the results of such an assessment may not necessarily parallel the individual's behavior in a naturalistic context, where the demand characteristics for approaching the feared object is not likely to be as high.

In using *self-monitoring* as an assessment device, reactivity becomes a most salient issue. In fact, although self-monitoring was originally devised as an assessment device, it soon became recognized as comprising an essential ingredient of many behavior change programs. The fact that reactivity does occur should not be too surprising, especially in light of the frequent clinical observation that feedback can alter behavior. Athough reactivity does occur, the direction, extent, and duration of the change can vary with the target behavior and the duration of the self-monitoring itself (Mahoney & Thoresen, 1974). As in contrived situational tests, the reactive effects of self-monitoring probably depend on the voluntary nature of the behavior in question (e.g., study behavior versus interpersonal anxiety). Furthermore, the question of whether the behavior will increase or decrease as a function of self-monitoring will, no doubt, vary with the perceived value of the behavior in question. In a study on the frequency of face touching, Nelson et al. (1975) found that even with attempts to experimentally manipulate expectancy for direction of change (i.e., increase, decrease, no change), the behavior pattern was found to decrease among subjects in all three conditions. Related to this finding is the effect of motivational variables, an issue studied by Lipinski et al. (1975). They found that the use of monetary incentives for reducing face touching further increased the reactivity associated with the self-monitoring and that self-observation of smoking behavior was reactive only for subjects who were motivated to stop smoking.

Until various parameters associated with the reactivity of self-monitoring have been discovered, the use of such a procedure for assessment purposes remains in doubt (see Ciminero, Nelson, & Lipinski, this volume).

UNRESOLVED CONCEPTUAL AND RESEARCH ISSUES

In concluding our overview of basic issues in behaviorial assessment, we would like to raise some additional considerations yet to be answered by behaviorally oriented researchers and clinicians. Many of these issues are practically and conceptually complex and clearly present a challenge to the ingenuity of behavioral assessors.

Comparative Validity of Behavioral and Traditional Assessment

In light of the growing interest in behavioral assessment procedures, it is somewhat surprising to find that virtually no research has been carried out to compare their validity and predictive efficiency with more traditionally oriented methods. When one considers that problems with the validity and reliability of many traditional assessment procedures were, to a large extent, responsible for the rejection of traditional models of human functioning, this lack of comparative research is even more surprising. Although a few isolated studies have tended to support a more behaviorally oriented approach to assessment (Goldfried & Kent, 1972), there are insufficient findings at present to draw any firm conclusions regarding the comparative validity of both orientations. Just as one can view behavior therapy as a broad orientation for approaching the full gambit of clinical problems, so can one construe behavioral assessment as providing clinical psychology with a new paradigm for measuring human functioning. As has been demonstrated with various behavior therapy procedures, the acceptance of a behaviorally oriented approach to assessment by clinical psychology in general is not likely to occur until it can be shown that it does a better job than that which is currently available.

Standardization of Behavioral Assessment Measures

As we indicated earlier in this chapter, behavioral assessment in clinical practice is based to a great extent on the conceptual ability and clinical intuitiveness of the particular assessor. Even in the case of research applications of behavioral assessment, one typically finds that assessment procedures focusing on a given target behavior differ from study to study. For example, assessment of assertiveness through role playing typically varies according to the content of the situation used, the duration of the role-played interaction (i.e., single response versus extended interaction), as well as the very mode of role playing itself (e.g., face-to-face versus interaction with a tape recorder). In light of such variations, it seems essential to us that greater emphasis be put on publishing the full details of idiosyncratic assessment procedures used in the various research studies. For example, when role-playing procedures are used, scoring procedures, details on the content of the associates' behavior, exact instructions given to the subject, as well as a full description of the situations used all too often are not reported. Although this may be more a function of editorial resistance to long articles, it nonetheless poses a serious problem in comparing various procedures.

A question yet to be answered is whether such procedural variations make a difference. In this regard, comparative research on the validity of our assessment procedures is clearly needed (e.g., Jeger & Goldfried, 1976). Only after such research is done can we hope to develop standardized measures that, in turn, would allow for clearer interpretation and generalization of research findings across outcome studies. Furthermore, standardized measures will provide us with comprehensive sets of normative data needed to assess clinically meaningful behavior change.

Difficulty Level of Behavioral Measures in Outcome Research

There is a potentially important and yet unstudied interaction inherent in most clinical outcome research, namely, the interaction between difficulty level of the task presented to the subject with the potency of the therapeutic intervention employed. This issue can be most clearly illustrated in the case of speech anxiety. Situation tests of speech anxiety may vary by virtue of the size and composition of the audience, the preparation period given to the subject, the length and topic of the speech, as well as other variations that can contribute to the potential aversiveness of the situation. That public-speaking situations can be differentially anxiety arousing is apparent to any behavior therapist who has ever constructed a desensitization hierarchy. In any given outcome study, however, the researcher typically decides on a fixed level of aversiveness and employs this task within pretesting and posttesting. The assumption is that if the therapies differ in their effectiveness, differential change will appear at posttest. However, if the situation test employed is too "difficult," the researcher runs the risk that his therapeutic intervention procedure may not be extensive or powerful enough—at least as it is typically employed within the context of an outcome study—to reflect any differential change. Conversely, if the test is too "easy," then even the less potent interventions may seem to be comparably effective. At present there are no parametric studies that focus on this most crucial issue.

Absence of Theoretical Framework

In the attempt to establish a different paradigm for understanding and modifying human functioning, behavior therapists have discarded much of personality theory as such and instead have maintained that any given behavior pattern may more profitably be understood within the current environmental context. This orientation is reminiscent of the view Skinner presented some years back when he questioned the necessity for theories of learning (Skinner, 1950). Thus, rather than employing theoretical conceptualizations such as need for achievement or self-actualization, behavior therapists have instead sought to determine the functional relationship involved with any given response. To say that each person's behavior will vary from situation to situation, however, is just as naive as asserting that everything an individual does may be understood in terms of his personality structure. The true state of affairs undoubtedly lies somewhere between these two extremes.

For the most part the variables that are currently the target of behavioral assessment procedures have been selected on a pragmatic, rather than theoretical, basis. Behavioral measures of assertiveness are popular because of the existence of assertion-training procedures. When we call an individual "unassertive," however, we are making some low-level theoretical inference that behavioral consistencies exist across a range of situations. Presumably this consistency is mediated by some sort of more general capability to respond in specified ways.

As we have noted earlier in this chapter, much has yet to be done in deriving a set of constructs that would be useful in behavioral assessment. Although Mischel (1973) has offered some tentative proposals for the relevant dimensions of human behavior on which we might focus, we instead favor the methodology described by Bem and Allen (1974) that attempts to keep theory construction very closely tied to functional relationships observed at an idiographic level. The existence of such a theoretical framework can provide us with important guidelines for deciding on the targets for our assessment procedures.

The Scope of Behavioral Assessment

Just as we are unwilling to define behavior therapy according to its available pool of techniques, we find it short-sighted and limiting to define behavioral assessment as being equivalent to the currently employed methods. Although we readily acknowledge that there are certain assessment procedures more likely to be associated with behavioral assessment (e.g., role playing, self-monitoring), behavioral assessors also use procedures employed by clinicians and researchers of other orientations, such as the interview (Linehan, in press).

From a comprehensive viewpoint, behavioral assessment might best be conceptualized as involving a sampling of the individual's responses to various aspects of his environment. If one accepts this broader vantage point, however, it is easy to point to certain traditional assessment techniques that are consistent with a behavioral orientation. As an example, take, of all tests, the Rorschach. One approach to interpreting the Rorschach involves a scoring procedure based on a sample approach, whereby the inkblots are conceptualized as perceptual-cognitive stimuli and the protocol is scored along the dimension of perceptual differentiation and integration. In essence, the behaviorally oriented assessor using the Rorschach for this purpose would be saying to himself: "In presenting this set of ambiguous stimuli to the subject, I am attempting to obtain a sample of his ability to take something that is vaguely structured and impose on it a certain cognitive order." Although the objection may be made that the ten Rorschach inkblots represent a somewhat unique sample of stimuli, this does not necessarily make their use "nonbehavioral." In fact, one may make this comment about the many currently available behavioral assessment techniques that suffer from poor content validity. Apart from the conceptual arguments associated with the use of the Rorschach as a perceptual task, the fact of the matter is that the actual validity of this particular scoring system has been most impressive (Goldfried, Stricker, & Weiner, 1971).

The question of whether certain traditional procedures might be useful for behavioral assessment is even more apparent in the clinical setting. Take the example of a teenage client who is unwilling to talk about what might be bothering her but might be willing to offer the clinician a sample of her concerns more indirectly by means of the Thematic Apperception Test (TAT). The argument that the empirical status of the TAT does not justify such use of the test may also apply to some of the behavioral assessment procedures employed in clinical practice, such as the interview. More often than not, one hears the behavior therapist justifying the use of certain assessment procedures on the grounds that "it is clinically useful" and that its utility is consistent with the general behavioral orientation. But what if we suggest that the TAT might be employed to induce an otherwise inarticulate client to talk about relevant material by first soliciting less anxiety-producing verbalizations and then making successive approximations to discussions of target problems?* Meichenbaum (1976)

* This potential use of the TAT was suggested by Diane Jacobstein, a graduate student at Catholic University.

has also suggested use of TAT-like pictures in the assessment of a client's cognitive behavior in target situations. He reports unpublished findings of Meijers that such a procedure is effective in discriminating between socially withdrawn and socially outgoing children.

In summary, the level of methodological sophistication of many of our clinical assessment procedures clearly indicates a need for greater refinement and research. We suggest, however, that it is premature to discard assessment techniques simply because they do not fit the conventional stereotype of behavioral assessment.

ETHICAL ISSUES IN BEHAVIORAL ASSESSMENT

A great deal has been written about the ethical problems associated with behavior therapy. Although such ethical concerns are probably no different from those inherent in any approach to therapeutic intervention, behavior therapists have been particularly sensitive to the moral decisions in selecting the goals and methods of therapy. By contrast, few concerns have been raised regarding the ethics of behavioral assessment.

In the context of outcome research, review committees frequently exist to protect the welfare of the participating subject. Subjects must offer their informed consent, and safeguards typically exist against subjecting individuals to dangerous procedures. An important and yet frequently unnoticed ethical concern associated with behavioral assessment in outcome research deals with the specific targets for change. For example, in utilizing role-playing assessment to evaluate the effectiveness of assertion training, the question of what is "appropriately assertive" clearly involves a value judgment. Does one include a scene depicting a man coming home from work, expecting a "nice home-cooked meal," only to find that his wife has been busy all day and has had time to prepare only a TV dinner? Is it appropriate to include an item requiring a subject to ask for a third cup of coffee of a waiter who is too busy to even begin serving individuals at other tables? Or should subjects be encouraged to express their true feelings about a gift they dislike when a friend has gone to great lengths to purchase it for them? Such decisions clearly extend well beyond the limits of our behavioral assessment technology.

In the context of clinical assessment, an ethical concern must be the validity of the assessment procedures used to identify target behaviors for change and to specify the controlling variables. Given both the monetary and personal costs involved in most therapies, the behavior therapist is ethically required to use those assessment procedures with the best evidence of validity. The time and cost of using procedures with good psychometric properties is frequently cited as the rationale for relying on more questionable assessment techniques. It is entirely possible, however, that the cost of the more time-consuming procedures would well be less than the cost of inappropriate therapy done on the basis of inaccurate assessment. Although much easier on the therapist, it is essential that the behavioral assessor not be lulled into the 50-minute hour approach to assessment.

SUMMARY

The emergent interest in behavioral assessment brings with it a number of issues that need to be considered to ensure that the field will develop in a manner that is methodologically sophisticated and clinically useful. This chapter focuses on several of these issues, including the conceptualization of what is to be measured and relevant strategies for test construction. Although behavioral researchers have taken a somewhat different tack in the development of measures, psychometric issues associated with assessment per se nonetheless remain critical. This chapter discusses some of the difficulties in establishing criterion-related validity for behavioral measures, and deals with the particularly unique relevance that content validity has in behavioral assessment. The implications of using theoretical constructs in a behavioral framework are discussed, together with methods of establishing the construct validity of measures. Although such issues as observer bias and reactivity have been studied extensively, there nonetheless remain numerous other potential sources of method variance yet to be investigated. The existence of many unresolved conceptual and research issues suggests that far greater attention must be paid to the training of potential researchers in behavioral assessment.

REFERENCE NOTES

1. Linehan, M. M., & Glasser, J. *Effects of situational context on reported difficulty of assertive behavior*. Unpublished manuscript, Catholic University of America, 1975.
2. Galassi, J. P., & Galassi, M. D. *A factor analysis of a measure of assertiveness*. Unpublished manuscript, West Virginia University, 1973.

REFERENCES

American Psychological Association, American Educational Research Association, and National Council on Measurement in Education. *Standards for educational and psychological tests.* Washington, D.C.: American Psychological Association, 1974.

Arkowitz, H., Lichtenstein, E., McGovern, K., & Hines, P. The behavioral assessment of social competence in males. *Behavior Therapy*, 1975, **6,** 3–13.

Bem, D. J., & Allen, A. On predicting some of the people some of the time: The search for cross-situational consistencies in behavior. *Psychological Review*, 1974, **81,** 506–520.

Bernstein, D. A. Situational factors in behavioral fear assessment: A progress report. *Behavior Therapy*, 1973, **4,** 41–48.

Bernstein, D. A., & Nietzel, M. T. Procedural variation in behavioral avoidance tests. *Journal of Consulting and Clinical Psychology*, 1973, **41,** 165–174.

Bolstad, O. D., & Johnson, S. M. Self-regulations in the modification of disruptive classroom behavior. *Journal of Applied Behavior Analysis*, 1972, **5,** 443–454.

Borkovec, T. D., Stone, N. M., O'Brien, G. T., & Kaloupek, D. G. Identification and measurement of a clinically relevant target behavior for analogue outcome research. *Behavior Therapy*, 1974, **5,** 503–513.

Campbell, D. T., & Fiske, D. W. Convergent and discriminant validation by the multitrait-multimethod matrix. *Psychological Bulletin*, 1959, **56,** 81–105.

Cautela, J. R., & Kastenbaum, R. A reinforcement survey schedule for use in therapy training and research. *Psychological Reports*, 1967, **20,** 1115–1130.

Cone, J. D. The relevance of reliability and validity for behavioral assessment. *Behavior Therapy*, in press.

Cone, J. D., & Hawkins, R. P. (Eds.). *Behavioral assessment: New directions in clinical psychology.* New York: Brunner-Mazel, in press.

Dickson, C. R. Role of assessment in behavior therapy. In P. McReynolds (Ed.), *Advances in psychological assessment.* Vol. 3. San Francisco: Jossey-Bass, 1975.

Ebel, R. Must all tests be valid? *American Psychologist*, 1960, **15,** 546–553.

Eisler, R. M., Hersen, M., Miller, P. M., & Blanchard, E. B. Situational determinants of assertive behavior. *Journal of Consulting and Clinical Psychology*, 1975, **43,** 330–340.

Eisler, R. M., Miller, P. M., & Hersen, M. Components of assertive behavior. *Journal of Clinical Psychology*, 1973, **24,** 295–299.

Endler, N. S., Hunt, J. McV., & Rosenstein, A. J. An S–R Inventory of Anxiousness. *Psychological Monographs*, 1962, **76,** (17, Whole No. 536).

Endler, N. S., & Okada, M. A multidimensional measure of trait anxiety: The S–R Inventory of General Trait Anxiousness. *Journal of Consulting and Clinical Psychology*, 1975, **43,** 319–329.

Fixsen, D. L., Phillips, E. L., & Wolf, M. M. Achievement place: The reliability of self-reporting and peer-reporting and their effects on behavior. *Journal of Applied Behavior Analysis*, 1972, **5,** 19–30.

Flowers, J. V. Behavior modification of cheating in an elementary school student: A brief note. *Behavior Therapy*, 1972, **3,** 311–312.

Freedman, B. J. *An analysis of social-behavioral skill deficits in delinquent and nondelinquent adolescent boys.* Unpublished doctoral disseration, University of Wisconsin, 1974.

Galassi, J. P., DeLo, J. S., Galassi, M. D., & Bastien, S. The college self-expression scale: A measure of assertiveness. *Behavior Therapy*, 1974, **5**, 165–171.

Gambrill, E. D., & Richey, C. A. An assertion inventory for use in assessment and research. *Behavior Therapy*, 1975, **6**, 550–561.

Gay, M. L., Hollandsworth, J. G., & Galassi, J. P. An assertiveness inventory for adults. *Journal of Counseling Psychology*, 1975, **4**, 340–344.

Geer, J. H. The development of a scale to measure fear. *Behaviour Research and Therapy*, 1965, **13**, 45–53.

Goldfried, M. R. Behavioral assessment. In I. B. Weiner (Ed.), *Clinical methods in psychology*. New York: Wiley-Interscience, 1976.

Goldfried, M. R., & Davison, G. C. *Clinical behavior therapy*. New York: Holt, Rinehart, & Winston, 1976.

Goldfried, M. R., & D'Zurilla, T. J. A behavioral-analytic model for assessing competence. In C. D. Spielberger (Ed.), *Current topics in clinical and community psychology*, New York: Academic, 1969.

Goldfried, M. R., & Kent, R. N. Traditional versus behavioral personality assessment: A comparison of methodological and theoretical assumptions. *Psychological Bulletin*, 1972, **77**, 409–420.

Goldfried, M. R., & Pomeranz, D. M. Role of assessment in behavior modification. *Psychological Reports*, 1968, **23**, 75–87.

Goldfried, M. R., & Sprafkin, J. N. *Behavioral personality assessment*. Morristown, N. J.: General Learning Press, 1974.

Goldfried, M. R., Stricker, G., & Weiner, I. B. *Rorschach handbook of clinical and research applications*. Englewood Cliffs, N.J.: Prentice-Hall, 1971.

Goldsmith, J. B., & McFall, R. M. Development and evaluation of an interpersonal skill-training program for psychiatric inpatients. *Journal of Abnormal Psychology*, 1975, **84**, 51–58.

Hagen, R. L., Craighead, W. E., & Paul, G. L. Staff reactivity to evaluative behavioral observations. *Behavior Therapy*, 1975, **6**, 201–205.

Hastings, J. E. *Cardiac and cortical responses to affective stimuli in a reaction time task*. Unpublished doctoral dissertation, University of Wisconsin, 1971.

Hersen, M., & Bellack, A. (Eds.). *Behavioral assessment: A practical handbook*. New York: Pergamon, 1976.

Jeger, A. M., & Goldfried, M. R. A comparison of situation tests of speech anxiety. *Behavior Therapy*, 1976, **7**, 252–255.

Johnson, W. *People in quandaries*. New York: Harper & Row, 1946.

Johnson, S. M., & Bolstad, O. D. Reactivity to home observation: A comparison of audio recorded bevavior with observers present or absent. *Journal of Applied Behavioral Analysis*, 1975, **8**, 181–185.

Johnson, S. M., Christensen, A., & Bellamy, G. T. Evaluation of family intervention through unobtrusive audio recordings: Experiences in bugging children. *Journal of Applied Behavioral Analysis*, 1976, **9**, 213–219.

Jones, R. R., Reid, J. B., & Patterson, G. R. Naturalistic observation in clinical assessment. In P. McReynolds (Ed.), *Advances in psychological assessment*. Vol. 3. San Francisco: Jossey-Bass, 1975.

Kent, R. N., O'Leary, K. D., Diament, C., & Dietz, A. Expectation biases in observational evaluation of therapy change. *Journal of Consulting and Clinical Psychology*, 1974, **42,** 774–780.

Klorman, R., Weerts, T. C., Hastings, J. E., Melamed, B. G., & Lang, P. J. Psychometric description of some specific-fear questionnaires. *Behavior Therapy*, 1974, **5,** 401–409.

Lang, P. J. Fear reduction and fear behavior: Problems in treating a construct. In J. M. Shlien, H. F. Hunt, J. D. Matarazzo, & C. Savage (Eds.), *Research in psychotherapy*. Washington, D.C.: American Psychological Association, 1968.

Lang, P. J. The application of psychophysiological methods to the study of psychotherapy and behavior modification. In A. E. Bergin & S. L. Garfield (Eds.), *Handbook of psychotherapy and behavior change: An empirical analysis*. New York: Wiley, 1971.

Lang, P. J., Melamed, B. G., & Hart, J. A. A psychophysiological analysis of fear modification using an automated desensitization procedure. *Journal of Abnormal Psychology*, 1970, **76,** 220–234.

Libet, J. M., & Lewinsohn, P. M. Concept of social skill with special reference to the behavior of depressed persons. *Journal of Consulting and Clinical Psychology*, 1973, **40,** 304–312.

Linehan, M. M. The behavioral interview. In J. D. Cone and R. P. Hawkins (Eds.), *Behavioral assessment: New directions in clinical psychology*. New York: Brunner-Mazel, in press.

Lipinski, D. P. Black, J. L., Nelson, R. O., & Ciminero, A. R. The influence of motivational variables on the reactivity and reliability of self-recording. *Journal of Consulting and Clinical Psychology*, 1975, **43,** 637–646.

Lipinski, D. P. & Nelson, R. O. The reactivity and unreliability of self-recording. *Journal of Consulting and Clinical Psychology*, 1974, **42,** 118–123.

MacCorquodale, K., & Meehl, P. E. On a distinction between hypothetical constructs and intervening variables. *Psychological Review*, 1948, **55,** 95–107.

MacDonald, M. *A behavioral assessment methodology applied to the measurement of assertiveness*. Doctoral dissertation, University of Illinois, 1974.

MacPhillamy, D. J., & Lewinsohn, P. M. Measuring reinforcing events. *Proceedings of the 80th Annual Convention of the American Psychological Association*, 1972, **7,** 399–400. (Summary)

Mahoney, M. J., & Thoresen, C. E. *Self-control: Power to the person*. Monterey, Calif.: Brooks-Cole, 1974.

Mariotto, M. J., & Paul, G. L. A multimethod validation of the inpatient multidimensional psychiatric scale with chronically institutionalized patients. *Journal of Consulting and Clinical Psychology*, 1974, **42,** 497–508.

McFall, R. M., & Lillesand, D. B. Behavior rehearsal with modeling and coaching in assertion training. *Journal of Abnormal Psychology*, 1971, **77,** 313–323.

McFall, R. M., & Martson, A. An experimental investigation of behavior rehearsal in assertive training. *Journal of Abnormal Psychology*, 1970, **6,** 295–303.

McFall, R. M., & Twentyman, C. T. Four experiments in the relative contributions of rehearsal, modeling, and coaching to assertive training. *Journal of Abnormal Psychology*, 1973, **81,** 199–218.

McReynolds, P. (Ed.). *Advances in psychological assessment.* Vol. 3. San Francisco: Jossey-Bass, 1975.

Meichenbaum, D. H. A cognitive-behavior modification approach to assessment. In M. Hersen & Bellack (Eds.), *Behavioral assessment: A practical handbook.* New York: Pergamon, 1976.

Miller, B., & Bernstein, D. Instructional demand in a behavioral avoidance test for claustrophobic fears. *Journal of Abnormal Psychology*, 1972, **80,** 206–210.

Mischel, W. *Personality and assessment.* New York: Wiley, 1968.

Mischel, W. Toward a cognitive social learning reconceptualization of personality. *Psychological Review*, 1973, **80,** 252–283.

Moos, R. H. Behavioral effects of being observed: Reactions to a wireless radio transmitter. *Journal of Consulting and Clinical Psychology*, 1968, **32,** 383–388.

Nelson, R. O., Lipinski, D. P., & Black, J. L. The effects of expectancy on the reactivity of self-recording. *Behavior Therapy*, 1975, **6,** 337–349.

O'Leary, K. D , & Kent, R. N. Behavior modification for social action: Research tactics and problems. In L. Hamerlynck, L. C. Handy, & E. J. Mash (Eds.), *Behavior change: Methodology, concepts, and practice.* Champaign, Ill.: Research Press, 1973.

Patterson, G. R., Ray, R. S., Shaw, D. A., & Cobb, J. Manual for coding of family interactions, 1969. Available from ASIS/NAPS, c/o Microfiche publications, 305 E. 46th Street, New York, N.Y. 10017. Document —01234.

Paul, G. L. *Insight versus desensitization in psychotherapy.* Stanford: Stanford University Press, 1966.

Paul, G. L. Tobias, L. L., & Holly, B. L. Maintenance psychotropic drugs in the presence of active treatment programs: A "triple-blind" withdrawal study with long-term mental patients. *Archives of General Psychiatry*, 1972, **27,** 106–115.

Purcell, K., & Brady, K. Adaptation to the invasion of privacy: Monitoring behavior with a miniature radio transmitter. *Merrill-Palmer Quarterly of Behavior and Development*, 1966, **12,** 242–254.

Rabin, A. I. Projective methods: An historical introduction. In A. I. Rabin (Ed.), *Projective techniques in personality assessment.* New York: Springer, 1968.

Rathus, S. A. A 30-item schedule for assessing assertive behavior. *Behavior Therapy*, 1973, **4,** 398–406. (a)

Rathus, S. A. Instigation of assertive behavior through video-tape-mediated assertive models and directed practice. *Behaviour Research and Therapy*, 1973, **11,** 57–65. (b)

Redfield, J., & Paul, G. L. Bias in behavioral observation as a function of observer familiarity with subjects and typicality of behavior. *Journal of Consulting and Clinical Psychology*, 1976, **44,** 156.

Reid, J. B. Reliability assessment of observation data: A possible methodological problem. *Child Development*, 1970, **41,** 1143–1150.

Risley, T. R., & Hart, B. Developing correspondence between the non-verbal and verbal behavior of pre-school children. *Journal of Applied Behavior Analysis*, 1968, **1,** 267–281.

Romanczyk, R. G., Kent, R. N., Diament, C., & O'Leary, K. D. Measuring the reliability of observational data: A reactive process. *Journal of Applied Behavior Analysis*, 1973, **6,** 175–184.

Rosenthal, R. *Experimenter effects in behavioral research.* New York: Appleton-Century-Crofts, 1966.

Skinner, B. F. Are theories of learning necessary? *Psychological Review*, 1950, **57,** 193–216.

Smith, R. E., Diener, E., & Beaman, A. L. Demand characteristics and the behavioral avoidance measure of fear in behavior therapy analogue research. *Behavior Therapy*, 1974, **5,** 172–182.

Taplin, P. S., & Reid, J. B. Effects of instructional set and experimenter influence on observer reliability. *Child Development*, 1973, **44,** 547–554.

Wachtel, P. Psychodynamics, behavior therapy and the implacable experimenter: An inquiry into the consistency of personality. *Journal of Abnormal Psychology*, 1973, **82,** 324–334.

Wiggins, J. S. *Personality and prediction: Principles of personality assessment.* Reading, Mass.: Addison-Wesley, 1973.

Wolpe, J., & Lazarus, A. A. *Behavior therapy techniques.* New York: Pergamon, 1966.

CHAPTER 3

A Psychologically Based System of Response Classification

HENRY E. ADAMS, JOSEPH A. DOSTER, and KAREN S. CALHOUN

During a critical period of development, the advancement of psychology as a science is impeded by the absence of a comprehensive system of classification. In its place exists a multitude of antiquated, narrowly defined systems that service nearly as many theoretical models. The resulting state of affairs is one marked by controversy and conflict over explanatory theories when, in fact, there is varying consensus as to the basic, phenomenological units to which these theories apply. Already too much effort has been invested in buttressing or defending classificatory schemes that are widely recognized as grossly inadequate and ill conceived. In so doing, psychology has failed to confront the fundamental need of any science for a comprehensive system of classification that unifies and transcends specialty areas. Taxonomic theory provides clear and specific methodology for the establishment of systems of classification. Until agreement can be reached on basic units, scientific nomenclature, and eventually explanatory laws, psychology will continue to exist only as a poorly organized collection of observations, hypotheses, inferences, and opinions.

The first and fundamental step in the study of behavior, including abnormal behavior, is the grouping of observations into an organized scheme so as to make sense of the bewildering array of response patterns. Classification is the basis of any science because it is the process of identification of a phenomenon so that events can be measured and communication can occur between scientists and professionals. In the medical profession, for example, this process is called diagnosis. Diagnosis involves a system of taxonomy in which observations are gathered and judgments are made in order to place events into categories. Scientific classification schemes are the outcome of controlled observations or established general laws such as the Mendeleyev periodic table. A workable classification system evolves and develops through guesswork, hunches, and assumptions as research progresses. Indeed, the preliminary construction of class systems has contributed considerably to the discovery of new events as well as to theoretical development such as the discovery of new elements in the periodic table. In any case, during the early stages a classification scheme should be influenced by observations rather than theoretical postures.

It has been suggested that the classification or diagnosis of people and their behavior is unnecessary, harmful, and degrading. For example, Rogers (1951) states that categorizing people into preselected categories, which he views as arbitrary and unnatural, is unnecessary. He indicates that the causes of normal or abnormal behavior are certain perceptions or ways of perceiving present circumstances. Therefore, the individual is the only one who has the potential of knowing fully the dynamics of his perception and his behavior. Rogers also feels that by classifying or diagnosing an individual the clinician interferes with his communication with the individual and distorts the nature of the person. Consequently, classification is not conducive to knowledge or treatment, according to Rogers.

A similar argument against classification is the assumption that each individual or response pattern is unique—consequently, classification is a meaningless activity. Although both of these assumptions may be valid, any science, including psychology, searches for common elements in events in order to integrate these events into a conceptual scheme. A classification system is a conceptual model of the real world that ignores many unique features of responses or individuals. Whether a particular model is justified is determined by how accurately the model facilitates the prediction, control, or understanding of behavior.

Although there is validity to both Rogers' and the uniqueness positions, there is no logical alternative to classification. Classification involves discriminations between events, people, and behaviors. Language and communication are classification. When an individual makes an observation, judgment, or communication about an event, he is engaging in classification. Statements such as "He is tall," "She is attractive," "The professor is a poor teacher," "Bill is irresponsible," and similar judgments about people are classificatory statements at an informal level because they involve ordering events or people into categories. It is inappropriate or even impossible to eliminate all classification endeavors even though current classification schemes are unsatisfactory.

Classification is the first step in the measurement of an event. As a matter of fact, classification can be conceived of as a type of nominal scale where events are placed into different categories that are arbitrarily defined. Assessment comprises those activities that accomplish the classification enterprise by introducing the technology of measurement. Classification is a conceptual scheme of a particular aspect of the universe, and assessment is the practical and technical method of implementing such classification schemes.

The immediate purpose of classification is to develop a means of communication among scientists and/or among clinicians, whereas the long-range goal of classification is to provide a vehicle for research, particularly with regard to the understanding of parameters. In the initial stages, classification does not explain a phenomenon, it only identifies it. Nevertheless, classification is the first step in the growth of knowledge because phenomena must be defined before they can be investigated and understood. This chapter reviews briefly the criticisms of the psychiatric classification system of deviant behaviors, provides a survey of the principles of classification illustrating how the medical classification system of deviant behavior violates classification principles, proposes a behavioral classification system, and discusses the implications of the new system.

UTILITY OF THE AMERICAN PSYCHIATRIC ASSOCIATION CLASSIFICATION SYSTEM

The American Psychiatric Association classification system (DSM-II, 1968) has often been referred to as the "medical model of abnormal behavior." However, the similarities between the classification of physiological disorders used by physicians and psychological disorders used by psychiatrists may be more apparent than real. A diagnosis of a medical disorder is based on a deviation from normal physiological functioning. This deviation may be either a difference in degree (e.g., high blood pressure) or kind (e.g., ulcerative colitis). The point is that medical diagnosis is based on known norms of physiological functioning developed from a standard physiological classification system. A physician does not classify in terms of the individual but in terms of responses of a physiological system such as the cardiovascular system. An individual has dysuria; he is not a dysuric. Infrequently, we may find individuals referred to as diabetics, hemophiliacs, and so on. This slippage in referring to the person by his disease seems to occur more often when the disorder is chronic, persistent, incurable, and/or requires long-term monitoring and changes in the person's life style. Under these conditions and with time, it may very well seem to others that the person is his disease. Furthermore, an individual may have a disorder of the cardiovascular system, but this does not necessarily imply disorders of the nervous system, skeletal-motor system, or other physiological systems. Indeed, the strength of functioning of other physiological systems may influence treatment of the afflicted system. An individual may have several medical disorders, but the physician does not necessarily assume a common underlying cause. The psychiatric classification system uses the same terminology as the medical classification system but not the same principles of classification.

The first question in evaluating any classification scheme is the reliability of the system. In other words, are individuals or responses reliably placed into the correct categories? Can clinicians agree on this sorting? Numerous studies have investigated the reliability of the psychiatric classification system. Zubin (1967) has examined this question both in terms of consistency of diagnosis over time and the agreement between two or more clinicians. In both cases, there is usually moderate agreement (rarely above 80 percent) between raters when broader classes of disorders such as organic brain syndrome, functional psychoses, and neuroses are diagnosed. However, when specific categories within these broad classes are used, the agreements fall below 50 percent. Although the violation of a number of basic classification principles is responsible for this state of affairs, the particular violations ensuring low reliability are the use of overlapping and inadequately defined categories. Zigler and Phillip's (1961b) study of 793 patients clearly exemplifies the diagnostic dilemma created by traditional psychiatric nomenclature. Their results showed that patients who are assigned to different diagnostic categories frequently show the same symptomatology. Table 3–1 indicates that even purportedly salient symptoms of categories do not adequately discriminate them from other categories. Thus a patient's diagnosis reveals surprisingly little information about his behavior. Other evidence also demonstrates that an individual's particular symptoms (behavior) are not highly related to his diagnosis—a strange situation indeed (Zubin, 1967). Ward, Beck, Mendelson, Mock, and Erbaugh (1962) examined the causes of a diagnostic disagreement among four experienced psychiatrists on 40 of 75 cases. Five percent of the case disagreements were attributable to inconsistencies on the part of the patient's behavior from one interview to another. Inconsistent behavior on the part of the examiners accounted for 32.5 percent of case disagreements. Over half of this disagreement occurred because symptoms received different weights in the diagnostic decisions. A huge 62.5 percent of diagnostic disagreements occurred as a result of inadequacies in the psychiatric taxonomy. These inadequacies included overly specific categories for nonspecific case pictures, identifying a predominant category when several categories applied, and inadequate definition of criteria for diagnostic categories.

The lack of reliability of the psychiatric classification system also has been illustrated in research with individuals labeled as "schizophrenic." A recently published evaluation by NIMH (1974) of the studies concerned

Table 3–1. Percentage of individuals in total sample and in each diagnostic category manifesting each symptom (From E. Zigler and L. Phillips, Psychiatric diagnosis and symptomatology. *Journal of Abnormal and Social Psychology*, 1961, *63*, 69–75. Copyright (1961) by the American Psychological Association. Reprinted by permission.

Symptom	Total Hospital (N = 793)	Manic-Depressive (N = 75)	Psychoneurotic (N = 152)	Character Disorder (N = 279)	Schizophrenic (N = 287)
Depressed	38	64	58	31	28
Tense	37	32	46	33	36
Suspiciousness	35	25	16	17	65
Drinking	19	17	14	32	8
Hallucinations	19	11	4	12	35
Suicidal attempt	16	24	19	15	12
Suicidal ideas	15	29	23	15	8
Bodily complaints	15	21	21	5	19
Emotional outburst	14	17	12	18	9
Withdrawn	14	4	12	7	25
Perplexed	14	9	9	8	24
Assaultive	12	5	6	18	5
Self-depreciatory	12	16	16	8	13
Threatens assault	10	4	11	14	7
Sexual preoccupation	10	9	9	6	14
Maniacal outburst	9	11	6	7	12
Bizarre ideas	9	11	1	2	20
Robbery	8	0	3	18	3
Apathetic	8	8	8	4	11
Irresponsible behavior	7	3	7	9	7
Headaches	6	7	10	4	5
Perversions (except homosexuality)	5	0	5	10	2
Euphoria	5	17	2	2	5
Fears own hostile impulses	5	4	9	5	2
Mood swings	5	9	5	4	4
Insomnia	5	11	7	3	5
Psychosomatic disorders	4	7	6	3	5
Does not eat	4	9	4	2	4
Lying	3	0	1	7	0
Homosexuality	3	3	3	8	2
Rape	3	0	3	8	1
Obsessions	3	8	3	1	4
Depersonalization	3	4	1	0	6
Feels perverted	3	0	3	1	5
Phobias	2	4	5	0	2

with the diagnosis of schizophrenia suggests that the probability of bein diagnosed as schizophrenic is much higher in the United States than i other countries, varies from state to state, from hospital to hospital, be tween wards within the same hospital, or in the same situation over tim Apparently, the best predictor of whether an individual will be labele "schizophrenic" is where the clinician was trained and the nature of h theoretical orientation rather than the individual's behavior.

Although the behavior of the individual is of minor concern in dia nosis, it has been demonstrated (NIMH, 1974) that well-defined beha

ioral rating scales increase the accuracy of diagnosis. These scales probably have not been used because they do not agree with preconceived notions of clinicians about neurosis, psychosis, or other disorders, and these theoretical notions greatly vary.

As a matter of fact, within the medical classification system diagnosis itself seems to be highly related to local customs and conventions. Temerlin (1968) has demonstrated how this problem may develop. He made a sound-recorded tape of an interview between a psychiatrist and a supernormal man—a professional actor who was given the role of a man who had effective work habits and a good relationship with the interviewer; who was self-confident and secure without being arrogant, guarded, or grandiose; and who was heterosexual, married, and in love with his wife; and who consistently enjoyed sexual intercourse. The reason given for the interview was that the model was a physical scientist who had read a book about psychotherapy and wanted to discuss it with a psychiatrist. The tape was heard by psychiatrists, clinical psychologists, and graduate students who were then instructed to rate the individual being interviewed as psychotic, neurotic, or mentally healthy. A number of different conditions were given to various subgroups of these mental health professionals. In the first condition no suggestion was given as to the mental health of the individual, or the raters were told that they were listening to an employment interview. Even then one third of the raters indicated that the man was neurotic, but none indicated that he was psychotic. In the next condition a prestige figure gave a suggestion of mental health, resulting in 100 percent of the raters indicating that the individual was mentally healthy. When a prestige suggestion of psychosis or neurosis was given, the supernormal individual was consistently judged as psychotic or neurotic. This study illustrates that the set the clinician has before actually seeing a client frequently determines the diagnosis.

A related question is whether the presenting symptoms or a particular diagnosis are useful in the selection of a treatment program or other psychiatric decisions. For example, in medicine a diagnosis of acute appendicitis determines the physician's treatment plan—usually surgery. In psychiatry does a diagnosis of paranoid schizophrenia determine how the client's problem will be treated? According to Bannister, Salmon, and Leiberman (1964) the answer is no. Other investigators (Mendel & Rapport, 1969) have found that the severity of psychopathology is unrelated to the decision for psychiatric hospitalization. Their findings indicated that hospitalization was likely to occur if the person had a prior history of hospitalization and if he were seen for admission during hours other than the daytime shift (9:00 A.M. to 5:00 P.M.) or on weekend shifts. Persons with prior hospitalization or those who appeared on evenings or weekends

showed no greater severity of symptoms than their counterparts. Similarly, Wenger and Fletcher's (1969) survey of commitment hearings found that the absence of legal counsel at the hearing, rather than the person's behavior, was a substantial factor in decisions to admit the person to a state mental hospital. Contrary to the severity of symptoms portrayed in diagnostic categories involving psychosis or mental deficiency, Pfeiffer, Eisenstein, and Dobbs (1967) report that a surprisingly large percentage of patients with either diagnosis are judged competent to stand trial. Since clinical decisions such as correct treatment programs are among the major purposes of a classification system in abnormal psychology, it would appear that classification of individuals in the current classification system is largely meaningless.

The essence of the question regarding the American Psychiatric Association classification system is whether abnormal people can be distinguished from normal people or, as Rosenhan (1973) puts it, can the "sane be distinguished from the insane?" Rosenhan conducted a study in which eight "sane" people gained admission to twelve different hospitals solely by stating that they had heard voices. They exhibited no other unusual behavior. They mentioned hearing voices only until they had been admitted to the hospital. On admission all these cases, with the exception of one, were given the diagnosis of "schizophrenia." They were discharged with a diagnosis of "schizophrenia in remission." On no occasion were they ever detected by the professional staff as being other than real patients. They were suspected only by other patients, usually because the pseudopatients were taking notes of their experiences and observations. Notwithstanding the outraged responses in *Science* and the *Journal of Abnormal Psychology,* the results of the experiment seem clear—it is not possible to differentiate between individuals who are "sane" and those who are "insane" using the psychiatric classification system. In addition, Rosenhan demonstrated that, once labeled insane, other people's perception of the individual and his behavior changed. He noted that once a label was applied it was so powerful that many of the normal behaviors of a pseudopatient were overlooked entirely or profoundly misinterpreted. Apparently the psychiatric label has a life and influence of its own.

The consequences of a diagnosis using the current classification system has been frequently criticized as being a catastrophe to the individual. For example, Laing (1960) has stated that diagnostic labeling can be a dehumanizing and antitherapeutic activity which results in pernicious, self-fulfilling prophecies. Sarbin (1967) referred to this as a transformation of social identity associated with social degradation and a loss of status. Szasz (1966) discussed this problem in terms of an adverse exercise of illegal social power over individuals. Ullmann and Krasner (1969) also discussed the fact that labeling an individual as "mentally ill" is a way of maintaining social control and, once labeled, the individual is expected to behave in accordance with the psychiatric diagnosis. In essence, the consequences of the diagnostic enterprise can be described as attaching a stereotype to an individual and then forcing him to behave in accordance with the stereotype. This occurs in spite of the fact that, as Rosenhan (1973) has noted, psychiatric diagnosis may be in the mind of the observer and not in the characteristics of the behavior. The consequences of a psychiatric diagnostic label are so harmful to the individual that the only reasonable alternatives would appear to be to eliminate the classification system or to devise a better one.

PRINCIPLES OF CLASSIFICATION

Within the field of psychology is the unique situation of a scientist attempting to formally classify and explain an activity in which he is engaging and which occupies a significant niche within the domain of human behavior. Taxonomy, or the theory and method of classificatory construction, is a formalization of the behaviors that psychologists refer to as concept formation and linguistic representation. This formalization requires strict adherence to explicit methodology on the part of the taxonomist as he constructs a scientific classificatory system. The present section reviews the principles and procedures of taxonomy to illustrate the problems that confront taxonomists and the basis on which classificatory systems initially can be evaluated.

A fundamental assumption underlying the behavior of taxonomists is that differentiation and order exist in the sets of phenomena that are the particular domain of each field of science (Kety, 1965). To assume otherwise would limit the activities of scientists to observations of unique and random events. A belief in the natural order of phenomena must not be confused with the artificial representations or inventions of taxonomists that we call classificatory systems. Such devices are the theoretical constructions of a science and for any given phenomena there are many alternative systems by which the basic data may be organized. The evolution and acceptance of a classification scheme will depend on the technological advancement and available knowledge of a science, the purposes of the classifier and the utility of the system, and the eventual predictive and explanatory value of the system (Bruner, Goodnow, & Austin, 1965; Kelly, 1955; Plutchik, 1968).

Classification divides a specified set of phenomena into mutually exclusive and jointly exhaustive subsets. The specified set is the realm of events that a classificatory system defines for scientific investigation. The specified set also has been called the "focus and range of convenience" of a system (Kelly, 1955) or the "universe of discourse" (Hempel, 1959). The specification of set may involve any variable phenomena including animate or inanimate objects and abstract constructions (Hempel, 1959; Mayr, 1952). Thus the phenomena for classification may be insects, minerals, situations, or theories of personality. Finally, the specification of set establishes the range of events that is relevant to a system and defines unitarily the nature of events under investigation. For example, the specification of set as "political ideologies" limits the range of membership by excluding other ideologies—for example, religions—and unifies the mutually exclusive subsets of various political ideologies into one superordinate set.

Kraepelin's classificatory system, the precursor to the *Diagnostic and Statistical Manual* of the American Psychiatric Association, fulfilled this basic requirement of taxonomic method with his "diseases-in-man" definition for a universe of discourse. Specifically, to define the set as mental diseases afflicting people excludes nondisease phenomena while unifying the mutually exclusive subordinate types of mental disorders that are diagnosed for individual cases. Although lip service is still paid to the diseases-in-man model, and some (Ausubel, 1961) argue for a broader, more flexible definition of disease, a cursory observation of the DSM-II fails to suggest a unifying definition for the superordinate set. Within recent years the Kraepelinian system has had additions of subsets that are defined by personal values (e.g., the inadequate personality), environmental conditions (e.g., situational stress reactions), developmental events (e.g., reactions of adolescence), formal laws of a social system (e.g., dyssocial reaction), hypothetical personality traits (e.g., asthenic personality), the observable behavior of the case (e.g., runaway reaction), or causes of damage to the brain (e.g., meningococcal meningitis).

The development of a classificatory system begins with the construction of lower order categories of what Bruner et al. (1965) refer to as an "alpha taxonomy." This level of classification provides the basic terminology or the operational definitions of a science. The construction of alpha taxonomy requires a thorough description of the observable attributes of phenomena within the specified set (Bruner, Goodnow, & Austin, 1965; Kety, 1965; Mayr, 1952; Plutchik, 1968; Robbins, 1966; Stengel, 1959). Eventually a careful specification is made of the "intrinsic attribute properties" of phenomena that distinguish as many mutually exclusive subsets as is possible. The adequacy of care that is given to specifying the defining properties of subsets will directly affect the reliability of the system when applied. The homogeneity of subsets or their exclusiveness from one another rests in the decision processes of the taxonomist as he proposes the defining properties of each subset; it cannot be considered a result of the phenomena under investigation (Zigler & Phillips, 1961a). Developmentally, the construction of lower order categories defined by observable attributes precedes quantitative measurement (Eysenck, 1952) and the establishment of higher order categories whose classifying principles have an empirical or theoretical base (Bruner, Goodnow, & Austin, 1965; Hempel, 1959; Mayr, 1952).

A statement of the defining properties of subsets establishes which attributes at what values are necessary requirements for class membership. The definition of subsets at the alpha level of taxonomy can form either conjunctive or disjunctive categories. Unfortunately, the frequent choice of taxonomists in the behavioral sciences has been the disjunctive category, which largely contributes to the problems in diagnostic agreement or inter-rater reliability and, in turn, to the problems of validity and experimental replication. This is because membership in a disjunctive category (Bruner, Goodnow, & Austin, 1965) requires only that some of the attributes are present at some value in order that the phenomena be given membership. To understand more fully the implications that arise with use of disjunctive categories one may simply examine the defining properties of *Obsessive-Compulsive Neurosis* as given by the DSM-II (1968). This disorder is:

". . . characterized by the persistent intrusion of unwanted thoughts, urges, or actions that the patient is unable to stop. The thoughts may consist of single words or ideas, ruminations, or trains of thoughts often perceived by the patient as nonsensical. The actions vary from simple movements to complex rituals such as repeated handwashing. Anxiety and distress are often present either if the patient is prevented from completing his compulsive ritual or if he is concerned about being unable to control himself." (p. 40)

Membership in this category requires the presence of a thought, an urge, or an action, alone or in combination. A second requirement is that the presence of the event is unwanted by the patient. A third requirement is that the patient is unable to terminate the presence of the event. Fourth, there may or may not be present the patient's perception that the unwanted, unprevented thought is nonsensical. Whether the patient views his actions or urges as nonsensical has no relevance as a defining property of this category. Fifth, anxiety and distress may or may not be present depending on whether one or both of two conditions occur—the prevention of the action or concern about self-control. Three statements of attribute value also appear in the definition. They are "persistent," "single words—trains of thoughts," "simple movements—complex rituals." For the interested reader Table 3–2 indicates how 34 clearly discriminable attribute combinations occur that will meet membership requirements for the *Obsessive-Compulsive Neurosis* without regard for the value of attributes. The patient afflicted with only unwanted, unprevented actions occupies the same diagnostic category as the patient afflicted with unwanted, unprevented thoughts, perceived as nonsensical by him, and with anxiety elicited by concern over the loss of self-control. The burden placed on the diagnostician for deciding which of the attributes at what values must be present to warrant this diagnosis is apparent. Frequently, the presence of other attributes as symptoms results in a secondary diagnosis. With the possibility of thirty-four different clinical pictures (with other symptoms possibly present), there is highly undifferentiated or heterogeneous grouping of patients into one diagnostic category.

A solution to the arbitrariness of disjunctive categories is the statement of empirically derived rules that specify which intrinsic attribute properties are interchangeable and at what values. At present, this is typically an informal decision in which each diagnostician establishes his own rules for what is the necessary and sufficient condition for class membership. A less easily resolved problem is the heterogeneous nature of the category and the implications this has for research on etiology and treatment.

The alternative, and the ideal for scientific classification at the alpha level of taxonomy, is the conjunctive category. The construction of conjunctive categories (Bruner, Goodnow, & Austin, 1965) requires the joint occurrence of the specified attributes at specified values as the necessary and sufficient condition in order for a phenomenon to qualify for membership in that class. The absence of one or more attributes or a change in value of an attribute would disqualify the phenomenon from class membership.

For the purpose of demonstration, disregard the notion that we are classifying people and that the data language is ambiguous, and look at a statement of defining attributes approximating the conjunctive type of category:

"The compulsive neurosis is characterized by the persistent intrusion of unwanted actions that the patient is unable to stop. The actions may consist of simple or complex motor responses that are perceived by the patient as nonsensical. Anxiety and distress are present when the patient is prevented from completing his motor activity."

Such a definition gives a much more homogeneous grouping of patients, assuming that additional attributes or symptoms are irrelevant to diagnosis. Overlooking other features of the clinical picture often occurs so as to provide a tidy diagnosis—and this is not a violation of classificatory principles. The selection of relevant and irrelevant attributes of phenomena for

Table 3–2. Thirty-four Different Clusters of Symptoms Qualify for Membership in the Obsessive-Compulsive Disorder Based on the DSM-II Definition

Cluster Number	Persistent Intrusion of: Thoughts	Urges	Actions	Unwanted by Patient	Unable to Stop	Patient Perceives Thoughts as Non-sensical	Concern About Self-Control	Prevention of Ritual	Anxiety
1	+	−	−	+	+	+	−	0	−
2	+	−	−	+	+	+	+	0	+
3	+	−	−	+	+	−	−	0	−
4	+	−	−	+	+	−	+	0	+
5	−	+	−	+	+	0	−	0	−
6	−	+	−	+	+	0	+	0	+
7	−	−	+	+	+	0	−	+	+
8	−	−	+	+	+	0	−	−	−
9	−	−	+	+	+	0	+	+	+
10	−	−	+	+	+	0	+	−	+
11	+	+	−	+	+	+	−	0	−
12	+	+	−	+	+	+	+	0	+
13	+	+	−	+	+	−	−	0	−
14	+	+	−	+	+	−	+	0	+
15	+	−	+	+	+	+	−	+	+
16	+	−	+	+	+	+	−	−	−
17	+	−	+	+	+	+	+	+	+
18	+	−	+	+	+	+	+	−	+

19	+	−	+	+	+	−	+	−	+
20	+	−	+	+	+	−	+	+	+
21	+	−	+	+	+	−	−	+	+
22	+	−	+	+	+	−	−	−	−
23	−	+	+	+	+	0	+	−	+
24	−	+	+	+	+	0	+	+	+
25	−	+	+	+	+	0	−	+	+
26	−	+	+	+	+	0	−	−	−
27	+	+	+	+	+	+	+	−	+
28	+	+	+	+	+	+	+	+	+
29	+	+	+	+	+	+	−	+	+
30	+	+	+	+	+	+	−	−	−
31	+	+	+	+	+	−	+	−	+
32	+	+	+	+	+	−	+	+	+
33	+	+	+	+	+	−	−	+	+
34	+	+	+	+	+	−	−	−	−
Number of Clusters that Show Attribute	24	18	24	34	34	12	17	12	23

\+ Attribute Present
− Attribute Absent
0 Attribute Nonapplicable

defining a category and determining class membership is a decision of the taxonomist. The utility and validity of this decision must stand the test of empirical investigation.

There are several points that must be taken into account when establishing the defining properties of scientifically meaningful categories. First of all, formal statements of the observable attribute properties that are a necessary and sufficient condition for membership in classes are reached through scientific convention or agreement (Bruner, Goodnow, & Austin, 1965; Kety, 1965). Kety exhorts that the behavioral sciences follow the lead of biology by imposing similar strict standards that differentiate "valid phenomena and primary data" for classification from "inferences and hypotheses." Adherence to strict standards has not characterized the development of the DSM-II. Decisions about the existence and defining properties of mental disorders cannot continue to follow the whim of a majority, as with the in-out-in-again pattern of neurasthenic neurosis, or to be subject to sociopolitical pressures, as with homosexuality. When inferences define the properties of classes, the heuristic value of the system may be compromised. In other words, the inferred property explains itself rather than encourages the search for empirical evidence to substantiate the inference. Indeed, some definitions may limit investigation so as to find only supportive evidence. An example of this problem can be found in the widely adopted class of responses termed "self-stimulatory behavior." This class may include head banging, rocking, head swaying, and many others. A differentiation of behaviors that are not self-stimulatory is not clear. Nevertheless, theoretical inference (e.g., head banging is self-stimulating) is treated as an attribute property that both describes and explains head banging. This appears to be a conclusion based on predicate logic rather than scientific method. Self-stimulation is a behavior. Head banging is a behavior. Therefore, head banging is a self-stimulatory behavior.

A second point regarding the defining properties of categories, and one that is essential to any classificatory scheme, is that the properties are clearly defined so that they can be "reliably stated" and "uniformly applied" by others (Bruner, Goodnow, & Austin, 1965; Plutchik, 1968; Zigler & Phillips, 1961a). The clarity with which the defining properties of categories are stated can be no better than the adequacy of the language employed by a science to describe the phenomena. At alpha taxonomy, terms are selected from the scientific vocabulary that represent or describe those observable properties that distinguish members of one class from members of other classes. Both Robbins (1966) and Hempel (1959) note that the use of operational definitions for scientific terms has had wide support within the scientific community. However, Hempel (1959) qualifies his own endorsement of operationism by requiring that terms be admitted to scientific nomenclature that (1) need the performance of several different operations to define fully the property in question, or (2) represent directly observable properties that do not involve a testing procedure. In the earlier example of obsessive-compulsive neurosis, it was noted that "persistent" is an attribute value that enters into the diagnostic decision although the term fails to specify the frequency or the duration of an unwanted thought or action that justifies class membership. Similar imprecision is found in other psychological terms such as "unperceptive," "lack of or poor judgment," "constriction of interests," "poverty of thought," and the like. Some psychological terms denote different behavioral attributes. For example, irritability may define the reactivity of sensory receptors, designate an emotional state, or connote social behavior.

A third factor to be considered when constructing formal categories is what Bruner et al. (1965) refer to as the "degree of definingness" of an attribute. This is the degree to which a change in the value of an attribute affects a change in class membership. For example, intelligence is a defining attribute of the disorder *Mental Deficiency,* and changes in the value of this attribute affect the subclass to which a patient is assigned. The subclass *Mild Mental Deficiency* is defined by IQs of approximately 70 to 85, *Moderate Mental Deficiency* is defined by IQs of approximately 50 to 70, and *Severe Mental Deficiency* is defined by IQs below 50. Similar changes in values of attributes seem to differentiate *Manic Reaction* into the subclasses *Hypomania, Hypermania,* and *Delirous Mania.* The chronological age of a patient represents a critical value change of an attribute that distinguishes adjustment reactions of infancy, childhood, adolescence, and late life. However, in the latter two examples the specification of value in relationship to class membership is not as precise as in *Mental Deficiency.*

A fourth factor that needs attention in the statement of formal categories is the distinction between intrinsic attribute properties of classes and what Zigler and Phillips (1961a) refer to as "extraclassificatory attributes." The latter are phenomena that have been found empirically to correlate with the former. However, class correlates are not the equivalent of defining attributes and serve poorly in this role. One may consider, for example, the number of "personality trait" measures that correlate with the various psychophysiological and addictive disorders. The significant, but nevertheless low, relationships observed would not warrant the inclusion of personality traits as defining properties of these disorders. The likelihood of this type of error increases when disjunctive categories are defined. Class correlates have had frequent use as screening devices in making decisions about whether a more thorough assessment is advantageous to diagnosis. A patient who mispronounces "methodist episcopal" may be examined for general paresis. However, this mispronouncement is regarded as a correlated sign rather than a defining property of the disorder. Clearly, many other disorders may account for this mispronouncement so that its value as a screening device is quite limited, as most of these devices are. At alpha taxonomy the construction process involves the description of observable phenomena, and its purpose is to aid the search for empirical generalizations and, eventually, explanatory laws and theories. The value of extraclassificatory attributes lies in the information they add beyond the intrinsic attribute properties of classes, which in turn suggests inferences and hypotheses that, when explored empirically, may lead to general laws and theories.

With the establishment of explanatory laws and theories, there is a concurrent shift of emphasis in taxonomy from categories based on the intrinsic attribute properties of phenomena to a hierarchy of categories defined by abstract principles. Indeed, the position of several authors (Bruner et al., 1965; Hempel, 1959; Robbins, 1966; Stengel, 1959) either implicitly or explicitly stated has been that a true taxonomic system evolves only when superordinate categories are specified whose classifying principles are founded in a comprehensive system of explanatory laws or theories. Whereas the aim of alpha taxonomy is to distinguish as many subclasses as possible, at beta taxonomy (Bruner et al., 1965) the aim is to organize these subclasses into higher order categories on the basis of a relationship that applies uniformly to all members of a class (Bruner et al., 1965; Hempel, 1959; Mayr, 1952). The scientific terms selected to define categories at this level no longer refer to directly observable phenomena but rather to abstract processes.

The structure of categories at higher levels of systematization fits Bruner's (1965) definition of relational categories. These categories are somewhat more complicated than those previously mentioned, because their construction involves the specification of a relationship between defining properties. The necessary and sufficient condition for class membership is determined by the relationship between defining properties and is not based solely on their presence. Examples of relational categories derived from clinical research are those offered by Wolpe (1963) as proximation phobias and remoteness phobias. Diagnosis of proximation phobia is based on the relationship that anxiety increases as the distance from a feared object, situation, or person decreases. Diagnosis of remoteness phobia is determined by the relationship that anxiety increases as the distance from a safe point or person increases. Thus in both instances the presence of the defining properties of anxiety and stimulus does not satisfy the requirements for class membership. Wolpe reports that the two classes show different responses to desensitization treatment with respect to the patterning of progress.

An important notion to remember about classificatory systems is that the membership of superordinate categories will be heterogeneous in terms of the defining properties of their subclass members but uniform with respect to the principle that relates the defining properties (Zigler & Phillips, 1961a). Wolpe (1963) was able to subsume a number of specific and descriptively different types of phobias within each of his relational categories. The extent to which a classificatory system employs categories of this sort will depend on the status of laws and theories within a science to account for the phenomena that are their concern. On this matter of status, Kety (1965) is quite clear in his warning about theoretical inference and hypothesis and their specification prematurely as classifying principles. He states:

"A useful system of classification does not permit [incorporate] inferences which beg important questions and which it is the very purpose of the classification to help solve. An effective nosological system should stimulate inferences and aid in their testing but not incorporate them [as classifying principles] until they are established by accepted rules of scientific evidence." (p. 192)

ASSUMPTIONS AND AIMS

The first step in building a classification system that meets the stated criteria is the selection of phenomena to be classified. These should be simple, clearly definable, and readily agreed on as representing the field of study in question. The classification system proposed and presented by us (see Table 3–3) meets the basic requirements of taxonomic method and many other needs in our science. Psychology has been defined as the study of behavior and thus the phenomena of psychological classification are behaviors. This system is capable of classifying all behaviors, rather than merely listing all possible responses, which could not be exhaustive and probably would not be useful because of the lack of organization. We have chosen as a method of organizing behaviors a scheme of response systems similar to the classification system used in physiology. The system is called a Psychological Response Classification System (PRCS). Unlike the DSM-II, the proposed system classifies responses rather than people. By defining a unitary set of phenomena, the eliciting stimuli, responses to treatment, theoretical inferences, and so on have been placed in their proper perspective—as empirical questions or eventual explanatory laws. The PRCS does not try to solve the dilemma of the DSM-II by spelling out more specifically the combination of symptoms to be found in syn-

Table 3–3. Psychological Response Classification System

Response Systems	Definition	Response Categories	Definition
Motor	Activity of the muscles and glands involved in physical behavior but exclusive of the meaning or content of those activities	Oculo-motor Facial Throat Head Limb Trunk	
Perceptual	Activities involving detection, discrimination, and recognition of environmental stimuli	Visual Auditory Gustatory Vestibular Visceral Olfactory Kinesthetic Cutaneous	
Biological	Behaviors associated with basic body needs arising from specific biochemical conditions or unusually strong peripheral stimulation that can impair the well-being or health of the individual if not satisfied	Hunger Thirst Elimination Sex Sleep Respiration Harm avoidance	
		Acquired physical dependencies (intake of substances into the body that change the biochemistry of the physiological sys-	

		tems so that the presence of these substances are required to avoid physiological or psychological distress)	
Cognitive	Behaviors indicating the processing of information	Information selection	Attending, orienting, focusing, and scanning of internal and external stimuli
		Information retrievel	Behavior that indicates the reproduction of prior experiences with specific stimuli
		Conceptualization	Sorting and classification of information
		Reasoning	Deriving hypotheses from selected information
Emotional	Activity of tissues and organs innervated by the autonomic nervous system which is associated with specific behavior patterns and specific subjective experiences of the individual	Anxiety Euphoria Dysphoria Anger Affection	
Social	Reciprocal actions of two or more individuals	Coercive	Activities whose intent or effect is the coercion of another
		Coercion eliciting	Activities whose intent of effect is coercion by another

(*continued*)

Table 3-3 (Continued)

Response Systems	Definition	Response Categories	Definition
		Submissive	Activities whose intent or effect is compliance (coercion accepting) to another
		Submission resisting	Activities whose intent or effect resists compliance to another
		Nurturance	Activities whose intent or effect is extention of benefits to another
		Nurturance withholding	Activities whose intent or effect is the withholding of benefits from another
		Succorance	Activities whose intent or effect is reception of benefits from another
		Succorance-Refusing	Activities whose intent or effect is that of refusing benefits from another

dromes presumed to exist, or by empirical study of the correlates of symptomatic behavior (Zigler & Phillips, 1961a). The removal of the heterogeneity at the alpha level of taxonomy has responded to the needs of a science rather than to a particular theoretical posture. This system encourages the empirical investigation of theoretical disagreements rather than obscuring or excluding them.

There are several advantages to such a system. Not only is it simple, coherent, and exhaustive (capable of handling all potential, operationally defined responses), but it excludes intervening variables and is relatively theory free. The response systems used are based on those informal areas that have become differentiated in psychology as the field has developed. These seem to have been useful distinctions in the study of behavior. The system is based on observation rather than inference, thus providing a format through which those in various areas can communicate and also a basis upon which correlational and theoretical developments can be made (beta level taxonomy). It is equally suitable for all theories (e.g., psychopathology, personality) to use as a base of phenomena, rather than having one theory defining a set of phenomena convenient only to that theory. Thus individuals of different theoretical persuasions can better communicate. The system is open-ended and allows a flexibility not approached by the disease model of abnormal behavior. New data can be incorporated with ease as better organization and definitions become available through research.

The proposed system has several specific aims. One is to take arbitrary assumptions regarding distinctions between normal and abnormal responses out of the alpha level of classification. Unless it is empirically demonstrated to be otherwise, abnormal behavior is considered to be an extension of normal behavior and similar in kind. Many difficulties have arisen from attempts to classify "symptoms" as distinct from nonsymptomatic behavior. It is not the proper role of an alpha level classification scheme to make value statements about what is normal and abnormal. Abnormal behavior can be defined only in the context of what is normal, which is an empirical question.

Terminology of the PRCS

If the study of behavior is to progress, consistency must be reached in the scientific labels applied to psychological phenomena. One of the major aims of the proposed system is to facilitate the application of the labeling process to behaviors rather than to individuals. The dehumanizing labeling effect of classification systems has been severely criticized by those of many widely diverse theoretical backgrounds and has been the impetus for suggestions that the process of classification be abandoned entirely. By making it clear that only specific responses are being labeled in nonevaluative terms, rather than the entire individual cast as schizophrenic, phobic, or whatever, the necessary process of classification is made both more useful and more humane.

The Heuristic Value of the PRCS

An additional aim of the proposed classification system is to differentiate the definitions of observations from their measurement and explanations. The confusion of these elements characterizes the DSM-II categories with the exception of *Mental Deficiency.* The definitions of phenomena to be observed must be such that most workers in the field can agree on them and use them as a basis for further study. The suggested system consists of phenomena for which definitions have largely been developed and agreed upon in prior work. In some cases, much work has gone into observation and measurement of the parameters of these behaviors which can be incorporated into the development of norms and the search for intercorrelations. The assessment of these responses will necessarily involve measurement along five major parameters: frequency, amplitude, duration, latency, and threshold. These parameters should not be confused with assessment instruments. Assessment involves the practical and technical methods of implementing classification. Greater precision in description is also offered by this approach. Organized in this way, the system indicates deficiencies in the knowledge of certain areas that have been obscured in the past by armchair approaches. Thus it is to be expected that technological advancement in measurement and assessment will be stimulated.

This system is proposed as a starting point, not an end. It is not assumed that response systems are either related or independent, since this is an empirical question. These relationships must be investigated in order to progress to the beta level of taxonomy, which may change the direction of research in abnormal behavior. Much research effort has been wasted in attempts to differentiate groups on the basis of different diagnostic labels. It should be much more fruitful to look instead at specific disturbances of response patterns and examine their etiology, correlates, and modification.

Discussion

Many months ago during a lunchtime conversation the three of us happened on the topic of a recent text on abnormal psychology that purported to emphasize a psychological approach. We were dismayed to note that the text proceeded from a scathing criticism of the DSM-II to adopting the system as a method for organizing the research literature. This is but another example of psychologists' inability or unwillingness to rid their science of the nemesis of the mental disease concept. As psychology has attempted to establish itself as an independent discipline—and succeeded —we have largely ignored the data base on which to build our science. The most salient reason that we could find or others have given for retaining the DSM-II is the void that would remain by its absence. Ausubel (1961) implied a return to the Dark Ages should we abandon the DSM-II disease concept. The issue then is whether psychology as a science is capable of filling this void. From our deliberations then and now we believe the answer to be yes. Psychologists in a quasiformal manner have divided the study of behavior into categories and subcategories producing sufficient information on which to develop a formal taxonomy.

It should be emphasized that the PRCS is not a finished product, but it is our contention that the principles applied should be used in developing a behavior classification system. We experienced a great deal of difficulty in agreement about operational definitions of the categories and subcategories of the cognitive and the social response systems. Other definitions, such as the biological and perceptual response systems, were somewhat easier and, in the case of some of the subcategories, were fairly obvious. For that reason, some of the subcategories in Table 3–3 were not operationally defined. A major problem was whether subsystems should be defined as unipolar or bipolar constructs. In other words, are elation and depression two opposite anchoring points of a single dimension of behavior or two separate dimensions of behavior? It was decided to use unipolar constructs rather than bipolar constructs because this allows for empirical answers to these questions. In any case, the classification system can be improved by more creative thinking, systematic observation, or empirical evidence on these issues.

To be meaningful, classification must indicate appropriate methods of measurement. In the present classification system, it is obvious that an evaluation of an individual's behavior cannot be accomplished with global assessment instruments such as the Rorschach or the Minnesota Multiphasic Personality Inventory. Appropriate clinical assessment requires a stimulus complex, response measures, and, in some cases, indices of the consequences of behavior. A major reason that empirical or behavioral assessment has been and will be more successful than traditional clinical assessment is the concern with eliciting stimuli in the assessment process. For this reason, modern clinical assessment would be wise to attend to the procedures and laws developed in psychophysics.

Stimuli are independent variables that must be manipulated along some stimulus dimension in order to observe changes in behavior. This procedure will require, in the long run, more formal classification of simple and complex stimulus patterns, independent of the classification of behavior. The classification of stimuli should be in terms of the physical dimensions of stimulus complexes. This topic has been discussed in detail by Bowers (1973) and Mischel (1968). In any case, it is logical to assume that the appropriate stimuli to assess sexual behavior should be erotic stimuli rather than inkblots. In a similar manner, one would not attempt to assess audition by varying temperature. Nevertheless, a decision that behavior is maladaptive may be based on the fact that responses are elicited by stimuli that do not ordinarily cause such behavior or vice versa. Examples are anxiety about heights or sexual responses to chickens. This type of behavior may be a function of either a decreased response threshold or increased response amplitude.

The dependent variable in behavior assessment is the response pattern. Response patterns should be evaluated in terms of the characteristics of measurement. In other words, the parameters of measurement are the frequency, amplitude, duration, latency, and threshold of the responses. Only if a response category or subcategory is delineated in accepted units of measurement will it be meaningful as a vehicle for communication and research among behavioral scientists.

Theoretically, it is desirable to have indices of all three channels of behavior assessment (i.e., self-report, behavioral observations, and physiological indices). It is always a happy occasion when all three indices indicate a similar conclusion, but it is not unusual for this not to be the case. There are a number of reasons for these discrepancies, some of which will be illustrated in later chapters. These discrepancies in response measure should not always be considered error variance. As a matter of fact, discrepancies between the three channels of measures may provide a valuable source of information and reflect intrinsic rather than extrinsic variance. One example is the individual who attempts to avoid social situations. On assessment it may be determined that the individual reports concern about interacting with groups and demonstrates behavioral avoidance but has no significant change in autonomic nervous system indices. A closer examination may reveal that this individual is not a social phobic but an individual who has deficits in social skills, a finding first indicated by a lack of extreme arousal in social situations.

Although it is desirable to utilize all three indices, in the case of some response systems one index is more important than another. For example, in the cognitive response system, self-report indices are crucial, whereas physiological indices are not available or not well understood. However, this state of affairs is rapidly changing. For example, Livanov (1962) observed the pair synchronization of biopotentials of human brain cortex during states of rest and mental work. While the subject was sitting at rest, results showed the regions of the brain to be uncoupled or substantially undifferentiated. Widespread coupling or synchronization of activity among regions occurred after a mental task was presented and during the interval of problem solving. Following the solution of the problem, cortical activity returned to the resting state. The findings of Aslanov (1970) with an obsessive-compulsive patient and of Gavrilova (1970) with a schizophrenic patient show greater synchronization of cortical activity than is expected or found among normals during the resting state.

Investigation of the consequences of a response is technically an inquiry about the cause of behavior. As a result, consequences of a response when included in assessment and classification of behavior beg the question of etiology, as noted by Kety (1965). The consequences of behavior are either associated with the development and maintenance of a response pattern or the maintenance of a response that has been initiated by other events (i.e., secondary gains). An example of the former is the phobia and of the latter, the conversion reaction, as described by Brady and Lind (1961). Although the clinician or researcher may assess behavior and its consequences concurrently, conceptually these events must be differentiated. Every clinician or researcher has certain theoretical positions or hypotheses about events that give rise to, maintain, or are the consequences of behavior. To evaluate these hypotheses, intuitions, or hunches with confidence, the clinician must conceptually differentiate these events from the behavior itself. By so doing, a variety of hypotheses—whether they represent different professional opinions or paradigmatic differences—can be systematically tested. As there should be a classification system for behavior, so should there be independent classifications of stimulus patterns and of causal factors, such as proposed by Hebb (1966). Independent classification systems for the three different types of phenomena (i.e., stimulus events, behavioral events, and consequences) are necessary to objectively generate knowledge about behavior.

THE STATISTICAL APPROACH TO ABNORMAL BEHAVIOR

There are two major methods of empirically developing criteria for accurately identifying abnormal behavior: extreme variation from typical behavior in a single response, and response clusters that differ in kind from those ordinarily observed in the majority of the population. In the first case a prerequisite is the development of norms including between-subjects and within-subject variations from which the population parameters of various categories and subcategories of response systems are determined. This approach would be similar to methods used in developing standards for intellectual performance or other psychological tests. However, in the present system the assumption should not be made that behavior is independent of the situation. In other words, situations are manipulated rather than held constant in order to observe changes in behavior. Behavior of a given individual should be evaluated as a function of relevant events as well as compared to the behavior of others. The method for developing norms should be based on single case designs (i.e., an individual's responses to various stimulus situations) replicated across a representative sample of the population. In addition, it must also be demonstrated that extremes of such behavior patterns are associated with extra-class correlates that are maladaptive or handicapping to the individual. To use another analogy, norms of blood pressure are known. Extremes of blood pressure (i.e., essential hypertension) are associated with malfunction of the individual's physiology and resulting handicaps for the person. In this case, there is a variation in degree of cardiovascular function rather than in kind, which may be associated with development of more severe physiological disorders (i.e., extra-class correlates).

The second class of abnormal behavior is functional clusters of responses not ordinarily observed in other individuals. Three criteria are necessary for establishing functional clusters, which can be considered relational categories. These criteria are: (1) simultaneous or consecutive variations in two or more response patterns; (2) covariation of responses rather than functionally independent multiple target behaviors; and (3) extra-class correlates that indicate such behavior patterns handicap or impair psychological functioning. The first two criteria establish the existence of the phenomenon, and the third criterion establishes the validity of the concept. In establishing norms for the functional clusters of responses, it must be determined that this class of behavior is not typically observed in the majority of people. The approach to establishing such categories would be multivariate analysis or multiple baseline designs across situations with the purpose of establishing that responses are related rather than independent. An example of such a relational class was noted by Wahler (1975) who found covariation within children's behavioral repertoires that were extremely stable over time and could be used to characterize each child. He also found that these behavior clusters were situation specific and that if a child was considered deviant in a setting, his problem behavior *always appeared in the obtained behavioral cluster*. Barlow (1974) made a similar observation in the case of a transsexual who exhibited gender role deviation, homosexual arousal, and an absence of heterosexual arousal. Initial treatment procedures to increase heterosexual arousal and decrease homosexual arousal failed. A successful treatment program was then carried out to increase male gender role behaviors. The treatment program for heterosexual arousal was then reinstigated and resulted in further increases in masculine role behavior, although no therapeutic attempt to accomplish this goal was being used at that time. Both of these studies illustrate that, in the case of specific problem behaviors, there are responses that covary and can be used to define such disorders. Furthermore, attempting to modify one of these responses may be unsuccessful if the prime response is not manipulated, since changes in the prime response elicit change in secondary responses. As Wahler (1975) noted, changes in the secondary responses may be desirable or undesirable, which raises the issue of positive and negative side effects of treatment programs. In addition the behavior labeled as a problem behavior may be a covariate of other responses and could be more readily changed by what Wahler calls "indirect modification."

With regard to traditional psychiatric disorders such as schizophrenia, to establish the validity of the concept, it must be demonstrated that responses such as associative difficulties, autism, ambivalence, and affect disorders covary to cause gross psychological impairment. The existence of schizophrenia as a phenomenon must be empirically established. The current confusion about schizophrenia may be because it has not been empirically demonstrated that such a phenomenon exists, resulting in a questionable basis for research into etiology and treatment methods. Perhaps the most frequent and unproductive quest in experimental psychopathology is the search for behavioral, etiological, and prognostic correlates of traditional psychiatric syndromes. Although the results may often show statistically significant differences between groups, the contribution or meaningfulness of these differences to psychological knowledge is a separate issue. The point is aptly made by Payne (1960) when he states:

> ". . . there has been an extremely unfortunate tendency for psychologists to regard psychiatric diagnostic labels as of fundamental importance to a scientific analysis of mental abnormality. Countless studies attempt to find objective correlates of these labels. Thus, instead of investigating, for example, the nature and causes of slowness of problem-solving a psychological variable which can be accurately defined and measured, and clearly related to other psychological variables, psychologists have concerned themselves with investigating the performance on batteries of tests individuals whom psychologists have labelled 'schizophrenic.'" (p. 196)

This is not to say that the concept of syndrome is meaningless but rather that the establishment of syndromes requires a different experimental approach. For example, research may show more frequent incidences of autistic thinking among a schizophrenic group than a nonpatient group. The statistical difference may indicate also that the use of autistic thinking as a diagnostic sign yields undesirably high rates of false positives and false negatives. The consequences of redistributing patient and nonpatient subjects into groups that are defined by the presence and absence of autistic thinking and that are then compared on other attributes is that a substantial gain of information may be made about autistic behavior. When and if we gain confidence in our knowledge of psychological concepts such as association, autism, ambivalence, and affect, we can then investigate their conjoint effect as a syndrome. However, if the patient group is constituted in such a way that there is a 52 percent incidence of associative difficulties, a 38 percent incidence of autism, a 14 percent incidence of ambivalence, and a 75 percent incidence of affective disturbance, then results will probably yield poor answers to otherwise good questions.

PRACTICAL IMPLICATIONS

Thus far in this chapter we have emphasized the potential contributions of the PRCS to theoretical and empirical advancements, giving a perhaps unintended impression that the practical advantages of the system are yet to develop. The mental health professionals reasonably may inquire, "Why should I go beyond a description or labeling of presenting complaints, symptoms, or targeted behaviors to classify these phenomena when, by its infancy and tentativeness, the PRCS seems to offer no more utility than the DSM-II?" From a preliminary search of our case experiences and the literature of abnormal psychology, we find that classification on the basis of the PRCS has a number of interesting results.

Many of the behaviors that we encountered in our clinic cases or from published case studies were assigned effortlessly to the categories and subcategories of the PRCS. A number of terms that denote abnormal behavior also denote normal behavior (e.g., giggling). However, in the abnormal literature such terms appear with qualifiers such as inappropriate, insufficient, inadequate, persistent, pervasive. There are also a number of formal terms (e.g., hyperesthesia) that suitably denote systems (e.g., perceptual) and subsystems (e.g., cutaneous). Usually the prefix of these terms qualifies the deviancy of the behavior.

Psychologists have differentiated and elaborated the behaviors of categories and subcategories in unequal proportions. For example, the literature abounds with research on anxiety or depression, but an article on affection is a rare one indeed. A substantial number of psychological terms, although popular in usage, seem to obfuscate important assessment questions. Clinical labels such as overinclusiveness, rumination, poverty of thought, or impaired judgment can each describe several different behaviors that belong to different subcategories of the Cognitive Response system. The PRCS requires more elaborate specification of behavior and thus more incisive evaluation on the part of the assessor. The client who reportedly has "poor judgment" on closer examination may show deviations of reasoning or of information selection.

In addition to the assignment of behaviors to appropriate categories on the basis of their attribute properties, the PRCS requires finer descriptions of the attribute values of these behaviors. The qualifications of a person's anger as overreactive or inappropriate conveys little information about the evaluator's observations. The clinical judgment may be based on what seems to be too low a threshold for the emotional response relative to the stimulus situation, too great an amplitude of the emotional response, or an inordinately long duration of responding.

The PRCS also encourages the clinician to establish the presence or absence of relationships between subcategories of the same or different response systems for each client. For example, an individual who complains of persistent, uncontrollable, and unwanted thoughts about bodily odors may seem a likely candidate for a DSM-II diagnosis of *Obsessive-Compulsive Reaction.* Security in this clinical impression may increase with the knowledge that the client bathes and changes to clean clothes with reasonable or more than reasonable frequency and has no bodily odors that are detectable to the examiner. Both client and therapist may conclude that the worry is nonsensical and proceed with treatment of a cognitive disorder. Although assessment may adequately evaluate whether the person fulfills the requirements for membership in a DSM-II category, nevertheless, assessment may be incomplete with respect to the client's complaint. Assessment of the perceptual response system of olfaction with an olfactometer may find hyperosmia (low threshold) on the part of the client to certain or many odors. This would not be an unlikely occurrence if the client were female, since females tend to be more sensitive to odors.

The PRCS parallels a current trend in the literature of experimental psychopathology and treatment methodology. With increasing frequency researchers compare and report on the relative success of treatment with adequately described, observable behaviors. The effect of this trend is the recent growth of innovative methods in clinical assessment and treatment that complement the PRCS but detract from whatever is the utility of the DSM-II.

To recapitulate our points, the utility of the PRCS in clinical practice is that:

1. It allows the clinician an opportunity to test the degree of definingness of the popular data language of psychology.

2. It shows that many psychological terms or concepts must be replaced or defined further so as not to obscure important diagnostic differences or produce ambiguous professional communication.

3. It makes the presence or absence of relationships among response syndromes a clinical decision based on case observation rather than a theoretical assumption.

4. It provides the clinician with a convenient model by which to organize and evaluate the usefulness of various assessment devices and treatment methodologies that are relevant to each response system and subsystem.

5. It reflects the progress or lack of progress of psychology with respect to the generation of information pertinent to response systems and subsystems.

In conclusion, several points should be made about classification systems, including the present one. A classification system should not impose inferences about etiology or appropriate treatment methods. However, a classification system of behavior is a necessary prerequisite for such inquiries. An adequate classification initially requires some theoretical assumption following the principles of classification, then a massive empirical research effort to expand, develop, revise, or discard the system. Until an adequate classification system for behavior is developed, the current confusion regarding abnormal and normal behavior will persist.

REFERENCES

American Psychiatric Association. *Diagnostic and statistical manual of mental disorders* (2nd ed.). Washington, D.C.: American Psychiatric Association 1968.

Aslanov, A. S. Correlation between cortical potentials in patients with obsessive neuroses. In V. S. Rusinov (Ed.), *Electrophysiology of the central nervous system*. New York: Plenum, 1970.

Ausubel, D. P. Personality disorder *is* disease. *American Psychologist*, 1961, **16,** 69–74.

Bannister, D., Salmon, P., & Leiberman, D. M. Diagnosis-treatment relationships in psychiatry: A statistical analysis. *British Journal of Psychiatry*, 1964, **110,** 726–732.

Barlow, D. H. The treatment of sexual deviation: Toward a comprehensive behavioral approach. In K. S. Calhoun, H. E. Adams, & K. M. Mitchell (Eds.), *Innovative treatment methods in psychopathology*. New York: Wiley, 1974.

Bowers, K. S. Situationalism in psychology: An analysis and a critique. *Psychological Review*, 1973, **80,** 307–336.

Brady, J. P. & Lind, D. L. Experimental analysis of hysterical blindness. *Archives of General Psychiatry*, 1961, **4,** 331–339.

Bruner, J. W., Goodnow, J. J., & Austin, G. A. *A study of thinking.* New York: Science Editions, 1965.

Eysenck, H. *The scientific study of personality.* London: Routledge & Kegan Paul, 1952.

Gavrilova, N. W. Spatial synchronization of cortical potentials in patients with disturbances of association. In V. S. Rusinov (Ed.), *Electrophysiology of the central nervous system.* New York: Plenum, 1970.

Hebb, D. O. *A textbook of psychology.* Philadelphia: Saunders, 1966.

Hempel, C. G. Introduction to problems of taxonomy. In J. Zubin (Ed.), *Field studies in the mental disorders.* New York: Grune & Stratton, 1959.

Kèlly, G. A. *A theory of personality: The psychology of personal constructs.* New York: Norton, 1955.

Kety, S. S. Problems in psychiatric nosology from the viewpoint of the biological sciences. In M. M. Katz, J. O. Cole, & W. E. Barton (Eds.), *The Role and methodology of classification in psychiatry and psychopathology.* Chevy Chase, Md.: National Institute of Mental Health, 1965.

Laing, R. D. *The divided self: A study of sanity and madness.* Chicago: Quadrangle, 1960.

Livanov, M. W. Information processing in the nervous system. In *Proceedings of the 22nd International Congress of Psychological Science*, Leiden, Amsterdam: Excerpta Medica Foundation, 1962.

Mayr, E. Concepts of classification and nomenclature in higher organisms and microorganisms. *Annals of the New York Academy of Science*, 1952, **56,** 391–397.

Mendel, W. M., & Rapport, S. Determinants of the decision for psyçhiatric hospitalization. *Archives of General Psychiatry*, 1969, **20,** 321–328.

Mischel, W. *Personality and assessment.* New York: Wiley, 1968.

National Institute of Mental Health, *Schizophrenia Bulletin, Issue No. 11*, Washington, D.C.: Government Printing Office, 1974.

Payne, R. W. Cognitive abnormalities. In H. J. Eysenck (Ed.), *Handbook of abnormal phychology.* New York: Basic Books, 1960.

Pfeiffer, E., Eisenstein, R. B., & Dobbs, E. G. Mental competency evaluation for the federal courts: I. Methods and results. *Journal of Nervous and Mental Diseases*, 1967, **144,** 320–328.

Plutchik, R. *Foundations of experimental research.* New York: Harper & Row, 1968.

Robbins, L. L. A historical review of classification of behavior disorders and one current perspective. In L. D. Eron (Ed.), *The classification of behavior disorders.* Chicago: Aldine, 1966.

Rogers, C. R. *Client-centered therapy.* Boston: Houghton Mifflin, 1951.

Rosenhan, D. L. On being sane in insane places. *Science*, 1973, **183,** 250–257.

Sarbin, T. R. On the futility of the proposition that some people can be labeled "mentally ill." *Journal of Consulting Psychology*, 1967, **31,** 447–453.

Stengel, E. Classification of mental disorders. *Bulletin of the World Health Organization*, 1959, **21,** 601–663.

Szasz, T. S. The psychiatric classification of behavior: A strategy of personal constraint. In L. D. Eron (Ed)., *The classification of behavior disorders*. Chicago: Aldine, 1966.

Temerlin, M. K. Suggestion effects in psychiatric diagnosis. *Journal of Nervous and Mental Disease*, 1968, **147,** 349–353.

Ullmann, L. P., & Krasner, L. *A psychological approach to abnormal behavior*. Englewood Cliffs, N.J.: Prentice-Hall, 1969.

Wahler, R. G. Some structural aspects of deviant child behavior. *Journal of Applied Behavior Analysis*, 1975, **8,** 27–42.

Ward, C. H., Beck, A. T., Mendelson, M., Mock, J. E., & Erbough, J. K. The psychiatric nomenclature. *Archives of General Psychiatry*, 1962, **7,** 198–205.

Wenger, D. L., & Fletcher, C. R. The effects of legal counsel on admissions to a state hospital: A confrontation of professions. *Journal of Health and Human Behavior*, 1969, **10,** 66–72.

Wolpe, J. Quantitative relationships in the systematic desensitization of phobias. *American Journal of Psychiatry*, 1963, **119,** 1062–1068.

Zigler, E., & Phillips, L. Psychiatric diagnosis and symptomatology. *Journal of Abnormal and Social Psychology*, 1961, **63,** 69–75. (a)

Zigler, E., & Phillips, L. Psychiatric diagnosis: A critique. *Journal of Abnormal and Social Psychology*, 1961, **63,** 607–618. (b)

Zubin, L. Classification of the behavior disorders. *Annual Review of Psychology*, 1967, **18,** 373–406.

CHAPTER 4

Instrumentation for Behavioral Assessment

JOHN D. RUGH and ROBERT L. SCHWITZGEBEL

Human sensory abilities allow observation of only a small fraction of the stimuli or energy in our environment. The eye, for example, is capable of detecting only an extremely small portion (0.000,000,09 percent) of the light energy (electromagnetic radiation) that surrounds us. Likewise our hearing, taste, and smell are limited to sampling only an incredibly small portion of physical events. Aside from the limitations in bandwidths of stimuli that can be perceived, the human sensory system is limited in sensitivity and discriminability. Physical stimuli of insufficient amplitude will go unnoticed. Similarly, stimuli that do not differ by a minimal quanta will not be differentiated.

Even when the energy of a stimulus is within the spectrum and of an intensity that is detectable, the human sensory system cannot always be relied on to provide an "accurate" description of a physical phenomenon. Our perceptions are subject to a variety of biases. The extensive literature on perceptual illusions, sensory adaptation, perceptual defense, habituation, signal processing, memory, and response bias demonstrate that the human being is a unique and limited instrument for recording physical events.

Certain frailties of the human perceptual system have been compensated for by human creativity in the form of technology. Sensory instrumentation has been developed to extend the accuracy and range of our observations. Weight, time, and motion can be measured with increasing precision and repeatability—for example, it is now possible to measure events that are only 10^{-16} of a second apart (Cannon & Jensen, 1975).

The preparation of this chapter was supported in part by NIH research grant No. 5 RO1 MH20315, awarded by the National Institute of Mental Health, PHS/DHEW.

The application of instrumentation specifically to the study of human behavior has been a relatively recent undertaking. Instrumentation in both the psychology clinic and the laboratory is still at a relatively primitive level compared to that in the physical sciences and in medical practice. Part of the lack of technological sophistication in psychology is due to the widespread belief that variables of interest to psychology are not subject to direct physical measurement. Such concepts as *ego strength* and *drive* are admittedly not subject to direct observation even with the most sophisticated instrument. Considerable debate properly continues over which concepts are of most value in understanding human behavior. There has been a recent trend, however, away from abstract concepts with no physical correlates to visually observable behavioral patterns, stimulus situations, and response topographies. Bachrach (1962), for example, has suggested that all psychological measurements must ultimately have some physical referent. Furthermore, he asserted that phenomena that cannot be physically measured should not be considered as scientific data.

Obviously the role of instrumentation in psychology will continue to depend on the discipline's conceptualization of its professional tasks and related methodologies. Behavioralists, psychophysiologists, and physiological psychologists who have concerned themselves with the manipulation of stimulus events and precise measurement of response characteristics are, in general, favorably disposed toward instrumentation.

In contrast, social psychologists and psychotherapists who are interested in love, hate, fear, aggression, anxiety, and so forth are less inclined to use instrumentation. These variables may, of course, be inferred from measurable phenomena. "Anxiety" may be operationally defined by certain levels of galvanic skin response, heart rate, and blood pressure. Such definitions are not without difficulties, however. First, investigators seldom use the same set of parameters to define a concept operationally. There are simply no widely accepted operational definitions. Second, there are more concepts floating around than there are easily measured physiological or behavioral properties. This situation results in the same physical measurements being used to define several quite different concepts. Hence the majority of measurable parameters cannot be used as exclusive indicants of any one specific emotional, cognitive, or behavioral concept.

When a parameter or group of parameters is used as an indicant of a hypothetical construct, an effort is usually made to arrange stimulus conditions such that alternative interpretations are minimized. For example, if the GSR is to be used as an indicant of "stimulus novelty," the investigator will arrange the subject's environment such that experimentally irrelevant stimuli are either eliminated or controlled. The subject will not be allowed to exercise physically, to breathe deeply, or to be presented stimuli that might be considered as fear evoking. Only the variable of stimulus novelty will be manipulated. In practice, however, it is quite difficult to assure that only "stimulus novelty" is responsible for the observed change. The investigator can never be totally sure that some of the novel stimuli may not be perceived by the subject as fearful or sexual, which would also produce a change in the GSR. This is the kind of thing that leads to "noise" in the recorded data, which is so frustrating to the experimenter but which may reflect important biological or social response patterns in the subject. "Noise" is not an inherent characteristic of recorded data itself—it is our evaluative judgment of the *quality* of such data. Behavior therapy has for the most part avoided the problems of laboring over hypothetical constructs and the meaning of observed behavioral changes by viewing behavioral events as behavioral events and nothing more. But this epistemological orientation does not eliminate the problem of "noise"—that is, of uninterpretable signals. One obvious strategy is to record patterns of responses over a larger time span or in more situations, while at the same time systematically filtering out those responses that occur at frequencies or magnitudes we arbitrarily decide in advance are too trivial. Instrumentation can sometimes help accomplish this task.

A wide range of behavioral assessment devices has been developed for specific behavioral responses. Unfortunately, technical reports are scattered in several journals, some of which are not commonly read by psychologists. Table 4–1 provides a selected bibliography of technical reports and of reviews of techniques. The reports are classified with respect to the response measured. The table does not include all published articles; an attempt was made to select only articles that describe recently developed techniques, provide unique methodolgy, or critically review several techniques. A less selective list was published earlier (Schwitzgebel & Schwitzgebel, 1973). The references are intended to serve as a guide to investigators contemplating the measurement of a particular behavior and allow them to benefit by the accomplishments (and errors) of others.

BASIC INSTRUMENTATION CONCEPTS

Although an astronomer need not understand the technology of lens-grinding to use a telescope, an understanding of the basic principles of his instrument is valuable. This knowledge allows the user to interpret more accurately the information provided by the instrument and to understand the limitations of the device. Several instruments for behavioral analysis are commercially available and may be employed without a technical knowledge of the principles of operation. But very often an appropriate

Table 4–1. Selected Behavioral Assessment Systems and Methodologies

Response	Selected References	Apparatus Description
Aggression	Geen & Stonner (1971)	An electromechanical readout device for communication of shock intensity and correct response. Includes a latency timer.
Anal sphincter pressure	Kohlenberg (1973)	Sphincter pressure indicated on water column connected to a fluid-filled balloon inserted in rectum.
Blood alcohol concentration	Sobell & Sobell (1975)	Inexpensive commercial device "MOBAT" estimates blood alcohol concentration via expired breath.
Blood flow	Greenfield et al. (1962)	Review of methods.
	Woodcock (1974)	
Blood pressure	Hinman et al. (1962)	A portable occlusive type device.
EEG	Shagass (1972)	Review of techniques and characteristics.
	Weiss (1972)	An integrated circuit differential amplifier.
	Waite (1973)	Alpha brain wave feedback device.
EMG	Basmajian (1967)	Review of techniques and characteristics.
	Goldstein (1972)	
	Ball (1969)	An integrated circuit differential amplifier.
	Waite (1975)	An inexpensive, complete EMG biofeedback device.
Equilibrium-stability	Shipley & Harley (1971)	Linear differential transformer senses movement of platform.
	Terekhov (1974)	Strain gauges on platform detecting movement associated with standing instability.
Eye-foot coordination	Mikaelian (1972)	A mirror-visual system.
Eyelid (blinking)	Grant et al. (1952)	A wire connected to eyelashes controls a potentiometer.
	Osborne et al. (1974)	Electrodes above eyebrow and below checkbone to measure EMG associated with blink.
Eye movement (EOG)	Haith (1969)	Corneal reflection method using TV camera and infrared light sources (suited for infant).

	Clark (1975)	Eye movement and direction of gaze detected by analysis of two reflections (Purkinje images).
	Russo (1975)	Eye position monitored by limbus reflection.
	Vaughan (1975)	Eye orientation using corneal reflection (closed circuit TV and minicomputer system).
Fetal EEG	Peltzman et al. (1973)	Describes an electrode system for intrauterine use on human fetus.
Galvanic skin response	Welford (1969)	Constant current device with built-in calibration methods.
	Lykken & Venables (1971)	Excellent review of GSR methodology and terminology; suggestions for standard procedures.
	Yonovitz & Kumar (1972)	Resistance-sensitive audio oscillator provides change in audio frequency as skin resistance changes.
	Edelberg (1972)	Review of techniques and principles.
Gross motor movement	Schulmann & Reisman (1959)	Self-winding wristwatch worn on arm and ankle.
	Goldman (1961)	Ultrasonic transducer worn on wrist.
	Barrett (1962)	Body movements detected by magnetic pick-up mounted on a chair.
	Herron & Ramsden (1975a)	Review of radio telemetry monitoring techniques of body movement.
	Siegel & Sameroff (1971)	Pressure transducer in mattress detects infant movement.
	Schroeder (1972)	Transducers mounted on hand tools indicates tool usage and workshop productivity.
	Elwood (1972a)	A commercial Doppler effect sonic movement detector.
	Dabbs & Clower (1973)	
Head movement (infant)	Vietze et al. (1974)	Pressure changes in an air pillow under infant's head triggers pressure-sensitive switches.
Head posture	Ball et al. (1975)	Mercury switch mounted on earphone detects duration of head tilting.
Heart rate	Guha et al. (1974)	Internal organ movement detected by changes in induced electrical field (experimental technique).
	Jernstedt & White (1974)	An integrated circuit bioelectric amplifier and a photo-plethysmographic amplifier.

Table 4–1. (Continued)

Response	Selected References	Apparatus Description
Illusion movement	Coren & Girgus (1972)	Compares the efficiency of five methods of measurement.
Locomotor activity	Herron & Ramsden (1967b)	An FM transmitter mounted in heel of shoe detects pressure changes.
Mastication	Kawamura (1964)	Review of electromyographic methods.
	Kavanagh & Zandler (1965)	Radio transmitter mounted in tooth detects bite information.
	Rugh (1971)	Small radio transmitter mounted in eye glasses transmits movement of temporalis muscle.
Micturation	Fried (1974)	Moisture-detection circuit transmits a tone to FM receiver.
	Kashinsky (1974)	A resistance-sensitive amplifier detects moisture on clothing and sounds alarm (inexpensive).
Nasality in speech	Roll (1973)	Piezo-electric crystal taped to nose detects nasal vibrations.
Oral forces	Rugh & Solberg (1972)	Strain gauges on bite element detect biting forces. (Review of other methods.)
Oral hygiene	Evans et al. (1968)	A chemical disclosing agent dyes red the plaque on teeth which may be photographed.
Penile erection	Barlow et al. (1970)	Mechanical strain gauge detects penis circumference (analog output).
Personal interaction	Stuart (1970)	A timer, recorder, and counter device to assess positive interaction.
	Thomas et al. (1970)	Electromechanical communication system (SAM) employs switches and lights for interaction between two people and monitor station.
Psychomotor skills	Fleishman (1954, 1958)	Electromechanical devices are used in Fleishman's classic studies.
	Michon & Koutstaal (1969)	Instrumented car to monitor driver movements.
	Trumbo (1969)	Review of methods and apparatus.

Pupil dilation	Hess (1965)	Photographic method.
	Loweth (1973)	Photodetectors sense amount of infrared light reflected from iris. A continuous monitoring technique.
Respiration	Gundersen (1971)	Thermocouple probes mounted near nose and mouth detect temperature changes caused by breathing.
	Levy & Helmer (1973)	Pressure on a speaker transducer is varied by string tied around subject's chest.
Salivation	Brown (1970)	Review of salivation as a psychophysiological response and methods of measurement.
Speech (fundamental frequency)	Shriberg (1971)	Commercial wave analyzer used to determine voice frequency characteristics.
Stomach acidity	Whitehead et al. (1975)	pH electrode in tube swallowed by subject.
Stomach motility	Wenger et al. (1957)	Magnetometer senses movement of magnet swallowed by subject.
	Edwards et al. (1967)	Review of techniques and new approaches.
Toothbrushing forces	Heath & Wilson (1974)	Strain gauges mounted on toothbrush handle detect forces.
Vertical separation (jaw)	Laird et al. (1971)	Jaw opening detected by recording induced voltage in coil mounted on lower teeth from coil mounted on maxilla teeth.
Vocalization	Siegel & Sameroff (1971)	Microphone, amplifier, filter, gate and digital counter indicate duration of vocalization.

device is not available, and the investigator must develop his own tools or modify an existing instrument to fit his needs. Furthermore, when an abundance of appropriate options exist (e.g., commercial oscillographs), a knowledge of basic instrumentation principles will make the investigator a wiser consumer.

Instruments designed to aid in behavioral assessment are basically energy-conversion devices. They detect and transform energy from its original form to a form that is quantifiable, more easily analyzed, or more intelligible to the investigator. An instrument may perform several functions as Figure 4–1 illustrates. A physical event is detected through the use of a transducer or sensor. The transducer usually transforms the event into an electrical signal that can be easily processed. Signal processing may increase or decrease the signal's amplitude, such as amplifying the minute electrical signals of the brain. It may also involve expansion or reduction of the temporal spacing of events. Circadian rhythms, for example, may be more easily understood when the time scale over which they naturally occur is compressed. A filtering or discrimination process is commonly used to eliminate unwanted aspects of a signal or to detect certain characteristics of interest. For example, filtering is used in the plethysmograph in Figure 4–1 to rid the low-frequency heart signal of unwanted 60 Hz. interference. Signal processing may sometimes involve converting a signal to a radio frequency such that it may be transmitted to distant recording stations.

After the signal is processed, it is typically displayed or stored in a manner to facilitate analysis. Examples of displays include oscilloscopes, speakers, and indicator lights. Storage devices include tape recorders, chart recorders, cameras, and computer printouts.

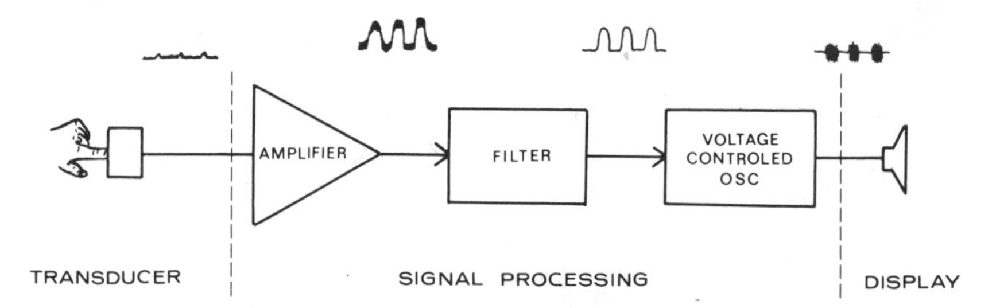

Figure 4–1. Block diagram of a plethysmograph that provides an auditory indication of heart rate. A photo cell and light source transducer are used to detect blood volume changes in the finger. The signals are then amplified, filtered, and used to modulate a voltage-controlled audio oscillator that drives a speaker.

Instrumentation designed to evaluate human behavior varies in complexity from simple timing mechanisms designed to measure response latencies, to complex self-branching interactive computing devices that provide a stimulus, record a response, and then provide another stimulus dependent on the nature of the preceding response. Common to each device, however, is the conversion of energy from one form to another; a transducer is the first and necessary system component.

Transducers

Transducers have been developed that detect at least six physical parameters: (1) mechanical, (2) electric, (3) magnetic, (4) thermal, (5) optical, and (6) chemical. In behavioral analysis the response to be monitored must be defined in terms of one or more of these physical properties in order to be detected.

Mechanical Transducers

A large number of behavioral responses involve movement of the body or movement of the air surrounding the body. Thus it is not surprising that mechanical transducers are by far the most popular sensing devices employed in behavioral assessment. Switches, potentiometers, accelerometers, microphones, and strain gauges are examples of mechanical transducers that can be used to measure responses involving changes in force, torque, pressure, sound, acceleration, flow, and distance. The switch is the simplest yet most versatile type of mechanical transducer. It is available in well over a thousand styles, a few of which are pictured in Figure 4–2. A switch can usually be found that can transform the movement associated with a reponse into an electrical impulse which then defines the response. The major limitation of employing a switch to monitor behavior is that it usually provides only binary information, that is, it is either open or closed. Other transducers such as potentiometers (pictured in Figure 4–3), strain gauges, microphones, variable capacitors, and variable inductors may be used to provide analogue or continuous information. The binary switch can indicate the presence or absence of a response. However, an analogue transducer can provide information regarding the magnitude of a response.

The selection of a transducer to sense a particular response will depend, in part, on the physical characteristics of the response. Eye blinks, for example, have been recorded using a delicate switch that operates by a very small amount of pressure. At the other extreme, human biting, which may reach 350 pounds of force, requires a very rugged strain gauge transducer.

Figure 4–2. Switch-type mechanical transducers: (A) rotary, (B) slide, (C) push-button, (D) foot, (E) ribbon, (F) toggle, and (G) mercury tilt. Switch types not pictured include magnetic reed, lever, knife, rocker, and micro.

Electrical Transducers

A considerable amount of human behavior can be quantified by recording electrical signals generated by the body. Eye movement, gastric motility, mental activity, heart rate, and frowning are all examples of events having measurable electrical correlates. The minute electrical signals accompanying such muscular activity or neural processes can be detected through the use of electrodes attached to the skin. Electrodes transfer bioelectric activity to an amplifier and recording system. Next in popularity to mechanical transducers, electrodes are widely used as a transducer device in behavioral assessment.

Recording electrodes are structurally quite simple. An electrode is typically a flat piece of metal and a lead wire. The principles underlying their function, however, are quite complex. Geddes (1972) has provided an in-depth review of different types of electrodes and the problems related to their use. A wide variety of recording electrodes is available commercially. Thus investigators are seldom required to construct their own. Commercial electrodes range from small needle electrodes for monitoring single-unit activity to large surface types for electrocardiography applications. Lists of

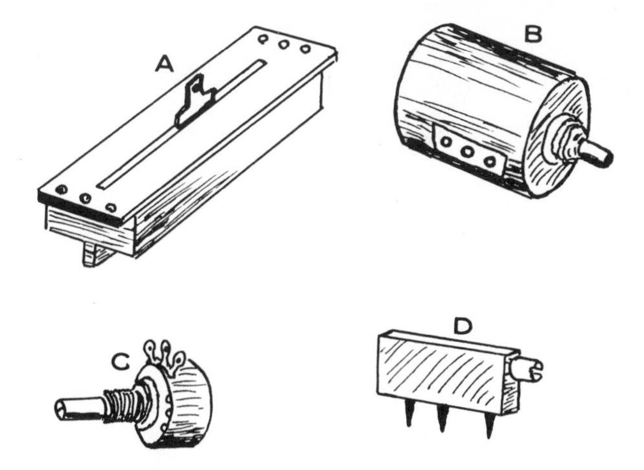

Figure 4–3. Potentiometer type mechanical transducers: (A) slide, (B) ten-turn wirewound, (C) carbon, and (D) miniature ten turn.

suppliers are available in published buyers' guides (e.g., Martin, 1974; Sidowski, 1975; Sommer, 1974).

It is generally held that electrodes made of silver and silver chloride have greater stability of electrode potential, fewer electrical artifacts, and lower contact impedance than simple silver electrodes. Many clinicians, however, prefer to use a silver electrode because it is much easier to care for. Electrodes are usually used with an electrode paste, an electrolyte, which helps to make contact between the metal electrodes and the skin. One of the most important considerations in using electrodes is to keep the electrode–subject impedance as low and as stable as possible. Low impedances (less than 10 kΩ) can usually be achieved by cleaning the skin and "rubbing in" the electrode paste.

Electrodes may also be used to provide a stimulus to the organism. The requirements of stimulating electrodes are not as exact as those for recording electrodes, and electrode paste is not usually required. Pulsed electrical current applied through electrodes placed over muscles can be used to elicit involuntary contraction of a muscle group. Alternatively, electrodes may be employed to deliver aversive shock.

Thermal Transducers

Behavioral events accompanied by a change in temperature may be detected through the use of a temperature-sensitive transducer. Thermistors and thermacouples are the most frequently employed temperature trans-

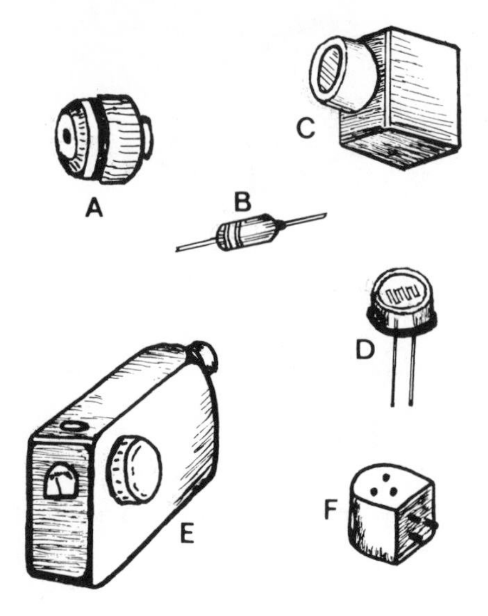

Figure 4–4. Miscellaneous transducers: (A) sonic transducer, (B) diode temperature transducer, (C) photo-relay device, (D) photo cell, (E) sound level meter, and (F) magnetic transducer.

ducers. However, the characteristics of many semiconductor devices such as diodes (see Figure 4–4) are also temperature dependent, and thus they may be employed as transducers. Thermistors are the simplest to use and are available as beads or probes of various dimensions. The thermistor transducer decreases in resistance as the temperature increases. The change in resistance is usually converted to a change in current or voltage, which can then be processed.

Temperature transducers have not been widely employed in the analysis of human behavior. They may, however, be quite useful. A small bead thermistor placed in or near the nasal passage can provide a convenient means of monitoring breathing patterns. As the warm air is expelled from the body, the thermistor heats. Conversely, it cools when the subject inhales. Temperature measurements are also of value in charting the menstrual cycle, which may be related to emotional patterns. The use of temperature biofeedback in the treatment of migraine headaches (Sargent, Green, and Walters, 1973) involves a novel and practical application of thermal transducers. The small size of thermistors makes them ideally suited for monitoring if the response of interest is correlated with a change in temperature.

Optical Transducers

Optical or photoelectric transducers basically convert changes in light energy to usable electrical signals. These transducers offer considerable versatility in the analysis of human behavior. Their chief advantage is that they can be used to monitor behavioral events without physically contacting the body, thus they do not physically disrupt the response being measured.

Common optical transducers include phototransistors, photodiodes and photocells or solar cells (see Figure 4–4). When exposed to light, the latter two transducers generate a voltage that can then be amplified and recorded. Phototransducers and photodiodes are semiconductor devices that change their resistive characteristics when exposed to light. Phototransducers can be used in digital or analogue applications whenever a behavior can be defined by or converted to a change in reflected or transmitted light intensity. When visible light may confound the measurement, infrared photodetectors may be employed.

The plethysmograph in Figure 4–1 uses a phototransducer to detect changes in light intensity resulting from variation in blood volume in the finger. Another application includes the recording of eye blinks. When a photosensitive device is placed such that it receives a reflected light from the eye, closing the eyelid results in a reduction of the reflected light and thus a change in the phototransducer's output. A similar application is involved in monitoring sweat gland activity. The presence of moisture on the skin increases the amount of light reflected by the skin, which may be detected by a phototransducer. Optical transducers are commercially available in sizes as small as a pinhead.

Chemical Transducers

Information processing within the body is accomplished through electrical and chemical changes. Behavioral assessment methodologies have, unfortunately, been generally limited to an examination of electrical correlates of behavior. The inattention to chemical changes accompanying emotional, cognitive, and behavioral events may be due to the complexities of biochemical analysis and to the limited knowledge most psychologists have of chemistry. Approximately 20 years ago, Rosenzweig, Krech, and Bennett (1958) noted the lack of collaboration between the behavioral and biochemical sciences, and they urged the development of more joint efforts.

Some chemical measurements can be made quite simply. The pH of a solution, for example, can be measured with the use of organic dyes, which when mixed with the solution indicate the acid-base balance by means of changes in color. Litmus and phenolphthalein are examples of such dyes. Some behavior therapists have used these dyes to indicate soiling by a child during toilet-training programs. More accurate measurements may be made through the use of chemical electrodes. When a metal is placed in a solution, an electrical potential results owing to the rearrangement of ions. Different metals (or membranes) provide different potentials depending on the specific ions in the solution and the nature of the metal or membrane employed. Based on these principles, measurement of pH, PCO_2 and pO_2 can be accurately made. A simple monitoring system would require only a specific ion electrode, a reference electrode, a high-input impedance amplifier, and a recorder to indicate the electrical potential between the two electrodes.

A number of ion-specific electrodes have been developed (Moody and Thomas, 1971) and many are commercially available. Small *in vitro* catheter electrodes are available (Beckman Instruments Co.) that can be used over long periods to measure blood pH. The recent developments of intragastric pH telemetry capsules (Kitagawa, Nishigori, Murata, Nishimoto, and Takada, 1966) may provide a suitable method of indexing emotionality. Wolf (1965) has noted that stomach hypofunction was associated with the feelings of fright, depression, and attitudes of being overwhelmed, whereas hyperfunction was apparently associated with aggressive attitudes, anger, and resentment.

Chemical electrodes have been used in measurments of the pH of electrolytes used in electrodermal recording. These investigations indicate that the magnitude of electrodermal response is affected by the acidity of the electrolyte used. Edelberg (1972) reported that the greatest response occurs at pH 7. At pH 3 the amplitude was reduced by 30 percent.

Magnetic Transducers

The measurement of magnetic energy has not received wide attention in the study of human behavior. Magnetic transducers, however, like optical transducers, need not contact the body, and thus they offer the advantage of minimal physical interference. Whenever there is a flow of electrical current, a magnetic field exists. The electrical activity of the brain, for example, produces a magnetic field detectable through sensitive magnetic transducers.

Measurement of magnetic fields can be made using the ordinary compass. The compass is merely a magnetized needle that balances itself magnetically with respect to the earth's geomagnetic field. The strength of an unknown magnetic field can be measured by observing the degree to which a compass's needle is deflected from the earth's north–south field, which is a known quantity.

Instruments designed to measure magnetic fields are called gaussmeters or fluxmeters. They usually involve magnetoresistive transducers or a coil of wire as a sensing element. As a coil of wire is moved through a magnetic field or a magnetic field is varied about a coil of wire, a voltage is induced into the coil that is measurable. A number of magnetic transducers are commercially available. However, few are well suited for behavioral research.

Magnetoresistive transducers function on the principle that most metals increase in electrical resistance when exposed to a magnetic field. Hall-effect transducers, which can be made very small, employ semiconductor materials that change their electrical characteristics when subjected to a magnetic field.

Measurement of the magnetic field produced by electrical activity of the brain is very difficult. Measurements must be made in carefully shielded rooms because the magnetic fields are very small. A magnetocardiograph has been developed to detect magnetically the activity of a human heart (Trends, 1971). The prototype device is very large and, owing to the extraneous magnetic noises on the earth's surface, reportedly had to be used in the bottom of an abandoned mine shaft!

Although the measurement of magnetic energy generated by the body may not prove to be a useful technique for some time, the effects of external magnetic forces on human behavior may also be of interest. Friedman, Becker, and Bachman (1967) have reported increased reaction times in human subjects when they are exposed to 5 to 10 gauss magnetic fields. Also Persinger (1969) found that rats exposed prenatally to low-intensity magnetic fields differed significantly from controls in ambulatory and defecation behavior in an open-field situation. Becker and his co-workers have reported finding a significant correlation between natural geomagnetic intensity and admission rates to psychiatric hospitals (Becker, Bachman, and Friedman, 1961). As man's technological accomplishments generate more and more magnetic fields in our environment, it may be wise to monitor such influences.

In circumstances allowing for the generation of a magnetic field, magnetic measurements may also be of use in monitoring body movements. Stomach motility, for example, has been recorded by having the subject swallow a small permanent magnet (Wenger, Henderson, and Dinning, 1957). A magnetic transducer was placed next to the subject to sense the changes in magnetic flux associated with movement of the magnet inside the subject's stomach. Barrett (1962) arranged a chair in which the involuntary tics of a patient induced current in a magnet coil which, in turn, triggered noise as an aversive feedback.

SIGNAL PROCESSING

The information detected by transducers is typically in the form of an electrical signal that may be processed by a variety of analogue or digital circuits. The nature and amount of signal processing required is quite variable and depends on the response being measured and the nature of the analysis desired. Measurements of reaction time, for example, may require only that a timing mechanism be activated. The measurement of alpha brain waves, on the other hand, will require considerable filtering and signal conditioning. A number of different types of signal-conditioning devices are commercially available.

The development of operational amplifiers and digital integrated circuits has greatly reduced the size and price of signal processing devices. The wristwatch calculator pictured in Figure 4–5 is an example of the miniaturization now possible employing integrated circuit technology. Recently microprocessors have been developed that perform the function of a computer's central processing unit. These devices are the size of a stick of chewing gum. Ten years ago such processing would have required a room full of equipment. Unfortunately, many technological accomplishments are slow to be applied to the behavioral sciences. The majority of companies manufacturing equipment specifically designed for behavioral analysis are small in size, the market is limited, and highly technical manufacturing techniques are not economically feasible.

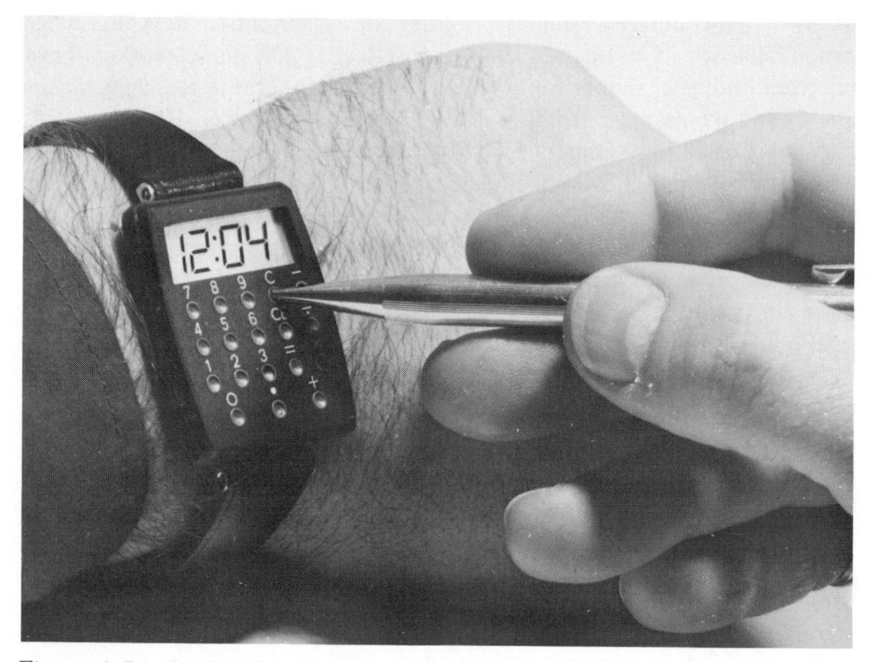

Figure 4–5. Combination wristwatch calculator (courtesy of Chomerics Inc., Woburn, Mass.).

A description and graphic illustration of input-output functions of common signal-processing circuits is provided in Tables 4–2 and 4–3. These signal-processing circuits may be employed for converting the output of a transducer to usable information. Some transducers require signal-processing devices with special input characteristics. The measurement of bioelectric events such as EMG and EEG requires amplifiers with high input impedance, low noise, and preferably a differential input with high common mode rejection characteristics. The signal processors in Table 4–2 are basically analogue circuits. Analogue processing would normally be employed with transducers that provide analogue information. Digital processing circuits as illustrated in Table 4–3 would accompany digital transducers (such as a switch). Note, however, that circuits are available that convert digital signals to analogue signals and vice versa.

The wide range of signal-processing capabilities indicated in Tables 4–2 and 4–3 allow the investigator considerable versatility. Two or more of the circuits are frequently connected such that several functions are performed. The computer is made in this way. Obviously, extremely complex signal processing can be performed by interconnecting several circuits. A knowledge of the basic function of these circuits coupled with a block diagram as in Figure 4–1 should allow the investigator with no engineering background to acquire a basic understanding of how an instrument works. The investigator need not be able to design each circuit; however, he should have a basic knowledge of what is happening to a signal inside his instruments.

Many signal processing modules are commercially available. Heath/Schlumberger Scientific Instruments (available through Heathkit), for example, markets both digital and analogue modules that perform many of the functions indicated in Tables 4–2 and 4–3. With a minimal amount of training the user can construct specialized signal-processing devices using these versatile modular building blocks. This mode of solving instrumentation problems is ideal for users whose interests or requirements constantly change. Users whose measurement requirements are less diversified will usually find it less expensive to purchase a complete system designed solely for a particular need.

Considerable attention has been given to the development of interactive computer systems for signal processing in behavioral assessment. Cole, Johnson, and Williams (1975) have discussed design considerations of an on-line assessment system, and Johnson, Gianetti, and Williams (1975) have described such a system installed at a Veterans Administration Hospital. The hospital computer system is used to administer personal questionnaires and various personality and pathology scales to incoming patients. Each test is computer analyzed, and the results are printed for

Table 4–2. Analog Signal Processing Circuits

Circuit	Input	Output	Function
Amplifier (AM)			Increases the amplitude of a signal.
Amplitude modulator			Varies the amplitude of a carrier wave (a) according to the amplitude of another wave (b).
Attenuator			Decreases the amplitude of a signal.
Automatic gain control			Maintains a constant output amplitude independent of input variations.
Chopper			Interrupts a current at regular intervals (usually to facilitate amplification).
Clipper			Limits the amplitude (positive or negative) of a signal.
Demodular (AM)			Operates on a carrier wave to recover the original wave.
Differentiator			Measures the rate of change of a signal.

Filter	Selects frequencies or suppresses noise.
Frequency modulator (FM)	Varies the frequency of a carrier wave according to the amplitude variation of another wave.
Integrator	Performs time integration of a signal.
Inverter	Reverses the polarity of a signal.
Logarithmic amplifier	Produces an output that is a logarithmic function of its input.
Phase shifter	Shifts the phase (fraction of the period that has elapsed as measured from some fixed point) of a signal.
Voltage controlled oscillator	Produces an oscillating output whose frequency is determined by input voltage.
Window discriminator	 Gives a fixed output voltage whenever the input is between two preset levels.

Table 4–3. Digital Signal Processing Circuits (Inputs are Either in a "High" or "Low" Logic State)

Circuit	Input	Output	Function
AND Gate			Produces high output only when all inputs are high.
Divider			Provides on output pulse for every fixed number of input pulses.
Inverter			Reverses logic state of input.
Monostable multi-vibrator (one-shot)			Gives an output pulse of predetermined duration for an input trigger signal of any duration.
NOR gate			Provides a low output when any of several inputs is high.
OR gate			Produces high output when any of several inputs is high.
Pulse-shaper			Produces a square pulse for input pulse of arbitrary shape.
Schmitt trigger			Generates an output pulse only when the input voltage exceeds a preset value.

clinical review. Diagnostic information and treatment programs may be stored in computer memory to guide and evaluate therapeutic programs.

A console for computer-administered psychological tests has been described by Space (1975). The console includes three visual displays, one auditory channel, and provisions for two subject-response modes. Elwood (1972b) has reported that automated administration of the Wechsler Adult Intelligence Scale (WAIS) provides very similar results to those obtained when the scale is administered personally.

Investigators intending to employ computers should acquaint themselves with the journal, *Behavior Research Methods and Instrumentation,* edited by J. Sidowski, which carries many informative articles on computer applications. The reviews of Borko (1962), Hunt (1969), and Lang (1969) should also be examined for applications of computers in behavioral assessment. Lader and Law (1974) have provided a discussion of the applications of digital computing techniques in psychophysiology.

Radio telemetry is another from of signal processing that has considerable potential. Behavioral or physiological information may be telemetered by a wire (telephone lines) or through the use of radio transmitters and receivers to distant recording equipment. Radio telemetry systems are useful when the subject's range of movement is large or when movement would be restrained by direct wiring. Jacobson, Kales, Lehmann, and Zweizig (1965), for example, employed radio telemetry equipment to study the EEG of sleepwalking subjects. Radio telemetry may also be useful when it is desirable that the subject be unaware of the recording. Thackray and Orne (1968) telemetered GSR data without the subject's awareness in a study designed to examine the effect of subject awareness on the detection of deception. Rugh (1971, 1972) described the construction and use of a radio telemetry system to monitor human chewing behavior without the subject's awareness. A tiny FM transmitter mounted in the side frame of eye glasses transmitted movement of the temporalis muscle to receiving equipment in an adjacent room. Herron and Ramsden (1967b) described a transmitter circuit that was mounted in the heel of a subject's shoe to monitor locomotor activity.

Investigators contemplating the use of radio telemetry in the analysis of human behavior will find the review papers by Coleman and Toth (1970), Schwitzgebel and Bird (1970), Miklich, Purcell, and Weiss (1974), and Miklich (1975) useful. For the technically sophisticated, Mackay's (1970) book on biomedical telemetry is useful inasmuch as many of the circuits designed for medical applications can be converted to behavioral applications. Numerous telemetry systems are commercially available from $200 up. Suppliers can be found listed under "telemetry systems" in the buyers' guides previously mentioned.

STORAGE AND DISPLAY DEVICES

Processed signals must be converted to some form of energy intelligible to the equipment user. As with signal processing, the type of display or recording device employed will depend in part on the nature of the response being measured. For example, a strain gauge dynamometer measuring handgrip forces generates an analogue signal requiring an analogue display. A DC voltmeter calibrated in pounds force would provide a convenient display. If a permanent record is required, a DC chart recorder could be used. Digital signals may require only an indicator light display. Prior to selecting a recording device, the investigator should be able to specify the exact parameters of interest and have a clear idea of how the information will be used. Display and storage devices differ with respect to several characteristics that make them very useful in some applications but quite useless in others. In selecting a display or storage device, factors such as portability, ease of operation, flexibility, frequency response, battery versus 110 volt AC operation, sensitivity, input impedance, and reliability should be considered.

Storage Devices

Popular data storage devices include tape recorders, paper tape cumulative or event recorders, polygraph or chart recorders, digital printers, and computer memory banks. A variety of these devices is commercially available in various sizes, prices, and specifications. Audio tape recorders continue to be among the most popular storage devices because they are relatively inexpensive and portable. Schoggen (1964) described a specially designed microphone and face mask to use with a portable tape recorder for taking field notes.

With a few external circuits, the inexpensive tape recorder can be adapted to a number of behavioral applications. The low-frequency response of most audio tape recorders is poor. However, if the input is frequency or pulse modulated, low-frequency signals can be recorded. Sulmar and Eisenberg (1975) have described the construction of an FM analog to a digital converter that can be used to store and play back low-frequency and DC signals on cassette tape recorders. This converter is capable of recording low-frequency bioelectric signals such as GSR and heart rate. The authors report that up to 900,000 bits of information may be stored on a 30-minute cassette tape. Brown (1971) has published an excellent review of the requirements and problems encountered in recording low-frequency biological signals. Investigators using tape recorders for this purpose might avoid serious technical problems by reviewing Brown's article.

An inexpensive telephone conversation monitor can be built using a cassette tape recorder and a simple control circuit described by Breindel (1974). The device not only automatically records conversations but records the dialed numbers. This same device could also be wired to an intercom system to record human verbal interaction in clinical or industrial settings.

The typical cassette recorder is limited to 60 minutes of continuous recording time. If, however, an auxiliary timer activates a recorder periodically for short intervals, the variables of interest can be sampled for days, weeks, or even months. Bernal, Gibson, Williams, and Pesses (1971) have described the adaptation of a commercial timer to activate a tape recorder at given time intervals during a day in order to record a mother's rate of commanding her children. The authors reported a high positive relationship between data recorded via the automated sampling device and that of a human observer. The timing device described by Bernal et al. (1971) was a large 110-volt AC electromechanical device that could now be made much smaller by incorporating integrated circuit timers. The timer circuit diagrammed in Figure 4–6, for example, can be built in a small package and has the advantage of being battery powered. With the component values specified in Figure 4–6, the timer will activate a tape recorder for a duration of 5 seconds every one minute. Using a 60-minute tape, a

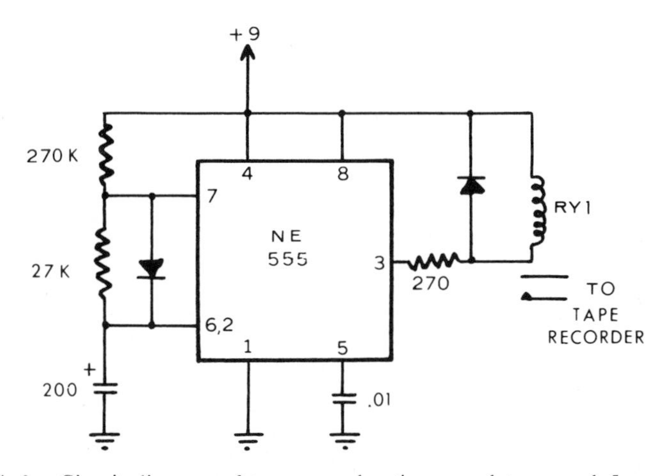

Figure 4–6. Circuit diagram of tape recorder timer used to record 5-second samples of data every 60 seconds. Closure of relay contacts is used to energize a battery operated tape recorder. Sampling time may be adjusted by varying the values of resistors R1, R2, and capacitor C1. Relay RY-1 is a calectro DI–962 or equivalent. Resistance values are in ohms except where noted otherwise. Capacitance values are in μf. A 9-volt transistor battery may be used to power the timer circuit.

12-hour period can be sampled and recorded. This timer circuit and a tape recorder have been used by the senior author of this chapter to sample and record GSR activity in sleeping subjects.

Audio tape cassettes are commercially available (Westinghouse Health Systems, Pittsburgh) that contain preprogrammed questions relative to a patient's medical history. The patient responds to taped questions by pushing appropriate buttons on a console. This system is capable of branching, depending on the patient's response. Such a system might be adapted to obtain standardized behavioral information on new patients or to chart with less interviewer bias the progress of patients being treated.

Videotape and time-lapse photography are becoming popular data-recording techniques. Although they allow the investigator to record the topology of behavior, videotape or photographic records have the disadvantage of ultimately requiring manual scoring by human viewers. Ekman and Friesen (1969) have noted this problem and have described the use of a computer system to help analyze video data.

Wilmer (1967), Alger (1969), and Berger (1970) have reviewed applications of videotape recorders in the clinical setting. Frequently a brief videotape is made during therapy sessions and played back immediately for the patient's viewing. Long-term patient improvement may be documented by reviewing tapes recorded at regular intervals during therapy. Eisler, Hersen, and Agras (1973) evaluated videotape methods to study nonverbal interaction (smiling and looking) of married couples. They report that live ratings and viewer ratings from videotapes were highly correlated and point out that one of the advantages of videotape is that additional behaviors can be rated on repeated replays. Time-lapse photography is useful when the events under study occur slowly over long periods. Patterning or changes in behavior may be more easily recognized when the interval over which the events naturally occur is compressed. Sanders and Paine (1972) have published a list of manufacturers supplying time-lapse equipment.

Data-recording devices such as digital printers, chart recorders, and computer memory banks are useful when the behavior being studied is sufficiently limited in scope. Digital printers can be used to obtain a paper tape record of numerical data such as time intervals, total responses, or the amplitude of an analogue signal. The use of a digital printer, however, usually requires considerable peripheral logic and/or control circuitry. Chart recorders, variously called polygraphs and oscillographs, provide a continuous record of DC or low-frequency AC signals. They seldom require external control circuitry, and some recent models are battery operated. The frequency response of chart recorders usually limits their application to signals less than 100 Hz. Event recorders typically are usable only with digital information. They provide a paper tape record of digital events as a function of time. Such devices have been widely used in behavioral psychology to record switch closures that indicate a specific response such as a bar press. The instruments are relatively inexpensive and provide permanent, complete records that can be analyzed with respect to parameters such as interresponse interval, total responses, and response frequency.

Display Devices

When permanent records of process signals are not required, information may be briefly examined on display devices such as digital panel meters, oscilloscopes, speakers, mechanical counters, or TV monitors. Such devices are typically less expensive than the recording devices discussed in the preceding section, and permanent records may be made by hand if required. Simple hand-held mechanical golf counters can be used to tally behaviors manually (Lindsley, 1968; "Communication," 1974). Mahoney (1974) has described a wrist counter made of leather and beads fashioned to appear as contemporary jewelry. Such a device may be more quiet and aesthetically appealing than a golf counter. Speakers, earphones, or vibra-tactile devices are useful indicators particularly when visual displays are inconvenient. Speakers and earphones generally have low-frequency response characteristics. However, low-frequency signals can be converted to frequency modulated audio tones and thus made audible. Several commercial biofeedback devices employ this technique to make audible low-frequency brainwave signals.

The oscilloscope has been a particularly useful tool in physiological recording techniques. The basic oscilloscope displays, on a cathode ray tube, the voltage of a signal as a function of time. It is capable of displaying extremely high-frequency signals because it is not limited by mechanical arms or levers as is the chart recorder. Permanent records may be made from the oscilloscope through photographic techniques. A few portable battery-operated oscilloscopes are now being manufactured that may extend the usefulness of these devices.

COMMERCIAL EQUIPMENT

Commercially developed products in behavioral psychology are typically quite expensive because of the limited market. The cost of development, materials, construction, advertising, documentation, and repair typically bring the price up to 20 times the cost of the component parts. The consumer is thus paying $1000 for a device the parts of which cost $50. Commercial products are, however, frequently more rugged, versatile, and aesthetically pleasing than homemade devices. In many cases the professional appearance of a device may be a critical factor in its acceptance by a patient. Innovative equipment users occasionally cut costs by finding a mass-produced popular item than can be adapted for behavioral measurements. The use of a commercial ultrasonic burglar alarm by Elwood (1972a) and by Dabbs and Clower (1973) to measure body movement is an excellent example of adapting a consumer item for behavioral assessment. A brief description of commercially available devices is provided in Table 4–4. Many of these devices were originally designed for measurement in other fields but have potential for behavioral research.

Table 4–4. Descriptive of Commercial Instruments with Application in Behavioral Assessment

Instrument	Description
Accelerometer	Transducer sensitive to rate of change in velocity of a moving mass.
Algesimeter	Device to measure pain threshold.
Ammeter	Device to measure flow of electrical current.
Amplifier	System to increase the magnitude of some physical parameter (voltage, power, pressure).
Audio analgesia	Device that provides an audio signal for the purposes of analgesia.
Audiometer	Device to measure acuteness of hearing.
Biofeedback devices	Instruments that display physiological signals to the person whose body is generating the signals.
Biothesiometer	Device to measure vibration perception thresholds.
Calorimeter	Device to measure heat loss.
Cardiotachometer	Instrument to measure heart rate.
Chronometer	Device to measure accurately periods of time.
Colorimeter	Instrument to measure color of light.
Compimeter (Diopsimeter)	Device to measure a field of vision.
Decibel meter	Device to measure sound levels.
Dolometer	Device to measure subjective pain levels.
Dynamometer	Instrument for measurement of force.
Electrocardiograph (ECG, EKG)	Device to measure electrical potentials of the heart muscles.
Electroencephalograph (EEG)	Instrument to measure the electrical activity of the brain.
Electrogastrograph	Device to measure gastric motility.
Electrogoniometer	Apparatus to measure the angular positions of the limbs of the body.
Electromyograph (EMG)	Instrument to measure the electrical activity of of the muscles.
Electronystagmograph (ENG)	Device for measurement of eye movement induced by electrical stimulation.

Table 4-4. (Continued)

Instrument	Description
Electroretinograph (ERG)	Device to measure electrical activity of the human retina to light stimulation.
Ergodynamograph	Device for recording work associated with muscular contraction.
Esthesiometer	Device to measure touch sensibility.
Evoked response audiometer	Device that detects changes in EEG activity evoked by auditory stimuli.
Galvanic skin resistance device	Instrument that measures the DC resistance of the skin.
Kinesthesiometer	Instrument to measure a person's ability to perceive his own body positioning.
Magnetoencephalograph (MEG)	Device to record the magnetic radiation of the brain.
Opthalmograph	Photographic device to record movements of the eye during reading.
Plethysmograph	Device to measure changes in blood volume, usually employing a light source and photodetector.
Pneumograph	Device for recording respiratory movements (respirometer).
Spectrum analyzer	Device to measure the frequency versus power spectrum of an electrical signal.
Stabilograph	Device for measuring human motor response instability.
Tachistoscope	Device to present visual stimuli at brief intervals.
Transducer	Device that transfers energy between two or more systems (frequently the conversion of energy from one form to another).

The selection of an appropriate instrument is often a difficult challenge for the mental health professional who frequently lacks technical education. Relying on the experience of others is often necessary and even when a person is technically knowledgeable, the task of equipment selection is not simple. Many equipment manufacturers do not provide adequate technical specifications in either their advertising literature or instruction manuals. We recently evaluated 44 items of advertising literature and 38 equipment instruction manuals of biofeedback devices. Twenty-one of the 44 pieces of advertising literature failed to provide specifications on the device's input impedance and other critical parameters that a potential user should consider when selecting a device. Furthermore, an examination of 38 equipment instruction manuals indicated that 28 of these did not provide technical specifications. Table 4–5 provides a list of characteristics of

Table 4–5. Factors to Consider in Selecting EMG and EEG Biofeedback Devices[a]

Factors	
Input impedance	Filter bandwidth
Warranty period	Circuit (potted?)
Common mode rejection	Built-in speaker
Sensitivity	Instruction book
Noise level	Clear and easy to understand
Min. detectable signal	References
Raw EMG gain control	Specifications clearly noted
Calibrated threshold control	Safety hazards discussed
Feedback volume control	Theory of operation
Log meter readout EMG	Device aesthetics (how would you feel about showing the device to your patients?)
Price (There is not necessarily a relationship between quality and price.)	Human factors
Preamplifier output jack	Controls clearly marked?
60 Hz. notch filter	Controls easy to turn in a relaxed state?
Weight and size (portability)	Type of feedback
Battery life (rechargeable?)	Raw EEG
Battery test function	FM
Electrode test function	AM
Complexity	Integrator
Input offset voltage	

[a] These characteristics are not listed in order of importance nor are they comprehensive.

biofeedback devices that the potential buyer may want to consider prior to purchasing a device. The relative importance of each factor will depend on the specific application of the device.

The availability of technical specifications is necessary not only for an intelligent selection of equipment but is also required to develop an adequate technical description of the apparatus in research reports. Authors of research papers *must* be able to specify clearly the characteristics of the equipment they have employed.

Even when specifications are provided by manufacturers, they are often inadequate. Unfortunately, standardized procedures are not used for obtaining equipment specifications. Each manufacturer may choose from a variety of measurement techniques to arrive at technical specifications describing his apparatus. Quite naturally, most manufacturers will select the method that makes their equipment appear favorable. It is thus often necessary to ask the manufacturer to supply details of his testing procedures. The user may be wise to make the purchase of the device contingent on such documentation. The purchaser should also request at the time of purchase schematic diagrams of the device to facilitate repairs.

INSTRUMENT STANDARDIZATION AND ERROR

A major problem in laboratory and clinical practice is the inability of a researcher or therapist to replicate the results of others. This failure is sometimes owing to an unwitting alteration or omission of a procedural detail that was not specified. When partial standardization of procedures can be accomplished through the use of instrumentation, the probability of valid and reliable replication should improve, assuming comparable instruments are used. Questions must be asked: How comparable are the data recorded by different devices? What are the sources and magnitude of errors that can be expected from the use of commercially available devices?

Schwitzgebel and Rugh (1975) recently published comparative test data on 13 alpha biofeedback devices. All the devices were evaluated by the same test procedures. Large variability was found between devices manufactured by different companies. Input impedance was found to vary from 500 ohms to greater than 2 megohms, which would provide output amplitude differences of over 90 percent. Furthermore, variations in filter characteristics between instruments were found that would cause errors as great as 11 dB in output amplitude. Differences between equipment parameters of this magnitude do little to help standardize assessment procedures. The use of poorly designed or nonstandardized devices would result in very little consistency in amplitude measurements of alpha waves. These findings point to the fallacy of assuming that instrumentation in itself produces "hard" and valid data.

Tursky and O'Connell (1966) surveyed users of electrodermal recording equipment and found wide disagreement in the procedures employed. For example, with respect to pretreatment of the skin prior to recording, 15 different procedures were reported from 26 different investigators. Brown (1967) has proposed standard nomenclature and techniques for many psychophysiological measures that should be carefully reviewed by equipment users. The report does not solve all standardization problems; however, it is a move in the right direction.

Theory building has traditionally been a highly praised endeavor. The development of a new tool for behavioral analysis can serve many of the same functions as the development of a new theory. An innovative tool provides a new perspective from which to view a series of seemingly unrelated behaviors. It may make philosophic speculations testable and open new avenues of research. However the tool cannot and should not be viewed as a replacement for theory in directing research projects. Etzioni (1975) recently commented on a potential pitfall in the use of high-speed computerized research techniques. He claimed that rapid data processing "practically eliminates the time once allotted to examining the findings, reflecting on their implications and evolving hypotheses." The fear is that it will become too easy simply to gather and analyze more meaningless data rather than spend time thinking about the data's relevance. Ideally, automation and instrumentation should free the investigator for *more* reflection, not *less*.

Behavioral instrumentation has the potential for standardizing, improving, and distributing certain aspects of mental health care more widely and economically. However, the uncritical, indiscriminate, and unstandardized use of instrumentation may lead to false hopes, commercial exploitation, and meaningless reams of data.

REFERENCES

Alger, I. Therapeutic use of videotape playback. *The Journal of Nervous and Mental Disease*, 1969, **148,** 430–436.

Bachrach, A. J. *Psychological research: An introduction* (2nd ed.). New York: Random House, 1962.

Ball, R. L. Amplifier for electromyographic signals. *American Journal of Physical Medicine*, 1969, **48,** 116–118.

Ball, T. S., McCrady, R. E., & Hart, A. D. Automated reinforcement of head posture in two cerebral palsied retarded children. *Perceptual and Motor Skills*, 1975, **40,** 619–622.

Barlow, D. H., Becker, R., Leitenberg, H., & Agras, W. S. A mechanical strain gage for recording penile circumference change. *Journal of Applied Behavior Analysis*, 1970, **3,** 73–76.

Barrett, B. Reduction in rate of multiple tics by free-operant conditioning methods. *Journal of Nervous and Mental Disease*, 1962, **135,** 187–195.

Basmajian, J. V. *Muscles alive: Their functions revealed by electromyography* (2nd ed.). Baltimore: Williams & Wilkins, 1967.

Becker, R. O., Bachman, C. H., & Friedman, H. Relation between natural magnetic field intensity and the increase of psychiatric disturbances in human population. International Conference on High Magnetic Fields, Massachusetts Institute of Technology, Cambridge, Mass., 1961.

Berger, M. M. (Ed.). *Videotape techniques in psychiatric training and treatment.* New York: Brunner-Mazel, 1970.

Bernal, M. E., Gibson, D. M., Williams, D. E., & Pesses, D. J. A device for automatic audio tape recording. *Journal of Applied Behavior Analysis*, 1971, **4,** 151–156.

Borko, H. (Ed.). *Computer applications in the behavioral sciences.* Englewood Cliffs, N.J.: Prentice-Hall, 1962.

Breindel, G. Ordinary cassette recorder can be full-time phone monitor. *Economics*, March 21, 1974, 98.

Brown, G. H. Magnetic tape recorders for low-frequency biological signals: A discussion. *BioMedical Engineering*, 1971, **6,** 348–350.

Brown, C. C. A proposed standard nomenclature for psychophysiologic measures. *Psychophysiology*, 1967, **4,** 260–264.

Brown, C. C. The parotid puzzle: A review of the literature on human salivation and its applications to psychophysiology. *Psychophysiology*, 1970, **7,** 66–85.

Cannon, W. H., & Jensen, O. G. Terrestrial timekeeping and general relativity—A discovery. *Science*, 1975, **188(4186)**, 317–328.

Clark, M. R. A two-dimensional purkinje eye tracker. *Behavior Research Methods and Instrumentation*, 1975, **7,** 215–219.

Cole, E. B., Johnson, J. H., & Williams, T. A. Design considerations for an on-line computer system for automated psychiatric assessment. *Behavior Research Methods and Instrumentation*, 1975, **7,** 195–198.

Coleman, R., & Toth, E. The adaptation of commercially available radio control equipment to behavior therapy. *Journal of Applied Behavior Analysis*, 1970, **3,** 221–222.

"Communication." *Journal of Applied Behavior Analysis*, 1974, **7,** 446.

Coren, S., & Girgus, J. S. A comparison of five methods of illusion measurement. *Behavior Research Methods and Instrumentation*, 1972, **4,** 240–244.

Dabbs, J. M., & Clower, B. J. An ultrasonic motion detector, with data on stare, restriction of movements, and startle. *Behavior Research Methods and Instrumentation*, 1973, **5,** 475–476.

Edelberg, R. Electrical activity of the skin: Its measurement and uses in psychophysiology. In N. S. Greenfield & R. A. Sternbach (Eds.). *Handbook of psychophysiology*. New York, Rinehart, & Winston, 1972.

Edwards, A. E., Hill, R. A., & Treadwell, T. Improvements in the magnetometer technique of measuring gastric motility. *Psychophysiology*, 1967, **4,** 116–118.

Eisler, R. M., Hersen, M., & Agras, W. S. Videotape: A method for the controlled observation of nonverbal interpersonal behavior. *Behavior Therapy*, 1973, **4,** 420–425.

Ekman, P., & Friesen, W. V. A tool for the analysis of motion picture film or video tape. *American Psychologist*, 1969, **28,** 240–243.

Elwood, D. L. A device to record gross motor movements in human subjects. *Behavior Research Methods and Instrumentation*, 1972, **4,** 315–316. (a)

Elwood, D. L. Validity of an automated measure of intelligence in borderline retarded subjects. *American Journal of Mental Deficiency*, 1972, **77,** 90–94. (b)

Etzioni, A. Effects of small computers on scientists. *Science*, 1975, **184,** 93.

Evans, R. I., Rozelle, R. M., Lasater, T. M., Bembroski, T. M., & Allen, B. P. A new measure of effects of persuasive communications: A chemical indicator of toothbrushing behavior. *Psychological Reports*, 1968, **23,** 731–736.

Fleishman, E. A. Dimensional analysis of movement reactions. *Journal of Experimental Psychology*, 1958, **55,** 438–453.

Fleishman, E. A. Dimensional analysis of psychomotor abilities. *Journal of Experimental Psychology*, 1954, **48,** 437–454.

Fried, R. A device for enuresis control. *Behavior Therapy*, 1974, **5,** 682–684.

Friedman, H., Becker, R. O., & Bachman, C. H. Effects of magnetic fields on reaction time performance. *Nature*, 1967, **213,** 949–956.

Geddes, L. A. *Electrodes and the measurement of bioelectric events*. New York: Wiley, 1972.

Geen, R. G., & Stonner, D. An extended apparatus for measuring aggression in humans. *Behavior Research Methods and Instrumentation*, 1971, **3,** 197–198.

Goldman, J. A look at human measurements in industry. In L. E. Slater (Ed.), *Interdisciplinary clinic on the instrumentation requirements for psychophysiological research*. New York: Fiev, 1961.

Goldstein, I. B. Electromyography. In N. S. Greenfield & R. A. Sternback (Eds.), *Handbook of psychophysiology*. New York: Holt, Rinehart, & Winston, 1972.

Grant, D. A., Schipper, L. M., & Ross, B. M. Effects of intertrial interval during acquisition on extinction of the conditioned eyelid response following partial reinforcement. *Journal of Experimental Psychology*, 1952, **44,** 203–210.

Greenfield, A. D. M., Whitney, R. J., & Mowbray, J. F. Methods for the investigation of peripheral blood flow. *British Medical Bulletin*, 1962, **19,** 101–109.

Guha, S. K., Tandon, S. N., & Khan, M. R. Electrical field plethysmography. *Biomedical Engineering*, 1974, **9,** 510–514.

Gundersen, J. Graphic recording of breathing rate using a simple thermocouple system. *Biomedical Engineering*, 1971, **6,** 208–210.

Haith, M. M. Infrared television recording and measurement of ocular behavior in the human infant. *American Psychologist*, 1969, **24,** 279–283.

Heath, J. R., & Wilson, H. J. Forces and rates observed during in vivo toothbrushing. *Biomedical Engineering*, 1974, **9,** 61–64.

Herron, R. E., & Ramsden, R. W. Continuous monitoring of overt human body movement by radio telemetry: A brief review. *Perceptual and Motor Skills*, 1967, **24,** 1303–1308. (a)

Herron, R. E., & Ramsden, R. W. A telepedometer for the remote measurement of human locomotor activity. *Psychophysiology*, 1967, **4,** 112–115. (b)

Hess, E. H. Attitude and pupil size. *Scientific American*, 1965, **212,** 400–411.

Hinman, A. T., Engel, B. T., & Bickford, A. F. Portable blood pressure recorder: Accuracy and preliminary use in evaluating daily variations in pressure. *American Heart Journal*, 1962, **63,** 663–668.

Hunt, E. Conversational computing systems as laboratory instruments. *American Psychologist*, 1969, **24,** 199–202.

Jacobson, A., Kales, A., Lehmann, D., & Zweizig, J. R. Somnambulism: All night electroencephalographic studies. *Science*, 1965, **148,** 975–977.

Jernstedt, G. C., & White, W. F. Cardiovascular response measures with simple integrated circuit amplifiers. *Psychophysiology*, 1974, **11,** 211–215.

Johnson, J. H., Giannetti, R. A., & Williams, T. A. Real-time psychological assessment and evaluation of psychiatric patients. *Behavior Research Methods and Instrumentation*, 1975, **7,** 199–200.

Kashinsky, W. Two low cost micturation alarms. *Behavior Therapy*, 1974, **5,** 698–700.

Kavanagh, D., & Zandler, H. A. A versatile recording system for studies of mastication. *Medical Electronics Biological Engineering*, 1965, **3,** 291–300.

Kawamura, Y. Recent concepts of the physiology of mastication. In P. M. Stable (Ed.), *Advances in oral biology*. Vol. I. New York: Academic, 1964.

Kitagawa, K., Nishigori, A., Murata, N., Nishimoto, K., & Takada, H. A new radio capsule with micro glass electrode for the telemetry of the gastrointestinal pH and its clinical use. *Digest* of 6th International Conference on Medicine and Biological Engineering, 1966, 216–217.

Kohlenberg, R. J. Operant conditioning of human anal sphincter pressure. *Journal of Applied Behavior Analysis*, 1973, **6,** 201–208.

Lader, M., & Law, L. The use of digital techniques in psychophysiological research. *Psychophysiology*, 1974, **11,** 372–381.

Laird, W. R. R., Davies, E. H., Manson, G., & Fraunhofer, J. A. Measurement of occlusal tooth separation by means of electrical field variations. *Bio-Medical Engineering*, 1971, **6,** 504–508.

Lang, P. J. The on-line computer in behavior therapy research. *American Psychologist*, 1969, **24,** 236–239.

Levy, J. K., & Helmer, R. J. A pneumographic transducer based on a small moving-coil loudspeaker. *Behavior Research Methods and Instrumentation*, 1973, **5,** 9–10.

Lindsley, O. A reliable wrist counter for recording behavior rate. *Journal of Applied Behavior Analysis*, 1968, **1,** 77–78.

Loweth, H. A device for continuous monitoring of pupil dilation. *Behavior Research Methods and Instrumentation*, 1973, **5,** 473–474.

Lykken, D. T., & Venables, P. H. Direct measurement of skin conductance: A proposal for standardization. *Psychophysiology*, 1971, **8,** 656–672.

Mackay, R. S. *Bio-medical telemetry* (2nd ed.). New York: Wiley, 1970.

Mahoney, K. Count on it: A simple self-monitoring device. *Behavior Therapy*, 1974, **5,** 701–703.

Martin, J. N. *Dictionary buyers' guide: Medical electronics and equipment news.* Radnor, Pa.: Chilton, 1974.

Michon, J. A., & Koutstaal, G. A. An instrumented car for the study of driver behavior. *American Psychologist*, 1969, **24,** 277–303.

Mikaelian, H. H. A technique for measuring eye-foot coordination without visual guidance. *Behavior Research Methods and Instrumentation*, 1972, **4,** 17–18.

Miklich, D. R. Radio telemetry in clinical psychology and related areas. *American Psychologist*, 1975, **30,** 419–425.

Miklich, D. R., Purcell, K., & Weiss, J. H. Practical aspects of the use of radio telemetry in the behavioral sciences. *Behavior Research Methods and Instrumentation*, 1974, **6,** 461–466.

Moody, G. J., & Thomas, J. D. R. (Eds.). *Selective ion sensitive electrodes*. Watford, England: Merrow, 1971.

Osborne, G., Roach, T., Gendreau, L., & Gendreau, P. An electrode hookup for eyelid conditioning. *Behavior Research Methods and Instrumentation*, 1974, **6,** 416–418.

Peltzman, P., Goldstein, P. J., Battagin, R., & Markevitch, B. A simple electrode to record fetal EEG for optimal signal analysis. *Behavior Research Methods and Instrumentation*, 1973, **5,** 395–399.

Persinger, M. A. Open-field behavior in rats exposed prenatally to low intensity–low frequency, rotating magnetic field. *Developmental Psychobiology*, 1969, **2,** 168–171.

Roll, D. L. Modification of nasal resonance in cleft-palate children by informative feedback. *Journal of Applied Behavior Analysis*, 1973, **6,** 397–403.

Rosenzweig, M. R., Krech, D., & Bennett, E. L. Brain chemistry and adaptive behavior. In H. F. Harlow & C. N. Woolsey (Eds.), *Biological and biochemical bases of behavior*. Madison: University of Wisconsin Press, 1958.

Rugh, J. D. A telemetry system for measuring chewing behavior in humans. *Behavior Research Methods and Instrumentation*, 1971, **3,** 73–77.

Rugh, J. D. Variation in human masticatory behavior under temporal constraints. *Journal of Comparative and Physiological Psychology*, 1972, **80,** 169–174.

Rugh, J. D., & Solberg, W. K. The measurement of human oral forces. *Behavior Research Methods and Instrumentation*, 1972, **4,** 125–128.

Russo, J. E. The limbus reflection method for measuring eye position. *Behavior Research Methods and Instrumentation*, 1975, **7,** 205–208.

Sanders, R. M., & Paine, F. Time lapse automation. *Journal of Applied Behavior Analysis*, 1972, **5,** 110.

Sargent, J. D., Green, E. E., & Walters, E. D. Preliminary report on the use of autogenic feedback training in the treatment of migraine and tension headaches. *Psychosomatic Medicine*, 1973, **35,** 129–135.

Schoggen, P. Mechanical aids for making specimen records of behavior. *Child Development*, 1964, **35,** 985–988.

Schroeder, S. R. Automated transduction of sheltered workshop behaviors. *Journal of Applied Behavior Analysis*, 1972, **5,** 523–525.

Schulmann, J. L., & Reisman, J. An objective measurement hyperactivity. *American Journal of Mental Deficiency*, 1959, **64,** 455–456.

Schwitzgebel, R. L., & Bird, R. M. Sociotechnical design factors in remote instrumentation with humans in natural environments. *Behavior Research Methods and Instrumentation*, 1970, **2,** 99–105.

Schwitzgebel, R. L., & Rugh, J. D. Of bread, circuses and alpha machines. *American Psychologist*, 1975, **30,** 363–370.

Schwitzgebel, R. L., & Schwitzgebel, R. K. (Eds.). *Psychotechnology: Electronic control of mind and behavior*. New York: Holt, Rinehart, & Winston, 1973.

Shagass, C. Electrical activity of the brain. In N. S. Greenfield & R. A. Sternbach (Eds.), *Handbook of psychophysiology*. New York: Holt, Rinehart, & Winston, 1972.

Shipley, R. E., & Harley, R. J. A device for estimating stability of stance in human subjects. *Psychophysiology*, 1971, **7,** 287–292.

Shriberg, L. D. A system for monitoring and conditioning modal fundamental frequency of speech. *Journal of Applied Behavior Analysis*, 1971, **4,** 337–339.

Sidowski, J. B. Buyers' guide. *American Psychologist*, 1975, **30,** 445–468.

Siegel, L., & Sameroff, A. Monitoring system for infant movement, vocalization and nurse interaction. *Behavior Research Methods and Instrumentation*, 1971, **3,** 305–306.

Sobell, M. B., & Sobell, L. C. A brief technical report on the MOBAT: An inexpensive portable test for determining blood alcohol concentration. *Journal of Applied Behavior Analysis*, 1975, **8,** 117–120.

Sommer, R. G. Guide to scientific instruments. *Science*, 1974, **186,** 9–162.

Space, L. G. A console for the interactive on-line administration of psychological tests. *Behavior Research Methods and Instrumentation*, 1975, **7,** 191–193.

Stuart, R. B. A cueing device for the acceleration of the rate of positive interaction. *Journal of Applied Behavior Analysis*, 1970, **3,** 257–260.

Sulmar, J., & Eisenberg, J. Build a portable analog/digital memory translator. *Popular Electronics*, 1975, **7,** 27–30.

Terekhov, Y. A system for the study of man's equilibrium. *Biomedical Engineering*, 1974, **9,** 478–480.

Thackray, R. I., & Orne, M. T. Effects of the type of stimulus employed and the level of subject awareness on the detection of deception. *Journal of Applied Psychology*, 1968, **52,** 234–239.

Thomas, E. J., Carter, R. D., Gambrill, E. D., & Butterfield, W. H. A signal system for the assessment and modification of behavior (SAM). *Behavior Therapy*, 1970, **1,** 252–259.

"Trends and techniques." *Biomedical Engineering*, 1971, **6,** 318.

Trumbo, D. Instrumentation in motor skills research. *American Psychologist*, 1969, **24,** 289–292.

Tursky, B., & O'Connell, D. N. Survey or practice in electrodermal measurement. *Psychophysiology*, 1966, **2,** 237–240.

Vaughan, J. On-line, real-time recording of eye orientation using the corneal reflection method. *Behavior Research Methods and Instrumentation*, 1975, **7,** 211–214.

Vietze, P., Foster, M., & Friedman, S. A portable system for studying head movements in infants in relation to contingent and noncontingent sensory stimulation. *Behavior Research Methods and Instrumentation*, 1974, **6,** 338–340.

Waite, M. Build a musçle feedback monitor. *Popular Electronics*, 1975, **7,** 39–42.

Waite, M. Build an alpha brain wave feedback monitor. *Popular Electronics*, 1973, **3,** 40–45.

Weiss, M. S. An inexpensive wideband high gain, physiological amplifier. *Physiology and Behavior*, 1972, **8,** 1183–1184.

Welford, N. T. A constant current skin resistance coupler. *Psychophysiology*, 1969, **5,** 724–726.

Wenger, M. A., Henderson, E. B., & Dinning, J. S. Magnetometer method for recording gastric motility. *Science*, 1957, **125,** 990.

Whitehead, W. E., Renault, P. F., & Goldiamond, J. Modification of human gastric acid secretion with operant-conditioning procedures. *Journal of Applied Behavior Analysis*, 1975, **8,** 147–156.

Wilmer, H. A. Practical and theoretical aspects of videotape supervision in psychiatry. *Journal of Nervous and Mental Disease*, 1967, **145,** 123–130.

Wolf, S. *The stomach.* New York: Oxford University Press, 1965.

Woodcock, J. P. Plethysmography. *Biomedical Engineering*, 1974, **9,** 406–417.

Yonovitz, A., & Kumar, A. An economical, easily recordable galvanic skin response apparatus. *Behavior Therapy*, 1972, **3,** 629–630.

PART TWO

General Approaches to Behavioral Assessment

CHAPTER 5

Behavioral Interviews

VICTOR MEYER, ANDRÉE LIDDELL, and MAUREEN LYONS

Interviewing in relation to assessment and diagnosis has tended to be criticized by many as being too subjective and unlikely to be reliable and valid. This was particularly true of those who advocated standardized tests as screening devices prior to patients' being processed into treatment. The long and often acrimonious debate between advocates of statistical as opposed to clinical methods in diagnostic labeling became irrelevant when the diagnostic labels they sought to reach with ultimate accuracy were shown to be inappropriate for planning therapeutic action, particularly when the action is based on psychological theories (e.g., learning theories).

Orthodox diagnosis of classical descriptive psychiatry was not rejected because such categorization is entirely wrong. It has repeatedly been demonstrated that, under suitable conditions, impressive reliability is obtainable. Unfortunately, there is ample evidence that psychiatric diagnosis does not predict either treatment or prognosis. The quality and quantity of the symptoms on which these diagnostic categories are most often based have failed to predict the behavior and attitude of either the patients or persons near to them regarding admitted or noticed incapacity and requests for therapeutic intervention. Other factors must be influential in making these people come forward to ask for help with their problems and in determining the help they eventually receive. Therapists must, therefore, seek to identify these factors and to investigate alternative frameworks to the conventional psychiatric model to accommodate such identifications.

Behavior therapists have generally focused narrowly on the most objective description of presenting complaints—their development and maintenance. At least this could be seen to be directly related to planning the therapeutic intervention. The problem behavior is usually reduced into as many components as are measurable. However, this extreme reductionism needs to be reversed at some point if the individual is to leave the clinic as an integral person whose therapeutic gains are to be maintained outside it and under his own control. Few behavior therapists have attempted to arrive at a conceptual system that approaches and systematically investigates the whole person in behavioral terms. Kanfer and Saslow (1965, 1969) are notable exceptions, and their suggestion for carefully detailed "behavioral analyses/diagnoses" must be acknowledged as an important influence on others who share the same concern.

The diagnostic interview plays a crucial part in relation to the type of wide-spectrum behavior therapy practiced by us (Meyer and Liddell, 1975). In training, it was thought to be one of the most important skills to impart (Meyer, Sharpe, Liddell, & Lyons, 1975). However, interviewing as a method of gathering and assessing relevant information must be justified and suspicions allayed as to its utility in relation to ongoing behavior therapy. Furthermore, a viable conceptual system or schema that will direct interviewing toward fulfilling its therapeutic aims must be demonstrated.

Interviewing as a Method

Too often interviewing has been criticized because of the type of data it tried to accumulate rather than as a method per se. For instance, Fisher, Epstein, and Harris (1967) showed that psychiatrists were unable to predict the efficacy of Peace Corps Volunteers in Ghana because the dimensions they assessed were unrelated to the real-life situations rather than because interviewing produced inaccurate data. On the other hand, Spitzer and Endicott (1973) were able to demonstrate their ability to assess several areas of psychopathology as accurately by interviews as by standardized tests. Goldberg (1974) in his recent review of objective tests and measures concluded that clinical decisions are usually made "subjectively" by the clinician since superior actuarial data are unavailable in the present state of things. A behavior therapist will also need to process and act on even the most objective type of information if he is to consider the individual needs of his patient. Behavior therapy is not envisaged as a selection of well-defined techniques into which patients will be "objectively" fitted but rather, as Kanfer and Saslow (1965) described, an "action-oriented approach" whereby the therapist and the patient develop and maintain a mutual relationship with the ultimate aim of developing, guiding, and encouraging the patient's self-control and independence.

It is thought that the best method to develop a mutual relationship between the patient and therapist is through a series of interviews in which the behavioral analysis of the patient proceeds through a flexible though logical and goal-directed sequence that will be detailed later. To maintain this relationship, the behavioral interview occupies the central point of all therapeutic activities, whether in terms of initial description or clarification of the presenting complaint, planning of the therapeutic program or its regular monitoring leading to eventual discharge and independence. It is considered most important for the patient and the therapist to be in close and direct communication, for the patient to be allowed to verbalize his own problems in his own way, and for the therapist to communicate his hypotheses as to the origins, maintenance, and possible modification of the problems. It is fully realized that the patient can structure his own world only as he sees it or because of his needs to see it thus. Nevertheless, for a mutual relationship the patient must be made to feel that he is the central point of reference from which all further investigation will proceed and this only with his full cooperation and understanding. Other sections of this book are a credit to the ingenuity of behavior therapists in developing an appropriate technology to enhance objectivity in behavioral measures. These methods must remain adjuncts to the interaction between patient and therapist; technology on its own can only create ambiguity and uncertainty in the patient (Rachman & Philips, 1975).

SCHEMA FOR BEHAVIORAL INTERVIEWING

Any attempt to give a schema for psychiatric interviewing may give the impression of inflexibility and uniformity as, for instance, is apparent in the usual format proposed in textbooks aimed at clinicians. The aims of all psychiatric history taking are the same—that is to conceptualize the patient and his problems—but the objectives can differ considerably. Although patients are usually asked to give an account of themselves, often in chronological order, the framework under which the therapist operates determines such things as how much time is spent on the early days, how early those days are, which relationships are specifically explored, what are considered to be neurotic traits, and how meticulously all these are recorded. This framework also influences whether the data are recorded verbatim or translated into jargon, and/or interpreted. In general the phrasing of the questions is the key to the therapist's understanding as well as a reflection of the type of relationship he is attempting to establish with his patient. A schema is proposed in Figure 5–1 and its contents elaborated and discussed below.

Point of Entry

When meeting a patient for the first time, the therapist must decide how to begin to accumulate relevant information. Some therapists are unconcerned about the presenting symptoms and aim to establish some sort of positive relationship that revolves around an understanding of the patient's

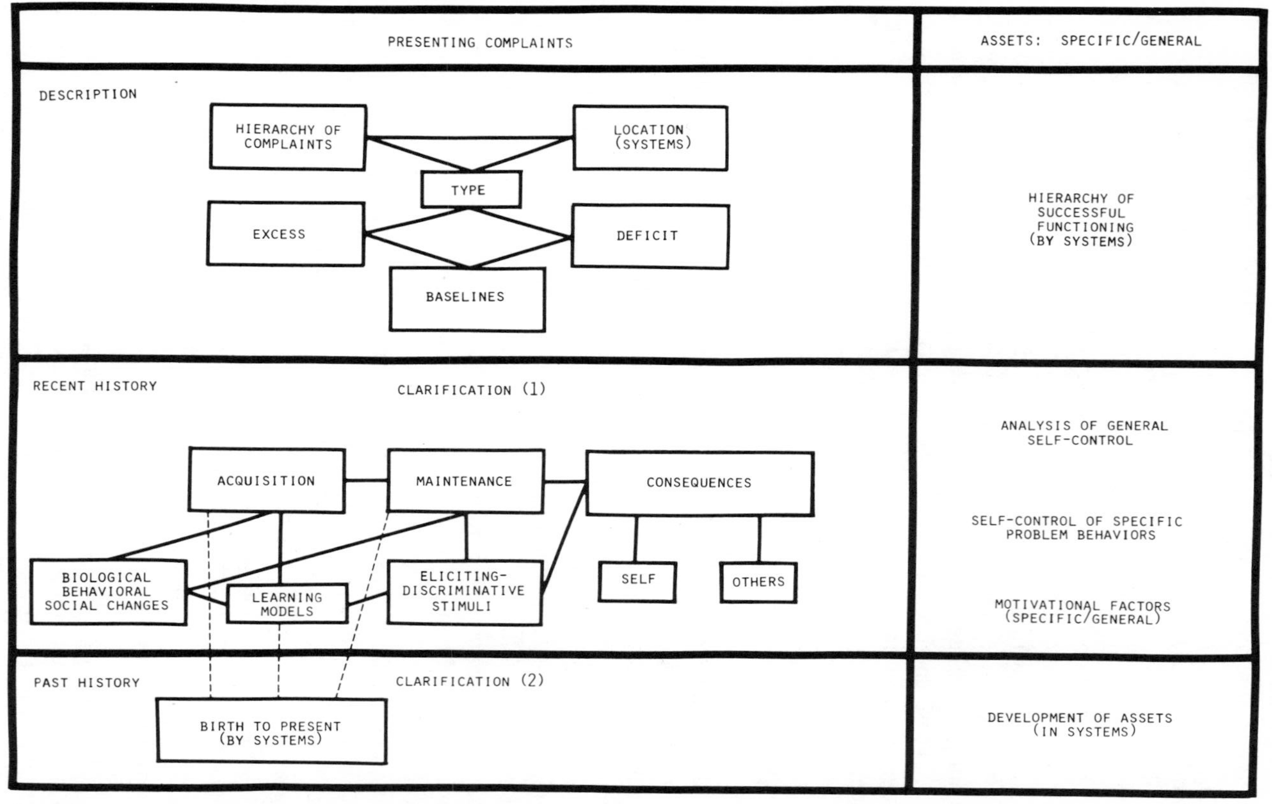

Figure 5–1. A schema for behavioral interviews.

overall functioning or philosophy of life. Others, although concerned with the presenting complaint, view it as a sign of a deeper or more hidden conflict that must be understood and eventually resolved if the overt symptoms are to disappear. This latter conceptualization will direct the therapist to seek a suitable interpretation of the symptoms presented to him. The behavior therapist is unashamedly concerned with quickly finding an operational definition for the patient's presenting complaint; the relationship he develops with his patient will be based on mutual understanding and agreement in developing therapeutic goals. In any case, since it is common for patients to be almost exclusively concerned with their presenting complaints, discussions particularly relevant to their problems should facilitate an easy and productive relationship.

Logic of Schema

It must be stressed that the above schema is only a guide to behavioral interviewing, and rigid sequential adherence should be discouraged. The areas graphically represented in Figure 5–1, although logically sequenced into a type of flow diagram, should be viewed as foci for interviewing. These foci include the description of the complaint and its recent and past history alongside information about the patient's general and specific assets and should at the same time include enough information to enable the therapist to conceptualize his patient as a whole person who has recognizable assets as well as deficits. The diagram could have been drawn as a series of concentric circles with the presenting complaint at its center and the other information relating to recent and past history radiating outward, interspersed with the general and specific assets of the patient. It will be up to the therapist eventually to structure the information he has obtained from his patient. Such diagrams are to be viewed as an aid to this reconstruction rather than as a format for the ongoing interview.

Presenting Complaint

Style of Interview and Description of Problem

Since so much will depend on the behavioral interview for a satisfactory relationship between patient and therapist and their mutual understanding of the presented problems, the therapist must develop the sensitivity required by all skilled interviewers. In a practical book for clinicians Bernstein, Bernstein and Dana (1974) presented a most helpful overview of interviewing techniques particularly designed to make interviewers aware of the methods they use in responding to their patients and vice versa and listed conditions for effective interviewing. These conditions are of particular interest to all potential interviewers and can be adopted freely as guidelines for conducting behavioral interviews. Five such conditions were listed: (1) attentiveness, viewed as a quality generated by the interviewer in which he neither talks too much nor too little but shows his interest and encourages the patient to express himself, (2) rapport, which from the therapist is an indication of genuine interest in the patient's problem and is demonstrated by courtesy and respect that encourage ease and confidence from the patient, (3) freedom from interruption, which can further encourage the previous conditions by arranging to keep consultations exclusively for the patient, (i.e., telephone and other interruptions are to be kept to a minimum if they cannot be totally excluded), (4) psychological privacy, which is different from geographical privacy and defined as an attitude of the therapist in which he shows undivided interest and concern, (5) emotional objectivity, a quality essential to every therapist although difficult to develop in all circumstances because it primarily involves control of subjective feelings that the therapist may experience in his interaction with the patient (this is not to be equated with coldness or attempts to hide or control all spontaneous reactions but more with a mature acceptance of the patient). These conditions will be encouraged by verbal as well as nonverbal modes of communication.

The language used by both patient and therapist will nevertheless be their prime mode of communication. The questions a behavior therapist asks will be aimed at gaining a clear and unambiguous description of the presenting complaint. Ullmann and Krasner (1969) suggest the use of the "what" type of questions rather than the "why" type of questions, which would be more appropriate to therapists with a Freudian orientation. We would add "how," "when," and "where" types. If the patient has many complaints, he will be asked to describe his main complaint (in his own words) first. Questions should lead on logically from the therapist's constant attempts at structuring the information on which he tests his hypotheses about the patient. Some patients will automatically see their problems in behavioral terms, but others are more likely to see them as vague feelings of, for instance, inadequacy, depression, general dissatisfaction, or anxiety. In such cases the behavior therapist must teach his patient self-observation directed to the description of specific behavior occurring in specific contexts. This is not always so easy with patients who expect or want answers to "why" questions, but the therapist should take every opportunity to explain his approach in terms that will be understandable to the patient concerned. He must also dispel misunderstandings as to both his and the patient's expected roles, the most common misconception deriving from the patient's acceptance of a sick role that conflicts with the setting and fulfilling of realistic treatment goals. We think these goals can be successfully achieved only through full awareness on the patient's part and mutual cooperation.

Davison and Neale (1974) pointed out that models in abnormal psychology were less structured than the models of other sciences, including other areas of psychology. Leaving all questions of validity or merit aside, we have found various models helpful in conceptualizing patients' problems. No single model has explained all problems and sometimes a complaint needs more than one paradigm for conceptualization. The model the therapist adopts determines the way in which he directs the interview. For instance, in a case of phobia the therapist can test for Mowrer's Two-Factor Theory (1950) as well as look for evidence of other forms of learning (such as imitation, latent learning), cognitive factors (such as coping statements [Meichenbaum, 1973]), and constitutional predisposing factors. In turn the clinician's own observation should lead him to modify existing inadequate models as well as to formulate alternative models in appropriate areas.

Type and Location of Presenting Complaint

The broadest way to conceptualize a problem is to see it as either a behavioral *excess* or a behavioral *deficit*. With the problem conceptualized, further refinement is attempted with a view to taking appropriate measures. An organizing theory being adopted by many therapists who want to see their patients as complete persons and within their own environment is that which usually goes under the name of "general systems theory." For more elaborate treatment of this framework the reader is referred to Sundberg, Tyler, and Taplin (1973) and Miller (1971). One of the most appealing characteristics of this theory to the behavior therapist is the possibility of taking as one's unit of observation a defined set of interacting variables rather than being confined to single elements. For instance, in a unit such as marriage or a family, one can observe and modify complex interacting variables in addition to the single elements. The systems within which the individual moves are interrelated and also follow a hierarchy. Miller (1971) delineated seven levels of living systems: (1) the cell system—represented by individual cells within the body, (2) the organ system—represented by such systems as the nervous system, the alimentary systems, (3) the organismic system—which is *the* individual, (4) the groups system—represented by family, occupational, and recreational groupings, (5) the organizational system—represented by industrial, professional or social agencies. Levels 6 and 7 extend the systems from mainly national to international systems. Systems 2, 3, and 4 as defined above are of the greatest interest to behavior therapists. Locating the presenting complaint within one of these systems will determine the type of measure and intervention taken. Reconceptualizing these systems in their simplest form it can be said that the complaint may fit into one of these three types: (1) Its effects are shown within a well-defined aspect of the individual's total functioning, that is, fears, addictions, (2) many aspects of the individual's total functioning are affected, that is, more pervasive intrapersonal difficulties, and (3) its effects encompass external groupings, that is, problems involving work, family, or other interpersonal relationships. However, complaints may not be so easy to categorize, and intervention may be directed at more than one of these areas.

Before the presenting complaint can be assessed, a suitable operational definition must be obtained from the patient. The definition will involve both qualitative and quantitative aspects. Qualitative aspects are usually easier for the patient to recall than quantitative aspects, which will require more directed guidance. The therapist asks how the patient would describe the complaint, subsidiary questions being aimed at its behavioral components. For instance, exactly what changes does the patient observe in himself when he feels excessive anxiety, what form does any marital disagreement take? The levels of measurement will be determined by the operational definition of the complaints, but even if the highest levels of measurement were possible, as is evident in the other chapters of this book, once again it must be emphasized that the implications of these measurements must be made clear to the patient, often at a much simpler level. However, some form of baseline is essential in order to set goals and assess ongoing progress toward these goals, but these baselines must be understood by both therapist and patient. It is also obvious that the less complex the unit of behavior, the more likely it is to be accurately measurable, but this can be of value only if it also reflects equally well the presenting complaints. Some behavior therapists prefer problems for which there are obvious and strong measures. We would prefer not to limit our role so rigidly, and we would attempt to deal with complex as well as simple units of measurement. When feasible, baselines should include measures relating to such dimensions as frequency, intensity, and duration.

Recent History (Clarification 1)

Once the problem or problems have been described and assessed, a systematic search is made for antecedents and consequences. The patient is questioned initially as to the first time he noticed his problem—whether he remembers where he was, what he was doing, who was there at the time—to determine any remembered features of the total situation in which an undesired behavior appeared or a desired behavior stopped occurring. It is particularly rewarding for the behavior therapist to be able to fit a problem within one or more well-known models, but even if this is not possible, he can use the information obtained to systematically change certain aspects of the total problem situation empirically and let the results guide his next step.

After the possibility of directly related events is investigated, the presence of indirectly related events is similarly investigated. This is done in terms of systems 2, 3 and 4 discussed earlier and listed in Figure 5–1 under rubrics of biological, behavioral, or social changes with the assumption that such changes may predispose the individual to resort to maladaptive strategies.

Precision in identifying the variables maintaining the maladaptive behavior is crucial, since it is from these that a therapeutic program will be devised to modify the target behavior or behaviors. The analysis will be dictated by the well-established principles accumulated from the experimental literature. These principles have been clearly expounded in a number of recent books giving guidelines for behavioral analyses (Blackman, 1974; Karen, 1974; Liberman, 1972). It is obviously not so easy to identify or control all independent variables in the clinic as it is in the laboratory, but the developing clinical literature testifies to the ingenuity and patience of behavior therapists when faced with clinical problems. In our schema we suggest a close scrutiny of the variables that are eliciting and discriminative stimuli, contingency related conditions (when possible), and the consequences such behavior brings to both the patient and those near him. This is the area of investigation that would most benefit from independent adjuncts that might include both standardized and nonstandardized measures to enhance objectivity. One such adjunct we have found particularly useful is interviewing a person who is near or "significant" to the patient (and often likely to be influenced by the problem behavior) or someone who knows the patient well. This part of the analysis of the presenting complaints may eventually lead both therapist and patient to view several complaints as functionally similar or forming part of the same problem.

Past History (Clarification 2)

Nobody would deny that past events have some influence on present behavior, but some behavior therapists reject all such considerations because the data obtained is retrospective. Learning histories vary considerably from individual to individual because objects and events that make up the environment are unique to each individual, resulting in a wide range of respondent behavior. We feel that the behavior therapist will gain a great deal by listening to abstract relevant data from the past of his patients. It is undoubtedly of more interest with pervasive intrapersonal difficulties than with patients who have circumscribed problems. In our experience, the amount and the depth of past history sought are related to a lack of clarity or definition in the recent history.

We have also felt that information sought from the past should be focused on the presenting complaint and should further illuminate it. Masters and Johnson (1970) advocated histories related to the sexual value systems of their patients as necessary before realistic treatment could begin. We see most complex problems as being related to value systems needing greater understanding. For instance, occupational and vocational problems are maintained by their own value systems. In these complex problems, we also advocate an assessment of the patient's attitudes and values.

Assets

This line of investigation is motivated by our need to see the individual as a whole person as well as directly relevant in using assets to maximize good functioning generally. Personality theories and assessment directly based on such theories have been of disappointingly little value to the therapist because the dimensions isolated and measured have little to do with response to therapy (Mischel, 1968). The behavior therapist is of necessity interested in areas of good functioning, self-control, and motivation because these can be utilized during treatment and are likely to ensure the maintenance of treatment gains during the posttreatment period (e.g., using obsessional tendencies to their best advantage).

General Assets

A thorough analysis of the individual and of all the systems in which the patient is involved will reveal the areas in which the patient is experiencing maladaptive behavior, but it should also reveal other areas in which the patient's personal strengths may be put to use. In a particular system, other people in the patient's present or past may also provide strengths that can be utilized in achieving the goals for treatment. Goals must be mutually agreed on with the patient. Therefore, if other people close to the patient are also to be involved, their cooperation and consent to the specified goals must also be sought if that system is to work to the patient's advantage (e.g., a husband should agree enthusiastically to his wife's changed occupational goals). Other areas where the problems are slight can be rectified early in treatment, and this early success can increase the motivation of the patient in areas of greater stress, where systems may have broken down entirely (i.e., minor marital discord could be rectified, and this increase in harmony could lead to a greater confidence on the patient's part, which could extend into other interpersonal relationships).

Specific Assets

The therapist should investigate the way in which the patient has previously tried to control or modify maladaptive behavior and with what success his attempts were met. The therapist is equally interested in knowing how much control the patient is able to exert in different areas of his life.

Motivational factors are of utmost importance in all therapeutic endeavor. One should try to establish motivational strength by noting how frequently, readily, and in what way the patient has dealt with setbacks. Is the patient reliant on others for reinforcement and feedback, or can he be his own reinforcer? Assets formed during early developmental periods that are not being used at present may be revived and may assist in treatment. The possibility of developing new assets as well as maximizing existing ones should always be considered.

Only such a comprehensive analysis of the individual's assets, real and potential, in addition to his problem areas will give rise to a complete picture of the individual and provide clues as to how to treat him most efficaciously.

CASE ILLUSTRATION

To illustrate the above schema, we include a transcript of a behavioral interview conducted by the senior author with a depressed 71-year old inpatient at a London teaching hospital, who was referred for assessment. This case has been selected because it is not typical of those usually referred for behavior therapy. Therefore it demonstrates the use of such a procedure in an atypical case. The interview was carried out in the presence of twelve clinical psychologists for teaching purposes.

THERAPIST: Sit down, I prefer to have you on my left hand side. Well, these are all professional people; it is confidential.

PATIENT: You need not worry about that.

THERAPIST: I would like you to talk about your problems and then see whether there is any way we could help you. In fact, your doctor was coming to see me about you because, as you probably know, there are various schools of thought in this field and they were thinking about coming to me to see if my tricks can help you.

PATIENT: What are your tricks?

THERAPIST: I'll explain to you. First of all, we have to find out what your problem is. You have been on this ward how long now?

PATIENT: Since the end of January.

THERAPIST: End of January. All right, and you came with what problem? What was your original complaint?

PATIENT: The thing is it came on so suddenly, I just do not know.

THERAPIST: You know what came suddenly?

PATIENT: The depression.

THERAPIST: Can you tell me what you mean by depression?

PATIENT: Just one day I did not want to get up and go to work.

THERAPIST: You did not want to go to work.

PATIENT: I am a retired pensioner.

THERAPIST: I see, and you stay in bed and what do you feel there?

PATIENT: I feel that things are getting worse and worse, everything is an effort.

THERAPIST: Let us go through it. Are you interested in anything at the moment?

PATIENT: Unfortunately, I have got no emotional feelings at the moment.

THERAPIST: No interest, what do you enjoy?

PATIENT: If I could enjoy something, I would be a happy man, enjoy something for ten minutes a day. I enjoy nothing at all, unfortunately.

THERAPIST: Do you eat?

PATIENT: Very litte.

THERAPIST: Weight loss?

PATIENT: I have not really troubled . . .

THERAPIST: Has there been any loss of weight?

PATIENT: I could not say.

THERAPIST: Eating, does it mean anything to you?

PATIENT: No.

THERAPIST: How do you sleep?

PATIENT: Now that is the amazing thing, I can sleep and sleep and sleep.

THERAPIST: Is the problem getting up, waking up?

PATIENT: Yes.

THERAPIST: So that is one thing that you can enjoy?

PATIENT: Sleeping, yes, because I am unconscious, I do not know what is going on.

THERAPIST: But in that period before you go to sleep, when are you drowsy?

PATIENT: That is the unfortunate thing, there is no period when I am awake nor asleep.

THERAPIST: You mean to say you put your head on the pillow and what happens in that period of time before you fall asleep, what are you thinking about?

PATIENT: How I am going to feel tomorrow.

THERAPIST: So looking at any day there is nothing in front?

PATIENT: Nothing.

THERAPIST: You are not looking forward to anything at all?

PATIENT: Nothing at all.

THERAPIST: Would you take your life?

PATIENT: If I had the opportunity.

THERAPIST: Have you seriously considered it?

PATIENT: I certainly have.

THERAPIST: Do you sometimes weep when you are on your own?

PATIENT: I have done the last couple of times.

THERAPIST: Okay. So how long have you been depressed like that?

PATIENT: Since March of this year. Depressed about my life, I mean.

THERAPIST: You said that you came here first in January of this year?

PATIENT: I noticed it getting worse.

THERAPIST: Is it the first time in your life that you noticed this depression?

PATIENT: No.

THERAPIST: Then the first time in your life, how long ago?

PATIENT: Going back 25 years, just after the war.

THERAPIST: Okay. Just after the war. You have no idea why you feel like that?

PATIENT: None at all.

THERAPIST: You seem to have no energy either?

PATIENT: That is correct.

THERAPIST: Are you very slow in your movements?

PATIENT: Painfully slow.

THERAPIST: What about thinking, is it an effort to think?

PATIENT: No, I am clear in my head, I know white is white and black is black.

THERAPIST: So your thought processes are as clear and as fast as ever, but do you still daydream?

PATIENT: I like to.

THERAPIST: What do you daydream about?

PATIENT: Being well again.

THERAPIST: Do you blame yourself for the way that you are?

PATIENT: No, because I do not know why it has happened, how it has come about.

THERAPIST: Do you think that you deserve it?

PATIENT: No, I do not think that I deserve it.

THERAPIST: Do you sometimes think that you are a worthless man?

PATIENT: I know I am a worthless man.

THERAPIST: Why?

PATIENT: Because I have got a sick wife at home and I went home yesterday and could only help her with very, very little.

THERAPIST: So you are married?

PATIENT: Yes.

THERAPIST: Got any children?

PATIENT: Yes, you see I married twice and the second time that I married, I married a young person not half my age.

THERAPIST: How old are you?

PATIENT: Seventy-one.

THERAPIST: Your wife?

PATIENT: Thirty-four.

THERAPIST: You are retired, so you do not work?

PATIENT: I had to work to sort of supplement my income. I had a little pension from work. We could manage quite nicely and now this lot has cropped up. Why it has cropped up, I do not know.

THERAPIST: Could you give me an idea of how you spent your time before you came here?

PATIENT: Got up in the morning, got my breakfast, couple of days work a week.

THERAPIST: Half days?

PATIENT: Full days.

THERAPIST: Enjoyed it?

PATIENT: Very much.

THERAPIST: What did you do?

PATIENT: Two days as a serviceman.

THERAPIST: And on those days that you did not work?

PATIENT: Used to help the wife very, very much indeed. Unfortunately, she has had a very severe illness.

THERAPIST: What is it?

PATIENT: Well, woman trouble, you know.

THERAPIST: Did she have a hysterectomy?

PATIENT: That is the next thing they are talking about; that is taking the womb away is it not?

THERAPIST: Have you got any emotional feeling toward your wife?

PATIENT: Let us say responsibility.

THERAPIST: Here is the problem in a nutshell: nothing interests you?

PATIENT: Correct.

THERAPIST: You might as well stay in bed?

PATIENT: Exactly.

THERAPIST: Let us go back, when you enjoyed life, you can recall that? What did you particularly enjoy?

PATIENT: Music.

THERAPIST: Now does it mean anything to you?

PATIENT: Nothing means anything to me.

THERAPIST: Let's go back soon after the war started. What did you enjoy doing during the war? I remember that period very well; I enjoyed myself very much indeed.

PATIENT: I was in the Air Force.

THERAPIST: So was I. Which part? Bomber Command? Fighter Command?

PATIENT: A little command called *X*.

THERAPIST: Where were you stationed?

PATIENT: (Town) for a time.

THERAPIST: In the forces did you enjoy life?

PATIENT: Yes.

THERAPIST: What did you particularly enjoy?

PATIENT: It is difficult to say, just life in general.

THERAPIST: I am trying to see you as a youngster in the Air Force. What sort of bloke were you, can you recall?

PATIENT: Happy-go-lucky sort of person.

THERAPIST: Happy-go-lucky sort of person. Lots of friends or a few close friends?

PATIENT: A fair amount of friends.

THERAPIST: Girl friends?

PATIENT: Eh . . . no.

THERAPIST: You were not a ladies' man, were you? What about drink, did you like to have a pint?

PATIENT: Oh, yes.

THERAPIST: Good sense of humor?

PATIENT: Pretty good.

THERAPIST: You see, when you talk about it, you begin to smile; when you think about it, you begin to cheer up a bit. Just think about, what suddenly stopped you enjoying life?

PATIENT: That I would like to know myself.

THERAPIST: Shall we try to find out?

PATIENT: Yes.

THERAPIST: Will you help me?

PATIENT: I certainly will.

THERAPIST: Life was all right in the forces, then you came out. What did you do?

PATIENT: Went back to my old job.

THERAPIST: Which was?

PATIENT: I was working in a warehouse at that time.

THERAPIST: How did you see the job after your war experience, was it still a good job, an exciting job or boring?

PATIENT: Well, it was boring after a time.

THERAPIST: What did you do, did you leave it or did you stick it?

PATIENT: Because they ran a pension scheme, I stuck it.

THERAPIST: Then you did a job you did not enjoy. When you came out of the forces, how old were you? Thirty years back you must have been a little over 40?

PATIENT: That is right.

THERAPIST: Were you married, at what age did you marry?

PATIENT: At 26.

THERAPIST: Married before the war. How many children?

PATIENT: Two.

THERAPIST: Can you describe your marriage, what was it like?

PATIENT: Like a lot of marriages during the war, it went off the rails.

THERAPIST: What about, anything?

PATIENT: My first wife had a kiddie and we decided to hush it up, pretend it never happened. But it never really worked, she never wanted me in the first place.

THERAPIST: Why did you marry her?

PATIENT: Because I was very much in love with her.

THERAPIST: You fell in love with her. When men fall in love, they compare the current partner with previous partners, they find something different, something better, they say that it is. What was so wonderful about her that swept you off your feet?

PATIENT: Her looks probably.

THERAPIST: Looks. Did you have a good contact with her right from the start, could you discuss things, do things together?

PATIENT: Oh, yes.

THERAPIST: What did you like doing with her.

PATIENT: Same as with the second one, I suppose.

THERAPIST: What did you enjoy doing in the past? We are not talking about sex, I am talking about social life together.

PATIENT: It was the early days of wireless and that, and that was about all.

THERAPIST: Did you listen to ITMA?

PATIENT: Yes.

THERAPIST: What else did you do? Did you take her out? Pictures?

PATIENT: Yes.

THERAPIST: Holidays, did you go together?

PATIENT: Yes.

THERAPIST: So life was fun then, and what went wrong in the first marriage?

PATIENT: She never really wanted to marry me to tell you the truth. It was only through her mother saying "give him a chance." In other words, she married me out of sympathy.

THERAPIST: So gradually you felt rejected?

PATIENT: I suppose so.

THERAPIST: And what happened, did you divorce your wife or did she divorce you?

PATIENT: She divorced me.

THERAPIST: On what grounds?

PATIENT: Cruelty.

THERAPIST: How could she, had she married a cruel man?

PATIENT: No.

THERAPIST: How could she do it on the grounds of cruelty?

PATIENT: I did not trouble to defend the case.

THERAPIST: And that was at what age? How old were you when she divorced you?

PATIENT: My memory has gone, I have got no idea at all.

THERAPIST: Roughly, how long were you married, 10 years, 20 years?

PATIENT: Divorced after about 20 years, I suppose.

THERAPIST: In this period during the war, did you see your wife at weekends? Did you come home gladly to see your wife?

PATIENT: Yes, we were bombed out, you see.

THERAPIST: You lived in (town) right? And your wife came to stay with you in (town).

PATIENT: For a little while, till she went back to relatives.

THERAPIST: Well, now, it is difficult for me to understand one thing. You married your wife and you felt that you loved her; she married you out of pity. Why did she take such a long time, 20 years, before she decided to get away from you? When a woman marries and very quickly discovers it does not work, she makes at least an attempt to make another go at life. Your first wife spent 20 years with you. Can you understand this?

PATIENT: I can understand the dates, yes.

THERAPIST: How many children did you have?

PATIENT: Three but really two; the third one was a war child.

THERAPIST: Do you see your children?

PATIENT: Not at all now.

THERAPIST: Do you know what happened to your wife? You are not in contact with her at all?

PATIENT: No, only through the court.

THERAPIST: Was she the same age as you or younger?

PATIENT: Two years younger.

THERAPIST: So you, in fact, coexisted with her all right. Sexually?

PATIENT: No, not a great amount.

THERAPIST: Was she disinterested or were you disinterested?

PATIENT: She was more disinterested.

THERAPIST: You do not know what happened to her at all when she divorced you. Do you know if she married again?

PATIENT: No, she has not.

THERAPIST: Was she a good mother?

PATIENT: Yes.

THERAPIST: Sometimes during your first marriage you must have been unhappy?

PATIENT: Yes, I suppose I was.

THERAPIST: Did you experience any of these depressive feelings then?

PATIENT: No.

THERAPIST: You are still struggling, trying to make a go of things, so you had a goal in life. You got divorced; what happened then? When you married for the second time, what age were you?

PATIENT: Fifty-one, I think.

THERAPIST: Your wife was 21?

PATIENT: No, 22.

THERAPIST: Now, why did you marry her, do you know why?

PATIENT: No.

THERAPIST: You did not love her, did you? Out of pity?

PATIENT: Probably.

THERAPIST: What was wrong with her?

PATIENT: I do not know.

THERAPIST: Did she work at the time that you met her?

PATIENT: She was working at the same place as me.

THERAPIST: Did she have lots of friends when you met her?

PATIENT: No, she was a very isolated girl, an only child.

THERAPIST: Shy, reserved?

PATIENT: No, really the other way. She was pushed by her parents into dancing.

THERAPIST: Was she an unhappy girl?

PATIENT: No, she was a very happy girl.

THERAPIST: But rather isolated. Did it bother you that she was 30 years younger than you?

PATIENT: Not at that period, no.

THERAPIST: How did the marriage develop? Was it a successful one?

PATIENT: Of course, most people were against it, against the age barrier. All they said in the finish was "you have made your bed, you have got to lie in it."

THERAPIST: What was the most difficult aspect of your marriage? I realize the age barrier, what else? How do you get on together?

PATIENT: Marvellously.

THERAPIST: Enjoyed doing things together?

PATIENT: Used to, but since January everything is dead in me. Mind you, she has nursed me through this before twice. This is the fourth bad depression that I have had; I seem to get these depressions every five years.

THERAPIST: So the first depression was when?

PATIENT: Probably 1948.

THERAPIST: The divorce—right?

PATIENT: No, a bit before.

THERAPIST: So you were still married, but your marriage was on the rocks, out of the forces into a boring job. When did you realize that your wife was contemplating a divorce? Surely before things happened? Was she faithful to you?

PATIENT: Except for this odd occasion.

THERAPIST: Okay. First depression, how long did it last?

PATIENT: Six weeks.

THERAPIST: What did you get, tablets?

PATIENT: No, electric treatment.

THERAPIST: Did you recover?

PATIENT: Yes.

THERAPIST: Second one?

PATIENT: Same again, six weeks.

THERAPIST: Third one, six weeks again. Electric treatment?

PATIENT: Yes.

THERAPIST: Who treated you?

PATIENT: No idea, I cannot remember.

THERAPIST: Fourth one is the current one since January. This one is lasting much longer now, it is not six weeks. You have had your electrical treatment and pills and nothing has happened. When did you retire, how long ago? At 65 I suppose, that is, six years ago. So you have spent all your time in the same job? Do you regard yourself as a success workwise?

PATIENT: No.

THERAPIST: Any financial hardship?

PATIENT: No, but there will be very shortly.

THERAPIST: Why?

PATIENT: Because the money is running out.

THERAPIST: Your savings are running out? And your wife, does she work?

PATIENT: Unfortunately, she cannot do anything at the moment because of this operation. We do not seem to be very educated people; we do not know very much about this social security business.

THERAPIST: You can get advice on this from our social workers here.

PATIENT: You see, my wife is in such a state, she cannot go anywhere by public transport; she has to go everywhere by taxi.

THERAPIST: When did she start having these troubles?

PATIENT: Some time this year.

THERAPIST: So when you look at your life, you have no job because you are not in a fit state to work, your wife is sick, you have to take care of her and you can hardly take care of yourself. Is there any relationship going on between you and your wife? Do you still enjoy her company?

PATIENT: To be honest, no.

THERAPIST: She is in a pretty bad state. How does she feel about you?

PATIENT: She feels very, very sorry for me up to such a point that she is getting like I am.

THERAPIST: In this 13 years of your marriage do you still feel the same way about your wife as you did originally, or has there been any changes?

PATIENT: I have no emotional feelings whatsoever.

THERAPIST: But originally you did?

PATIENT: Of course.

THERAPIST: When did you lose this emotional feeling for her?

PATIENT: Not only for her, but for everybody and everything.

THERAPIST: The last time you came into hospital, you were married to your wife, did you lose your feelings then?

PATIENT: Not to such a degree as now.

THERAPIST: You do not know why you lost these feelings? Do you think that she feels the same way about you?

PATIENT: She is very concerned.

THERAPIST: Has she been a good wife to you?

PATIENT: Very good.

THERAPIST: Is she interested sexually?

PATIENT: She would be.

THERAPIST: Did you have a good sex life with her?

PATIENT: Pretty good; we did until the beginning of this year.

THERAPIST: Why?

PATIENT: Just became impotent.

THERAPIST: Do you think you became impotent and then started losing all your feelings or that you became depressed and then became impotent?

PATIENT: Became depressed, then became impotent.

THERAPIST: Does your wife complain about it, does she miss it?

PATIENT: She says she does not, but being human she would do.

THERAPIST: Let us go back a little bit, can you describe your mother to me?

PATIENT: I was very fond of my mother.

THERAPIST: What was she like, what was characteristic about her?

PATIENT: She died at the age of 51 with cancer, sir.

THERAPIST: What sort of woman was she?

PATIENT: Very warm, lively.

THERAPIST: Affectionate?

PATIENT: Very.

THERAPIST: Loved you?

PATIENT: Definitely.

THERAPIST: Were you the only one or did you have brothers and sisters?

PATIENT: I had four sisters.

THERAPIST: Were you the eldest one, youngest, or the middle?

PATIENT: The second eldest.

THERAPIST: Who was preferred by your mother? Did she show any preferences?

PATIENT: No, she did not show any preferences.

THERAPIST: Was she just, fair in treating you?

PATIENT: Yes.

THERAPIST: Could you predict when you would be punished by her?

PATIENT: I never knew her do any punishing, except telling off.

THERAPIST: Were you such a good boy?

PATIENT: No, I just got away with it, I suppose.

THERAPIST: So you had a good relationship with her?

PATIENT: Yes, sir.

THERAPIST: So you loved her, trusted her, respected her?

PATIENT: Yes.

THERAPIST: And your father?

PATIENT: Father was a stern man, sir, he was a different kind of person.

THERAPIST: Stern, strict?

PATIENT: Strict, yes. Not that I saw much of him; he used to work till nine o'clock at night.

THERAPIST: What did he do?

PATIENT: He was a shop assistant. On Saturday, well, he got home and well, you probably used to see him at weekends.

THERAPIST: Were you close to him?

PATIENT: Fairly, I suppose.

THERAPIST: Well, respect with fear or respect with affection?

PATIENT: Respect with fear, though he never laid a hand on me.

THERAPIST: How did your parents get on together?

PATIENT: Not too well, sir.

THERAPIST: Do you know why?

PATIENT: Financial trouble.

THERAPIST: Was that the whole story? Was that the only trouble? Was there an age difference?

PATIENT: Only a couple of years.

THERAPIST: Usually when a marriage does not work out, it is not the finances. It is something else, and the finances just add to the problem. Were there any other problems? Do you think they were happily married?

PATIENT: No, they were not happy people.

THERAPIST: How old were you when your mother died?

PATIENT: Twenty-six.

THERAPIST: And your father?

PATIENT: He died about 70.

THERAPIST: Did you maintain contact with him?

PATIENT: Yes.

THERAPIST: He was very strict but fair; was he a reliable man?

PATIENT: Yes, very.

THERAPIST: Were they faithful to each other?

PATIENT: Definitely, in those days . . .

THERAPIST: When you say he was strict, how did he demonstrate this strictness?

PATIENT: I had to go to church on Sunday, you know, morning, afternoon, and evening.

THERAPIST: And did you rebel, or did you go obediently?

PATIENT: I suppose I used to rebel at times.

THERAPIST: Are you a religious man now?

PATIENT: No, sir.

THERAPIST: Your mother, was she a religious person as well?

PATIENT: No.

THERAPIST: Who was the boss in the family?

PATIENT: Father would be the boss.

THERAPIST: But who was the real boss?

PATIENT: My father was the real boss.

THERAPIST: Did he have any preferences for one of your sisters, or was he again very fair?

PATIENT: I think he was pretty fair.

THERAPIST: So how do you remember your early childhood?

PATIENT: That's going back a bit, is it not?

THERAPIST: Yes, it is, of course. For that period, a normal childhood? No bad memories?

PATIENT: Not particularly, no.

THERAPIST: Do you remember any illnesses in early childhood apart from the normal childhood illnesses?

PATIENT: No.

THERAPIST: Did your mother tell you that you had some problems, like food fads or temper tantrums, something like that?

PATIENT: No.

THERAPIST: You were surrounded by women, weren't you? Your youngest sister, how old was she when you were about 10?

PATIENT: She wasn't born.

THERAPIST: So there was a gap between you. What was the age range?

PATIENT: The eldest is one year ten months older than me, the youngest is about 60 years old.

THERAPIST: How do you get on with your sisters? Do you contact them?

PATIENT: One comes up to see me, and the others, well, I do not know why we did not all go to pieces.

THERAPIST: What do you mean go to pieces?

PATIENT: Well, my eldest sister just can't understand why I got in a condition like this; she has got no time for it.

THERAPIST: Are they all right, all your sisters?

PATIENT: Fine.

THERAPIST: No problems. Do you remember your father getting moody sometimes?

PATIENT: No.

THERAPIST: Was he always all right, no problems and your mother too, was she all right, no problems?

PATIENT: Well, finances.

THERAPIST: Except for finances. But did you suffer because of financial problems? Did you have enough food, clothing? Materially were you taken care of?

PATIENT: Yes.

THERAPIST: You stayed at school from the age of what?

PATIENT: Five to fourteen.

THERAPIST: How do you remember that period?

PATIENT: I just detested school, I am a bad scholar.

THERAPIST: Why?

PATIENT: I cannot spell.

THERAPIST: Why do you make such a point of your spelling? Lots of people cannot spell.

PATIENT: Let's face it, people are good at something. I was never good at anything.

THERAPIST: You mean at school, you were always the last one in the class?

PATIENT: Average.

THERAPIST: Average, that is all right then. Do you recall anything unpleasant in your early schooldays? I am trying to picture you at school, how were you? Good, obedient or rather a slightly naughty boy?

PATIENT: I was a goody, goody.

THERAPIST: Popular?

PATIENT: I think so.

THERAPIST: Made fun of?

PATIENT: Not that I know of.

THERAPIST: Nickname?

PATIENT: Not at school.

THERAPIST: What about problems at school, did the teachers like you?

PATIENT: I think so.

THERAPIST: Games, participated in all activities?

PATIENT: I came at the wrong time for playing games, sir; the war came.

THERAPIST: The war started. Did you have any bad experiences during the war itself, the first one?

PATIENT: Dead scared during the Zeppelin raids.

THERAPIST: Did you have any bad experiences during the second one?

PATIENT: Certainly did, but it did not worry me then.

THERAPIST: No problems at school really. I suppose no one told you about sex in the family. It was a dirty word?

PATIENT: Yes.

THERAPIST: Where did you learn about it?

PATIENT: The usual way.

THERAPIST: What was the usual way in those days?

PATIENT: Somebody knew something and said something and so on, and so on.

THERAPIST: What did you feel about it when you learned about sex? What was your attitude to it when you learned about it?

PATIENT: (no answer, long pause).

THERAPIST: Do you know what I am trying to find out? Did you think it was something very fantastic, something pleasant, sinful, something matter of fact, at the very beginning, when you were a little boy?

PATIENT: My brain has gone, I cannot answer these.

THERAPIST: All right, you left school, we know something about that. I would like to know the following. Can you give me some idea of what was your ideal girl when you were 16, 17, 18? Did you have a picture of an ideal girl?

PATIENT: A picture?

THERAPIST: We all have a picture of an ideal partner.

PATIENT: You see, my brain is dim, I understand what you mean but I cannot express myself.

THERAPIST: Well, when you married your wife you were 26. Before you were 26, you had met some girls. Did you have lots of girlfriends or just a few?

PATIENT: Just a few.

THERAPIST: Do you remember any girl with whom you had a much longer relationship than just a casual one, before you married? Was there a girl you went out with for a long time?

PATIENT: No.

THERAPIST: No, so there were other casual girlfriends before that. I would like to know how you treated your girlfriends. Were you a gentleman or a bit naughty?

PATIENT: A bit naughty at times.

THERAPIST: And you cannot recall what sort of a type?

PATIENT: We used to call them the sporty type in those days.

THERAPIST: Your first wife, you said that she was vivacious, full of life. Was she pretty?

PATIENT: That was the trouble!

THERAPIST: Why do you say that was the trouble?

PATIENT: Other people seem to make passes at them, don't they?

THERAPIST: Are you a jealous man?

PATIENT: Would be, yes.

THERAPIST: How soon, that would be extremely useful information, did you start realizing your wife did not return the affection you gave her?

PATIENT: I should say, pretty well the day we got married.

THERAPIST: So for 20 years you were married realizing this?

PATIENT: Yes, I know it does not seem to make sense.

THERAPIST: Did she make you very unhappy occasionally?

PATIENT: Yes, occasionally.

THERAPIST: What did you do? Did you argue, talk about it, or did you just withdraw?

PATIENT: Just withdrew.

THERAPIST: Has it always been your way of dealing with problems?

PATIENT: I'm afraid I cannot take responsibility, I do know that.

THERAPIST: So very easy when problems just pile up. I have already asked you if you experienced, during your marriage, some of the depression that you are experiencing at the moment. You cannot remember?

PATIENT: No.

THERAPIST: Your two children, were they planned?

PATIENT: No.

THERAPIST: Your wife, was she very displeased about it when she got pregnant?

PATIENT: No, I do not think so, just accepted it as the normal thing.

THERAPIST: Did you want children?

PATIENT: Certainly.

THERAPIST: I see, and your wife, was she a good mother then?

PATIENT: Yes.

THERAPIST: Did she keep a good house?

PATIENT: Quite good.

THERAPIST: Houseproud?

PATIENT: She was clean and tidy.

THERAPIST: You said she was not very much interested in sex, but was she interested in sex with other men?

PATIENT: That I would not know, sir.

THERAPIST: But she was not faithful to you?

PATIENT: Only on that one occasion, she said, during the war.

THERAPIST: Did you forgive her?

PATIENT: Of course.

THERAPIST: Can you please help me? I have one little problem about your second wife. You said that she was a gay person when you met her, full of life, happy, why did she marry you? You said you married her out of pity, but I still do not see what you pitied in her.

PATIENT: She was that type of kiddie . . .

THERAPIST: It is difficult to talk about it?

PATIENT: That is difficult.

THERAPIST: And, as you know, those things that are difficult for you to talk about are important for me to know. I would very much like to know why your wife married you and why you married her.

PATIENT: There used to be a press office in (tube station). It used to be an old workhouse I think. We were walking past there one day, there were people shuffling up to the railings begging for cigarettes. I said to her, "I hope I never get like that," and she said to me, "You never will, I'll see to that."

THERAPIST: Did she have parents?

PATIENT: Yes.

THERAPIST: How did she get on with them?

PATIENT: Very well, I think, but the mother is a very dominating woman.

THERAPIST: Was she totally inexperienced when you married her?

PATIENT: No.

THERAPIST: Was she experienced?

PATIENT: Very much so.

THERAPIST: But why did you pity her, that is what I do not understand? You suggest she was not unhappy. If I could understand that, I would have a clue to your problem. Probably you do not understand yourself. I believe to understand why you feel the way that you do, something has happened, is happening in this marriage. Do you follow? On top of that, I think that it is very important that you are not working and that your wife is ill. Other things are beginning to pile up on you right now, but I think, much more important, something is going on in your marriage which really hurts you. This is my assumption.

PATIENT: The assumption is that I now cannot give her what we used to have.

THERAPIST: Yes, you either had something in the very beginning that you don't have now; something that happened in your first marriage is happening now and this adds to your problems and probably, if this could be sorted out, you would not feel the way you do, do you see what I mean?

PATIENT: I see what you mean, but I am answering as truthfully as I can.

THERAPIST: Try to make me feel better by telling me why you felt sorry for your wife. If a man feels sorry for a woman, one supposes it is because she is very, very poor or lonely or miserable, something is wrong and it is lovely to be able to protect someone. It is a nice feeling.

PATIENT: Beautiful.

THERAPIST: Beautiful, I agree, but then you do not suggest that your wife needed any pity because she was perfectly all right. This is what is difficult for me to understand, do you follow?

PATIENT: I do!

THERAPIST: But still I do not understand why your wife wanted to marry you, never mind the age difference, because I always ask the same question of anybody, I would like to understand. There are a variety of reasons why people marry.

PATIENT: Probably, I had been on my own for 10 years and then she came along and seemed a gay, vivacious sort of child. That is just what happened.

THERAPIST: But it is not very common that a girl marries a man nearly 40 years older. There must be a good reason for it.

PATIENT: She was not pregnant or anything.

THERAPIST: I am not suggesting that.

PATIENT: No, but that could be the reason.

THERAPIST: Let me put it this way. There is a girl who never had a father; now she is looking for a father figure. She is happy with a man like that. Right. Another one, supposing a girl had a very, very bad experience with men and wants to marry a nice, safe man who will appreciate her and who will treat her well. You see what I mean. I am trying to find out why your wife decided to marry you. Did she ever tell you?

PATIENT: No.

THERAPIST: So you just asked her if she'd marry you and she said yes, as simple as that?

PATIENT: As simple as that, or she might even have broached the subject herself, "I'd like to marry somebody like you." I pointed out the age factor.

THERAPIST: Yes, and what did she say?

PATIENT: "If I had a few years with you, I'd be happy."

THERAPIST: And you didn't question it any further?

PATIENT: No.

THERAPIST: And do you know anything about her past, her childhood? Do you know her parents?

PATIENT: Yes.

THERAPIST: Are they nice people.

PATIENT: Her mother was a caretaker for a doctor, and her father worked on the railway.

THERAPIST: So at the moment, the relationship between you is not very good?

PATIENT: Not at this moment. More so on her side, as I say. I'm callous, no emotional feelings.

THERAPIST: When a man tells me he has no emotional feelings over someone as dear to him as his wife, one possibility is that the wife hurt him very badly?

PATIENT: No, because I've got it for my daughter, I've got it for everybody.

THERAPIST: Well, I still maintain that I have no other way to understand your problem. Let me put it this way. You've had a very good life as a child, protected by your mother, well taken care of. You had a very strict father who tended to impose very high standards, principles, and you were never well prepared to stand up for yourself, how to deal with problems, you would rather withdraw. You were rather an unassertive, nice kindly man and I expect, as well, a bit of a romantic. You idealized women. Your mother was a very good woman, so you tended to look for a sort of ideal woman and you plunged into this marriage when you thought you'd found an ideal woman and you got rejected, it didn't work out. You were in trouble and you'd never been prepared to deal with it. You put everything into this marriage. You expected her to be your ideal woman, and when she wasn't, your world collapsed for you. Not only that, but she didn't care very much.

PATIENT: But I was a lot better in between.

THERAPIST: When did you feel better?

PATIENT: Every fifth year, it seems to be.

THERAPIST: Yes, what I am trying to tell you is that the trouble started here. It must have been a fantastic disappointment to you. The world collapsed.

PATIENT: Yes.

THERAPIST: I would expect it to fluctuate up and down. I would expect you to feel better if your wife became slightly better predisposed toward you. You would feel better straight away. And also I expect that you have high standards. When you do something, you want to do it well or you won't touch it. That's what I mean by not being able to take responsibility. Now you lived on your own for 13 years, right?

PATIENT: Ten years.

THERAPIST: And you weren't very happy. Do you remember that period? Did you live with your parents or on your own?

PATIENT: On my own.

THERAPIST: In a bedsitter?

PATIENT: Yes.

THERAPIST: Did you have any friends during that period?

PATIENT: Yes, I mean I can't understand. During that period, I was all right. I never had any problem.

THERAPIST: You led a bachelor's life, no involvement?

PATIENT: That's right.

THERAPIST: Then you met this girl, your second wife, and I bet you felt much better. By the way, the marriage at the beginning was working much better, at least, this is what you suggest. Sex was all right too. And then, things started going wrong again?

PATIENT: I got these depressions.

THERAPIST: You see, you tried to suggest to me that depression creates these problems for you, and I'm trying to suggest that the problems created these depressions. So we think differently about it. You are trying to convince me that you have periodic depressions every five years. But not during your period of bachelorhood. What I am suggesting to you is that for you the greatest stress, let me put it this way, that you were very much interested in a good close relationship with another person, a close relationship in which you feel secure and loved, accepted and appreciated. When you went into this relationship, it didn't work out. You got out of it eventually, no involvement. But if that period of being single was such a wonderful period, you wouldn't have touched another women with a barge pole, would you? You are still looking for a close relationship with another human being. That's why you went into this marriage. I think something else: It didn't work out because she married you out of pity. You were genuinely involved, but you went into this one hoping you could create a wonderful relationship by offering somebody needing protection, care and protection. You thought if you did this, you would get in return the affection, appreciation that you expect. My hypothesis is that it didn't work out and depression returned. On top of that, your retirement didn't help very much. On top of that, your wife's illness hasn't helped very much. On top of that, you're an active person, you've always worked, you begin to face financial problems. But I think at the beginning of it something happened in your second marriage. I'll understand if you say, yes, but don't want to talk about it. You see what I mean, the way I think about you. I do not believe that you have recurrent depressions for organic reasons or whatever it is. There are experiments, by the way, which show that if a person who has never been able to deal with stress, to cope with problems or responsibilities, have these piling up on them, they just give up and become depressed. Animals behave in a similar way. Do you see what I mean? If I look at you the way I want to look at you, there is a chance to help you. But if you tell me, "It's every five years a depression, doctor," then it's very difficult to help, because the only treatments for an organic type of depression are pills, electrical treatment. If they do not eliminate it, what else do you do? But if there is a psychological problem in your marriage, then there's a possibility that one can help you psychologically. Do you understand?

PATIENT: Yes.

THERAPIST: You see, if you look at your style of life right from childhood, I cannot help but think along these lines. You see, in your family, no one gets depressed. You see, if you had said your father or your mother got depressed, I would think it's possible that you have a basic predisposition, but there is no such evidence. You lead a good life—you are a "goody, goody." No problem until your first marriage. I assume that a problem is going on in your marriage right now, you don't feel as secure as you used to, that's why you're depressed. You think about it, because if they ask me, suppose the professor comes to me and says, "Let's see if you can help." I would say, "Yes, I can help, if I get the right information." Because if you force me to think that the depression just recurs and has nothing to do with your problems, then I cannot help because pills are the answer. You see what I mean? Now, how many times since January have you returned to this hospital?

PATIENT: Twice.

THERAPIST: What precipitated this return to the hospital?

PATIENT: My wife was finding it difficult to cope, the second time my wife had to go into hospital, so she couldn't look after me.

THERAPIST: Tell me, is your wife very good at caring for you when you need it?

PATIENT: I know, I get her down now.

THERAPIST: But is she a good nurse, good at taking care of you?

PATIENT: She would do, but she's not in a position herself at the moment.

THERAPIST: I understand, but before, during your third depression?

PATIENT: Yes, she used to come over to the hospital pretty well every day. It was a long journey in those days; she never had any of this trouble she's got now.

THERAPIST: Okay. I understand. Does she become more affectionate when you are in trouble? You know, some women do when their husband suffers or is ill. Much more affectionate. Is your wife like that?

PATIENT: I would say, yes.

THERAPIST: Do you think she still loves you?

PATIENT: Yes, I'm sure she does.

THERAPIST: But it's difficult for her to express it because of her illness? Can you trust her implicitly? Remember that she is now 34. You suggest that she's an attractive women. You said "The trouble with my first wife, she was too pretty, other men looked at her." Do men look at this wife?

PATIENT: They certainly do.

THERAPIST: Is she pretty?

PATIENT: She's beautiful.

THERAPIST: Do other men look at her?

PATIENT: Certainly, they do.

THERAPIST: Do you trust her?

PATIENT: Yes.

THERAPIST: You have no grounds to suspect that she has been unfaithful to you? Why I'm so suspicious about it is because, already, you have had this experience.

PATIENT: Yes.

THERAPIST: You are more likely to be suspicious with the second one. I think it's unfair of me to press for this information, I wish you would come out with it, it would sort of make me happier. Either I'm right or wrong, I don't know. This is my opinion at the moment. But if I'm right, I could try to help you. Do you understand? I see that it is very difficult for you to talk about it. When I ask you a question that is difficult for you to answer, you get muddled up and you say you can't remember. This is probably not an ideal place to talk about it. Probably we'll have to sit down alone and have a chat and if you feel like crying, have a good cry, it will help. When you feel like talking to me, you tell your doctor that you would like to talk to me, then I will see you on my own, the two of us. It's probably too difficult for you to talk in front of these people. Thank you very much for coming.

Conclusion

It is hoped that this somewhat long interview demonstrates in a clear way the uses of this type of behavioral analysis. We aimed to demonstrate that the interview was goal directed and directive but that at all times the therapist was sensitive to all responses from the patient. In spite of the presence of twelve other people, psychological privacy was maintained because the therapist focused all his attention on the patient in a way that appeared to convince the patient of the genuineness of his efforts in seeking to discover how he, the patient, functioned in a total way (including his assets and deficits).

Rapport was established quickly and maintained throughout the interview. Points that were unclear to the patient were elucidated. As soon as hypotheses had been sufficiently formulated, they were presented to the patient for discussion, and he was put in the position of feeling free to accept, reject, or modify them. An examination of the patient's value system took place in a situation designed to afford ease, acceptance, cooperation, and confidence.

Questions moved from the general to the specific in a logical sequence and a large number of "what" type of questions were asked; inductive reasoning was used throughout the interview. Events needing greater clarification in the present led to an emphasis on gaining details of interpersonal relationships in the patient's early history. This afforded a greater understanding of the many facets and dimensions of the patient's personality. We would hope that the reader can conceptualize a multidimensional person from the behavioral interview and not merely a selection of habits or symptoms viewed in isolation.

REFERENCES

Bernstein, L., Bernstein, R. S., & Dana, R. H. *Interviewing: A guide for health professionals* (2nd ed.). New York: Appleton-Century-Crofts, 1974.

Blackman, D. *Operant conditioning: An experimental analysis of behaviour* London: Methuen, 1974.

Davison, G. C., & Neale, J. M. *Abnormal psychology: An experimental clinical approach*. New York: Wiley, 1974.

Fisher, J., Epstein, L. J., & Harris, M. R. Validity of the psychiatric interview. *Archives of General Psychiatry*, 1967, **17,** 745–750.

Goldberg, L. R. Objective diagnostic tests and measures. *Annual Review of Psychology*, 1974, **25,** 343–366.

Kanfer, F. H., & Saslow, G. Behavioral analysis. *Archives of General Psychiatry*, 1965, **12,** 529–538.

Kanfer, F. H., & Saslow, G. Behavioral Diagnosis. In C. M. Franks (Ed.), *Behavior therapy: Appraisal and status*. New York: McGraw-Hill, 1969.

Karen, R. L. *An introduction to behavior theory and its applications*. New York: Harper & Row, 1974.

Liberman, R. P. *A guide to behavioral analysis and therapy*. New York: Pergamon, 1972.

Masters, W. H., & Johnson, V. E. *Human sexual inadequacy*. London: Churchill, 1970.

Meichenbaum, D. H. Cognitive factors in behavior modification: Modifying what clients say to themselves. In C. M. Franks & G. T. Wilson (Eds.), *Annual review of behavior therapy theory & practice*. New York: Brunner-Mazel, 1973.

Meyer, V., & Liddell, A. Behaviour therapy. In D. Bannister (Ed.), *Issues and approaches in the psychological therapies*. London: Wiley, 1975.

Meyer, V., Sharpe, R., Liddell, A., & Lyons, M. The nature of behavior therapy and the training of behavior therapists. *European Journal of Behavioural Modification and Analysis*, 1975, **1,** 49–57.

Miller J. G. The nature of living systems. *Behavioral Science*, 1971, **16,** 277–301.

Mischel, W. *Personality and assessment*, New York: Wiley, 1968.

Mowrer, O. H. *Learning theory and personality dynamics*. New York: Ronald, 1950.

Rachman, S. J., & Philips, C. *Psychology & medicine*. London: Temple Smith, 1975.

Spitzer, R. L., & Endiocott, J. The value of the interview for the evaluation of psychopathology. In M. Hammer, K. Salzinger & S. Sutton (Eds.), *Psychopathology: Contributions from the social behavioral and biological sciences*. New York: Wiley, 1973.

Sundberg, N. D., Tyler, L. E., & Taplin, J. R. *Clinical psychology: Expanding horizons* (2nd ed.). New York: Appleton-Century-Crofts, 1973.

Ullmann, L. P., & Krasner, L. *A psychological approach to abnormal behavior*. Englewood Cliffs, N.J.: Prenctice-Hall, 1969.

CHAPTER 6

Self-Report Schedules and Inventories

DONALD L. TASTO

When self-report measures are administered for purposes of assessing the nature and degree of clinical problems, it is usually assumed that the self-ratings are measures, albeit less than perfect, of some other observable behavioral phenomena. If a client with instructions to rate fears checks "very much" after the item "nonpoisonous snakes," it is generally assumed that this rating bears some relationship to the behaviors that such a person would engage in when confronted in real life by a nonpoisonous snake. The person who rates "very much" would be expected to display more avoidance behavior in the presence of a snake than the person who rates "not at all." Likewise, if a person estimates that it takes him 45 minutes to fall asleep at night, the assumption is made, typically with some degree of trepidation on the part of the experimenter, that such a rating would correlate with the data that EEG measures would yield under laboratory conditions. And if a person reports the symptoms typically associated with a tension headache, it might well be assumed that, in the absence of being able to observe a headache, such a complaint represents an underlying physiological process that is at least potentially measurable and which, independent of self-report, would define the headache. For purposes of basic research, direct measurements of behavioral phenomena taken independently of self-report would be required for a strict application of the philosophy of science to behavioral investigations. However, the pursuit of such a goal for the assessment of clinical problems could prove to be inappropriate as well as problematic.

To illustrate, suppose a man complaining of frequent headaches presents himself to a therapist, and the therapist decides to measure the headaches independently of the patient's self-report. From a purely clinical perspective, measurement that is independent of the patient's report is superfluous: If the therapist's independent measure, whether it be physiologically or behaviorally based, were correlated perfectly with the subject's self-report, such alternative measurement would be unnecessary. Insofar as it correlates less than 1.0 with self-report, and if the therapist uses his independent measure as the true criterion for the presence of a headache, he will conclude that his patient has a headache at times when his patient claims not to have one and, conversely, he will conclude at times that his patient does not have a headache when in fact his patient claims to have one. As the correlation between the patient's report and the therapist's measures decreases, the discrepancy between the patient's claim and that of the therapist increases.

It is understandable historically how verbal reports came to be looked on as something less than the best predictor of other human behavior. Yet in the realm of clinical practice, *the operational criteria for the existence of problems are self-reported verbalizations.* If a patient says there is a problem, then there is a problem. And conversely, when the patient claims there is no problem, then there is no problem. Therapeutic intervention is considered to be progressing to the extent that the patient (and others who may also be involved) report that things are better and, conversely, therapeutic intervention may be considered to be of no value or even harmful as a result of the patient's (and sometimes others') report. With the exception of behaviors that are illegal and consequently defined as problems independently of the patient's view, it is the patient's complaint of anxiety, depression, insomnia, or the like that defines whether a problem exists for clinical purposes. When a problem exists, it means that decisions involving the use, nonuse, or termination of treatment programs are called for.

Self-report, however, does not have to be limited to the assessment of unreliable verbalizations in response to unstructured, open-ended questions. It is because of the problems inherent in subjective and unsystematic forms of assessment that self-report inventories and schedules were developed. The fact that self-report defines the problem for clinical purposes should not be a cue for discouragement but rather a signal for the development of a sophisticated psychometric approach to the measurement and validation of self-report.

NORMATIVE DATA AND THERAPEUTIC JUDGMENTS

It would be pleasant to report that the solutions to problems of self-report schedules and inventories amount to no more than the collection of additional data for purposes of standardizing, item analyzing, and factoring such inventories on a variety of clinically relevant populations. If it were then known what the means, variance, factor structure, and so on looked like on a particular scale for a given subset of the population, a therapist would know the relative status of any particular person by reference to the normative ratings.

Problems arise, however, in regard to what is *done* with that information. If a 30-year-old, white, middle-class male rates a 1.0 (meaning "not at all") to the item "worms" on the Fear Survey Schedule (FSS), a therapist would most likely find no need to pursue treatment to this item since the average rating for this item by that population is slightly more than 1.0. This person's rating of his own fear of worms was slightly under average. If this same person rates a 2.0 (meaning "a little") to the item "harmless spiders," he would be only slightly above the mean. Under these conditions a therapist may not consider the person's rating on this item to indicate a need for therapeutic assistance. One reason for this judgment might be that, although the patient's rating was slightly above average, if indeed his fear were average or normal for this population, a rating of 2.0 would be the closest he could come because raw score ratings are in discrete numbers (i.e., 1.0, 2.0, 3.0, 4.0, 5.0). A rating of 1.0 would have placed him considerably below the mean and a rating of 3.0 considerably above. Another reason for this judgment could be that, apart from what the norms are, the rating is low, and the face validity meaning attached to the 2.0 is "a little," which a therapist may judge to be of little or no relevance to this person's adaptation to the world.

If, however, a 20-year-old, white, middle-class female rates 4.0 (meaning "much") to the item, "feeling rejected by others," she would be closer to the average rating for this population than she would be using any other raw score rating. However, the therapeutic decision may be to deal with such a concern in therapy and, if this be the case, deviance from the mean rating would not be the *criterion* for such a decision. The fact that the rating is high, regardless of the average rating, could indicate that a real problem exists. The fact that a real problem exists for many does not dilute the intensity of it for an individual. Importance is not to be confused with deviation from the mean.

The issue that arises is a question of the extent to which normative data are helpful. If the purpose is descriptive, normative data are necessary for making such statements as, "Women report less fear of being with a member of the opposite sex than men do." If the purpose is proscriptive, factors in addition to normative data must be considered. The determination of the most appropriate treatment typically requires input from several sources.

FACTORS AND TOTAL SCORES

It is not infrequent that investigators studying the outcome of therapeutic procedures have used inventories that purportedly measure reactions to a rather heterogeneous group of items. Changes in total raw scores on these measures have then been viewed as providing an index of the effects of treatment. It may be that on any given instrument empirically distinct factors exist within a pool of items and, if so, it would not be known how many items load per factor. For example, a total raw score on the Fear Survey Schedule might be used as an index of change resulting from therapeutic procedures designed to alleviate social anxiety. However, it may be that the changes implied by many items are simply not susceptible to such a treatment procedure. If it turned out that there was a specific type of social anxiety factor that changed as a result of treatment whereas other factors that were empirically independent did not change, the use of a total raw score would be highly questionable. In fact, such a criterion might serve only to mask the real effects of treatment. This hypothetical factor, by definition, would be composed of items that had considerable overlap of variance, and, to the extent that each is measuring the same thing, the actual number of items measuring it is unimportant. However, a total raw score on the FSS is susceptible not only to ratings on individual items but also to the actual number of items comprising the factors or clusters. Since the number of items loading on a factor may be quite arbitrarily decided on or accidently arrived at, it is quite possible that any total score may be disproportionately influenced by a totally irrelevant dimension. When the total score is used as a measure of therapeutic outcome, it becomes necessary to consider how the various factors and their item populations are reflected in any observed change.

THE FEAR SURVEY SCHEDULE

The Fear Survey Schedule has been used clinically and experimentally since 1956. The various forms of the FSS that have emerged over the last two decades are composed of stimulus items, ranging in number from 50 to 122, to which subjects rate their fears on a five-point or seven-point scale. Akutagawa (1956) developed the FSS-1, which is composed of 50 items that he thought represented the more commonly occurring fears. Geer (1965) empirically constructed the FSS-11, which consists of 51 items that were derived from open-ended questionnaire data. Whereas the FSS-11 was empirically constructed for research purposes, Wolpe and Lang (1964) developed the FSS-111 from their own clinical observations. This scale consists of 72 items and was intended for clinical purposes.

Wolpe (1973, pp. 283–286) has presented an 86-item FSS, Wolpe and Lang (1969) have published a 108-item FSS, and Braun and Reynolds (1969) combined items from various forms that resulted in a 100-item FSS.

Although several studies reported later have used the 122-item FSS, its exact origin is somewhat unclear. It appears that Peter Lang developed this form in 1963 but did not publish it. It was then obtained in 1969 by a personal communication to Frank Lawlis (cited in Lawlis, 1971), who was then at the Arkansas Research and Rehabilitation Center in Fayetteville, Arkansas. Lawlis was working with Charles Truax on a large NIMH grant at that time and, among other instruments, the 122-item FSS was being routinely administered to the patients (neurotics, psychotics, and patients with behavior disorders) of a national sample of psychologists and psychiatrists. The items for this form appear in Tasto and Hickson (1970) and in Lawlis (1971).

The FSS has been used in a great number of empirical studies. However, several different forms of the instrument have been employed, and some investigators have further modified these existing forms. It is interesting to note that there are 18 fears in common between Geer's (1965) FSS-11 and Akutagawa's (1956) original FSS-1, and there are 20 fears in common between the FSS-11 and Wolpe and Lang's (1964) FSS-111. Because of investigators' idiosyncratic modifications of the FSS and because of the far-from-perfect overlap of items among various FSS forms, the interpretation of the research discussed in this chapter must be somewhat tentative.

It was in response to the problems of using total FSS scores as well as curiosity about the factor structure of self-reported fears and anxieties that led to several factor analytic studies of the different forms of the FSS.

Rubin, Katkin, Weiss, and Efran (1968) factor analyzed the 51-item FSS-11 (Geer, 1965) separately for men and women and subjected their findings to a replication on a new sample of men and women. The two samples and the two sexes constituted four groups for four separate analyses. The three factors that consistently emerged for all four groups were: fear of water, death and illness, and interpersonal events. A fourth factor—discrete stimuli—emerged in all but the first female group. Rubin, Lawlis, Tasto, and Namenek (1969) factor analyzed the 122-item FSS and arrived at five conceptually pure factors: (1) fears related to small animals, (2) fears of the precipitators and manifestations of hostility, (3) moralistically related fears, (4) fears of isolation and loneliness, and (5) fears of anatomical destruction and physical pain. Using a 0.35 correlation of an item with its factor as the criterion for inclusion, a 40-item FSS was constructed.

Braun and Reynolds (1969) combined items from other fear surveys and developed a 100-item fear inventory, which was then factor analyzed. Although they reported 21 interpretable factors for each sex and 16 factors common to both sexes, some factors had so few items (as low as one and two) as to be of dubious clinical utility. The major areas of fear in this study, however, were social criticism, medical intervention, sudden noises, cars, and death. These investigators compared their number of factors (21) extracted from the 100-item inventory with the number of factors (three to four) by Rubin et al. (1968) on the 51-item FSS and suggested that the number of factors was perhaps a function of the number of items. This interpretation must, however, remain highly suspect, particularly since Rubin et al. (1969) found only five factors emerging from the 122-item FSS.

Bernstein and Allen (1969), like Rubin et al. (1968), factor analyzed the FSS-11 with the following factors emerging: live organisms, death and illness, social interaction, and social evaluation. The FSS-111 (Wolpe & Lang, 1964) was factor analyzed by Landy and Gaupp (1971), and the following four factors were consistent on the two samples: fear of animate nonhuman organisms, interpersonal events, the unknown, and noise and medical-surgical procedures. The same instrument was factor analyzed by Merbaum and Stricker (1972) with factors emerging separately for men and women. For men the factors were fears of aggression, travel, harmless animals, bodily insults, and unreality whereas for women they were fears of bodily insult, social rejection, harmless animals, public display, aggression, disability, and confinement.

The use of college students as subjects for psychological research has brought the generalizability of results into question. All the above factor analyses were performed on data obtained from college students. Although there are no reported factor analyses of normal (noncollege student) adults, three factor analytic studies of disturbed populations deserve comment. Lawlis (1971) factor analyzed the 122-item FSS using responses from psychiatric subjects diagnosed as psychotic, neurotic, and as having behavior disorders. The factors that emerged from the pooled subject populations were fears related to losing status and adequacy socially, fears relating to small animals, and fear relating to disease.

In contrast to Lawlis's (1971) discovery of only three factors in a psychotic population, Rothstein, Holmes, and Boblitt (1972) found 16 factors to emerge from a factor analysis of psychiatric patients' responses to the FSS-111, and each of these factors accounted for less than 5 percent of the variance. Bates (1971) obtained 17 factors on the FSS-111 with neurotic male veterans whereas Meikle and Mitchell (1974), using a population of phobics, found 21 factors on the FSS-111, although they concluded that only two of these were genuine factors.

It appears that the factor structure for self-reported fears is a somewhat unsettled issue for psychiatric populations. If, however, we consider only the studies done with college students, a moderately consistent picture begins to emerge. It is true that different investigators have named their factors differently and that, if one were to look only at the factor names, confusion about factor structure might occur. Nevertheless, a look at the specific item loadings for the different studies suggests that a significant proportion of between-study variance is accounted for by the different names investigators have chosen to describe their factors rather than by large differences in factor composition. Inspection of the items and factors across the studies seems to indicate that among college students there is a fair degree of factor stability and that the most frequently occurring clusters are (1) fears related to small animals, (2) fears associated with death, physical pain, and surgery, (3) fears about aggression, and (4) fears of interpersonal events. The fear of interpersonal events is sometimes broken down into the components of social evaluation versus social interaction. These factors appear to emerge more or less in this fashion whether the analyses are done separately by sex or on data pooled for the sexes. Conclusions about the factor structure for psychiatric populations must remain somewhat tentative pending further studies; and, of course, we can make no statements at all concerning the structure of fear response in a normal, noncollege population.

Reliability

No study has had as its sole purpose the investigation of the reliability of FSS items. The reliability data presented here are therefore drawn from studies conducted for other reasons. Geer (1965) found internal consistency estimates of the FSS-11 to be 0.939 overall: 0.928 for females and 0.934 for males. Hersen (1971) found internal consistency coefficients on the FSS-111 to be 0.97 overall: 0.97 for males and 0.97 for females. Braun and Reynolds (1969) found test-retest reliabilities on a 100-item FSS over a 10-week period to be 0.88 for males and 0.85 for females. Suinn (1969) found the test-retest reliability of a modified FSS to be 0.72 when five weeks elapsed between the two administrations. Tasto and Suinn (1972) determined test-retest reliabilities for the five factors that emerged from the Rubin et al. (1969) factor analysis as well as for total scores on a 122-item FSS. Although somewhat lower than those reported by Braun and Reynolds (1969), reliability tended to be moderately high (generally in the 0.70s). Conspicuously low, however, was the reliability of 0.27 for men's ratings on the "fears of isolation and loneliness" factor.

Normative Data

There is not an overabundance of normative information on the FSS, and that which is available has been obtained exclusively on college students. Geer (1965) has presented means and item with total score correlations for the FSS-11. It is clear from his data as well as those of others (Hersen, 1971; Lawlis, 1971; Tasto & Hickson, 1970) that women generally rate themselves as more fearful than men. Whether this is a result of differential social desirability affecting the way men versus women admit to fear or whether women are actually more afraid (as defined by some measure other than self-report) cannot be determined from existing data.

Tasto and Hickson (1970) developed separate norms for men and women for the 122-item FSS. Each item was scaled by a z score transformation with a constant of 3 added to every z score. A therapist, by converting a raw score to a scaled score of this nature, would be able immediately to determine how many standard deviations from the mean a subject's rating for each item would be because the mean in scaled score form would always by definition be 3.0 and the standard deviation 1.0. For example, if a subject gave a raw score of 4.0 and this converted to a scaled score of 5.2, this rating would be 2.2 standard deviations above the mean. Likewise, if a subject rates a 1.0 and this rating converts to a scaled score of 1.8, this rating would be 1.2 standard deviations below the mean. Although such a procedure allows the therapist to assess relative standings for an individual on specific items or on the total score, it does not help the therapist to assess areas of concern that might be defined by factors emerging from factor analyses. Since by definition items that form a factor are correlated with one another, it would not be unreasonable to expect that, if a patient has anxiety associated with one item from the factor, anxiety is also associated with other items comprising that factor.

In an attempt to deal with this issue as well as the previously discussed problems of using total scores, Tasto, Hickson and Rubin (1971) combined the scaling of the Tasto and Hickson (1970) study and the five factors of the Rubin et al. (1969) factor analysis to form a profile of how subjects compare on the factors. The items from the five factors of Rubin et al. (1969) were scaled and totals converted to T scores. Thus a therapist would convert each raw score rating to a scaled score and total the scaled scores for each of the five factors separately. Table 6–1 presents the items for each of the five factors with the scaled scores corresponding to raw score ratings of from 1.0 to 5.0 on each item. In scaled score form, the mean of each item is 3.0 and the standard deviation is 1.0. The summation of the scaled scores for the items within each factor forms the factor totals that are plotted on a profile sheet in a fashion similar to that used for the MMPI. By referring to the side of the profile sheet, which is marked in T scores and which appears in Figures 6–1 and 6–2, it becomes clear how a subject compares to a reference group on each factor. (In T score form, the mean is 50.0 and the standard deviation is 10.0.) Such instrumentation is probably of most clinical utility for assessing *where* and the *degree to which* anxiety exists.

To use changes on such an instrument from pretherapeutic to post-therapeutic intervention as an index of therapeutic effectiveness might be appropriate provided the therapist has some indication as to what changes on the different factors would be expected as a function of time. Tasto and Suinn (1972) administered the 122-item FSS to subjects on two occasions separated by a 10-week period to assess whether changes without

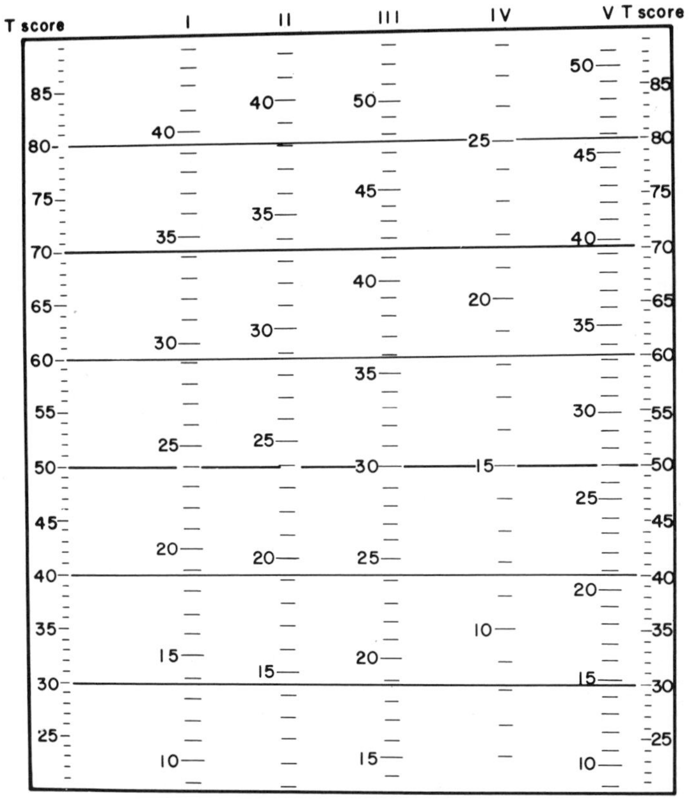

Figure 6–1. Fear Survey Schedule profile, college males. [From D. L. Tasto, R. Hickson, and S. E. Rubin, Scaled profile analysis of fear survey schedule factors. *Behavior Therapy,* 1971, *2,* 543–549. Copyright (1971) by Academic Press. Reproduced by permission.]

Table 6–1. Factors with scaled scores. [From D. L. Tasto, R. Hickson, and S. E. Rubin, Scaled profile analysis of fear survey schedule factors. *Behavior Therapy*, 1971, *2*, 543–549. Copyright (1971) by Academic Press. Reproduced by permission.]

	Men					Women				
Factor I: Fears related to small animals										
1 Worms	2.70	6.32	9.93	13.55	17.17	2.31	3.25	4.19	5.13	6.07
2 Mice or rats	2.22	3.54	4.86	6.18	7.50	1.72	2.43	3.13	3.84	4.55
3 Bats	2.04	3.31	4.57	5.84	7.11	1.61	2.43	3.24	4.06	4.88
4 Crawling insects	2.25	3.66	5.06	6.47	7.87	1.84	2.59	3.34	4.09	4.84
5 Cemeteries	2.45	3.85	5.25	6.64	8.04	2.03	2.84	3.65	4.46	5.27
6 Harmless spiders	2.22	3.17	4.11	5.06	6.01	1.60	2.28	2.95	3.62	4.30
7 Harmless snakes	2.25	3.10	3.95	4.79	5.64	1.70	2.33	2.95	3.58	4.20
8 Flying insects	2.31	3.81	5.30	6.80	8.30	2.03	2.79	3.55	4.31	5.07
Factor II: Fears of Precipatators and manifestations of hostility										
9 One person bullying another	1.60	2.50	3.40	4.30	5.20	1.49	2.30	3.11	3.92	4.73
10 Feeling angry	2.13	3.14	4.15	5.16	6.17	2.15	2.93	3.72	4.50	5.28
11 Angry people	1.73	2.83	3.92	5.02	6.12	1.40	2.33	3.25	4.18	5.10
12 Loud voices	2.23	3.37	4.52	5.66	6.80	2.25	3.37	4.48	5.60	6.72
13 Feeling disapproved of	1.38	2.41	3.44	4.47	5.50	.94	1.85	2.75	3.65	4.55
14 Sick people	1.81	2.90	3.99	5.08	6.17	1.84	2.76	3.68	4.60	5.52
15 Losing control	1.77	2.62	3.47	4.32	5.17	1.63	2.40	3.18	3.96	4.74
16 Feeling rejected by others	1.31	2.26	3.21	4.16	5.11	.88	1.71	2.54	3.37	4.21
Factor III: Moralistically related fears and sexual fears										
17 Thoughts of having a defective child	1.63	2.39	3.15	3.91	4.67	1.46	2.19	2.91	3.64	4.36
18 Thoughts of suicide	2.19	2.96	3.74	4.51	5.29	2.21	2.91	3.62	4.32	5.02

19 Homosexual thoughts	2.19	2.91	3.63	4.35	5.08	2.24	2.89	3.53	4.17	4.82
20 Sexual inadequacy (impotence or frigidity)	2.27	3.06	3.85	4.63	5.42	2.14	2.83	3.51	4.20	4.88
21 Thoughts of being mentally ill	2.05	2.89	3.73	4.57	5.41	1.98	2.73	3.49	4.24	4.99
22 Leaving the gas on	2.01	2.89	3.77	4.64	5.52	1.90	2.64	3.38	4.12	4.85
23 Masturbation	2.50	3.59	4.68	5.77	6.86	2.32	3.06	3.81	4.55	5.30
24 Giving off an offensive odor	1.58	2.45	3.32	4.19	5.06	1.52	2.28	3.05	3.82	4.58
15 Leaving home	2.24	3.69	5.14	6.59	8.04	2.23	3.06	3.81	4.55	5.30
26 Being punished by God	2.02	2.68	3.35	4.01	4.68	1.69	2.35	3.02	3.69	4.35
Factor IV: Fears of isolation and loneliness										
27 Darkness	2.44	3.94	5.44	6.94	8.44	2.12	2.98	3.83	4.68	5.54
28 Being alone	2.37	3.80	5.23	6.66	8.09	1.92	2.83	3.74	4.64	5.55
29 Being in a strange place	1.92	3.30	4.69	6.08	7.47	1.57	2.73	3.89	5.05	6.22
30 Going alone into a dark theater	2.57	4.39	6.22	8.04	9.86	2.16	2.97	3.78	4.60	5.41
31 Entering a room where other people are already seated	1.84	3.18	4.52	5.86	7.20	1.77	2.84	3.91	4.98	6.05
Factor V: Fears of anatomical destruction and physical pain										
32 Human blood	2.36	3.54	4.72	5.90	7.08	2.02	2.77	3.53	4.28	5.04
33 Animal blood	2.49	4.01	5.53	7.05	8.56	2.05	2.86	3.68	4.49	5.31
34 Open wounds	1.66	2.79	3.91	5.04	6.16	1.52	2.43	3.33	4.23	5.14
35 Witnessing surgical operations	2.05	2.90	3.76	4.61	5.46	1.73	2.40	3.08	3.75	4.43
36 Seeing other people injected	2.36	3.89	5.43	6.96	8.50	2.13	3.11	4.09	5.08	6.06
37 Dead animals	2.29	3.61	4.92	6.23	7.54	1.82	2.67	3.51	4.36	5.21
38 Dead people	1.66	2.65	3.64	4.63	5.62	1.37	2.07	2.77	3.46	4.16
39 Medical odors	2.16	3.45	4.73	6.02	7.30	2.15	3.06	3.97	4.88	5.80
40 Receiving injections	2.08	3.44	4.81	6.17	7.53	1.91	2.79	3.68	4.56	5.44

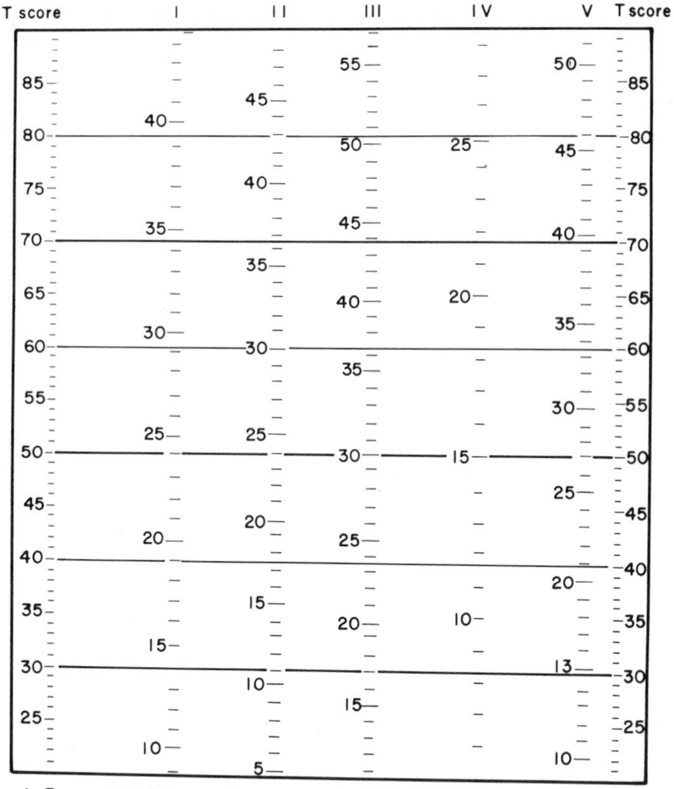

I Fears related to small animals.
II Fears of the precipitators and manifestations of hostility.
III Primitive moralistically related fears and sexual fears.
IV Fears of isolation and loneliness.
V Fears of anatomical destruction and physical pain.

Figure 6–2. Fear Survey Schedule profile, college females. [From D. L. Tasto, R. Hickson, and S. E. Rubin, Scaled profile analysis of fear survey schedule factors. *Behavior Therapy*, 1971 *2*, 543–549. Copyright (1971) by Academic Press. Reproduced by permission.]

therapeutic contact occur in sufficient degree to warrant a correction factor when using the instrument as an index of change. On some factors and on total score, moderately small yet statistically significant decreases do occur over time. Suinn (1969) supports the finding that a decrease in total score occurs over time. However, replications of this study are needed to assess the stability of total and factor changes due to nonspecific variables.

If a therapist has accounted for change that may occur over time, an assessment technique that measures a person's relative standing on fear factors may be potentially helpful in testing for the generalization of fear reduction that may occur as a result of treatment. Because items within a factor are correlated, it would be interesting to test whether, if fear is reduced to one item within a factor, the reduction generalizes to other items in the factor, and, if so, whether the generalization is greater within a factor than between factors. Such information would be clinically valuable and is as of yet unavailable.

Validity

Although a test may be reliable and yet invalid, it cannot simultaneously be valid and unreliable because the validity of a test cannot exceed the square root of its reliability. Reliabilities for the FSS, both test-retest and internal consistency, are quite respectable. Although the studies that shed light on the validity of the FSS have not especially had the establishment of validity as their major purpose, several studies have provided relevant data.

Construct Validity

To establish the construct validity of a given test, it can be correlated with performance on another test that itself is considered to be a valid measure of the construct in question—for example, anxiety. Suinn (1969) found correlations of 0.49 and 0.38 between scores on the FSS and scores on the Test Anxiety Scale (Sarason, 1957). Grossberg and Wilson (1965) found a 0.46 correlation between the FSS and the Manifest Anxiety Scale (1953) (MAS) although Lang and Lazovik (1963) found a much higher correlation ($r = 0.80$) between the FSS and the MAS. Geer (1965) found correlations of 0.39 and 0.55 between FSS total scores and MAS scores for men and women respectively. In this study the FSS correlated with Welsh's A-Scale (Welsh, 1956) (0.42 for men and 0.57 for women), with a measure of social desirability (Ford, 1964) (0.23 for men and 0.27 for women), and with the Emotionality Scale of Bendig's Pittsburgh Scales (1962) (0.40 for the sexes combined).

The issues involved with construct validity for behavioral assessment are somewhat unique, not in regard to statistical approaches but in regard to which tests are relevant for establishing construct validity—a point at the foundation of the *raison d'etre* of behavioral assessment. The need for developing new assessment approaches for behavior therapy stems from the fact that traditional psychological tests, which emanated from the more psychodynamic approaches of psychotherapy, are simply not relevant to the type of assessment required for behavior therapy. Such tests as the Rorschach, TAT, and MMPI did not seem to be measuring what behavior therapists were concerned about measuring and subsequently treating.

Since the field of behavior therapy assessment is in its infancy, an important question of construct validity centers around the question of what tests might be appropriately used as validity checks. Also germane to the issue is just what high correlative relationships between indices yielded by behavioral assessment techniques and dynamically oriented measures might mean.

Let us assume for the moment that in regard to the assessment of fears and anxieties the behavior therapist is more interested in assessing specific reactions to discrete stimuli than in the assessment of anxiety that might be described as a trait or contributor to overall drive. Procedures such as systematic desensitization seem to be more appropriate to the treatment of fear reactions to specific stimuli. Presuppositions about the state/trait controversy notwithstanding, the face validity of the FSS, which was developed to assess specific fear reactions, would suggest that it is more appropriate for the assessment goals of the behavior therapist than is the MAS, which is composed of items drawn from the MMPI and which was subsequently used to measure anxiety as a trait. Since the FSS was the first psychometric attempt to assess specific fear responses as a diagnostic aid for behavior therapy, it is understandable why investigators may wish to correlate this new instrument with preestablished measures. On the other hand, since the FSS came about because other tests were inadequate as assessment devices for behavior therapy, there is no particular reason either for demanding or expecting high correlations between it and previously existing tests. If the FSS were to correlate perfectly with any measure whose limitations were in part responsible for the development of the FSS, the FSS by definition would suffer from the same limitations. If we considered the coefficient of correlation between the FSS and some other measure to begin dropping from 1.0 toward 0.0, the overlap between the two measures would begin to decrease. The problem, however, is that in the absence of an independently established criterion, the optimal relationship is not only unspecifiable but probably not relevant.

This commentary is not meant to imply that investigators have been exerting fruitless efforts on studying construct validities of the FSS and other behavioral measures. The point is that when a new self-report measure is being developed because previous instruments do not measure what is desired, studies of construct validity that depend on those same instruments are probably not the most efficacious method of establishing validity.

Criterion-Related Validity

The establishment of criterion-related (which includes what used to be referred to as concurrent validity and predictive validity) for self-report measures seems to be a more appropriate approach to establishing the validity of new psychometric instrumentation. Criterion-related validity may be established by correlating the test in question to performance on some other task. When, for example, the assumption is made that a behavioral measure is a valid index of therapeutic change, correlating a self-report measure with a behavioral measure will yield a criterion-related validity coefficient. Several therapy studies to be discussed later have provided behavioral measures as well as FSS self-report data.

The component of criterion-related validity for a new measure may have merit depending on the purposes for which it is to be used. If an investigator developed a social skills test for the purpose of identifying those persons who would perform adequately in administrative positions requiring refined diplomatic abilities, prediction would be of utmost concern. If, on the other hand, an investigator developed a social skills test for the purpose of assessing specific deficits in social skills and additionally to provide a dependent variable that would be sensitive to the effects training in social skills, the assessment of the concurrent component of criterion-related validity would be most germane (i.e., data on the relationship between the test and some behavioral measure of social skills).

In many of the earlier parametric studies of systematic desensitization, a version of the FSS was administered to experimental and control groups before and after treatment. Although required statistical assumptions frequently were not checked, analyses of difference scores from pretreatment to posttreatment often constituted the base from which inferences about therapeutic effectiveness were drawn. The purpose of these studies was essentially to establish the effectiveness of systematic desensitization and variants of this procedure—not to assess the validity of the assessment measures. When research involves testing, treating, and retesting, it is necessary to assume that either the test or the treatment is valid and, given this assumption, it is then possible to assess the validity of the other. In most studies that have employed treatment, the assumption has been made that the FSS as well as other measures were valid indicators of change and that effectiveness of the treatment techniques, rather than the validity of the observations, constituted the purposes of the research. Probably the assumption that was actually made was that the behavioral measures in such studies provided the ultimate criteria of effectiveness and that, since the self-report measures tended to go along with the behavioral measures, they must also be valid measures of change. A purview of the literature (Paul, 1969) on systematic desensitization and its various modes of application would unquestionably suggest that, regardless of the manner by which therapeutic outcome has been measured, systematic desensitization is an effective technique for reducing fear responses to specific stimuli. If we turn things around and now make the assumption that the treatment is effective, it becomes possible to look at the validity of the FSS from the viewpoint of those studies whose original purpose was to assess the effectiveness of treatment while assuming the validity of the measures. We will now assume that the treatment is valid and look at the validity of the instruments.

Lang and Lazovik (1963) employed systematic desensitization to treat snake-phobic subjects. They found on posttesting that subjects who had successfully completed treatment showed decreases in their self-ratings of fear, in particular their ratings to the snake item on the FSS, as well as decreases in their behavioral avoidance of snakes. Behavioral and self-report data were again obtained at a six-month follow-up. The results of the follow-up, taken together with other data from the study, led the authors to conclude that changes in self-report measures and behavioral measures do not tend to occur simultaneously and that typically "subjective report lags behind overt behavior" (p. 178). This conclusion, if true, would lend credence to the theory that changes in self-concept, self-description, subjective perceptions, and so on are the result of changes in behavior rather than vice versa. After treatment for a phobia perhaps a person must have several behavioral approach experiences with the stimulus before he is willing to label himself as "not afraid of it." Although such a conclusion would be congruent with current psychological thinking, the data are not without inconsistency.

In a sequel to their first study, Lang, Lazovik, and Reynolds (1965) showed that, as a result of systematic desensitization, significant changes occurred on behavioral measures as well as on self-report measures. If self-report does lag behind behavioral measures and if it becomes more consistent with behavioral measures only after experience, it would be expected that the self-report data would show less change than the behavioral data. It is not possible to compare directly the magnitude of FSS changes with that of behavioral measures. However, since the *N* is usually equal for both, it is possible to compare significance levels provided that the distributions of behavioral and self-report measures are similar. In the Lang et al. study cited above it is interesting that changes on the behavioral measures yielded greater statistical significance than did changes on the total FSS scores. However, changes on the "snake" item alone from the FSS yielded greater significance than either the behavioral measures or the total score. It is possible that the limited range on a single item might in part be responsible for the significance level of the item exceeding the significance level for the behavioral measures. However, subjects' responses to the single item, which is more accurately the behavioral measure's counterpart than is the total FSS score, did not in this study appear to lag behind their behavioral measures. That the total FSS score should significantly change at all, given the total number of items, suggests that some generalization of fear reduction occurs across stimuli.

In studying the components of reciprocal inhibition, Cooke (1968) desensitized subjects who were rat phobics. Although total FSS score data were not presented, it appeared that, when subjects who completed the hierarchy were compared against those who did not and against controls, the behavioral measures and self-ratings to the FSS "rat" item significantly changed as a result of intervention. The significance levels for both measures were quite similar.

Cotler and Garlington (1969) tested for the generalization effects of fear reduction from snakes to other small animals. Both the behavioral measures and the responses to the FSS tended to lend support for generalization. With some reservations about conclusions due to the control data, the pretherapy to posttherapy changes for the "snake" item yielded significance at 0.01, for the total FSS score 0.01, and for the behavioral avoidance test 0.05.

Robinson and Suinn (1969) found that when desensitizing spider phobics, the significance of change was comparable for a behavioral approach task and for self-ratings on the spider item. The statistical significance of change for the total FSS score, however, was somewhat lower. Schroeder and Dietrich (1973) found behavioral measures, but not total FSS scores, to change as a function of systematic desensitization for snake-phobic women. They did not present data on the "snake" item.

Willis and Edwards (1969) found in treating mice phobics that a systematic desensitization group was superior to an implosive therapy group or a control group and that there were no significant differences between the latter two groups. The FSS total score, the FSS "mice" item, and the behavioral avoidance measure all reflected the differential effectiveness of treatment at the 0.01 level for each comparison on each measure.

Everaerd, Rijken, and Emmelkamp (1973) found total FSS scores and behavioral measures to change with about the same level of statistical significance when using flooding or "successive approximation" in the treatment of agoraphobia. The tendency, however, was for the effect on behavioral measures to be more significant than on the FSS total score.

Ritter (1969) offers data that might be interpreted as lending minor support for the notion that self-report lags behind behavioral changes. He found that a significant difference on a behavioral measure (0.05) occurred when only 15 minutes of standard systematic desensitization was administered to acrophobics. However, the procedure failed to produce significant changes on total FSS scores or on the "height" item from the FSS. Because this study did not employ desensitization for more than 15 minutes, because other variants on the standard administration of systematic desensitization did not produce any significant changes on behavioral or FSS scores, and because there were only four subjects per group, this study cannot be interpreted as offering overwhelming support for the theory that subjective report lags behind behavioral experience.

Whatever the case for perceptual "lag," the weight of the research suggests that as a function of therapeutic intervention (at least, systematic desensitization), changes on self-ratings to specific items occur when overt behaviors change. Furthermore, the magnitude of the statistical significance for self-rated changes to *specific* stimuli is about the same as for behavioral measures. The preliminary suggestion of Lang and Lazovik (1963) concerning the temporal relationship between behavioral changes and self-report changes, although not defeated, does not find more than partial support from the literature cited above.

As every good psychologist knows, the James-Lange theory of emotion purports that the labeling of emotional states is temporarily preceded by behavior. A man does not run because he is afraid; he is afraid because he is running. Although James and Lange did not discuss what happens to the behavior-emotion relationship when therapy eliminates a fear, they might have described the mechanism involved in the improvement of a client who successfully completed systematic desensitization for a snake phobia as, "He is not afraid because he approaches the snake," or "He is relaxed because he approaches the snake." His description of himself as "not afraid" is contingent on his behavioral approach to the snake.

It may well be that behavioral experience is necessary before a person changes his subjective ratings. The temporal relationship between behavioral measures and self-report measures of therapeutic change, however, has not been systematically manipulated or studied. What is necessary is a study that desensitizes phobics and then manipulates the order in which posttreatment behavioral and self-report measures are taken. If it should turn out that subjects do not rate themselves as relaxed or unafraid following desensitization until they have had the behavioral experience of approaching the stimulus object, parametric studies investigating the effects that time and number of behavioral experiences have on self-ratings would be in order. More specific information on the relationship between behavioral measures and self-report would be of value to the clinician, particularly when behavioral measures are not convenient or not possible.

All these studies can be interpreted as yielding criterion-related validity and some degree of construct validity for self-ratings to specifically treated items on the FSS. With a somewhat lower degree of confidence, we might view changes in total score on the FSS as an index of the effectiveness of treatment programs designed to eliminate phobic behavior. Changes in total score also relate to the issue of the generalization of anxiety reduction, a topic to be discussed later.

It is fortunate that studies have been done relating FSS changes to behavioral measures on problems when this is possible. It would be very difficult, for example, to relate changes in FSS scores to behavioral measures in the case where people have been treated for examination anxiety. The observable behaviors of test anxiety, other than verbal complaints from test-anxious subjects, are hard to specify. Since the validity of FSS ratings has been established in the case of other anxiety-provoking stimuli, it would be reasonable to expect that decreases on the FSS that might occur following treatment of examination anxiety would reflect the effectiveness of treatment if decreases attributable to nonspecific factors over time are accounted for.

In regard to test anxiety, Suinn (1968), Garlington and Cotler (1968), and Ihli and Garlington (1969) have all reported significant total FSS changes as a result of systematic desensitization for test anxiety. In addition, Garlington and Cotler have reported a significant decrease on the "test anxiety" item from the FSS. In contrast to these findings, Crighton and Jehu (1969) found that, although other self-report measures changed as a result of systematic desensitization for "test anxiety," total scores on the FSS failed to do so.

Baker, Cohen, and Saunders (1973) found FSS total scores to change as a function of treating acrophobia. A group that was given standard desensitization with a therapist did not differ on posttreatment FSS scores from a "self-directed desensitization" group. The latter group, which essentially learned desensitization by tapes, showed a further drop in FSS total scores from postreatment to an eight-month follow-up, whereas the "therapist" group maintained gains only at follow-up. A behavioral measure was not used. However, these results were corroborated by a variety of other measures.

The overall conclusion regarding systematic desensitization and the FSS is that the FSS total score appears to show some decrease as a result of treatment directed toward a specific phobia. The fact that some decrease occurs during the period of therapy, however, cannot be unequivocally interpreted as reflecting effective treatment because decreases do occur as a result of nonspecific factors. Decreases on specifically treated FSS items occur more reliably and they appear to follow closely, if not define, the effectiveness of intervention. The literature in this respect is almost suggestive of the phrase that a colleague once uttered: "If you want to know what is wrong with a patient, you should ask him." The literature to date would indicate that, in the absence of behavioral measures, the therapist who judges therapeutic success by looking at changes on specific FSS items may do so with a fair degree of confidence—confidence that changes in the patient's self-report and changes in a behavioral measure, if the latter were available, would be closely related.

Generalization Effects

Changes in the FSS total score that do occur, but with a lower probability value than the individually treated items, may be interpreted as indicating that the effects of desensitization are not confined to the one item for which desensitization was conducted but rather that there is some generalization of anxiety reduction to other items. In an attempt to predict which items would be most sensitive to generalization, Lang (1969, pp. 163–165) presented data on the generalization of desensitization as a function of the correlation of items with the target item. He and his colleagues administered the FSS to groups of subjects before and after treating them for a snake phobia. On a separate sample the correlations of each item with the snake item were determined as were changes from pretest to posttest on all items for the treated group. Their data showed that the generalization of anxiety reduction from a treated fear to untreated fears is a direct monotonic function of the correlation between the untreated fears and the treated one. The amount by which an untreated phobia benefits from treatment for another phobia is directly related to how much variance the treated phobia accounts for in the untreated phobia.

That generalization is related to the similarity between untreated items and treated items further suggests that generalization of anxiety reduction should be greater within analytically derived factors of the FSS than between factors. More studies are needed to assess the degree of generalization, to determine those stimuli that are most amenable to the effects of generalization, and to discover whether generalization, once begun, will increase from posttreatment to various stages of follow-up.

Other Considerations of FSS Validity

Although most of the studies relating to the validity of the FSS have been done in conjunction with an evaluation of the effects of systematic desensitization, there are other perspectives on validity in the literature worth noting. For example, in an exploratory study that may have implications for the predictive power of the FSS in regard to prognosis, Scrignar, Swanson, and Bloom (1973) treated airplane-phobic patients and suggested that multiple fears as indicated by high total scores on the FSS were associated with treatment failure in two of the nine cases.

Geer (1966) has shown that, if subjects are divided on the basis of high versus low ratings to the "speaking in front of a group" item from the

FSS and if expectancy of having to speak after performance of a task is manipulated, judges who were naive to the conditions rated high-fear subjects and low-fear subjects differently on the formal aspects of verbal production.

Adams (1971, 1972) has shown that total FSS scores and factor scores for 10 of the 16 factors derived from the Rothstein, Holmes and Boblitt (1972) factor analysis drop as a function of psychiatric hospitalization. To conclude that decreases in the FSS are an index of the benefits of psychiatric hospitalization presupposes that psychiatric hospitalization is beneficial. Although this topic has generated a great deal of unresolved controversy, it might on the surface make sense that self-rated fear decreases in the non-threatening environs of the hospital. What is needed are follow-up data relating FSS changes to recidivism rates. If increases in FSS scores following hospitalization are predictive of rehospitalization, further validity data would be added to the nomological network of the FSS.

Begelman and Hersen (1973) administered the FSS to both schizophrenics and normals. They gave a behavioral approach task toward snakes to half of each group while the other half served as controls. Then the FSS was readministered. Correlations between the two administrations of the FSS and between the first administration of the FSS and the actual approach behavior strongly support the notion that schizophrenics are not very accurate at judging their fears in the absence of behavioral experience. However, their self-assessments became significantly more accurate as a result of direct exposure to phobic stimuli. Normals were apparently more accurate in reporting fears prior to the actual experience since they did not revise their ratings following exposure to the snake. The implication of this study is that while normals (i.e., nonschizophrenics) may yield high concordance between self-ratings and behavioral measures, caution must be exercised when studying the fears of schizophrenics. Both behavioral and self-report measures of their fears should be taken whenever possible, and the fact that the former may be useful in modifying the latter should not be overlooked.

Zeisset (1968) studied the effects of systematic desensitization and relaxation-plus-application training on interview anxiety in neurotic and functionally psychotic inpatients. Among other self-report measures, the FSS scores dropped significantly as a result of these treatment approaches. Zeisset also reported a lack of correlation between self-report measures and a behavioral measure developed specifically for this study. This finding is consistent with that of Begelman and Hersen (1973), which showed a lack of relationship between self-report and behavioral measures prior to behavioral experience in a hospitalized population but not in a normal population.

Weiss, Katkin, and Rubin (1968) studied subjects who had scored high or low on the "fear of death" factor, which was derived from the Rubin et al. (1968) factor analysis of the FSS. They found that exposure to a film on fatal disease detrimentally affected subsequent motor performance of subjects scoring high but not of subjects scoring low on the factor. Since the factor analytic studies of the FSS have not produced completely consistent results in terms of factor composition, more studies of this type are needed to establish the validity of specific factors. The consistency of factor loadings must be established by continued sampling. Factor validities, however, must be established by relating them to criteria that are independent of the factors.

Although it appears that the FSS can be used as a valid index of change for nonhospitalized phobics, data on the validity of the instrument with other populations strongly suggests that it would be inappropriate to assume consistent applicability across populations. More data on pathological populations and normal adult populations (in contrast to the more easily obtained and more frequently utilized college population) would be helpful in expanding the nomological network of the FSS.

OTHER SELF-REPORT MEASURES

Social Anxiety

Although earlier attempts had been made at assessing social anxiety (Dixon, deMonchaux, & Sandler, 1957; Sears, 1967), Watson and Friend (1969) developed two social anxiety scales that appeared more relevant to the assessment and evaluation needs of behavior therapy. Since behavior therapists typically treat specific reactions to specific situations and since it appears that anxiety scales asking specific questions about specific situations have greater predictive validity than scales that ask about a variety of situations (Endler & Hunt, 1966), Watson and Friend (1969) constructed their instruments with the hope that each would measure a homogeneous construct.

Their Social Avoidance and Distress (SAD) scale is a series of 28 true-false questions about how subjects feel in a variety of social contexts and what social situations they tend to avoid. The Fear of Negative Evaluation (FNE) scale is a series of 30 true-false items that describe situations of real or potentially negative evaluation by others. As one measure of homogeneity, correlations were obtained between each item and the total score for the two scales. The average correlation for the FNE was 0.72 and for the SAD it was 0.77. As a second measure of homogeneity the

KR-20 was applied and 0.94 coefficients emerged for both scales. As the result of three validity studies Watson and Friend (1969) concluded:

> People high in SAD tended to avoid social interactions, preferred to work alone, reported that they talked less, and were more worried and less confident about social relationships, but were more likely to appear for appointments. Those high in FNE tended to become nervous in evaluative situations, and worked hard either to avoid disapproval or gain approval. (p. 448)

Endler, Hunt, and Rosenstein (1962) developed the S–R Inventory of Anxiousness (SRIA) as a measure of trait anxiety. On this instrument a subject rates on a 5-point scale 14 modes of response to 11 different situations. For example, one situation is "You are starting off on an automobile trip." The subject would rate on a five-point scale with the anchor points being "not at all" and "very much" 14 reactions to each situation. Examples of the reactions are "heart beats faster," "get an uneasy feeling," "perspire," and so on. Since there are 14 responses to 11 situations, the total number of items is 154. Because the SRIA has been used in behavior therapy practice and research, it is mentioned in this chapter. However, because it was developed as a more general measure of trait anxiety and is thus not in the mainstream of behavioral assessment, it will not be reviewed in detail.

In a study of dating behavior, Arkowitz, Lichtenstein, McGovern, and Hines (1975) have provided independent validity data on the SAD, the FNE, and the SRIA. These measures correlated among themselves from 0.58 to 0.71, and all three significantly ($p < 0.001$) differentiated high-frequency daters from low-frequency daters. In addition, the self-report measures were significantly correlated with several behavioral measures as well as peer ratings of social skill.

Using data from a social performance task in conjunction with results reported by others (Weiss, 1968; Lewinsohn, Weinstein, & Shaw, 1969; Libet & Lewinsohn, 1973), Arkowitz et al. (1975) have appropriately pointed to "the need for more refined behavioral analysis of interactional sequences . . . " (p. 3). That is, if subjects are placed in an experimental situation requiring social interaction, the assessment of the interaction must consider not only the responses of the target subject but also the behaviors of others in the situation. The data would indicate that interaction variables are considered by subjects when they rate themselves and by peers when they rate others. It would, therefore, seem reasonable for experimenters to attend to them also.

In an attempt empirically to construct a self-report measure of social anxiety, the Social Anxiety Inventory was developed (Richardson & Tasto,

1976). We wrote to all members of the Association for the Advancement of Behavior Therapy and published a note in *Behavior Therapy* requesting social anxiety hierarchy items that practicing clinicians have used. The response to this request was almost overwhelming. We eliminated duplicate items and rewrote others so that all items followed the same format and could be answered by men and women whether married or single. This was particularly necessary with items involving heterosexual contact, but the rewriting did allow us to have one form for all subjects. The result was a 166-item questionnaire that was given to 395 subjects and submitted to factor analyses. Seven conceptually clear factors emerged and were named as *fears*: (1) disapproval or criticism, (2) social assertiveness and visibility, (3) confrontation and anger-expression, (4) heterosexual contact, (5) intimacy and interpersonal warmth, (6) conflict with or rejection by parents, and (7) interpersonal loss.

We are currently adding more items to extend some of the factors and collecting more data in order to cross-validate these factors. Following this systematic replication of our initial analysis, studies directed at scaling, item analysis, and validity will be in order. As with the Fear Survey Schedule factors, it would be predicted that, if anxiety is reduced to an item within a given factor, the generalization of anxiety reduction should be greater for other items within that factor than for items on other factors.

Although the self-report measures of social anxiety discussed here may be of value in identifying situations that elicit anxiety, there is the broader diagnostic issue of anxiety-suppressed behaviors versus behavioral deficits leading to anxiety. In spite of the fact that the determination of the relative contribution of factors is critical to effective treatment, this issue has been the focus of much speculation but no psychometric development.

It is possible that a person who reports being anxious in a given social situation is responding to a learning history in which certain social situations have gained the capacity to elicit anxiety. This person may or may not have in his repertoire the social behaviors to deal with the situation. If he does have the appropriate social behaviors but is simply too anxious to engage them, the goal of therapeutic intervention would be to eliminate the anxiety directly by some procedure such as desensitization, implosion, or the like. Suppose, however, that the problem centers more on a behavioral deficit or performance anxiety, that is, this person does not know how to conduct himself, what to say, how to gesture, and so on, and it is the inability to perform socially that leads to anxiety. If social deficit is the problem, therapeutic intervention should be directed at supplying, developing, and teaching this person new social skills.

Diagnosing the maintaining causes of social anxiety as a prerequisite to effective therapy is of critical importance. Suppose that our hypothetical patient's social anxiety was caused by social skill deficit. He has taken all of the social anxiety scales described above, and his therapist has astutely assessed the specific social situations that elicit anxiety. If the therapist did not make a diagnosis of behavioral deficit versus conditional anxiety but simply proceeded to employ systematic desensitization to these situations, little progress toward alleviating the anxiety would be expected because the patient's anxiety is directly evoked, not by the social circumstance, but by his own behavioral deficit. If it should happen that during the desensitization sessions the patient serendipitously focuses on his own deficit and imagines a state of relaxation to it, the expected result would be that he can now remain relaxed in the situation but with no more social adeptness than before therapy.

It is easy to be fooled when questioning a patient about this issue. For example, a female college student may say, "I want to get mad at my father every time he complains about my boyfriend, but the reason I cannot get mad is because the thought of getting mad at my father makes me too anxious." In reaction to such a statement the therapist may conclude that this woman has the requisite behavioral skills but that they are simply held in check by an excessive amount of conditioned anxiety. If, however, the therapist were to pursue a line of questioning in more detail and ask the client what words she would actually *say* if she were to become angry at her father, she may simply not know. Saying that she would like to get mad may reflect more the effect she would like to have on her father than an accurate knowledge of the specific verbalizations that would achieve this effect.

This line of diagnostic inquiry must come to a very concrete level of specificity. It is important to discover whether clients really have the verbalizations and behaviors at their disposal that are necessary to achieve the desired social effects or whether their descriptions are vague generalities of how they would ideally like to see themselves. The development of self-report measures that would help to accomplish this step in diagnosis is a major challenge in the area of social anxiety.

Assertiveness

For the purpose of assessing assertive behavior, the Rathus Assertiveness Schedule (RAS), consisting of 30 items, (Rathus, 1973a) was developed. Subjects rate on a 6-point scale the degree to which each statement is characteristic of them. The items are scored in such a way that the higher the total score, the more assertive the subject. In the initial report on this scale, test-retest reliability over a two-month period was 0.78, and split half reliability was 0.77. It appears from these data that self-ratings of assertiveness are relatively stable and that the items comprising this instrument are quite homogeneous.

Initial validity data were obtained by correlating subjects' scores on the RAS with ratings of the subjects by others who knew them. Self-ratings of assertiveness correlated positively with others' ratings on the factors of boldness, outspokenness, assertiveness, aggressiveness, and confidence. RAS scores correlated negatively with ratings of "niceness" and did ot correlate "with scales indicative of intelligence, happiness, fairness and so on. . . ."

In a second validity study, subjects were asked how they would respond to a series of questions that were related to assertiveness. Their answers were recorded and independently rated for assertiveness. A 0.70 correlation was obtained between these ratings and RAS scores.

Rathus (1973b) has shown that RAS scores increase as a function of assertion training. One might expect that subjects who were more assertive would also be less anxious, at least in the training situation. Interestingly enough, however, Fear Survey Schedule scores did not show a significant concommitant change, that is, as self-reports of assertiveness increased following assertion training, self-reported fear did not significantly decrease. Although nonsignificant FSS changes were in the predicted direction, the magnitude of these changes ought to be larger if, as Wolpe (1973) purports, assertiveness and anxiety are antagonistic responses. Morgan (1974) has corroborated the findings of Rathus (1973b) by showing that there is very little common variance between the FSS and the RAS.

Although further data relating *changes* on the RAS to *changes* on behavioral ratings would be desirable to substantiate the validity of change scores resulting from intervention, preliminary data on the RAS indicate that it possesses sufficient reliability and validity to be clinically useful.

Because the implementation of assertion training is rapidly expanding, the potential uses of the RAS, both as a diagnostic instrument and as an evaluation tool, are many and varied. Because assertion training is being used for such varied subpopulations as women's groups, men's groups, alcoholics, drug addicts, ulcer patients, and college students, the most obvious need for the RAS at present is the collection of normative data on various subgroups. A determination of the factor structure of assertive behaviors, investigated separately by subpopulations, is more than an academic exercise since what is considered effective assertive behavior in one group or subset of the population may be considered aggressive and ineffective in another. Such information would seem to be of importance to the development and evaluation of training programs.

McFall and Lillesand (1971) constructed the 35-item Conflict Resolution Inventory (CRI) as a measure of assertiveness. Each item describes a situation involving an unreasonable request and asks subjects whether they would refuse the request and how they would feel about their response. Preliminary data suggest that scores on this scale are quite sensitive to behavioral rehearsal when it is geared toward the development of refusal behaviors.

Whereas the CRI is highly specific to refusal behaviors, Galassi, DeLo, Galassi, and Bastien (1974) developed the 50-item College Self-Expression Scale (CSES) as a more general measure of assertive behavior. The items were written to measure positive assertiveness (expressing love, admiration, approval, etc.), negative assertiveness (expressing justified anger, dissatisfaction, annoyance, etc.), and self-denial (overapologizing, excessive interpersonal anxiety, exaggerated concern for others, etc.). These investigators' data have indicated that college men rate themselves as slightly more assertive than do college women. Test-retest reliabilities for total scores were 0.89 and 0.90. For purposes of establishing construct validity, the CSES was correlated with several scales of the Adjective Check List (Gough & Heilbrun, 1965). Positive correlations were obtained between the CSES and the following scales from the Adjective Check List: Number checked, Defensiveness, Favorable, Self-confidence, Achievement, Dominance, Intraception, Heterosexuality, Exhibition, Autonomy, and Change. Negative correlations were found with the Unfavorable, Succorance, Abasement, Deference, and Counseling Readiness scales. Low, yet statistically significant, correlations were obtained between supervisor ratings and self-ratings. In another study (Galassi & Galassi, 1973), correlations of greater significance and slightly greater magnitude were obtained between residence hall counselor ratings and self-ratings of assertiveness.

Exactly what should be measured with assertiveness scales is a question whose answer is perhaps less than obvious. If we consider assertive behavior to be subsumed under the superordinate concept of adaptive or effective behavior, the precise definition of the assertive behavior involves judgments not completely amenable to empirical analysis. If one were to take a firm stance against buying a used automobile from a salesman whose business ethics seemed less than laudable, most people (with perhaps the exception of the salesman) would consider the refusal behavior to be assertive, effective, and adaptive; and, conversely, if this person were to acquiesce to the pressures of the salesman and buy the car, most people would consider this to be nonassertive, ineffective, and maladaptive. On the other hand, suppose that a waiter in a restaurant brings a man his steak too well done. The customer in a loud, offensive tone, with words that would be censored from the *Tonight Show,* tells the waiter to take it back and bring another. This in turn angers the waiter who, in a passive aggressive way, engages in delay tactics that have the effect of postponing the customer's gratification. The delay in turn further angers the customer, and the end result is an angry waiter, an outraged customer, and a delayed steak. Alternatively, the customer, on cutting into his overly done steak, may smile and politely tell the waiter he knows that it is not his fault but the steak is not quite right. The waiter, rather than feeling angry, may feel apologetic in response to the customer's approach and wish to please the customer by bringing him another steak as quickly as possible. Under these conditions neither waiter nor customer is angry and the goal, having the steak prepared correctly, is achieved more *effectively*.

In the first alternative the customer would have been considered assertive and in the second he would have been considered effective. If the goal of assertion training is the development of assertive behavior and if the customer had just completed an assertiveness training program, he would probably be judged by others and rated by himself as more assertive in the first mode of behavior than in the second. If the concept of assertive behavior is dilineated so that the criteria for assertive behavior can be specified in terms of effectiveness (i.e., achieving what one wants within the bounds of social appropriateness), then the development of instrumentation for measuring assertive behavior must be geared toward the assessment of social effectiveness. Although the concept of effectiveness rather than assertion per se is not new, it is by no means uncommon for assertiveness trainers to teach their clientele to make assertive responses under a variety of circumstances and then to consider their task completed. This seems to be particularly true with the recent emergence of assertion training *groups*. The major point is that people who are beginning to acquire the ability to be assertive can frequently defeat themselves through their abandonment of the stated goals toward which their assertiveness was directed. Indiscriminant assertiveness is simply not intelligent behavior. In regard to assessment, therefore, adaptation and effective control over one's environs should be considered in the development of instrumentation to measure the individual's successful incorporation of a repertoire of assertive behavior.

Depression

Although depression is clearly a major clinical problem, very little behavior therapy research has been published on the treatment of depression and even less on its assessment. The Depression Adjective Check List (DACL) (Lubin, 1965) is one of the few existing scales shown to be sensitive to behavioral treatment programs for depression. This scale consists of 32 adjectives to which subjects rate "applies to me" or "does not apply to me." Twenty-two of the adjectives, if rated applicable, load in the depressive direction and ten load in the nondepressive direction. There are four forms for males and four for females. Each form is comprised of different adjectives, which makes daily monitoring less influenced by the previous day's ratings. Normative data on the scales allow for standard score conversions that make it possible to make comparisons across the different forms. The scale appears to be reliable (Anton, Note 1). It differentiates psychiatric patients carrying a depressive diagnosis from those carrying other diagnoses, and it differentiates depressed people from normals (Lewinsohn & Libet, 1972). Its major limitation is that it appears to be inadequate in differentiating severe from moderate levels of depression.

Anton (Note 1) has shown that the DACL scores change very significantly in depressed subjects as a function of treatment. Her treatment program involved a cognitive behavioral approach in which depressed subjects were trained to anticipate as well as engage in pleasant activities. The beneficial changes that occurred on the DACL immediately after treatment were maintained at one week following the termination of treatment. At the time of writing this Chapter, her follow-up data had not yet been collected. It is interesting to note that the DACL scores remained stable and virtually unchanged for her no-treatment control and placebo-control groups.

The dearth of instrumentation on the measurement of depression is paralleled by the lack of treatments of established effectiveness. Historically, it seems that the development of assessment instrumentation has followed the development of treatment procedures. One reason for this may have to do with a unique behavioral aspect of depression. Depression as seen by behaviorally oriented psychologists (Burgess, 1969; Lazarus, 1968) involves a lack of reinforcement in one's environment. A lack of reinforcement leads to extinction, and extinction is behaviorally characterized by a lack of behavior. Many of the psychopathologies are defined by excessive behaviors that ought to be eliminated, and the focus of diagnostic assessment is on the measurement of these behaviors. The observable behavioral phenomenon that operationalizes depression, however, is a lack of behavior rather than a surplus. Perhaps measuring the relative absence of behaviors, or of anything for that matter, is a somewhat more difficult task than measuring the excessive frequency (or presence) of some undesirable behavior. Whatever the cause or combination of causes may be for the paucity of research, it is clear that further investigations of the treatment and assessment of depression are indicated.

Acrophobia

Baker, Cohen, and Saunders (1973) have reported on the use of the Acrophobic Questionnaire (AQ) for assessing fear of heights. This questionnaire consists of 20 situations such as "standing next to an open window on the third floor," "walking on a footbridge over a highway," and the like. The items can be rated on 7-point scale for the degree of anxiety each situation would elicit and rated on a three-point scale for the tendency to avoid each situation. These investigators found split-half reliabilities to be 0.82 when subjects rated how much anxiety each item produced and 0.70 when they rated how much they would wish to avoid each situation. The anxiety and avoidance ratings correlated 0.73 with each other. Test-retest reliabilities over a 3-month period were 0.86 for anxiety ratings and 0.82 for avoidance ratings. Some validity data for the AQ were also presented by the investigators. They treated acrophobics with standard desensitization or self-directed desensitization and found significant decreases in AQ scores for these groups in comparison with waiting-list controls. Other measures followed this pattern.

It appears that the AQ is a reliable and valid measure of acrophobia that can be used for both assessment and evaluation. Many empirical studies on procedures designed to alleviate phobias have employed small animals, particularly snakes and mice. One reason for this has been the relative ease of obtaining both self-report and behavioral measures on small animals. Since the AQ does appear to be reliable and valid and since behavioral measures of response to height can be obtained with relative ease (particularly in cities with tall buildings), acrophobia may offer an attractive research alternative to snake and mice phobias. This might especially be true when one has depleted the supply of a particular type of phobic. From 1969 to 1971 so many snake-phobic subjects at Colorado State University were experimentally treated that it was almost impossible to find a volunteer subject on campus with a high fear rating of snakes!

A CASE STUDY IN SELF-REPORT MEASUREMENT

An example of the need for, and subsequent development of, psychometric instrumentation in behavior therapy can be seen in recent work on dysmenorrhea (menstrual pain). Tasto and Chesney (1974) used muscle relaxation and visualization of imagery related to dysmenorrhea in treating women who complained of menstrual problems. The outcome data, measured by the Symptom Severity Scale, indicated that some subjects were benefiting from treatment whereas others were not. The question arose as to whether there might be two types of dysmenorrhea and that, if so, perhaps our program was effective with one type and not with the other. We went back to the literature on dysmenorrhea and discovered that Dalton (1969) had proposed two separate types of dysmenorrhea, namely, spasmodic and congestive. She described *spasmodic* dysmenorrhea as pain that begins on the first day of menstruation and may be experienced as spasms that can lead to vomiting or fainting. The pain is limited to the back, inner sides of the thighs, and lower abdomen. *Congestive* dysmenorrhea occurs during the premenstrual cycle and may be experienced as increasing heaviness or dull aching pains in the lower abdomen, breasts, and ankles. Lethargy, depression, and irritability may also characterize this type.

Dalton hypothesizes that the hormonal substrate of the two different types involves the relative balance of estrogen and progesterone levels with progesterone raised above estrogen in the spasmodic type and estrogen raised above progesterone in the congestive type. Although she believes that there is a physiological basis for the two types, she also claims that the two types can be diagnosed on the basis of a clinical interview. Our thinking was that, if two distinct types exist and if a clinical interview can reliably separate the two types, psychometric instrumentation could potentially be developed that would be at least as reliable and valid as a clinical interview.

In a sequal to the first study of 1974 we set about to construct an instrument that distinguished between the two types (Chesney & Tasto, 1975a). We constructed 51 items that seemed to reasonably distinguish between the verbal symptoms that Dalton reports as characteristic of the spasmodic and congestive types. Women who reported menstrual difficulties were asked to respond to these items, which were in turn subjected to a factor analysis. When items with less than a 0.35 factor loading were discarded, 25 items remained. Of these, 12 were characteristic of Dalton's description of spasmodic dysmenorrhea, and 12 were characteristic of congestive dysmenorrhea. The remaining item consisted of a description of the two types and asked the subject to indicate the type most characteristic of her. These 25 items were administered to a new sample of women reporting menstrual difficulties, and the result of the second factor analysis was that the same items loaded on the same factors as was the case for the first sample.

The questionnaire was administered twice to each sample, and test-retest reliabilities of the items were obtained. Each of the 25 items constituting the final set had a test-retest reliability of 0.65 or greater, and the average coefficient based on z score transformation was equal to 0.78.

The items are scored on a five-point scale ranging from "never" to "always." Extreme answers are ipsative in that, given a population of women with dysmenorrhea, a score toward one end or the other of the five-point scale loads on one type of dysmenorrhea or the other. For example, if a women rates "always" to the item, "I feel depressed for several days *before* my period," this would weigh in the direction of the congestive type. If another woman, however, were to rate "never" to this item, her response, given that she experiences menstrual difficulties, would not be neutral but would load in the direction of the spasmodic type. On this particular item the reason a "never" response would load in the direction of the spasmodic type is that the symptoms of the spasmodic type do not begin several days before the period but typically coincide with the beginning of the period.

Because of the ipsative nature of the individual items, it was possible to score the items on the congestive factor in the reverse order of the spasmodic items so that a high total score reflected a tendency toward spasmodic type and a low score a tendency toward the congestive type. In doing this, we expected that a continuum from congestive to spasmodic would emerge from the subjects' ratings. This was not so much because of any underlying theory about dysmenorrhea as such but because behavioral phenomena typically distribute themselves in a unimodal fashion from one end of a continuum to the other. In contrast to our expectation, all subjects on the three samples we now have score at the extremes, either high or low but not in the middle. Within the spasmodic range and within the congestive range, subjects' ratings appear to represent an underlying continuity. However, abrupt discontinuity between the two distributions occurs. At this stage of our research, it appears that Dalton's theory about the existence of two types of dysmenorrhea has been confirmed as well as our assumption that they can be distinguished with psychometric instrumentation.

The resultant instrument is entitled the Menstrual Symptom Questionnaire (MSQ) and it appears with its directions for scoring in Table 6–2. Since we had reason to believe that treatment consisting of muscle relaxation plus imagery of menstrual scenes would be more effective with the spasmodic type than with the congestive type, we conducted a factorial study to assess treatment effectiveness (Chesney & Tasto, 1975b). Women who reported menstrual symptoms were administered the MSQ and divided into spasmodic and congestive types based on the results of this test. Each of these two groups was further divided into three subgroups by random assignment to a behavior therapy program, a pseudotreatment program or a waiting list control condition. This formed a 2 (type) × 3 (treatment) factorial structure comprised of six groups. As a measure of symptomology, the Symptom Severity Scale (SSS) (Chesney & Tasto, 1975b) was administered to all subjects before and after the treatment period. The post-treatment measures were obtained long enough after the termination of treatment to ensure that each woman had at least two periods.

The results indicated that on SSS measures from pretesting to post-testing the waiting list controls, whether spasmodic or congestive, showed a

Table 6–2. Items on the Menstrual Sympton Questionnaire. [From M. A. Chesney and D. L. Tasto, The development of the menstrual symptom questionnaire. *Behaviour Research and Therapy*, 1975, *13*, 237–244. Copyright (1975) by Pergamon Press. Reproduced by permission.]

Item*	Never (1	Rarely 2	Sometimes 3	Often 4	Always 5)	Type of dysmenorrhea:† S = Spasmodic C = Congestive
1. I feel irritable, easily agitated, and am impatient a few days *before* my period.	N	R	S	O	A	(C)
2. I have cramps that *begin* on the first day of my period.	N	R	S	O	A	(S)
3. I feel depressed for several days *before* my period.	N	R	S	O	A	(C)
4. I have abdominal pain or discomfort which begins one day *before* my period.	N	R	S	O	A	(S)
5. For several days *before* my period I feel exhausted, lethargic or tired.	N	R	S	O	A	(C)
6. I only know that my period is coming by looking at the calendar.	N	R	S	O	A	(S)
7. I take a prescription drug for the pain *during* my period.	N	R	S	O	A	(S)
8. I feel weak and dizzy *during* my period.	N	R	S	O	A	(S)
9. I feel tense and nervous *before* my period.	N	R	S	O	A	(C)
10. I have diarrhea *during* my period.	N	R	S	O	A	(S)
11. I have backaches several days *before* my period.	N	R	S	O	A	(C)
12. I take aspirin for the pain *during* my period.	N	R	S	O	A	(S)
13. My breasts feel tender and sore a few days *before* my period.	N	R	S	O	A	(C)
14. My lower back, abdomen, and the inner sides of my thighs *begin* to hurt or be tender on the first day of my period.	N	R	S	O	A	(S)
15. *During* the first day or so of my period, I feel like curling up in bed, using a hot water bottle on my abdomen, or taking a hot bath.	N	R	S	O	A	(S)
16. I gain weight *before* my period.	N	R	S	O	A	(C)
17. I am constipated *during* my period.	N	R	S	O	A	(C)
18. *Beginning* on the first day of my period, I have pains which may diminish or disappear for several minutes and then reappear.	N	R	S	O	A	(S)
19. The pain I have with my period is not intense, but a continuous dull aching.	N	R	S	O	A	(C)
20. I have abdominal discomfort for more than one day *before* my period.	N	R	S	O	A	(C)
21. I have backaches which *begin* the same day as my period.	N	R	S	O	A	(S)
22. My abdominal area feels bloated for a few days *before* my period.	N	R	S	O	A	(C)
23. I feel nauseous *during* the first day or so of my period.	N	R	S	O	A	(C)
24. I have headaches for a few days *before* my period.	N	R	S	O	A	(S)

25. TYPE 1‡

The pain begins on the first day of menstruation, often coming within an hour of the first signs of menstruation. The pain is most severe the first day and may or may not continue on subsequent days. Felt as spasms, the pain may lessen or subside for awhile and then reappear. A few women find this pain so severe as to cause vomiting, fainting or dizziness; some others report that they are most comfortable in bed or taking a hot bath. This pain is limited to the lower abdomen, back and inner sides of the thighs.

TYPE 2

There is advanced warning of the onset of menstruation during which the woman feels an increasing heaviness, and a dull aching pain in the lower abdomen. This pain is sometimes accompanied by nausea, lack of appetite, and constipation. Headaches, backaches, and breast pain are also characteristic of this type of menstrual discomfort.

The type that most closely fits my experience is TYPE ———

* On the first 24 items *Ss* were instructed to indicate the degree-to which they experience the symptom by selecting one of five response choices [Never (N), Rarely (R), Sometimes (S), Often (O), and Always (A)].

† The first 24 items are characteristic of either spasmodic or congestive dysmenorrhea. The type of dysmenorrhea indicates the order of scoring for each item. Items designated as S (Spasmodic), score as indicated by numbers 1–5. Items designated as C (Congestive), reverse scoring. On item 25, if *S* checks Type 1, score 5; if *S* checks Type 2, score 1.

‡ On the twenty-fifth item, *Ss* were instructed to read the descriptions of two types of menstrual discomfort and select the type that most closely fits their experience.

slight, but nonsignificant, increase in reported symptomology. The pseudotreatment groups, whether spasmodic or congestive, showed slight but statistically nonsignificant decreases in reported symptomology. (A Rogerian colleague did not like for this group to be entitled "pseudotreatment" because it was essentially a client-centered group that discussed personal problems associated with dysmenorrhea.) When behavior therapy involving muscle relaxation and imagery of menstrual scenes was used with congestive types, no significant improvement occurred. However, when the same procedures were applied to the spasmodic types, a dramatic decrease in reported symptomology occurred that was of both statistical and clinical significance.

The conclusion was that this particular behavior therapy approach is effective with women suffering from spasmodic dysmenorrhea but not for women suffering from congestive dysmenorrhea. It is, therefore, necessary to determine which type of dysmenorrhea a person is suffering from before initiating treatment. It is relatively simple to use the highly reliable MSQ for such purposes. To diagnose and then treat may sound like the medical model in psychology revisited, but that may not be all bad if differential diagnosis leads to differential prognosis as a function of a given treatment procedure.

The step currently being taken in this case study is the initiation of an efficient treatment program for dysmenorrhea at the student health center on campus. The concept is that a woman who complains of menstrual problems will take the MSQ. This can be quickly scored and, if a given woman's score indicates that she is of the spasmodic type, she will learn relaxation and have menstrual imagery presented via audio tape. Women who score in the congestive range will at least not waste their time engaging in an ineffective program. Since the implementation of this program is only beginning, we have no evaluative data to present as of yet. However, it does illustrate the need for developing self-report inventories and questionnaires that are specifically developed to contribute to the analysis and treatment of specific problems.

POTPOURRI

The following are brief descriptions of other self-report measures that have been used for assessment in behavior therapy:

Cautela and Kastenbaum (1967) developed the Reinforcement Survey Schedule (RSS) to assess reinforcers in one's environment. The items on the RSS are divided into four sections, and they essentially ask subjects what situations and activities they like and how much they like them. In their development of the RSS the investigators conceived of this scale as a valuable aid in identifying positively reinforcing stimuli that might potentially have control over operant behavior under a variety of situations. Cautela, Kastenbaum, and Wincze (1972) have shown that "juvenile offenders preferred items associated with relationships with loved ones; non-offenders preferred items associated with being right or being praised" (p. 261). However, little research on the ideographic use of the RSS has been done.

Lazarus (1968) regards depression as a matter of "inadequate or insufficient reinforcers" (p. 84). The depressed individual is on an extinction schedule that results in a decrease of behaviors. Significant reinforcers such as money, love, status, or security may have been lost. Or the loss may have been more subtle such as a loss of youth, a loss of bodily functioning, or the anticipation of a nonreinforcing state. To the extent that psychotherapy for depression involves identifying and utilizing reinforcers to energize behavior, the RSS may be of value in helping both the patient and therapist in this regard.

In his major books on behavior therapy, Wolpe (1958, 1969, 1973) has described the use of the Willoughby Personality Schedule. This test was derived from the Clark-Thurstone Inventory and consists of 25 items that center around social anxiety, emotional sensitivity, and the ability to be assertive. Examples of items are "Do you keep in the background on social occasions?" "Are you happy and sad at times without knowing why?" "Do you lack self-confidence?" These items are then rated on a five-point scale ranging from 0 (meaning "No," "Never," "Not at all," etc.) to 4 (meaning "practically always," "entirely," etc.).

Wolpe (1958, pp. 218–219) presents Willoughby scores on patients taken before and after psychotherapy based on reciprocal inhibition. Assertion, desensitization, use of the sexual response, relaxation, and other approaches had been used to treat a wide variety of problems. For patients who were judged by Knight's (1941) criteria to be "apparently cured," the Willoughby scores dropped from a mean of 45.2 before treatment to a mean of 12.2 after treatment. The group judged to be "much improved" changed from a mean of 44.8 to a mean of 25.6. Wolpe has arbitrarily defined the "normal" upper limit to be 20.0. It will be interesting if these results are substantiated upon further investigation since the "apparently cured" group with a mean of 12.2 falls well within this limit whereas the mean of the "much improved" group is 5.6 points from this limit.

Although Wolpe presents no control group data on the Willoughby Personality Schedule, Baker, Cohen, and Saunders (1973) have shown that as a function of systematic desensitization for acrophobia, whether treatment was self-directed or conducted by a therapist, Willoughby scores dropped significantly in comparison with those of a waiting list control. The waiting list controls' scores showed a slight, although not statistically significant, increase from pretest to posttest.

The initial data-based indications on the Willoughby Schedule suggest that the scores are sensitive to the effects of behavior therapy and that further data are needed to refine and specify its appropriate uses.

Wolpe (1969, 1973) has also described the use of the Bernreuter Self-Sufficiency Inventory for purposes of assessing dependency and assertive problems. This scale consists of 60 items that are simply answered "yes" or "no." Examples of items are: "Have books been more entertaining to you than companions?" "Do you want someone with you when you receive bad news?" "Do you dislike finding your way about in strange places?" "Do you experience periods of loneliness?" Scoring 1.0 or 0.0 is keyed to the face validity nature of the items, and a total score is the summation of the 1.0s.

Wolpe suggests that a normal score falls between 24.0 and 42.0 and that a score below 20.0 is possibly indicative of overdependency, agorophobia, or lack of self-sufficiency. Although the face validity of the items appears to be high, asking expert judges the direction each item should be scored might result in interrater reliabilities of less than 1.0, which may be why the scoring key differs on four items between the 1969 (p. 290, errata) and the 1973 (p. 290) editions of Wolpe's *The Practice of Behavior Therapy*.

The Fear Thermometer that was initially used by Walk (1956) requires subjects to rate on a 100-point scale their subjective fear in the presence of a phobic stimulus. Although the fear thermometer is not a schedule or inventory as such and thus extensive coverage of it does not fall within the domain of this chapter, it is a self-report index of fear that has been used rather extensively. As examples, see Rachman (1965), Lomont and Edwards (1967), Willis and Edwards (1969), and Schroeder and Dietrich (1973). Its reliability, validity, and utility indicate that it should be useful in quantifying subjective responses of fear to specific stimuli.

CONCLUSION

At the risk of stating the obvious, we must conclude that the development of self-report measures for behavioral assessment has only just begun. A great deal of research effort is still needed before the clinical potential of self-report measurement in behavior therapy is reached. The instruction and validation of reliable instrumentation are relevant to theory construction as well as to the evaluation of treatment effects. Although progress has been made in the assessment of specific phobic reactions, the major challenges for behavioral self-report measurement lie ahead.

It is clear that a more refined measurement of social anxiety is needed. However, of particular relevance to the social area is the development of diagnostic instrumentation that distinguishes stimulus-bound social anxiety from anxiety that arises as a result of social skill deficit. Once this distinction can be made, how does one quantify the deficit for purposes of monitoring therapeutic progress? Measuring the lack of something may be a bit more tricky than measuring an excessive amount of something. This same problem applies to measuring the lack of behaviors involved with depression—another problem characterized by a dearth of instrumentation.

The measurement of assertive behavior, particularly when assertive behavior is subordinated to the concept of effective behavior, is still another area in which needs outweigh its present assessment resources. The self-report aspects of psychophysiological disorders is a relatively untouched area that needs psychometric quantification. However, as long as the researcher and clinician keep in mind that it is the patient's self-report that usually establishes the existence and defines the parameters of clinical problems, the technology of self-report will emerge as a critically important and perhaps indispensable mode of behavioral assessment for psychotherapy research and practice.

REFERENCE NOTE

1. Anton, J. L. *Approaches to the self-management of depression*. Paper presented at the National Conference on Behavioral Self-Control, Salt Lake City, 1975.

REFERENCES

Adams, J. Change on the fear survey schedule during psychiatric hospitalization. *Journal of Clinical Psychology*, 1971, **27**, 533–535.

Adams, J. Change on 16 fear factors during psychiatric hospitalization. *Journal of Behavior Therapy and Experimental Psychiatry*, 1972, **3**, 91–95.

Akutagawa, D. A. *A study in construct validity of the psychoanalytic concept of latent anxiety and a test of projection distance hypothesis*. Unpublished doctoral dissertation, University of Pittsburgh, 1956.

Arkowitz, H., Lichtenstein, E., McGovern, K., & Hines, P. The behavioral assessment of social competence in males. *Behavior Therapy*, 1975, **6**, 3–13.

Baker, B. L., Cohen, D. C., & Saunders, J. T. Self-directed desensitization for acrophobia. *Behaviour Research and Therapy*, 1973, **11**, 79–89.

Bates, H. D. Factorial structure and MMPI correlates of a fear survey schedule in a clinical population. *Behaviour Research and Therapy*, 1971, **9**, 355–360.

Begelman, D. A., & Hersen, M. An experimental analysis of the verbal-motor discrepancy in schizophrenia. *Journal of Clinical Psychology*, 1973, **29**, 175–179.

Bendig, A. W. The Pittsburgh scales of social extroversion-introversion and emotionality. *Journal of Psychology*, 1962, **53,** 199–209.

Bernstein, D. A., & Allen, G. I. Fear Survey Schedule (II): Normative data and factor analysis based upon a large college sample. *Behaviour Research ana Therapy*, 1969, **7,** 403–407.

Braun, P. R., & Reynolds, D. N. A factor analysis of a 100-item fear survey inventory. *Behaviour Research and Therapy*, 1969, **7,** 399–402.

Burgess, E. P. The modification of depressive behaviors. In R. D. Rubin & C. M. Franks (Eds.), *Advances in behavior therapy*. New York: Academic, 1969.

Cautela, J. R., & Kastenbaum, R. A Reinforcement Survey Schedule for use in therapy, training, and research. *Psychological Reports*, 1967, **20,** 1115–1130.

Cautela, J. R., Kastenbaum, R., & Wincze, J. P. The use of the Fear Survey Schedule and the Reinforcement Survey Schedule to survey possible reinforcing and and aversive stimuli among juvenile offenders. *The Journal of Genetic Psychology*, 1972, **121,** 255–261.

Chesney, M. A., & Tasto, D. L. The development of the menstrual symptom questionnaire. *Behaviour Research and Therapy*, 1975, **13,** 237–244. (a)

Chesney, M. A., & Tasto, D. L. The effectiveness of behavior modification with spasmodic and congestive dysmenorrhea. *Behaviour Research and Therapy*, 1975, **13,** 245–254. (b)

Cooke, G. Evaluation of the efficiency of the components of reciprocal inhibition psychotherapy. *Journal of Abnormal Psychology*, 1968, **73,** 464–467.

Cotler, S. B., & Garlington, W. K. The generalization of anxiety reduction following systematic desensitization. *Behaviour Research and Therapy*, 1969, **7,** 35–40.

Crighton, J., & Jehu, D. Treatment of examination anxiety by systematic desensitization or psychotherapy in groups. *Behaviour Research and Therapy*, 1969, **7,** 245–248.

Dalton, K. *The menstrual cycle*. New York: Pantheon Books, 1969.

Dixon, J. J., deMonchaux, C., & Sandler, J. Patterns of anxiety: The phobias. *British Journal of Medical Psychology*, 1957, **30,** 34–40.

Endler, N. S., & Hunt, J. McV. Sources of behavioral variance as measured by the S–R Inventory of Anxiousness. *Psychological Bulletin*, 1966, **65,** 336–346.

Endler, N. S., Hunt, J. McV., & Rosenstein, A. J. An S–R inventory of anxiousness. *Psychological Monographs*, 1962, **76,** (17, Whole No. 536).

Everaerd, W. T. A. M., Rijken, H. M., & Emmelkamp, P. M. G. A comparison of "flooding" and "successive approximation" in the treatment of agoraphobia. *Behaviour Research and Therapy*, 1973, **11,** 105–117.

Ford, L. H. A forced-choice, acquiescence-free, social desirability (defensiveness) scale. *Journal of Consulting Psychology*, 1964, **28,** 475.

Galassi, J. P., DeLo, J. S., Galassi, M. D., & Bastien, S. The College Self Expression Scale: A measure of assertiveness. *Behavior Therapy*, 1974, **5,** 165–171.

Galassi, J. P., Galassi, M. D., & Litz, M. C. Assertive training in groups using video feedback. *Journal of Counseling Psychology*, 1974, **21,** 290–294.

Garlington, W. K., & Cotler, S. B. Systematic desensitization of test anxiety. *Behaviour Research and Therapy*, 1968, **6,** 247–256.

Geer, J. H. The development of a scale to measure fear. *Behaviour Research and Therapy*, 1965, **3,** 45–53.

Geer, J. H. Effect of fear arousal upon task performance and verbal behavior. *Journal of Abnormal Psychology*, 1966, **71,** 119–123.

Gough, H. G., & Heilburn, A. B. Jr. *The adjective check list manual.* Palo Alto, Calif.: Consulting Psychologist Press, 1965.

Grossberg, J. M., & Wilson, H. K. A correlational comparison of the Wolpe-Lange Fear Survey Schedule and Taylor Manifest Anxiety Scale. *Behaviour Research and Therapy*, 1965, **3,** 125–128.

Hersen, M. Fear scale norms for an in-patient population. *Journal of Clinical Psychology*, 1971, **27,** 375–378.

Ihli, K. L., & Garlington, W. K. A comparison of group vs. individual desensitization of test anxiety. *Behaviour Research and Therapy*, 1969, **7,** 207–209.

Knight, R. O. Evaluation of the results of psychoanalytic therapy. *American Journal of Psychiatry*, 1941, **98,** 434–446.

Landy, F. L., & Gaupp, L. A. A factor analysis of the Fear Survey Schedule–III. *Behaviour Research and Therapy*, 1971, **9,** 89–93.

Lang, P. J. The mechanics of desensitization and the laboratory study of human fear. In C. M. Franks (Ed.), *Behavior therapy: Appraisal and status.* New York: McGraw-Hill, 1969.

Lang, P. J., & Lazovik, A. D. Experimental desensitization of a phobia. *Journal of Abnormal and Social Psychology*, 1963, **66,** 519–525.

Lang, P. J., Lazovik, A. D., & Reynolds, D. J. Desensitization, suggestibility, and pseudotherapy. *Journal of Abnormal Psychology*, 1965, **70,** 395–402.

Lawlis, G. F. Response styles of a patient population on the Fear Survey Schedule. *Behaviour Research and Therapy*, 1971, **9,** 95–102.

Lazarus, A. A. Learning theory and the treatment of depression. *Behaviour Research and Therapy*, 1968, **6,** 83–89.

Lewinsohn, P. M., & Libet, J. Pleasant events, activity schedules, and depressions. *Journal of Abnormal Psychology*, 1972, **79,** 291–295.

Lewisohn, P. M., Weinstein, M. S., & Shaw, D. A. Depression: A clinical research approach. In R. D. Rubin and C. M. Franks (Eds.), *Advances in behavior therapy.* New York: Academic, 1969.

Libet, J. M., & Lewinsohn, P. M. Concept of social skill with special reference to the behavior of depressed persons. *Journal of Consulting and Clinical Psychology*, 1973, **40,** 304–312.

Lomont, J. F., & Edwards, J. E. The role of relaxation in systematic desensitization. *Behaviour Research and Therapy*, 1967, **5,** 11–25.

Lubin, B. L. Adjective checklists for measurement of depression. *Archives of General Psychiatry*, 1965, **12,** 57–62.

McFall, R. M., & Lillesand, D. B. Behavior rehearsal with modeling and coaching in assertion training. *Journal of Abnormal Psychology*, 1971, **77,** 313–323.

Meikle, S., & Mitchell, M. C. Factor analysis of the fear survey schedule with phobics. *Journal of Clinical Psychology*, 1974, **30,** 44–46.

Merbaum, M., & Stricker, G. Factor analytic study of male and female responses to the fear survey schedule. *Journal of Behavior Therapy and Experimental Psychiatry*, 1972, **3,** 87–90.

Morgan, W. G. The relationship between expressed social fears and assertiveness and its treatment implications. *Behaviour Research and Therapy*, 1974, **12,** 255–257.

Paul, G. L. Outcome of systematic desensitization I: Background, procedures, and uncontrolled reports of individual treatment. In C. M. Franks (Ed.), *Behavior therapy: Appraisal and status*. New York: McGraw-Hill, 1969.

Rachman, S. Studies in desensitization: I. The separate effects of relaxation and desensitization. *Behaviour Research and Therapy*, 1965, **3,** 245–252.

Rathus, S. A. Instigation of assertive behavior through videotape-mediated assertive models and directed practice. *Behaviour Research and Therapy*, 1973, **11,** 57–65. (a)

Rathus, S. A. A 30-item schedule for assessing assertive behavior. *Behavior Therapy*, 1973, **4,** 398–406. (b)

Richardson, F. C., & Tasto, D. L. Development and factor analysis of a social anxiety inventory. *Behavior Therapy*, 1976, **7,** 453–462.

Ritter, B. Treatment of acrophobia with contact desensitization. *Behaviour Research and Therapy*, 1969, **7,** 41–45.

Robinson, C., & Suinn, R. M. Group desensitization of a phobia in massed sessions. *Behaviour Research and Therapy*, 1969, **7,** 319–321.

Rothstein, W., Holmes, G. R., & Boblitt, W. E. A factor analysis of the fear survey schedule with a psychiatric population. *Journal of Clinical Psychology*, 1972, **28,** 78–80.

Rubin, B. M., Katkin, E. S., Weiss, B. W., & Efran, J. S. Factor analysis of a fear survey schedule. *Behaviour Research and Therapy*, 1968, **6,** 65–75.

Rubin, S. E., Lawlis, G. F., Tasto, D. L., & Namenek, T. Factor analysis of the 122-item Fear Survey Schedule. *Behaviour Research and Therapy*, 1969, **7,** 381–386.

Sarason, I. Test anxiety, general anxiety, and intellectual performance. *Journal of Consulting Psychology*, 1957, **21,** 485–490.

Schroeder, H. E., & Dietrich, R. R. Transfer of fear reduction through systematic desensitization. *Behaviour Research and Therapy*, 1973, **11,** 137–141.

Scrignar, C. B., Swanson, W. C., & Bloom, W. A. Use of systematic desensitization in the treatment of airplane phobic patients. *Behaviour Research and Therapy*, 1973, **11,** 129–131.

Sears, D. O. Social anxiety, opinion structure and opinion change. *Journal of Personality and Social Psychology*, 1967, **7,** 142–151.

Suinn, R. M. The desensitization of test-anxiety by group and individual treatment. *Behaviour Research and Therapy*, 1968, **6,** 385–387.

Suinn, R. M. The relationship between fears and anxiety: A further study. *Behaviour Research and Therapy*, 1969, **7,** 317–318.

Tasto, D. L., & Chesney, M. A. Muscle relaxation treatment for primary dysmenorrhea. *Behavior Therapy*, 1974, **5,** 668–672.

Tasto, D. L., & Hickson, R. Standardization, item analysis, and scaling of the 122-item fear survey schedule. *Behavior Therapy*, 1970, **1,** 473–484.

Tasto, D. L., Hickson, R., & Rubin, S. E. Scaled profile analysis of fear survey schedule factors. *Behavior Therapy*, 1971, **2,** 543–549.

Tasto, D. L., & Suinn, R. M. Fear Survey Schedule changes on total and factor scores due to nontreatment effects. *Behavior Therapy*, 1972, **3,** 275–278.

Walk, R. D. Self ratings of fear in a fear-invoking situation. *Journal of Abnormal and Social Psychology*, 1956, **52,** 171–178.

Watson, D., & Friend, R. Measurement of social-evaluative anxiety. *Journal of Consulting and Clinical Psychology*, 1969, **33,** 448–451.

Weiss, R. L. Operant conditioning techniques in psychological assessment. In P. McReynolds (Ed.), *Advances in psychological assessment*. Palo Alto, Calif.: Science and Behavior, 1968.

Weiss, B. W., Katkin, E. S., & Rubin, B. M. Relationship between a factor analytically derived measure of a specific fear and performance after related fear induction. *Journal of Abnormal Psychology*, 1968, **73,** 461–463.

Welsh, G. S. Factor dimensions A and R. In G. S. Welsh & W. G. Dahlstrom (Eds.), *Basic reading on the MMPI*. Minneapolis: University of Minnesota Press, 1956.

Willis, R. W., & Edwards, J. A. A study of the comparative effectiveness of systematic desensitization and implosive therapy. *Behaviour Research and Therapy*, 1969, **7,** 387–395.

Wolpe, J. *Psychotherapy by reciprocal inhibition*. Stanford: Stanford University Press, 1958.

Wolpe, J. *The practice of behavior therapy*. New York: Pergamon, 1969.

Wolpe, J. *The practice of behavior therapy* (2nd ed.). New York: Pergamon, 1973.

Wolpe, J., & Lang, P. J. A fear survey schedule for use in behavior therapy, *Behaviour Research and Therapy*, 1964, **2,** 27–30.

Wolpe, J., & Lang, P. J. *Fear Survey Schedule*. San Diego, California: Educational and Industrial Testing Service, 1969.

Zeisset, R. M. Desensitization and relaxation in the modification of psychiatric patients interview behavior. *Journal of Abnormal Psychology*, 1968, **73,** 18–24.

CHAPTER 7

Self-Monitoring Procedures

ANTHONY R. CIMINERO, ROSEMERY O. NELSON,
and DAVID P. LIPINSKI

A popular behavioral assessment procedure requires individuals to record various aspects of their own behavior. With this procedure, which is generally labeled self-monitoring, self-recording, or self-observation, individuals may be asked to record the occurrences of a specified behavior as well as the events that precede and follow the behavior. The frequency of the behavior and the specification of the antecedent and consequent events that may control the behavior provide some of the basic information needed for behavioral assessment.

Before describing various methods of collecting and using self-recorded data for assessment purposes, the question of what actually constitutes self-monitoring should be addressed. In a discussion of *self-observation* in relation to self-control strategies, Thoresen and Mahoney (1974) have analyzed self-observation into various components. The first phase is that of discrimination, in which the individual must decide whether a behavior has or has not occurred. This discrimination may be in response to various interoceptive or exteroceptive stimuli. The next phase in self-observation they describe consists of recording *and* charting the specific behavior being observed. This can actually be viewed as two separate steps in the self-observation procedure since individuals may be asked to record various aspects of their behavior without being required to chart these data on a graph. Recording one's own behavior without charting it can appropriately be referred to as the *self-recording* or *self-monitoring* phase in self-observation. During this phase the individual simply engages in some action that produces a record of his own behavior. The actual charting or graphing of the behaviors that have been recorded can be viewed as a separate step

The authors wish to thank Linda R. Hay for reviewing an earlier version of this chapter.

which, for the sake of clarity, might be referred to as *self-charting*. The final phase in Thoresen and Mahoney's conception of self-observation is the data analysis phase. During this phase, the individual evaluates his behavior, which is represented by the self-recorded data, in relation to standards that the individual has set for himself.

From this analysis it is clear that self-monitoring is only one component of the total self-observation process. Although the present chapter will deal briefly with issues relating to self-observation in general, the prime concern will be with self-monitoring procedures in particular and with the problems in the reactivity and reliability of self-recorded data. The first section of the chapter describes the methods and devices used for self-monitoring. The second and third sections deal respectively with the issues of reactivity and reliability.

HISTORY AND USE OF SELF-MONITORING

The procedure of observing and recording one's own behavior is not a new technique. Thoresen and Mahoney (1974) reported that Benjamin Franklin had a detailed method for recording his own behavior in 13 response categories. Kazdin (1974b) noted that self-observation was used historically in psychology in psychophysical research and by the structuralists under the label of introspection.

Although current self-monitoring methods may be related to historical procedures, the purposes of contemporaneous self-recording techniques are quite different. Three current uses of self-observation can be delineated. First, self-observation can be utilized during preliminary stages of behavioral assessment to obtain baseline frequencies of proposed target behaviors and to explicate the functional relationship of the target behavior to environmental antecedents and consequences. If self-monitoring is used during the preliminary stages of behavioral assessment, the subject would need to record not only the occurrence of the target behavior but also the events that precede and follow the behavior. A functional analysis of the relationship of the behavior to its controlling variables is often a prerequisite for developing a successful treatment strategy.

After the target behavior has been selected and a treatment program implemented, self-monitoring must continue in order to fulfill the second purpose of self-recording. Here, the data obtained during the therapy phase are compared with data obtained during the baseline phase in order to evaluate the effects of the treatment program.

In both of the above cases the primary utility of self-monitoring lies in its assessment or data collection function. A third purpose of self-monitoring is to produce behavior change. Many studies, to be detailed later, have demonstrated that the act of recording one's own behavior is reactive in that it produces changes in the frequency of the behavior. Thus self-monitoring may be used as a method to measure some dependent variable or as a therapeutic strategy to produce behavioral changes.

The current increased interest in the use of self-monitoring is related to various developments in contemporary behavior therapy. One characteristic of behavior therapy is its concern with producing empirically verifiable behavior changes in the client's own environment. Trained observers have been used to collect data in the natural environment (Patterson, 1971a), but the use of such observers is often impractical, and the addition of strangers to the environment may produce reactive changes in the observed behavior. In contrast, having a client collect data on himself through self-monitoring is less expensive and more convenient. In addition, as Kazdin (1974b) has pointed out, self-monitoring may produce a more representative sample of data. Whereas external observers have access to only a sample of incidents in the client's life, the client himself has access to the entire population of incidents.

A second trend in behavior therapy is a change in emphasis from external control of behavior to self-control in which clients direct their own therapeutic programs (Bandura, 1969; Goldfried & Merbaum, 1973; Kanfer & Phillips, 1970; Mahoney & Thoresen, 1974; Thoresen & Mahoney, 1974). Self-monitoring is integral to many self-control programs, either as a data collection technique or as a therapeutic strategy.

Finally, there is an increased interest in covert events as target behaviors (Homme, 1965). With present-day technology, the only procedure possible to collect data on thoughts, urges, or fantasies is to have the client self-observe and self-record these events. Covert events are "private" by their very nature; other events, such as excretion or sexual behavior, are private by convention. Since external observation would most likely produce very reactive changes in these private target behaviors, self-monitoring may be the only practical means of data collection in these cases.

SELF-MONITORING PROCEDURES

Self-monitoring may be used to collect data both on response frequencies and on the variables that control these response frequencies. The first two portions of this section will delineate procedures for selecting data-recording methods in each of these two categories. Next is a description of specific devices and techniques that can be used to collect self-recorded data. Finally, procedures that may be used to initiate and maintain clients' self-recording behaviors are proposed.

Methods of Self-Recording Target Behaviors

A decision must be made about how each target behavior can best be recorded. The recording method selected must be easy to implement, must produce a representative sample of the target behavior, and must be sensitive to changes in the occurrence of the target behavior. As will be demonstrated, for different types of target behaviors, there are different preferred recording methods.

Frequency counts have been the most usual data collection method both in the laboratory and in naturalistic settings (Skinner, 1953). To self-monitor frequency, each occurrence of a response is recorded. The unit of time during which the frequency count occurred is noted, and a response rate (i.e., the number of responses per unit time) is calculated. This procedure, which is often referred to as *event sampling,* is especially useful when the target behavior is discrete, is relatively low in frequency, and is of a short duration (e.g., smoking cigarettes or cursing).

An alternative method of self-monitoring can be used if the target behavior is composed of a finite response class, such as cleaning the house or completing a list of assignments. In these cases, a percentage measure may be used, in which the denominator is the number of components comprising the finite response class, and the numerator is the number of components successfully completed.

A different type of percentage measure may be used for discriminated operants, that is, behaviors that occur only in the presence of a clearly specified antecedent. The denominator contains the number of opportunities to perform the target behavior, (e.g., the number of times a person who is trying to reduce his smoking rates is offered a cigarette by another person), and the numerator contains the number of times the behavior occurs.

A duration measure is more appropriate when the behavior to be recorded is not discrete and instead varies considerably in its duration (e.g., studying, practicing a musical instrument, talking on the telephone, or watching television). With these behaviors, it may be more useful to self-record the amount of time the individual engages in the behavior, rather than the frequency of the behavior. Watson and Tharp (1972, p. 82) suggested a rather pragmatic way of deciding whether one should record frequency or duration data: If it is easy to record separate occurrences of the response, record frequency data; if the behavior can occur for long periods at a time, record the duration of the responses.

There are two other situations when frequency data are difficult to obtain via self-recording. First, Mahoney and Thoresen (1974) note that covert behaviors may "run together" such that there is no clear onset or offset of the behavior. Thus it might be impossible to self-record discrete occurrences of these responses (e.g., self-deprecating thoughts, urges to engage in inappropriate behavior). A second situation when it may be difficult to obtain self-recorded frequency data is when the behavior occurs at very high rates. Here it is not that a person could not record the frequency of the behavior; instead, the individual simply may not be willing to record every occurrence of the response over an extended period of time.

Under these circumstances when there are technical or practical problems associated with collecting frequency data, *time-sampling* procedures may be useful. These methods have been used in behavioral research for several years and offer a convenient method for collecting self-recorded data. One variation of this method is to divide time into intervals (e.g., one-hour units) in which the person simply records whether the behavior occurred during each interval. Mahoney and Thoresen (1974, p. 31) have referred to this as "all-or-none" measurement since the individual simply indicates whether the behavior occurred at all during an interval. The behavioral records used in this procedure simply indicate the intervals in which the behavior occurred *at least once.* With this method one can graph the percentage of time samples in which the behavior occurred to get an indication of the strength of the response. It is clear that much information is lost with this procedure since the intervals that are scored "positive" (i.e., containing at least one occurrence of the response) may not indicate comparable frequencies of the response.

Other methods can be used to help provide more information than the "all-or-none" measure. Instead of simply recording the presence or absence of a response during an interval, the individual can "rate" each interval on the basis of how frequently the behavior occurred. For example, Stumphauzer (1974) reported a 4-point scale on which a behavior is rated 0, 1, 2, or 3 depending on whether the behavior occurred "never, occasionally, often, or very frequently." Again data are lost when this system is compared to a frequency count, but the information loss is not as great as that in an "all-or-none" measurement system.

An additional procedure that combines time sampling and event techniques can be used when one is recording a high-rate discrete behavior. A person is asked to record the frequency of the response only during certain time periods. For example, one might be asked to record the frequency of hair pulling during certain times of the day (e.g., 10:00 to 11:00 A.M., 4:00 to 5:00 P.M.). There is a major problem with this technique in that behavior may fluctuate at certain times of the day, and one can easily get a biased picture of the strength of the behavior unless one records from a representative sample of time intervals. One way to help assure a relatively unbiased sample is to collect data from several intervals (a minimum of three per day) and to vary the specific time intervals in which the data are recorded.

Another self-recording procedure that is viable for high-frequency behaviors is spot checking. A timer (e.g., a kitchen timer or a parking meter timer) can be set on a variable-interval schedule by the subject or by an associate. When the timer rings, the subject notes whether or not he was engaging in the target behavior. A percentage measure is calculated in which the denominator is the number of times the timer rang, and the numerator is the number of times the target behavior was occurring when the timer rang.

Another indication of behavioral strength that can be used in conjunction with other self-recorded measures or in place of them is based on some *outcome measure.* Instead of actually measuring the response in question, one measures some correlated outcome of the behavior. One of the best examples of such a measure comes from weight-control studies when a change in body weight is used as an indication of a change in eating behavior (e.g., Mahoney, Moura, & Wade, 1973). Similar approaches have used class grades as an outcome of study behavior (Johnson & White, 1971), fingernail length as a measure of nail biting (McNamara, 1972), and hair length as a measure of hair pulling (McLaughlin & Nay, 1975). Certain physiological outcome measures have also been used. For example, carbon monoxide in the breath has been used to indicate smoking (Lando, 1975), blood-alcohol levels to measure drinking (Miller, Hersen, Eisler, & Watts, 1974), and urine analysis to detect drug usage (Goldstein & Brown, 1970). Outcome measures can be quite useful in behavioral assessment, and it is hoped they will be developed further and used more extensively in the future.

Methods of Self-Recording Antecedents and Consequences

In contrast to the various options for collecting data on the target behavior, the methods for assessing antecedent and consequent events by means of self-recording are quite limited. Generally individuals are asked to indicate with a narrative description or with a coding system what happened before and after the response occurred. These approaches provide a sample of the antecedents and consequences of the response being monitored.

Occasionally, there is a one-to-one relationship between a behavior and a set of environmental events. For example, a spouse may report that each argument begins with the other spouse's mishandling of financial affairs. However, the typical case is not as clear or consistent as this. Generally, a client will report a variety of antecedents and consequences. One reason why it may be difficult to identify reinforcing events is that many behaviors in naturalistic settings are maintained on an intermittent schedule of reinforcement. Another problem with identifying reinforcers is that the behavior may be followed by covert self-reinforcement (Kanfer, 1970) or by delayed reinforcing consequences.

More consistency can sometimes be found when antecedent events that may be functioning as discriminative stimuli are recorded. The stimulus control of a response may be well established even though the current reinforcement schedule is quite thin. Therefore, the identification of the discriminative stimuli controlling the behavior may be easier than the identification of the reinforcing consequences. Watson and Tharp (1972) suggested recording procedures in which individuals count the occurrences of behavior in specific situations such that the behavior and setting events are directly tied together in the recording system. These procedures frequently can aid in determining what antecedent events influence the behavior. They reported an example when a woman used such a system to code the situations in which she smoked. From a sample of her records, it could be seen that a high percentage of her smoking was related to eating and social situations.

During the preliminary stages of behavioral assessment, the clinician will often have to make an educated guess about the antecedent and consequent events maintaining the target behavior. However, an analysis relating the behavior to its controlling variables is important in devising a treatment strategy. Shapiro (1966) recommended a hypothesis-testing approach in which the clinician makes his best guess about what is controlling the behavior. Continued monitoring of the strength of the target behavior during interventions will confirm or reject the clinician's choice of a treatment procedure.

Self-Monitoring Devices

The devices used in gathering self-recorded data are quite crude when compared to the technologically sophisticated equipment used in many laboratory settings. There are, however, several criteria that should be considered when one selects a self-monitoring device. Watson and Tharp (1972) suggest that the primary consideration is that the device be available when the target behavior occurs. In many cases, then, the device must be portable so that it can be carried or worn by the individual. Typically, the self-monitored data must be recorded as the target behavior occurs in order for the data to be accurate. A second criterion is that the self-recording device be easy to use. If the person cannot understand how to use the apparatus, either no data will be recorded or the collected data will be unreliable or invalid. A third consideration is the cost of the self-recording apparatus. Although most of the devices we will describe are very economical, the cost factor may become more crucial as more sophisticated devices (e.g., telemetric recording systems) are developed. A final consideration in the selection of a self-monitoring device is its obtrusiveness. The device per se may function as a discriminative stimulus for the client to make the self-recording response. If the self-monitoring device is not sufficiently obtrusive, the client may forget to record the target behavior. On the other hand, if the device is conspicuous, persons other than the client may attend to the self-recording apparatus. Attention from others may reinforce or punish the self-recording responses depending on the client and the nature of the target behavior. Given these four considerations—accessibility, ease of use, cost, and obtrusiveness—a variety of self-monitoring devices will be described.

Paper-and-Pencil Techniques

The first major category of self-monitoring devices can be classified as *paper-and-pencil techniques*. Basically these are procedures in which an individual is asked to record on paper various aspects of his behavior. The data collected can range from a simple count of the frequency of the response to a more complete narrative description of the client's behavior. What the individual is asked to record will depend on what information the clinician already has from other assessment procedures (e.g., interviews, questionnaires) and what information is still needed. For example, the therapist may want only some measure of the strength of the behavior to determine the effects of some treatment intervention. In this case the client might be asked only to count the frequency of the response. At other times the variables maintaining a behavior may be quite obscure and potentially important as far as a treatment plan is concerned. One would want information on what events precede and follow the response as well as a measure of strength of the behavior. If this were the case, the client might be asked to collect a frequency count and to record what happened before and after each occurrence of the response. Again it should be emphasized that what a client is asked to record depends on what the clinician needs to know.

One relatively popular paper-and-pencil device is the *behavioral diary*. This is typically used when a clinician needs information about the controlling variables as well as the strength of the response. Clients are usually asked to record in a notebook or on cards when and where the behavior occurred, and what happened before and after the response. The usefulness of this method of assessment will depend on the specificity and objectivity of the reports. If the reports are very subjective, the information collected may not be very helpful.

	SUN		MON		TUE		WED		THU		FRI		SAT	
	AM	PM	AM	PM	AM	PM	AM	PM	AM	PM	AM	PM	AM	PM
12:00														
1:00														
2:00														
3:00														
4:00														
5:00														
6:00														
7:00														
8:00														
9:00														
10:00														
11:00														
TOTAL														

Figure 7–1. A paper-and-pencil device for self-recording.

There are more structured self-report forms that can be used by clients to help ensure that objective data are recorded. Several examples of these can be found in recently published behavior modification books (e.g., Patterson, 1971b; Stuart & Davis, 1972; Zifferblatt, 1970). These forms serve a function similar to that of the behavioral diary in that they are also aimed at collecting information about the variables controlling the behavior as well as data that would indicate response strength.

Another common paper-and-pencil device is a simple three-by-five-inch *self-monitoring card.* Because of space limitations, these cards generally are used to collect frequency counts or ratings of behavior. Although clinicians frequently use a plain three-by-five-inch card, more structured forms may help in the data collection procedure. Stumphauzer (1974) described a card on which daily ratings or frequency tallies could be recorded on four different behaviors. Figure 7–1 shows another form that has been found useful in collecting frequency or time-sampled data. Each day of the week is listed across the top of the card with hours of the day listed along the left side. Each day is further subdivided into A.M. and P.M. hours so that every hour during the week is represented on the form. By counting with tally marks, a subject can record several occurrences of a response within the space provided for each hour. The name of the client, the date, and the behavior being recorded can all be recorded on the other side of the card. Like other self-monitoring cards, it meets the criteria of being an economical, portable, and easy-to-use recording device.

A paper-and-pencil device that may be used by children to self-monitor their own behavior is Kunzelmann's countoon (1970), as described in detail by Thoresen and Mahoney (1974). The countoon utilizes a pictorial sequence so that the child may record events that precede the target behavior, the incidence of the target behavior, and consequences that follow the target behavior.

A final paper-and-pencil device commonly used in self-monitoring procedures is the *behavior graph* (Mahoney & Thoresen, 1974). Individuals are asked to chart their behavior on a sheet of standard graph paper. The graph is generally set up such that time (e.g., days) is represented along the horizontal axis and some measure of behavior strength (e.g., frequency or duration) is represented on the vertical axis. Each data point on the chart will indicate the strength of the response at the time of observation.

The behavior graph is useful not only for directly recording a response when it occurs but also for storing the data collected on other self-monitoring devices. Watson and Tharp (1972) discussed the importance of transferring self-recorded data to a storage record and suggested that a graph could be used as a storage device. Thus an individual who is recording the frequency of a response with tally marks on a three-by-five-inch card can transfer his daily frequency to a graph. In this fashion a single data point will represent the rate of the response for a particular day. In addition the slope of the line connecting consecutive data points will indicate whether the strength of the behavior is increasing, decreasing, or remaining stable. It should be cautioned that since this type of feedback possibly can provide conditioned reinforcement for changes in behavior (e.g., seeing a decrease in weight may reinforce changes in eating behavior), the data collected or stored by means of self-charting may be quite reactive, as is described below. However, it should be noted that the speculation that self-charting adds to the reactivity of self-monitoring has not been confirmed experimentally.

Mechanical Counters

Various *mechanical counters* that are manually operated comprise the second major category of self-monitoring devices. These counters are typically used to collect frequency data. One of the more popular devices is a golf-stroke counter that can be worn on the wrist (see Lindsley, 1968). This type of counter (see Figure 7–2) is portable, easy to use, relatively inexpensive, and for the most part unobtrusive. Multiple wrist counters could be used if the individual is to self-record multiple behaviors, as was done by Hannum, Thoresen, and Hubbard (1974). In addition to the wrist counter, there is a variety of pocket-sized golf-stroke counters that are available at most sporting good stores. The "Knit Talley," a counting device described by Sheehan and Casey (1974), is also a very inexpensive and portable means of collecting frequency data (see Figure 7–3).

A novel manually operated counting device is the "Ristkountr," described by K. Mahoney (1974). This apparatus (see Figure 7–4) consists of a miniature abacus that is worn on a leather wristband resembling handcrafted leather jewelry. The advantages of this device are its inconspicu-

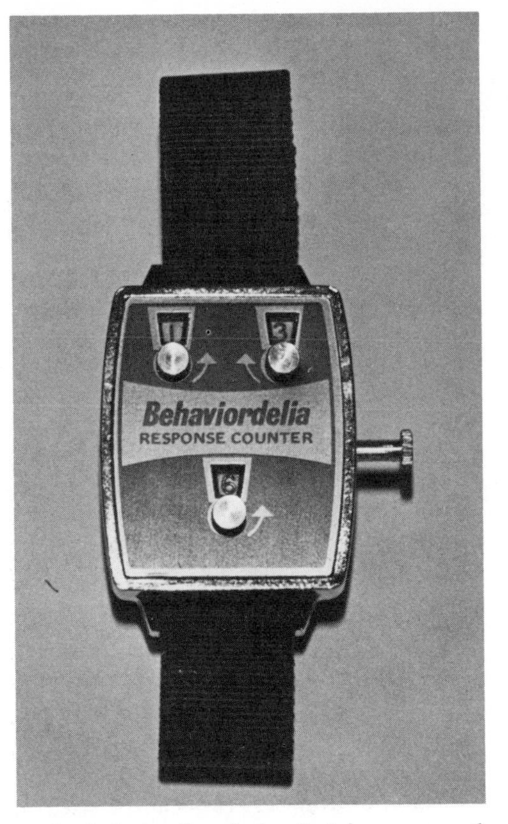

Figure 7–2. A mechanical counting device that is worn on the wrist. (The *Response Counter* is available for $5.95 from: Behaviordelia, Inc., P. O. Box 1044, Kalamazoo, Michigan 49005.)

ousness in comparison to other devices and the fact that several different events can be monitored simultaneously.

Timing Devices

Timing devices offer a third method for self-monitoring, and as might be expected, these devices are generally used to collect duration data. Mahoney and Thoresen (1974) described how an electric clock with a switch installed in the cord can be used as a timing device. The example they use is that of a student who can set the time at twelve o'clock and switch the clock on whenever he is studying. At the end of certain time periods (e.g., days or weeks) he can record on a paper-and-pencil device how much time has been spent studying. If a switch is not available, the

Figure 7–3. The *Knit Talley* (Available from Boye Needle Company, 4343 N. Ravenswood Ave., Chicago, Illinois 60613.)

person can simply plug the clock in when he begins the activity and pull the plug out when he stops. In this fashion a person can still obtain the cumulative duration of the behavior for a given period. Although the electric clock is useful for behaviors that occur in a fixed setting (e.g., studying at a desk), this device is limited in that it is not portable enough to be used in a variety of settings. There are other options if a portable timing device is needed. For example, some stopwatches are capable of providing the cumulative duration of a response for up to an hour. Many wristwatches also have elapsed time indicators or dials that can be set to tell how much time has been spent in an activity (see Katz, 1973). With both of these procedures the data have to be transferred to a paper-and-pencil storage device. Although the stopwatch and wristwatch are portable and easy to use, the major drawback is their cost.

Portable timing devices—for example, a kitchen timer or a parking meter reminder (Foxx & Martin, 1971)—can be used in the spot-check self-recording procedure as described on page 200. For high-frequency

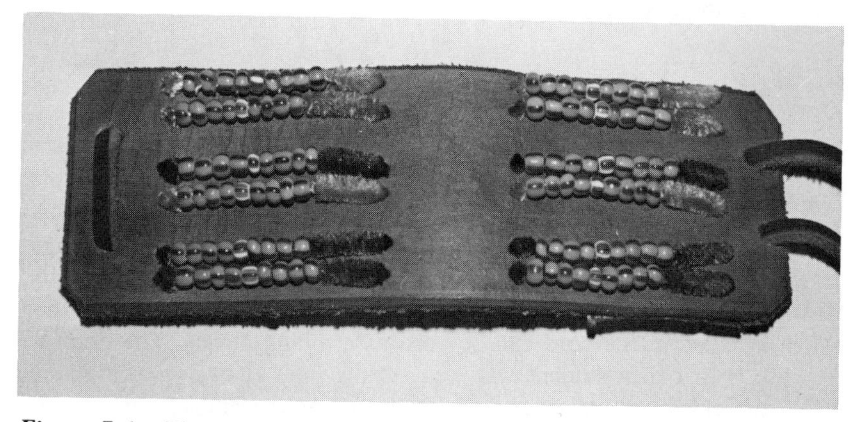

Figure 7–4. The *Ristkountr* (Available from Encor–R.K., 116 South 42nd Street, Omaha, Nebraska 68131.)

behaviors, the client notes whether or not the behavior was occurring when the timer (set on a variable-interval schedule) rang.

Electronic Devices

The final group of self-recording devices can be categorized as *electronic devices.* Video and audio tape-recording equipment can be used so that clients can self-monitor their behaviors at future times when they are not also engaging in other, possibly competing, behaviors. Thomas (1971) reports that teachers successfully self-monitored and changed aspects of their teaching behaviors by observing video tapes of their classroom behavior. Other electronic devices automatically record the subject's responses if the client wears or utilizes the apparatus. For example, Azrin and Powell (1968) have developed a cigarette case that automatically records the number of times it is opened. If the subject takes only one cigarette at a time and takes cigarettes only from this cigarette case, an automatic recording of the number of cigarettes smoked is produced. Similarly, Azrin, Rubin, O'Brien, Ayllon, and Roll (1968) developed an apparatus that automatically counts the number of times a subject assumes an inappropriate posture, given that the subject is wearing the apparatus. Schwitzgebel and Kolb (1974) describe a variety of other automated devices that, given the subject's cooperation, record specific aspects of his behavior. Some of the examples that they describe include a gravity-sensitive watch to measure hyperactivity (Schulmann & Reisman, 1959), ultrasonic speakers worn by the individual to measure body movements (Goldman, 1961), and radio telemetry to record conversations (Soskin & John, 1963). The obvious limitation to the widespread use of electronic devices is their cost. In addition these devices usually provide data only on the behavior itself, not on its antecedents or consequences.

Some miscellaneous methods of recording that do not fit into any of the groups listed above have been reported. Watson and Tharp (1972) reported some very simple methods of self-monitoring. One client transferred pennies from one pocket to another, each penny representing one occurrence of the target behavior. Another person moved toothpicks from one compartment of her purse to another to record her behavior. As Watson and Tharp (1972) indicated, the variety of self-monitoring devices is limited only by the ingenuity of those developing such techniques.

Procedures To Initiate and Maintain Self-Monitoring

The clinician must make many decisions that may facilitate or hinder the client from engaging in self-monitoring.The clinician in consultation with the client must select a recording method that is appropriate for the target behavior in question. For example, if a frequency count is suggested for a high-frequency behavior, the client may cease self-monitoring because of the excessive burden imposed by counting a high-frequency behavior. Alternatively, if the clinician had proposed a time-sampling or spot-checking procedure, the client may have continued to self-monitor. As noted, the accessibility, ease of use, cost, and obtrusiveness of the self-monitoring device may influence whether the client uses it.

The clinician must train the client in the use of the self-monitoring device. Behavioral rehearsal in which the therapist models the use of the self-monitoring device and then has the client practice its use while receiving feedback from the therapist may be used to train the client. Periodic retraining may be required to ensure that the individual continues to follow the same self-monitoring procedure.

The clinician must realize that certain clients will self-monitor whereas others will not. A complex self-recording system, including the recording of several behaviors as well as their antecedents and consequences, may be arranged for an obsessive-compulsive client, whereas other clients may need to have trained observers or outcome measures serve to collect their data. The clinician may also need to use "placebo power" to convince the patient that self-monitoring is a necessary aspect of the person's successful treatment. Frequent contacts by telephone or by mail can be used to prompt the person to maintain self-monitoring, to gather daily or near-daily data, and to reinforce socially the person for data collection.

These variables and several others have been found to control differentially the reactivity and reliability of self-monitoring. The reactivity and reliability of self-recording are crucial when it is used as an assessment device.

REACTIVE EFFECTS OF SELF-MONITORING

The presence of a trained observer has been demonstrated to be reactive in that behavior changes occur in the person being observed (Arsenian, 1943; Bechtel, 1967; Mercatoris and Craighead, 1974). This reactivity is understandable since the presence of an observer alters the usual stimulus situation, thereby producing behavior changes. Similarly, when an individual begins to self-observe his own behavior, there is also a change in the usual stimulus situation. The changes in the client's behavior produced by self-monitoring are labeled the *reactive effects* of self-recording. Reactive effects have been demonstrated in case studies, in within-subject experimental designs, and in between-subject experimental designs. In addition the therapeutic changes produced by self-monitoring have been compared with changes produced by alternative treatment strategies.

Reactive Effects in Case Studies

Several case studies have been reported suggesting that the introduction of self-monitoring altered the frequency of the target behavior. Rutner and Bugle (1969) had a schizophrenic patient self-record the frequency of her auditory hallucinations. During the three days of self-monitoring, her reported frequency of hallucinations decreased from 181 to 10. After these first three days, the patient's reported frequencies were placed on public display, and the ward staff was requested to praise the lack of reported hallucinations. Although reported hallucinations did decrease to zero by the sixteenth day of self-monitoring, it is impossible to separate the effects of self-recording and the social reinforcement that was introduced after the third day.

Ernst (1973) had a patient self-record on a golf counter the frequency of lip and mouth biting. Compared with the state of her mouth prior to the self-monitoring, the patient reported significant tissue repair during the week of self-monitoring. Additional decreases in mouth biting were self-recorded when wrist counter presses were used to cue relaxation responses.

In combination with a behaviorally-oriented group therapy session that met weekly, Sobell and Sobell (1973) had six alcoholics record all instances of alcoholic drinking on Alcohol Intake Sheets. After five months, four subjects maintained controlled drinking and a fifth subject remained abstinent. Confirmation of the self-reported drinking was obtained for four of the six subjects through collaterals in the patients' environments.

Maletzky (1974) had five patients self-monitor on wrist counters the frequencies of their repetitive, unwanted behaviors. Self-recording decreased the frequencies of the undesirable behaviors in all five cases. Discontinuation of self-counting increased the frequencies, and reinstatement of self-recording produced further decrements. No procedures were utilized to estimate the subjects' self-recording accuracy.

Within-Subject Experimental Designs

Utilizing a single case design, Leitenberg, Agras, Thompson, and Wright (1968) found that a claustrophobic patient increased the time she spent in a small dark room when she used a stopwatch to calculate the amount of time per trial that she spent in the room. No increases per trial were found when the patient was not provided with the stopwatch.

Herbert and Baer (1972) had two mothers use wrist counters to self-record attention to appropriate child behaviors while in their homes. Independent observers in the home reported that self-recording increased maternal attention and appropriate child behaviors. During the reversal phases of this experiment, attention to appropriate child behaviors stabilized rather than reversed. Reinstatement of self-recording produced further increments in maternal attention.

Lipinski and Nelson (1974b) had trained observers monitor the face-touching frequency of college students in a classroom situation from behind a one-way mirror throughout the experimental conditions. Self-recording of face-touching significantly reduced its frequency below baseline levels, whereas a return-to-baseline condition reinstated its frequency.

Using a modified multiple baseline design across several behaviors of one tiqueur, Thomas, Abrams, and Johnson (1971) concluded that self-recording reduced the frequency of multiple tics, most noticeably a verbal tic. However, the patient was praised for low self-reported frequencies, and systematic desensitization was employed prior to the self-monitoring of the other two tics. Hence it is not possible to attribute the therapeutic effects to self-monitoring alone. Using another patient who also displayed Gilles de la Tourette's syndrome, Hutzell, Platzek, and Logue (1974) employed a multiple baseline design for neck jerks and vocalizations. Their results replicated Thomas et al. findings (1971)that the frequency of tics can effectively be reduced by self-recording. In addition, Hutzell et al. (1974) found that these results generalized to the patient's home environment and were maintained during a one-year follow-up.

Hendricks, Thoresen, and Hubbard (Note 1) used a multiple baseline design to demonstrate that teachers can employ self-monitoring to increase the frequencies of positive classroom behaviors, both verbal and non-verbal, as independently assessed by observers. A third class of behaviors, negative commands, was unchanged by self-recording. Thomas (1971) also used a multiple baseline design with teachers. Self-monitoring from videotapes altered the teachers' classroom behaviors; they subsequently delivered more tokens and made more behavior-specific praise statements.

Two experiments are reported by McKenzie and Rushall (1974), one utilizing a multiple baseline design and the other, a reversal design. Both studies showed that swimmers could utilize self-monitoring and public display of these self-recordings to reduce absenteeism, tardiness, and early departures from swimming practice; conversely, total number of laps swum during practice increased through self-monitoring.

Between-Subject Experimental Designs

Johnson and White (1971) used a between-subjects design to assess the effects of college students' self-monitoring on their course grades. There were three groups of subjects: those who monitored their study activities, those who monitored their time spent dating, and a no-treatment control group. The weekly grades of the group self-monitoring studying were superior to the control group; the mean grades of the group self-monitoring dating, however, fell between the means of the other two groups and did not differ significantly from either of them. In addition to concluding that self-recording produced reactive effects in study activities, the authors speculate that collateral effects may have been produced by the self-monitoring of dating, a behavior that may not be independent of study time.

Comparative Studies

With the target behavior of fingernail biting, Horan, Hoffman, and Macri (1974) had subjects participate in various experimental conditions, namely, baseline self-monitoring of placing a finger in the mouth, self-monitoring plus self-punishment by a rubber band snap on the wrist, and self-monitoring plus covert self-reward. Since experimental conditions were confounded with sequence effects, it is not possible to evaluate separately the treatment phases. The entire treatment sequence, however, was successful in producing gains in nail length and improved cosmetic appearance of the hands.

Nelson, Lipinski, and Black (1976a) compared the effectiveness of a token economy with retarded adults' self-monitoring in increasing the frequencies of three desirable target behaviors: Converation in the dining room, participation in recreational lounge activities, and tidiness in the bedrooms. A comparison among the six experimental conditions, which included two baseline phases, three token economy phases, and a self-recording phase, revealed that the greatest increases for all three desirable target behaviors occurred during the self-monitoring condition.

In comparison with the superior results of self-monitoring found in the above study, Emmelkamp (1974) using between-subjects designs, found self-recording to be equally effective to other techniques in the treatment of agoraphobia. Emmelkamp and Ultee (1974) found self-monitoring of the time spent outdoors to be as efficacious as differential reinforcement by therapist praise for longer excursions. Similarly, Emmelkamp (1974) found that self-recording of time spent outside was as effective as imaginal and in vivo flooding in reducing agoraphobia, with both techniques superior to a no-treatment control group. A combined flooding and self-observation treatment produced greater gains on some dependent measures than either treatment used alone.

In contrast to these positive effects found for self-monitoring, self-recording of weight and eating habits does not seem to be as effective as alternative treatment strategies in reducing weight. Mahoney et al. (1973) found that after four weeks, self-monitoring plus self-reward produced greater weight loss than self-monitoring (of weight and of eating habits) alone or an information control group. Similar results were reported by M. J. Mahoney (1974): Self-monitoring (of weight and of eating habits) was not as effective as self-monitoring plus self-reward for weight loss or self-monitoring plus self-reward for improvements in eating habits. Stollack (1967) found that therapist feedback was important in producing weight loss through self-recording of eating habits. Self-recording subjects who received such therapist feedback lost more weight than subjects who self-recorded eating habits but had no regular therapist contact. Romanczyk (1974) demonstrated that the specific nature of the target behavior to be self-recorded influenced subsequent weight loss: Self-recording of daily weight and of daily caloric intake produced greater weight loss than self-recording of daily weight without records of caloric intake.

In summary, the self-recording by subjects of their own behavior may cause the behavior to change in frequency. These reactive effects of self-monitoring have been demonstrated in case studies, in within-subject experimental designs, and in between-subject experimental designs. Comparisons of self-recording with other therapeutic techniques have shown that for at least some target behaviors, self-recording is as effective or more effective than other techniques.

Variables Influencing the Reactivity of Self-Monitoring

Not all studies that employed self-recording report reactive changes. Kazdin (1974b) reviews several case reports in which self-monitoring failed to produce therapeutic changes. Jackson (1972) had a depressed housewife self-record and self-reinforce housekeeping activities, but no change in the frequency of activities or in the self ratings of depression resulted. M. J. Mahoney (1971) reported a case in which self-monitoring of obsessional ruminations failed to alter their frequency over a two-week period. Self-recording of hair pulling by a young woman also did not produce a reduction in frequency (Bayer, 1972). As noted, Mahoney has failed to find that self-recording of weight and of eating habits produces significant weight loss (Mahoney et al., 1973; M. J. Mahoney, 1974). McNamara (1972) found no differences among six groups of nail-biting subjects in terms of increased nail length: self-monitoring of nail biting, self-monitoring of an incompatible response of finger tapping, and self-monitoring of an incompatible response of pulling the hand from the lips produced no differences from control groups who did not self-monitor. Given the seemingly inconsistent results produced by self-recording, it is important to consider the variables that control the reactivity of self-recorded data.

Valence of the Target Behavior

Kanfer (1970) had speculated that the direction of reactive changes produced by self-monitoring would be determined by the valence of the response being self-recorded. Thus the self-monitoring of positive behaviors would cause them to increase in frequency, whereas the self-monitoring of negative behaviors would cause them to decrease in frequency. Kanfer's speculation has since been experimentally confirmed. Broden, Hall, and Mitts (1971) found that self-recording produced increases in the classroom study behavior of an eighth-grade girl, whereas self-recording produced decreases in inappropriate talking-out in the classroom by an eighth-grade boy. In both cases the findings were corroborated by a trained observer who was recording data throughout all phases, including a pre-self-recording baseline phase. Using adult retarded subjects, Nelson, Lipinski, and Black (1976a) found that self-monitoring a socially desirable behavior (conversation in the recreation lounge) increased its frequency, whereas self-monitoring an undesirable behavior (face-touching) decreased the frequency of this response for three of the five subjects. In addition to these studies conducted in naturalistic settings, Kazdin (1974a) experimentally manipulated the valences assigned to self-reference statements with laboratory subjects assigned a Taffel task (Taffel, 1955). For subjects who had been given positive valences, self-monitoring increased self-reference statements; conversely, self-monitoring decreased these statements in subjects who had been given negative valences. In another laboratory experiment, Cavior and Marabotto (1976) permitted subjects to select their own positively and negatively valenced behaviors within the response class of verbal behaviors. Consistent with other findings, self-recording increased the frequency of positive behaviors and decreased the frequency of negative behaviors.

Motivation

Related to the valence the subject perceives to be attached to the self-monitored behavior is his motivation to alter the target behavior. The contribution of motivation to the reactivity of self-monitoring has been especially noted with regard to smoking. McFall and Hammen (1971) used subjects all of whom were motivated to reduce their cigarette smoking. All four groups of subjects did decrease their smoking, regardless of the specific behavior recorded: self-recording of cigarettes smoked, self-recording of successfully resisted urges to smoke, and self-recording of the minimum of 20 successfully resisted urges to smoke. In contrast, when McFall (1970) used as subjects students who happened to be smokers and who were not necessarily motivated to reduced their smoking, self-monitoring of the number of cigarettes smoked actually increased rates of smoking; self-monitoring of resisted urges to smoke did decrease smoking frequency. Lipinski, Black, Nelson, and Ciminero (1975) reported a study specifically comparing the effects of cigarette self-monitoring on motivated smokers (subjects who signed up for an experiment to reduce smoking) versus nonmotivated smokers (subjects who signed up for an experiment for smokers). Self-recording decreased smoking for the motivated group only. Self-monitoring may effectively change behavioral frequencies only if the subject accepts the behavioral valence and believes a behavior change to be desirable.

Expectancy

The latter statement is somewhat confirmed by Nelson, Lipinski, and Black (1975) who investigated the effects of experimenter-given expectancies regarding direction of behavior change to be produced by self-monitoring. Different groups of college student subjects were told that by self-recording, the frequency of face touching in a classroom situation would be expected to increase, decrease, or remain the same. Despite questionnaire data indicating that all groups accepted their expectancies, the face touching for all groups, including a no-expectancy control group, decreased in frequency from baseline levels. All data were collected by trained observers from behind a one-way mirror. Thus personal valences and motivation may have overridden experimenter-given expectancies regarding direction of behavior change.

Goals

The effectiveness of self-monitoring in producing reactive changes was enhanced by the setting of performance goals in a experiment reported by Kazdin (1974a). Using a Taffel task, subjects who were given a specific goal of the number of self-reference statements they were to make and to self-record made more such statements than a self-monitoring group who were not provided with a specific goal. In fact, 30.6 percent of the former group actually achieved the goal.

Reinforcement and Feedback

Kazdin (1974a) provided feedback to some subjects during the very act of self-monitoring by permitting them to see the counter displaying their self-recorded responses. These subjects used more self-recorded, self-referent pronouns than a group of subjects for whom the counter displays were covered.

In addition to having all their subjects set behavioral goals for themselves, Kolb, Winter, and Berlew (1968) investigated the effects of social reinforcement on meeting these goals. Half of the subjects met weekly for

10 weeks and were encouraged to discuss their self-monitored progress; the other half also met but did not discuss their individual projects. More change was reported in the group receiving social reinforcement on their progress. Nelson et al. (1976a) had adult retarded subjects self-record the frequency of either talking, touching environmental objects, or face touching. The subjects were then given token reinforcement that they believed to be contingent on self-recorded changes in the frequency of these responses. Compared to the self-monitoring baseline, reinforcement plus self-monitoring increased the frequencies of talking and object touching for all five subjects in their respective groups, and decreased the frequency of face touching for four of the five subjects in the third group. Lipinski et al. (1975) similarly found that compared with baseline self-monitoring, differential monetary reinforcement of decreases in self-monitored face touching produced further decrements in the frequency of this response in college students in a classroom setting. Thus reinforcement or feedback given contingently on reactive changes further enhances the therapeutic utility of self-recording in producing behavior change.

Nature of the Target Behavior

Varying response classes that can be self-monitored seem to be differentially sensitive to the reactive effects of self-recording. Hayes and Cavior (in press) compared the relative reactivity of self-monitoring in three target behaviors. The self-recording of face touching was more reactive than the self-recording of verbal nonfluencies. Both of these behaviors changed more through self-recording than verbalizations containing value judgments. Peterson, House, and Alford (Note 2) similarly found self-monitoring to be more reactive when the target behavior was nonverbal (i.e., face touches) than when it was verbal (i.e., the particular phrases "you know" and "and all that"). Romanczyk (1974) found that self-recording produced greater weight loss if the responses being monitored were daily weight and daily caloric intake than if the response was daily weight alone. Even within a single target behavior, varying the self-recording instructions may alter the reactive effects produced. McFall (1970) reported that when smoking students were instructed to record the number of cigarettes they smoked, their smoking rate increased; conversely, if the students were told to self-monitor resisted urges to smoke, their smoking rate decreased. Using a crossover design, Gottman and McFall (1972) similarly found that self-monitoring of classroom participation produced increases in talking, whereas self-monitoring of unfulfilled urges to participate produced decreases in the rate of oral class participation. Thus the specific choice of the target behavior to be self-monitored may differentially affect the reactivity of the results.

Number of Target Behaviors Concurrently Self-Monitored

Hayes and Cavior (in press) had subjects concurrently self-monitor one, two, or three target behaviors. Using a change ratio as a dependent measure, they found that the reactive effects of self-recording were greatest when only a single behavior was self-monitored.

Schedule of Self-Monitoring

Using college students studying for the Graduate Record Examination by using teaching machines, Mahoney, Moore, Wade, and Moura (1973) found that continuous self-monitoring of correct answers produced longer study sessions than intermittent self-monitoring.

Timing of Self-Monitoring

In a case study Rozensky (1974) had a subject vary the timing of her self-monitoring in relation to her cigarette smoking. After a baseline estimate of her smoking rate, she was first asked to self-record the time and place of smoking *after* smoking the cigarette. During the next phase, she was asked to self-record the smoking data *before* consuming the cigarette. Although the timing conditions are confounded with sequence effects, the results suggest that self-monitoring prior to smoking produced greater decrements in smoking than self-monitoring after smoking. These results were confirmed by Bellack, Rozensky, and Schwartz (1974), who used a group design with the dependent measure of weight loss. They found that self-monitoring of food intake information prior to its consumption produced greater weight loss than self-monitoring the same type of information after food intake. These results verify Kanfer's (1970) speculation that self-monitoring responses that precede the occurrence of the target behavior may be more effective because the self-monitoring responses are interpolated into a response chain and provide an alternative behavior. Conversely, postoccurrence self-recording cannot affect the target behavior on that trial.

Cavior and Marabotto (1976) had some subjects self-monitor their behaviors on videotape prior to participation in a test session. In comparison with subjects who self-monitored negatively valenced behaviors during the test session, presession videotaped self-recording produced greater reductions in the negatively valued responses. In this case the reason for these effects may differ from breaking the response chain, the explanation offered in the studies previously discussed. During videotaped self-monitoring, the subjects may be able to attend more fully to their responses because they have no competing behaviors to perform.

Summary

Although a great many studies have demonstrated that self-recording causes behavior changes, other studies that employed self-monitoring did not find these reactive effects. Many of the variables that differentially affect the reactivity of self-monitoring were examined, including the valence of the target behavior, the subject's motivation to alter the target behavior, the setting of performance goals, performance feedback and reinforcement, the nature of the target behavior, the number of target behaviors concurrently self-recorded, the schedule of self-recording, and the timing of self-monitoring. A therapist should consider these variables when using self-monitoring as a therapeutic technique in order to maximize its reactive effects.

Longevity of Reactive Effects of Self-Monitoring

To examine the long-term effects of self-monitoring, a self-recording experimental phase must be followed by a return-to-baseline phase in which the subjects no longer self-monitor but in which data are collected on the target behavior. In McFall's (1970) return-to-baseline condition, he found one of the few long-lasting effects of self-recording. Even though subjects no longer self-monitored their resisted urges to smoke, their cigarette consumption in the one-week return-to-baseline phase did not increase to baseline levels. Most studies, however, report ephemeral effects produced by self-recording. Broden et al. (1971) found that behaviors returned to baseline levels when their two students ceased self-recording. Herbert and Baer (1972) found their results to stabilize but not to continue to improve when mothers stopped self-recording their attention to appropriate child behaviors. Students returned to their baseline levels of face touching when they no longer self-monitored this response (Lipinski & Nelson, 1974b; Nelson et al., 1975).

One of the reasons proposed for these ephemeral results is that the self-recording device per se may function as a discriminative stimulus controlling the occurrence of the target behavior (Maletzky, 1974). To facilitate generalization from the self-recording phase to the non-self-recording phase, Maletzky (1974) had his subjects gradually withdraw the wrist counters that seemed to be controlling the decreases in their undesirable behaviors; the time for which the subjects wore the wrist counters was gradually reduced. To accomplish a similar generalization goal, Broden et al. (1971) had a teacher praise a girl's classroom study behaviors while the girl was self-monitoring these responses. In contrast to a previous return-to-baseline phase, the teacher's praise was able to maintain high rates of study behavior even though self-monitoring had ceased.

Additional variables that may determine the longevity of the reactive effects produced by self-monitoring merit investigation. Some of these variables include the history of the target behavior (behaviors performed for many years may be more resistant to long-term reactive changes than relatively new behaviors), the duration of self-monitoring (self-monitoring for longer periods of time may produce longer lasting results than shorter periods of self-monitoring), and the schedule of self-monitoring (intermittent self-monitoring may be more resistant to extinction than continuous self-monitoring).

Theoretical Accounts of the Reactivity of Self-monitoring

As noted earlier in this chapter, the presence of an external observer has been demonstrated to cause reactive changes in the behavior of the persons being observed, possibly because of the change in the usual stimulus situation. Since self-monitoring also produces reactive changes, a parallel process may occur, that is, self-recording causes reactive changes because the person observing himself also alters the usual stimulus situation. Several studies have compared the reactive changes produced by external observation versus self-observation. Kazdin (1974a) found that although self-monitoring and other-monitoring groups used the target pronouns more than a no-monitoring group, the two monitoring groups did not differ from each other. Similarly, Cavior and Marabotto (1976) found no difference between self-monitoring and external agent monitoring in producing changes in subject-selected target behaviors. Conversely, Ciminero, Graham, and Jackson (Note 3), utilizing a single-case design, noted that greater reactive effects were produced by self-recording than by obtrusive recording by another person. Their design permitted an assessment of changes in the external observer's behavior and found that the behavior of one observer also decreased in frequency, as did the subject's. Nelson, Lipinski, and Black (1976b) compared decreases in face touching producd by the presence of an external observer versus self-observation. Self-observation produced greater decrements than did the external observation.

Given the results of these latter two studies, under at least some conditions, it appears that the reactivity of self-monitoring may be due to variables other than self-observation. Kanfer (1970) has proposed a three-stage mediational model that may account for the reactivity of self-recording. The person first self-observes, then self-evaluates his responses in accordance with norms established during his learning history. Positively evaluated behaviors then increase in frequency through the subject's self-reinforcement, whereas negatively evaluated behaviors decrease in frequency through the subject's self-punishment.

In contrast to Kanfer's mediational explanation of the reactivity of self-monitoring, Rachlin (1974) offers an operant explanation. Rachlin proposes that consequences one gives oneself function not as reinforcers or as punishers to alter response frequencies but function, rather, as cues. These cues signal the ultimate external consequences for engaging in the target behavior. For example, Ferster, Nurnberger, and Levitt (1962) propose that the ultimate aversive consequences for overeating are unique to each client. It is these external consequences that serve to change response frequencies. Rachlin (1974) notes that self-monitoring may also serve a cueing function by making the subject aware of the environmental consequences that then alter response frequencies.

Regardless of the explanations offered for the reactivity of self-monitoring, the behavior changes that self-recording can produce have been documented many times. In addition to this therapeutic function of self-monitoring, self-recording is also important in the assessment of behavior.

ACCURACY OF SELF-MONITORING

As noted in the beginning of this chapter, self-recording is a frequently used assessment technique in behavior therapy and research. One reason for this use of self-monitoring is the behavioral emphasis on the situational-specificity of responses that necessitates assessment in the natural environment as well as in clinical settings. Although trained observers could be used in the natural environment to record the frequencies of some behaviors, trained observers are costly and reactive (Lipinski & Nelson, 1974a) and may obtain a less representative sample of behavior than the subject himself could obtain (Kazdin, 1974b). Some target behaviors are not available for external observation, namely, covert behaviors (e.g., thoughts, urges, and fantasies), and private behaviors, (e.g., sexual behavior). For these categories of target behaviors, self-monitoring may be the only feasible means of data collection.

In a clinical situation self-recording may be used during two stages of the assessment process. During the initial assessment phase, when the client and therapist are deciding on the target behavior and its controlling variables, the subject may self-record the frequency of a proposed target response and also note its antecedents and consequences. In later assessment phases, when decisions have been reached regarding the target behavior and a therapeutic strategy, the subject may continue to self-monitor only the target behavior in order to evaluate the effectiveness of the treatment techniques being utilized.

In addition to the assessment functions of self-monitoring within a clinical situation, self-recording is often used to provide the dependent measure in research projects, especially research in the self-control area (Goldfried & Merbaum, 1973; Kanfer & Phillips, 1970; Mahoney & Thoresen, 1974; Thoresen & Mahoney, 1974). The rationale for this use of self-recording is similar to the reasons stated above, namely, the cost and reactivity of trained observers and the nonavailability of many target behaviors to external monitoring. As has been discussed, however, self-recording is also reactive and may possibly have therapeutic effects of its own. Hence if self-recording is being used to collect dependent measures, then an experimental control is required to evaluate separately the reactive effects of self-monitoring and therapeutic effects produced by other treatment techniques. When a between-group experimental design is being used, Nelson and McReynolds (1971) and Jeffrey (1974) have suggested the use of a self-monitoring-only control group. In comparison with this and other control groups, the therapeutic effect of other treatment techniques may be assessed while still utilizing self-recording to monitor the dependent variable. When a within-group experimental design is used, Jeffrey (1974) proposes an *ABCABC* design, in which *A* is an independently assessed baseline, *B* is self-monitoring only, and *C* is self-monitoring plus an additional treatment strategy. If a reversal design is impractical or not feasible, Jeffrey (1974) notes that a multiple baseline design in which the *ABC* procedure is applied sequentially to different subjects, behaviors, or situations (Hall, Christler, Cranston, & Tucker, 1970) is a suitable alternative.

Jeffrey (1974) proposed that an independently assessed baseline be obtained prior to the subject's self-recording of the target behavior. The reason for this is the reactivity of self-monitoring: If a self-recording phase is considered as baseline data, the reported frequency of the target behavior is most likely altered from its pre-self-monitoring rate. Although an independently assessed baseline may be ideal, this procedure is impractical in many situations and impossible for covert target behaviors. At these times the initial self-monitored data may be utilized as an artificial baseline against which to evaluate further changes produced by additional treatment techniques. Another alternative is to have the subject estimate the pre-self-recording occurrence of the target behavior. Berecz (1972), for example, had his subjects provide a prebaseline estimate of the number of cigarettes they smoked per day prior to another baseline where they self-recorded their smoking rates. As might be predicted from the reactivity of self-recording, the self-recorded levels were lower than the prebaseline estimates. The use of independent observations, however, permits not only the recording of baseline frequencies prior to reactive changes produced by self-recording but also permits the accuracy of the self-recorder in monitoring his own behavior to be evaluated.

Problems in the Use of Self-Monitoring in Assessment

Reactivity

The reactive effects produced by self-recording comprise its primary therapeutic utility. On the other hand, as noted above, this reactivity interferes with the assessment functions of self-recording. A self-recorded baseline cannot be assumed to represent the same behavioral frequencies as occurred before self-recording was initiated. Hence a self-recorded baseline at best is an artificial baseline against which only further changes produced by other techniques, which include self-monitoring and other variables, can be evaluated. Other alternatives to the interference that the reactivity of self-monitoring produces in the assessment of baseline frequencies are, as described above, pre-self-recording estimates of baseline frequencies or the use of trained observers. Lipinski et al. (1975), for example, utilized a two-stage baseline. The subjects, who were college students in a classroom setting, were observed by trained observers from behind a one-way mirror. These observers obtained a baseline frequency of the subjects' face touching. The effects of reinforcement contingent on decreases in face touching or increases in accuracy were subsequently evaluated against both the independent observers' and the self-recording baselines. Self-recording produced a decrease in face touching below levels observed during the independent observers' baseline; differential reinforcement further decreased face touching below the self-recorded baseline.

Low Accuracy

The assessment function of self-recording is hampered by the reactivity of self-monitoring. The assessment function is further hindered by a frequent lack of accuracy found in the data collected by self-recorders as compared with data collected by other observers. The term *interobserver agreement* or *accuracy* is preferred over the term *reliability* adopted from traditional testing theory, but in either case, the concept is that two observers are able to produce comparable sampling estimates by utilizing the same observation procedures in the same setting (Johnson & Bolstad, 1973). In several studies the data collected by self-recorders have been compared with the data collected by other observers. In some cases high interobserver agreement was found and in other cases poor interobserver agreement was noted.

Kazdin (1974b) reviewed several self-monitoring studies that reported either high or low self-recording accuracy. He tentatively suggested that adult subjects may be more accurate self-recorders than children. Mahoney et al. (1973) found a high correspondence (0.938) between college students' self-monitoring of reviewing procedures in preparation for an examination and an unobtrusive reliability measure. Azrin and Powell (1969) found a 98 percent agreement between hospital employees' records and self-reported pill taking. Using smoking as the target behavior, Ober (1968) reported a correlation of 0.94 between self-reports and friends' reports of subjects' smoking. McKenzie and Rushall (1974) found that swimmers' and experimenters' counts of the number of laps swum agreed 100 percent.

In contrast many other studies report relatively low agreement between self-recordings and independent observations. McFall (1970) had college student smokers self-record their smoking rates, while nonsmoking peers simultaneously and unobtrusively observed these rates. Over 70 days of observation, the interobserver agreement was 0.61. For the two mothers in Herbert and Baer's study (1972), the rates of agreement between their self-recordings of their attention to appropriate child behaviors and independent observers' recordings of these behaviors were 46 percent and 43 percent, respectively. For the two teachers who self-recorded three different target behaviors in a multiple baseline design, Hendricks et al. (Note 1) found the percentage of agreement between their self-recordings and external observations to range from 41 percent to 87.8 percent. Cavior and Marabotto (1976) found that when college student subjects self-monitored their verbal behaviors in a dyadic situation, their agreement with trained observers was 0.37.

In addition to the poor accuracy of self-monitoring reported in the above studies that utilized adult subjects, other experiments have found that children are also inaccurate in their self-recording as compared with external observations. Risley and Hart (1968) graphically depicted the low correspondence between children's self-reports of their nonverbal behavior and the frequency of their behavior as measured by observers. Broden et al. (1971) reported that while the overall agreement between a student's self-recordings of her study behavior and the observer's recordings were fairly high, there were very large day-to-day discrepancies in their recordings. Fixsen, Phillips, and Wolf (1972) found that boys' reports on the cleanliness of their own rooms agreed with peer reports 76 percent; conversely, the boys' self-reports and their reports on their peers' rooms agreed with adult observers' reports 50 percent.

Variables Controlling the Accuracy of Self-Monitoring

Simkins (1971b) proposed several reasons for the discrepancies that have been reported between self-recordings and external recordings. First, the external observers may receive better training in making observations than do self-observers. In addition the external observers may possibly be under stronger contingencies to produce accurate recordings. The external observers and the self-observers may be using different response criteria in noting the occurrence of a response. Finally, the self-recorders may have concurrent prepotent responses that interfere with their ability to self-monitor accurately.

Some of Simkins' ideas have been subjected to experimental investigation. These and other studies help to explain the variable accuracy of self-monitoring reported in the experiments cited above. These studies also provide suggestions to maximize the accuracy of self-recording so that it may adequately serve assessment functions.

Nature of the target behavior

In an initial study in which college student subjects self-monitored a class of verbal responses, namely praise words, Bailey and Peterson (Note 4) reported rates of agreement between self-recorders and external observers to be 51.6 percent when the subjects were informed of reliability assessment and 37.7 percent when they were unaware. By comparing their data on verbal responses to Lipinski and Nelson's (1974b) data on face touching (86 percent when subjects were informed of reliability assessment, 52 percent when unaware), Bailey and Peterson proposed that verbal responses may be more difficult to self-record accurately than face touches. This suggestion was confirmed in a later study by Peterson, House, and Alford (Note 2) who found higher accuracies for self-recorded face touches (64.3 percent agreement) and lower accuracies for self-recorded verbal responses (31.4 percent agreement for the phrase "and all that," and 0 percent agreement for the phrase "you know"). Cavior and Marabotto's (1976) accuracy measure for the self-recording by college students of their verbal responses was similar, namely 0.37. Hayes and Cavior (in press) however, found that for at least one class of verbal responses, namely, value judgments, self-monitoring was quite accurate. In their study the correlations between self-monitored scores and those determined by external raters were 0.87 for face touching, 0.40 for value judgments, and 0.00 for speech nonfluencies. Thus these results indicate that different classes of target behaviors may be relatively easy or difficult to self-monitor accurately. The data suggest that verbal responses may be among those responses that are more difficult to self-monitor accurately.

Concurrent response requirements

Although Cavior and Marabotto (1976) found low accuracy (0.37) of self-recording when the subjects attempted to self-monitor their verbal behavior while engaging in a dyadic interaction, their accuracy increased to 0.89 when given the opportunity to self-monitor their verbal behavior from videotapes. One interpretation of these findings is that in the dyadic interaction, the subjects were engaged in concurrent responses and hence could not accurately self-record.

Three experiments have confirmed that the accuracy of self-monitoring is decreased when subjects are required to perform concurrent responses (Epstein, Miller, & Webster, 1976; Epstein, Webster, & Miller, 1975). A similar paradigm was followed in each of these studies. Subjects made fewer errors in their self-monitoring of respiration when they engaged in self-monitoring alone (error rate in one study was 4 percent; in other studies, the mean proportion of errors was 0.28 and 0.28) than when they engaged in a concurrent operant task of lever pressing in addition to self-monitoring of respiration (error rate rose to 9.5 percent in one study; in other studies, the mean proportion of errors rose to 0.72 and 0.49, respectively). These results suggest that people are able to self-monitor most accurately when other tasks do not interfere with their self-observation and/or self-recording.

Awareness of accuracy assessment

A series of studies have demonstrated that self-recorders are more accurate in their self-recordings when they are aware that their accuracy is being monitored by external observers than when their accuracy is monitored covertly. Lipinski and Nelson (1974b) found that the accuracy of self-recorded face touching was 0.52 when subjects were unaware of reliability assessment; the accuracy increased to 0.86 when subjects were made aware of reliability checks. In two similar studies, Nelson et al. (1975) found that awareness of reliability checks increased the accuracy of self-recorded face touches from 0.55 to 0.81, and Lipinski et al. (1975) found a comparable increase from 0.46 to 0.67. These results have been replicated with verbal responses by Bailey and Peterson (Note 4), who found that awareness of reliability checks increased accuracy of self-recorded praise words from 37.7 percent to 51.6 percent. Similarly, Santogrossi (Note 5) reported that children's discrepancies between self-recording of correct reading responses and the external observers' recording were decreased when either a teacher or a peer also monitored the children's reading response. Comparable efforts were obtained by either teacher or peer monitoring.

These findings that self-recorders are more accurate when aware of reliability checks parallel results found with trained observers. Romanczyk, Kent, Diament, and O'Leary (1973) found that the reliability for trained observers aware of reliability assessment and of the specific reliability checker was 0.77; reliability dropped to 0.53 under overt assessment with an unidentified assessor; reliability was reduced to 0.33 when the observers were unaware of reliability assessment. Reid (1970) found that observer reliability dropped from a median of 0.76 to 0.51 when observers were led to believe that accuracy was no longer being assessed. Taplin and Reid (1973) found that the level of reliability fell from 0.81 on the last day of observer training to 0.65 on the first day of covert reliability assessment.

Thus when self-monitoring is to be used to collect data in a naturalistic setting, the evidence suggests that more accurate self-recordings will be obtained if subjects are informed that another person will be checking their accuracy. This procedure was used by Tokarz and Lawrence (Note 6), who had insomniacs self-monitor their time of falling asleep and awakening. With the insomniacs' knowledge of this possibility, roommates were used to assess periodically and covertly the insomniacs' accuracy.

Reinforcement for accurate self-monitoring

Several studies have demonstrated that the accuracy of self-monitored responses increases if reinforcement is made contingent on accurate self-recordings. The low correspondence Risley and Hart (1968) initially found between children's verbal and nonverbal behavior was increased by reinforcement contingent on correspondence as evaluated by external observers. Fixsen et al. (1972) found that peer and self-reports of room cleanliness was initially 76 percent, with token reinforcement for agreement increasing the reliability to 86 percent. The cheating behavior of a sixth-grade girl was significantly reduced when her weekly grades were made contingent on daily accurate self-evaluation (Flowers, 1972). Using retarded adult subjects, Nelson et al. (1976a) reported that the accuracy of self-monitoring was increased by reinforcement contingent on accuracy for two of three target behaviors. The self-monitored accuracy of touching environmental objects increased from 0.70 to 0.92, and the self-monitored accuracy of face touching increased from 0.45 to 0.82 (the self-monitored accuracy of talking, however, remained identical, 0.73). Lipinski et al. (1975) differentially rewarded some subjects for decreases in self-recorded face touching and other subjects for increases in the accuracy of their self-recordings of face touches. Compared with a baseline self-monitoring accuracy of 0.67 (awareness of reliability assessment), the former group increased their accuracy to 0.72, and the latter group increased their accuracy to 0.84. Although their subject's initial accuracy in self-monitoring the phase "you know" was 0 percent, Peterson et al. (Note 2) found that reinforcement contingent on accurate self-monitoring increased the accuracy to 50.1 percent.

Summary

The research cited above suggests that verbal responses may be among the more difficult to self-record accurately. It has also been shown that when subjects are engaged in concurrent responses, the accuracy of their self-monitoring decreases. Conversely, accuracy is increased by awareness of reliability assessment and by reinforcement contingent on accurate self-recording. If self-recording is to be used to collect data in a clinical situation, the accuracy of the self-monitoring may be maximized if clients are asked to self-record when they are not overly busy with other behaviors, if a reliability assessor in the natural environment is utilized, and if reinforcement is made contingent on the congruence of the self-monitored data and the data of the reliability assessor. It is also assumed that adequate training in the actual self-recording task is necessary to obtain data that is clinically relevant and accurate.

Relationship between the Accuracy and Reactivity

Simkins (1971a, 1971b) and Nelson and McReynolds (1971) have engaged in a debate on whether the accuracy and reactivity of self-monitoring can be investigated as separate research issues. Nelson and McReynolds (1971) suggest that even though self-recording may be very unreliable, its reactive effects may be consistent. This suggestion has been experimentally corroborated by Broden et al. (1971), Fixsen et al. (1972), Herbert and Baer (1972), and Lipinski and Nelson (1974b), all of whom demonstrated that self-recording produced reactive effects even though the self-monitoring itself was inaccurate as compared with external observations. Hayes and Cavior (in press) concluded that the accuracy of self-monitoring was not correlated with the magnitude of its reactive effects. Although the accuracy of self-monitoring was greatest for face touching, less accurate for value judgments, and poorest for verbal nonfluencies, reactivity was greatest in face touching followed by nonfluencies and value judgments respectively.

The question then arises: If subjects are not accurately self-monitoring, what is the mechanism by which the reactive changes produced by self-monitoring occur? Peterson et al. (Note 2) have suggested that a minimal level of accuracy is necessary before reactivity occurs. They base this suggestion on their data with the self-monitoring of the phrase "you know": When accuracy was 0.00, no reactivity occurred; only when training and reinforcement increased the level of accuracy did reactivity occur. An alternate suggestion is that subjects may sometimes self-observe their own behavior but fail to make the actual self-recording response. Simkins (1971b) has noted the distinctiveness of the target behavior versus the self-recording response of counting the occurrence of the target behavior. Self-monitoring may be reactive even though inaccurate if a subject self-observes his or her own responses yet fails to make the self-recording response.

CHAPTER SUMMARY

Self-monitoring consists of the discrimination of a response, the recording of its occurrence by the subject, and subsequent evaluation of these data by the subject. A variety of self-recording devices and procedures were described. Self-monitoring has been used to fulfill two functions. One function is to collect data in the natural environment when the use of trained observers is impractical or impossible. The accuracy of self-monitoring is of great concern when self-recording is fulfilling this assessment function. The second function of self-monitoring is therapeutic in that changes occur in the self-recorded target behavior. The reactivity of self-monitoring is of foremost concern when self-recording is fulfilling this therapeutic function. Experiments delineating the variables that differentially affect the reactivity and accuracy of self-monitoring were summarized, and corresponding suggestions were made to maximize either its therapeutic or assessment functions.

REFERENCE NOTES

1. Hendricks, C. G., Thoresen, C. E., & Hubbard, D. R., Jr. *The effects of behavioral self-observation training on elementary teachers*. Unpublished manuscript, Stanford University, 1973.
2. Peterson, G. L., House, A. E., & Alford, H. F. *The accuracy and reactivity of self-monitored conversational behavior*. Paper presented at the meeting of the Southeastern Psychological Association, Atlanta, March, 1975.
3. Ciminero, A. R., Graham, L. E., & Jackson, J. L. *A comparison of obtrusive and self-recording procedures*. Paper presented at the meeting of the Southeastern Psychological Association, Atlanta, March 1975.
4. Bailey, M. I., & Peterson, G. L. *Reactivity and accuracy of self-monitored verbal responses*. Manuscript submitted for publication, 1975.
5. Santogrossi, D. A. *Self-reinforcement and external monitoring of performance on an academic task*. Paper presented at the Fifth Annual Conference on Applied Behavior Analysis in Education, Kansas City, Kansas, October 1974.

6. Tokarz, T., & Lawrence, P. S. *An analysis of temporal and stimulus factors in the treatment of insomnia*. Paper presented at the meeting of the Association for Advancement of Behavior Therapy, Chicago, 1974.

REFERENCES

Arsenian, J. Young children in an insecure situation. *Journal of Abnormal and Social Psychology*, 1943, **38,** 225–249.

Azrin, N. H., & Powell, J. Behavioral engineering: The reduction of smoking behavior by a conditioning apparatus and procedure. *Journal of Applied Behavior Analysis*, 1968, **1,** 193–200.

Azrin, N. H., & Powell, J. Behavioral engineering: The use of response priming to improve prescribed self-medication. *Journal of Applied Behavior Analysis*, 1969, **2,** 39–42.

Azrin, N., Rubin, H., O'Brien, F., Ayllon, T., & Roll, D. Behavioral engineering: Postural control by a portable operant apparatus. *Journal of Applied Behavior Analysis*, 1968, **1,** 99–108.

Bandura, A. *Principles of behavior modification.* New York: Holt, Rinehart, & Winston, 1969.

Bayer, C. A. Self-monitoring and mild aversion treatment of trichotillomania. *Journal of Behavior Therapy and Experimental Psychiatry*, 1972, **3,** 139–141.

Bechtel, R. B. The study of man: Human movement and architecture. *Transaction*, 1967, **4,** 53–56.

Bellack, A. S., Rozensky, R., & Schwartz, J. A comparison of two forms of self-monitoring in behavioral weight reduction program. *Behavior Therapy*, 1974, **5,** 523–530.

Berecz, J. Modification of smoking behavior through self-administered punishment of imagined behavior: A new approach to aversive therapy. *Journal of Consulting and Clinical Psychology*, 1972, **38,** 244–250.

Broden, M., Hall, R. V., & Mitts, B. The effect of self-recording on the classroom behavior of two eighth-grade students. *Journal of Applied Behavior Analysis*, 1971, **4,** 191–199.

Cavior, N., & Marabotto, C. Monitoring verbal behaviors in dyadic interaction. *Journal of Consulting and Clinical Psychology*, 1976, **44,** 68–76.

Emmelkamp, P. M. G. Self-observation versus flooding in the treatment of agoraphobia. *Behaviour Research and Therapy*, 1974, **12,** 229–237.

Emmelkamp, P. M. G., & Ultee, K. A. A comparison of "successive approximations" and "self-observation" in the treatment of agoraphobia, *Behavior Therapy*, 1974, **5,** 606–613.

Epstein, L. H., Miller, P. M., & Webster, J. S. The effects of reinforcing concurrent behavior on self-monitoring. *Behavior Therapy*, 1976, **7,** 89–95.

Epstein, L. H., Webster, J. S., & Miller, P. M. Accuracy and controlling effects of self-monitoring as a function of concurrent responding and reinforcement. *Behavior Therapy*, 1975, **6,** 654–666.

Ernst, F. Self-recording and counterconditioning of a self-mutilative compulsion. *Behavior Therapy*, 1973, **4,** 144–146.

Ferster, C. B., Nurnberger, J. I., & Levitt, E. B. The control of eating. *Journal of Mathetics*, 1962, **1,** 87–109.

Fixsen, D. L., Phillips, E. L., & Wolf, M. M. Achievement Place: The reliability of self-reporting and peer-reporting and their effects on behavior. *Journal of Applied Behavior Analysis*, 1972, **5,** 19–30.

Flowers, J. V. Behavior modification of cheating in an elementary school student: A brief note. *Behavior Therapy*, 1972, **3,** 311–312.

Foxx, R. M., & Martin, P. L. A useful portable timer. *Journal of Applied Behavior Analysis*, 1971, **4,** 60.

Goldfried, M. R., & Merbaum, M. (Eds.). *Behavior change through self-control.* New York: Holt, Rinehart, & Winston, 1973.

Goldman, J. A look at measurements in industry. In L. E. Slater (Ed.), *Interdisciplinary clinic on the instrumentation requirements for psychophysiological research*. New York: Fier, 1961.

Goldstein, A., & Brown, B. W. Urine testing schedules in methadone maintenance treatment of heroin addition. *Journal of the American Medical Association*, 1970, **214,** 311–315.

Gottman, J. M., & McFall, R. M. Self-monitoring effects in a program for potential high school dropouts: A time-series analysis. *Journal of Consulting and Clinical Psychology*, 1972, **39,** 273–281.

Hall, R. V., Christler, C., Cranston, S., & Tucker, B. Teachers and parents as researchers using multiple baseline designs. *Journal of Applied Behavior Analysis*, 1970, **3,** 247–255.

Hannum, J. W., Thoresen, C. E., & Hubbard, D. R., Jr. A behavioral study of self-esteem with elementary teachers. In M. J. Mahoney & C. E. Thoresen, *Self-control: Power to the person*. Monterey, Calif.: Brooks-Cole, 1974.

Hayes, S. C., & Cavior, N. Multiple tracking and the reactivity of self-monitoring: I. Negative behaviors. *Behavior Therapy*, in press.

Herbert, E. W., & Baer, D. M. Training parents as behavior modifiers: Self-recording of contingent attention. *Journal of Applied Behavior Analysis*, 1972, **5,** 139–149.

Homme, L. E. Perspectives in psychology, XXIV: Control of coverants, the operants of the mind. *Psychological Record*, 1965, **15,** 501–511.

Horan, J. J., Hoffman, A. M., & Macri, M. Self-control of chronic fingernail biting. *Journal of Behavior Therapy and Experimental Psychiatry*, 1974, **5,** 307–309.

Hutzell, R., Platzek, D., & Logue, P. Control of symptoms of Gilles de la Tourette's syndrome by self-monitoring. *Journal of Behavior Therapy and Experimental Psychiatry*, 1974, **5,** 71–76.

Jackson, B. Treatment of depression by self-reinforcement. *Behavior Therapy*, 1972, **3,** 298–307.

Jeffrey, D. B. Self-control: Methodological issues and research trends. In M. J. Mahoney & C. E. Thoresen (Eds.), *Self-control: Power to the person.* Monterey, Calif.: Brooks-Cole, 1974.

Johnson, S. M., & Bolstad, O. D. Methodological issues in naturalistic observation:

Some problems and solutions for field research. In L. A. Hamerlynck, L. C. Handy, & E. J. Mash (Eds.), *Behavior change: Methodology, concepts, and practice*. Champaign, Ill.: Research Press, 1973.

Johnson, S. M., & White, G. Self-observation as an agent of behavioral change. *Behavior Therapy*, 1971, **2,** 488–497.

Kanfer, F. Self-monitoring: Methodological limitations and clinical applications. *Journal of Consulting and Clinical Psychology*, 1970, **35,** 148–152.

Kanfer, F. H., & Phillips, J. S. *Learning foundations of behavior therapy*. New York: Wiley, 1970.

Katz, R. C. A procedure for concurrently measuring elapsed time and response frequency. *Journal of Applied Behavior Analysis*, 1973, **6,** 719–720.

Kazdin, A. E. Reactive self-monitoring: The effects of response desirability, goal setting, and feedback. *Journal of Consulting and Clinical Psychology*, 1974, **42,** 704–716. (a)

Kazdin, A. E. Self-monitoring and behavior change. In M. J. Mahoney & C. E. Thoresen (Eds.), *Self-control: Power to the person*. Monterey, Calif.: Brooks-Cole, 1974. (b)

Kolb, D. A., Winter, S. K., & Berlew, D. E. Self-directed behavior change: Two studies. *Journal of Applied Behavioral Science*, 1968, **4,** 453–471.

Kunzelmann, H. D. (Ed.). *Precision teaching*. Seattle: Special Child Publications, 1970.

Lando, H. A. An objective check upon self-reported smoking levels: A preliminary report. *Behavior Therapy*, 1975, **6,** 547–549.

Leitenberg, H., Agras, W. S., Thompson, L. E., & Wright, D. E. Feedback in behavior modification: An experimental analysis in two phobic cases. *Journal of Applied Behavior Analysis*, 1968, **1,** 131–137.

Lindsley, O. R. A reliable wrist counter for recording behavior rates. *Journal of Applied Behavior Analysis*, 1968, **1,** 77–78.

Lipinski, D. P., Black, J. L., Nelson, R. O., & Ciminero, A. R. The influence of motivational variables on the reactivity and reliability of self-recording. *Journal of Consulting and Clinical Psychology*, 1975, **43,** 637–646.

Lipinski, D. P., & Nelson, R. O. Problems in the use of naturalistic observation as a means of behavioral assessment. *Behavior Therapy*, 1974, **5,** 341–351. (a)

Lipinski, D. P., & Nelson, R. O. The reactivity and unreliability of self-recording. *Journal of Consulting and Clinical Psychology*, 1974, **42,** 118–123. (b)

Mahoney, K. Count on it: A simple self-monitoring device. *Behavior Therapy*, 1974, **5,** 701–703.

Mahoney, M. J. The self-management of covert behavior: A case study. *Behavior Therapy*, 1971, **2,** 575–578.

Mahoney, M. J. Self-reward and self-monitoring techniques for weight control. *Behavior Therapy*, 1974, **5,** 48–57.

Mahoney, M. J., Moore, B. S., Wade, T. C., & Moura, N. G. M. The effects of continuous and intermittent self-monitoring on academic behavior. *Journal of Consulting and Clinical Psychology*, 1973, **41,** 65–69.

Mahoney, M. J., Moura, N. G., & Wade, T. C. The relative efficacy of self-reward, self-punishment, and self-monitoring techniques for weight loss. *Journal of Consulting and Clinical Psychology*. 1973, **40,** 404–407.

Mahoney, M. J., & Thoresen, C. E. *Self-control: Power to the person*. Monterey, Calif.: Brooks-Cole, 1974.

Maletzky, B. M. Behavior recording as treatment: A brief note. *Behavior Therapy*, 1974, **5,** 107–111.

McFall, R. M. Effects of self-monitoring on normal smoking behavior. *Journal of Consulting and Clinical Psychology*, 1970, **35,** 135–142.

McFall, R. M., & Hammen, C. L. Motivation, structure, and self-monitoring: Role of nonspecific factors in smoking reduction. *Journal of Consulting and Clinical Psychology*, 1971, **37,** 80–86.

McKenzie, T. L., & Rushall, B. S. Effects of self-recording on attendance and performance in a competitive swimming training environment. *Journal of Applied Behavior Analysis*, 1974, **7,** 199–206.

McLaughlin, J. G., & Nay, W. R. Treatment of trichotillomania using positive coverants and response cost: A case report. *Behavior Therapy*, 1975, **6,** 87–91.

McNamara, J. R. The use of self-monitoring techniques to treat nail biting. *Behaviour Research and Therapy*, 1972, **10,** 193–194.

Mercatoris, M., & Craighead, W. E. Effects of nonparticipant observation on teacher and pupil classroom behavior. *Journal of Educational Psychology*, 1974, **66,** 512–519.

Miller, P. M., Hersen, M., Eisler, R. M., & Watts, J. G. Contingent reinforcement of lowered blood/alcohol levels in an outpatient chronic alcoholic. *Behaviour Research and Therapy*, 1974, **12,** 261–263.

Nelson, C., & McReynolds, W. Self-recording and control of behavior: Reply to Simkins. *Behavior Therapy*, 1971, **2,** 594–597.

Nelson, R. O., Lipinski, D. P., & Black, J. L. The effects of expectancy on the reactivity of self-recording. *Behavior Therapy*, 1975, **6,** 337–349.

Nelson, R. O., Lipinski, D. P., & Black, J. L. The reactivity of adult retardates' self-monitoring: A comparison among behaviors of different valences, and a comparison with token reinforcement. *The Psychological Record*, 1976, **26,** 189–201. (a)

Nelson, R. O., Lipinski, D. P., & Black, J. L. The relative reactivity of external observations and self-monitoring. *Behavior Therapy*, 1976, **7,** 314–321. (b)

Ober, D. C. Modification of smoking behavior. *Journal of Consulting and Clinical Psychology*, 1968, **32,** 543–549.

Patterson, G. R. Behavior intervention procedures in the classroom and in the home. In A. E. Bergin and S. L. Garfield (Eds.), *Handbook of psychotherapy and behavior change: An empirical analysis*. New York: Wiley, 1971. (a)

Patterson, G. R. *Families*. Champaign, Ill.: Research Press, 1971. (b)

Rachlin, H. Self-control. *Behaviorism*, 1974, **2,** 94–107.

Reid, J. Reliability assessment of observation data: A possible methodological problem. *Child Development*, 1970, **41,** 1143–1150.

Risley, T. R., & Hart, B. Developing correspondence between the non-verbal and verbal behavior of preschool children. *Journal of Applied Behavior Analysis*, 1968, **1,** 267–281.

Romanczyk, R. Self-monitoring in the treatment of obesity: Parameters of reactivity. *Behavior Therapy*, 1974, **5,** 531–540.

Romanczyk, R. G., Kent, R. N., Diament, C., & O'Leary, K. D. Measuring the reliability of observational data: A reactive process. *Journal of Applied Behavior Analysis*, 1973, **6,** 175–184.

Rozensky, R. H. The effect of timing of self-monitoring behavior on reducing cigarette consumption. *Journal of Behavior Therapy and Experimental Psychiatry*, 1974, **5,** 301–303.

Rutner, I. T., & Bugle, C. An experimental procedure for the modification of psychotic behavior. *Journal of Consulting and Clinical Psychology*, 1969, **33,** 651–653.

Schulmann, J. L., & Reisman, J. M. An objective measurement of hyperactivity. *American Journal of Mental Deficiency*, 1959, **64,** 455–456.

Schwitzgebel, R. K., & Kolb, D. A. *Changing human behavior: Principles of planned intervention*. New York: McGraw-Hill, 1974.

Shapiro, M. B. The single-case in clinical-psychological research. *The Journal of General Psychology*, 1966, **74,** 3–23.

Sheehan, D. J., & Casey, B. Communication. *Journal of Applied Behavior Analysis*, 1974, **7,** 446.

Simkins, L. A rejoinder to Nelson and McReynolds on the self-recording of behavior. *Behavior Therapy*, 1971, **2,** 598–601. (a)

Simkins, L. The reliability of self-recorded behaviors. *Behavior Therapy*, 1971, **2,** 83–87. (b)

Skinner, B. F. *Science and human behavior*. New York: Macmillan, 1953.

Sobell, L. C., & Sobell, M. B. A self-feedback technique to monitor drinking behavior in alcoholics. *Behaviour Research and Therapy*, 1973, **11,** 237–238.

Soskin, W., & John, V. P. The study of spontaneous talk. In R. Baker (Ed.), *The stream of behavior*. New York: Appleton-Century-Crofts, 1963.

Stollack, G. E. Weight loss obtained under different experimental procedures. *Psychotherapy: Theory, Research, and Practice*, 1967, **4,** 61–64.

Stuart, R. B., & Davis, B. *Slim chance in a fat world: Behavioral control of obesity*. Champaign, Ill.: Research Press, 1972.

Stumphauzer, J. S. *Daily behavior card*. Venice, Calif.: Behaviometrics, 1974.

Taffel, C. Anxiety and the conditioning of verbal behavior. *Journal of Abnormal and Social Psychology*, 1955, **51,** 496–501.

Taplin, P. S., & Reid, J. B. Effects of instructional set and experimenter influence on observer reliability. *Child Development*, 1973, **44,** 547–554.

Thomas, D. R. Preliminary findings on self-monitoring for modifying teaching behaviors. In E. A. Ramp & B. L. Hopkins (Eds.), *A new direction for education: Behavior analysis*, Vol. 1. Lawrence: University of Kansas, 1971.

Thomas, E. J., Abrams, K. S., & Johnson, J. B. Self-monitoring and reciprocal inhibition in the modification of multiple tics of Gilles de la Tourette's syndrome. *Journal of Behavior Therapy and Experimental Psychiatry*, 1971, **2,** 159–171.

Thoresen, C. E., & Mahoney, M. J. *Behavioral self-control*. New York: Holt, Rinehart, & Winston, 1974.

Watson, D. L., & Tharp, R. G. *Self-directed behavior: Self-modification for personal adjustment*. Monterey, Calif.: Brooks-Cole, 1972.

Zifferblatt, S. M. *Improving study and homework behaviors*. Champaign, Ill.: Research Press, 1970.

CHAPTER 8

Analogue Measures

W. ROBERT NAY

The careful assessment of client-targeted behaviors prior to treatment planning has been recommended for a number of years (e.g., Kanfer & Saslow, 1965), but it is only in recent years that behavior assessment strategies themselves have become the focus for systematic evaluation. Although a number of excellent reviews of assessment alternatives have been presented in the literature at various times (Weick, 1968; Wright, 1967), most have failed to focus on important methodological issues. More recent reviews (Goldfried & Kent, 1972; Lipinski & Nelson, 1974) have provided an initial structure for evaluating behavioral assessment methodologies, and systematic evaluations of behavioral assessment procedures have begun to appear in the literature (Jones, Reid & Patterson, 1975; Nay & Kerkhoff, 1974; Romanczyk, Kent, Diament, & O'Leary, 1973).

Directly monitoring a client's behavior in the natural environment seems to be the most valid approach to information gathering. However, there are a significant number of limitations to this approach. First, there is the very real possibility that the observer's presence may contaminate the environment in some fashion, thus producing an invalid sample of behavior (e.g., Patterson & Harris, Note 1). Second, whereas the ordinary classroom environment physically restricts client behavior to a single setting and is thus ideal for direct observational procedures, it is clear that such settings as homes, institutional cottages or wards, or out-of-door conditions place important restrictions on any observational effort. In placing two observers in a cottage setting consisting of between 25 and 30 delinquent adolescents (Nay, 1974), it was impossible to monitor each girl's behavior on a continuous basis because the subjects moved freely about the cottage (e.g., to their rooms, to their recreation room, etc.). In attempting to follow a particular subject throughout the setting using a one-to-one observation strategy, it became obvious that the obtrusiveness of the observer was greatly enhanced, leading to questionably valid data collection. In response to this problem the two observers were posted at either end of a large recreation room area, and during the observation period all girls were required to be in attendance. In addition, television and playing of records, which made it impossible for the observers adequately to hear client verbal interactions, were prohibited. Such unfortunate restraints on client behavior become necessary as clients move freely about the settings or perhaps engage in behaviors that interfere with observational strategies. Many investigators have had to resort to similarly restrictive observational requirements (e.g., Patterson, Cobb, & Ray, 1973). Third, direct observation in the natural environment may be quite costly and impractical for the practicing behavior therapist. Most reports of behavior intervention that appear in the literature employ a team of well-trained observers (often university undergraduates) who conduct systematic observations in specially constructed or assigned settings. Although such systematic and comprehensive efforts are to be commended, most treatment settings are unable to supply necessary personnel and most therapists cannot spend six to eight hours a week in a home, classroom, or cottage conducting a comprehensive behavioral analysis. Whenever I present elaborate direct observational strategies to teachers, school psychologists, ward personnel, and others in workshop settings, I am most often met with rather realistic responses such as: "I have a caseload of some 300 children; where am I going to find the time to go into the home?" "With all the other demands placed on my time, I cannot justify the time and cost required." Although it is easy for the research-minded behavior analyst to criticize such approaches as "resistant" or "unsystematic," it is obvious that many change agents cannot or will not employ direct observational strategies in the natural environment. Last, because the observer has no control over the natural environment, client behaviors may be determined by a host of transient situational variables such that the conditions of data collection vary considerably across observational sessions. Thus a large number of data collections is necessary to obtain a valid and reliable assessment of the consistencies that client behavior displays over time.

As an alternative, investigators have increasingly employed in the clinical/research setting analogue situations that require the client/subject to respond to stimuli that simulate those found in the natural environment. Although such analogue measurements also raise questions about validity and observer effects, they do provide the change agent with a less costly and more practical alternative means of collecting information regarding particular target behaviors under highly controlled conditions. Goldfried and Kent (1972) suggested that the change agent could require the client to role play "his response as if he were actually in the situation in question" (p. 414) as one of three alternatives in assessing a client's behavior. An increasingly diverse array of analogue measures have been employed in the literature, and these will be the focus of the present discussion.

Although most analogues require the client to respond to some stimulus that may also be found in the natural environment, the means of presenting such stimuli, as well as the modalities of responses monitored, have varied considerably. While most require the client to "respond as you usually would to the following situation," some place the client in novel situations to test the limits of the client's response repertoire; and in some cases an assessment of how the client handles preprogrammed responses is undertaken. To determine the current status of the analogue as an assessment method, six major journals in which a majority of behavioral assessment and therapeutic approaches are reported were surveyed from 1972 through early 1975. When a particular investigation employed an analogue as an assessment tool, a careful description of its characteristics was noted as well as information as to subject characteristics, the setting in which the analogue was employed, those behaviors measured in the analogue, as well as other pertinent information. The results of this survey are presented in Table 8–1.

Five distinctive categories of analogue measurement emerged from this review. Each category will be briefly described, and its rationale as an assessment tool will be considered. Following a presentation of representative examples from the literature, the major defining characteristics of that analogue will be presented. The advantages as well as limitations of each category will also be summarized. Following this presentation, validity and reliability assessment as related to the analogue will be discussed and supported by the literature where possible. Finally, the current status of the analogue as a behavioral assessment alternative will be evaluated.

ANALOGUE CATEGORIES

Paper-and-Pencil Analogues

Description

Perhaps the least costly and most readily administered analogue requires the respondent to endorse how he would respond to a stimulus situation presented in written form. Much like the paper-and-pencil tests employed in the academic setting, this approach requires the client to make a written statement of what he would say and/or do in response to the stimulus scene, or requires him in some way to endorse one of an array of written response alternatives that immediately follow the stimulus situation (e.g.,

Table 8–1. Methodological Summary of Analogue Employment

Study	N	Subject Description[a]	Analogue Description	Setting[b]	Assessment Instrument[c]
Paper and Pencil					
Young, Rimm, & Kennedy (1973)	40	F-UG Subassertive	69 multiple choice	U	S–R; C–V–B
Nay (1975)	77	Mothers of behavior problem children	25 item multiple choice problem situations	U	
Audio Tape					
Goldstein et al. (1973)	90	M + F psychoneurotic outpatients	50 interpersonal-independence relevant situations	C	C–V–B
Arkowitz, Lichtenstein, McGovern, & Hines (1975)	35	20 M UG high-frequency dating, 15 M UG low-frequency dating	10 social situations	U	C–V–B
Nay (1975)	77	Mothers of behavior problem children	12-item audio tape analogue use of time-out procedures with 5-year-olds	U	C–V–B
Videotape					
Dublin & Berzins (1972) (1972)	72	36 M + F, UG; "As" 36 M + F UG; "Bs"	Tape of "patient" in psychothreapy—*S* asked to respond "helpfully"	U	C-V-B

		Enactments			
Toepfer, Reuter, & Maurer (1972)	48	24 mother-child pairs; behavior management	Mothers commanded child to perform simple motor responses	U	C–V–B; C–P–B
Sobell, Schaefer, & Mills (1972)	49	26 M alcoholics, 23 M normal drinkers	Drinking sessions in realistic experimental bar	C	C–P–B
Bugental, Love, & Kaswan (1972)	30	20 "disturbed" families, 10 normal families	Videotaped with discussing in waiting room	C	C–V–B
Parsons & Alexander (1973)	40 40	G + B delinquents and families	Discussed accuracy of perceptual tasks	C	C-V-B.
Miller, Hersen, Eisler, & Hemphill (1973)	30	M alcoholic inpatients	Ss judged 6 beverages' (3 alcoholic) taste dimensions	C	Amount of alcohol consumed
Herbert et al. (1973)	12	4 B, 2 G, 6 Mothers	Mothers tried to have child perform tasks assigned	Cl	C–P–B
Eisler, Hersen, & Agras (1973a)	12	6 married couples, M patients at VA hospital	Discussion	C	C–P–B
Eisler, Hersen & Agras (1973b)	24	12 married couples	Discussed selected topic	C	C–P–B
Carter & Thomas (1973)	2	1 married couple	Discussed 4 assigned topic	C	C–V–B
Alexander (1973)	52	Families of 30 G + B delinquents, 22 G + B G + B normals	Discussed "several" topics	JC	C–V–B;
Williams & Brown (1974)	24	12 M alcoholics, 12 M normal drinkers	Groups of 4 M allowed to drink ad lib in realistic setting	C	C–P–B

(Continued)

Table 8–1. (continued)

Study	N	Subject Description[a]	Analogue Description	Setting[b]	Assessment Instrument[c]
Role play					
Woy & Efran (1972)	35	12 F; 23 M UG speech phobic	*Ss* gave speech with at least 13 observers	C	C–P–B
Serber (1972)	1	M, subassertive	Role played situation with *E* as prospective employer	C	C–P–B
Fancher, McMillan, & Buchman (1972)	30	M, UG	6 simulated phone conversations	U	A + E
Doster (1972)	60	M, UG	*Ss* read script of "volunteer interview with realism"	U–C	C–V–B
Miller, Hersen, Eisler, & Hilsman (1973)	16	8 M alcoholics, 8 M social drinkers	5 social situations with *E* who was antagonistic and critical	C C	C–V–B; P
Karst & Most (1973)	80	M + F UG speech phobic	*Ss* gave 2-minute autobiographical speech; every other *S* had an audience	U	S–R–; P
Hersen, Eisler, & Miller (1973)	50	M psychiatric subassertive	Behavioral Assertiveness Test (BAT): 14 interpersonal encounters requiring assertive behavior		C–P–B; C–V–B
Haase & Markey (1973)	36	28 M UG, 8 F UG socially anxious	*Ss* approached *E* until comfortable distance	VA	C–P–B
Eisler, Hersen, & Miller (1973)	30	M psychiatric patients, subassertive	BAT; used 5 of 14 situations	C	C–V–B; C–P–B

Study	N	Subjects[a]	Situation	Setting[b]	Assessment[c]
Bloomfield (1973)	8–10	M + F subassertive	Therapists and Ss role-play assertive situations and switched roles	C	C–V–B
Borkovec, Fleischman, & Caputo (1973)	34	17 M UG high social; 17 M UG low social anxiety	2 confederates and 1 S interacted and discussed	U	C–V–B
Nau, Caputo, & Borkovec (1974)	73	F UG fear of snakes	Ss role-played effects particular therapy would have on them re fear of snakes	U	C–P–B
Kifer, Lewis, Green, & Phillips (1974)	6	3 parent-child pairs; behavior management	Pairs role played parent-child conflict situation	Cl	C–V–B
			Pairs discussed trouble areas	H	
Hersen, Eisler, & Miller (1974)	50	M psychiatric patient, low low assert	Behavioral Assertiveness Test (BAT)	C	C–V–B C–P–B
Goldfried & Trier (1974)	27	17 M, UG; 10 F, UG speech phobic	Ss presented 4-minute speech before live audience	U	C–V–B; C–P–B
Borkovec, Wall, & Stone (1974)	60	M + F, UG speech phobic	Ss gave 3 short speeches	U	S–R; P; C–V–B
Borkovec, Stone, O'Brien, & Kalpoupek (1974)	46	M, UG socially anxious	Ss talked to female assistants	U	S–R; P; C–P–B
Arkowitz, Lichtenstein, McGovern, & Hines (1975)	35	20 M, UG high-frequency dating 15 M, UG low-frequency dating	In vivo conversation with confederate and telephone call to confederate	U	C–V–B; C–P–B

[a] Subject abbreviations: M-male; F-female; C-children; G-girls; B-boys; UG-undergraduate.

[b] Setting abbreviations: C-clinic; U-university; Cl-classroom; H-home; JC-juvenile court; VA-V.A. Hospital.

[c] Assessment abbreviations: C–V–B—coded verbal behavior; C–P–B—coded physical behavior; S–R—self report; P—physiological; A–E—attitudes and emotions.

true or false; multiple choice). Most often, the stimulus situation depicts some ordinary event of relevance that occurs in the client's natural environment. For example, a paper-and-pencil analogue evaluating a client's repertoire of assertive responses might present a scene that calls for assertiveness (e.g., "You are standing in line in a supermarket waiting to be checked out, when a rather loud and aggressive man pushes by you and takes the place in front of you. Please write down what you would say and/or do in response to this situation."). Instructions might require the respondent make his written response in terms of what he would currently do if this were to happen to him or perhaps to respond as he believes he "ideally" should do. In fact the client may be required to make his response in terms of both instructions.

Rationale

In requiring the respondent typically to make a written response to stimulus situations presented in a paper-and-pencil format, this approach obviously does not permit the assessor to observe any overt verbal or physical representation of the client's behavior. Primarily this analogue enables the assessor to determine the way the client sees himself responding within the constraints of the instructions (e.g., "Your usual way," "The ideal way"). In many instances when client knowledge of what to do within such situations is deemed a prerequisite to client practice in the natural environment, the paper-and-pencil approach provides a scorable, quantifiable assessment of knowledge or information. Thus before a change agent could expect a client to appropriately employ a systematic approach such as time-out procedure with her child, the client must have knowledge of each of the component parts of the procedure as well as what is called for when the child responds in a particular way. A paper-and-pencil analogue would enable the assessor economically to determine the parent's knowledge of correct responses prior to requiring enactment in the clinical or natural settings.

Examples

There are few reports in the literature of paper-and-pencil analogues being employed in clinical behavioral assessment, in contrast to their frequent employment in the academic realm. Representative of this approach is a workbook developed by Becker, Englemann, and Thomas (1971), which might be employed by the change agent to train teachers in behavior management procedures. Each unit of instruction in the workbook is followed by paper-and-pencil assessments of the teacher's knowledge of important procedures. One of the approaches the authors employ is an analogue that requires an open-ended written response. ("For each of the following, specify what you could do or say to deal with the situation." For example: "Marie talks up loudly like the rest of the group. She has done this rarely in the past." p. 151) Another alternative requires that the respondent endorse one of an array of prelisted alternatives. In constructing a questionnaire to assess a parent's knowledge of the procedural steps of time-out procedure following a group training program, Nay (1975) employed analogue items in an 18-item multiple-choice questionnaire. One example of these items, calling for the parent to circle the appropriate response, is presented below.

You have just provided your child with information as to what you want him to do (i.e., "Johnny, go empty the trash!") and the child says: "No!" In using time-out procedures, you would now:

a. *firmly* tell him to do it again
b. reason with him that if the trash isn't taken out it will make the house an unsanitary place, and ask him again
c. place him in time out
d. slap his face and reprimand him for "talking back"
e. warn him that if he doesn't take out the trash immediately, he will have to go to time out

Defining characteristics

The following characteristics apply to the paper-and-pencil analogue:

1. Stimulus situations are presented in a written format, and responses are most often written, although they may be verbal or physical.
2. A stimulus scene that calls for a response is typically presented, followed by a written or verbal suggestion or cue (e.g., tone) that a response should be made.
3. Two alternative response modalities are typically employed. In the first the respondent is asked to describe what he would do in response to the stimulus situation in an open-ended fashion. In some cases he is specifically cued to describe what he would say and what he would physically do in response to the same. In the second format the respondent endorses one or more of an array of responses already prelisted on the response sheet. This multiple-choice format has the distinct advantage that it forces the respondent to discriminate from among an array of fixed choices, thus making quantitative scoring much easier. The open-ended format, owing to the highly subjective nature of the responses it elicits, is perhaps more useful when the assessor wishes to know precisely what the respondent would do or say, expressed in his own language and not limited by a set of fixed response categories. Scoring of open-ended responses can be accomplished by constructing a scoring system that defines the content

of responses appropriate to each stimulus scene, perhaps providing examples of responses that will receive full or partial credit. These responses can best be predetermined by a series of "expert" judges, with inclusion based on agreement criteria. It is particularly important that the reliability of such a scoring system be established by determining the percentage agreement or correlations achieved by multiple scorers of each analogue item.

4: To achieve uniformity of administration, respondents can be given a time limit within which to make responses. Should such a time limit be employed, it is obvious that it must be carefully geared to the writing and verbal skills of the respondents, particularly when open-ended responses are required.

Advantages and disadvantages

Paper-and-pencil analogues can be administered to large numbers of respondents at a given sitting, which is perhaps their major advantage. They can be administered by virtually any staff member capable of handing out the instruments and reading a set of instructions. In addition, the administration requires no bulky equipment and can be accomplished in any clinical or natural setting. Another important advantage is the ease with which paper-and-pencil responses can be quantified, particularly when the multiple choice response format is employed. It is conceivable that respondents could make their multiple-choice/true-false responses on computer scanning sheets that would make scoring and statistical analysis most convenient.

Regarding disadvantages, a stimulus scene presented in written form can be far removed from the natural situation the scene depicts. Although we know that a written description of a situation, or in fact dialogue, can often evoke emotional responses in the reader (e.g., the popular novel), a written description is obviously not the best representation of the stimulus. The presentation of the scene in auditory, visual, or audiovisual format, or in some natural context is a much better approximation of the stimulus situation. If in fact the assessor is interested in how the respondent will respond to a particular stimulus in the natural environment, then it makes good sense that the stimulus item should approximate that environment if a valid representation of the respondent's behavior is to be elicited. Although the respondent who can actively and vividly obtain a cognitive image of a written stimulus scene would be a more ideal candidate for a paper-and-pencil analogue, it is obvious that this format is not ideal when a close approximation of the natural event is desirable. Stimuli presented in a written format have been found to elicit much different responses from similar stimuli presented in an auditory format

(Nay, 1975). Also it is obvious that a respondent's written description of what he would do within a situation may be very divergent from what he would actually do when faced with the situation in the natural environment. Thus the validity of the paper-and-pencil analogue response, when correlated with responses actually made to the criterion natural stimulus, is questionable and should be assessed.

A paper-and-pencil format primarily taps a respondent's knowledge of what to do, and it may well be important for the behavioral change agent to assess client knowledge prior to exposing the client to real-life situations (e.g., Patterson, Cobb, & Ray, 1973). However, it is my experience that clients who know precisely what to do in response to the behavior of a child, for example, are often unable to respond in appropriate fashion when interacting with that child in the natural environment. Unfortunately, the correlations of paper-and-pencil measures with overt behavioral indices have varied considerably in the literature (Mischel, 1968).

Thus the paper-and-pencil analogue is an efficient, easily administered, and readily quantifiable approach to assessing a respondent's information regarding some procedural topic. The extent to which the analogue scenes predict responses typical of everyday functioning remains to be seen and may depend on the client's ability to "get into" the scene (e.g., visualization) and on the extent to which the written stimulus carefully describes a scene typical of the natural environment. Finally, this measure is greatly limited because the assessor is not provided with the opportunity to observe the respondent's overt verbal and physical behavior in response to the stimulus situation, and this behavior may be very far removed from a written description or multiple-choice endorsement.

Audiotape Analogues

Description

In contrast to a written format, the audiotape analogue presents stimulus items in an exclusively auditory format. A narrator typically describes a scene on an audiotape (e.g., "You have had a long and hard day at the office, and all you want to do is come home and relax. When you arrive, your wife comes over to you and says . . . . ") followed by an actor making some verbal statement appropriate to the scene (e.g., wife: "Why do you always come home so late? You're irresponsible! Now, I want you to go and immediately fix that shelf you promised to fix."). In this example calling for an assertive response, some form of auditory cue on the tape (e.g., a tone) signals the respondent to make a verbal and/or physical response to the situation. The verbal responses of actors on the audiotape are constructed to duplicate, to the extent possible, those persons relevant to the respondent's natural environment, and the analogue items proper are typically preceded by written or verbal instructions that carefully define what the respondent is to do. One or two examples often precede the scored analogue items, so that the respondent has a chance to practice making responses in this somewhat unusual format.

Rationale

Because the audiotape analogue approximates the kind of verbal responses that others in the natural environment make to the respondent, it may provoke respondent verbal and physical behavior more consonant with ordinary behavior than the paper-and-pencil approach and provides the assessor with a sample of overt behavioral responses that may then be coded using some systematic format.

Examples

The audiotape format has become increasingly popular in recent years owing to the ease of administration and the kind of overt behavioral responses it evokes. To assess the extent to which 90 psychiatric patients could employ an independent response to an array of ordinary social situations, Goldstein, Martens, Hubben, Van Belle, Schaaf, Wiersma, and Goedhart (1973) developed 50 interpersonal situations presented on audiotape. An example of such a situation is: "It is Friday afternoon, five o'clock, and you are about to go home from work. Your boss appears and says: 'We've just received some work we didn't expect. It must be completed. Everybody will have to work overtime' " (p. 34). The tape then asks for the subject's answer.

In employing these analogue situations in treatment, Goldstein et al. (1973) exposed an experimental group of patients to a modeling situation in which the patients heard a model making an independent response to each of 30 of the situations. Thus the stimulus scene was presented, with an appropriate model's response following. Over an additional 10 situations, the patients were presented with two response alternatives and required to choose the one that most closely represented what they would say in the situation. When a patient displayed an independent response, he was reinforced by the experimenter, whereas dependent responses elicited no reinforcement. Following treatment, patients were required again to make open-ended responses to analogue situations similar to those presented at baseline. A 5-point rating scale was employed to judge pretreatment and posttreatment free responses, with rating categories ranging from independent to clearly dependent. Four graduate student judges obtained an interjudge reliability coefficient of 0.85 in employing this scale. Although the authors emphasized the importance of in vivo follow-up tests, they did not assess their patients in the natural environment to determine the generality of analogue responses to natural settings.

As another example, Arkowitz, Lichtenstein, McGovern, and Hines (1975) employed this format with a population of high-frequency and low-frequency daters in an undergraduate population. Interested in determining discrepancies between the groups across behavioral measures of social competency (latency of responses from auditory signal to respond, number of words omitted), the authors employed a Taped Situation Test (TST) in which the subjects' response to 10 social situations were recorded on an audiotape. The authors state: "Each situation was introduced and described by a male voice (e.g., 'At a party, you go over to a girl and ask her to dance.'). A female voice then read a line of dialogue (e.g., 'I'm not really much of a dancer.') The male had to respond aloud after a prerecorded signal (e.g., 'Actually, neither am I. Why don't we just talk instead?')" (p. 5). The authors found this technique could significantly discriminate between low-frequency and high-frequency daters, suggesting its validity as a measure of social competence.

Defining characteristics

The following define the audiotape approach:

1. Following a set of instructions describing how responses are to be made, a series of situations that approximate criterion natural situations are introduced by means of a narrative, typically followed by a verbal statement of some person in the scene. Most typically, the actor who makes this statement attempts to approximate in content, style, and tone of voice some relevant criterion person in the natural environment. Thus if the analogue situation attempts to simulate a child responding to his parent, a child actor of similar age may be employed to make the recorded response. Ideally, audiotape or videotape recordings of relevant client responses in the natural environment can be employed as a model for actors, so that an exact replication is achieved in producing the audio tape scenes. Thus comprehensive specimen audio or video tape records (Wright, 1967) could be made in the natural environment, and the specific scenes included in the analogue then chosen from among the ordinary interactions recorded. Provided that the specimen sampling is representative of those interactions that occur in the population of interest, the analogue situations chosen are also representative of that population.

2. Although the respondent is typically required to make a verbal (and perhaps even a physical) response to the auditory stimulus, written responses of an open-ended or multiple-choice nature may also be required, particularly if a more quantifiable scoring system is desirable. In their

treatment phase Goldstein et al. (1973) presented their patients with a forced choice between a dependent or independent response, which was prerecorded on cards presented to the patients. Nay (1975) required a written open-ended response to audiotape analogue scenes as a means of administering the measure to a group of subjects. Obviously any written response to an auditory stimulus is subject to the same limitations as the paper-and-pencil analogue format.

3. Responses may be time limited, being signaled by a cue on the audiotape to ensure an immediate response (Goldstein et al., 1973; Nay, 1975), or respondent determined. In the latter case a respondent signals the analogue administrator that he is through making his response, indicating that the next analogue scene can then be presented.

Advantages and disadvantages

An audiotape analogue presents the respondent with a more natural segment of behavior and typically elicits an overt response, yet it holds many of the advantages of administration and quantifiability displayed by the paper-and-pencil analogue. These are the major advantages of this approach. An audiotape presentation does not require that the assessor be present, and audiotape recordings of the responses made to each of the analogue stimuli can be scored at a later, more convenient time. This approach offers considerable flexibility in that it can be administered either in a clinical or natural setting. Also the test constructor has the option of making the stimulus scenes highly idiosyncratic to a particular client, or of a general nature to assess the competencies of some larger group of clients. Because of the structured nature of the stimuli to which the client must respond, repeated audiotape analogue assessments throughout treatment provide a standardized and uniform measure of client progress in an economical fashion. Finally, should a stimulus situation attempt to approximate the ordinary background sounds or perhaps special auditory effects found in the natural environment (e.g., the sounds of traffic; a high level of background noise such as could be found in a playroom, nursery, or playground setting; and so on), the audiotape medium is limited only by the creativity of the analogue constructor (and perhaps by his skill in employing audio gear).

The exclusive presentation of auditory stimuli limits a stimulus scene to verbalizations or other setting-produced noises and does not permit the respondent to see the stimulus person or background stimuli that may ordinarily be present in the natural environment. An array of investigators (e.g., Kiesler & Bernstein, Note 2) have stressed the importance of paralinguistic and other behaviors that are often concomitants of verbal communications (e.g., body language), and it is obvious that such nonverbal communications can cue the recipient as to the appropriate response to the situation. The stern command of a father directed toward his son takes on a much different meaning when it is accompanied by a smile or a wink. However, the audiotape approach unfortunately would not permit the inclusion of such nonverbal accompaniments. Although this limitation may be overcome by a verbal narrative introducing a scene, it is obvious that a purely verbal stimulus is severely lacking in the kind of communicative cues most often present in the ordinary situation. If the assessor wishes to maximize a respondent's attention to the stimulus person's voice or the content of his speech, an audiotape presentation is most desirable.

As a vehicle for training, as in the Goldstein et al. (1973) investigation, the limitations of an audiotape analogue approach are more evident. In attempting to foster more appropriate and independent communications on the part of a group of psychiatric patients, these authors exposed clients to models making appropriate responses in an audiotape format. Because these clients were trained to respond only to the content and voice characteristics of the stimulus persons, without being exposed to attendant paralinguistic and kinesic information, it is possible that they learned to respond exclusively to the verbal aspects of a communication while failing to discriminate other important communicative cues. Although I know of no data to support this possibility, it seems desirable to train clients to respond to the comprehensive communication process in all its subtleties, rather than having them respond exclusively to the content of some verbal communication. One of the most difficult aspects of training clients in social skill behavior is the promotion of appropriate discriminations when the client is faced with a complex and often paradoxical array of verbal and nonverbal communications.

These limitations stated, it is obvious that hearing the verbalization of a stimulus person is a much closer approximation of the natural environment than reading about a stimulus situation in a paper-and-pencil format, and it is a step in the direction of simulating the kinds of stimuli that occur naturally.

Videotape Analogues

Definition

Similar to an audiotape analogue, a videotape format presents the respondent with stimulus scenes that have been previously recorded on videotape. Thus an audio and video component is presented to the respondent. As with the audiotape format, a narrator typically introduces a scene and provides directions to the respondent for each segment of behavior to which the client is asked to respond. An actor is often, presented looking face forward, as if to the viewer. The actor talks and makes responses to the viewer (camera) that require the respondent to reciprocate. At its extreme, the stimulus person and respondent could actually carry on a conversation of sorts, limited only by the extent to which the presentation medium is programmed to emit alternative actor responses. Most typically, the actor behaves in some fashion (e.g., makes a statement, asks a question, engages in some behavior calling for a response), and the respondent is cued to make a response. Although this response could be a written one, most typically the respondent is asked to make an overt behavioral response.

Rationale

The videotape format maximizes the congruence between the stimulus presentation and the criterion situation in the natural environment without employing live models or in vivo role playing. This approach has the economy and flexibility as well as the standardized format of the analogues previously discussed, but it more closely approximates an ordinary stimulus situation. In addition it broadens the array of verbal and particularly nonverbal stimuli that may be presented as part of the stimulus configuration.

Examples

Although numerous investigators have required clients to make approach-like responses to slides visually depicting stimuli that provoke avoidance responses (Hamilton & Schroeder, 1973; McReynolds & Tori, 1972), no example could be found of a videotape analogue employed as an assessment device in a behavioral change effort. Dublin and Berzins (1972) employed a videotape analogue of "patient" behavior to assess the differential manner in which "A" and "B" therapist-type undergraduate students would respond to an analogue patient. The authors describe the construction of various scripts employed to produce the videotapes. The scripts were enacted by college professional actors, and attempts were made to depict the passage of time realistically as the enactments were recorded on the videotape (e.g., changes of apparel appropriate to the season, different lengths of beard stubble on different days). Thus every attempt was made to present these actors as real-life clients.

Defining characteristics

The following define the videotape approach:

1. In contrast to the exclusively audio approach, both the verbal and visual components of the stimulus person's behavior are presented to the respondent. In presenting visual material it becomes critically important

that the actor master the appearance and array of nonverbal behaviors that accompany the verbal communication, and that the background materials appearing in the scene (e.g., props) approximate the criterion environment. Only a careful assessment of the visual features of the criterion setting, as well as careful observation of the criterion person's behavior, can ensure that the videotape produced validly represents the natural environment.

Although responses to the videotape can be written, it is highly unlikely that the assessor would choose this as the primary format for the respondent. Ideally the respondent's behavior should be videotaped to provide a complete record of responses, which can then be systematically observed and coded at a later time. The distinct advantage of a videotape recording of responses is that observers do not have to be physically present in the environment to observe the respondent's behavior, which might reduce observer effects. Of course responses can be observed and coded by independent coders via closed circuit television, as an alternative means of immediate and independent assessment. It has been my experience that it is very costly and time consuming, as well as impractical, to employ reliable observers on an immediate basis for such observational efforts, and that a videotape recording permits coding to be postponed until a more convenient time. In addition, particularly if nonverbal as well as verbal respondent behaviors are to be coded, it may be impossible for the direct observer systematically to scan the array of events of interest and make reliable observations on an immediate basis. It is generally most difficult for an observer to process and record more than three or four social behaviors occurring simultaneously. Thus the observational strategy and level of sophistication of the observers may well predict whether a video tape record is profitable.

Another advantage of the videotaped record is that it can be reviewed with the respondent at a future time and may be important if feedback and additional training are goals of treatment. Thus in the example presented students can observe a videotape recording of their responses to the analogue situation and even code their own behavior as a means of requiring them to focus on important verbal and nonverbal aspects of their enactment. The videotape can be paused and replayed as necessary, and such a videotape feedback can be a prelude to additional exposure to modeling and role-playing efforts.

2. As with any analogue, responses may be time limited or free with respect to time. Because of the extraordinary requirement that the respondent talk to a person on a television screen, instructions for responding should be carefully described, following a general description of the nature of such an analogue. As with the audiotape approach, it is most

desirable that practice items be included in the videotape presentation to assess the degree to which the respondent has mastered the task. It makes sense that many individuals experience difficulty when asked to make responses to an inanimate object. In addition this kind of task may require that the client be able to role-play and even requires certain imaginal abilities (e.g., in terms of "getting into" the scene) that some clients may not have adequately developed. The assessor must be certain that the client is comfortable with the task and can adequately perform the task prior to employing such an instrument as an assessment tool. To the extent that the client's responses are colored by the awkwardness of the situation or inhibited by anxiety or other situation-produced intrinsic events, the client's responses may represent an invalid record. In addition, as with any assessment device, the analogue constructor must be certain that the instructions do not demand certain kinds of responses that may delimit the client/subject's options in responding. For example, if the instructions require that the respondent do or say something for each analogue scene, this may very well preclude appropriate nonresponding (e.g., ignoring a child's tantrum).

Advantages and disadvantages

It is most unfortunate that the videotape analogue approach has been so infrequently employed in the literature. This approach has distinct advantages when compared with the frequently employed audiotape format. One of its most important advantages is the fact that an array of nonverbal behaviors as well as the setting characteristics can be incorporated into the video portion of an analogue presentation. Another is its exclusive utility when nonverbal behaviors are of relevance.

Among disadvantages, it is much more costly to produce a videotape than merely to record voices with an audiotape. A videotape demands that the criterion environment be duplicated in the production, thus requiring an array of props and materials relevant to the setting. This may be impractical. In addition actors must be carefully trained to portray the characters described in scripts, which requires careful attention to nonverbal as well as verbal behaviors. Although it would seem that the video tape approach is optimal, the necessary resources (e.g., equipment, actors, props, production expertise, etc.) may make this approach impractical.

The visual components presented in a videotape may confound the client's ability to get into the scene, particularly if any elements of the visual array are not consonant with the ordinary setting. Thus if parents were asked to respond to an analogue child as if he were their own, they may be able to get into the scene better by imagining that the child heard on an audiotape is their own. A child presented on a videotape is obviously not their own child and may make it difficult for them to comply with the instructions. Because no investigator has systematically compared video with audio analogues, or even looked at the role of certain respondent variables (e.g., ability to imagine, ability to role play), the relative utility of the two approaches for particular client groupings remains to be explored. In summary to the extent that a videotape analogue accurately depicts the criterion situation, and when nonverbal as well as verbal components of the situation are relevant to valid simulation of the scene, video tape offers a significant degree of flexibility not found in other formats.

Enactment Analogues

Description

Rather than presenting the stimulus situation by means of a written or recorded medium, the enactment analogue requires the respondent to interact with relevant stimulus persons or objects usually present in the natural setting within the clinical/laboratory setting. The assessor brings relevant stimulus persons or objects into the assessment setting so that client responses to those stimuli can be monitored. The emphasis is most often on the here and now (e.g., approach the dog [phobic stimulus] as closely as you can, carry on a conversation with your wife as you ordinarily would in the home), and the respondent is typically not required to play any role other than his own.

The most commonly employed enactment analogue found in the literature is the Behavioral Approach Test, originally employed by Lang and Lazovik (1963) to assess the degree to which fearful clients could approach a snake. The Behavioral Approach Test (BAT) has been so widely employed in the assessment of avoidant behaviors that this analogue measure has become the focus for an array of research efforts (e.g., Bernstein & Nietzel, 1973). In the vast majority of cases the phobic stimulus has been a snake, with the client instructed to complete as many of some fixed number of approach responses as is possible without experiencing anxiety (e.g., looking at the snake from a distance of 15 feet, touching the container that houses the snake, picking up the snake, etc.). As the client completes the approach task, his approach responses are given a numerical score, and his behavior is often coded to assess the degree of emotion he shows while he performs (e.g., Paul, 1966). Thus the BAT enables the assesor to quantify the degree to which a client can approach some feared stimulus array. For a thorough review of the various procedural alternatives available in constructing a BAT analogue, the reader is referred to Bernstein and Nietzel (1973) as well as to the chapter by Borkevec,

Weerts, and Bernstein (this volume). Because of this coverage, examples of enactment analogues other than the BAT will be presented here.

Rationale

In the course of assessment it is often desirable to observe the manner in which a client interacts with important persons or objects found in the natural environment. A client's child, spouse, parents, or other important persons may be importantly related to some targeted client behavior. When we speak of objects, we are often talking about one of the array of potential physical objects or animals that clients may come to avoid owing to their previous learning histories. Although it may not be practical or feasible to observe such persons and/or objects in the natural setting, the assessor can use the enactment approach to observe a client's responses to these stimuli in a contrived setting that is more convenient and less costly. While the analogue approaches we have previously discussed present the stimulus material through some medium, the enactment analogue assumes that a much more valid sample of client responses can be obtained when the client is directly exposed to the stimuli. It is obvious that seeing a televised portrayal of a snake, person, or some social situation will not be as natural as directly confronting these stimuli, and in this sense the enactment approach is a much better simulation of the natural environment. To the extent that the enactment elicits responses consonant with those elicited by criterion stimuli, this approach has many advantages over direct observation in the natural setting.

Examples

Most non-BAT enactments have been directed at reproducing the behavior of various members of the family constellation in clinical settings (see Table 8–1). In such analogues certain members of the family are asked to interact as they normally would in a free situation (e.g., Bugental, et al., 1972; Eisler, et al., 1973a, 1973b; Herbert, Pinkston, Hayden, Loeman, Sajwaj, Pinkston, Cordua, & Jackson, 1973) or given some standaradized task (e.g., discuss a particular topic and reach consensus) that often requires clients to display relevant skills such as cooperation and attending to task (Alexander, 1973; Carter & Thomas, 1973; Parsons & Alexander, 1973; Toepfer, et al., 1972). Many investigators have required some enactment on the part of all the members of a family (e.g., Alexander, 1973; Bugental, et al., 1972; Parsons & Alexander, 1973); other enactment analogues have been directed at specific categories of parent-child interaction (Herbert et al., 1973; Toepfer et al., 1972; Hanf, Note 3) as well as spouse-spouse interactions in marital therapy (Carter & Thomas, 1973; Eisler et al., 1973a, 1973b).

As an example in comparing the communications of families containing a runaway or ungovernable adolescent with families that included normal adolescents, Alexander (1973) provided one of a series of discussion topics (e.g., "What are good parents?") for family members and asked them to talk about the topic. The discussion topic presumably required all members of the family to interact in offering opinions and information to others, while the experimenter had the opportunity to evaluate the frequency and type of interactions emitted and received by each family member. An array of specific communicative behaviors (verbal and nonverbal) could then be scored from the videotapes made as a record of the enactment.

It is obvious that in using this approach any topic that may elicit relevant targeted behaviors on the client's part (e.g., the way family members deal with aggression, offer sympathy, share information, etc.) can be employed, and an exhaustive array of behaviors can be coded either in vivo, or videotaped and later encoded. It is important that the topics given to family members for discussion be similar to those topics often focused on in the natural environment, so that a simulation of natural responding can be obtained. The kind of directions provided the clients predicts the response categories that will be observed in such a programmed interaction. Instructions directing family members to discuss a neutral topic (e.g., the current status of our schools) may well provoke a different class of behavioral categories than if they addressed a contemporary topic of personal interest (e.g., family finances, "who is boss in your family?", etc.). In addition, discussion of a topic is a different task from reaching consensus about some matter of personal interest e.g., ("Your task is to decide what you as a family will do together this weekend"). However, it may be that the specific instructions are outweighed by the family members' typical manner of communicating with one another, which will be displayed regardless of the task characteristics. These are empirical questions, and the few studies that have evaluated the role of demand characteristics in effecting analogue responses (e.g., Borkovec et al., 1974; Smith, Diener, & Beaman, 1974) have produced mixed and rather paradoxical results. If standardized analogues were repeatedly employed across clinical settings and carefully manipulated with regard to instructions, analogue characteristics, and subject population, some of these questions could be answered.

In teaching mothers to interact more effectively with their children by means of "bug in the ear" verbal promptings, Hanf (Note 3) both assessed and treated mothers in one of seven standard situations that fall within the enactment category. These standard situations were gleaned from the verbal reports as well as behavioral observations of a large grouping of mothers and were thought to represent those situations most frequently reported as being problematic. For example, mothers reporting difficulty in dealing with a child's attempts to seek continuous attention were asked to remain "occupied" in some task (e.g., read a magazine) while the child played alone. Or if a mother reported difficulty in eliciting compliance to requests, she was asked to play a game with her child in which she defined the rules and expected the child to follow them. The mother was provided with specific instructions regarding what she was to do and say to her child to set up the standard situation, and all mother-child pairs interacted in a playroom where they were observed and videotaped through a one-way mirror. Thus even though this standard situation was conducted in a clinical setting, it attempted to reproduce a mother-child event that occurred at some high frequency in the natural environment and potentially evoked problem behavior.

As a third example of using enactment, Eisler et al., (1973a) videotaped the interactive behaviors of married couples required to talk about a fixed topic in the dyadic situation. The authors were interested in comparing ratings made "live" in the situation with behavioral observations made from the videotapes. Both looking and smiling behaviors were systematically observed by four observers trained to acceptable levels of reliability. The couples were instructed to talk about feelings elicited by being observed and taped and also to think of topics they would like to discuss for the remainder of the session. Observers who made live observations of the couples showed reliabilities ranging from 83.15 to 100 percent agreement, with a mean of 93.8 percent across the six couples observed. Observers rating behaviors from a video monitor showed reliabilities ranging from 88.3 to 96.7 percent, with a mean of 94.3 percent across the six couples, suggesting that both means of recording elicited equally reliable encoding of behavior.

It makes sense that any analogue that evokes active verbal and/or nonverbal client behaviors can be employed as a treatment medium although the question of practice effects is raised by this procedure. For example, given that married couples learn to communicate in more appropriate ways in the analogue topic discussion, one could ask whether these behavioral gains would generalize to other discussion topics or to the free conversational situation. Very simply, do clients learn to behave appropriately within the specific confines of the analogue, or are they learning some skills of a general nature that will generalize to other situations? Perhaps those analogue situations employed for baseline and posttreatment assessment could differ with regard to content or in terms of other characteristics from the analogue situations employed in treatment (e.g., alternative topics, different instructions, etc.) to assess the generality of behavioral changes. Much like the alternative forms employed by the constructors of many paper-and-pencil tests, the analogue constructor could devise alternative formats from among the array of relevant scenes and/or situations and employ these alternate forms across baseline and treatment phases.

Unfortunately, most analogues are not assessed with regard to their reliability across administrations and are not standardized for employment across clinical settings.

Although the majority of non-BAT analogues have been directed at the interactions of family members, virtually any behavior that occurs in the natural environment can be duplicated in the clinical setting, given that relevant stimulus persons and/or objects are presented to the respondent. For example, to assess the drinking patterns of alcoholics who had voluntarily admitted themselves to an alcoholism treatment program, Williams and Brown (1974) permitted the subjects to drink in an analogue bar and lounge in the clinical setting. Their drinking patterns were compared to normal drinkers recruited from the local community. To construct this bar in the clinical setting, the authors went to great pains to ensure that the analogue setting included those elements present in community taverns. They were interested in assessing the quantity of alcohol consumed, preferences for certain drinks, and the size of a sip of alcohol, as well as the speed with which alcohol was ingested (ml of alcohol ingested per minute) across the alcoholic and control subjects. Staff members present in the setting were instructed to interact with the subjects in a friendly but uninvolved manner. They unobtrusively made recordings of subject drinking behavior over each period of four hours that the bar was open. The findings that alcoholic subjects ingested significantly more alcohol during the sessions, drank more rapidly (ml/minute), and typically took larger sips provide data of possible use in constructing training programs directed at altering the manner in which alcoholics consume beverages. This study is marked by the systematic and comprehensive fashion in which the experimenters constructed the analogue. Similar although less systematically tailored bar settings have been constructed by Sobell et al. (1972) and Miller et al. (1973) to sample similar drinking behaviors on the part of alcoholic patients. It is reasonable to assume that such attention to detail in simulating a naturalistic situation as complex as a bar will provoke client responses maximally similar to those provoked by a tavern setting in the community. Unfortunately, this question is an empirical one, and as will be pointed out in the sections to follow, few investigations have compared responses provoked by analogues that differ along the dimension of similarity with the criterion situation.

Defining characteristics

The following characteristics listed below apply to the enactment approach:

1. An ordinary stimulus found in the natural environment is presented in the contrived surroundings of the clinical setting. The vast majority of

investigators require the client to respond, both verbally and physically, as he ordinarily would in the natural setting, and it is clear that the response setting should permit the respondent readily to make whatever kind of response is ordinarily required in the situation.

2. Based purely on face validity, the degree of similarity to the natural setting should be positively related to the validity of responses obtained to the stimulus. It is important that careful observations, perhaps augmented by a complete videotape record of the natural setting, be employed to assist in the construction of the analogue, so that all important elements are present. If a husband and wife in the home situation never argue over finances or child rearing, then it is obvious that such topics may not elicit a valid record of ordinary interactive responses. A careful assessment of the criterion setting, perhaps augmented by a complete and comprehensive case history of the development of the targeted behavior ensure that the analogue represents what it is intended to represent.

3. This approach requires the client to respond in the here and now and in his own role. Although it is certainly possible that the assessor could require the client to respond in some atypical fashion (e.g., as you ideally would, as you wish you could, etc.) the idea of an enactment implies that an assessment of the current response repertoire is the primary focus. Because this approach does not require the client to role play, fantasize, visualize, or in some other fashion behave atypically, the enactment approach can be feasibly employed with a wider array of subjects than an analogue calling for such skills. Because it is straightforward and easy to construct, the enactment approach has been the most widely employed of analogue situations.

Advantages and disadvantages

The outstanding advantage of the enactment approach is that the assessor can systematically record the client's behavior in response to the actual stimuli of relevance, making this probably less artificial than the approaches described thus far. Regardless of the class of problematic natural stimuli, the creative assessor can typically devise an enactment situation that approximates them. If the client experiences some difficulty in communication skills with another person, that person may be asked to come in and interact with the client while the assessor collects data. If the client has difficulty in approaching or avoiding some object, the object itself can be brought into the clinical setting. When it is impossible to duplicate certain natural phenomena, some special setting may be constructed (e.g., the behavioral approach test) that may be handled as a "power" test (e.g., how long can you tolerate this situation? how close can you approach the snake? etc.). The enactment may be duplicated as many times as is relevant to assessment, and in fact, many investigators employ enactment analogues as a vehicle for treatment. Thus if the client experiences difficulty in interacting with his wife, he may be trained to interact more effectively using the methods of videotape feedback, modeling, role playing, cueing, contracting, and the like in an enactment requiring such interactions. Although it is obvious that the instructions may color the responses obtained, that the clinical setting may display certain characteristics not found in the natural environment, and that the client may adopt some intrinsic set (e.g., to behave in a socially desirable fashion), it is also clear that the assessor obtains a record of client responses to a standard stimulus over time. Such standardized replication of an assessment situation is typically impossible in the natural environment owing to the array of unsystematic and uncontrolled sources of variability that naturally occur in such settings. The advantages of savings in assessment time, cost, standardization, and ease of administration that apply to the previous analogues also apply to the enactment approach, and when the behavioral change agent cannot practically or feasibly go into the natural environment, these advantages become extremely important.

Because the clinical setting never perfectly duplicates the natural setting, the issue of validity is a potential limitation of any analogue assessment. However, with this in mind, the enactment approach, in presenting the criterion stimuli themselves and not some recorded or written representation of them, comes much closer to an approximation of the natural environment than those analogues previously discussed. Another disadvantage is the impracticality or impossibility of presenting certain environment stimuli in the clinical setting. To take avoidant behavior as an example, it may be impossible to present certain phenomena owing to their special features, immobility, size, or other characteristics. For the client who is fearful of crossing a bridge, exposing himself to water, approaching fire stimuli, or even avoidant of wide open spaces, it is difficult to see how such phenomena could be simulated in a clinic/laboratory situation. In such cases the investigator may be forced to assess the client in the natural environment or to carefully record such phenomena within videotape or film media and present those enactments in the clinical setting. A final practical limitation is the lack of control over important persons in the natural environment. Although the assessor may very well wish to enact a client's interactions with certain children, a spouse, or other family members, those parties may be unable or unwilling to participate in the clinical setting, and furthermore, such persons may not permit the assessor to come into the natural environment to make such assessments. In such cases the role-play approach to be discussed in the next section may be the only assessment medium of practical relevance. Finally, the client himself may be unwilling to tolerate an enactment (e.g. some phobic clients will not submit to any presentation of fear-arousing stimuli).

In summary, for most clients as well as for most criterion stimuli of importance the enactment approach offers a convenient, less costly alternative to assessment in the natural environment. The creative analogue constructor is limited only by the characteristics of the stimuli of relevance and the setting resources in constructing such enactments. Although any clinical enactment is certainly removed from the natural environment, this approach offers the advantage of standardization with regard to assessment conditions over time. If viewed as a test of the limits of the client's response repertoire, this approach is particularly worthy of consideration as a supplement to client verbal reports and paper-and-pencil responses.

Role-play Analogues

Description

When it is neither practical nor feasible to present criterion stimuli in the clinical setting, the client may be asked to visualize or covertly rehearse stimuli under certain standardized conditions, or he may be asked to overtly role play criterion situations with staff members and/or clients portraying persons of relevance. In employing such role-play procedures, it is obvious that the assessor's possibilities for reenacting naturally occurring phenomena, or for exposing the client to novel phenomena is greatly enhanced. The assessor is no longer limited by the particular characteristics of the stimulus items nor by the practical constraints that the client may place on the enactment. In fact, such role-play enactments are limited only by the assessor's ability to construct and present relevant replications and the client's ability to covertly and/or overtly role play.

Rationale

A host of investigators have employed role playing in both assessment and therapeutic endeavors, and in recent years the components of such replication procedures (Kanfer & Phillips, 1970) have been carefully scrutinized (e.g., Lira, Nay, McCullough, & Etkin, 1975; McFall & Twentyman, 1973). As with any analogue, a role play assumes that the responses a client emits in his portrayal are consonant with responses emitted to similar stimuli in the natural environment. Although role playing as an assessment device has not been systematically evaluated in the literature, the gains made as clients rehearse important behaviors in the clinical setting very often do translate to behavioral changes in the natural environment (Karst & Trexler, 1970; McFall & Lillesand, 1971). As with the analogues previously described, role playing can be standardized and instructions can be prerecorded (e.g., Lira et al., 1975) so that assessment takes place under highly similar conditions across time.

Examples

Role playing has most typically been employed to assess social skill behaviors. More specifically, investigators have employed such analogues in assessing assertive behavior (Eisler et al., 1973; Hersen et al., 1974; Macpherson, 1972; Serber, 1972) as well as avoidant behavior in the social situation (e.g., Borkovec et al., 1974; Goldfried & Trier, 1974). Another major focus has been the assessment of therapist skill behaviors (e.g., Doster, 1972; Nau et al., 1974). The vast majority of these studies has required the client/trainee to make overt verbal and non-verbal responses to actors portraying criterion persons of relevance. Most investigators have provided the respondent with instructions, either in written or audio form, as well as the opportunity to practice their enactments prior to assessment. Although an array of paper-and-pencil (e.g., Friedman, 1971) and audiotape analogues (e.g., McFall & Marston, 1970) has been used to assess client assertive behavior, the Behavioral Assertiveness Test developed by Eisler, Miller, and Hersen (1973) is the most widely employed role-play analogue. However, since this procedure is described in detail by Hersen and Bellack (this volume), it will not be presented here.

Hersen et al. (1974) assessed client responses to 10 scenes adapted from and based on the Behavioral Assertiveness Test. Although previous studies had both assessed as well as treated clients in the same scenes, this study is marked by the inclusion of training as well as generalization scenes. All 10 scenes were administered both prior to and following treatment, but the training (e.g., exposure to instructions plus modeling of appropriate assertive behavior) was carried out in only five training scenes, so that generalization to five generalization scenes could be assessed. Although it is most commendable that Hersen et al. (1974) have attempted to validate their analogue measure, most investigators employ role playing in a much more informal fashion. For example, Serber (1972) and Bloomfield (1973) directly role played with their clients in situations calling for assertive behavior. In these case studies the therapist presented a situation, played the role of some relevant person, and required the client to role play. Serber took the role of a prospective employer and required the subassertive client to try to convince him of the client's job qualifications. The interaction was videotaped and replayed for the client, which was followed by the therapist modeling appropriate assertive behaviors in the situation. Similarly Bloomfield, in working with outpatient schizophrenics, played the role of an array of persons to whom these clients had difficulty expressing assertive behaviors. These case examples are, unfortunately, more representative of the manner in which role playing is employed in the literature, and it is obvious that the therapist's active role in assessment may bias any recordings of client behavior. For example, following treatment the therapist may not play the role of provocateur as aggressively as prior to treatment. Whenever possible, it is most desirable for the therapist to employ actors other than himself as part of a role-play analogue assessment, and to employ behavioral observers who are "blind" as to specific targeted behaviors.

An assessment of client anxiety to the public speech situation is another frequent focus for role-play analogues. For example, to assess the role of expectancy as a component of the systematic desensitization process, Woy and Efran (1972) required subjects to give a speech in a room containing a contrived audience as well as three observers to assess the effects of differential treatments. Similarly, to assess the effects of two different kinds of relaxation training, Goldfried and Trier (1974) required that speech-anxious clients present a four-minute speech before a live audience in the clinical setting. Virtually the same approach was employed by Borkovec, Wall, and Stone (1974) to assess the role of false physiological feedback in reducing anxiety in the speech situation. Although the goals of each of these investigations differed somewhat, all investigators directly observed client verbal and nonverbal behaviors to assess anxiety (e.g., pauses, disfluencies), and Borkovec, Wall, and Stone (1974) included the monitoring of heart rate.

In one of the few investigations specifically directed at evaluating an analogue social situation, Borkovec, Fleischman, and Caputo (1973) attempted to determine whether a role-play analogue would discriminate groups of undergraduate students who described themselves as "socially anxious" and "socially nonanxious" across an array of dependent variable measurements. Seventeen subjects scoring in the upper (high anxious) and lower (low anxious) 25 percent on the Social Avoidance Distress Scale (Watson & Friend, 1969), were exposed to a role-play analogue that required increasingly involved interactions with confederate "peers." A paper-and-pencil self-report (5-point rating scale) of the amount of anxiety experienced during the session showed that high-anxious subjects experienced significantly more anxiety than did low-anxious subjects. Behavioral measurements of subject anxiety in the analogue situations (number of words produced per minute, number of overt anxiety signs produced per minute, number of speech disturbances per minute, during each of the three phases of the session) did not differentiate between the high-anxious and low-anxious subjects. The authors concluded: "In terms of self-report measures, the analogue social interaction of the present study appears to be a satisfactory situation for measurement of social anxiety. The subjects identified as socially anxious by questionnaire two months earlier reported both greater anxiety and a greater number of autonomic cues during the session than did low-anxious subjects" (p. 160). The authors advanced a number of hypotheses to explain the inconsistent findings for the behavioral measures.

A comprehensive evaluation of the role of covert stimuli (e.g., visualizations, fantasies, imagery) in assessment and treatment is beyond the scope of this chapter. However, it should be pointed out that virtually any criterion situation from the environment could be presented to the client covertly, through specific instructions (e.g., Try to vividly imagine yourself interacting with your wife. You're discussing . . . , etc.), and an array of client overt behavioral manifestations could be recorded (e.g., self-report, overt behavioral signs of anxiety, physiological, responses, etc.). Interestingly, few investigators have employed covert rehearsal as an assessment medium. Even for the very popular imaginal approaches to desensitization, most investigators have employed an overt behavioral approach test as the primary means of assessing client behavioral change (Bernstein & Nietzel, 1973). To the extent that such covert phenomena are a target for intervention (e.g., urges to smoke, negative self-statements, etc.), covert assessments can and should be performed, governed by standardized, audio taped instructions that set up the covert situation of interest. Such covert presentations of criterion stimuli are particularly relevant when it is impossible to simulate criterion stimuli in the clinical setting, or when the client is unable or unwilling to role play overtly. Perhaps investigators have been reticent to employ a purely covert presentation of stimuli because of the more general problem of reliability in the covert design (Nelson & McReynolds, 1971; Simkins, 1971), preferring instead to evaluate overt responses to clearly defined stimuli that can be directly observed.

Defining characteristics

The following characteristics apply to the role-play analogue approach:

1. Although actual stimuli relevant to a client's targeted problem behavior are not directly presented in the clinical setting, they are simulated in role-play situations that require the client to play his own role or the part of some other person. Usually a careful assessment of the criterion environment precedes the construction of roles, and the client is often encouraged to coach the actors in their portrayals of persons relevant to him. In some cases (e.g., Eisler, Hersen, & Miller, 1973) a series of predetermined and standardized role-play situations is presented to the client with careful instructions as to how he is to interact with the actor. The

assessor may often wish to expose the client to an array of novel situations to measure the extent of the client's response repertoire, and here the client may be asked to respond, "As you think you would," or "As you would like to respond," and so on. In fact a client can be exposed to two or more sets of differing instructions for a standard role-play scene. For example, the client can be asked to role play a given scene first as he would currently behave, and second, as he would ideally like to behave in the situation. This can provide information as to the client's goals in therapy, as well as useful data regarding the practicality of such goals in light of the client's current response repertoire. Most investigators have directly observed the client interacting in the analogue, but it is obvious that an array of self-report as well as physiological measures could be assessed both during and following the role enactment (e.g., Borkovec, Wall, & Stone, 1974).

2. The client is typically asked to play himself in the situation, but he can play the role of other important persons (e.g., his wife) as a means of assessing their role in his behavior and the manner in which he cognitively views them. When he plays himself, it can serve as a further measure of his response repertoire.

3. The client should be provided with explicit instructions regarding his activities and given the opportunity to practice getting into the role prior to formal assessment. Because clients may vary in their ability to act or role play, the assessor can permit the client to read from a script, practice role playing the behavior of characters on film or television, or perhaps respond to a more structured stimulus (e.g., audio or video tape analogues), as a training prelude to overt rehearsal. To the extent that the client's performance is limited by his ability to role play, the data gathered by this format will correspondingly be of limited utility.

Advantages and disadvantages

The outstanding advantage of the role-play analogue approach is that it provides much greater flexibility to the assessor in presenting criterion stimuli of relevance than the other analogues we have discussed. Any person in the client's environment is readily available by merely training an actor to portray that role. Objects that exist in the natural environment, that perhaps cannot be duplicated in the clinical setting, can be visualized or imagined to exist in a role-play scene. In addition the assessor has increased control over those stimulus persons or objects presented in the scene and may alter them to provoke particular client behaviors. In a pure enactment in which two married partners are asked to interact as they ordinarily would, the assessor has little control over how the client's husband and/or wife will respond. If the assessor is interested in how the client responds when his spouse is angry, an enactment may not provide an opportunity for this behavior to be observed. In contrast an actor's responses can be preprogrammed in some fashion to elicit client responses of interest. Also it may be relevant to assess the client's responses to persons who are deceased or not physically available to the setting. Although a client's verbal depiction of his relationship with his father may be a useful source of information, the client's training of an actor to portray his father and observation of the client role playing some interaction with his "father" provide the assessor with the opportunity to see how the client responded. Even if the client's responses are not valid representations of what happened in the past, they are a representation of how the client wishes to portray those events now and may provide useful information to the assessment agent. Additionally, role-play interactions can be carefully controlled by written or audiotape instructions and can be repeated as many times as are necessary during assessment.

The verbal and nonverbal responses provoked by role playing provide a rich record of client responses that may be directly recorded or videotaped for future coding or treatment use. Thus the assessor has total control over the characteristics of the stimulus, the number of presentations, and the timing of presentations, as well as instructions that may elicit client responses to the standard stimulus item.

Perhaps the major disadvantage of this approach is the potential lack of concordance between stimuli presented in the role-play situation and criterion stimuli found in the natural environment. Thus when an actor plays the role of the client's wife, the validity of the sample of responses elicited will depend on the actor's ability to portray the spouse accurately. In addition the ability of actors to engage consistently in such portrayals across time is another source of potential variability. Thus changes in client behavior across role-play analogue assessments may be more a function of differential actor behavior than of changes in the client's behavior. Furthermore, any role-play approach is limited by the client's ability to act. Many clients find this kind of situation difficult and atypical for them. The role-play analogue is not equally desirable for all clients. Unfortunately, I could find no research aimed at relating differential client characteristics to ability to role play. Given the increased employment of role play as an assessment vehicle, such research would make an obvious contribution.

ISSUES IN ANALOGUE ASSESSMENT

Validity

Traditional measures of personality and intellectual functioning presume to measure some construct (e.g., dependency, aggression, pure intelligence, etc.), although the criterion events they assess are not readily observable and must be inferred from the client's verbal report or from his observable behavior. By validity, we simply mean that a given measurement device adequately samples the criterion behaviors of interest. This process has typically involved the correlation of one paper-and-pencil measure with another paper-and-pencil instrument, both of which are assumed adequately to sample the criterion construct (Mischel, 1968). Such correlations do indeed depict similarities and dissimilarities between the response patterns elicited by such instruments, but it is not certain that they in fact tap the construct of interest. Many investigators have proposed an array of methods for validating the construct (Cronbach & Meehl, 1955; Sarason, 1966). As Goldfried and Kent (1972) have noted, behavioral assessment procedures are interested in sampling only targeted criterion behaviors that can be carefully and systematically defined, and not in inferring that these behaviors are indicative of some underlying construct or "personality" dimension. The task of validating a behavioral assessment instrument should be relatively straightforward, in that the measurement operations as well as the criterion behaviors (given that they are overt in nature) can be systematically defined in terms of behavioral referents. As a behavioral measure, an analogue situation attempts to sample behaviors *that presumably would be elicited by the criterion stimuli that the measure attempts to simulate.* An enactment analogue that requires mother-child interaction in the clinical setting should predict mother-child behavior that occurs in some natural setting (the criterion setting). At one end of the continuum we should expect that natural and clinical analogue responses would have 100 percent agreement. However, in practice this level of agreement is rarely reached for any behavioral assessment instrument. In fact, the degree of correlation that must exist between analogue measure and criterion behavior to define "minimally acceptable" is quite loosely defined for behavioral assessment instruments. In most cases investigators report the significance level of correlations between various response channels (e.g., between self-report, overt behavioral, and physiological measures). Although the correlation between such clinic/laboratory measures is often significant and quite pronounced (e.g., Bandura, Blanchard, & Ritter, 1969; Borkovec, Stone, O'Brien, & Kaloupek, 1974; Lira et al., 1975), very few investigators have systematically compared measurements in the clinical setting to criterion behaviors in the natural environment. If the goal of clinical analogue measurement is to predict functioning in natural environments, behavioral assessment approaches have not clearly advanced beyond the kind of traditional validation processes often criticized by the behaviorally oriented researcher (e.g., Kanfer & Saslow, 1965; Mischel, 1968). This finding is particularly appalling when one considers the relative ease with which criterion behaviors and their clinical analogue counterparts can be reliably observed (Jones et al., 1975; Lipinski & Nelson, 1974; Patterson et al., 1973; Paul, 1966).

Regarding clinic/laboratory assessments, the literature is extensive and has largely focused on the Behavioral Approach Test as a measure of avoidant behavior in "fearful" subjects (e.g., Bernstein, 1973; Borkovec & Craighead, 1971). Because the BAT has not been a primary focus of this chapter, clinical setting validation of other analogue measures will be presented. Taking measures of assertiveness as an example, Hersen et al. (1973) report an array of audio tape, enactment, and role-play analogues that have frequently been employed (see also Hersen and Bellack, this volume). In a majority of cases subject behaviors elicited in the analogue situation are compared with other clinical analogue responses, paper-and-pencil assertiveness tests, or written analogues. For example, McFall and Lillesand (1971) found that subjects' self-ratings of assertiveness on the Conflict Resolution Inventory (a 35-item paper-and-pencil measure of subjects' ability to "refuse" when this is appropriate) correlated relatively highly with their refusal behavior in a role-play analogue situation (0.69 in the pretest and 0.63 in the posttest phase of the experiment). In a validation attempt a 30-item paper-and-pencil self-report measure of assertiveness (Rathus Assertiveness Schedule (RAS), Rathus, 1973) was correlated with subjects' verbal responses to stimuli presented in what closely resembles an audiotape analogue format. In this analogue subjects were asked to describe "what they would do in situations in which assertive, outgoing behavior could be used with profit" (p. 402). For example, subjects were told: "You have worked very hard on a term paper and you receive a very poor grade, say a D or an F. What would you do?" If the subject says she would discuss it with her professor, she is further asked, "What if the professor is uncooperative or nasty?" (p. 402). Although the description of this procedure is somewhat vague (it was not clear whether the subjects merely described what they would do, or were asked to actually make a response appropriate to the situation), responses were audiotaped and scored by a series of judges according to a scoring system. Subjects' scores on the Rathus Assertiveness Schedule were then correlated with the behavior scored in response to the analogue, yielding an r of 0.70 ($p < 0.01$). The author concluded that the RAS scores were valid in terms of impartial raters' impressions of subject behavior.

While this finding shows that an analogue measure correlated highly with subjects' self-reports, Friedman (1971) and Hersen et al. (1973) have found the relationship between self-report and behavioral change to be "contradictory." It is difficult to make a general statement about such correlational data because of the lack of consistency in self-report measures employed and in the characteristics of the analogues themselves across studies. Eisler et al. (1973) are among a very few investigators who have repeatedly employed a standardized analogue measure (the Behavioral Assertiveness Test) across different groupings of clients and treatment interventions in an extended series of studies. This lack of consonance in analogue characteristics in the literature is a major drawback in defining the current status of the analogue, and such method variability (e.g., Campbell & Fiske, 1959) contributes to the divergent validity findings.

Although the vast majority of clinic-based validation efforts employ self-report/attitudinal measures as the criterion variable, only a few investigators have examined the relationship between analogue responses and physiological measures (Borkovec et al., 1974; Karst & Most, 1973; McFall & Marston, 1970). The Borkovec et al. investigation is an exceptional attempt at validation owing to its methodological sophistication and the multiple criterion variables employed. Interested in whether a role-play analogue requiring social interaction could discriminate between high-anxious and low-anxious subjects as defined by a Fear Survey Schedule, the authors evaluated an array of self-report, behavioral, and physiological measures. Twenty-three high-anxious and 23 low-anxious subjects were asked to interact with a confederate in a role-play analogue situation. The authors found that high-anxious subjects displayed significantly greater anxiety during the procedure than nonfearful subjects on three self-report measures. In addition, the confederate made behavioral ratings of subject anxiety (e.g., disfluencies, overt signs of anxiety), and these findings were mixed. Overt signs of anxiety, as well as the ratio of disfluencies to percentage of speaking time, failed to discriminate the two groups, but high-anxious subjects did tend to speak less during the session and were rated significantly lower in social effectiveness. Furthermore, high-anxious subjects displayed significantly greater physiological arousal. The vast majority of criterion variables indicated that this analogue measure could discriminate high-anxious from low-anxious individuals. Although a primary goal of this investigation was to determine the effects of high-demand and low-demand instructions on a second administration of the analogue, the overall findings thus suggested the validity of this measurement procedure when criterion measures of anxiety were assessed in the clinical situation. Such comprehensive validation across multiple criterion response modalities is rarely undertaken.

The fact that very few investigators have employed extra-clinical response modalities as the criterion variables for validating analogue measures may be explained in a variety of ways. It is very costly and sometimes impractical or unfeasible to assess such criterion behaviors in the natural environment. To validate a measure such as the Behavioral Assertiveness Test, the client's responses to each of the 14 interpersonal situations would have to be assessed in the natural environment in which they might ordinarily occur. Given unobtrusive measurement, the assessor has no control of these events in the natural setting and would have to wait for those situations (e.g., You buy something and the cashier hands you inappropriate change) to occur to assess the client's responses. If the client's responses correlated highly with his responses to that item on the Behavioral Assertiveness Test on a sufficient number of occasions, this item would be considered a valid elicitor of client behavior in that specific situation. It is obvious that validation of all the 14 items of this test would require extensive observations of client behavior, and it is difficult to see how such observations could be made in an unobtrusive fashion, given the diversity of situations depicted.

The ease with which such validation could be undertaken depends on the specific characteristics of the stimuli presented in the analogue and the class of responses elicited by it. Although it may be easy to validate analogues that simulate spouse-spouse, parent-child, or family interactive behaviors owing to the high probability that such behaviors will occur in the home setting, the problems for low rate, highly stimulus-specific events are obvious and restrict attempts at validation. In addition, it is hard to imagine that stimuli presented in a clinic-based analogue will be identically duplicated in the natural environment, and to the extent that there is divergence across the two stimulus classes, responses elicited may very well be divergent. Thus the question of comparability of analogue stimuli with their naturally occurring counterparts may be an important limiting factor in any attempt at analogue validation.

To the extent that analogue stimuli are systematically derived from an assessment of the criterion environment, the probability of their being comparable is enhanced. The issue of comparability most severely limits attempts at validating a standardized analogue used across large numbers of clients, given divergent criterion environments across clients. One way of getting around this limitation is to program criterion relevant events in the natural environment and to correlate responses elicited with responses to the concomitant clinical analogue. For example, McFall and Marston (1970) compared responses to a clinic-based analogue of assertiveness with client responses to a telephone conversation in which a "salesman" employed an array of high-pressure sales techniques in an attempt to induce subjects to subscribe to two magazines. Telephone calls were monitored and taped, and subjects' responses were rated in terms of their ability to refuse in an assertive fashion. The authors found that assertive behavior in the analogue correlated highly ($r = 0.76$) with subjects' ability to refuse the sales probe. This approach assured that the stimulus presented to clients in the natural environment (criterion) was identical across clients.

The relevance of validating analogues presented in the clinic with naturally occurring phenomena may depend on the goals of analogue measurement. If the assessor views the analogue as a probe or power test of the client's response repertoire and is not interested in making inferences about the natural setting, such validation becomes less meaningful. Thus an assessor may be interested only in determining a client's repertoire of positively reinforcing statements, facially expressive behaviors, or his ability to maintain eye contact in an interaction as a quantifiable assessment of the client's repertoire of social skills. This approach is based on the assumption that a client cannot respond beyond his repertoire. Even though the client may never be exposed to a situation requiring him assertively to maintain his place in line, each of these situations requires certain verbal and nonverbal skills that may be relevant to wide areas of the client's functioning in the natural environment.

Goldfried and D'Zurilla (1969) have developed a behavioral analytic method for constructing a behavioral test that seems to be ideally suited to the construction of analogues that realistically represent naturally occurring phenomena. The assumption of this approach is that the stimulus situations the analogue depicts must adequately represent and simulate those analogous situations found in the natural setting. As Goldfried and Kent (1972) point out: "For example, in surveying fear behavior, it is necessary to obtain measures of fear in situations which sample, in a representative manner, the population of potentially anxiety-producing situations. In selecting the stimulus items, then, the concept of content validity, as it has been traditionally applied to proficiency tests, becomes highly relevant for behavioral assessment" (p. 413). In their behavioral analytic method, the initial step involves selecting a pool of test items derived from a situational analysis.

In constructing an analogue of inappropriate behaviors displayed by a group of preschool children, for example, a situational analysis may be accomplished by having each mother describe in writing the problematic behaviors displayed by her child, supplemented by parental record keeping over a sufficient period of time. These data may then be augmented by direct behavioral observations of randomly selected parents interacting with their children in situations reported to be problematic, with all child behaviors encoded using a systematic recording format. When possible, the reports of both husband and wife can be employed to assess the reliability of parent self-reports across spouses. Following the gathering of this information, the situations that consistently elicit problematic behavior across self-report and direct observational data sources can then be carefully defined and retained in the stimulus pool. The items can then be resubmitted to the parents to be arranged in a hierarchy in terms of least to most troublesome, or along some other dimension of interest. Or the item pool can be submitted to an independent panel of judges who categorize those problematic situations that tend to cluster together and be similar, and those that tend to be discrete, so that a final selection of discrete, dissimilar items each tapping a divergent problematic situation of interest could be retained for the analogue. At this point items that have now been carefully defined can be put into virtually any written, recorded, enactment or role-play format, with every attempt made to simulate the manner in which they occur in the natural setting. This process insures that the items chosen are in fact representative of the natural setting, and provides the analogue constructor with sufficient information realistically to simulate each stimulus item on the analogue. This process greatly enhances the probability that behaviors elicited by the clinical analogue will be consonant with behaviors elicited by the criterion stimuli, and this can be readily determined by comparing analogue and criterion responses across large groupings of clients to determine their convergence.

Regarding the response measures employed as criterion variables in the validation process, it is wise for the analogue constructor to ensure that high correlations between response measures are not merely due to the similarity of the measurement techniques, called method or apparatus factors by Campbell and Fiske (1959). Campbell and Fiske urge that the level of contribution of the method of measurement, as opposed to target behavior variance, can be estimated by employing more than one method as well as more than one behavior in the validation process. The assessor then can assess not only convergence between similar methods (e.g., self-report instruments) intended to measure a particular behavior, but also between dissimilar measurement methods assessing the same behavior. This approach, called a multitrait-multimethod analysis, presents all the intercorrelations found when a number of behaviors are measured by each of several different measurement procedures. The matrix can then be evaluated to determine the extent to which the correlations obtained reflect convergence owing to common methods as opposed to convergence of the behavior across diverse evoking conditions.

To evaluate the validity of a role-play analogue in which subjects were asked to give a two-minute autobiographical speech about such topics as their current classes, their high school, family, home town, and so on, Karst and Most (1973) performed a multitrait-multimethod analysis for three measures of anxiety (two self-report measures of stress elicited by public speaking and finger sweat prints as a measure of physiological reactivity) evaluated prior to, during, and following the analogue speech. In evaluating the correlational matrix the authors were able to conclude that for the general self-rating and anchored self-rating measures, the components of anticipatory and performance stress level have some convergent validity (general self-rating and anchored self-rating are measuring the components) and some limited discriminant validity (the components of anticipatory stress and performance stress level can be differentiated as somewhat separate constructs). Further analysis of the matrix indicated that the finger sweat print did not correlate with either the general self-rating or anchored self-rating at any point, and this measure thus yielded the highest hetero-trait-monomethod correlations. The finger sweat print, then, seemed to be measuring the same process at different measurement periods, and that process was unrelated to the other measures. This kind of analysis could more clearly define the variability associated with measurement methods employed, and would enable the analogue to assess the validity of his measurement procedure more clearly.

In summary, although most behavioral analogues have been validated in the clinical setting, few investigators have correlated analogue responses with responses elicited by criterion natural stimuli. It was noted that there are a number of problems raised by employing natural phenomena as criteria within validation, but this strategy could readily be undertaken for many behaviors, most notably social interactive behaviors emitted in defined settings. The behavioral analytic method of Goldfried and D'Zurilla (1969) was suggested as an approach useful in constructing clinic-based analogue stimuli consonant with criterion natural stimuli. Finally, it was suggested that the methods employed to monitor client behavior in the analogue situation might themselves contribute to validity determinations. The multitrait-multimethod analysis presented by Campbell and Fiske (1959) was suggested as a means of determining the sources of variability in validating an analogue.

Reliability

Most investigators report interrater reliability data to assess the degree with which multiple assessors agree on the incidence of targeted behaviors elicited by the analogue. This determines the reliability of the rating system employed. To know that certain targeted behaviors of interest can be rated with reliability is an important finding and should be reported for each specific targeted behavior observed. However, such data do not assess the internal consistency of the analogue measure or its reliability across multiple analogue administrations. Goldfried and Kent (1972) make the point that "traditional personality tests and behavioral tests share many of the same methodological assumptions (e.g., reliability of scoring, adequacy of standardization)" (p. 410). However, most analogue constructors have not employed traditional measures of reliability in evaluating the utility of their instruments. Regarding internal consistency, constructors of traditional personality tests often assess the degree with which subgroupings of items of an instrument (e.g., odd and even items) correlate. None of the investigations reported in Table 8–1 assessed internal consistency in this fashion, with the exception of Nay (1975), who reported a split-half reliability coefficient of 0.81 for a paper-and-pencil analogue and 0.88 for an audio tape analogue. Although investigators often report internal consistency evaluations for self-report measures incorporating semantic differential or true-false responses (e.g., Rathus, 1973), it is unfortunate that such evaluations have not been reported for the analogues described here.

The consistency of responses elicited by an analogue across administrations (test-retest reliability) has been reported only by Weinman, Gelbart, Wallace, and Post (1972). The authors constructed a series of behavioral tasks (Behavior in Critical Situations Scale) to study the effects of assertiveness training for a population of hospitalized schizophrenic subjects. In an enactment analogue subjects were required to respond overtly to a series of situations calling for assertive behavior (e.g., subject reaction to being "short-changed" following the experimenter's promise to pay). The instrument was administered twice in a one-month period, producing a test-retest reliability of 0.72, which is certainly not impressive. However, it is laudable that such data were reported. An analogue should be a reliable elicitor of client behaviors to be useful in evaluating client behavioral change. If an analogue is administered in pretest and posttest fashion, as is typical of most investigations, it is most difficult to determine whether any changes that occur following treatment are due to the treatments administered or to the unreliability of the instrument. It seems that each of the categories of analogue presented in this chapter would be amenable to internal consistency and test-retest reliability assessments, given the highly structured way in which they are presented and the ease of administration that most of these instruments display. It is hoped that such data will be reported more frequently in the literature in the future.

ANALOGUES: CURRENT STATUS AND CRITIQUE

It is obvious that investigators are increasingly employing clinic-based analogues as defined in this chapter, probably owing to the ease and standardization of administration, as well as to the reduced cost of assessment these measures provide. The Behavioral Approach Test has been widely employed as an analogue of phobic behavior, but the present discussion and review of the literature indicates that a diverse and often highly idiosyncratic array of alternative analogues has been constructed and is being employed as measures of behavioral change in treatment. The five categories of analogues presented here each represents assessment possibilities that hold distinct advantages and disadvantages that should be considered prior to analogue construction. As one progresses from the paper-and-pencil analogue approach to those analogues involving enactments and role play, it is obvious that the costs of administration increase, while similarity of analogue stimuli to those found in the natural environment is concomitantly enhanced. Because of the paucity of research specifically directed at analogue characteristics, it is not currently possible to evaluate the relative validity and reliability of each of these analogue categories across targeted behaviors and client populations. Thus it is not clear whether choosing the more costly and time-consuming procedures in fact evoke a more valid and reliable sample of behavior than those approaches involving paper-and-pencil or media presentation.

Although reports of intercorrelations between divergent measures of analogue-evoked behavior are increasing in the clinical setting, the validity of responding to analogues as a predictor of behavior in the naturalistic setting has only rarely been reported in the literature. This is a serious omission.

The ease with which internal consistency as well as consistency across analogue administrations can be assessed makes it very difficult to understand the dearth of such evaluative assessment. Investigators are increasingly attuned to important methodological variables in designing research to assess various treatments, but the assessment of dependent variable behavior is often conducted with highly idiosyncratic instruments of questionable validity and reliability. It is hoped that by defining the current status of the behavioral analogue as an assessment instrument, this chapter will provoke additional research along the lines of the Arkowitz et al. (1975) and Borkovec, Stone, O'Brien, and Kaloupek (1974) investigations that are specifically directed to evaluating analogue components. Such research efforts may well result in the development of standardized, valid, and reliable analogue instruments that may be used comparably across clinical and research settings.

REFERENCE NOTES

1. Patterson, G. R., & Harris, A. *Some methodological considerations for observation procedures*. Paper presented at the American Psychological Association Annual Convention, San Francisco, 1968.
2. Kiesler, D. J., & Bernstein, A. J. *A communications critique of behavior therapies*. Unpublished manuscript, Virginia Commonwealth University, 1974.

3. Hanf, C. *A two-stage program for modifying maternal controlling during mother-child (M-C) interaction*. Paper presented at the Western Psychological Association meeting, Vancouver, B.C., 1969.

REFERENCES

Alexander, J. F. Defensive and supportive communications in normal and deviant families. *Journal of Consulting and Clinical Psychology*, 1973, **40,** 223–232.

Arkowitz, H., Lichtenstein, E., McGovern, K., & Hines, P. The behavioral assessment of social competence in males. *Behavior Therapy*, 1975, **6,** 3–13.

Bandura, A., Blanchard, E., & Ritter, B. Relative efficacy of desensitization and modeling approaches for inducing behavioral affective and attitudinal changes. *Journal of Personality and Social Psychology*, 1969, **13,** 173–199.

Becker, W. C., Englemann, S., & Thomas, D. R. *Teaching: A course in applied psychology*. Chicago: Science Research Associates, 1971.

Bernstein, D. A. Situational factors in behavioral fear assessment: A progress report. *Behavior Therapy*, 1973, **4,** 41–48.

Bernstein, D. A., & Nietzel, M. T. Procedural variation in behavioral avoidance tests. *Journal of Consulting and Clinical Psychology*, 1973, **41,** 165–174.

Bloomfield, H. H. Assertive training in an outpatient group of chronic schizophrenics: A preliminary report. *Behavior Therapy*, 1973, **4,** 277–281.

Borkovec, T. D., & Craighead, W. E. The comparison of two methods of assessing fear and avoidance behavior. *Behaviour Research and Therapy*, 1971, **9,** 285–292.

Borkovec, T. D., Fleischmann, D. J., & Caputo, J. A. The measurement of anxiety in an analogue social situation. *Journal of Consulting and Clinical Psychology*, 1973, **41,** 157–161.

Borkovec, T. D., Stone, N. M., O'Brien, G. T., & Kaloupek, D. G. Evaluation of a clinically relevant target behavior for analogue outcome research. *Behavior Therapy*, 1974, **5,** 503–513.

Borkovec, T. D., Wall, R. L., & Stone, N. M. False physiological feedback and the maintenance of speech anxiety. *Journal of Abnormal Psychology*, 1974, **83,** 164–168.

Bugental, D. E., Love, L. R., & Kaswan, J. W. Videotaped family interaction: Differences reflecting presence and type of child disturbance. *Journal of Abnormal Psychology*, 1972, **79,** 285–290.

Campbell, D., & Fiske, D. Convergent and discriminant validation by the multitrait-multimethod matrix. *Psychological Bulletin*, 1959, **56,** 81–105.

Carter, R. D., & Thomas, E. J. A case application of a signaling system (SAM) to the assessment and modification of selected problems of marital communication. *Behavior Therapy*, 1973, **4,** 629–645.

Cronbach, L. J., & Meehl, P. E. Construct validity in psychological tests. *Psychological Bulletin*, 1955, **52,** 281–302.

Doster, J. A. Effects of instructions, modeling and role rehearsal on interview verbal behavior. *Journal of Consulting and Clinical Psychology*, 1972, **39,** 202–209.

Dublin, J. E., & Berzins, J.. I. A–B variable and reactions to nonimmediacy in neurotic and schizoid communications: A longitudinal analogue of psychotherapy. *Journal of Consulting and Clinical Psychology*, 1972, **39,** 86–93.

Eisler, R. M., & Hersen, M. Behavioral techniques in family-oriented crisis intervention. *Archives of General Psychiatry*, 1973, **28,** 111–116.

Eisler, R. M., Hersen, M., & Miller, P. M. Effects of modeling on components of assertive behavior. *Journal of Behavior Therapy and Experimental Psychiatry*, 1973, **4,** 1–6.

Eisler, R. M., Hersen, M., & Agras, W. S. Videotape: A method for the controlled observation of nonverbal interpersonal behavior. *Behavior Therapy*, 1973, **4,** 420–425. (a)

Eisler, R. M., Hersen, M., & Agras, W. S. Effects of videotape and instructional feedback on nonverbal marital interaction: An analogue study. *Behavior Therapy*, 1973, **4,** 551–558. (b)

Eisler, R. M., Miller, P. M., & Hersen, M. Components of assertive behavior. *Journal of Clinical Psychology*, 1973, **29,** 295–299.

Fancher, R. E., McMillan, R., & Buchman, N. A. Interrelationships among accuracy in person perception, role-taking, and the A–B variable. *Journal of Consulting and Clinical Psychology*, 1972, **39,** 22–28.

Friedman, P. H. The effects of modeling and role-playing on assertive behavior. In R. D. Rubin, H. Fensterheim, A. A. Lazarus, & C. M. Franks (Eds.), *Advances in behavior therapy*. New York: Academic, 1971.

Goldfried, M. R., & D'Zurilla, T. J. A behavioral-analytic method for assessing competence. In C. D. Spielberger (Ed.), *Current topics in clinical and community psychology*. Vol. 1. New York: Academic, 1969.

Goldfried, M. R., & Kent, R. N. Traditional versus behavioral personality assessment: A comparison of methodological and theoretical assumptions. *Psychological Bulletin*, 1972, **77,** 409–420.

Goldfried, M. R., & Trier, C. S. Effectiveness of relaxation as an active coping skill. *Journal of Abnormal Psychology*, 1974, **83,** 348–355.

Goldstein, A. P. Martens, J., Hubben, J., Van Belle, H. A., Schaaf, W., Wiersma, H., Goedhart, A. The use of modeling to increase independent behavior. *Behaviour Research and Therapy*, 1973, **11,** 31–42.

Haase, R. F., & Markey, M. J. A methodological note on the study of personal space. *Journal of Consulting and Clinical Psychology*, 1973, **40,** 122–125.

Hamilton, M., & Schroeder, H. E. A comparison of systematic desensitization and reinforced practice procedures in fear reduction, *Behaviour Research and Therapy*, 1973, **2,** 649–652.

Herbert, E. W., Pinkston, E. M., Hayden, M., Loeman, S., Sajwaj, T., Pinkston, S., Cordua, G., & Jackson, C. Adverse effects of differential parental attention. *Journal of Applied Behavior Analysis*, 1973, **6,** 15–30.

Hersen, M. Self-assessment of fear. *Behavior Therapy*, 1973, **4,** 241–257.

Hersen, M., Eisler, R. M., & Miller, P. M. Effects of practice, instructions and modeling on components of assertive behavior. *Behaviour Research and Therapy*, 1973, **2,** 443–451.

Hersen, M., Eisler, R. M., & Miller, P. M. An experimental analysis of generalization in assertive training. *Behaviour Research and Therapy*, 1974, **12,** 295–310.

Hersen, M., Miller, P. M., & Eisler, R. M. Interactions between alcoholics and their wives: A descriptive analysis. *Quarterly Journal of Studies on Alcohol*, in press.

Jones, R. R., Reid, J. B., & Patterson, G. R. Naturalistic observations in clinical assessment. In P. McReynolds (Ed.), *Advances in psychological assessment, Vol. III*. San Francisco: Jossey-Bass, 1975.

Kanfer, F., & Phillips, J. *Learning foundations of behavior therapy*. New York: Wiley, 1970.

Kanfer, F., & Saslow, G. Behavior analysis: An alternative to diagnostic classification. *Archives of General Psychiatry*, 1965, **12,** 529–538.

Karst, T. O., & Most, Robert. A comparison of stress measures in an experimental analogue of public speaking. *Journal of Consulting and Clinical Psychology*, 1973, **41,** 342–348.

Karst, T. O., & Trexler, L. D. Initial study using fixed role and rational emotive therapy in treating public speaking anxiety. *Journal of Consulting and Clinical Psychology*, 1970, **34,** 360–366.

Kifer, R. E. Lewis, M. A., Green, D. R., & Phillips, E. L. Training predelinquent youths and their parents to negotiate conflict situations. *Journal of Applied Behavior Analysis*, 1974, **7,** 357–374.

Lang, P. J., & Lazovik, A. D. Experimental desensitization of a phobia. *Journal of Abnormal and Social Psychology*, 1963, **66,** 519–525.

Lipinski, D., & Nelson, R. Problems in the use of naturalistic observation as a means of behavioral assessment. *Behavior Therapy*, 1974, **5,** 341–351.

Lira, F., Nay, W. R., McCullough, J. P., & Etkin, M. The relative effects of modeling and roleplaying in reducing avoidance behaviors. *Journal of Consulting and Clinical Psychology*, 1975, **43,** 608–618.

Macpherson, E. L. Selective operant conditioning and de-conditioning of assertive modes of behavior. *Journal of Behavior Therapy and Experimental Psychiatry*, 1972, **3,** 99–102.

McFall, R. M., & Lillesand, D. B. Behavior rehearsal with modeling and coaching in assertion training. *Journal of Abnormal Psychology*, 1971, **77,** 313–323.

McFall, R. M., & Marston, A. R. An experimental investigation of behavior rehearsal in assertive training. *Journal of Abnormal Psychology*, 1970, **76,** 295–303.

McFall, R. M., & Twentyman, C. T. Four experiments on the relative contribution of rehearsal, modeling, and coaching to assertion training. *Journal of Abnormal Psychology*, 1973, **81,** 199–218.

McReynolds, W. T., & Tori, C. A further assessment of attention-placebo effects and demand characteristics in studies of systematic desensitization. *Journal of Consulting and Clinical Psychology*, 1972, **38,** 261–264.

Miller, P. M. Hersen, M., Eisler, R. M., & Hemphill, D. P. Electrical aversion therapy with alcoholics: An analogue study. *Behaviour Research and Therapy*, 1973, **2,** 491–497.

Miller, P. M., Hersen, M., Eisler, R. M., & Hilsman, G. Effects of social stress on operant drinking of alcoholics and social drinkers. *Behaviour Research and Therapy*, 1974, **12,** 67–72.

Mischel, W. *Personality and assessment*. New York: Wiley, 1968.

Nau, S. D., Caputo, J. A., & Borkovec, T. D. The relationship between credibility of therapy and simulated therapeutic effects. *Journal of Behavior Therapy and Experimental Psychiatry*, 1974, **5,** 129–133.

Nay, W. Comprehensive behavioral treatment in a training school for delinquents. In K. Calhoun, H. Adams, & K. Mitchell (Eds.), *Innovative treatment methods is psychopathology*. New York: Wiley, 1974.

Nay, W. R. A systematic comparison of instructional techniques for parents. *Behavior Therapy*, 1975, **1,** 14–21.

Nay, W. R., & Kerkhoff, T. Informational feedback in training behavioral coders. *Psychological Reports*, 1974, **35,** 1175–1181.

Nelson, C., & McReynolds, W. Self-recording and control of behavior: A reply to Simkins. *Behavior Therapy*, 1971, **2,** 594–597.

Parsons, B. V., Jr., & Alexander, J. F. Short-term family intervention: A therapy outcome study. *Journal of Consulting and Clinical Psychology*, 1973, **41,** 195–201.

Patterson, G., Cobb, J., & Ray, R. A social engineering technology for retraining the families of aggressive boys. In H. E. Adams & I. P. Unikel (Eds.), *Issues and trends in behavior therapy*. Springfield, Ill.: Thomas, 1973.

Paul, G. L. *Insight versus desensitization in psychotherapy*. Stanford, Calif.: Stanford University Press, 1966.

Rathus, S. A. A 30-item schedule for assessing assertive behavior. *Behavior Therapy*, 1973, **4,** 398–406.

Romanczyk, R., Kent, R., Diament, C., & O'Leary, K. Measuring the reliability of observational data: A reactive process. *Journal of Applied Behavior Analysis*, 1973, **6,** 175–184.

Sarason, I. G. *Personality: An objective approach*. New York: Wiley, 1966.

Serber, M. Teaching nonverbal components of assertive training. *Journal of Behavior Therapy and Experimental Psychiatry*, 1972, **3,** 179–183.

Simkins, L. The reliability of self-recorded behaviors. *Behavior Therapy*, 1971, **2,** 83–87.

Smith, R. E., Diener, E., & Beaman, A. L. Demand characteristics and the behavioral avoidance measure of fear in behavior therapy analogue research. *Behavior Therapy*, 1974, **5,** 172–182.

Sobell, M. B., Schaefer, H. H., & Mills, K. C. Differences in baseline drinking behavior between alcoholics and normal drinkers. *Behaviour Research and Therapy*, 1972, **10,** 257–267.

Toepfer, C., Reuter, J., & Maurer, C. Design and evaluation of an obedience training program for mothers of preschool children. *Journal of Consulting and Clinical Psychology*, 1972, **39,** 194–198.

Watson, D., & Friend, R. Measurement of social-evaluative anxiety. *Journal of Consulting and Clinical Psychology*, 1969, **33,** 448–551.

Weick, K. Systematic observational methods. In G. Lindsey & E. Aronson (Eds.), *The handbook of social psychology*. Vol. 2, Reading, Mass.: Addison-Wesley, 1968.

Weinman, B., Gelbart, P., Wallace, M., & Post, M. Inducing assertive behavior in chronic schizophrenics: A comparison of socioenvironmental, desensitization, and relaxation therapies. *Journal of Consulting and Clinical Psychology*, 1972, **39,** 246–252.

Williams, R. J., & Brown, R. A. Differences in baseline drinking behavior between New Zealand alcoholics and normal drinkers. *Behaviour Research and Therapy*, 1974, **12,** 287–294.

Wright, H. *Recording and analyzing child behavior*. New York: Harper & Row, 1967.

Woy, J. R., & Efran, J. S. Systematic desensitization and expectancy in the treatment of speaking anxiety. *Behaviour Research and Therapy*, 1972, **10,** 43–49.

Young, E. R., Rimm, D. C., & Kennedy, T. D. An experimental investigation of modeling and verbal reinforcement in the modification of assertive behavior. *Behaviour Research and Therapy*, 1973, **11,** 317–319.

CHAPTER 9

Direct Observational Procedures: Methodological Issues in Naturalistic Settings

RONALD N. KENT and SHARON L. FOSTER

Two young children are fashioning an elaborate sand castle at the edge of the ocean. The summer sun accentuates the blue-green water, the children's colorful swimsuits, the white beach fringed with brown where waves have moistened the sand. Remembering a recent Kodak ad, you wish for a camera to record the scene permanently, so that even after your memory of the afternoon has waned, you can retain a perfect likeness of the children and the beach.

A photograph—the seemingly ideal record. And yet, as many professional photographers will readily tell you, no two pictures of the scene will ever be identical. Subtle changes in lighting, a minor tilt of the camera, the children's movements will alter the contrast and composition of the photograph. Even more striking differences will emerge if the photographs are taken with different equipment. Shot from a distance, a wide-angle lens will capture much of the beach without focusing on the children; a telephoto lens will reveal greater detail in the children's expressions but will blur the background seascape. Changing one's film and altering exposure times can heighten color, resolution, and light-shadow contrasts in the final product. Altering any of the many steps in the development process will emphasize the differences that can emerge in separate prints.

This research was supported by NIMH Grant MH21813. The authors would like to express their appreciation to Joyce Sprafkin, Ruth Shepard, K. Daniel O'Leary, and Donald Hartmann for their helpful suggestions and editorial assistance on this chapter. The authors are also indebted to Margaret McCarthy for continued assistance and secretarial services in the preparation of this manuscript.

In the same way that a photograph is often casually accepted as a mirror of the scene it depicts without the realization that the final picture is a product of the equipment, photographer, and developing process as well as the scene itself, many investigators and practitioners in all areas of behavioral science have embraced observation recording as the purest possible scientific portrayal of behavior. On the surface viewing and immediately recording the behavior one wishes to study seem to provide an unequivocal, lasting measure of actual events. Until recently this view has largely prevailed, and observational data have been championed as a presumably objective, reliable, nonreactive picture of human behavior.

Although sophisticated discussions of variations in observational technology had appeared in the psychological literature much earlier (e.g., Arrington, 1939, 1943), it was not until the late 1960s that the appearance of controlled evaluations raised serious questions regarding the truth of this assumption. Just as the choice of procedures alters a photograph, different observational strategies can influence the character and quality of the data they produce. In the same way that the wrong F-stop setting or a slight movement of the camera can blur or obscure relevant details in a photograph, unnoticed or uncontrolled features of observational recording can introduce sources of error and bias that, at best, introduce variability into an investigator's data and, at worst, render it uninterpretable or misleading.

Research findings can be no more valid or reliable than the measurement procedures on which they are based. The purpose of this chapter is to identify and evaluate a number of possible sources of data distortion under typical circumstances of observational recording in field experimental settings, drawing primarily from well-controlled recent investigations that best approximate these conditions. Neither the data currently available nor space considerations allow a comprehensive discussion of all aspects of observational recording. Rather, topics of immediate relevance to investigators employing observational procedures, particularly those assessing behavior change in naturalistic settings, will be emphasized.

Initial consideration focuses on possible biases in the actual collection of observational data, including the expectations of the observer, the reactivity of the observed, and the effects of utilizing videotapes and one-way mirrors as alternatives to placing an observer directly in the target setting. Subsequent sections highlight factors that have been shown to inflate artifactually estimates of the reliability of observational data, and compare various measures of observer agreement. Finally, research that suggests possible improvements in procedures for training observers and for evaluating and enhancing the validity of observational recordings is presented.

BIASES IN THE COLLECTION OF OBSERVATIONAL DATA

Expectation Biases

One of the earliest lines of methodological research on expectation bias in observational recording procedures stems from the work of Robert Rosenthal (summarized in Rosenthal, 1966, 1969). Rosenthal and his associates demonstrated that informing experimenters of predicted experimental findings results in biased observational recordings in tasks such as rating the amount of success or failure shown in photos of faces (Rosenthal, Friedman, Johnson, Fode, Shill, White, & Vikan-Kline, 1964), or counting the number of turns or contractions by planaria (Cordaro & Ison, 1963). Azrin, Holz, Ulrich, and Goldiamond (1961) had also reported a similar expectation effect in an attempt to replicate an earlier verbal conditioning study: Experimenters' ratings of opinion statements in conversations varied with the differential predictions of outcome they were given. Although it is true that the specificity of judgmental criteria in these studies was substantially less than that for recordings of behavior in most current behaviorally oriented investigations, it remained uncertain in the late 1960s whether the substantial expectation bias documented by Rosenthal and Azrin et al. was also characteristic of other behavioral recordings.

In 1967 Scott, Burton, and Yarrow reported data in the context of a treatment study that suggested that observers who are aware of treatment hypotheses may report data biased in the direction of their expectations. In this investigaiton the senior author and three uninformed observers tape-recorded a running description of the target child's behavior at various times and later rated his behavior from their tapes. A comparison of Dr. Scott's ratings with those of an uninformed observer revealed a significant difference, with the ratings of the senior author more strongly confirming the experimental hypothesis. Unfortunately, the use of only one informed observer, who clearly differed from the uninformed observers in several respects, made it impossible to determine the source of this bias.

On the basis of Rosenthal's findings and the suggestive data of Scott et al., Kass and O'Leary (Note 1) designed the first controlled evaluation of the extent to which knowledge of treatment hypothesis can affect the behavioral recordings of observers. In this study three groups of observers utilized a 9-category behavioral code for disruptive behavior that has been used in a variety of treatment and methodological studies by O'Leary, Kent, and their associates* to record the behavior of children from video-

* The nine categories of the O'Leary et al. code include out of chair, modified out of chair, touching others' property, inappropriate vocalization, playing, orienting (turning around), nonverbal noise, and time-off-task. A composite of these categories is also computed as an overall index of disruptive behavior (cf., O'Leary, Kaufman, Kass, & Drabman, 1970).

tapes taken in an experimental classroom. One group of observers was told to expect an increase in level of disruptive behavior from baseline to treatment phases of the study, whereas a second group was led to expect a decrease. No predictions were offered in the third group. In fact, all groups of observers viewed the same videotapes, which had been selected to show a substantial decrease from baseline to treatment. The results of this study suggested that substantial biases had resulted from the differential predictions of treatment effects. In general the group of observers for which an increase in disruptive behavior was predicted recorded a smaller decrease from baseline to treatment than the group for which a decrease was predicted. The conclusions that could be drawn from these results, however, were complicated by the unexpected finding that greater differences had existed among the three experimental groups during baseline than during treatment recordings.

A closer look at Kass and O'Leary's (Note 1) procedure shows that they had trained each of the three experimental observer groups separately, although identical descriptions of the behavioral code were utilized by the same experienced research assistant in all the training sessions. Although in retrospect this seems to be a major confound, it must be remembered that in 1969 applications of the same behavioral code by different observers in different studies and even in different laboratories were viewed as yielding comparable data.

To investigate further the dimensions of expectation bias, Kent (1972) designed a dissertation involving 40 observers who were randomly assigned to eight expectation conditions. To avoid the possible confound in the Kass and O'Leary study, all 40 observers were trained as a single large group for 40 hours over a 5-week period using videotape recordings. Although all observers were initially required to match their ratings with those of the trainer, subsequently each observer computed his or her reliability with a partner who was randomly assigned at the end of each observation period. By the end of the five weeks, it became clear that the average occurrence reliability computed among the 40 observers had reached its asymptote at a level of about 0.60.

This figure was discouragingly low. Because there was no evidence that high reliabilities could in fact be obtained among such a large group of observers, Kent assigned the observers to their respective experimental groups of five observers each and continued the training period. During these training sessions the five observers in each group continued to view videotapes, and then compared their recordings with one another. After only three days the average reliability among observers within their respective groups had increased to over 0.70, an acceptable level of agreement. Unfortunately, significant differences in the frequency of behavior recorded by the different groups had also emerged prior to any experimental manipulation.

It thus became clear that differences in recording among observer groups were completely and inextricably confounded with the experimental conditions to be imposed on each group. Far more important, it was evident that observers who are allowed to compare their recordings may develop a consensus regarding the behavioral categories that will differ from group to group. Thus any study in which groups of observers collect data only within a particular classroom or treatment condition may badly confound differences in use of the behavioral code with the variables under investigation. This effect, termed *consensual observer drift* (Johnson & Bolstad, 1973) will be discussed in detail in the section entitled Biases in Estimating Reliability.

A subsequent study by Kent, O'Leary, Diament, and Dietz (1974) further examined the effects of predicted results on the observational recordings of trained observers. To avoid the confounds encountered by Kass and O'Leary (Note 1) and by Kent (1972), 10 pairs of observers were trained until each observer became reliable with her partner. At this point observer pairs were randomly assigned to one of the two experimental conditions and began to attend separate observational sessions. At these times they viewed tapes labeled as the baseline and treatment phases of a study that had supposedly been done in a special class for disruptive children. The experimenters in one condition informed the observers that a decrease in disruptive behavior from baseline to treatment was predicted. In the other condition observers were told to expect no change. In reality the two groups viewed the same videotape recordings in which there was no difference between baseline and treatment tapes for any of the nine behavioral categories.

After all the observations had been completed, observers were given a postexperimental questionnaire that included the question, "What actually happened to the level of disruptive behavior from the baseline to the treatment condition in the videotapes your group viewed? (a) Increase; (b) Decrease; (c) No change." Responses to this question indicated that the observers' global evaluations of change were significantly related to the results predicted by the experimenters ($\chi^2 = 7.50$; $df = 1$; $p < 0.01$). Of the 10 observers for whom a decrease in level of disruptive behavior from baseline to treatment conditions was predicted, nine reported that they had actually seen a decrease. Seven of the 10 observers for whom no change had been predicted said they had seen no change.

An analysis of variance of the actual behavioral recordings on the nine categories contrasted markedly with these global ratings. Each of the nine observational categories, plus a composite score reflecting the total frequency of disruptive behavior recorded on the nine individual categories, was analyzed separately. These analyses revealed that expectation produced no significant main effects on any of the nine behavioral categories or on the composite measure. Expectation also failed to interact with other factors in the design. Thus the two expectation conditions failed to differentially affect different observer pairs, different "treatment" conditions, observations of different children, and observations on different days, as well as combinations of these four experimental factors.

Shuller and McNamara (Note 2) have recently corroborated these findings. In their investigation of the influence of trait labels on assessment ratings, behavioral observations of children were unaffected by manipulation of observer expectation, whereas global ratings of their behavior showed the same large biases found in the Kent et al. (1974) study.

Although these findings await additional controlled replications and extension in the context of actual behavioral change, utilizing adult targets of observation and observers other than college undergraduates, the results of these investigations support the conclusion that when no actual change in behavior occurs, knowledge by observers of predicted results may, in fact, not alter behavioral recordings. Global evaluations of change, on the other hand, are more likely to evidence substantial bias. This contrast suggests that a focus on operational definitions of specific aspects of behavior may help to reduce the influence of spurious factors such as predictions of change, thus mitigating expectation bias in observational recordings.

It is possible, however, that the knowledge of predicted results may combine with other factors in field experimental settings to produce biased results. An experimenter may, for example, on receiving data from individual observers immediately examine the data and openly make evaluative comments, expressing surprise, approval, or displeasure regarding the extent to which the data have fulfilled experimental predictions. This kind of feedback from an experimenter may in turn affect the nature of subsequent recordings.

O'Leary, Kent, and Kanowitz (1975) sought to determine whether biased observational recordings could be shaped by an experimenter's comments about the data. Four female observers were trained to utilize four of the behavioral categories employed in previous studies of Kent, O'Leary, and their associates—vocalization, playing, orienting, and noise. After training to a median reliability of 0.74 with the experimenter, the observers were told that they would then view videotapes representing the baseline and treatment phases of a study that had been recently completed. The experimenter explained that during the treatment phase, two of the categories of behavior, playing and noise, had been subject to a powerful token program and were predicted to dramatically decrease in frequency, whereas vocalization and noise were not expected to change. Each of the observers independently viewed the baseline and treatment videotapes, which in fact showed no change in any of the four categories. After each observation session, the experimenter examined and discussed each observer's data with her. During the treatment phase, the experimenter employed a shaping procedure in these discussions. When an observational recording reflected the predicted decreases in playing and noise, the experimenter made one of several positive statements, such as, "These tokens are really having an effect on (category)"; and "Dr. O'Leary will really be pleased to see the drop in the level of (category)." When an observer's data failed to reflect the expected reduction in behavior, he reacted negatively: "You don't seem to be picking up the treatment effect on (category)"; and "I don't think a graph of this data will reflect the decrease in the number of (category)."

An analysis of variance revealed that experimenter feedback coupled with predictions of treatment outcome produced highly significant effects on the observers' data. Both target categories, playing and noise, were recorded less during treatment than during baseline. Recordings of playing decreased 27 percent, whereas noise decreased 38 percent. In contrast, recordings of vocalization and orienting, the categories for which no change had been predicted, showed no significant changes during treatment.

This study suggests that a knowledge of predicted effects coupled with evaluative feedback from an investigator can produce significant biases in observational data. In this investigation experimenter responses to observational data were based on criteria that were more systematic and explicit than would be the case in field-experimental studies, thus possibly increasing the bias. However, other aspects of this investigation may well have lessened the impact of experimenter feedback. The duration of the treatment phase was only four days; in a typical intervention program it could have lasted at least 10 to 15 days, allowing considerably more opportunity for shaping of recordings. Furthermore, the limited number of observations and the use of recordings of videotapes, rather than live children, eliminated the possibility of prolonged contact of observers with the experimenter, the teacher, and the children. Such contact might have produced a greater commitment and *esprit de corps* among observers, resulting in greater motivation to produce "acceptable" data.

It is clear that circumstances conducive to shaping of behavioral recordings may actually occur in a variety of applied settings. Interaction of observers with faculty, graduate students, and applied personnel who convey enthusiasm as well as their own vested interest in a particular treatment program may have significant effects on the data obtained. Thus until further data are available concerning the parameters of this possible bias, it seems prudent to withhold evaluative treatment-related feedback from observers who are charged with collecting observational recordings.

Reactivity of Observational Procedures

The vast majority of investigations utilizing behavioral recording have introduced nonparticipant observers directly into the target setting, rather than utilizing cameras, mirrors, or other devices to conceal the collection of behavioral recordings. This procedure implicitly assumes that the behaviors of interest will remain unaltered despite the presence of an observer. The possibility that observer presence may alter the behavior of an individual who is observed has been a recurring source of concern over the last 25 years (Campbell & Stanley, 1963; Polansky, Freeman, Horowitz, Irwin, Papanis, Rappaport, & Whaley, 1949; Webb, Campbell, Schwartz, & Sechrest, 1966). Although certain authors have maintained that the reactive effects of observers in applied settings are likely to be negligible (Behrens & Sherman, 1959; Heyns & Lippitt, 1954; Selltiz, Jahoda, Deutsch, & Cook, 1959; Werry & Quay, 1969; Wright, 1967), other investigators, unwilling to assume either nonreactivity or habituation to observers, have applied a variety of technical innovations in the collection of in vivo behavioral recordings such as miniature radio transmitters worn by the subjects (Moos, 1968; Purcell & Brady, 1965; Soskin & John, 1963), portable observation booths (Burton, 1971; Gerwitz, 1952), and sunglasses worn by observers (Surratt, Ulrich, & Hawkins, 1969). It remains unclear, however, whether even these attempts to reduce the impact of observers are sufficient.

Roberts and Renzaglia (1965) were among the first to investigate directly the effects of external monitoring on the behavior of individuals under observation. Counselor-client conversations were recorded either openly with an obtrusive tape recorder or secretly by a hidden recording system. Results revealed that the relative amounts of time that counselor and client spoke during sessions as well as six out of seven categories of counselor behavior did not differ in the two conditions. However, other behaviors were affected by overt recording. Counselors made more interpretive statements when the tape recorder was present. In addition clients voiced more positive self-references when they knew their conversations were being recorded, whereas more negative self-directed comments emerged with covert recording.

In 1969 Surratt, Ulrich, and Hawkins presented suggestive evidence that the presence of an observer in a class setting may increase the frequency of "on task" behavior above the level observed by means of a concealed camera. However, the observer employed in that investigation had been previously involved in delivering tokens to this class for "on task" behavior. As Surratt et al. (1969) noted, the effects of observer presence may have resulted from that observer becoming a discriminative stimulus for "on task" behavior.

In two subsequent investigations, White (Note 3) studied the effects of observer presence on the interaction and activity level of mothers and their children in a simulated living room setting. Both investigations had the advantage of continual covert monitoring of family behavior from a concealed observation area during observer presence in and absence from the living room. Each mother was led to believe that her family would be observed only part of the time, since the observer was also required to watch another family in the next room. White reports lower rates of disruptive behavior for older children and less movement and change of location for all family members during the two half-hour periods when an observer was visible.

Unfortunately, White's investigation was significantly limited by the relatively brief duration of observation. In both studies behavior was recorded for four consecutive half-hour periods during which an observer was alternately absent from and present in the simulated living room. In contrast observational recording in child behavior modification research often involves the presence of an observer for 5 to 10 days during baseline alone. In view of the persistent suggestion that subjects adapt to the presence of observers, investigations encompassing more extensive periods of time seem particularly important.

Mercatoris and Craighead (1974) recently investigated the effects of observation on adult female retardates in a classroom setting. The design involved placing an observer in the classroom for 10 days, removing him for 10 days, reinstating him for five days, and removing him again for five days. All data were collected surreptitiously by means of a videotape camera. Mercatoris and Craighead reported that observer presence increased the frequency of teacher-student interaction; however, the percentage of appropriate behavior displayed by the students did not change.

Another recent study (Hagen, Craighead, & Paul, 1975) evaluated staff reactivity to evaluative behavioral observation on a research ward of a mental hospital. This investigation systematically varied the presence or absence of an observer while continuously recording staff and patient interactions with concealed microphones. It was found that neither the level nor the appropriateness of staff activity was significantly affected by the presence of the observer. Hagen et al. suggested that the absence of reactivity in this investigation might be attributed to three factors: extensive habituation to being observed over many weeks before the study began, frequent and highly unpredictable observation schedules, and a delay of feedback to staff that obscured the relationship between particular observers, observations, and evaluations. In addition they noted that high levels of interaction and appropriate staff behavior existed across experimental conditions. Especially in view of the improvement in reliability coefficients that consistently occurs when observers know the accuracy of their recordings will be assessed (see the section on biases in reliability estimates which follows), one wonders if different results might have emerged had Hagen et al. been working with a less conscientious staff.

An interesting albeit somewhat different approach to the issue of reactivity has been taken by Johnson and G. K. Lobitz (1974). In their view any situation in which an observer is recording behavior presents implicit demand characteristics that can influence the interactions of the observed individuals. For example, in a family in which a child has been referred for psychological assistance, parents may intentionally or unknowingly attempt to accentuate their child's misbehavior when observers are present during the pretreatment assessment to "prove" that the child needs therapy. By asking normal families alternately to make their children look either "good" or "bad," Johnson and G. K. Lobitz found significant differences in both parent and child behavior: Deviant child behavior, negative parental responses, and parental commands were higher on "bad" days than on "good" days. W. C. Lobitz and Johnson (Note 4) later replicated and extended this finding by observing families that included a child whom the parents considered to present significant behavior problems, as well as normal control families. Although their methodology differed slightly from the first study, the results confirmed and extended the generality of Johnson and G. K. Lobitz's (1974) findings.

Although these studies demonstrate that the response set of parents *can* bias observational data, they provide no indication as to how common this form of reactivity actually *is* in the applied settings in which observation is commonly employed. To illuminate the naturally occurring parameters of reactivity, we must return to the controlled evaluation of reactivity to outside observers described earlier (i.e., Hagen et al., 1975; Mercatoris & Craighead, 1974; Roberts & Renzaglia, 1965; White, Note 3). It should be noted that although three of those four studies reported significant effects due to the presence of the observer, only a small proportion of the behaviors recorded in the investigations were actually affected. These findings are consistent with pilot data from three separate studies by Kent, O'Leary, and their associates. In these studies an observer was systematically introduced and withdrawn in a special class setting while recordings of student and teacher behavior were obtained from behind a one-way mirror. Occasional significant effects of the magnitude reported by other investigators have been evidenced. However, substantial difficulty has been encountered in replicating these effects across studies.

The previous studies all employed outside observers to evaluate the effects of reactivity. It is not uncommon, however, for a researcher or clinician to ask a parent or teacher to observe and record the behavior of a referred child. It is not unreasonable to hypothesize (as some have) that individuals under observation should deviate less from their usual behavior patterns when the observer is an ordinary part of the everyday environment.

Hay, Nelson, and Hay (Note 5) cast doubt on this assumption in their examination of the effects of participant observation on teacher and student behavior. Independent observers recorded the behavior of elementary school teachers and students for a 5-day baseline period, then for five days during which each teacher simultaneously recorded the behavior of two target childlren in his or her classroom. One target child had been referred for disruptive behavior; the other had not. Independent observers also collected data on one referred and one nonreferred child who served as controls and were not observed by the teachers. Other than recording their observations whenever a kitchen timer rang (approximately once every four minutes over a one-hour period [cf. Kubany & Sloggett, 1973]), teachers were instructed to continue their regular classroom routines. The results of the study were intriguing. Teacher promptings to target children increased significantly when the teachers began to collect data on these students; target children were also prompted more than control children during this period. Rates of teacher praise and criticism did not change. Referred and nonreferred target children showed significantly more change in appropriate behavior than did control children. Nonreferred children showed significant changes in passive behavior relative to their non-observed controls, while referred children showed similar changes in disruptiveness. The direction of these changes varied from child to child—some showed increases in the particular category, others showed decreases—and visual inspection of the data indicated that the direction was not correlated with the child's referral status. Unfortunately, it was impossible to tell whether these changes were owing to teacher observation per se, the changes in teacher behavior, or some combination of the two.

On the basis of available evidence there seems little reason to doubt that the presence of an observer may, in fact, affect the behavior of those he observes. But the number of factors determining the magnitude and direction of behavior change may be so great that manifest reactivity is scattered and almost completely unpredictable. Although current research warns that some behavioral recordings may be affected by the presence of an observer, there is also the strong suggestion that a variety of other behaviors will be virtually unaffected by in vivo observational procedures.

Current investigations have only begun to untangle some of the specific factors that can contribute to reactivity to observation. Martin, Gelfand, and Hartmann (1971) found that same-sexed peer observers facilitated children's imitative aggression in a free-play situation compared to the amount of aggression they displayed when adults or opposite-sexed peers were present. Mash and Hedley (1975) indicate that the experience of either pleasant or negative interactions with an adult can respectively enhance or decrease children's later performance on a simple motor task when that adult is present. Other investigators have presented data that suggest that reactivity may interact with level of test anxiety in children (Cox, 1966, 1968) and adults (Ganzer, 1968); however, these results are not entirely consistent (Martens, 1969). Unfortunately, the artificiality of the settings and tasks employed in all these studies (with the exception of Martin et al., 1971) may greatly limit the applicability of their conclusions to the study of reactivity in applied settings.

It is clear that future research must probe the issue of reactivity in greater depth with a wider variety of populations in naturalistic assessment situations. This is particularly necessary for adult populations. Influencial investigators in the fields of marital counseling (e.g., Weiss, Hops, & Patterson, 1973) and depression (e.g., Lewinsohn, 1974; Lewinsohn & Shaffer, 1971) already use observational measures as routine parts of their clinical and research assessment batteries, yet research on adult reactivity in these circumstances is virtually nonexistent. Four other general aspects of in vivo observation also provide interesting topics for future research: characteristics of the subject (e.g., hyperactive versus withdrawn; show-off versus shy); physical and behavioral characteristics of the observers (e.g., male versus female; amount of eye contact); characteristics of the observed behaviors (e.g., overt versus subtle); and characteristics of the environment (e.g., particular contingencies in effect, amount of structure).

Until the determinants of reactivity to observation are further investigated, perhaps the best that an investigator can do is to utilize alternate methods of data collection whenever feasible on a spot-check basis. Thus an investigator who primarily utilizes observers placed in the situation of interest might occasionally obtain covert recordings with a videotape camera or tape recorder that could be operated by remote control. Allowing for naturally occurring fluctuations in behavior, a comparison of the recordings obtained by this less obtrusive procedure with the observational recordings obtained in vivo would provide an estimate of reactivity. Use of this procedure assumes, of course, that the necessary apparatus is available in the target setting and that comparable measures can be obtained utilizing automatized and in vivo recording procedures.

Observational Media

A variety of potential benefits is associated with the use of alternatives to direct in vivo observation. Observation mirrors (which conceal the presence of an observer from those whose behavior is recorded) present a number of advantages even if the subjects are aware of the observation procedures. Concealing the observer can eliminate the influence of observer characteristics as well as any distraction that might be owing to observer activity, such as the use of a stopwatch and recording materials. In addition interpersonal contact between the observer and the observed (e.g., eye contact, facial reactions) is eliminated.

The use of videotape recordings provides additional advantages. As will be shown in a subsequent section, assessing the reliability of observational data is a procedure that, in and of itself, may actually inflate reliability estimates. Videotape recordings or closed-circuit television can provide unobtrusive records of ongoing behavior and thus a covert method of evaluating the recordings of in vivo observers. Furthermore, the use of a behavioral code by individual observers or groups of observers may vary dramatically over time, as evidenced by observer drift. Possible confounds with this "instrument decay" could be eliminated by collecting all data on videotapes, then presenting the tapes to observers in random or counterbalanced sequences. Finally, videotape recordings can provide the basis for a variety of methodological evaluations of observational recording procedures.

In view of the many possible improvements in observational methodology that videotapes offer, it is of interest to investigate the extent to which recordings of behavior from videotape apparatus are, in fact, comparable to recordings obtained in vivo. The extent to which substantial differences exist will undoubtedly limit the generalizability of conclusions drawn from laboratory analogs in which videotaped—rather than in vivo—behavior is recorded by observers. Similarly the research utility of videotapes as the basis for raw data will depend to a large extent on the fidelity of recordings, the reliability with which they can be coded, and the practical limitations of the medium itself.

Lovaas, Koegel, Simmons, and Long (1973) reported the use of videotape recordings in providing spot checks on the reliability of observers who recorded the behavior of autistic children over an extended behavioral treatment program. Observers who were unfamiliar with both the children and the treatment procedures were trained to record five categories of behavior: self-stimulation, appropriate speech, echolalia, nonverbal social behavior, and appropriate play. They then rated videotapes that had been filmed at various points throughout the program. Because pre- and post-treatment videotapes were viewed in random order, the potential biasing effects resulting from increased familiarity with the experiment and/or the experience of observing children progress through an orderly treatment intervention were lessened. Lovaas et al. indicated that data recorded by both the experienced and the naive (spot check) observers showed the same pre-post trends. However, the authors do not report actual reliability coefficients and do acknowledge differences in absolute frequencies recorded for some of the categories. They attribute these differences to reduced fidelity of the videotape recordings, particularly for speech and facial expression.

Eisler, Hersen, and Agras (1973) more systematically compared in vivo observations of nonverbal marital interactions (looking and smiling) with simultaneous ratings of the same couple's behavior using a videotape monitor in an adjacent room. Reliabilities obtained by pairs of observers utilizing each media did not differ substantially. Similarly Hawn, Brown, and LeBlanc (Note 6) found that observations of nonverbal teacher behavior showed equivalent average reliabilities whether made in vivo, from continuous videotapes, or by switching the videotape on and off at regular 10-second intervals. In contrast teacher and student verbal behavior was consistently more reliably recorded in vivo than by continuous videotape. The on-off procedure improved reliabilities to in vivo levels, suggesting that modifications in recording procedures can improve the quality of data obtained from videotaped recordings. Conclusions drawn from both these studies are limited, however, by the investigators' omission of reliability coefficients that indicated the extent to which observational recordings concurred across different media.

Kent, Dietz, Diament, and O'Leary (in press) compared the effects of different observational media on observational recordings of nine categories of disruptive behavior in a special class setting. During observation sessions, three groups of three observers recorded the behavior of children simultaneously in vivo, through a one-way mirror, and by closed-circuit television. The composition of each observer group and the observers' assignment to the three media were carefully counterbalanced so that each observer computed reliability with a variety of other observers and recorded behavior using each of the media. Significant differences in levels of recorded behavior among media occurred on only one category, vocalization. For this category, in vivo observers recorded frequencies approximately 60 percent higher than did observers utilizing either mirror or television. Because the category of noise (roughly defined as nonverbal sounds, such as tapping a pencil) was not similarly affected, the authors ascribed this finding to the difficulty reported by Lovaas et al. (1973) and Hawn et al. (Note 6) in obtaining sufficient fidelity to discriminate speech, rather than a general liability for categories involving the detection of sound. It is interesting to note that the recordings of observers who had a great deal of prior experience with either in vivo, television, or mirrors did not differ from those produced by observers with substantially less experience with the same medium.

There were, however, slight differences in the occurrence reliabilities obtained for each of the three media. The average reliability for the composite of the nine categories was 0.71 in vivo, 0.69 behind the mirror, and 0.65 by television. These are similar to the differences between continuous videotape and on-the-spot observation reported by Hawn et al. (Note 6). Lower reliabilities emerged from comparisons among observers recording the same events but using different media. The average reliability of the composite score was 0.58 between in vivo and mirror, 0.55 between in vivo observation and television, and 0.50 between mirror and television.

Two aspects of these results are quite encouraging. The three media produced equivalent behavioral frequencies for eight out of nine code categories, and difficulties in recording the ninth—verbal behavior—may possibly be offset by turning the videotape monitor off at regular intervals (Hawn et al., Note 6), or by replaying the tape. Furthermore, the within-media reliabilities were reduced less than 0.06 by employing mirror and television instead of in vivo recording, a difference that is probably of little consequence in most applied investigations. In general this suggests that observation mirrors and closed-circuit television may provide acceptable alternatives to in vivo observation. Unfortunately, more substantial decreases in reliability, ranging from 0.05 to 0.21, emerged when recordings in different media were compared. These decreases imply that although television, one-way mirrors, and in vivo observation can provide equivalent data when employed throughout the entirety of a study, interchanging the media may result in a lack of uniformity in obtained data. Investigators who intend to use videotapes to make unannounced spot-check reliability assessments with in vivo observers may therefore be advised to evaluate the between-media comparability of their particular observation measures before utilizing this procedure.

It should be noted that the use of videotape equipment does entail certain logistic limitations. To reduce obtrusiveness, cameras must be placed in a fixed location for the duration of an observation period; lighting and microphone arrangement may also restrict the flexibility and fidelity of the medium (Herbert, 1970; Weick, 1968). Furthermore, in vivo observers are (for the most part) not subject to sudden breakdowns. Nonetheless, the clear methodological advantages of lessening or eliminating potential biases in observational recording seem to more than justify considering such alternatives to in vivo recordings.

Reducing Biases in Data Collection

All the evaluations presented here suggest that the investigator employing behavioral observations may be surprisingly immune to the potential expectation biases that have plagued other methods of data collection. Based on the few unconfounded studies of expectation bias in observational procedures (e.g., Kent et al., 1974; Shuller & McNamara, Note 2), it is possible to state that knowledge by observers of the predicted effects of treatment may be insufficient to significantly bias observational recordings that utilize highly specific behavioral codes. This is particularly fortunate as it is often difficult, if not impossible, to conceal treatment onset and the intended direction of change from observers who are familiar with a particular field setting.

Other evidence, however, highlights the necessity of limiting feedback to observers regarding the success of particular manipulations. The study by O'Leary, Kent, and Kanowitz (1975) indicates that observers may quickly and dramatically modify their application of a behavioral code when given consistent evaluative feedback. This is unfortunate, as the present authors formerly found it highly desirable, both from an educational and motivational point of view, to involve undergraduate research assistants in an ongoing discussion of treatment. Although this practice should be discouraged, in certain cases observers must be involved in continuing discussions of treatment results as, for example, when resident staff or graduate students also double as observers for budgetary reasons. In these cases it is critical to employ naive observers on a spot-check basis (cf., Lovaas et al., 1973) to evaluate whether behavioral observations have been biased.

The possibility of reactivity to the presence of an observer and to the demand characteristics of observational assessment remains largely unresolved. This is particularly disturbing because scattered and unpredictable effects of observer presence are sometimes of substantial magnitude. As a precautionary measure, the obtrusiveness of an observer should be reduced in any way possible. Observers who dress and behave in an inconspicuous manner seem less likely, on an a priori basis, to have continued effects on the behaviors of interest.

Although it may appear that personnel already present in a particular field setting could best record behavior unobtrusively while continuing their daily tasks, Hay et al. (Note 5) have shown that the recordings of participant observers can also suffer from reactive effects on both the observer and the observed, as well as from a lack of reliability. However, Hay et al. do not indicate whether the teachers in their study ever received any practice with the observational code and/or performance feedback during training. The poor reliabilities they reported could thus be owing either to training or performance deficits. The magnitude of reactivity found in the Hay et al. study implies that although outside observers are in most cases more obtrusive and create more logistical problems than on-the-scene participant observers, the data they produce may be paradoxically more generalizable to conditions when an observer is not present. Clearly, though, the parameters of participant observation are far from defined. Hay et al.'s investigation must be replicated with different populations and experimental conditions before conclusive statements on the merits and liabilities of outside observers and their participant counterparts can be made.

It is important that outside observers should not interact with the person they are observing any more than absolutely necessary, nor should they be involved in any phase of the treatment program themselves (Mash & Hedley, 1975; Surratt et al., 1969). Finally, it is helpful to provide persons who are to be observed with an acceptable and nonthreatening rationale for the activities of observers and to allow a substantial amount of time for subjects to habituate to their presence.

Comparative evaluations of observation media (Eisler et al., 1973; Kent, Dietz, Diament, & O'Leary, in press; Hawn et al., Note 6) suggest that both one-way mirrors and videotape may prove useful in evaluating and eliminating biases associated with in vivo observational recordings. Particularly in view of the low-cost availability of portable observation booths and videotape recording apparatus, utilization of this technology may be available to large numbers of investigators in the foreseeable future. It would be particularly fortunate if in vivo data could be routinely supplemented by videotapes periodically collected throughout the course of a variety of applied studies (cf. Lovaas et al., 1973). Such control data would not only provide a clear evaluation of the quality of in vivo observational data obtained but would in addition generate a growing data bank regarding the behaviors, coding systems, treatment populations, and settings most likely to yield biased data.

BIASES IN ESTIMATING RELIABILITY

When observational recording procedures are employed, frequent estimates of the similarity of simultaneous judgments are obtained from pairs of observers. These samples of observer agreement or correlation are referred to as *reliability* and provide the basis for assertions that behavioral recordings are the replicable product of well-specified recording procedures, rather than the idiosyncratic judgments of several observers. Either an experimenter, an observer trainer, or a member of a group of observers may serve as the assessor and compare his or her own ratings with those of the other observers to compute reliability.

Reliability coefficients are intended to reflect the quality of behavioral recordings obtained throughout a particular project or investigation. Unfortunately, the assessment of observer reliability typically occurs under a set of circumstances that may enhance the reliability estimate. The observer not only knows when evaluations will occur but also has experience from training or from previous reliability assessments in comparing his or her recordings with those of the assessor. Recent research has suggested that reliabilities obtained in this fashion may be substantially and spuriously enhanced. Likewise, differences in the actual situations viewed by observers can produce differentially reliable recordings of behavior.

Complexity Factors Influencing Reliability

The possibility that all behaviors, individuals, and interactions cannot be observed with equal reliability has received surprisingly little attention in the literature on observer reliability. On an intuitive basis it seems obvious that some situations will be easier to observe than others. Recording subcategories of verbal behavior, for example, will be facilitated if the speaker enunciates clearly. Coding family interaction will be more difficult when two simultaneous discussions are occurring than when everyone is quietly playing a card game.

Jones, Reid, and their colleagues have empirically investigated the possibility that more complex situations are less reliably observed than simpler situations (Jones, Reid, & Patterson, 1974; Reid, Skinrud, Taplin, & Jones, Note 7). They define complexity as a "measure of the number of discriminations required of an observer during a data collection session" (Jones et al., 1974). Negative correlations ranging from −0.52 and −0.75 were consistently obtained in a number of studies in which observers' percentage agreement scores were correlated with complexity scores derived from the observers' data. Furthermore, certain situational and subject factors were related to complexity. Observational recordings revealed greater complexity during sessions immediately before or after a reliability session than during sessions when a second observer was present for a reliability check. In addition observations of children showed greater complexity than observations of parents (Jones et al., 1974).

The consistency of this relationship between complexity and reliability led Jones and his associates to conclude that reliability coefficients will be misleading when complexity differs systematically between reliability and nonreliability sessions. This bias may be attenuated, to some extent, by sampling reliability widely across subjects, situations, and experimental conditions. Once the data are collected, complexity levels for assessment and nonassessment sessions can be compared. If these levels differ significantly, reliability coefficients can then be weighted according to the level of complexity of the data on which they are based.

Although these data are intriguing, their implications for observational procedures are still tentative. The 28-category interaction code used by Jones et al. (1974) was designed to be exhaustive, that is, any behavior should be scorable under one of the category definitions. A measure of complexity has yet to be derived for nonexhaustive and/or less complex codes, let alone tested to see if the relationship between complexity and reliability can be generalized to other observational measures. Sources of differences in complexity, both in behavior and in recordings, are still largely unspecified. Nonetheless, the findings of Jones et al. (1974) are striking and merit further in-depth study.

The issue of complexity has been investigated from a different vantage point—that of code complexity—by Mash and McElwee (1974). In an analogue study observers used one of two exhaustive codes to score verbal behavior from audiotapes. One code contained four categories; for the other, each category was subdivided, yielding a total of eight. Reliability was computed between observers and a criterion protocol (a single recording established a priori as a standard of comparison for reliability computation) for each of the tapes. Results indicated that significantly better reliabilities were obtained with the code with fewer categories. A second finding of this study, confirmed by a subsequent replication (Mash & Makohoniuk, 1975), revealed that repeated initial training with a tape recording of interaction that occurred in a highly predictable fashion resulted in poorer agreement on a subsequent tape than did training with unpredictable interaction. Extrapolations from these laboratory analogues to the naturalistic circumstances of observational assessment must be made cautiously. Observers rated only two 6.5-minute tapes through the entirety of these studies (each was rated four to six times) and were never given performance feedback on their ratings. Pretraining was limited to 10 minutes. In addition the increase in the number of categories in this study effectively meant that observers were required to make finer discriminations among the *same* pool of behaviors, rather than attending to a greater number of different classes of behavior. Despite these limitations, these analogue studies have opened an empirical door into areas previously neglected and subject only to speculation.

It has also been noted anecdotally that observers "do better" once they are accustomed to a particular setting or group of individuals. Johnson and Bolstad (1973), for example, state:

"Our observers are convinced that calibration (reliability) scores obtained on a single day of observation are probably lower than would be obtained over two or more days of observation. The reason for this belief is that the calibrator would logically have more difficulty in adapting to each new home environment and identifying the subjects of observation on the first day in the home than on subsequent days." (p. 26)

We have noted a similar phenomenon with observers whose preliminary training included both in vivo and videotape observations of a small laboratory classroom. Reliability typically drops dramatically during initial observations in normal public school classrooms and subsequently increases after a few practice sessions in the new environment. Additional controlled research aimed at sorting out the situational factors responsible for these fluctuations will be of importance both practically and theoretically.

Knowledge of Reliability Assessment

Reid (1970) was the first to report "a possible methodological problem" in the reliability assessment of observation data. Reid trained 11 student observers in the application of a 33-category observational code. All observers viewed videotapes of mother-child interaction during the training stage and, after reaching an acceptable level of reliability with criterion protocols, were told that they would rate additional tapes but that their recordings would not be evaluated further. In reality covert reliability assessments were conducted throughout the study by comparing the observers' recordings with the criterion protocols. Reid reported that observers demonstrated an average drop of 25 percentage points in their agreement with the criterion from the end of training and overt reliability assessment to the very first day of covert assessment.

In a subsequent study Taplin and Reid (1973) investigated the effects of three "instructional sets" as determiners of observer accuracy in recording. Eighteen undergraduates were trained to record the interactions of a group of three mothers and their four children from a series of videotapes. After training the observers were divided into three groups and given different instructions. The first group was told that the experimenter would not evaluate their data collection. The second group, termed the *random-check group,* was told that any part of their work might be checked by the experimenter at a subsequent time. Finally, the third group of observers was told that they would be spot checked on occasion but that the evaluation of their recordings would be obvious when it occurred. In reality reliability was later computed for every session, regardless of instructions, using standard criterion protocols for each of the videotapes.

The results of the Taplin and Reid (1973) investigation were clear and compelling. The random-check group maintained the highest consistent level of agreement with criterion ratings. The no-check group maintained an intermediate level of reliability throughout the study. The spot-check group evidenced the lowest reliability measures for every session except those during which overt evaluations were performed. Taplin and Reid conclude:

"The major thrust of the findings . . . is to point to the danger of assuming that unmonitored observational data are reliable. Instead of being established a priori, the reliability of observational data ought to be empirically demonstrated. Without such demonstrations, the accuracy of observational data can only be a matter of faith." (p. 553)

Familiarity with the Assessor

Romanczyk, Kent, Diament, and O'Leary (1973) hypothesized that estimates of observer reliability are inflated not only by awareness that an assessment is taking place but also by knowledge of the identity of the observer with whom recordings will be compared. This would be the case, for example, if observers adjusted their rating criteria to match the idiosyncratic ways in which each assessor interpreted the behavioral code. To test this hypothesis, Romanczyk et al. assessed the reliability of five trained observers with each of two assessors under two experimental conditions. During the overt assessment condition, observers were told that either Keith or Laurie (the two assessors) would check their reliability at the end of the session. During covert assessment, observers were not told that reliability would be assessed. Throughout the study, both assessors simultaneously recorded behavior at all times with each observer whose reliability was being measured.

One purpose of the study was to determine if observers would change their style of observation to match the unique ways that different assessors applied the behavioral code. For this reason the definitions of four of the nine categories of the behavioral rating code were modified so that each assessor used stable but different observational criteria. As a result of these modifications, the code employed by Keith produced higher frequencies of vocalization and noise than the code employed by Laurie. For example, in employing the modified definitions of vocalization, Keith recorded even the softest verbalizations and any "mouthings" the child might make, whereas Laurie recorded only the louder vocalizations and ignored humming, whispering, and sighing. To balance the design of the study, the behavioral code was further modified so that Laurie recorded greater frequencies of playing and orienting than did Keith. These differential observational criteria were defined in great detail to maintain a moderately high correlation between the assessors' ratings across experimental conditions.

For 2½ weeks prior to the experimental conditions, Laurie and Keith employed their respective versions of the modified code and at regular intervals computed reliability with each observer a median of four times (range two to four). At these times the assessor and the observer jointly determined the number of agreements and disagreements and calculated the reliability coefficient. These four reliability computations provided the only opportunity for observers to note the unique observational criteria being employed by the two assessors. At no time did either assessor overtly contrast his or her rating criteria with that of the other.

After the study had ended, the protocols of both assessors were used to measure the reliability of the observers during all sessions of both overt and covert assessment conditions. Across the eight days of the study, reliabilities on the modified categories averaged 0.77 with the identified assessor and 0.53 with the unidentified assessor. It is clear from these data that when differences exist among assessors in the application of an observational code, observers are able to match those differences.

In addition Romanczyk et al. (1973) replicated the findings of Reid (1970) and Taplin and Reid (1973) that reliability estimates are substantially lower when observers are unaware of assessment. An average occurrence reliability of 0.77 with overt assessment by a known assessor diminished to an average of 0.33 when reliability was covertly checked. This investigation clearly implies that overt reliability assessment performed at regular intervals throughout a study may not reflect the actual consistency of observation records done on a day-to-day basis. Thus studies reporting reliabilities between 0.70 and 0.80 during overt assessment may be generating data that are in reality substantially less reliable.

Consensual Drift Among Observer Groups

In describing the evolution of expectation research earlier in this chapter, Kent's (1972) dissertation research was described. Recall that 40 observers were trained in a large group, then divided into smaller groups for three additional 1½-hour training sessions. Examination of data from these groups for the subsequent 4-day period revealed that intergroup reliabilities had substantially improved. Unfortunately, during the short period of training in small groups, each observer group had apparently developed enough minor modifications in the application of the behavioral code to produce significant differences in the frequencies with which seven of the nine observational categories were recorded. It seemed clear that the magnitude of these differences would have been sufficient to distort treatment effects had these groups been assigned to view different treatment conditions at this point. Furthermore, the instability of these differences eliminated the possibility of developing "individual equations" to adjust the ratings of each group to make them comparable to one another.

For these reasons the subsequent evaluation of expectation bias (Kent, O'Leary, Diament, & Dietz, 1974) was specifically designed to assess as well as control the confound of consensual observer drift. Twenty observers were trained for 10 hours to match the recordings of an experimenter. The observers were then randomly paired and were told to compare their recordings only with those of their partners. After each pair had practiced recording behavior and comparing their observations for five hours, reliability (computed for each pair) for three consecutive observation periods averaged 0.72. At this point pairs of observers were randomly assigned to the two expectation conditions and continued to record behavior from videotapes for a period of eight days.

The design of this study allowed an evaluation not only of expectation bias but also of the extent to which behavioral recordings were affected by differences in recording between pairs of raters. Five factors were included in this design: expectation (predicted decrease in disruptive behavior versus no change), phase of the supposed study that had been videotaped (baseline versus treatment), identity of the target child, observation session, and observer pair. Analyses of variance revealed that recordings of three of the nine categories (playing, orienting, and noise) were significantly influenced by the main effects produced by differences among observer pairs. Furthermore, the observer pair factor was involved in a number of significant interactions with other factors in the design.

To the extent that different observer pairs generate differing behavioral recordings, reliabilities calculated within a pair of observers should be greater than reliabilities calculated between pairs of observers. This was, in fact, the case. An analysis of variance indicated significant differences in estimates of reliability as a function of computation within versus between pairs of observers ($F = 8.939$, $df = 1, 18$, $p < 0.05$). Overall, the reliabilities that resulted when observations of partners were compared averaged nine percentage points higher than reliabilities computed between recordings of individuals who had not been paired with each other.

Johnson and Bolstad (1973) described an unpublished study by DeMaster and Reid that corroborated these findings. The observers in this investigation were divided into 14 pairs and assigned to one of three feedback conditions in which they discussed the accuracy of their observations of videotape segments. In the first group observers scored and discussed their recordings using a previously established criterion protocol as a standard of comparison. In the second group pairs of observers discussed and compared their recordings with each other without a criterion standard, whereas the third group neither computed reliabilities nor discussed their recordings. DeMaster and Reid found that within-pair reliability scores across groups were higher than agreement scores calculated either with the criterion protocol or between observers who were not in the same pair. Further analyses revealed that the criterion protocol group obtained higher within-pair reliabilities than the observer pairs, which outperformed the no-reliability group. Basing their conclusions on this finding, Johnson and Bolstad recommend "recalibrating" observers throughout a study by means of ongoing training sessions using videotaped materials for which criterion protocols have been established.

The bulk of this evidence points to the conclusion that reliability estimates calculated from the data of observers who have trained and rated behavior as a team provide inadequate and inflated measures of the uniformity with which a behavioral code has been applied throughout a study employing different observer groups. A corollary problem results from the sometimes significant differences in actual frequencies of behavior that are recorded—frequencies on which statistical analyses and investigatory conclusions will be based. This issue is further compounded, as Johnson and Bolstad (1973) indicate, by the results of the Romanczyk et al. (1973) investigation: "It is possible for observers to produce one kind of consensual drift with some calibrators and an opposite consensual drift with others" (Johnson & Bolstad, 1973, p. 24). Suggestions for mitigating these difficulties will be discussed in a later section of the chapter.

Cheating Among Observers

In field-experimental evaluations of behavioral treatment procedures, observers often record behavior in the treatment setting on a regular basis unaccompanied by the principal investigator. Under these conditions pairs of observers are periodically asked to observe the same behaviors simultaneously and to compute a reliability coefficient. Implicit in this request is the desire of the experimenter to obtain accurate and high measures of agreement. This arrangement provides the opportunity for observers intentionally or carelessly to improve their reliabilities rather than disappoint their supervisor. This can be accomplished either by communicating with one another during the process of behavioral recording, by modifying the recordings during reliability computations to increase the level of agreement, or by making computational errors that spuriously inflate the reliability coefficient.

An early study by Azrin et al. (1961) lends credence to these possibilities. In attempting to replicate another investigator's work on verbal conditioning, the investigators assigned students the task of carrying out the experimental procedures, only to discover later that some of the students had deliberately fabricated their data to fulfill their assignment and to please the experimenters. It should be noted, however, that the undergraduate students in this study worked alone and received virtually no supervision in conducting their experiments.

Observers in applied studies, in contrast, are usually supervised on a regular basis and work in teams, thus discouraging actual fabrication of data. Nonetheless, O'Leary and Kent (1973) have reported two pilot studies that illustrate the enhancement of reliability measures by ambitious undergraduates. During the initial training period of the first study, 12 observers recorded behavior from videotapes and computed reliabilities while an experimenter was in the room. This lessened the possibility that observers might discuss and modify their recordings during reliability computation. In fact it was emphasized that any observer caught cheating would fail the course in child behavior modification research in which they were all enrolled. During the final six days of training, however, O'Leary and Kent arranged for the experimenter to be called from the room for one of the two daily 12½-minute observation and reliability computation sessions. In contrasting reliabilities obtained for these six days in the presence and absence of the experimenter, O'Leary and Kent found average occurrence reliabilities of 0.66 during the absence of the experimenter and 0.55 during the experimenter's presence. This difference illustrated a systematic tendency for reliabilities to be higher during the period when observers were unsupervised.

In a second investigation (O'Leary & Kent, 1973) two groups of five pairs of observers recorded the behavior of children from videotapes and calculated reliability with their partners after one out of every four observation periods. The observers were supervised during the observation sessions by two experimenters who stressed that communication and modifying recordings were strictly forbidden but who did not closely monitor the actual arithmetic of reliability computations. After the study had ended, O'Leary and Kent evaluated the observers' calculations of reliability for mathematical errors. The average occurrence reliability computed by observers had been 0.66 over the eight days of observation, in contrast with an average of 0.58 computed by the experimenters. This tendency toward errors in computation could spuriously inflate a reported level of agreement.

Sources of Bias in Combination

Investigations cited thus far suggest that assessment of observer reliability typically occurs under a set of advantageous circumstances. The occurrence of a reliability-check session is quite obvious, and the observer also has had prior experience comparing recordings with the particular assessor. Thus an observer has the opportunity to modify his coding behavior during reliability assessment, for example, by attending more carefully (Reid, 1970) and attempting to approximate the recording style of the assessor (Romanczyk et al., 1973). In addition when several groups of observers are involved in a project and the observers serve as assessors for one another, reliability is routinely computed among observers in the same group, rather than among observers in different groups. If, over time, group differences in recording have emerged, reliability computed within groups will be systematically higher than measures computed among observer groups (O'Leary & Kent, 1973). Finally, reliability is frequently assessed without the presence of the experimenter or another monitor, which allows the possibility of interobserver influence or miscalculations during reliability assessment (O'Leary & Kent, 1973). These characteristics of reliability assessment in field experimental settings—knowledge of assessment and assessor, absence of the experimenter, and calculation of reliability within groups—may be predicted to yield reliability estimates that are spuriously inflated. A study by Kent, Kanowitz, O'Leary, and Cheiken (in press) extended earlier investigations by examining the cumulative effects of these factors in a single study and over an extended period of time.

These investigators trained 12 undergraduates as a group in the use of the nine-category observation code employed in earlier studies. During training, all 12 observers reached an overall level of occurrence reliability of 0.70 with each other. After training, the 12 observers were randomly divided into three groups of four members each and were told that all future computation of reliability and discussion of disagreements in recording would occur only within their respective groups. The experimenter stressed the importance of maintaining accurate recordings at all time and emphatically discouraged any copying of another observer's recordings.

Data were collected on 22 days across an 8-week period. During each day, observers viewed three 12½-minute videotape segments. All 12 observers viewed each videotape simultaneously, each group from its respective row of chairs in the room. When a reliability assessment had been announced, each group of observers adjourned immediately after viewing that videotape segment to the room provided for that group. There each group member computed his or her reliability with the assessor, and disagreements in recordings were discussed.

During each 2-day period, the observers viewed six videotaped segments under six observation conditions. The six conditions were determined by a two-by-three matrix that combined two observation conditions (i.e., experimenter present or absent during the observation period) with three different levels of information provided to the observers. Observers were either (1) not told that their reliability would be checked, (2) told that reliability would be assessed but were not provided with the identity of the assessor who was later selected from the experimental group, or (3) told that reliability would be assessed and were provided with the identity of which member of the group would serve as the assessor. Each of the six experimental conditions occurred 11 times during the 22 days of the study.

After all observations had been collected, occurrence reliabilities among observers within each group were calculated for recordings generated under each of the experimental conditions. In addition, reliabilities were computed between observers in different groups. Analysis of the data was limited to descriptive rather than inferential statistics because the latter are complicated by such factors as the likely nonnormal distribution of reliability coefficients and complex interdependencies in the data matrix.

Kent et al. (in press) reported that knowledge of assessment and assessor increased occurrence reliability over the no-knowledge condition an average of 10 percentage points (ranging from one to 38 points) on the nine behavioral categories. Absence of the experimenter increased reliability on individual categories an average of six points (range two to 14). Computation of reliability within the observer group increased reliability an average of 11 points (range three to 22) over between-group computations. Every experimental factor without exception produced inflated reliabilities on each of the nine behavioral categories.

A subsequent analysis evaluated the increase in reliability estimates produced by the experimental factors in combination. That combination of factors predicted to produce the highest reliability—knowledge of assessment and assessor, absence of experimenter, and computation of reliabilities within the observer group—was compared with that combination of factors predicted to produce the lowest reliability—no knowledge of assessment or assessor, experimenter present, and computation of reliability between the groups. The effect of the experimental factors in combination ranged from an inflation of 0.04 for the category *modified out-of-chair* to 0.66 for the category *touching.* On the average the experimental factors in combination increased reliability 28 points, from 0.50 to a respectable 0.78. These data unquestionably indicate that high reliabilities obtained under typical conditions of assessment may be extremely misleading.

Reducing Biases in Reliability Assessment

Wiggins (Note 8) has reflected the results of investigations of biases in reliability assessment:

"It makes a certain amount of sense. We all work a little bit harder when the boss is around. Our opinions are perhaps a shade closer to the boss's in his presence. And we are more accurate in describing events that have been observed by others than we are in recounting exploits that cannot be verified." (pp. 5–6)

How then can we make human observers less subject to the influence of these understandable characteristics? Procedural modifications in reliability assessment arrangements could contribute to more accurate estimates of observer agreement. Most important, observers should be informed that reliability checks will be performed covertly on a regular basis, rather than being specifically told each time an assessment session occurs. Unobtrusive reliability checks could be arranged, for example, if an experimenter who continually monitors observers throughout a study also covertly checks reliability on occasion. This solution would be useful only if the experimenter's behavior were consistent during regular monitoring and reliability checks; otherwise, observers would soon realize that their accuracy was being evaluated. An alternate arrangement could be employed when observers are simultaneously collecting data on several individuals in the same setting. Each observer could be given a schedule specifying the subject to be observed during a particular time interval; these schedules would be prearranged to provide for occasional simultaneous observation of the same behavior by two observers. By comparing recordings during overlapping observations, the experimenter could later determine the level of agreement. A potential difficulty with this arrangement is that observers, if motivated to do so, could easily determine from one another which observation intervals had been designated for reliability assessment and could respond as they would during an overt reliability evaluation.

An additional difficulty in obtaining unbiased data lies in the tendency for an observer's interpretation of a behavioral code to evolve such that it more closely matches that of observers with whom he is working. Thus when observers are divided into different groups, different modifications of the code may emerge. These modifications seem to have an unpredictable effect on frequencies of behaviors recorded by observers and therefore must be differentiated from potential systematic biases owing for example, to experimenter feedback to an observer. Eliminating information regarding the results of reliability assessment might eliminate this consensual drift. More likely, however, each observer would then develop unique modifications of the behavioral code.

It is clearly unwise to confound individual observers or groups of observers with different experimental conditions. In between-subject designs one could employ a single group of observers to record data from all treatment groups. Alternately, several groups of observers could be rotated periodically from one treatment group to another. Neither of these procedures guarantees that the recordings from a particular experimental condition will represent comparable applications of the behavioral code at any two points in time. On the other hand, each procedure does ensure that the data from each treatment group will be equally affected by any modifications in the behavioral code that do occur.

Even in single-group, within-subject designs the possibility exists that observers may drift in their application of a behavioral code, yielding data recorded during one experimental condition that is incomparable with data from a subsequent phase. In within-subject designs the critical comparison is between an experimental condition instituted at one time and a second condition instituted at some later point. To alleviate drift in this type of investigation, a number of independent observer groups could be used across all experimental phases. For example, if each condition lasted a week or longer, a different group of observers could be employed on each day of the week. Drift among groups would thus add to the variation in data from each condition but would not distort comparisons between the conditions. Alternately, the behavior of the target individual or group could be videotaped throughout the experiment and these recordings later rated in random order. When this is impractical, a smaller number of videotapes could be filmed at random times during each experimental condition. Ratings of these tapes would provide a measure of the validity of trends revealed across time by in vivo behavioral recordings (e.g., Lovaas et al., 1973).

As an alternative to these methods of equalizing the effects of observer drift across groups and conditions, Johnson and Bolstad (1973) recommend that observers frequently retrain throughout an investigation by periodically rating videotape segments and then comparing their recordings with preestablished criterion protocols. This, they suggest, would help allay observer drift by establishing a set of stable standards for all experimental conditions. Although this type of retraining is potentially quite useful, in light of the Romanczyk et al. (1973) findings that observers may use a behavioral code quite differently as a function of different circumstances of assessment, the additional precautionary measures suggested above are advisable even in the context of frequent recalibration.

Selecting a Reliability Measure

The method of computing reliability is an important determiner of the magnitude of the reliability coefficient and, therefore, of the conclusions reached about the quality of one's data. Selection of an appropriate and psychometrically acceptable measure of the similarity of observational recordings is an exceedingly complex matter, and a variety of methods is available. The present discussion is intended to provide a number of guidelines for the reader who must interpret levels of reliability reported in published articles, and for the research investigator who wishes to compare the general advantages and liabilities of different available approaches.*

For our purposes here we will consider reliability computation as a determination of the similarity of recordings by pairs of observers at a particular time. These same procedures can also be employed to evaluate the consistency with which an individual observer applies a behavioral code over time (e.g., by obtaining periodic ratings of the same videotape). The "accuracy" of an observer can also be computed using these methods if an experimenter has access to a criterion measure or protocol that he is willing to view as "truth." The bulk of the present discussion will concern the often used *interval* recording methods in which the presence or absence of individual behaviors is recorded during successive short intervals of time. Alternate methods of recording behavior, such as counting the *frequency* with which behavior occurs or measuring the *duration* of each instance of the target behavior will be considered separately.

As a first step in calculating reliability, an experimenter must determine the units of data to be employed. When observers are recording a number of different categories of behavior simultaneously, reliability may be calculated for the individual categories and/or for composite measures (i.e., sums of some or all of the categories). In addition, reliability can be calculated on the basis of short intervals within a particular observation session or by combining these intervals and using only the overall total frequency of a given behavior for that session.

The most important guideline in calculating reliability for a research report is that the data points that serve as the units of a statistical or graphic analysis must themselves be evaluated in terms of reliability. Thus an investigator who analyzes individual session frequencies for each of three treatment conditions must determine the reliability for each session, combining individual subjects' data in each treatment. The investigator considering these same data at a more molecular level by looking at patterns in each subject's data during each observation session must determine

* Much of the material concerning reliability computation presented in this section is based on an excellent manuscript by Donald Hartmann (in press).

the reliability of those units of data. An experimenter analyzing only a composite measure of a number of behavioral categories need only determine the reliability of the composite. If any of the individual categories are analyzed separately, the reliability of those specific categories must also be determined.

In addition to analysis of the reliability of units of data to be presented in research reports, the investigator may be interested in computing the reliability of smaller units of data. The purpose of this may be to refine a code, to train or provide feedback to observers, or to aid in preliminary evaluations of small subsets of data. These analyses are primarily for the experimenter's benefit. Although it is appropriate to present them as supplementary information in a research report, the computation of such measures primarily serves to provide guidance in determining and, if necessary, taking steps to enhance the quality of data.

Two general types of reliability measures will be considered here. Hartmann (in press) terms these "trial" and "session" reliability measures. *Trial* measures utilize data recorded during small intervals of time in an individual observation session as the basic units of analysis. *Session* reliability measures are based on the total number of intervals in which a particular behavior was recorded, the total frequency of the behavior, or the total duration of occurrence during each individual session.

Four basic types of trial reliability measures have been reported recently. In describing these methods of computation, we will utilize a two-by-two matrix for representing the simultaneous recordings of two observers (see Table 9–1). Cell A of this matrix represents the number of intervals in which the recordings of both observers reflected the occurrence of a particular behavior. Cell *D* represents the synchronous recordings of nonoccurrence. Cell *B* represents those intervals in which Observer 1 rated the target behavior while Observer 2 recorded a nonoccurrence. Cell *C* is the

Table 9–1. Frequency Matrix for the Simultaneous Recordings of Two Observers

		Observer 1	
		Occurrence of Target Behavior	Nonoccurence of Target Behavior
Observer 2	Occurrence of Target Behavior	*A*	*C*
	Nonoccurence of Target Behavior	*B*	*D*

converse of Cell B. Thus Cells A and D represent agreement on the respective occurrence and nonoccurrence of a particular behavior, and Cells B and C represent disagreement.

The first and most common measure of reliability in current literature has been termed *agreement reliability* (Hartmann, in press). This is a measure of agreement on both occurrence and nonoccurrence of the defined behaviors. Computationally, the agreement measure involves summing A and D and dividing that sum by the total $(A + B + C + D)$. As will be noted later, this measure is greatly dependent on chance agreement among observers.

A second type of measure is *occurrence reliability,* computed by dividing A by the total $(A + B + C)$. This measure is appropriate when an investigator is primarily concerned with the rate of occurrence of behavior, especially when this rate remains relatively low throughout the study. When a target behavior occurs infrequently, agreement reliability will yield high reliability coefficients largely as a function of observers' chance agreements on the nonoccurrence of the behavior. If analyses are based on the frequency with which the target behavior occurred, high reliability in recording the absence of that behavior is not particularly relevant. Under this circumstance computation of agreement reliability is appropriate.

A variation of occurrence reliability is used to assess reliability in recording nonoccurrence, computed by dividing D by the total $(B + C + D)$. This is used when the nonoccurrence of a particular behavior or group of behaviors is not only low in frequency but also represents the focus of investigation. This might be the case, for example, if an investigator wished to use the absence of a number of observable physical reactions as an index of speech anxiety. In this case a measure of the reliability of observers in recording nonoccurrence would be most appropriate.

All the measures described thus far are, in fact, inflated to some extent by chance agreements among observers on the occurrence and/or nonoccurrence of behaviors. Computation of chance agreement on the occurrence of behavior involves multiplying $(A + B)$ by $(A + C)$ and dividing the product by the total $(A + B + C + D)$. Using this formula, if two observers record the occurrence of behavior during 60 percent of the observation intervals, their chance agreement in Cell A will be 0.36. Only reliability scores that exceed that figure can be viewed as reflections of observers' nonchance agreement in recording. Similarly, chance agreement on the nonoccurrence of behavior can be determined by multiplying $(B + D)$ by $(C + D)$ and dividing the product by $(A + B + C + D)$. Thus if the target response were not recorded 90 percent of the time, observers would agree by chance alone on the nonoccurrence of that behavior during 81 percent of the intervals. Finally, when an occurrence-nonoccurrence reliability measure is employed, chance agreement on both occurrence and nonoccurrence inflates reliability estimates. Thus if two observers both recorded 60 percent occurrence and 40 percent nonoccurrence for a particular target behavior, the chance level of agreement would be 0.36 for occurrence and 0.16 for nonoccurrence, yielding a total chance agreement of 0.52.

Cohen (1960) has described a statistic named *kappa,* which represents an agreement measure for both occurrence and nonoccurrence of behavior, corrected for chance agreement among observers (Cohen, 1960; Everitt, 1968; Fleiss, 1971; Fleiss, Cohen, & Everitt, 1969). This statistic corrects the formula for agreement reliability by subtracting chance agreement on occurrence and on nonoccurrence from both the numerator and denominator. The computation of kappa for the agreement reliability measure can be expressed with the following formula:

$$K = \frac{\left[A - \frac{(A+B)(A+C)}{A+B+C+D}\right] + \left[D - \frac{(B+D)(C+D)}{A+B+C+D}\right]}{\left[A - \frac{(A+B)(A+C)}{A+B+C+D}\right] + B + C + \left[D - \frac{(B+D)(C+D)}{A+B+C+D}\right]} \tag{1}$$

Variations of this statistic can be employed for either occurrence or nonoccurrence reliability measures by subtracting appropriate chance agreement correction figures from the numerators and denominators. For occurrence reliability, the formula is:

$$K_{occ} = \frac{A - \frac{(A+B)(A+C)}{A+B+C}}{\left[A - \frac{(A+B)(A+C)}{A+B+C}\right] + B + C} \tag{2}$$

For nonoccurrence reliability, the computation is expressed by:

$$K_{nonocc} = \frac{D - \frac{(B+D)(C+D)}{B+C+D}}{B + C + \left[D - \frac{(B+D)(C+D)}{B+C+D}\right]} \tag{3}$$

In our opinion investigators reporting agreement on occurrence, nonoccurrence, or occurrence and nonoccurrence of behavior must employ this correction if reliability estimates are to reflect the quality of their data accurately. For the agreement reliability measure the level of chance agreement is lowest when behaviors are recorded by both observers during one out of every two observation intervals and increases rapidly as the rate of recorded behavior either rises above or falls below the 50 percent level. In contrast, occurrence reliability measures are increasingly inflated as the frequency of occurrence increases from zero to 100 percent occurrence. Thus occurrence reliability is inflated only 1 percent when behaviors are recorded by both observers in 10 percent of the intervals. This figure rises to 81 percent when behaviors are recorded during 90 percent of the intervals. Conversely, nonoccurrence reliability is inflated very little at very high rates of behavior and dramatically inflated at very low rates. This differential inflation implies that uncorrected reliabilities for different experimental conditions may not be comparable if the actual frequency of a behavior changes across conditions. The use of kappa effectively eliminates this problem.

A number of investigators have recently begun to employ the two-by-two correlation coefficient, *phi* (ϕ), to evaluate trial data. This statistic is a Pearson product-moment correlation for dichotomous variables and thus possesses many advantageous psychometric properties. Some of these will be enumerated in a later discussion of the use of the product-moment correlation coefficient as an estimate of session reliability. The computational formula for phi is:

$$\phi = \frac{(A \times D) - (B \times C)}{\sqrt{(A + B)(C + D)(A + C)(B + D)}} \tag{4}$$

It should be noted that the value of phi (a measure of trial reliability) also indicates the likely lower limit for the level of a product-moment correlation between observers computed on the basis of session frequencies (Gelfand & Hartmann, 1975). In general the absolute values for kappa (computed for agreement reliability) and phi correspond closely.

When frequency or duration measures are collected during small intervals in an observational session, either agreement reliability or kappa can be employed to assess the level of agreement. Observers who count the number of verbalizations made by a child during consecutive 20-second intervals might record, for example, frequencies ranging from zero to five. Agreement could be measured by dividing the number of exact agreements (i.e., the number of intervals in which frequency tallies were identical) by the number of agreements plus disagreements. Particularly if there were a high proportion of recordings of a given frequency (e.g., zero), it would be desirable to subtract the cumulative chance agreement from the numerator and denominator of this fraction, as was demonstrated earlier with kappa. Thus if both observers recorded frequencies of zero for 40 percent of the intervals, one for 20 percent, two for 10 percent, three for 10 percent, four for 10 percent, and five for 10 percent, the cumulative chance agreement would be $0.16 + 0.04 + 0.01 + 0.01 + 0.01 = 0.24$. If exact agreement was 75/100, adjustment for chance agreement in this case would yield $51/76 = 0.67$.

Unfortunately, the use of exact agreement reliability with either frequency or duration measures obtained during consecutive recording intervals does not discriminate between recordings that are slightly different and those that are extremely discrepant. Both instances are simply scored as disagreements. The use of ranges of durations in the computation of agreement (e.g., durations of 0 to 4, 5 to 9, 10 to 14, and 15 to 19 seconds) would enhance absolute agreement levels, but it is inappropriate unless the experimental data are analyzed in the same fashion (e.g., with durations of 0 to 4 seconds represented by a single value). Perhaps the best alternative when distributions of obtained frequencies or durations meet the requirements of parametric statistics is to determine the Pearson product-moment correlation between pairs of observers across consecutive recording intervals.

At this point, we will turn to session reliability measures calculated on the basis of the total number of intervals of occurrence or nonoccurrence, the total frequency, or the total duration of occurrence during an entire observation session. A measure of session reliability that has enjoyed considerable popularity, particularly in the early days of behavior modification, involves computing session totals from each of the two observers and then dividing the smaller by the larger total to yield a *percentage agreement* score. The use of this measure is singularly unfortunate and fails to provide much information regarding the similarity of ratings by two observers. Not only is there no measure of chance agreement, but in addition this statistic is heavily dependent on the specific rate of behavior in the session in which it is calculated (Hartmann, in press). It is, therefore, strongly recommended that this statistic not be employed even for preliminary data analyses. Only if this statistic is low can a valid conclusion be reached, namely, that the data are of poor quality. Alternately, the statistic can be quite high while reflecting neither agreement nor correlation between two observers.

The most traditional measure of session reliability is the product-moment correlation (r), based on the paired scores of observers for a number of sessions that are jointly observed. This statistic is appropriate for recordings of interval, frequency, and duration measures and has a variety of advantages associated with its status as a parametric statistic. The r^2 provides an accurate appraisal of the proportion of variance among session scores accounted for by correspondence between recordings of different observers. Additionally, r indicates the degree of linear association between two observers' scores. Systematic biases that operate linearly (e.g., a repeated tendency for one observer to record higher levels of behavior than another) will be masked by r but can be easily discerned by using a t test to examine the extent to which the two sets of scores differ (Hartmann, in press). When session totals represent the unit of analysis in a study utilizing observational data, the product-moment correlation coefficient is frequently the most appropriate measure of reliability.

Reporting Observational Reliability

A recent paper by Meighan (Note 9) raises a salient and uniformly neglected point regarding reports of observer reliability. Meighan notes that it is common practice to calculate only a mean reliability based on a number of reliability estimates. But since the distribution of reliability coefficients is quite likely to be negatively skewed, the best description of central tendency in a sample of reliabilities is probably the median rather than the mean.

When the median reliability is based on periodic reliability checks rather than on continuous evaluation of the data throughout an investigation, it is also desirable to calculate and report a confidence interval defining the possible range of values of the true reliability of all the data. Drawing on scientific tables discussed by Diem (1962), Meighan presents a procedure for describing this type of confidence interval. According to the nonparametric statistic on which these tables are based, it is necessary for an investigator to obtain a minimum of six reliability coefficients to be 95 percent confident that the extreme reliabilities define the possible range of the true reliability. As additional reliabilities are included, the extreme high and low reliabilities may be discarded in defining this range. Routinely specifying a confidence interval in the description of reliability levels is considerably more informative than simply presenting a single median or mean, as is currently common practice.

STEPS TOWARD BETTER OBSERVATIONAL DATA

Issues in Training

The rare descriptions of methods used to train observers that are scattered through research reports reveal a wide variety of training procedures. These include training observers to approximate the ratings of one or more trainers and, less commonly, training to agreement with criterion protocols. Equally common is a combination of instruction by research assistants with discussion and consensus among observers who will be recording and computing reliability together. In a very real sense this kind of "consensual training" implies that observers are simply refining and synthesizing their mutual interpretations of a written description of the behavioral definitions until adequate levels of agreement are reached.

A study by Wildman, Erickson, and Kent (1975) specifically compared two different procedures for training observers. Four pairs of observers were trained as a group by an experimenter who answered questions about the code and whose ratings were used for reliability assessments (experimenter-trained). Another four pairs trained without an instructor by discussing their recordings and working together to achieve consensus (self-trained). Observers used the O'Leary nine-category code for disruptive classroom behavior (O'Leary, Kaufman, Kass, & Drabman, 1970). After seven one-hour training sessions, all observers viewed six 40-minute videotapes. Reliability measures were taken both overtly and without the observers' awareness and computed within and between observer pairs for each of the two groups. Although there were no overall differences in mean reliabilities reported for each of the two groups after training, the group trained by the experimenter recorded significantly more disruptive behaviors than did the self-trained group. In addition the variance in the number of disruptive behaviors recorded by the experimenter-trained group was significantly less than the variance of the self-trained group ($F = 1.75$; $df = 95.95$; $p < 0.01$).

With equal training the same level of reliability was demonstrated by both experimenter- and self-trained groups. Unfortunately, such indications of reliability are frequently taken as evidence that adequate data are being collected. The fact that different rates of behavior were recorded, however, reveals that different interpretations of the behavioral code were being employed. This might not be critical if the difference between the two groups' recordings were consistent, so that the same conclusions could be drawn from either set of data when recordings from different experimental conditions were compared. This was probably not the case: Observers who trained each other generated significantly more variable data than the experimenter-trained group, suggesting increased error in the behavioral recordings of the self-trained group.

Two additional studies further describe the role of training experiences as determiners of subsequent behavioral recordings. Mash and McElwee (1974) and Mash and Makohoniuk (1975) examined the effects of training with audiotapes that showed different patterns of conversation. During training, observers used a verbal interaction code to rate tapes scripted to depict either repetitious (predictable) or unpredictable sequences of the various code categories. In both studies performance on a second tape improved after training with unpredictable interactions, whereas performance worsened if training had been with predictable tapes. This performance decrement apparently occurred because observers trained with predictable tapes mistakenly recorded the patterns they had repeatedly observed during prior training. In addition observers who had been specifically informed in advance that there was a pattern in the interactions omitted more "codeable" behavior during training than did uninformed observers (Mash & Makohoniuk, 1975), regardless of whether the predicted pattern was actually present in the tape. These data imply that training materials or situations should be selected to provide variable and nonpatterned interaction sequences to enhance the quality of posttraining data.

Consistent use of a behavioral code in retraining observers throughout an investigation is as necessary as consistency during the initial training phase. It is clear from the data on observer drift that observers who discuss their ratings with one another modify their original rating style over time (Kent, Kanowitz, O'Leary, & Cheiken, in press). Because the important comparisons in an extended study often involve consecutive treatments and/or measures of change across lengthy periods, it is critical that observers utilize a behavior code in a uniform fashion throughout the investigation. Even with a single trainer, the very real possibility remains that the trainer's implementation of the code will vary during the course of the study.

The availability of a standardized set of criterion ratings for use with videotaped material in initial training and later retraining might eliminate some of these difficulties. However, establishing a criterion protocol means that an investigator must designate one set of recordings as a standard. More often than not, the selection is arbitrary. In an attempt to establish more specific, empirically founded guidelines for this procedure, the senior author collected a large number of videotapes of children in a special class setting. Between 10 and 12 trained observers then rated each of these tapes. Ratings were subsequently processed by a computer program that generated a criterion protocol for each tape. To produce the final protocols, the program in essence eliminated each instance of behavior that was not recorded by a substantial proportion of the observers. This established a criterion measure that reflected an empirically derived consensus among a large group of raters.

The criterion protocols generated by computer-based decisions can actually be used to operationally define the different categories of a behavioral code. Because the criterion protocols eliminate particular exemplars of individual codes that simply cannot be recorded reliably, the operationalization of the behavioral code is not necessarily identical at a conceptual level to the written description of the code. Rather, criterion protocols reflect refinement and elaboration of this description based on an empirical evaluation of consensus in recording each occurrence of a behavioral category during each specific recording interval.

Criterion protocols can be utilized in initial training and subsequent recalibration of observers throughout extended periods of observation, providing a source of consistent and continued feedback. Furthermore, when standard protocols are produced by systematic selection of those behaviors to be classified as "occurrences," the same standard of consensus can be applied for all categories of behavior. Pilot data from our own laboratory indicate that this procedure has yielded behavioral categories of highly similar reliability, an attribute of considerable methodological value.

Jones et al. (1974) discussion of the complexity of observed interactions underscores the need for careful selection of practice observation situations during training and recalibration. In the context of their 28-category family interaction code, more complex interactions are consistently coded with lower reliability than are simpler interactions. This implies that observers trained to be reliable only with low-complexity situations will produce less reliable data when they encounter sessions with more complex interactions. Training with videotapes that represent the full range of complexities the observers are likely to encounter can mitigate this problem. Observer competence throughout training can be assessed by computing reliabilities for various complexity levels; continued training would be necessary only for those levels where reliability was unacceptable. Similarly, the subsequent performance decrement after training with predictable interaction sequences (Mash & McElwee, 1974; Mash & Makohoniuk, 1975) could be allayed by arranging training tapes purposely selected for variability rather than consistency in patterns of target behavior.

Finally, videotapes and criterion protocols are clearly transportable and durable in ways that individual trainers are not. Thus the development of a number of such operational descriptions of behavioral codes could provide the potential for truly replicable measures from different laboratories and at different times.

VALIDITY CONSIDERATIONS IN OBSERVATIONAL RECORDING

Evaluating Validity

"The validity of a test concerns *what* the test measures and *how well* it does so. In this connection, we should guard against accepting the test name as an index of what the test measures. Test names provide short, convenient labels for identification purposes. Most test names are far too broad and vague to furnish meaningful clues to the behavior area covered, although increasing efforts are being made to use more specific and operationally definable test names. The trait measured by a given test can be defined only through an examination of the objective sources of information and empirical operations utilized in establishing its validity. . . . Moreover, the validity of a test cannot be reported in general terms. No test can be said to have 'high' or 'low' validity in the abstract. Its validity must be determined with reference to the particular use for which the test is being considered." (Anastasi, 1968, p. 99)

This paragraph was written by Anastasi in 1968 as an introduction to her consideration of validity issues in traditional psychological testing. Substituting the words "behavioral code" or "category" for "test," and "behavior" for "trait," this quotation could be equally applicable to behavioral observation procedures. Nonetheless, the concept of validity has been largely ignored in observational methodology, perhaps because the high face validity of behavioral definitions tends to obscure more complex validity considerations (Johnson & Bolstad, 1973; Jones et al., 1974).

The concept of validity has been subdivided and redefined in a variety of ways by theoreticians, measurement experts, and investigators (see, for example, *APA Standards of Tests and Measurements,* 1966; Campbell & Fiske, 1959; Cronbach, 1970; Johnson & Bolstad, 1973; Wiggins, 1973). Underlying these formulations are the two basic questions implied by Anastasi: (1) What does the measurement instrument actually assess? and (2) How well does it accomplish its purpose? The simplicity of these questions belies the complexities involved in attempting to provide definitive answers. The few validity studies using observational codes that are presented below represent attempts to approach the questions from a variety of methodologies and perspectives.

The answer to the first question will obviously be dependent on the actual formulation of the behavioral code, independent of its later application as an assessment tool. A number of authors have speculated on the influence of different types of category definitions and sampling procedures on data obtained (e.g., Bijou, Peterson, & Ault, 1968; Hutt & Hutt, 1970; Lipinski & Nelson, 1974; Weick, 1968; Mash, Note 10). Nevertheless, the development of observational criteria for recording a particular category of responses (e.g., verbalizations) seems to remain a unique and nonsystematic enterprise for each individual investigator. Efforts to enhance the adequacy of observational codes in representing a full range, or an unbiased sample, of relevant behavioral phenomena are rarely reported. There is currently little systematic or empirical attention to such aspects of code development as identification of the subset of behavioral manifestations of a particular general category of responses (e.g., aggression), determination of relevant behavioral characteristics of the behavior(s) of interest (e.g., frequency versus intensity versus duration), or development of specific observational criteria. More often than not, such basic measurement decisions seem to reflect the whim or habits of the individual investigator.

Some investigators have sought to validate behavioral definitions by evaluating the response of relevant persons to representative behaviors. Jones et al. (1974) describe a code employed to measure "deviant" and "nondeviant" behavior in family interactions. To determine whether categories labeled a priori as deviant in fact represented behaviors that parents found disturbing, mothers were given written descriptions of the 28 behavior categories of child behavior. They then rated each description according to how annoying the behavior was to them. Ratings of deviant behaviors were significantly higher than ratings of nondeviant categories, indicating that the a priori labels and parental ratings strongly concurred. This result was strengthened by the lack of overlap in annoyance ratings for deviant and nondeviant behaviors.

Johnson and Bolstad (1973) describe a second study evaluating the validity of the same code. They postulate that parents would respond negatively more often after deviant child behaviors than after positive behaviors. Inspection of observers' recordings revealed that deviant categories were, in fact, followed more frequently by negative parental consequences than were nondeviant categories.

Most recently there have been scattered reports of relationships between observational recordings and other methods of assessment. These investigations address the issue of how well a code meets the assessment purposes for which it was designed, and a significant positive relationship between two different measures is often interpreted as substantiation of the validity of both. Jones et al. (1974) described an unpublished study by Hendriks that evaluated the correlation between their behavioral code and parental responses on an adjective checklist. Mothers' ratings of items that formed the aggression factor of the checklist correlated significantly with baseline frequencies of seven of 14 observational categories of deviant behavior. Patterson (1974) also found that the total deviant behavior score obtained for referred children using the same code correlated significantly with parents' daily reports of the problem behaviors for which the child had been referred.

Finally, several investigators have reported validation of observational codes on the basis of discrimination among criterion groups. Werry and

Quay (1969) developed a behavioral code to assess the behavior of four groups of children: two classes of conduct-problem children after at least one semester of special class placement, another group of conduct-problem children prior to special class placement, and normal control children. Statistical comparisons were then made among the four groups for each code category. To suit the research purposes of the investigators, the code should be able to (1) reflect pretreatment differences between referred and nonreferred children, and (2) show change that occurs as a function of treatment. Significant differences found on the majority of categories between normal controls and conduct-problem children observed before special class placement satisfied the first requirement. The second was tentatively confirmed by the fact that data from observations of children during special class placement did not differ from data for the normal controls but did differ from pretreatment data for referred children. These conclusions were unfortunately limited by the absence of pretreatment data for the two treated groups.

Following a similar strategy, Johnson and Bolstad (1973) refer to the Johnson and G. K. Lobitz (1974) investigation to provide evidence that their "total deviant behavior" score is a meaningful index of a child's overall misbehavior. In this study parents were instructed to make their children look either "good" or "bad" on alternate days. No additional instructions were provided. The data revealed that total deviant behavior scores were significantly higher on bad days than on good days and thus indicated that their code could reflect changes in behavior related to particular interventions (in this case, instructions to parents). Weiss, Hops, and Patterson (1973) also use data reflecting change, but as a function of therapy, in supporting the validity of a marital interaction observational code.

It should be noted that extensive validity evaluations may be virtually impossible, practically speaking, for investigators who employ observational methods with $n = 1$ research designs. This is especially true for treatment studies in which unique target behaviors may be defined for each client immediately prior to baseline data collection. Nonetheless, alternative measures of target behaviors can and should be collected in these cases to aid in assessing the validity of one's measures.

Enhancing Validity

Validity is typically evaluated on a post hoc basis once an observational system has been established and is in use. Although these evaluations provide some indication of the quality of obtained data, they shed little light on the factors that can influence the utility of behavioral measures. The strategies and choices of investigators throughout the initial development of an observational system will clearly affect the extent to which their data adequately reflect the phenomena of interest and concur with alternate measures of the same behaviors. It should thus be possible to isolate and define procedures which, if used during the actual formulation of a behavioral measure, will enhance the probability that later evaluations will provide satisfactory validity indices.

The senior author recently had the experience of attempting to measure disruptive behavior in an open classroom setting, using a code that had been developed for highly structured classrooms. It rapidly became clear that many of the behaviors considered to be inappropriate and disruptive in a structured class setting were in fact typical of normal students in open classrooms. It thus became necessary to develop new categories and refine old ones to reestablish the discriminability of the observational measure. Teachers in local open classrooms were asked to select children they considered disruptive and others who were average in order to obtain criterion samples of behavior. The tentatively refined behavioral categories were then employed on a number of occasions to observe both samples of children. Several *t* tests were utilized to determine if the data for each category revealed significant differences between the two samples.

When a particular behavioral category failed to discriminate significantly between disruptive and normal children, the means and standard deviations for both samples were examined. In some cases the mean frequency of a particular category was so low for both samples that significant differences would not be expected. Under these circumstances additional exemplars of that conceptual category were sought in order to increase recorded frequencies, rather than requiring the more extensive data collection sometimes necessary to produce stable discriminative measures with low-frequency behavior. In other cases when no significant differences were found between the groups, high levels of recorded behavior for both disruptive and normal children suggested that the categories might be refined to be less inclusive and to focus on the two groups of behaviors most likely to differentiate normal and disruptive children. In yet other cases the means for the two groups were quite different, but the standard deviations were sufficient to eliminate significance. In these circumstances an attempt was made both to eliminate responses common to both groups and to seek additional behaviors that would be appropriate to the category and were likely to be unique to disruptive children.

The subjective judgments of persons highly familiar with the open classroom were particularly crucial in developing this new code. In generating new behavioral exemplars of disruptive children and eliminating others common to normal children, the senior author drew heavily on the experience of observers who had spent many hours in these settings. Ultimately the use of criterion samples provided an empirical and unequivocal basis for determining on an a priori basis the functional utility of the observational code in discriminating between populations of interest.

As noted previously, investigators often utilize a combination of several categories as an index of a broader class of behaviors, such as deviance, anxiety, or hyperactivity. In the typical method of calculating this kind of score the frequencies, durations, or number of intervals of occurrence of target behaviors are simply summed without a differential weighting reflecting the importance of individual categories. Thus in measuring disruptive behaviors in the classroom, for example, forms of severe aggression may be summed with more innocuous behaviors, such as getting out of seat or speaking to a neighbor. Clearly the "disruptiveness" of one aggression may be equal to the occurrence of many less serious behaviors. Statistically treating all responses as equivalent may thus weaken the validity of the total.

Kent, O'Leary, Coletti, and Drabman (Note 11) employed the judgment of experts as a criterion to obtain differential weightings of the nine categories of a code for disruptive behavior. Five classroom teachers were asked to view a number of videotapes that had been previously rated by trained observers. After viewing each of ten 12½-minute videotape segments, the teachers provided a global rating of the level of disruptiveness of individual children on a zero to 100 scale. Kent et al. (Note 11) reported that the correlation of the unweighted sum of nine categories with the teacher ratings was 0.65, accounting for approximately 40 percent of the variance. Using a multiple regression procedure, the investigators calculated the differential weightings for each of the nine categories that would maximize the correlation between the composite score and teacher ratings. This raised the overall correlation to 0.95. It was true, however, that these weights were uniquely suited to ratings by the initial sample of five teachers and were unlikely to equally enhance correlations between the composites and ratings made by alternate samples of teachers. Therefore, the investigators obtained global ratings of the same videotapes from a second set of five teachers, and employing the weightings based on ratings by the first set of teachers, they obtained a correlation of 0.85. Thus by utilizing the judgments of experts to differentially weight the nine categories behavior, the proportion of variance accounted for by the composite score had increased from 40 percent to well over 70 percent, even with a cross-validation sample. Whether these weightings will improve the code's ability to discriminate between behavior of problem and normal children in more naturalistic classroom settings has yet to be empirically evaluated. Nonetheless, the procedure offers a promising method of refining an observational code to approximate more closely a criterion measure—in this case, teacher judgments.

Because the investigators employing observational assessment procedures have only recently become sensitive to the issue of validity, validity considerations will probably continue to pose complex empirical issues for observational methodology for a number of years. This discussion has sampled and summarized a few of these complexities. The interested reader who wishes to explore the topics of validity and its first cousin, generalizability, in greater depth is referred to Cronbach, Gleser, Nanda, and Rajaratnam (1970), Jones et al. (1974), Johnson and Bolstad (1973), Mash (Note 10), and Wiggins (1973), as well as classic testing literature, such as Anastasi (1968).

CONCLUSION

In the late 1960s there was a virtual absence of controlled investigations of methodological biases in observational recording despite the growing popularity of these measures. Methodological studies during the last decade have begun to fill this void. Their results have yielded both good and bad news. The good news is well documented in the early sections of this chapter. Behavioral observation procedures in the majority of cases seem to be largely unobtrusive, unaffected by the expectations of the examiner, and compatible with a variety of recent technical innovations, such as videotape recording. The bad news is that investigators seem to have grossly overestimated the ease with which reliable, replicable, and valid behavioral recordings can be obtained. Behavioral recordings can be influenced by a variety of situational factors, many of which are currently undefined.

To date the bulk of methodological research has focused on simple evaluations of the presence or absence of error and bias in applications of recording procedures. The next several years are likely to witness an emphasis on solutions to existing difficulties, particularly in the areas of observer training and behavioral code development. Furthermore, as forecast by Hartmann (in press), there is likely to be an important and productive convergence of research on observational recording with the more traditional testing literature.

It is clear that behavioral observation procedures are associated with advantages as well as liabilities not shared by other psychological and behavioral assessment procedures (cf. Goldfried & Kent, 1972). This may account for the exciting fact that the number of investigators actively engaged in methodological research on observational procedures has increased dramatically in only the last two or three years. Considering the quality and volume of research being generated, substantial technological and theoretical advances in this area during the next few years seem a virtual certainty.

REFERENCE NOTES

1. Kass, R. E., & O'Leary, K. D. *The effects of observer bias in field-experimental settings.* Paper presented at Symposium "Behavior Analysis in Education," University of Kansas, Lawrence, Kansas, April 9, 1970.
2. Shuller, D. Y., & McNamara, J. R. *Expectancy factors in behavioral observation.* Manuscript submitted for publication, 1975.
3. White, G. D. *Effects of observer presence on family interaction.* Paper presented at the meeting of the Western Psychological Association, Anaheim, California, 1973.
4. Lobitz, W. C., & Johnson, S. M. *Parental manipulation of the behavior of normal and deviant children.* Unpublished manuscript.
5. Hay, L. R., Nelson, R. O., & Hay, W. M. *Some methodological problems in the use of teachers as behavior observers.* Paper presented at Southeastern Psychological Association, Miami, Florida, May 1974.
6. Hawn, J., Brown, G., & LeBlanc, J. M. *A comparison of three observation procedures: Consecutive intervals on-the-spot, consecutive intervals from video tape, 10-sec-on, 10-sec-off from video tape.* Paper presented at American Psychological Association, Montreal, August 1973.
7. Reid, J. B., Skinrud, K. D., Taplin, P. S., & Jones, R. R. *The role of complexity in the collection and evaluation of observation data.* Paper presented at the American Psychological Association, Montreal, August 1973.
8. Wiggins, J. S. *The quality of observational data: Discussion.* Paper presented at a symposium on the Quality of Observational Data, Western Psychological Association, San Francisco, April 1974.
9. Meighan, M. *Percentage agreement scores as estimations of nonparametric observer reliability.* Research training paper No. 70, Bureau of Child Research, Kansas Center for Mental Retardation and Human Development, Kansas City, Missouri, March 1975.
10. Mash, E. J. *Behavior modification: A developmental perspective.* Manuscript submitted for publication, 1975.
11. Kent, R. N., O'Leary, K. D., Coletti, G., & Drabman, R. S. *Increasing the validity of an observational code: An empirical methodology.* Manuscript in preparation, 1975.

REFERENCES

American Psychological Association. *Standards for educational and psychological tests and measures.* Washington, D.C.: American Psychological Association, 1966.

Anastasi, A. *Psychological testing* (3rd ed.). Toronto: Macmillan, 1968.

Arrington, R. E. Time-sampling studies of child behavior. *Psychological Monographs*, 1939, **51.**

Arrington, R. E. Time sampling in studies of social behavior: A critical review of techniques and results with research suggestions. *Psychological Bulletin*, 1943, **40,** 81–124.

Azrin, N. H., Holz, W., Ulrich, R., & Goldiamond, I. The control of the content of conversation through reinforcement. *Journal of the Experimental Analysis of Behavior*, 1961, **4,** 25–30.

Behrens, M. L., & Sherman, A. Observational research with emotionally disturbed children: Session I. *American Journal of Orthopsychiatry*, 1959, **29,** 243–248.

Bijou, S. W., Peterson, R. F., & Ault, M. H. A method to integrate descriptive and experimental field studies at the level of data and empirical concepts. *Journal of Applied Behavior Analysis*, 1968, **1,** 175–191.

Burton, R. V. An inexpensive and portable means for one-way observation. *Child Development*, 1971, **42,** 959–962.

Campbell, D. T., & Fiske, D. W. Convergent and discriminant validation by the multitrait-multimethod matrix. *Psychological Bulletin*, 1959, **56,** 81–105.

Campbell, D. T., & Stanley, J. C. *Experimental and quasi-experimental designs for research*. Chicago: Rand McNally, 1963.

Cohen, J. A coefficient of agreement for nominal scales. *Educational and Psychological Measurement*, 1960, **20,** 37–46.

Cordaro, L., & Ison, J. R. Observer bias in the classical conditioning of the planaria. *Psychological Reports*, 1963, **13,** 787–789.

Cox, F. N. Some effects of test anxiety and presence or absence of other persons on boys' performance on a repetitive motor task. *Journal of Experimental Child Psychology*, 1966, **3,** 100–112.

Cox, F. N. Some relationships between test-anxiety, presence or absence of male persons, and boys' performance on repetitive motor task. *Journal of Experimental Child Psychology*, 1968, **6,** 1–12.

Cronbach, L. J. *Essentials of psyshological testing* (3rd ed.). New York: Harper & Row, 1970.

Cronbach, L. J., Gleser, C. G., Nanda, H., & Rajaratnam, N. *The dependability of behavioral measures*. New York: Wiley, 1970.

Diem, K. (Ed.). *Documenta Geigy: Scientific tables* (6th ed.). Ardsley, N.Y.: Geigy Pharmaceuticals, 1962.

Eisler, R. M., Hersen, M., & Agras, W. S. Videotapes: A method for controlled observation of non-verbal interpersonal behavior. *Behavior Therapy*, 1973, **4,** 420–425.

Everitt, B. S. Moments of the statistics Kappa and weighted Kappa. *British Journal of Mathematical and Statistical Psychology*, 1968, **21,** 97–103.

Fleiss, J. L. Measuring nominal scale agreement among many raters. *Psychological Bulletin*, 1971, **76,** 378–382.

Fleiss, J. L., Cohen, J., & Everitt, B. S. Large sample standard errors of Kappa and weighted Kappa. *Psychological Bulletin*, 1969, **72,** 323–327.

Ganzer, V. J. Effect of audience presence and test anxiety on learning and retention in a serial learning situation. *Journal of Personality and Social Psychology*, 1968, **8,** 194–199.

Gelfand, D. M., & Hartmann, D. P. *Child behavior analysis and therapy*. New York: Pergamon, 1975.

Gerwitz, J. L. Plans for construction of a portable one-way observation booth. *Child Development*, 1952, **23,** 307–314.

Goldfried, R. M., & Kent, R. N. Traditional versus behavioral personality assessment: A comparison of methodological and theoretical assumptions. *Psychological Bulletin*, 1972, **77,** 409–420.

Hagen, R. L., Craighead, W. E., & Paul, G. L. Staff reactivity to evaluative behavioral observations. *Behavior Therapy*, 1975, **6,** 201–205.

Hartmann, D. P. Considerations in the choice of interobserver reliability estimates. *Journal of Applied Behavior Analysis*, in press.

Herbert, J. Direct observation as a research technique. *Psychology in the Schools*, 1970, **7,** 127–138.

Heyns, R., & Lippitt, R. Systematic observational techniques. In G. Lindzey (Ed.), *Handbook of social psychology*. Vol. 1. Cambridge, Mass.: Addison-Wesley, 1954.

Hutt, S. J., & Hutt, C. *Direct observation and measurement of behavior*. Springfield, Ill.: Thomas, 1970.

Johnson, S. M., & Bolstad, O. D. Methodological issues in naturalistic observation: Some problems and solutions for field research. In L. A. Hamerlynck, L. C. Handy, & E. J. Mash (Eds.), *Behavior change: Methodology, concepts, and practice*. Champaign, Ill.: Research Press, 1973.

Johnson, S. M., & Lobitz, G. K. Parental manipulation of child behavior in home observations. *Journal of Applied Behavior Analysis*, 1974, **7,** 23–32.

Jones, R. R., Reid, J. B., & Patterson, G. R. Naturalistic observation in clinical assessment. In P. McReynolds (Ed.), *Advances in psychological assessment*, Vol. 3. San Francisco: Jossey-Bass, 1974.

Kent, R. N. Expectancy bias in behavioral observation. Unpublished doctoral dissertation, State University of New York, Stony Brook, N.Y., 1972.

Kent, R. N., Dietz, A., Diament, C., & O'Leary, K. D. A comparison of observational recordings *in vivo*, via mirror, and via television. *Child Development*, in press.

Kent, R. N., Kanowitz, J., O'Leary, K. D., & Cheiken, M. Observer reliability as a function of circumstances of assessment. *Journal of Applied Behavior Analysis*, in press.

Kent, R. N., O'Leary, K. D., Diament, C., & Dietz, A. Expectation biases in observational evaluation of therapeutic change. *Journal of Consulting and Clinical Psychology*, 1974, **42,** 774–780.

Kubany, E. S., & Sloggett, B. B. Coding procedure for teachers. *Journal of Applied Behavior Analysis*, 1973, **2,** 339–343.

Lewinsohn, P. M. A behavioral approach to depression. In R. J. Friedman & M. M. Katz (Eds.), *The psychology of depression: Contemporary theory and research*. Washington, D.C.: V. H. Winston & Sons, 1974.

Lewinsohn, P. M., & Shaffer, M. The use of home observations as an integral part of the treatment of depression: Preliminary report and case studies. *Journal of Consulting and Clinical Psychology*, 1971, **37,** 87–94.

Lipinski, D., & Nelson, R. Problems in the use of naturalistic observation as a means of behavioral assessment. *Behavior Therapy*, 1974, **5,** 341–351.

Lovaas, O. I., Koegel, R., Simmons, J. Q., & Long, J. S. Some generalization and follow-up measures on autistic children in behavior therapy. *Journal of Applied Behavior Analysis*, 1973, **6,** 131–167.

Martens, R. Effect of an audience on learning and performance of a complex motor skill. *Journal of Personality and Social Psychology*, 1969, **12,** 252–260.

Martin, M. F., Gelfand, D. M., & Hartmann, D. P. Effects of adult and peer observers on boys' and girls' responses to an aggressive model. *Child Development*, 1971, **42,** 1271–1275.

Mash, E. J., & Hedley, J. Effect of observer as a function of prior history of social interaction. *Perceptual and Motor Skills*, 1975, **40,** 659–669.

Mash, E. J., & Makohoniuk, G. The effects of prior information and behavioral predictability on observer accuracy. *Child Development*, 1975, **46,** 513–519.

Mash, E. J., & McElwee, J. D. Situational effects on observer accuracy: Behavior predictability, prior experience, and complexity of coding categories. *Child Development*, 1974, **45,** 367–377.

Mercatoris, M., & Craighead, W. E. The effects of non-participant observation on teacher and pupil classroom behavior. *Journal of Educational Psychology*, 1974, **66,** 512–519.

Moos, R. H. Behavioral effects of being observed: Reactions to a wireless radio transmitter. *Journal of Consulting and Clinical Psychology*, 1968, **32,** 383–388.

O'Leary, K. D., Kaufman, K. F., Kass, R. E., & Drabman, R. S. The effects of loud and soft reprimands on the behavior of disruptive students. *Exceptional Children*, 1970, **37,** 145–155.

O'Leary, K. D., & Kent, R. Behavior modification for social action: Research tactics and problems. In L. A. Hamerlynck, L. C. Handy, & E. J. Mash (Eds.), *Behavior change: Methodology, concepts, and practice*. Champaign, Ill.: Research Press, 1973.

O'Leary, K. D., Kent, R. N., & Kanowitz, J. Shaping data collection congruent with experimental hypotheses. *Journal of Applied Behavior Analysis*, 1975, **8,** 43–51.

Patterson, G. R. Interventions for boys with conduct problems: Multiple settings, treatments, and criteria. *Journal of Consulting and Clinical Psychology*, 1974, **42,** 471–481.

Polansky, N., Freeman, W., Horowitz, M., Irwin, L., Papanis, N., Rappaport, D., & Whaley, F. Problems of interpersonal relations in research on groups. *Human Relations*, 1949, **2,** 281–291.

Purcell, K., & Brady, K. Adaptation to invasion of privacy: Monitoring behavior with a miniature radio transmitter. *Merrill-Palmer Quarterly*, 1965, **12,** 242–254.

Reid, J. B. Reliability assessment of observation data: A possible methodological problem. *Child Development*, 1970, **41,** 1143–1150.

Roberts, R. R., Jr., & Renzaglia, G. A. The influence of tape recording on counseling. *Journal of Counseling Psychology*, 1965, **12,** 10–16.

Romanczyk, R. G., Kent, R. N., Diament, C., & O'Leary, K. D. Measuring the reliability of observational data: A reactive process. *Journal of Applied Behavior Analysis*, 1973, **6,** 175–184.

Rosenthal, R. *Experimenter effects in behavioral research*. New York: Appleton-Century-Crofts, 1966.

Rosenthal, R. Interpersonal expectations: Effects of the experimenter's hypothesis. In R. Rosenthal & R. L. Rosnow (Eds.), *Artifact in behavioral research*. New York: Academic, 1969.

Rosenthal, R., Friedman, C. J., Johnson, C. A., Fode, K. L., Shill, T. R., White, C. R., & Vikan-Kline, L. L. Variables affecting experimenter bias in a group situation. *Genetic Psychological Monographs*, 1964, **70,** 271–296.

Scott, P. M., Burton, R. V., & Yarrow, M. R. Social reinforcement under natural conditions. *Child Development*, 1967, **38,** 53–63.

Selltiz, C., Jahoda, M., Deutsch, M., & Cook, S. W. *Research methods in social relations*. New York: Holt, Rinehart, & Winston, 1959.

Soskin, W. F., & John, V. P. The study of spontaneous talk. In R. G. Barker (Ed.), *The stream of behavior*. New York: Appleton-Century-Crofts, 1963.

Surratt, P. R., Ulrich, R. E., & Hawkins, R. P. An elementary student as a behavioral engineer. *Journal of Applied Behavior Analysis*, 1969, **2,** 85–92.

Taplin, P. S., & Reid, J. B. Effects of instructional set and experimenter influence on observer reliability. *Child Development*, 1973, **44,** 547–554.

Webb, E. J., Campbell, D. T., Schwartz, R. D., & Sechrest, L. *Unobtrusive measures: Nonreactive research in social sciences*. Chicago: Rand McNally, 1966.

Weick, K. E. Systematic observational methods. In G. Lindsley & E. Aransen (Eds.), *The handbook of social psychology* (2nd ed.) Vol. 2. Reading, Mass.: Addison-Wesley, 1968.

Weiss, R. L., Hops, H., & Patterson, G. R. A framework for conceptualizing marital conflict. In L. A. Hamerlynck, L. C. Handy, & E. J. Mash (Eds.), *Behavior change: Methodology, concepts, and practice*. Champaign, Ill.: Research Press, 1973.

Werry, J. S., & Quay, H. C. Observing the classroom behavior of elementary school children. *Exceptional Children*, 1969, **35,** 461–476.

Wiggins, J. S. *Personality and prediction: Principles of personality assessment*. Reading, Mass.: Addison-Wesley, 1973.

Wildman, B. G., Erickson, M. T., & Kent, R. N. The effect of two training procedures on observer agreement and variability of behavior ratings. *Child Development*, 1975, **46,** 520–524.

Wright, H. F. *Recording and analyzing child behavior: With ecological data from an American town*. New York: Harper & Row, 1967.

CHAPTER 10

Psychophysiological Procedures

WILLIAM M. KALLMAN and MICHAEL FEUERSTEIN

Psychophysiological measurement is a relatively new procedure in applied psychology and behavioral assessment. Psychophysiology is the study of the relationship between physiological and psychological events in the intact organism. As with all forms of measurement, the goal of psychophysiology is quantification; in this case it is the physiological response that is being quantified. This differs from the area of physiological psychology where overt behavior is typically the dependent variable and manipulation of a physiological system represents the independent variable. Psychophysiological measurement can thus be defined as *the quantification of biological events as they relate to psychological variables.*

This chapter will briefly review some of the instrumentation and methods used in psychophysiological assessment. The emphasis will be on the interpretation of physiological measures in terms of biological events and their relationship to psychological variables. There is a brief introduction to the basics of instrumentation in psychophysiology and an overview of the biological bases of the various response measures. The major goal of the chapter is to provide the reader with a methodology for psychophysiological assessment that is applicable to the initial assessment, treatment evaluation, and outcome assessment of particular behavioral disorders. The emphasis is on the identification and control of psychobiologically relevant stimuli to assure valid and reliable data that can be used as an important channel of measurement in the comprehensive behavioral assessment.

The utilty of psychophysiological measurement in behavioral assessment is dependent on several factors. First, because of the complexity and expense of physiological recording instruments, physiological measures should provide information that cannot be obtained as reliably or efficiently by other means. Second, some aspect of the physiological response must be uniquely related to a psychological variable in such a way that the measure is of use in predicting and modifying behavior. In an applied setting the psychophysiological measure should suggest to the practitioner something about the selection and evaluation of an appropriate intervention for change. Finally, as with all assessment tools, psychophysiological measures must have an adequate degree of reliability and validity to permit the use of these measures across time, situations and individuals.

History of Psychophysiological Assessment

The study of the relationship between physiology and behavior is a part of the earliest history of psychology. In the first English-language physiological psychology textbook, Ladd (1887) noted that the relationship between the autonomic nervous system (ANS) and emotion was so well known that it required no further discussion in his book. Despite Ladd's "definitive" statement, there has been much interest in the relationship between biological events and psychological variables since the late nineteenth century.

One of the early theories of the relationship between biological events and "emotional" experiences was proposed by William James (1890) and Carl Lange (1885). The James-Lange theory, as it is now known, proposed that emotion is the subjective experiencing of an autonomic nervous system response. It was proposed that the ANS responded automatically to environmental events and that the perception of the ANS response led to the experiencing of "emotion." Stated simply, the James-Lange theory suggests that "we do not run because we are afraid of a stimulus, rather we are afraid of a stimulus because we perceive ourselves to be running."

In 1915 Cannon challenged the James-Lange theory, noting that the physiological response of the organism is an "all-or-none" phenomenon. According to Cannon, the ANS responds in too diffuse a fashion to permit the perception of the many specific emotions for which we have labels. Darrow (1929) reviewed the literature dealing with physiological and psychological variables and concluded that there were two distinct patterns of response for external, environmental stimuli and internal, ideational stimuli. External stimuli (i.e., light, noise, etc.) produce changes in the peripheral physiological systems such as increased electrodermal activity and cephalic vasodilation with peripheral vasoconstriction. In contrast "mental activity" produces changes in more centrally located autonomic systems such as heart rate and blood pressure.

Darrow's work represents the traditional attempt of psychologists to identify specific patterns of physiological activity that could be related to a definite psychological event. Through the 1930s and 1940s psychologists and physiologists continued to search for specific physiological patterns associated with different psychological variables. It was not until the 1950s that psychologists were able to further differentiate emotions on the basis of physiological responses. Ax (1953) first demonstrated that there are two distinct physiological response patterns to elicited "fear" and "anger." Since Ax's classic work, there have been several attempts to differentiate various emotions on the basis of physiological response patterns (Averill & Opton, 1968). Although Ax's specific findings have been replicated (e.g., Schachter, 1957), recent interpretations of the use of physiological measures to identify specific emotional patterns suggest that this approach has failed to provide information useful in identifying and modifying behavior disorders. The theoretical issues involved in the use of psychophysiology in behavioral assessment will be discussed further in a later section of this chapter.

INSTRUMENTATION IN PHYSIOLOGICAL MEASUREMENT

Students and practitioners are often awed by the sight of a large physiograph. The numerous knobs and dials give the instrument a look of complexity and authority that often leads to avoidance or misuse on the part of the practitioner. There is nothing complex about a physiograph, but there are many details that must be considered to ensure valid and reliable recordings.

The basic concept of the physiograph can be understood by analogy with the common stereo component system found in the home. The record has a groove that has mechanical ridges pressed on it. The stylus converts the physical distortions on the surface of the record to an electrical signal that is amplified and converted back to a mechanical signal at the speaker.

Physiological recording instrumentation works on a similar principle. The components are an input transducer (e.g., electrodes or specialized sensors), amplifier (preamplifier and driver amplifier), and an output transducer for converting the amplified electrical signal into a useable visual or auditory form (See Figure 10–1).

There are numerous ways to measure physiological responses. Each is determined by the physical characteristics of the biological response and the available technology. Brown (1972) describes two basic types of physiological responses: bioelectric potentials and responses derived from physical characteristics of the organism. In the case of bioelectric potentials, the living organism acts as a transducer in that it converts a physical or chemical process within the organism into an electrical potential. Conducting electrodes can then be used to directly input this signal to an amplifier. The second type of response is the mechanical or physical re-

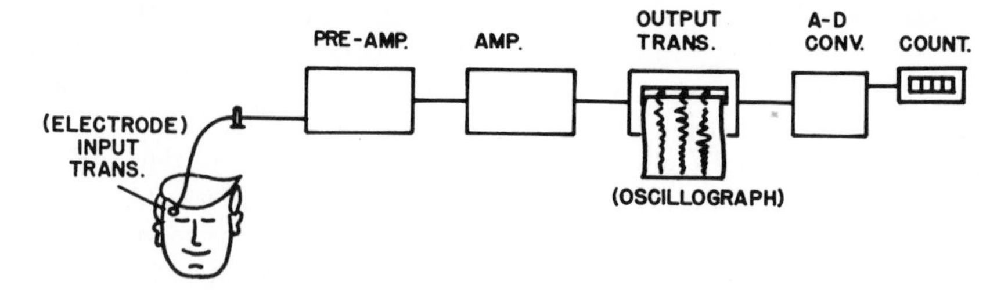

Figure 10–1. Schematic representation of a typical psychophysiological recording system.

sponse (i.e., volume, rate, strength, etc.). These responses are analogous to the mechanical ridges on the phonograph record. They must be converted to an electrical signal, amplified, and then reconverted to a non-electrical signal.

There are various degrees of complexity in instrumentation depending on the level of measurement and type of biological response. Although the minimal instrumentation necessary for most clinical applications consists of an input transducer (or electrode), an amplifier, and an oscillograph (pen writer), the task of analyzing psychophysiological records is tedious and often less than reliable. Therefore, it is desirable to utilize some means of reducing the physiological measure to a readable format. There are several methods used to automatically reduce data, although the basic concepts are the same in all cases. The most elementary reduction technique is the conversion of the physiological response to a digital format by means of an analogue-to-digital (A–D) converter. An A–D converter is simply a device that outputs a discrete pulse that is directly related to the amplitude of a continuous but variable input (i.e., Schmidt triggers, level slicers, window discriminators, etc.). The second type of device for reducing data is an integrator. This instrument averages ongoing biological responses and presents either an average response level or a cumulative record of activity for a fixed period. Peripheral data reduction devices are discussed more fully by Rugh and Schwitzgebel (this volume).

There are variations on these devices that become complex and costly, ranging all the way to complete computer systems for on line analysis of any preprogrammed aspect of the physiological response. However, for use in assessment of behavioral disorders, the simplest system of a transducer, amplifier, and output transducer with a basic data reduction device is usually adequate.

Although the conceptualization of psychophysiological instrumentation is not complex, there are numerous technical details that must be considered to obtain valid and reliable measures. It is beyond the scope of the present chapter to cover all the specific aspects of recording methodology. Excellent discussions of these issues can be found in Brown (1967), Greenfield and Sternbach (1972), and Venables and Martin (1967).

Biological amplifiers are an integral part of any laboratory where the assessment of psychophysiological responses is undertaken. These amplifiers permit the recording of extremely small electrical or mechanical changes within the organism. Table 10–1 summarizes the physiological response systems and the instrumentation necessary to measure each response. The table presents a brief summary of the electrical characteristics of the biological responses and the devices used to measure them. The best source of information on the characteristics of a particular bioamplifier is the instruction manual supplied by the manufacturer. Thorough familiarity with the measurement instrument is the best way to avoid many problems with interpretation of the physiological record. As Table 10–1 indicates, biological signals may be recorded directly by electrodes or derived through the use of transducers. Regardless of the origin of the signal, there are two basic types of amplifiers used in psychophysiological measurement —the preamplifier and the driver amplifier. The preamplifier is considered the first stage of amplification. That is, the input cable originating from the subject is interfaced initially to the preamplifier coupling or connection. Preamplifiers boost the recorded signal, but the type of preamplifier input coupling will determine the characteristics of the response that it receives. A direct coupling (DC) input will pass only unidirectional electrical signals to the preamplifier, thus permitting the recording of slow biological responses. Conversely, a capacitor-coupled (AC) input will filter out the DC portion of the signal and permit the passing of the rapidly changing, bidirectional aspects of the signal. Input coupling is critical in that it may completely change the interpretation of the measured response. For example, the electrodermal response (see next section) is composed of a tonic (DC) and phasic (AC) component that can be recorded from the same set of elecrodes by passing the signal through separate AC and DC input couplers.

Psychophysiological responses are generally characterized by their frequency [cycles per second or Hertz (Hz)] and magnitude (amplitude-voltage). Specific preamplifiers are used to record these parameters with minimum distortion. In addition to the coupling characteristics described above, amplifiers are usually classified by the degree of amplification (gain) and their frequency characteristics (frequencies at which they can operate with maximum gain and minimum distortion of the signal).

Most preamplifiers are equipped with external sensitivity or gain controls (analogous to the volume control on a stereo) that permit the oper-

Table 10–1. Characteristics of Biological Response Systems and Appropriate Psychophysiological Instrumentation

Response System	Psychophysiological Response	Physiological Basis of Response
Somatic	Electromyogram (EMG)	Muscle action potentials
Cardiovascular	Electrocardiogram (EKG)	Action potentials of cardiac muscle during contraction.
	Blood Pressure (BP)	Systolic: Force of blood leaving the heart. Diastolic: Residual pressure in the vascular system.
	Blood Volume (BV)	Tonic level of blood in the tissue.
	Blood Volume Pulse (BVP)	Phasic level of blood with each cardiac contraction.
Electrodermal	Skin Resistance Level (SRL) and Response (SRR)	Source of signal is uncertain. Current theories favor sweat gland activity.
	Skin Conductance Level (SCL) and Response (SCR)	Reciprocal of SRR and SRL.
	Skin Potential Response (SPR)	Unclear. Probably represents changes in membrane potentials.
Central Nervous System	Electroencephalogram (EEG)	Electrical activity of cortical neurons.
	Average Evoked Response (AER)	Same as EEG in response to identifiable stimulus.
	Contingent Negative Variation (CNV)	Same as EEG, appears during preparatory responses.
Gastric	Stomach motility	Peristaltic movement of stomach.
	Stomach pH	Level of acidity of stomach contents.
Specialized Responses	Sexual	
	Male (penile circumference)	Engorgement of penis with blood.
	Female (vaginal blood volume or pulse)	Engorgement of vagina with blood.
	Temperature	Probably vasomotor and sweat gland activity.
	Respiration	Inhalation and exhalation of air.

Table 10–1. (continued)

Response	Electrical and/or Physical Characteristics	Quantifiable Aspects of the Response
EMG	Bioelectric potential, uvolt—mvolt, fast AC	Amplitude or cumulative activity.
EKG	Bioelectric potential, mvolt, slow AC	Rate, liability/stability.
BP	Physical—electrical characteristics depend on the transducer used. Typically use occlusion cuff and auditory pickup.	Systolic/diastolic pressure, mm of Hg.
BV BVP	Physical—typically a photoplethysmograph is used.	Amplitude, lability/stability.
SRL SRR	Exosomatic electric current or voltage. Measure is change in resistance to applied current or voltage.	Absolute level for SRL. Frequency or magnitude of SRR.
SPR	Bioelectric potential, mvolt, slow AC	Frequency or magnitude.
EEG	Bioelectric potential, uvolt—mvolt, AC	Amplitude, frequency or power spectrum.
AER	Bioelectric potential, mvolt, slow AC	Amplitude and latency of specific components.
CNV	Bioelectric potential, mvolt, DC	Magnitude and latency.
Motility	External: uvolt—mvolt, fast AC Internal: Physical event, characteristics depend on transducer.	Frequency and strength of contraction.
pH	Transducer sensitive to hydrogen ions.	pH
Penile	Physical—electrical characteristics depend on transducer, usually strain gauge—mvolt, DC.	Percentage of full erection.
Vaginal (BVP) (BV)	Physical—photoplethysmograph.	Amplitude, lability/stability.
Temperature	Physical—thermistor or thermocouple.	Absolute temperature or difference between two sites.
Respiration	Physical—typically strain gauge or temperature device at nostril.	Rate and depth.

Table 10–1. (continued)

Response	Instrumentation Characteristics	Useful Peripheral Reduction Apparatus
EMG	Wide-band, high-gain, AC-coupled preamplifier.	Average or cumulative integrator.
EKG	Low-frequency, AC- or DC-coupled preamplifier.	Cardiotachograph and A-D converter.
BP	Low-frequency, AC- or DC-coupled preamplifier.	Level detectors.
BV	DC-coupled preamplifier.	A–D converter.
BVP	AC-coupled preamplifier.	A–D converter.
SRL	DC-coupled preamplifier.	A–D converter.
SRR	Low-frequency, AC-coupled preamplifier.	A–D converter.
SPR	Low-frequency, AC-coupled preamplifier.	A–D converter.
EEG	High-frequency, wide-band AC-coupled preamplifier.	Integrator for gross measure of activity in selected frequency bands.
AER	Derived from averaging ongoing EEG.	Typically requires elaborate peripheral equipment to quantify for clinical use.
CNV	DC-coupled preamplifier. Derived from averaging of ongoing EEG.	AER and CNV are derived by computer or photographic averaging.
Motility	Same as somatic responses.	A–D converter.
pH	Typically recorded by telemetry.	A–D converter.
Penile	DC-coupled preamplifier.	A–D converter.
Vaginal (BV)	DC-coupled preamplifier.	A–D converter.
(BVP)	AC-coupled preamplifier	A–D converter.
Temperature	DC-coupled preamplifier.	Meter or digital temperature read-out device.
Respiration	Same as other strain gauge devices or temperature devices.	A–D converter.

ator to adjust the magnitude of the amplifier output for various levels of input signal strength. The frequency characteristics of a preamplifier are a function of the design of the amplifier and the filters within the circuit. As with the gain control, there are usually external filter settings on good quality bioamplifiers. These filters are divided into low or high frequency responses depending on whether they permit the selective passage of low or high frequencies. Additionally, many preamplifiers and driver amplifiers are equipped with a special notch filter that selectively filters out 60 Hz signals from external AC sources such as light fixtures and electrical wall outlets.

The second stage of amplification is executed by the driver amplifier, which further boosts the signal to a level sufficient to "drive" or operate the output transducer. Output transducers may take any form that will permit the conversion of the amplified electrical signal into some non-electrical form for recording and analysis. Typical output transducers include oscillographs, computers, behavioral programming equipment, or simple meter movements. The most common type of output transducer is the pen writer or oscillograph, which provides a continuous permanent record of the assessment session.

The discussion above provides only a brief introduction to the use of bioamplifiers. In addition to the manual that accompanies each measurement device the reader who is interested in a more detailed description of bioamplifiers is referred to Yanoff (1972) or Deifenderfer (1972).

BIOLOGICAL RESPONSE: PHYSIOLOGICAL AND ELECTRICAL CHARACTERISTICS

The choice of a physiological system in behavioral assessment is determined by several factors. In an applied setting the psychophysiologist is dealing with an intact organism. Therefore, measures must be taken externally or through a natural orifice of the body (e.g., mouth). Since most biological responses are too small to detect and interpret without elaborate instrumentation, recording is limited to those responses for which biomedical engineers have developed adequate measurement devices. Finally, the selection of a physiological response is often determined by historical precedent. As noted earlier, the James-Lange theory placed the physiological basis of emotion in the autonomic nervous system. The somatic response system is also involved in the expression of emotion. The influence of both the visceral and somatic systems is reflected by such phrases as "shaking in my boots," 'butterflies in my stomach," "my heart was pounding with fear," and "she blushed like a new bride." Tremors represent somatic activity (skeletal muscle responses) whereas gastric motility, heart rate, and peripheral vasomotor responses indicate involvement of the autonomic nervous system. Both these systems are in turn regulated by the central nervous system.

In this section the physiological response systems will be presented with an emphasis on the biological basis of each response and an introductory comment on the measurement of each. The majority of the information on the physiology of the response systems was taken from Mountcastle (1974) and represents only the briefest summary of the data. The interested reader should examine Mountcastle (1974) or a comparable physiology text for further information.

SOMATIC RESPONSE SYSTEM

The skeletal muscle system is a complex of effectors and affectors that innervate the muscle and supply the central nervous system with information regarding limb position, direction, force, and rate of movement. In the simplest form the action of skeletal muscle is initiated by the discharge of specialized nerve endings (Thompson, 1967). When physiological recordings of skeletal muscle activity are made with surface electrodes, it is the sum of numerous muscle action potentials (MAP) that is being measured (Goldstein, 1972). The amplitude and frequency of the electromyogram (EMG) is influenced by the number of individual motor units activated at any given time (Basmajian, 1962).

During the generation of an MAP, very small electrical potentials are produced at each neuromuscular junction. These bioelectric potentials, when summed across many individual muscle fibers, produce a signal that can be detected with surface electrodes and amplified by appropriate instrumentation. Because of the short duration of the MAPs and their small magnitude, a high-gain, fast-frequency, AC-coupled amplifier is necessary to record the EMG response.

VISCERAL RESPONSE SYSTEM

Visceral functions are controlled by the autonomic nervous system (ANS). The ANS is comprised of two distinct components—sympathetic and parasympathetic. Traditionally, the sympathetic nervous system (SNS) has been associated with activation of bodily functions and mobilization of energy, whereas the parasympathetic nervous system (PNS) is identified with the conservation of energy and inhibition of visceral activity

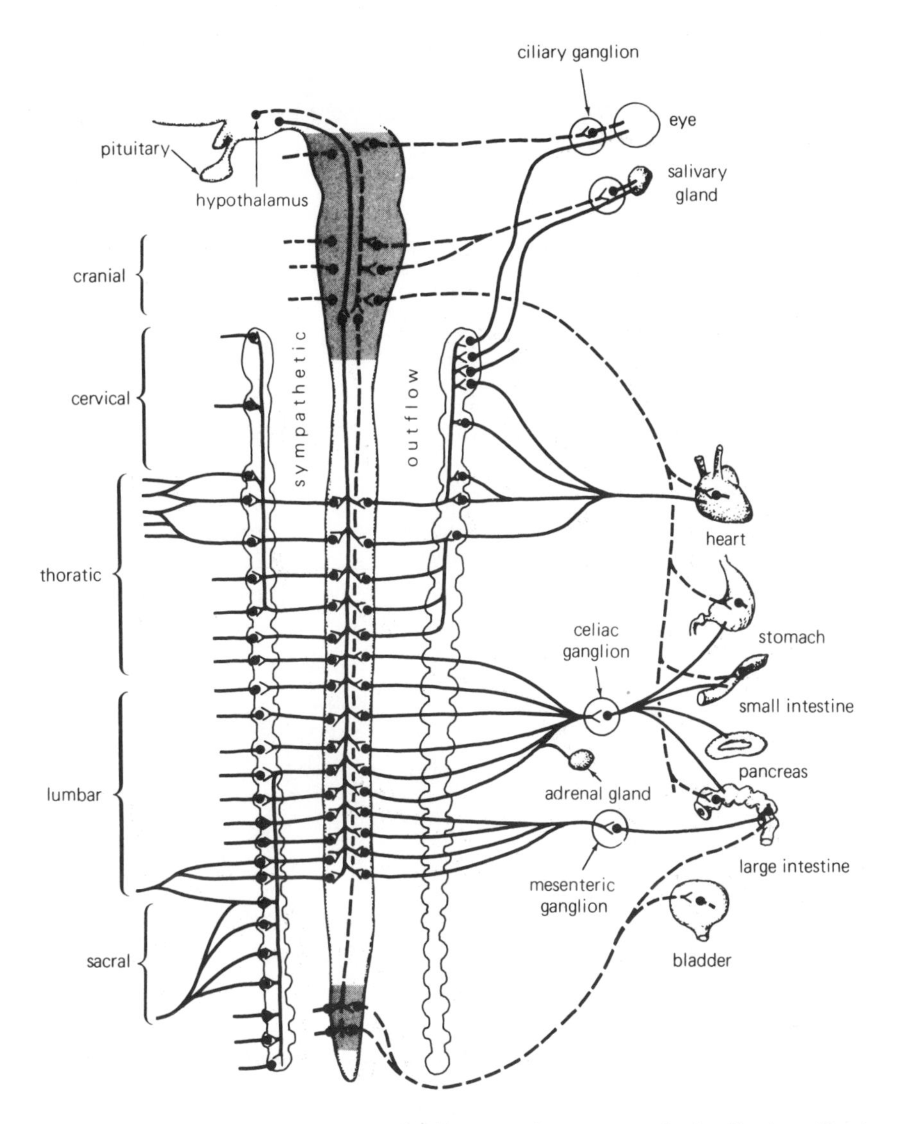

Figure 10–2. The sympathetic (solid lines) and parasympathetic (broken lines) divisions of the autonomic nervous system and their visceral connections. (From P. M. Milner, *Physiological Psychology,* copyright 1970 by Holt, Rinehart, & Winston, Inc. Based on original figure from E. Gardner, *Fundamentals of Neurology,* 6th edition. Philadelphia, W. B. Saunders Company, 1975, p. 268. Reproduced by permission).

(Thompson, 1967). Although this schema is an oversimplification, it is satisfactory as a general description of the function of the autonomic nervous system. As seen in Figure 10–2, the viscera are generally supplied by both the SNS and PNS, although the sweat glands and peripheral vascular system are thought to receive only sympathetic innervation (Thompson, 1967).

In addition to the anatomical distinction between the SNS and PNS, they are characterized by the presence of two different neurotransmitters at the postganglionic synapse. The SNS is said to be an adrenergic system because of the presence of noradrenalin or norepinephrine as the postganglionic neurotransmitter. In contrast the neurotransmitter substance of the PNS is acetylcholine, hence the system is frequently referred to as a cholinergic system. A typical ANS-visceral interaction is presented in Figure 10–3.

There is one notable exception to the division of adrenergic and cholinergic innervation. As noted above, the sweat glands receive only sympathetic innervation. However, the postganglionic neurotransmitter for the cutaneous sweat glands is acetylcholine, the PNS neurotransmitter.

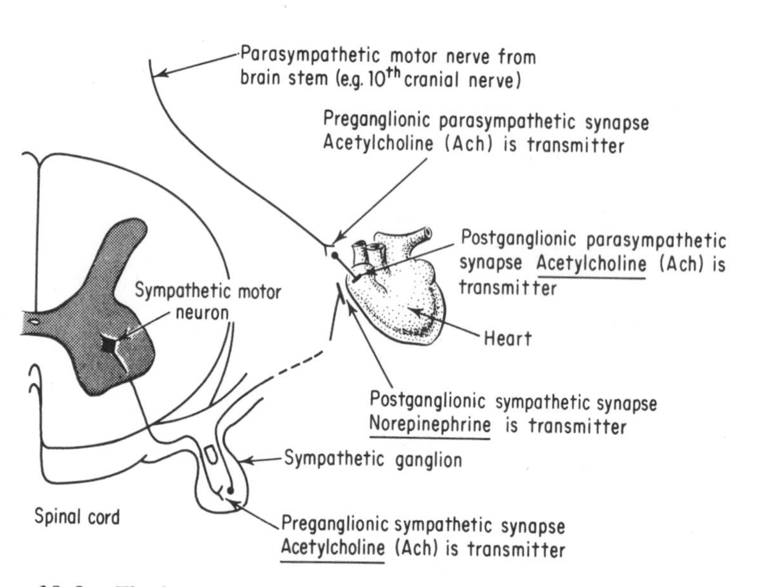

Figure 10–3. The interaction of the autonomic nervous system with cardiac functioning. Presented as a representative visceral-ANS interaction. [Figure 8.3 (p. 199) from *Foundations of Physiological Psychology* by Richard F. Thompson. Copyright © 1967 by Richard F. Thompson. By permission of Harper & Row, Publishers].

Cardiovascular Response System

Heart

The cardiac muscle contains internal pacing cells that stimulate the muscle fibers to contract even in the absence of any external innervation. The rate of firing of these internal pacing cells can be excited or inhibited by the action of sympathetic fibers from the cervical and thoracic region of the spinal cord and parasympathetic fibers of the vagus nerve, respectively (Milnor, 1974). Stimulation of the vagus produces cardiac deceleration (bradycardia), whereas blocking of vagal influences produces heart rate acceleration (tachycardia). Obrist, Lawler, Howard, Smithson, Martin, and Manning (1974) have suggested that the parasympathetic influences on heart rate are predominant, and sympathetic influences are active only during acute stress. Furthermore, the sympathetic influences appear to be independent of other somatic activities, whereas parasympathetic influences appear to be directly related to the overall level of somatic activity.

The clinical use of the electrocardiogram (EKG) entails careful placement of the recording electrodes on the surface because the waveform of the EKG is different at various recording sites (Milnor, 1974). For the purpose of the psychologist, the placement of the electrodes is generally not critical because the primary interest is in heart rate rather than the shape of the EKG waveform. The measurement of heart rate has traditionally been done with surface recording electrodes that measure the bioelectric action potentials produced by the cardiac muscle during contraction. As shown in Table 10–1, this method of measurement requires a low-frequency, AC-coupled preamplifier or a DC-coupled preamplifier. Stern (1974) has recently suggested that heart rate can be recorded more reliably with a photoplethysmograph on the earlobe.

Blood pressure

The cardiovascular system is most easily understood in terms of a hydraulic model. Blood pressure in the cardiovascular system is a function of numerous factors. Among the biological variables that influence blood pressure are: (1) viscosity of the blood, (2) plasticity of the blood vessels, (3) strength and rate of cardiac contractions, and (4) the volume of blood in the system in relation to the total volume of the blood vessels (Milnor, 1974a).

Systolic and diastolic blood pressure are the two components of the blood pressure response that are typically reported. Systolic blood pressure is the force with which the blood leaves the heart. It represents the pressure at which blood is forced into the atrium and out of the heart by contraction of the ventricle. The diastolic blood pressure represents the force with which the blood flows back to the heart and therefore is representative of the residual pressure in the vascular bed when the cardiac muscle relaxes (Milnor, 1974a).

Because of the complex nature of the blood pressure response there are several points in the cardiovascular system where the ANS can exert its influence. Changes in the rate or strength of cardiac contraction will produce changes in blood pressure. Constriction or dilation of the vascular beds will produce increases or decreases in blood pressure with constant heart stroke volume. Typically the cardiovascular system works as a unit to maintain homeostasis. Since decreases in blood pressure are frequently accompanied by increases in heart rate (Milnor, 1974b), a normally functioning cardiovascular system can show multidirectional changes in different components at any given time.

Blood pressure is a derived physical measure that must be recorded with a transducer that can change the physical event into an electrical signal for amplification. The most common device for recording blood pressure externally is the sphygnomanometer. This device includes an occlusion cuff that is used to stop both the arterial and venous blood flow in the periphery. In its simplest form the sphygnomanometer is used with a stethoscope that allows one to listen to the sound of the blood as it begins to flow in the limb following deflation of the occlusion cuff. The point at which the first heart sound (Korotkoff sound) is heard is the systolic blood pressure, and the pressure at which the last sound is heard is the diastolic pressure. Devices are available that will automatically inflate the occlusion cuff at fixed time intervals, and an auditory pickup (microphone) can be used to transfer the Korotkoff sounds to a physiological recording device. The bioamplification system characteristic is dependent on the type of transducer used.

Vasomotor Response

Vasomotor activity has been differentiated into two components, blood volume (BV) and blood volume pulse (BVP). Blood volume represents the absolute level of blood in the tissue and is considered to be the tonic component of the vasomotor response. The blood volume pulse represents the blood flow through the tissue with each cardiac contraction and represents the sum of the tonic blood volume and the phasic pulse volume (Brown, 1967).

Autonomic innervation of the blood vessels is poorly understood. The BV and BVP are a function of volume of blood in the system, strength of cardiac contraction, and diameter of the blood vessels. The latter is the most critical aspect of the vasomotor response for the typical measurement of this response in assessment. Dilation and constriction of the blood vessels is controlled by the autonomic nervous system. However, there is considerable debate as to whether there is both SNS and PNS innervation of this response. The current view presented in most textbooks is that there is only sympathetic innervation of the peripheral vascular system (e.g., Thompson, 1967). The direction of change following sympathetic activation of the blood vessels varies with location. For example, the orienting reflex is mediated by sympathetic activity, yet it is characterized by simultaneous vasoconstriction in the periphery and cephalic vasodilation (Sokolov, 1963).

Like blood pressure, blood volume and blood volume pulse are physical characteristics that must be converted to electrical signals for psychophysiological recording. The most common method for measuring BV and BVP is with a photoplethysmograph, a device that measures the light either transmitted through or reflected from a section of tissue. Because tissue is relatively transparent to light whereas blood is relatively opaque, the amount of light transmitted or reflected is directly proportional to the amount of blood in the underlying tissue. A DC-coupled amplifier will permit the recording of the relatively slow changes in blood volume whereas an AC-coupled amplifier will pass the faster changing BVP responses (Brown, 1967; Brown, Giddon, & Dean, 1965).

Electrodermal Response System

The electrodermal response (EDR) can be divided into two distinct classes of response—endosomatic and exosomatic. The endosomatic response is a bioelectrical potential and occurs in the absence of any applied external current. The exosomatic response is not a bioelectric potential but represents changes in skin resistance to an applied, external source of voltage or current. Endosomatic and exosomatic responses can be further divided into tonic and phasic components. In the past the terms GSR (galvanic skin response) and PGR (psychogalvanic skin response) have been used indiscriminately to describe different responses and procedures. To avoid confusion the Society for Psychophysiological Research has recommended adoption of the standard nomenclature described in Table 10–2.

Table 10–2. Standard nomenclature for electrodermal responses (EDR)

Tonic measure	Phasic measure
Skin resistance level (SRL)	Skin resistance response (SRR)[a]
Skin conductance level (SCL)	Skin conductance response (SCR)
Skin potential level (SPL)	Skin potential response (SPR)

[a] Historically the term nonspecific GSR has referred to the SRR.

The physiological basis of the EDR is uncertain. Theories have suggested such varied sources as muscle action potentials, vasomotor activity, changes in membrane potentials, and sweat gland activity. Currently the consensus is that the exosomatic responses reflect changes in sweat gland activity whereas endosomatic responses probably represent changes in the permeability of cell membranes in the skin (Edelberg, 1967, 1972).

The measurement of skin potential responses is a complex matter because of problems with electrode bias and polarization. As with all bioelectric potentials, the response can be picked up by external electrodes and amplified directly. The skin potential response is a relatively slow changing, biphasic response and should be amplified with a low-frequency, AC-coupled preamplifier.

The tonic and phasic component of the exosomatic response can be recorded from the same set of skin electrodes by using two independent amplifier coupling systems. A DC-coupled amplifier will allow the recording of the slow changing SRL whereas a low-frequency, AC-coupled preamplifier will permit the recording of the more rapidly changing SRR response. The frequently reported SCL and SCR are derived from the SRL and SRR by a reciprocal transformation. Edelberg (1967, 1972) has written several guides for the measurement of the EDR. His excellent chapters on the EDR should be consulted before attempting to use these measures in any assessment program.

Gastrointestinal Response System

There are many aspects of gastrointestinal activity that have been measured by the psychophysiologist. In the present section only gastric motility and stomach acidity (pH) will be discussed because they are the most frequently reported measures. A more complete discussion of measures of the gastrointestinal response system can be found in Wolff and Welsh (1972).

Everyone is familiar with the feeling of "butterflies" in the stomach. This common sign of emotionality is thought to be a function of increased stomach motility. In normal digestive functioning the smooth muscle of the stomach produces internal rhythmic electrical potentials at approximately 20-second intervals. These slow potentials can produce peristaltic movement, or contraction of the stomach wall, if followed by a secondary action potential. This secondary action potential can arise from several sources, including parasympathetic discharge through the Vagal nerve, circulating hormones, or internal reflexes (Hendrix, 1974). A crude measure of gastric motility can be obtained by recording the action potentials by external EMG electrodes. More refined measures can be derived indirectly by converting the physical contraction of the muscle into an electrical signal with an internal transducer (see Rugh & Schwitzgebel, this volume).

Acid content, or pH level, of the stomach has only recently become an area of interest to the psychophysiologist. The advent of ingestible transducers and telemetry techniques permits the monitoring of this response without the complicated intubation procedures necessary in the past (Mackay, 1967).

Hydrochloric acid is produced by the parietal cells of the gastric lining. These cells are stimulated to release acid by the interaction of neural stimuli and gastrin, a hormone produced in the pyloric anterum. Stimulation of acid secretion is initiated by the vagal nerve and stretch receptors in the lining of the stomach. Psychophysiological measurement of stomach acidity is accomplished by transducers that are sensitive to varying concentrations of hydrogen ions (pH) in the stomach (Hendrix, 1974).

CENTRAL NERVOUS SYSTEM

The electroencephalogram (EEG) represents a gross measure of the electrical activity of the cortex of the brain. More specifically, the EEG is a measure of the electrical potential difference between any two electrodes placed on the scalp. Because the EEG is recorded from surface electrodes it is believed to represent activity from a group of cortical neurons in the periphery of the electrode site.

The activity of the EEG is most often classified in terms of frequency or cycles per second—hertz (Hz). Several frequency ranges have been identified and given standard labels (Berger, 1933). The most widely investigated frequencies are alpha, beta, delta, and gamma. The alpha frequencies are between 8 and 12 Hz with an amplitude of 25 to 100 microvolts (μV). Beta rhythm, the second most common component of the adult EEG, has a characteristic frequency range of 13 to 30 Hz with an amplitude rarely exceeding 20 μV. The theta wave (found predominantly in children) has a frequency of 4 to 7 Hz with an amplitude of approximately 20 μV. The theta wave attenuates in amplitude and density after the age of 20 in humans. Delta wave activity is defined as frequencies of less than 4 Hz and is considered abnormal in the waking adult EEG. Finally, the gamma wave is used to describe all high-frequency (35 to 50 Hz) activity in the EEG. Although controversy in the area exists, various subjective states have been associated with the four frequency ranges (Grossman, 1973).

In addition to the traditional classification by frequency, a specialized waveform found over the sensorimotor cortex in man and cats has been described recently and is of interest because of its association with the inhibition of seizure activity. This waveform, termed the sensorimotor rhythm (SMR) is defined as having a frequency of approximately that of alpha but is differentiated by its location on the cortex (Sterman, 1973; Sterman, McDonald, & Stone, 1974).

In addition to the standard EEG patterns, there are two derived characteristics of cortical activity that have been related to psychological variables—the sensory averaged evoked response (AER), and the contingent negative variation (CNV). The sensory AER is the average of several specific segments of the EEG over time. These segments are time locked to the presentation of a sensory stimulus (usually visual, auditory, or somatosensory) and represent the averaged cortical response to the multiple presentation of a stimulus. Averaging is used to filter out the random patterns of electrical activity in the ongoing EEG and to provide what is believed to be a cortical response to environmental stimuli. Psychological variables such as expectancy and attention appear to influence the AER (Sutton, Tueting, Zubin, & John, 1967; Wilkinson, 1970). A more complete description of the AER is provided by Katzman (1964).

The contingent negative variation (CNV) is a slow, negative DC-potential shift in the EEG observed between the warning and response stimuli in a reaction time task (Walter, Cooper, Aldridge, McCallum, & Winter, 1964). As with the AER, the CNV is an averaged response. However, fewer signals are necessary to obtain a clear recording of the CNV.

The EEG and its derived characteristics (i.e., AER and CNV) are all electrical potentials produced by the neurons of the cerebral cortex. It is believed by certain investigators that these rhythmic electrical potentials represent excitability changes in cortical neurons. According to Brazier (1968), cortical responses may be the result of the several factors known to influence individual nerve cell activity.

SPECIALIZED RESPONSE SYSTEMS

Sexual Arousal

Sexual arousal in the male is evidenced by erection of the penis due to engorgement of the sexual organ with blood. This engorgement can be brought on by CNS-mediated cognitive processes or reflexively by direct stimulation of the genitalia. Innervation of the sexual organ is primarily parasympathetic. However, sympathetic fibers also produce erection and are primarily responsible for ejaculation (Koizumi & Brooks, 1974). Measurement of male sexual arousal is most easily accomplished with a strain gauge device that is sensitive to changes in circumference of the penis (Freund, 1963).

Female sexual arousal is mediated by similar neural systems. A physical characteristic of female sexual arousal is increased blood flow in the lining of the vagina (Masters & Johnson, 1966). This response is most commonly measured with a reflectance photoelectric transducer similar to the device used to measure BV or BVP (Sintchak & Geer, 1975).

Temperature

Skin temperature is regulated primarily by the vascular system of the underlying tissue. Typically skin temperature has a greater range than internal temperatures. The skin temperature is regulated by a complex system of temperature receptors in the skin and can be modified by changes in blood flow, sweat gland activity, or muscle activity (Hardy & Bard, 1974). Skin temperature can be measured directly with any temperature sensitive device (i.e., thermometer) or indirectly with a thermistor or thermocouple that translates temperature to an electrical signal for use with bioamplifier and recording systems. Some researchers have used skin temperature as an indirect measure of blood volume (e.g., Sargent, Green, & Walters, 1973).

Respiration

Inspiration and expiration of air in the process of breathing is controlled primarily by neurons in the medulla. Respiration depth and rate can be controlled automatically by the brainstem or voluntarily by the organism. Normal breathing is a function of rhythmic activity of the muscles of the diaphragm. In addition to normal breathing there are numerous respiratory reflexes that can be evoked by various chemical or physical agents (Lambertsen, 1974).

Psychophysiologists are typically interested in only the basic components of depth and rate of respiration. Since respiration is a physical process, its recording characteristics depend on the type of transducer employed. A strain gauge around the diaphragm can provide a measure of depth and rate of breathing. Temperature-sensitive devices such as a thermocouple or thermistor, when taped to the skin below a nostril, can also be used to obtain relative measures of both depth and rate of breathing since inhaled air is cooler than expired air. As with other temperature measures, a DC-coupled preamplifier is satisfactory.

Again, this section cannot serve as a complete guide to psychophysiological measurement. It is meant to be an overview of the most common psychophysiological response systems used in assessment. For the reader interested in adding the psychophysiological channel of measurement to their assessment procedures, several handbooks are available (Brown, 1967; Greenfield & Sternbach, 1972). In addition, the chapter by Geddes (1967) provides an excellent review of electrodes and transducers in psychophysiological measurement.

METHODS OF PSYCHOPHYSIOLOGICAL ASSESSMENT

Historically psychophysiological measurement has been used in clinical research to define specific patterns of biological responses for individual behaviors (affective, cognitive, and motor). Ax (1953) first described specific patterns of physiological responses for anger and fear. These patterns included greater increases in diastolic blood pressure, frequency of SRRs and frontalis EMG, and greater deceleration of heart rate for anger than for fear. Fearful subjects showed higher skin conductance levels (SCL) and respiratory rate than the anger group. Clearly the ability to differentiate classes of behavior disorders on the basis of physiological responses, as Ax reported with emotions, would be extremely important to the practicing clinical psychologist. However, little substantial progress has been made in this area since Ax's classic work.

Approaches to the identification of specific response patterns have varied. Some investigators have examined basal level responses between clinically defined groups (e.g., Hart, 1974; Venables & Wing, 1962) whereas others have evaluated the reactivity of these clinical populations to various types of stimulation (e.g., Lovallo, Parsons, & Holloway, 1973; Malmo & Shagass, 1952).

One of the underlying assumptions of the above approach is that behavior reflects a stable psychobiological state of the organism. This approach has typically dealt with the concept of an arousal continuum along which all behaviors can be classified (e.g., Duffy, 1962; Malmo, 1957). In a recent review of the arousal literature Alexander (1972) has sugested that the utility of this approach to psychophysiological assessment is questionable.

Recent evidence from psychophysiology and personality theory suggests that behavior is situation specific (Mischel, 1968). The concept of *situational specificity* implies that behaviors occur in a given environmental context and do not represent an underlying biological or personality trait. Therefore, the assessment of behavior and concomitant physiological responses is *valid only in relation to a specific set of stimulus events.*

In addition to situational specificity Lacey and Lacey (1970) have presented a case for response specificity or "response stereotypy." These authors suggest that each individual responds to a given stimulus event in an idiosyncratic manner. For example, one subject may show electrodermal reactivity whereas another may exhibit predominantly cardiovascular changes in response to the same stimulus event.

The concepts of situational and response specificity suggest a specialized approach to psychophysiological measurement in behavioral assessment. Situational specificity necessitates the evaluation of each organism's reactivity to an individualized complex of stimuli. For example, to assess a sexual disorder it is necessary to evaluate sexual arousal patterns in the presence of relevant sexual stimuli. In the case of a social phobic it is unlikely that the client will demonstrate unique physiological response patterns in a resting state. However, when exposed to a specific fearful stimulus (in vivo or cognitive), they may exhibit changes in autonomic activity. It is evident from these examples that an adequate behavioral interview is a necessary prerequisite for any psychophysiological assessment.

The concept of response specificity requires the sampling of multiple physiological systems to assure a valid assessment. Any individual may show responses in a specific biological modality, but this is a highly individualized phenomenon and the most responsive system for a given subject can be determined only during the assessment.

Assuming that the relevant stimulus events have been selected and the maximally responsive biological system has been identified, there are several other factors that must be considered to ensure a valid and reliable interpretation of the psychophysiological recording.

Artifacts

Many variables can alter the activity of a physiological response system. For the purpose of psychophysiological recording these variables can be divided into two broad classes—artifacts and psychobiologically relevant stimuli. Artifacts are defined here as *any change in a psychophysiological response system that is not attributable to a psychobiologically relevant stimulus*. This rather broad definition includes not only the traditionally defined sources of artifacts such as movement or electrical interference but the more subtle, environmental variables that can produce a false-positive interpretation of the psychophysiological record.

There has been a tremendous amount of research dealing with psychological variables that alter physiological response systems. However, Lacey's (1967) response specificity concept leads to the conclusion that there is no single biological system or group of systems that responds to only one psychological event. It is not the intent here to review all the literature on behavior-physiology relationships. A review of any major work on psychophysiology (e.g., Duffy, 1962; Greenfield and Sternbach, 1972; Martin, 1961) will convince the reader that almost any biological response system can and will respond to almost any psychological variable (cognitive, motor, or affective). The purpose of this section is to provide some information on those variables that produce artifacts in the psychophysiological record. These artifacts can be divided into two major categories: artifacts of instrumentation and recording, and artifacts of interpretation (false-positives or false-negatives).

Artifacts of instrumentation can be attributed primarily to two sources—the organism and the measurement environment. Organismic artifacts are primarily the result of movement. Any shift in the interface between the subject and the electrode or between the electrode or subject and the conductive medium (electrode paste) will cause an artifact in the record. To avoid movement artifacts, subjects should be kept as comfortable and immobile as possible. Some means of directly observing the subject is advisable so that movements preceding changes in the physiological record can be noted. In the case of small bioelectric potentials (i.e., EMG or EEG), movement artifacts become crucial, and even eye blinks will produce changes in the EEG or frontalis muscle tension record.

The major environmental source of instrumentation artifact is transient electrical fields in the test room. Because of the extreme sensitivity required for recording bioelectric potentials, even small, stray electrical signals can interfere with the recording. Electrical interference comes from AC wall outlets, fluorescent light fixtures, and peripheral electromechanical programming equipment. Electrical interference can be eliminated by electrically shielding the test chamber or by grounding the subject.

Artifacts of interpretation are more subtle yet more numerous and difficult to deal with than instrument artifacts. Significant changes may occur in any biological system in response to several variables other than those of clinical interest.

Any organism will orient, behaviorally and physiologically, to a novel stimulus (Sokolov, 1963). Although the orienting response habituates quickly, psychobiologically relevant stimuli habituate at a slower rate (Mangelesdorf & Zuckerman, 1975). Habituation is defined as a decrease in a physiological response with repeated stimulus presentations. To ensure that an organism's response is not due simply to the novelty of the stimulus it is often necessary to assess physiological reactivity over several sessions (Kallman, 1975).

Physiological systems are responsive to any change in ambient sensory levels. Starzl, Taylor and Magoun (1951) reported that auditory and tactile stimuli have a potent effect on the EEG pattern. Since then other sensory modalities have been shown to alter psychophysiological response systems. Noise, light, odors, tactile stimulation, and ambient temperature all affect biological response systems and can lead to a false-positive reading of the psychophysiological record. It is critical that ambient sensory levels be controlled during psychophysiological recording. The testing environment must be temperature controlled, sound treated and illuminated at a constant level within and between testing sessions.

During a test session there are necessary changes in sensory levels due to the changing of stimulus conditions from baseline to test periods. In this case, where sensory input is not constant and changes that produce an orienting response cannot be avoided, it is necessary to separate out the sensory and informational aspects of the relevant stimulus change. In Hebb's (1955) terms the "cue" function and "arousal" function of the stimulus must be differentiated. The cue function is that part of the stimulus that we have labeled psychobiologically relevant. "Cue" is the informational aspect of the stimulus that leads to a response different from that produced solely by the "arousal" value inherent in any sensory change. Finally, it should be noted that psychobiological relevance is not limited to those stimuli associated with undesirable behaviors or emotions. Averill and Opton (1975) reported that both pleasant and aversive situations produce changes in physiological responses. Stimuli that are chosen as neutral to control for the arousal function may also possess significant psychobiological information.

Assessment Cases

The following section includes several assessment cases from our records as examples of the methodological issues involved in psychophysiological assessment. These cases are limited in the range of response systems sampled and the type of problems evaluated. They are presented as illustrations of a general single-subject assessment procedure that is applicable to any problem. The mode of stimulus presentation may vary (i.e., in vivo or cognitive, visual or auditory, etc.), and the set of psychobiologically relevant stimuli will differ for each client, but the within and between sessions controls in the following examples will provide the practitioner with a framework within which any type of behavior problem or treatment program can be evaluated.

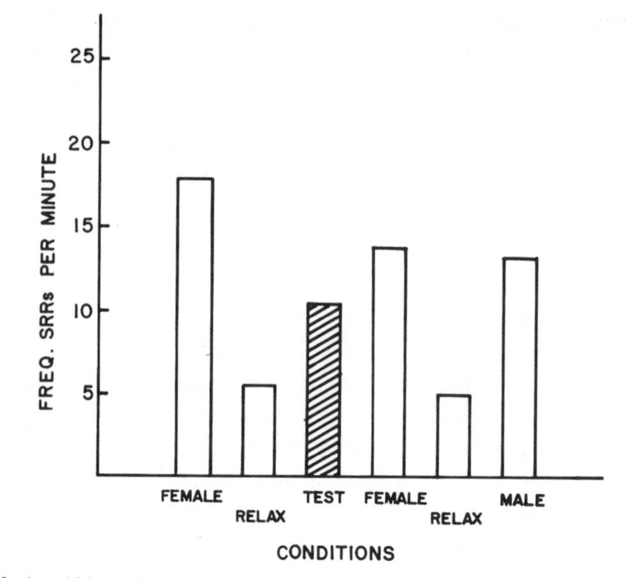

Figure 10–4. Skin resistance response of a social phobic during relaxation and social interaction with a female and male. Test condition represents introduction of a male peer with no interaction required.

The first case is that of a 23-year-old male with complaints of difficulty in relating to females. He reported anxiety associated with any type of heterosocial interaction but denied any problems in relating to male peers. The psychophysiological assessment plan involved measurement of the SRR during periods of relaxation and social interaction. Figure 10–4 shows that the resting level frequency of SRRs was relatively low. In contrast, during periods of interaction the level of physiological reactivity was noticeably higher. The difference in frequency of the SRRs between the two conditions (relaxation and interaction) is an example of the situational specificity of the biological response.

As an illustration of response specificity, Figure 10–5 presents changes in heart rate between neutral and psychobiologically relevant stimuli for two different clients. Client 1 was a 45-year-old male with multiple phobias. Client 2 was a 50-year-old male who complained of oversensitivity to criticism resulting in anxiety and depression. Each client was exposed to alternate presentations of neutral and psychobiologically relevant auditory stimuli in a single session. As Figure 10–5 illustrates, the first client demonstrates significant heart rate increases (stressful stimulus—baseline) across three assessment sessions whereas the second client shows very little heart rate reactivity in a session and habituation of the heart

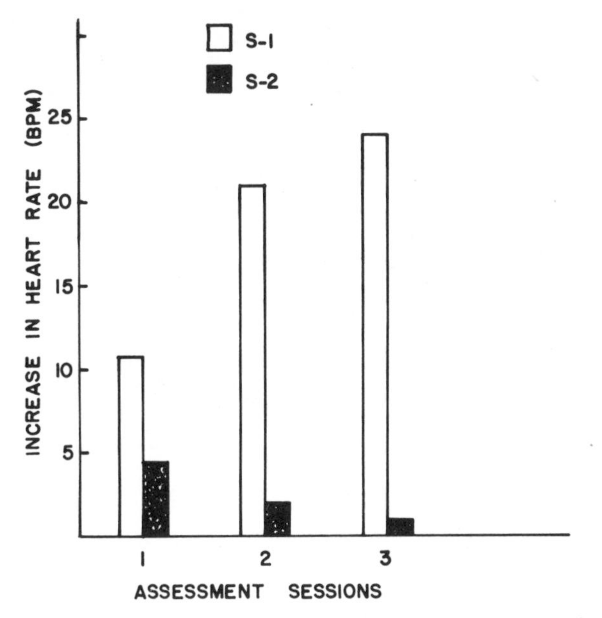

Figure 10–5. Increase in heart rate above baseline to fearful stimuli for two different clients. Client 1 shows increasing reactivity to the stimulus across sessions, whereas the second client shows habituation in the cardiac response system.

rate response across the three sessions. However, as seen in Figure 10–6, the second client did indicate psychophysiological reactivity in the electrodermal response system. Had heart rate been the only system sampled, it might have been concluded that the client's verbal report of anxiety and depression was not related to the stimuli being investigated.

Figures 10–4 and 10–6 depict the relevance of changes in sensory levels to psychophysiological reactivity. In the case summarized in Figure 10–4 there is both a sensory and informational (arousal and cue) change from relaxation to the introduction of a peer with instructions for the client to engage in social interaction. The test stimulus (hatched bar) represents the client's biological response to the introduction of a male peer into the environment without any expectancy of an occasion to interact. The presence of the peer alone resulted in an increase in the frequency of the SRRs. However, this increase was less than that seen during the presentation of a peer in the context of a social interaction.

Figure 10–6 represents an example of an attempt to control for the motor and sensory components of speech. The subject was instructed simply to verbalize neutral and depressive scenes. In the neutral verbalization conditions (three per assessment), with the exception of assessment session one, the frequency of SRRs was considerably less than in the de-

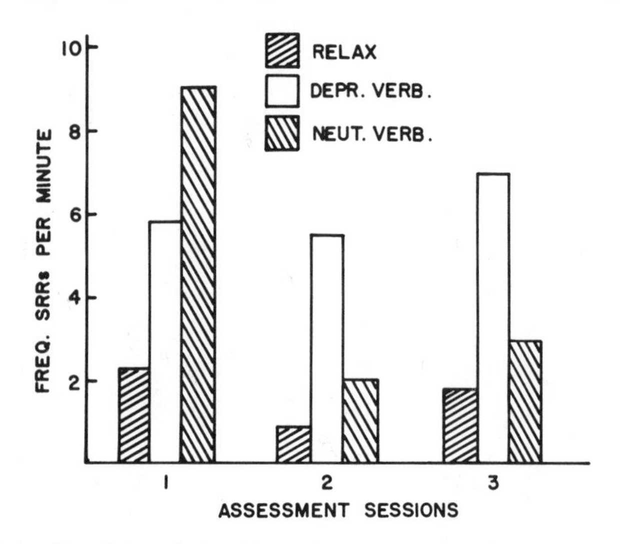

Figure 10–6. Reactivity of the skin resistance response for the second client in Figure 10–5. Although heart rate was not reactive to psychobiologically relevant stimuli, the skin resistance response was highly reactive.

pressive condition. However, the act of verbalization did result in an increase in reactivity. Without the use of a neutral verbalization condition the clinician would be unable to differentiate the arousal and cue functions of the depressive verbalization. Assessment session 1 in Figure 10–6 also demonstrates that positive as well as negative content may result in an increase in reactivity. The neutral scenes described by the client (e.g., going out to dinner) were apparently pleasant enough to elicit responses and hence could not be considered neutral from a psychobiological viewpoint.

Although the above cases illustrate specific aspects of a psychophysiological assessment methodology, the following is a case report of a comprehensive behavioral assessment utilizing all response channels (self-report, behavioral, and psychophysiological).

The subject was a 45-year-old male with complaints of chronic anxiety. Initially the client reported severe reactions to sudden noises that prevented him from operating an automobile (fear of someone blowing a horn) or working regularly at his trade (construction). Observations in the hospital indicated, however, that the problem was more global than a specific noise phobia. Based on information gathered in the intake interview, it appeared that the client's problem dated to a war incident involving an explosion and the death of a friend. However, this incident had occurred twenty years prior to the assessment, and there was no history of treatment for the anxiety during the interim. The stimuli involved in the anxiety could not be identified from the client's response to the Fear Survey Schedule because of a general response set to rank all stimuli as very fearful. The global nature of the client's complaint suggested a free-floating anxiety.

An initial assessment involved presenting the client with numerous audiotaped scenes consisting of specific events or objects in the environment (e.g., blood, automobiles, sports, etc.) as well as social interactions with family and peers. During this first assessment, physiological measures of blood pressure, respiration, and heart rate were taken. In addition, the subject was asked to rate the level of anxiety associated with each scene on a scale from 1 to 10 (1 = no anxiety, 10 = extreme anxiety).

As a consequence of this first session, three specific stimuli were identified that elicited high levels of heart rate reactivity and ratings of moderate to high anxiety on the self-rating scale.

The three stimuli that elicited a clear response were (1) blood, (2) being confined in a small room, and (3) a scene in which the subject was constantly surrounded by loud noises. The sensory value of the scenes was controlled within a session by having neutral scenes interspersed with the psychobiologically relevant stimuli. All the scenes were presented by a tape recorder with the sound-pressure level held constant. Figure 10–7 shows the subject's heart rate response on a beat-to-beat basis for the last minute of each 2-minute scene.

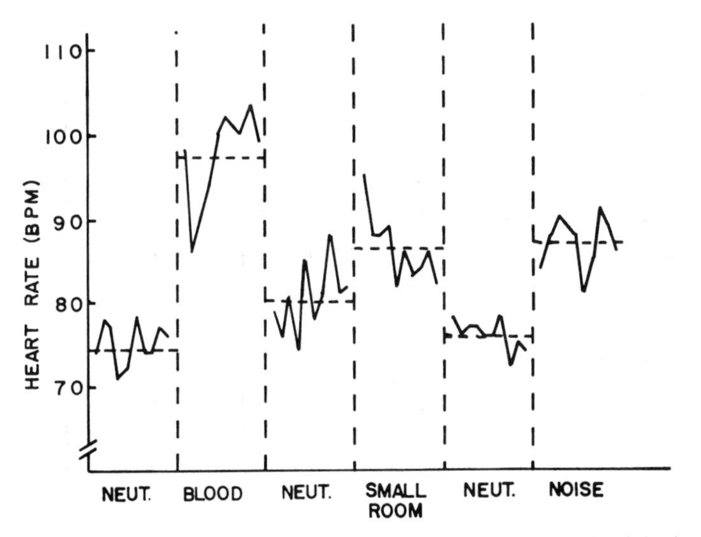

Figure 10–7. Beat-by-beat heart rate activity across several psychobiologic stimuli in a client with multiple phobias.

In the next phase of the assessment a behavioral avoidance task (BAT) was developed for each stimulus. For the blood stimulus the subject was asked to stand in a room with a blood-stained (vegetable dye) sheet. For the small room a closet three feet by three feet lit by a 75-watt overhead bulb was used. The noise task involved having the subject listen to a tape of random noises presented at a fixed volume. In each of the three behavior avoidance tests the subject was instructed to remain in the presence of the stimulus as long as he could. Time spent in the presence of each stimulus was used as a measure of fear. Finally, the subject was asked to rate his level of anxiety on a scale of 1 to 10 (1 = least anxious, 10 = most anxious) following each behavioral avoidance test. In Figure 10–8 the data for all three responses modalities for each of the three fearful stimuli is presented across five assessment sessions.

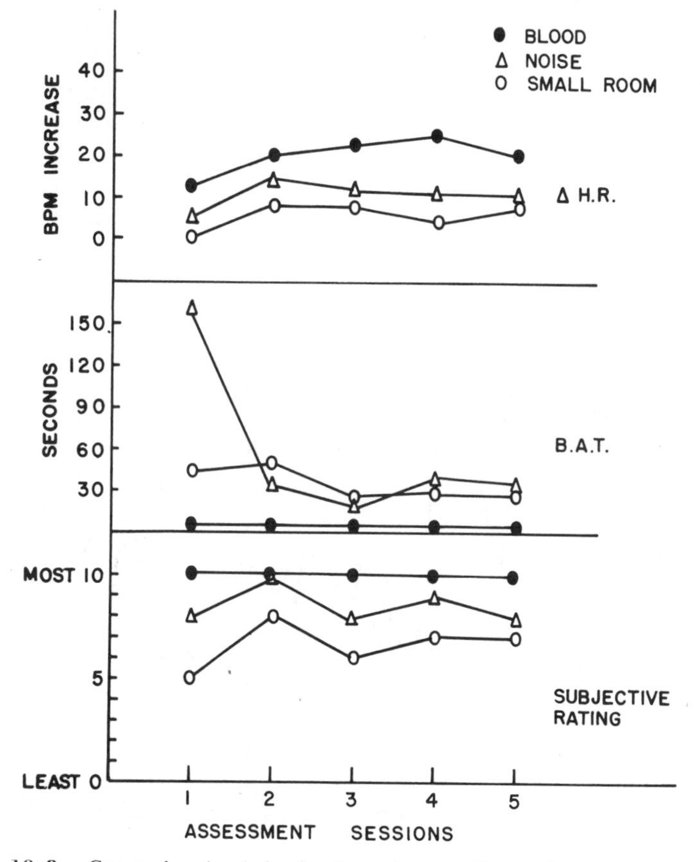

Figure 10–8. Comprehensive behavioral assessment. Comparison of three response modalities (physiological, behavioral and self-report) in a client with multiple phobias.

It is evident from Figure 10–8 that there was a highly stable response pattern for this subject across sessions. In addition, there is a gradient of responsivity that places the blood stimulus at a maximum level with loud noises being intermediate and small rooms being the least reactive stimulus. All the measurement modalities show a similar order of reactivity within and across sessions.

The value of the psychophysiological assessment in this case is clear. The client had been suffering with symptoms of severe anxiety for 20 years without seeking any professional intervention. He was reluctant to discuss this past experience, and he even distorted reports about his level of functioning during the interim period from the war incident to hospital admission. His avoidance of the fearful stimuli was so complete that verbal reports and self-rating measures were of little use in identifying the relevant stimuli. The primary fearful stimuli were rapidly identified by sampling the psychophysiological response mode. Further assessment in other modalities (self-rating and behavioral) supported the initial psychophysiological assessment and led to identification of specifiable stimulus events in an apparent free-floating anxiety.

CURRENT STATUS OF PSYCHOPHYSIOLOGICAL ASSESSMENT

In the introduction to this chapter three criteria were identified for evaluating the utility of psychophysiological measurement in behavioral assessment. First, does the biological response mode provide information that cannot be obtained as reliably or efficiently by other means? Second, is there a unique response that can be attributed to a psychological variable in such a way as to provide relevant information for prediction and modification of behavior? Finally, is there an adequate degree of reliability and validity for the psychophysiological assessment procedures?

Although the expense involved in psychophysiological recording is great when compared with other behavioral assessment methodologies, there is justification for its use. The measurement of physiological reactivity to environmental events is the only objective means of assessing a covert event. Although the level of sophistication at this point does not permit the specification of private events with any detail, it appears that even our gross measurement does allow the specification of psychobiologically relevant stimuli. This does not mean that psychophysiological measures are more valid or useful than behavioral or self-report measures. However, recording specific biological changes in response to controlled stimuli does provide information that can be of great value in the complete behavioral assessment. Although the specific relationships of physiological and psychological variables is poorly defined at present, there is adequate evidence of a direct relationship between physiological responses and both overt and covert stimuli (e.g., Averill & Opton, 1968, Black, 1970). Physiological measurement often provides information regarding psychobiologically relevant stimuli that cannot be obtained by other means.

There are a number of variables that affect all assessment modalities (e.g., demand characteristics, socioeconomic status, and educational level). However, autonomic and central nervous system responses appear to be less susceptible to voluntary distortion from demand characteristics and expectancies than other response modalities. Despite the new wave of data supporting learned self-control of biological functions, recent reviews (Blanchard & Young, 1974; Lynch & Paskewitz, 1971) suggest that self-control of autonomic and central nervous system functioning is only minimal at best. Physiological responses are not independent of expectancies and demand characteristics (Lazarus & Opton, 1966; Schacter, 1966), but volitional control of bodily responses is not as readily apparent in the physiological response mode as in the self-report and behavioral channels.

In terms of the second criterion for evaluation, the search for unique physiological response patterns for a given behavioral disorder has not been profitable (e.g., Martin, 1961; Alexander, 1972). Perhaps a redefinition of this criterion is necessary. Rather than searching for a pattern of responses that is unique to a clinically defined population (with all the problems of the clinical diagnostic system), it may be more useful to define uniqueness on an individual basis. Uniqueness in terms of *a response that is specific to the informational or cue content of a given stimulus* is a more acceptable criterion for evaluating psychophysiological assessment. When the arousal and cue functions of a stimulus are controlled, the presence of a differential physiological response indicates the psychobiological relevance of the stimulus.

What does the physiological response channel tell us about the selection of an appropriate behavioral intervention? As the limited examples presented demonstrate, psychophysiological assessment is a useful tool for identifying psychobiologically relevant stimuli. As part of the complete behavioral equation (Kanfer & Phillips, 1970), identification of relevant stimuli is critical. Psychophysiological measures also offer an objective evaluation of the second factor of the equation—organismic variables. Following identification of relevant stimuli and uniquely responsive physiological systems, appropriate counterconditioning procedures are readily instituted and evaluated throughout treatment by means of the physiological channel.

In a recent study (Suarez, Adams, & McCutcheon, in press) the psychophysiological reactivity of subjects to fearful stimuli was used to predict the outcome of different behavioral interventions (systematic desensitization versus implosion). This approach offers promise for the future use of the biological response channel to select an appropriate intervention on the basis of the state of the organism (e.g., arousal level) during assessment.

Finally, the problems of the reliability and validity of psychophysiological measures must be considered. Neither the reliability nor the validity of psychophysiological assessment has been firmly established by traditional criteria. Reliability between biological systems is poor with respect to the intersubject correlation (Martin, 1961; Martin & Stroufe, 1970) of psychophysiological responses. From the concept of response stereotypy (Lacey, 1967) it is concluded that the appropriate measure of reliability is intrasubject, repeated measures reliability. Lazarus, Speisman, and Mordkoff (1963) and Schnore (1959) have reported high levels of concordance between physiological response systems when they are evaluated within individual subjects. In an applied setting, when the individual client is the ultimate unit of investigation, reliability of psychophysiological records across stimulus presentations appears to be appropriate.

Evaluating the validity of psychophysiological measurement is difficult. In the past there have been many attempts to validate biological responses against objective and projective measures with differing degrees of success. Typically, with a standard psychometric instrument, measurements are not taken in a psychobiologically relevant environment. Since biological responses appear to be situation specific, this may account for the low level correlations between physiological responses and standard psychometric instruments. Lazarus and Opton (1966) have reviewed a procedure involving the concurrent measurement of subjective stress and psychophysiological responses in the presence of an ongoing stressful stimulus (film). They report higher correlations than are typical with comparisons of biological responses and standard psychometric instruments. When biological responses and self-report are evaluated concurrently in a relevant environment, they appear to be directly related, offering some degree of validity in terms of client complaints.

Additional validation of psychophysiological procedures must be accomplished through comparison of this channel with the behavioral response channel. Unfortunately, at present there is little information relating psychophysiological activity to overt behavior. One problem with concurrent measurement of biological and motor responses has been the necessity of restricting the subject's movement during physiological recording sessions. However, with the development of telemetry devices, recordings can readily be obtained from a subject interacting with his environment.

FUTURE DIRECTIONS

Although the search for physiological correlates of behavior is as old as psychology itself, the use of psychophysiological measures in clinical assessment is a relatively new endeavor. Perhaps it is the research in biofeedback procedures that has spurred the interest in the biological response mode. The interest in biofeedback is definitely responsible for the development of new, inexpensive bioamplifier systems for use in the practitioner's office. However, the use of psychophysiological assessment must still be considered to be in its formative stage.

Several important questions must be answered before psychophysiological measurement can reach its full potential as an assessment tool. Further validation of psychophysiological measures with other behavior is necessary before the role of situation specific biological responses in psychopathology is fully realized. Many of the behavioral assumptions inherent in a psychophysiological assessment have not been adequately tested. Second, the precision of psychophysiological recording will have to be further developed in terms of environmental and individual parameters that may interfere with accurate recordings. Finally, considerable effort needs to be directed toward the role various biological response patterns can play in the selection of appropriate behavioral interventions.

The use of direction of change in a physiological response system as an indicator of the relevance of a stimulus to the client has not been used to select clinical interventions. For example, the work of Klorman, Weisenfeld, and Austin (1975) suggested that one may differentiate the significance of a stimulus for an individual by determining if the change is in the direction of a defensive or orienting reaction. Clinically, this would allow the differentiation among neutral, aversive, and positive stimuli. Frequently an assessment does not make use of the difference between a stimulus that elicits a biological avoidance response and one that represents a positive value to the client. Although the magnitude of biological responding is specific to the individual, other aspects such as direction of change appear to be consistent across psychobiologically meaningful stimulus contexts.

As noted earlier, psychophysiological procedures provide an objective measure of covert events. Despite the gross level of analysis available with current methodology, it is clear that these procedures can be of benefit in the comprehensive behavioral assessment.

REFERENCES

Alexander, A. A. Psychophysiological concepts of psychopathology. In N. S. Greenfield & R. A. Sternbach (Eds.), *Handbook of psychophysiology*. New York: Holt, Rinehart, & Winston, 1972.

Averill, J., & Opton, E. M. Psychophysiological assessment: Rational and problems. In J. R. McReynolds (Ed.), *Advances in psychological assessment*. Vol. 1. Palo Alto, Calif.: Science and Behavior Books, 1968.

Ax, A. F. The physiological differentiation between fear and anger in humans. *Psychosomatic Medicine*, 1953, **15,** 433–442.

Basmajian, J. V. *Muscles Alive*. Baltimore: Williams & Wilkins, 1962.

Berger, H. Uber das elecktroenkephalogram des menchen. *Arkiv Fur Psychiatrie und Nervenkranken*, 1933, **99,** 555–574.

Black, P. (Ed.) *Physiological correlates of emotion*. New York: Academic, 1970.

Blanchard, E. B., & Young, L. D. Clinical applications of biofeedback training. *Archives of General Psychiatry*, 1974, **30,** 573–589.

Brazier, M. A. B. *The electrical activity of the nervous system* (3rd ed.) London: Pitman Medical, 1968.

Brown, C. C. Instruments in psychophysiology. In R. A. Greenfield & N. S. Sternbach (Eds.), *Handbook of psychophysiology*. New York: Holt, Rinehart, & Winston, 1972.

Brown, C. C. Techniques of plethysmography. In C. C. Brown (Ed.), *Methods in psychophysiology*. Baltimore: Williams & Wilkins, 1967.

Brown, C. C., Giddon, D. B., & Dean, E. D. Techniques of plethysmography. *Psychophysiology*, 1965, **1,** 253–266.

Cannon, W. B. *Bodily changes in pain, hunger, fear and rage*. New York: Appleton-Century-Crofts, 1915.

Darrow, C. W. Differences in the physiological reactions to sensory and ideational stimuli. *Psychological Bulletin*, 1929, **16,** 185–201.

Deifenderfer, A. J. *Principles of electronic instrumentation*. Philadelphia: Saunders, 1972.

Duffy, E. *Activation and behavior*. New York: Wiley, 1962.

Edelberg, R. Electrical activity of the skin: Its measurement and uses in psychophysiology. In N. S. Greenfield & R. A. Sternbach (Eds.), *Handbook of psychophysiology*. New York: Holt, Rinehart, & Winston, 1972.

Edelberg, R. Electrical properties of the skin. In C. C. Brown (Ed.), *Methods in psychophysiology*. Baltimore: Williams & Wilkins, 1967.

Freund, K. A. A laboratory method for diagnosing predominance of homo- or hetero-erotic interest in the male. *Behaviour Research and Therapy*, 1963, **1,** 85–93.

Gardner, E. *Fundamentals of neurology* (5th ed.). Philadelphia: Saunders, 1968.

Geddes, L. A. The measurement of physiological phenomena. In C. C. Brown (Ed.), *Methods in psychophysiology*. Baltimore: Williams & Wilkins, 1967.

Goldstein, I. B. Electromyography: A measure of skeletal muscle response. In N. S. Greenfield & R. A. Sternbach (Eds.), *Handbook of psychophysiology*. New York: Holt, Rinehart & Winston, 1972.

Greenfield, N. S., & Sternbach, R. A. (Eds.). *Handbook of psychophysiology*. New York: Holt, Rinehart, & Winston, 1972.

Grossman, S. P. *Essentials of physiological psychology*. New York: Wiley, 1973.

Hardy, J., & Bard, P. Body temperature regulation. In V. B. Mountcastle (Ed.), *Medical physiology* (13th ed.). St. Louis: Mosby, 1974.

Hart, J. D. Physiological responses of anxious and normal subjects to simple signal and non-signal auditory stimuli. *Psychophysiology*, 1974, **11,** 443–451.

Hebb, D. O. Drives and the C.N.S. (conceptual nervous system). *Psychological review*, 1955, **62,** 243–254.

Hendrix, T. R. Physiology of the digestive system. In V. B. Mountcastle (Ed.), *Medical physiology* (13th ed.) St. Louis: Mosby, 1974.

James, W. *The principles of psychology*. New York: Holt, 1890.

Kallman, W. M. *Physiological and behavioral responses to altered sensory levels and stress*. Unpublished doctoral dissertation, University of Georgia, 1975.

Kanfer, F. H., & Phillips, J. S. *Learning foundations of behavior therapy*. New York: Wiley, 1970.

Katzman, R. (Ed.). Sensory evoked response in man. *Annals of the New York academy of science*, 1964, **112,** 1–546.

Klorman, R., Weisenfeld, A. R., & Austin, M. L. Autonomic response to affective visual stimuli. *Psychophysiology*, 1975, **12,** 553–559.

Koizumi, K., & Brooks, C. McC. The autonomic nervous system and its role in controlling visceral activities. In V. B. Mountcastle (Ed.), *Medical physiology* (13th ed.) St. Louis: Mosby, 1974.

Lacey, J. I. Somatic response patterning and stress: Some revisions of the activation theory. In M. H. Appley & R. Trumbull (Eds.), *Psychological stress*. New York: Appleton-Century-Crofts, 1967.

Lacey, J. I., & Lacey, B. C. Some autonomic-CNS interrelationships. In P. Black (Ed.), *Physiological correlates of emotion*. New York: Academic, 1970.

Ladd, G. T. *Elements of physiological psychology*. New York: 1887.

Lambertsen, C. J. Respiration. In V. B. Mountcastle (Ed.), *Medical physiology* (13th ed.) St. Louis: Mosby, 1974.

Lange, C. G. *Orm sindsbevaegelser. et psyko. fysiolog. studie*. Copenhagen: Krøonar, 1885.

Lazarus, R. S., & Opton, E. M. The study of psychological stress. In C. D. Speilberger (Ed.), *Anxiety and behavior*. New York: Academic, 1966.

Lazarus, R. S., Speisman, J. C., & Mordokoff, A. M. The relationship between autonomic indicators and psychological stress: Heart rate and skin conductance. *Psychosomatic Medicine*, 1963, **25,** 19–30.

Lovallo, W. O., Parsons, O. A., & Holloway, F. A. Autonomic arousal in normal, alcoholic, and brain damaged subjects as measured by the plethysmograph response to cold. *Psychophysiology*, 1973, **10,** 166–176.

Lynch, J. J., & Paskewitz, D. A. On the mechanisms of the feedback control of human brain wave activity. *Journal of Nervous and Mental Disease*, 1971, **153,** 205–217.

Mackay, R. S. Telemetry and telestimulation. In C. C. Brown (Ed.), *Methods in psychophysiology*. Baltimore: Williams & Wilkins, 1967.

Malmo, R. B. Anxiety and behavioral arousal. *Psychological Review*, 1957, **64,** 276–287.

Malmo, R. B., & Shagass, C. Studies of blood pressure in psychiatric patients under stress. *Psychosomatic Medicine*, 1952, **14,** 82–93.

Mangelesdorf, A. D., & Zuckerman, M. Habituation to scenes of violence. *Psychophysiology*, 1975, **12,** 124–129.

Martin, B. The assessment of anxiety by physiological and behavioral measures. *Psychological Bulletin*, 1961, **58,** 234–255.

Martin, B., & Stroufe, L. A. Anxiety. In C. G. Costello (Ed.), *Symptoms of psychopathology*. New York: Wiley, 1970.

Masters, W., & Johnson, V. *Human sexual response*. Boston: Little, Brown, 1966.

Milner, P. A. *Physiological psychology*. New York: Holt, Rinehart, & Winston, 1970.

Milnor, W. R. Cardiovascular system. In V. B. Mountcastle (Ed.), *Medical physiology* (13th ed.) St. Louis: Mosby, 1974. (a)

Milnor, W. R. The electrocardiogram. In V. B. Mountcastle (Ed.), *Medical physiology* (13th ed.) St. Louis: Mosby, 1974. (b)

Mischel, W. *Personality and assessment*. New York: Wiley, 1968.

Mountcastle, V. B. (Ed.). *Medical physiology* (13th ed.). St. Louis: Mosby, 1974.

Obrist, P. A., Lawler, J. E., Howard, J. L., Smithson, K. W., Martin, P. L., & Manning, J. Sympathetic influences on cardiac rate and contractility during acute stress in humans. *Psychophysiology*, 1974, 11, 405–427.

Sargent, J. D., Green, E. E., & Walters, E. D. Preliminary report on the use of autogenic feedback training in the treatment of migraine and tension headache. *Psychosomatic Medicine*, 1973, **35,** 129–135.

Schachter, J. Pain, fear and anger in hypertensive and normotensives. *Psychosomatic Medicine*, 1957, **19,** 17–29.

Schachter, S. The interaction of cognitive and physiological determinants of emotional states. In C. D. Speilberger (Ed.), *Anxiety and behavior*. New York: Academic, 1966.

Schnore, N. M. Individual patterns of physiological activity as a function of task differences and level of arousal. *Journal of Experimental Psychology*, 1959, **58,** 117–128.

Sintchak, G., & Geer, J. A. A vaginal plethysmograph system. *Psychophysiology*, 1975, **13,** 113–116.

Sokolov, Y. N. *Perception and the conditioned reflex*. New York: Macmillan, 1963.

Starzl, T., Taylor, C., & Magoun, H. G. Collateral afferent excitation of reticular formation of the brain stem. *Journal of Neurophysiology*, 1951, **14,** 479–496.

Sterman, M. B. Neurophysiological and clinical studies of sensorimotor EEG biofeedback training: Some effects on epilepsy. *Seminars in Psychiatry*, 1973, **5,** 507–525.

Sterman, M. B., MacDonald, L. R., & Stone, K. R. Biofeedback training of sensorimotor electroencephalogram rhythm in man: Effects on epilepsy. *Epilepsia*, 1974, **15,** 395–416.

Stern, R. M. Ear lobe photoplethysmography. *Psychophysiology*, 1974, **11,** 73–75.

Suarez, Y., Adams, H. E., & McCutcheon, B. A. Implosion and systematic desensitization: Efficacy in subclinical phobics as a function of arousal. *Journal of Consulting and Clinical Psychology*, in press.

Sutton, S., Tueting, P., Zubin, J., & John, E. R. Information delivery in the sensory evoked potential. *Science*, 1967, **155,** 1436–1439.

Thompson, R. F. *Foundations of physiological psychology.* New York: Harper & Row, 1967.

Venables, P. H., & Martin, I. (Eds.) *Manual of psychophysiological methods.* Amsterdam: North-Holland, 1967.

Venables, P. H., & Wing, J. K. Level of arousal and the subclassification of schizophrenia. *Archives of General Psychiatry*, 1962, **7,** 114–119.

Walter, W. G., Cooper, R., Aldridge, V. J., McCallum, W. C., & Winter, A. L. Contingent negative variation: An electrical sign of sensorimotor association and expectancy in the human brain. *Nature*, 1964, **203,** 380–384.

Wilkinson, R. T. Evoked response correlates of expectancy during vigilance. *Acta Psychologia*, 1970, **33,** 402–413.

Wolff, S., & Welsh, J. D. The gastrointestinal tract as a responsive system. In N. S. Greenfield & R. A. Sternbach (Eds.), *Handbook of psychophysiology.* New York: Holt, Rinehart & Winston, 1972.

Yanoff, H. M. *Biomedical electronics.* Philadelphia: Davis, 1972.

PART THREE

Assessment of Specific Behaviors

CHAPTER 11

Assessment of Anxiety

THOMAS D. BORKOVEC, THEODORE C. WEERTS, and
DOUGLAS A. BERNSTEIN

This chapter deals with the assessment of anxiety, a problem familiar to everyone, but one whose definitional vagueness is perhaps second only to that of personality. Before discussing approaches to anxiety assessment, it is important to place this deceptively simple term in its historical and conceptual perspective.

ANXIETY AS A CONSTRUCT

We can begin by recognizing the prominent role played by anxiety in psychological theories. McReynolds (in press) has noted, "Virtually every theorist in personality and psychopathology has found it necessary to incorporate anxiety, in one form or another, in formulations with regard to the acquisition, stability, and change of human behavior . . . Further, anxiety has occupied this central position for 50 years." Indeed, every psychological theorist from Freud to Skinner has dealt in some fashion with anxiety, but the traditional focus on this construct seems to stem not from specification or discovery of its fundamental nature or function but from the fact that, as a term, it is sufficiently imprecise to encompass a wide range of behavioral phenomena that are, themselves, of interest and importance.

"Anxiety" entered the psychological lexicon as the English translation of Freud's *Angst,* a word he used to describe the negative affect and physiological arousal that is analogous to the consequence of having food stuck in one's throat (McReynolds, in press; Sarbin, 1964, 1968). Although Freud never specifically defined the unique identifying characteristics of *Angst,* the construct was nevertheless emphasized in his theory of the development of behavior and behavior disorder. Consequently, psychology and psychiatry were faced with the task of measuring and modifying a vague, ill-defined, and metaphorical variable that, over time, was reified (Sarbin, 1964) into a "thing" assumed to be of vital importance in the understanding of human behavior. It is important to note that, in the reification process, anxiety developed a "multiple personality." It has been viewed as transient emotional/physiological *behavior* (i.e., "He is anxious today"), a dispositional *trait* ("She is an anxious person"), and a cause or *explanation* of behavior (i.e., "He overeats because of anxiety"; "Her seductiveness is a defense against anxiety").

Consistent with the breadth of the construct, at least 120 specific procedures to measure anxiety had been developed (Cattell & Scheier, 1961) by the time theories of social learning in human behavior (upon which the assessments of anxiety discussed in this chapter are based) began to gain prominence. As we will see, these theories not only stimulated numerous additions to the anxiety assessment armamentarium but provided a new approach to the construct itself. Indeed, a new approach seemed to be needed. Mandler (1972, p. 361) summarized the situation in anxiety theory and research by noting, "We seem to be going around in circles, becoming more strident, leaving the field, but certainly not advancing knowledge significantly." Similarly, Sarason (1966, p. 63) has argued that ". . . the fruitfulness of our current formulations (about anxiety) has been exhausted."

The most obvious result of 50 years of theoretical and research activity focused on anxiety is the realization that definition or conception of anxiety as a unitary "thing" (be it emotional state, psychological trait, or underlying cause) is both inefficient and inappropriate. Instead, scientific psychologists have more recently come to view anxiety as a shorthand term that refers to a complex and variable pattern of behavior ". . . characterized by subjective feelings of apprehension and tension accompanied by or associated with physiological activation" (Paul, 1969b, p. 64), which occurs in response to internal (i.e., cognitive) or external (i.e., environmental) stimuli. Furthermore, it is clear that this complex construct is multidimensional, involving three separate but interacting response components, and that it is therefore measurable by three main channels. The first channel involves overt, *motoric behavior,* which occurs either as an observable consequence of increased physiological arousal (e.g., trembling or stuttering) or as a means of escape from or avoidance of certain stimuli. The second is the subjective or *self-report* channel, in which an individual may indicate informally (by reporting on current or past cognitions or arousal levels) or formally (i.e., through psychological test scores) the degree of anxiety he experiences, either as a rule (trait anxiety) or in response to specific situations (state anxiety) (Spielberger, 1966). The third response channel is that of *physiological arousal,* primarily involving activity of the sympathetic branch of the autonomic nervous system. Persons showing anxiety in this channel display changes in one or more indices such as electrodermal responses, heart rate, blood pressure, blood volume, respiration, muscle tension, pupillary response, and the like.

Anxiety research has highlighted the fact that data from one of the three anxiety response channels often do not correlate well with one from another (Lacey, 1959; Lang, 1968), directly indicating that there are individual differences in response patterns of anxiety that are functionally important in the maintenance and reduction of anxiety. A person who is anxious in relation to a particular stimulus situation may display strong reactions in only one or two channels (e.g., in self-report but not in overt behavior or physiological activity). In addition to the presence of individual differences, further discrepancies among measurement channels may occur as a function of the effects of current environmental variables on a particular response component. For example, a male college student may show intense physiological activity and a great deal of overt avoidance behavior in relation to large dogs but, because he does not wish to appear "foolish" or "unmasculine," he vigorously denies any discomfort. A person learning to sky-dive may display clear physiological arousal (and some avoidance behavior) before a jump, but that arousal may be interpreted by the individual as "excitement" or some other emotion (Schachter, 1964; Schachter & Singer, 1962), and thus no anxiety is reported. Finally, an individual who reports strong anxiety in relation to dentistry and displays clear autonomic arousal in the dentist's chair may show no overt avoidance behavior because of the anticipated positive consequences of receiving treatment. The individual difference factor will have implications for choice of treatment strategy, whereas the influence of environmental variables on response measurement suggests the need for careful research assessment procedures.

Obviously, then, whether a person is labeled "anxious" depends to a great extent on (1) the individual's anxiety response pattern and which anxiety channel is assessed, and (2) what social/situational, cognitive, consequential, or other potentially influential factors are operative (we will return to this point in some detail later). Many researchers in the field now recognize this problem and have at least begun to base statements about anxiety on measures that reflect all three channels and under conditions that minimize the influence of artifacts. However, because of the now-obvious complexity, multidimensionality, and elusiveness of the construct, some social learning theorists (e.g., Bandura, 1969; Krasner & Ullmann, 1973; Ullmann & Krasner, 1969; Ullmann, Note 1) have suggested that the term *anxiety* be abandoned so that we can focus instead on the stimulus conditions (external or internal) that result in behaviors labeled as anxiety and/or on its specific components (e.g., emotional arousal, avoidance behavior).

This new approach is based on the empirical evidence alluded to above, which indicates that the theoretical construct called *anxiety* does little to provide specific information about a person's behavior. The approach also assumes that, because anxiety is primarily a shorthand *description* of complex behavior, its reification and use as an *explanation* of maladaptive, irrational, or unusual behavior is inappropriate. Krasner and Ullmann (1973, pp. 98-99) put it this way: "We have to deal not with . . . anxiety, but with the conditions giving rise to anxiety. . . . The concept of anxiety is superfluous in dealing directly with people rather than with theories. In a clinical interaction we deal with what is being avoided, with what a person needs to learn or unlearn or relearn. . . . [The concept of anxiety] makes us think we know something when we do not and should be looking harder." Consistent with this thinking, the social learning (or behavioral) approach to anxiety and anxiety measurement focuses on clear specification of stimulus conditions and on objectively quantified responses to those stimuli rather than on the use of psychological tests designed to measure the presence of or changes in a generalized construct. This has, in turn, resulted in the development of anxiety management techniques based on social learning and designed to alter individuals' maladaptive response patterns to specific classes of stressful stimuli rather than being designed to eliminate anxiety. The success of these treatment procedures is then evaluated in terms of the magnitude of desirable changes in specified target behaviors (often in all three anxiety channels) that are assessed both before and after treatment.

Thus instead of continuing traditional attempts to define and measure a supposedly unitary anxiety construct, social learning theory has sought to better understand the nature of the response components of anxiety by attending to and extending research on the functional relationships between those components and the (internal and external) environment in which they appear. For example, the research of Lindsley (1951), Malmo (1966), and other physiological psychologists makes it clear that physiological responding is related, through the reticular activating system and the cerebral cortex, to the intensity of external and internal (i.e., cognitive) stimulation present. Strong stimulation results in high levels of response whereas minimal stimulation produces reduced arousal. Further research on the physiological dimension has shown that it is related quite directly to cognitive and motor learning and performance. In general behavioral efficiency on learning/performance tasks is very poor when an individual's physiological activity is extremely low, increases to some maximum level as cortical and autonomic activity increases, and then begins to deteriorate as this arousal is further elevated. The magnitude of physiological responding associated with optimal efficiency tends to be higher for relatively simple tasks and lower for more complex tasks. For example, a level of arousal that would not interfere with performance of a simple well-learned task such as turning on a light switch could badly disrupt the complex pattern of behavior associated with being interviewed for a job or giving an extemporaneous speech.

Research on the relationship between arousal and emotion provides an additional perspective from which to view anxiety. The individual experiencing relatively nonspecific and diffuse autonomic activity is likely to use past experience to interpret that arousal and label it as a particular emotion. Research on the relationships among physiological patterns, cognitive labeling, and the social and other cues that determine that labeling (e.g., Schachter, 1964) has partially clarified the operation of the labeling process and has also been very valuable in understanding both the role of the self-report channel of anxiety and the discrepancies between levels of physiological activity and verbal reports of distress that are so common (e.g., Lang, 1968).

Investigations of the kind just outlined support the basic assumption of the social learning approach to anxiety assessment, namely, that it is far easier to gain accurate information about the nature and function of anxiety by analyzing its components, the relationships among them, and their interaction with the environment than by dealing with the construct in global terms.

ASSESSMENT OF ANXIETY

As might be anticipated, the way in which psychologists historically go about measuring anxiety has been based largely on how the construct has been viewed. Researchers who saw anxiety as a global and transsituational personality characteristic have sought to develop *trait* anxiety assessments whereas those who emphasized the situation-specific aspects of anxiety have worked on construction of *state* anxiety instruments. Similarly, concern over the presence of unconscious anxiety fostered the use of "depth" (e.g., projective) assessments; assuming anxiety to be a clearly visible, conscious phenomenon made "surface" tests more appropriate. Furthermore, the degree to which assessments are focused on the cognitive, physiological, or motoric/behavioral channels of the anxiety construct has been a function of researchers' biases about the relative importance of those components. Thus the large number and great diversity of anxiety assessment procedures currently available (Cattell & Scheier, 1961; Levitt, 1967) is a reflection of the number of ways in which anxiety has been operationally defined.

Although the variety of specific anxiety measures is great, it is clear that, traditionally, clinical assessments have been focused primarily on state and trait anxiety as displayed in the self-report channel. These assessments have taken the form of projective tests (from which unconscious anxiety is inferred) and, more commonly, anxiety scales, inventories, and questionnaires of the true-false, forced-choice, rating-scale, and multiple-choice variety (see Levitt, 1967). The approach represented by such techniques has been called "sign oriented" (Goodenough, 1949) in that data from traditional self-report instruments ". . . are held to be significant only as they provide an index to or sign of otherwise unobservable personality predispositions or constructs" (McReynolds, in press).

In sharp contrast to traditional sign-oriented anxiety assessment, social learning theory has taken a sample-oriented approach. This means that, instead of interpreting test scores as *signs* of the degree or amount of anxiety a person possesses, arrangements are made to systematically observe the person's cognitive, physiological, and/or motor behavior in relation to specific anxiety-relevant environmental stimuli. The purpose of this type of assessment is to identify the environmental circumstances that result in the appearance of anxiety responses in one or more channels and furthermore, to collect information about the relationship between the magnitude of those responses and the nature or intensity of the antecedent conditions. Mischel (1971, p. 179) neatly summarized the approach by observing that the assessor oriented to social learning ". . . tries to observe what the person does, rather than to infer what he has or is. He searches for the stimulus conditions controlling or causing particular behavior patterns; he does not try to interpret the behaviors as indirect signs of the person's underlying motives and dispositions."

Thus from this point of view an individual's responses to a questionnaire designed to tap trait anxiety would be seen not as signs of anxiety level but as part of a behavior sample which, when combined with other observations of the subject's verbal and nonverbel behavior, simply provides a description of how he behaves during psychological testing. Since social learning theorists and practitioners are more interested in sampling behavior that occurs in relation to anxiety-relevant environmental stimuli other than traditional paper-and-pencil tests, they have been active in developing specialized procedures designed to collect such data in all three anxiety response channels. In the sections to follow we will explore the nature of and problems associated with these assessments of social learning anxiety.

Functional Analysis of Anxiety

It should be clear that, from a social learning perspective, the assessment of anxiety does not differ in principle from the functional analysis of any other target behavior. The definition presented earlier implies that there is no satisfactory or simple method of measuring anxiety. Rather, the clinician or research investigator needs to consider (1) the stimuli eliciting anxiety response components, (2) the types of components appearing in the individual or groups of individuals, and (3) the consequences of these components.

At the present time there is a marked discrepancy in emphasis and sophistication between clinical and research methods of anxiety assessment. That discrepancy is in part a function of differences between the usual goals of assessment procedures in the two settings. In the clinic functional analysis of the client's presenting problem is aimed primarily at the ideographically based development of a maximally efficient and efficacious therapy package, and only secondarily at systematic evaluation of treatment (or treatment component) effectiveness. On the other hand, anxiety measurement in research is ordinarily geared toward nomothetic quantification of anxious behavior and the changes in that behavior that occur owing to manipulation of experimental variables, including theoretically relevant subject or environmental characteristics as well as therapeutic techniques.

These goals need not be mutually exclusive, of course; both clinical and research endeavors stand to benefit from increasing attention to variables and issues that have often been ignored. For example, the use of more systematic, sophisticated, but still individual-oriented procedures for assessing anxiety in clinical settings would greatly facilitate the evaluation of current treatment practices and guide in their modification where needed. Similarly researchers need to become more acutely aware of the (often idiosyncratic) functional relationships that exist both among anxiety response components and between those components and an environment that can distort data generated by controlled experimentation.

Development of methods for measuring anxiety that go beyond response component quantification to address broader questions vital to complete functional analysis (e.g., Frankel, 1975; Hawkins, 1975) should become a research item of top priority in the near future. For the time being, however, much of the information relevant to adequate functional analysis of anxiety problems is available only through clinical interviews. Although the ultimate reliability and validity of data obtained in this way are established by the success or failure of treatment procedures based on them, careful development and use of objective measurements is to be encouraged whenever possible since, without precise outcome indices, the terms *success* and *failure* are vague and scientifically useless. Furthermore, increased use of objective, pretherapy anxiety assessment as a supplement to interview data can facilitate the appropriate a priori choice of therapeutic strategies.

With these considerations in mind, we begin our discussion of anxiety assessment by listing the questions to be dealt with in a clinical case through some combination of interviews and objective measures. The answers to these questions will provide the outline of a functional analysis of anxiety-related problem behavior with implications for treatment methods. We will then discuss various measurement methods born in the research laboratory and geared toward quantification of anxiety response components. The discrepancy between clinical assessment questions and the current research methods of anxiety measurement will be obvious. The main questions involved are summarized in Table 11-1 and discussed below.

Table 11–1. Questions relevant to a functional analysis of anxiety

Stimulus Class	Reaction	Consequence
Critical objects or events? Cognitions? Thoughts? Images?	Cognitive (Anticipatory?) Disruptions? Reports of Distress? Catastrophizing Self-Statements? Behavioral (Anticipatory?) Disruptions? Escape/Avoidance? Skill Deficit? Physiological (Anticipatory?) Disruption? Arousal? Mediated by Self-Statements?	Social and/or other Evironmental Reinforcement?

1. *What is the nature of the stimulus classes that elicit and/or signal anxiety response components in this presenting problem?* Information on this point is crucial not only because it provides a logical starting point for functional analysis but also because intervention techniques based on social learning are specifically designed to alter maladaptive anxiety responses as well as to train the client in cognitive, overt behavioral, and physiological responses that are more functional, adaptive, and rewarding. Since these goals are attained with respect to relatively specific stimulus situations known to produce strong discomfort, their clear identification becomes a prerequisite to treatment planning. Stimuli to be explored include both the fairly obvious external or distal variety (e.g., a dentist's office, large dogs, high places) and those that are internal or proximal (e.g., cognitive, imaginal, and verbal) representations of distal stimuli.

Furthermore, assessment should extend to response components of anxiety that occur in anticipation of as well as in direct response to proximal and distal stimuli. Finally, without inferring the operation of psychodynamic processes, it is important to recognize that generalization of anxiety responses can occur along semantic as well as more concrete stimulus dimensions (e.g., Hekmat, 1972; Staats, 1972; Staats & Staats, 1957). Thus words or concepts not obviously related to distal stimuli may develop arousal potential and complicate the assessment picture. Lazarus (1971), for example, reported that a claustrophobic's anxiety seemed to be based on fear of "suffocating" interpersonal relationships. Taken together, these points make it obvious that raw self-report and observational data from a client may present a varied, apparently inconsistent, and often confusing picture of the stimuli related to the problem behavior, and a great deal of clinical skill and careful assessment are required to identify the most basic and functional stimulus dimensions.

To the extent that anxiety reactions are elicited by cognitive stimuli, treatment may focus on imaginal techniques for presenting a stimulus (e.g., systematic desensitization); to the extent that cognitive mediators are absent, the use of such techniques is likely to be fruitless. Whenever possible, however, real-life exposure will ordinarily be employed to guarantee generalization of improvement from therapeutic contexts to the client's everyday life.

2. *What response components are functionally relevant to the presenting problem?* At the most global level, this question refers to the relative degree of disruption and/or distress manifested by cognitive, behavioral, and physiological reactions to anxiety-provoking stimuli. Reports of disruption or distress may be mediated by behavioral or physiological disruptions elicited by the stimulus situation. If the target problem has already been labeled by the client as involving anxiety, regardless of its basis, the cognitive response system has, by definition, been implicated. In the absence of other response components, however, the anxiety label may be inappropriate and susceptible to attribution instructions that indicate the veridical source of distress and lead to an appropriate relabeling of the emotional behavior (cf. Valins & Nisbett, 1971). In addition, interview questioning should focus on the self-produced proximal stimuli (what the client is imagining and/or saying to himself) occurring immediately before and after confrontation with the critical situation. Catastrophizing self-verbalizations may often facilitate the occurrence of an anxiety reaction; evidence of such behavior, obtainable mainly through the client's report, would suggest the possible implementation of rational-emotive (Ellis, 1973), self-instructional (Meichenbaum, 1974), or other cognitive training tactics (cf. Rimm & Masters, 1974).

Assessment of anxiety components must also include information about overt motor responses: What is the nature and strength of avoidance behaviors in problematic situations and to what extent would the individual's functioning be disrupted if avoidance were not possible? The presence of frequent avoidance behavior may, depending on other considerations, suggest the use of participant modeling or positive reinforcement programs for approach behavior. Furthermore, for reasons to be discussed later, it is essential to determine what adaptive overt responses would make the individual less anxious in the critical situation and the degree to which the client is skilled at making such responses.

Physiological response to feared situations should be assessed by focusing on whether disruptions or increases in physiological arousal occur and, if so, which response systems show the greatest change. The identification of a strong physiological reaction will imply a therapy procedure that, in part, attempts to provide the client with methods of reducing that reaction (e.g., relaxation or biofeedback training, self-instructional training for cognitively mediated reactions). Such information can be obtained indirectly through interviewing but, as we will see, more direct measures may also be employed.

3. *Does the client display an anticipatory anxiety reaction and, if so, what is its component structure and spatial/temporal, thematic, and semantic relationship to feared stimuli?* Clients frequently report that subjectively experienced anxiety, disrupted behavior, and/or physiological activity become increasingly probable as they approach critical situations. Determining the specific stimuli that elicit anticipatory responses is obviously related to Question 1 above but is particularly crucial because such information contributes to the development of an anxiety hierarchy for treatment techniques such as participant modeling, systematic desensitization, and other gradual exposure procedures. In addition, the occurrence of strong anticipatory reactions may signal the implication of cognitive mediators.

4. *Does the client's anxiety response pattern represent an inappropriately conditioned response to an objectively nonthreatening situation, or is it an appropriate reaction to situations that, for a variety of reasons, are harmful, dangerous, or punishing?* Although direct and/or vicarious learning processes underlie or facilitate the development of both kinds of problems, those in the former category are usually called *conditioned* whereas the latter are referred to as *reactive.* Thus in addition to all the information obtained with respect to Questions 1 through 3, one must also determine whether identified anxiety response components are appropriate or inappropriate, adaptive or maladaptive, "rational" or "irrational." Reactive anxiety very often appears in social-evaluative contexts when the individual's overarousal occurs as an appropriate reaction to actual stress conditions that themselves are partly a function of the person's own be-

havior. Consider, for example, the person who reports strong anxiety at parties as a result of actually having been ignored or insulted in those situations. If the person elicits these consequences because he is obnoxious, abusive, or otherwise socially unskilled, the anxiety problem is, in part at least, reactive.

Although repeated punishment may ultimately result in a conditioned anxiety response, identification of a reactive aspect of anxiety-related problems requires that training in relevant skills become part of a total treatment package. For the student who is anxious about tests because of poor study skills, for the person who avoids dating because of inadequate conversational skills, or for the husband or wife whose fear of coitus is based on lack of sexual sophistication, exclusive attention to the conditioned anxiety involved will be likely to provide only minimal and temporary decrements in discomfort (e.g., the student may be a bit more comfortable while failing examinations). Since response-contingent punishment or extinction will continue in the absence of appropriate skill training, the probability of renewed anxiety and avoidance is very high. Bandura (1971) made the same point by noting, "No psychological methods exist that can render an organism insensitive to the consequences of its actions" (p. 693).

General assessment of various behavioral skills is presented in other chapters of this volume. In the present context it is important only to mention the necessity of identifying or ruling out a skill deficit component in a presenting problem involving anxiety. Interview information and observation of the client in a role-played scene representing the feared situation will usually reveal the presence or absence of required skills. In the case of test anxiety, for example, the client's description of study habits and test-taking strategies may quickly alert the clinician to the necessity of study counseling procedures (e.g., Allen, 1971); role-played social encounters in the consulting room may reveal the lack of an appropriate social repertoire.

5. *What are the immediate and/or long-term consequences of each anxiety response component?* One or more aspects of anxiety may be more strongly controlled by their consequences than by proximal or distal eliciting or discriminative stimuli. For example, positive social reinforcement following fearful verbalizations, overt avoidance, and perhaps even autonomic reactions may play a role in the development, maintenance, and intransigence of the response components. When this is the case, a totally adequate intervention must include rearrangement of relevant response consequences in addition to (or instead of) other procedures for reducing anxiety.

Our review of laboratory-based methods of assessing social learning anxiety will focus almost entirely on Question 2 above, that is, the quantification of anxiety response components. Deemphasis of Questions 3 through 5 is dictated by the relative absence of experimentally validated procedures designed to address them. Question 1 (identification of anxiety-relevant stimulus classes) will be included to some extent by definition since the social learning approach to anxiety assessment stresses the relationship between specific environmental stimuli and response components. Thus measurement of responses is routinely obtained during controlled presentations of anxiety-provoking stimuli. This assumes, however, the prior identification of those critical stimuli.

Although observation of anxiety response in "natural" field settings is becoming more frequent in the clinical literature, the development and use of most measurement methodologies has occurred primarily under artificial laboratory conditions. The following review reflects this state of affairs, but it should be noted that a very real trade-off exists in choosing between "real world" and laboratory assessment environments. Although the validity of the former may be greater than that of the latter, it is often purchased at the price of reliability; the opposite can often be said of laboratory-based measures. Resolution of this dilemma will probably involve both adaptation of controlled techniques to field settings, perhaps by use of radiotelemetry (e.g., Butterfield, 1974; Miklich, 1975) or other sophisticated instrumentation, and alteration of relevant laboratory conditions and variables so as to increase their ecological validity (Brunswick, 1947; Orne & Holland, 1968). Later we will make some suggestions along these lines.

In nearly all the anxiety measurement systems to be described, exposure ordinarily involves increasing approach to a feared object or event, either in a temporal sense (e.g., a waiting period prior to presenting a speech followed by a signal to begin the speech) or in terms of physical proximity (e.g., bringing a feared object toward a client or instructing the client to approach the object), primarily by real life (in vivo) exposures but sometimes through imaginal exposures. In vivo exposures either involve presentation of the feared situation in the client's natural setting (e.g., speech presentation in a public-speaking class; Paul, 1966) or in a laboratory setting (e.g., asking the person to present a speech to research assistants; Borkovec, Wall, & Stone, 1974). Assessment of anxiety response components (overt behavioral, physiological, and cognitive) is ordinarily made prior to, during, and/or after the exposure task.

Methods of Anxiety Measurement

Behavioral Measures

Overt behavior responses have been the most heavily emphasized component of anxiety in the social learning literature and stems in part from both dissatisfaction with the reliability and validity of client reports of distress and from the emphasis on specific response alternations rather than "personality" change in early "behavior therapy" enterprises. Unfortunately, this overt behavioral emphasis has resulted in relative disregard of self-report data in outcome research literature; changes in the overt motor channel of anxiety shape conclusions regarding treatment efficacy, often regardless of data reported verbally. Thus although social learning therapists have long characterized the outcome of traditional therapy with the comment that the client still engages in the problem behavior but now knows why and feels better about it, an exclusively behavioral focus can and has resulted in the opposite, equally distressing state of affairs: The client may display less escape and/or avoidance behavior but still reports subjective anxiety. Obviously the clinical goal is to modify all relevant response systems. Thus reliability and validity problems associated with self-report measures in the research setting only underscore the need for more careful use of those instruments.

Overt behavior measures of anxiety are in any case important and influential components of anxiety research and are designed to reflect either the direct or indirect effect of ongoing physiological activity on observable behavior. As Paul and Bernstein (1973) have indicated, assessment of *direct* anxiety focuses on the observable effects of physiological events on behavioral functioning and/or the interference of arousal with performance. *Indirect* assessment involves measures of observable escape and avoidance of anxiety-provoking stimuli. In all instances measurement devices involve observation and recording of relevant behavior by mechanical instrumentation and/or trained observers. The variety of common measures of behavioral anxiety components is described below.

Direct observational measures. Assuming that the increased physiological activity elicited in anxiety-provoking situations will influence behavioral functioning, several anxiety outcome investigations have employed rating instruments that quantify the presence, intensity, or frequency of overt signs of anxiety. One of the most frequently used measures of this type is the Timed Behavioral Checklist (TBCL) developed by Paul (1966). Based on an earlier factor analytic study of anxiety signs in speech research (Clevenger & King, 1961), the TBCL was constructed to measure overt anxiety in a public-speaking situation and includes 20 behaviors reflecting both interference with performance (e.g., speech blocking or stammering) and the observable effects of arousal on behavior during the speech (e.g., pacing, swaying, foot shuffling, trembling, extraneous arm movement, hand tremors, facial tension, heavy breathing, perspiration, quivering voice). It is important to note that although the majority of these behaviors are frequently related in a fairly direct way to the intensity of the physiological response, the occurrence of some behaviors may be more reflective of avoidance behavior for particular individuals. Poor eye contact, especially during social interaction situations, represents the clearest example.

In Paul's (1966) investigation trained observers recorded the presence or absence of each behavior in eight successive 30-second intervals during class-related speech presentations. The total scores summed over 20 behaviors and eight time periods served as the overt anxiety index. Training of observers was conducted prior to the experiment and involved practice with both live and videotaped speech presentations. The resulting interrater reliability averaged 0.95 and remained high throughout the study. Six-week test-retest correlation was low but significant ($r = 0.37$). Unfortunately, the coefficient was calculated on the basis of all 67 subjects contacted in the outcome investigation so that the effects of treatment variables confound the relationship. Intercorrelations between TBCL scores and five other measures of anxiety (heart rate, palmar sweat, and three self-report measures) were nonsignificant prior to treatment but pretest-posttest change in the checklist score correlated significantly with improvement in all of the other measures.

The TBCL has been adapted for use in assessing a variety of other therapy analogue anxiety targets (e.g., social situations, Borkovec, Stone, O'Brien, & Kaloupek, 1974; snakes, Bernstein & Nietzel, 1974; insects, Fazio, 1972). Interrater reliability correlations have typically ranged from 0.71 to 0.96. Although higher reliabilities have been reported, they are based on agreement achieved during training sessions. Continued reliability checks are often absent from subsequent assessment periods even though some evidence (Bernstein, 1973) indicates that high "practice" agreement may not be maintained during actual testing periods. This is a problem for observational systems in general and for complex systems such as the TBCL in particular. Jones, Reid, and Patterson (1974) have pointed out that the presence or absence of a reliability checker can have a marked influence on behavioral ratings. Data obtained by a single observer must therefore remain tenuous, regardless of previously or periodically obtained reliabilities based on subsamples.

Other direct anxiety measures focus more specifically on the disruptive effects of overarousal on verbal behavior. For example, Dollard & Mowrer (1947) developed a content analysis system for determining client tension during therapy sessions. The resulting Discomfort-Relief Quotient is similar in concept to Mahl's (1956) speech disturbance ratio in which the number of speech disruptions (e.g., sentence corrections and incompletions, repetitions, stuttering, intruding incoherent sounds, slips of the tongue, omissions, use of "ah") is divided by the total number of words spoken. Mahl also scores the percentage of time spent in silence, an index thought to be sensitive to the client's arousal level. Interrater reliability for both measures can be quite high ($r = 0.94$ and 0.96; Mahl, 1956), especially if scoring is based on typed transcripts. In the original validation of the measures, Mahl found speech disturbances and silence to be significantly greater during anxious/conflicted segments of interviews than during defensive or low-anxious segments.

Attempts have recently been made to apply parts of Mahl's scoring system as a measure of anxiety in nontherapy social situations and, although the number of non-ah speech disturbances failed to discriminate high versus low self-reported socially anxious subjects, that measure was found to increase with progressively increasing stress in a social interaction situation (Borkovec, Fleischmann, & Caputo, 1973). Three-week test-retest reliability in a similar laboratory analogue social situation has indicated that the speech disturbance ratio score is fairly stable in the absence of treatment ($r = 0.75$, Borkovec et al., 1974a).

A review of relevant literature by Murray (1971) revealed that the relationship between anxiety and levels of word productivity is a complex one. In general, word production appears to display an inverted-U relationship with the degree of stress, reflecting the relationship of intensity of physiological activity and behavioral efficiency mentioned earlier. Thus it is obvious that the validity of word production as an indicant of anxiety will very much depend on an interaction between level of stress employed as well as the general disposition of the subject to react with anxiety to the stressor.

In addition to recording instances of performance disruption during exposure to feared situations, many researchers also attempt to measure the overall effectiveness, adequacy, or appropriateness of that performance. The most common example of this approach in the social learning literature is provided by recording the academic performance of test-anxious subjects (cf. Allen, 1972). The indices employed are numerous but generally of two types: in-class performance (e.g., quizzes, final exams, grade-point average) and scores on laboratory-based tests (e.g., portions in IQ tests, reading tests, problem solving). These measures are sometimes supplemented by nonreactive (Webb, Campbell, Schwartz, & Sechrest, 1966) assessment of other presumably anxiety-related aspects of test taking such as filling in nonessential information on test forms, messiness and disorganization of answer sheets, and the like (Johnson & Sechrest, 1968).

Researchers interested in social anxiety have also constructed laboratory performance tests for its assessment. For example, McFall and his associates (e.g., McFall & Marston, 1970; McFall & Twentyman, 1973) have employed behavioral role-playing tasks, extended interaction tests, and follow-up phone calls to assess the client's level of assertion in response to unreasonable requests. In the role-playing task individuals are asked to imagine themselves being confronted by various situations calling for an assertive response and to reply to the situation as they normally would. Interjudge agreement on ratings of tape-recorded responses on a five-point scale of degree of appropriate refusal has varied between 0.76 and 0.97. In the extended interaction and telephone follow-up an antagonist persists in making an unreasonable request of the subject whose responses are scored in terms of when and if acquiescence occurs. Interrater reliabilities for the latter two measures have not been reported. Borkovec et al. (1974) used a similar role-playing measure with socially anxious and nonanxious subjects. Performance was rated by a confederate on a seven-point effectiveness scale and, although interrater reliability was not assessed, the ratings significantly discriminated the two anxiety groups; three-week test-retest reliability was significant though low ($r = 0.38$).

Indirect behavioral measures. The most widely employed overt behavioral anxiety measures are indirect and involve quantification of subjects' escape/avoidance of feared stimuli. Escape/avoidance responses are assumed to be reinforced by anxiety reduction, and their intensity presumably reflects the strength of the mediating anxiety. As we will see, however, escape/avoidance behavior may also be a function of variables that are completely unrelated to the degree of arousal engendered by the target stimulus or situation.

Assessments of avoidance in clinical patients have often been made by therapist or independent assessor ratings of phobic avoidance. Common rating forms are modeled after Gelder and Marks (1966) and involve five-point scales of severity for phobic anxiety and avoidance, for both main phobia and total phobias. Unfortunately, the basis of the ratings often resides in client reports during interviews and thus present the same difficulties inherent in all self-report measures. Satisfactory interrater reliabilities among client, therapist, and independent rater scores are achievable (e.g., *r*s = 0.75 to 0.90, Watson & Marks, 1971), although they are not always found to be that high (e.g., *r*s = 0.53 to 0.74, Emmelkamp, 1974).

Under carefully controlled conditions escape/avoidance tests (usually called behavioral avoidance tests or BATs) can be a valid indirect measure of overt anxiety. This is fortunate because escape/avoidance is one of the most distressing components of clinical anxiety owing to its impact on the client's daily life. Evaluation of its presence and subsequent evidence of its modification are therefore often of the greatest clinical importance.

When the anxiety-provoking stimulus is a concrete object, presentation of that stimulus in a BAT is easily controlled by the experimenter, thus easing quantification of physical avoidance. The first systematic use of a

BAT was reported by Lang and Lazovik (1963). Snake-phobic subjects were requested to approach, touch, and handle a live snake prior to and after treatment; their minimum distance (in feet) from the animal or degree of interaction with it (e.g., touch, hold) were used as indices of fear.

Because fears of small animals are frequently reported in normal populations and because of the apparent simplicity of assessing such fear through BATs conducted under controlled conditions, scores of laboratory analogue studies similar to the Lang and Lazovik investigation have focused on this form of anxiety measurement (Bernstein & Paul, 1971). Avoidance scales that rank physical proximity to or intimacy of contact with feared objects in terms of numerical equivalents are rather easily constructed and have been used to measure degree of avoidance to rats, mice, dogs, water, sharp objects, spiders, and cockroaches, in addition to the often-employed harmless snake.

A related measure involves duration of exposure to the feared stimulus. For example, Miller and Bernstein (1972) asked self-reported claustrophobics to remain in a closed chamber for as long as they could and Rutner and Pear (1972) constructed an observational apparatus whereby subjects could control duration of visual exposure to a laboratory rat. Further refinement of BATs can be achieved by inclusion of latency data such as the amount of time between the beginning of the test and the point at which physical contact with the feared object is made (e.g., Bernstein, 1973; Borkovec, 1972). More detailed data can be collected by using tape-event recorders and other equipment to signal the initiation and/or completion of each BAT step and to provide a permanent record of interstep times. Studies obtaining latency information over a series of avoidance steps have found latency to be a positively accelerated increasing function of proximity (Levis, 1969; Borkovec & Craighead, 1971). In addition to providing a finer-grain analysis than simple approach (distance) scores, the combination of latency measures and distance scores has been found to correlate higher with self-report instruments than distance alone (Mac & Fazio, 1972).

Avoidance tests have also been used in more applied settings to measure less frequently encountered, though clinically relevant, anxiety. This usually involves instructing the client to engage in a series of ideographically defined, increasingly anxiety-provoking activities similar to the steps contained in BATs employed in analogue research. Thus acrophobics are asked to climb a ladder (Ritter, 1970), or persons who typically engage in obsessive-compulsive rituals are prevented from doing so during exposures to stimuli discriminative for such rituals (Rachman, Hodgson, & Marks, 1971). As in research projects, duration-of-exposure measures have also been used in clinical cases of agoraphobia (Everaerd, Rijken, & Emmelkamp, 1973) and other specific fears (Leitenberg, Agras, Butz, & Wincze, 1971) by recording the length of time clients remain in the presence of the feared stimulus before feeling uncomfortable.

As an observational measurement device, BATs require (and appear to have) substantial interrater agreement. Under controlled laboratory conditions, typical reliability coefficients are nearly perfect (e.g., $r = 0.99$, Borkovec, 1972). Although interrater correlations are ordinarily not included in clinical reports involving a BAT, it is likely that similar reliabilities are achievable because of the discrete and highly operational nature of the avoidance scale steps and the general accuracy of timing measurements.

Although the majority of BATs involve active movement by subjects in relation to feared stimuli, other measurement goals can be facilitated by the use of a passive avoidance test that allows the subject to remain in a stationary position. The most elaborate version of this procedure is the Phobic Test Apparatus (PTA), a subject- or experimenter-controlled mechanical device that systematically moves a feared object by fixed distances toward the seated testee (Levis, 1969; Miller & Levis, 1971). A less expensive alternative is for the experimenter simply to carry or push the feared object's cage or container toward the subject. The advantages of the passive avoidance test include (1) allowance for continuous physiological recording, which usually requires a relatively quiescent subject, (2) complete experimenter control (when desirable) over duration of stimulus exposure and approach progress, and (3) potential for automatic recording of interresponse latencies in subject-controlled tests.

The decision to use active or passive BAT procedures can be made on the basis of practicality or the type of data desired since it appears that the two approaches produce highly similar avoidance assessments. Borkovec and Craighead (1971) evaluated avoidance scores of analogue snake phobics exposed to (counterbalanced) repeated tests using either a PTA or the usual BAT conditions. Approach score correlations ranged from 0.87 to 0.95.

The stability of the BAT on untreated subjects has been variable, partly as a function of time between testings. Reliability coefficients range from 0.63 in Lang and Lazovik's (1963) five-week retest to 0.95 in Borkovec and Craighead's (1971) immediate retest.

The use of naturalistic field observations as a means of collecting data on relevant behaviors has been an ubiquitous tool in functional analytic research and treatment aimed at a wide range of targets, but it is almost never employed in research or treatment involving social learning approaches to anxiety-related problems. A rare exception is provided by

Bailey and Atchinson (1969) who applied time-sampling procedures (Ayllon & Azrin, 1968) to the assessment of obsessive-compulsive behavior. Attendants observed the target patient once an hour 14 times a day and recorded the presence or absence of handwashing behavior. Expansion and refinement of naturalistic (and perhaps unobtrusive) observation systems designed to assess anxiety components would be highly desirable because, although emphasis on laboratory measurement has fostered the development of relatively reliable anxiety assessment procedures, the ecological validity of such data will always remain somewhat questionable. This problem is of little concern to most therapy analogue researchers whose interests are focused on theoretical, procedural, and parametric research on fear and its modification (cf. Bates, 1970; Levis, 1970) but is of great moment to the practitioner because real-life change is the only clinically relevant variable. Thus although controlled assessment of clients in artificial laboratory situations can serve useful purposes, field assessment cannot be ignored. As we have seen, those assessments have typically been based on client self-report, but it is hoped that more extensive use of systematic observation and quantification of problematic behaviors occurring in the client's environment will become common anxiety assessment approaches in the future.

Self-Report Measures

Despite frequent criticism of self-report data, this channel of anxiety measurement is the only method of obtaining information regarding the cognitive-phenomenological component of anxiety. Self-report measures in the behavior therapy literature have basically involved one of two forms: (1) general questionnaries that require the respondent to rate the presence, absence, or degree of anxiety felt in response to a variety of items representing potential eliciting situations and (2) specific rating forms to assess the degree of discomfort experienced during recent exposure to an anxiety-provoking situation.

General fear questionnaire. Prototypic of the general fear questionnaire is the Fear Survey Schedule. Lists of commonly feared objects or events are presented, and the client simply indicates his estimated degree of fear of each situation on a several-point scale. Various forms have been constructed, ranging from Geer's (1965) 51-item research schedule to Wolpe and Lang's (1964) 120-item form for use with clinical patients (see Tasto, this volume). In research settings the typical use of the schedule has been to identify large numbers of subjects fearful of the same object or event. The questionnaire has thus primarily served as an initial screening device prior to ultimate selection of phobic subjects on the basis of their overt behavior during a laboratory exposure to the object. The principal use of the survey in clinical work has been to identify fears related to or in addition to the presenting problem. The claustrophobic, for example, who indicates intense fear of items reflecting social encounters, may be treated quite differently from one who fails to reveal this potentially central fear theme. The general questionnaires vary in the targets represented, from surveys of a variety of common objects and events to tests dealing with a common theme. Examples of the latter include Lang's Snake Questionnaire (cf. Klorman, Weerts, Hastings, Melamed, & Lang, 1974), Paul's (1966) Personal Report of Confidence as a Speaker (PRCS), Watson and Friend's (1969) Social Avoidance and Distress scale and Fear of Negative Evaluation scale, Endler, Hunt, and Rosenstein's (1962) S–R Inventory of Anxiousness, and Suinn's (1969) Test Anxiety Behavior scale. Each of these questionnaires includes items representing several instances of the same target fear, and the respondent obtains a total fear score based on the number of items reported to be anxiety producing.

A recent and detailed review of general questionnaires, with particular focus on the fear survey schedule, has been provided by Hersen (1973). In his article reliability of the schedule as well as its validity, factorial structure, sex and population differences, and relationship to various personality scales are presented. Consequently, we will not duplicate his efforts. Some of his conclusions, however, are similar to those that will be drawn below for specific fear rating scales: Internal consistency and test-retest reliabilities for the total scale have been relatively high; there has been an absence of long-term test-retest studies; moderate correlations exist between fear inventories and other self-report scales; correlations of surveys with behavioral and physiological measures are sometimes significant but often nonsignificant.

Specific fear rating scales. Analogous to the behavioral measures obtained during actual confrontation with the anxiety stimulus, specific fear ratings are routinely obtained just prior to, during, and/or just after test exposures and are designed to measure the cognitive anxiety component in direct response to the stimulus. These self-report measures may be divided arbitrarily into two types: (1) obtrusive rating scales that include items directly related to the feared stimulus and that ask the subject to indicate the amount of fear experienced during the exposure, and (2) less obtrusive scales that attempt to measure the subject's current discomfort with less explicit reference to the feared stimuli and/or their descriptors. Typical of the former is the Fear Thermometer (Walk, 1956), a 10-point scale on which the subject estimates the degree of his anxiety during the exposure task. Common examples of the latter type include the Affect Adjective Checklist and the Anxiety Differential.

By far the most frequent method of assessing momentary anxiety level in response to a feared stimulus is Walk's (1956) Fear Thermometer (FT) or derivatives thereof. Walk conducted two studies to validate this very direct method of anxiety assessment. Parachutist trainees were given the FT just prior to each of several mock tower jumps in the first study and after a series of jumps in the second study. Subjects scoring high and low on the FT scale were compared on behavioral performance ratings and success in completing the training program. In both studies FT scores discriminated quality of performance. Scores on the FT were significantly related to other self-report measures of fear. Analysis of prequestionnaire data indicated that the FT ratings were specific to the testing situation itself and did not reflect a general tendency among high scorers to admit fear.

The majority of behaviorally oriented therapy outcome studies have employed some form of the FT as one of their self-report instruments. The FT is the quickest test to administer and is applicable to any fear situation. Immediate test-retest correlations (*r*s = 0.94 to 0.98, Borkovec & Craighead, 1971) and reliability over several weeks (*r* = 0.75, Lang & Lazovik, 1963; *r* = 0.94, Trexler & Karst, 1972) have been generally quite high in studies of both snake phobia and speech anxiety. As mentioned earlier, phobic patient ratings of fear level have generally correlated highly with therapist and medical assessor ratings (e.g., 0.75 to 0.87, Watson & Marks, 1971).

In addition to ratings of anxiety level, numerous clinical investigations have collected client-recorded data on anxiety-motivated behavior. Examples include daily frequency counts on self-mutilating behavior (Ernst, 1973), frequency and duration of body washing (Rachman, Hodgson, & Marzillier, 1970), and frequency of ruminations (Stern, Lipsedge, & Marks, 1973).

Although relatively easy to obtain, the FT and self-recorded anxiety data are also the most direct request for reports of anxiety level and thus are most susceptible to demand effects and faking. We will return to this point in a subsequent section.

In contrast to direct self-report measures, ratings on instruments such as adjective checklists and the semantic differential apparently provide somewhat more subtle measures of anxiety. Zuckerman (1960) developed the Affect Adjective Check List (AACL) to measure fluctuations in state anxiety. Subjects simply checked adjectives that reflected how they generally felt ("general" form) and how they felt on the day of the test administration ("today" form). The 21 adjectives used evolved from a longer list of adjectives with face-valid connotations of anxiety, and they were selected on the basis of their ability to discriminate psychiatrically diagnosed anxiety cases from normals (Persky, Maroc, Conrad, & DenBreeijen, 1959) and to show changes under experimentally induced anxiety conditions (Levitt, DenBreeijen, & Persky, 1960). Checking any of the 11 "anxiety-plus" adjectives (e.g., afraid, desperate, shaky, tense) and failing to check any of the 10 "anxiety-minus" adjectives (e.g., calm, cheerful, loving, steady) contribute to a total anxiety score. Zuckerman's (1960) own reliability study on college normals revealed acceptable internal consistency in both "general" ($r = 0.72$) and "today" ($r = 0.85$) forms. One-week test-retest reliability was relatively high for the "general" form ($r = 0.68$) and low for the "today" form ($r = 0.31$). The latter result is to be expected since state anxiety level may fluctuate from week to week. In an attempt to validate the instrument Zuckerman administered the "today" form over several days prior to and after class examinations; significant increases in anxiety level were found on examination days relative to nonexam days.

The AACL has been employed in various outcome investigations (e.g., snake phobia, Kazdin, 1974; stressor films, Davidson & Hiebert, 1971), but although the measure has reflected overt behavioral changes in such studies, little additional evidence regarding its reliability and interrelationships with other measures has been provided.

The Anxiety Differential (AD) (Husek & Alexander, 1963), or modifications thereof, has been a frequently used self-report instrument in behavior therapy research. Like the AACL, the AD was developed as a verbal response measure of situational anxiety. The more specific goal was to create an instrument that would "(a) be of such a nature that subjects are unlikely to falsify their responses, (b) not be susceptible to response sets, (c) be scorable by an objective, nonjudgmental key, (d) be easily administered to groups of any size, (e) be short, and (f) be inexpensive" (Alexander & Husek, 1962, p. 326). The semantic differential technique of Osgood, Suci, and Tannenbaum (1957) was employed to measure the connotive (the affective feeling) meaning of cognition. Ratings of concepts simply involved checking bipolar scales of adjectives (e.g., loose–tight, deep–shallow). The concepts chosen to be rated in the AD were not clearly associated with anxiety (e.g., dreams, me, hands), thus making response faking difficult. Pilot work and hypotheses regarding the nature of anxiety resulted in 68 initial scale items (i.e., concepts and their respective bipolar adjective scales). Several experiments have been reported (Alexander & Husek, 1962; Husek & Alexander, 1963) documenting the sensitivity of the AD in discriminating anxious and nonanxious states, both within and between subject groups. Anxious subjects instructed to "fake good" have been found to display higher anxiety scores than a nonanxious control group. In a separate investigation, knowing the purpose of the test was unrelated to anxiety scores. Factor analysis of the scales revealed one large anxiety factor that correlated significantly with the Nowlis and Green (1959) adjective checklist for the measurement of momentary mood. Internal consistency of the items was found to be adequate in three separate studies. Various sets of adjective scales were developed, with different sets found to be differentially appropriate, depending on the type of design employed (e.g., pretest-posttest, pretest-posttest comparisons of experimental and control groups, or posttest-only comparisons).

Several studies involving both small animal phobias (e.g., Bernstein, 1973; Bernstein & Nietzel, 1974) and social-speech anxiety (e.g., Borkovec et al., 1974a; Goldfried & Trier, 1974; Paul, 1966; Woy & Efran, 1972) have employed the AD in its original form. In addition a similar semantic differential measure has been used by Bandura, Blanchard, and Ritter, (1969) and other researchers (e.g., Kazdin, 1974; Hekmat, 1972; Cautela, Flannery, & Hanley, 1974) in analogue therapy studies. In clinical settings Marks (1965; Watson & Marks, 1971) typically obtains patients' semantic differential ratings of the main phobic situation, a control fear situation, a neutral situation, the therapist, and psychiatrists. The instrument employed by Bandura and Marks and their associates differs from the original AD in that the feared stimulus itself is rated on bipolar adjective scales. Since this form is more obtrusive than the original AD, the potential influence of demand characteristics appears greater.

It should be pointed out that in the development and evaluation of the AD Husek and Alexander (1963) employed (1) films of surgical operations and highway accidents and (2) college examinations as the environmental stressors. Thus the AD may be most appropriate when target fears involve bodily injury or social evaluation. Other than the original data provided by Husek and Alexander, little additional information about the validity and reliability of the AD and its derivatives has been provided. Paul (1966) has reported a moderate seven-week test-retest correlation ($r = 0.54$) for his speech-anxious sample (treated and nontreated subjects). Three-week test-retest reliability among 47 nontreated socially anxious subjects has been found to be fairly high ($r = 0.78$, Borkovec et al., 1974a).

The specific self-report instruments discussed so far have focused on assessment of two of the three components of the anxiety response: phenomenological distress and the occurrence of anxiety-mediated overt behavior. However, subjective measures of the physiological component of anxiety have also been developed. Subjects simply report their awareness of several autonomic responses when they feel anxious. An early version of this type of instrument was reported by Mandler and his associates (Mandler & Kremen, 1958; Mandler, Mandler, & Uviller, 1958). Their

Questionnaire on the Perception of Feeling consisted of 28 items that request respondents to indicate the degree to which various bodily reactions occurred during two emotional states. The first 21 items (the Autonomic Perception Questionnaire, APQ) relate to subjective experiences when the person is anxious (e.g., muscle tension, changes in heart rate, sinking stomach); for each item, the subject checks a point on a continuous line whose ends represent absence versus intense presence of each bodily response. High and low perceivers are identified in terms of the sum of the 21 individual item scores. Although Mandler has employed a general form of the APQ ("When you are anxious, do you notice . . .?"), subsequent studies have also used a task-specific form ("During the test exposure, did you notice . . .?").

Mandler's investigations have shown that actual autonomic reactivity (heart rate, PGR, and respiration) to stress is related to the degree of perceived reactivity as measured by the APQ. In addition behavioral performance on a vocabulary test was unrelated to actual arousal but was significantly and negatively related to perceived arousal. Later investigations have found the APQ to be related to performance in heart-rate control tasks (Bergman & Johnson, 1971; Blanchard, Young, & McLeod, 1972) and the extinction (Borkovec, 1973) or paradoxical enhancement (Stone & Borkovec, 1975) of fear during test exposures to feared stimuli. Very little reliability data have been obtained on the APQ; its use in anxiety research is of relatively recent origin. One study did report a three-week test-retest correlation of 0.71 in a laboratory measurement of social anxiety (Borkovec et al., 1974a).

As will be apparent from the physiological measurement section to follow, individuals differ in the reactiveness of various autonomic responses. Some individuals, for example, respond to stress with large heart rate changes, whereas others react with maximal response in the gastrointestinal system. It would be reasonable to expect similar individual response stereotypes in self-reports of autonomic arousal, and this has been found to be the case. Borkovec (1976) factor analyzed the APQs of three separate samples of college students and found five replicated profiles of autonomic response patterning. Females tended to report responses involving (1) stomach activity and perspiration, (2) heart activity and muscle tension, or (3) a combination of heart and stomach activity. Males tended to respond with either (4) heart activity or (5) stomach activity and perspiration. Although Mandler (1972) found a weak but significant relationship between total APQ score and various autonomic measures, recent research suggests that stronger relationships may exist between more specific perceived and actual autonomic response systems. Edelman (1972), for example, exposed subjects to neutral and fearful imagery while heart rate and GSR were monitored; half of the subjects were high perceivers of heart rates, by their self-report, whereas half were high perceivers of GSR. Only the former showed significant heart rate increases to fearful images.

Physiological Measures

Activity in the physiological response channel is almost always included as an integral component of theories of emotions (Goldstein, 1968). Indeed, extreme peripheralist theories, such as the James-Lange theory, even equate emotions with the physiological events. Any attempt to examine the theoretically and clinically crucial emotion of anxiety must then expend considerable effort in evaluation of physiological responding, including both somatic and autonomic. This section will present a highlighted view of the empirical findings in physiological anxiety assessment.

Physiological anxiety assessment schemes often tacitly, and sometimes explicitly, assume that peripheral physiological measures provide a straightforward index of a massive and diffuse sympathetic arousal that serves to energize the overt responses of anxiety and to determine the phenomenological experience of fearfulness. The notion of far-ranging sympathetic activation as the prototypic physiological component of fear and anxiety states originated from Cannon's (1915) early formulation of fear as a somatic emergency reaction directed toward meeting the exigencies of physical exertion. Cannon specifically implicated adrenal medullary epinephrine (adrenalin) secretion as serving the metabolic requirement of active skeletal muscles and hormonally augmenting all sympathetic activity. If indeed the physiological reaction to threatening stimuli were to follow an arousal pattern of uniform increases in the varied sympathetic functions, then quantitative measurement of physiological anxiety respondents would in no way be problematical. Any one measure of autonomic activity (heart rate, skin conductance, blood pressure, plasma levels of epinephrine, etc.) could be interchanged with any other as an indicant of physiological "arousal." However, this relatively uncomplicated view of somatic responding has not survived empirical tests. Lacey (1959, 1967) in particular has marshalled evidence against unidimensional arousal, demonstrating repeatedly that complex and specific patterns of autonomic responses are elicited by specific stress stimuli. In addition, it is now clear that the ubiquitously found secretion of epinephrine is not subservient to muscle action but rather maintains the sugar supply to the brain (Smith, 1973). Thus although variants of unidimensional arousal theory do persist in the literature (e.g., Duffy, 1972) there is sufficient evidence against this conceptualization in its simple form to exclude it as a guide in any venture in assessing anxiety.

Fundamental issues of validity in the assessment of the physiology of anxiety are raised by the failure empirically to find a simple unidimensional arousal facet of physiological responding. These issues will be dealt with in detail later and will only be alluded to here. This section will simply review selected empirical data pertaining to the more frequently monitored physiological response systems, primarily heart rate and electrodermal activity. A more thorough earlier review of much of this literature may be found in Mathews (1971).

Cardiovascular responses. There are a large number of measures of cardiovascular functioning, including heart rate, systolic blood pressure, diastolic blood pressure, cardiac output, peripheral resistance, blood volume and flow, skin temperature, reactive hyperemia, and many others. They are all interrelated but not in a simple, positive, linear fashion, and thus they cannot be assumed to be interchangeable. Heart rate is by far the most frequently assessed cardiovascular output parameter, with blood pressure, blood volume, and skin temperature trailing well behind. The others are only rarely measured in psychological investigations, primarily owing to technical difficulties. Heart rate will receive the focus of attention here, because it has received the greatest empirical investigation and because it has received the greatest impirical investigation and because the relative ease of recording it is likely to prompt its selection in clinical schemes to assess anxiety. Electrodermal and somatic measures will be reported in this section when they are taken in conjunction with heart rate.

Heart rate can be continuously monitored preceding and during fear stimuli presentations. For all practical purposes, fear stimuli can be presented in only three modes: (1) in vivo, as in the BAT; (2) in fantasy, commonly through explicitly described or previously agreed on imagery scenes; and (3) pictorially, usually by slide projections. Each of these modes of presentation has its own influence on heart rate through the cognitive and motor demands of the setting. Thus comparison conditions involving low-fear stimuli should be included to control for these effects. Since many experiments do not include adequate comparison tasks, the reported accelerations in heart rate must be evaluated relative to absolute values and waveforms assumed to be generated by comparable neutral transactions.

Craighead (1973) recorded heart rate, as well as respiration rate, from snake-phobic subjects before and throughout Levis's (1969) procedure and apparatus for testing phobics. Prior to being informed that they would be placed in proximity to a snake, the subjects had a mean resting heart rate (after ten minutes of quiet sitting) of 85.03 beats per minute (B/M). Since mean resting heart rate in the general population is approximately

72 B/M, and healthy college students frequently rest well down in the sixties and below, the resting rate of over 85 represents mild heart rate arousal evoked by unspecified aspects of the experimental situation. Mean heart rate increased to 96.08 B/M at the point where each subject stopped advancing the snake toward herself. To put this increase in perspective, severe exercise results in a mean heart rate of approximately 130 B/M. A rate of over 96 can aptly be described as a "moderate" acceleration. Respiration rate doubled from a resting level of 20.28 cycles/M (compared to a general average of 12 cycles/M) to 41.13 cycles/M at the final test point. A comparison task involving increasing proximity to an emotionally neutral object would have eliminated nagging alternative interpretations based on possible physiological requirements of the general testing procedure.

Anxiety about public speaking performance was assessed and treated by Paul (1966), who included a 30-second sample of heart rate and a palmar sweat index just preceding public-speaking tests. At pretesting the heart rate average was 88.90 B/M for all groups; at posttesting, the heart rate fell slightly to 86.26 B/M for the treated groups. Only the desensitization group showed a significant heart rate decline, compared to a no-treatment control, with desensitized subjects dropping from 92.7 to 86.1 B/M. This test situation, then, appears to result in mild to moderately high levels of heart rate in anticipation of the actual stressor, and this heart rate response was not dramatically diminished by treatment. A comparison task of parallel cognitive and motor needs, although probably difficult to construct, would have been valuable. Alternatively, a group of relaxed public speakers would provide a useful control group.

Results of a recent experiment by Borkovec, Stone, O'Brien, and Kaloupek (1974) bring the heart rate responses attending public-speaking anxiety into considerably sharper relief. Male subjects with high and low social anxiety were administered an interaction task on two occasions separated by two to three weeks. Heart rate was monitored continuously from the time subjects were told they would be required to talk to a female confederate to the end of the interaction. Figure 11–1 presents the heart rate levels and waveforms for the two groups and tests. At the first point in the pretest, when subjects were waiting to begin the task, low-anxious subjects were resting at a relatively low 81.6 B/M, whereas high-anxious subjects were 10.8 B/M higher at 92.4 B/M. This separation was maintained throughout all phases of the test. The dramatic feature of the waveform is the sharp rise of over 20 B/M from the point of entrance of the confederate at phase 4 to the start of the interaction at phase 6 for both groups. It is tempting to speculate that this large time-locked acceleration represents a heart rate adjustment for perceptual-motor needs, whereas the consistent separation of heart rate between high-anxious and low-anxious groups reflects the anxiety aspects of the situation. However, it is intuitively obvious that the anticipatory period in those minutes immediately prior to interaction onset is also the most stressful time in the task, and thus the acceleration in this time frame may well partially represent a surge in anxiety. Again, as with Paul (1966), a comparison task requiring perceptual motor demands without the evaluative features of social interaction could resolve this interpretative ambiguity.

Continuing inspection of Figure 11–1, it is interesting to note that in the second testing the low-anxious subjects produced heart rates in the anticipatory period comparable in magnitude to those of high-anxious subjects. Experience with the stressor, then, differentially affected the anticipatory response compared to the reactive component in these subjects. Such an effect would be difficult to see with anything other than a dependent variable, such as heart rate, which can be continuously monitored to check the flow of events.

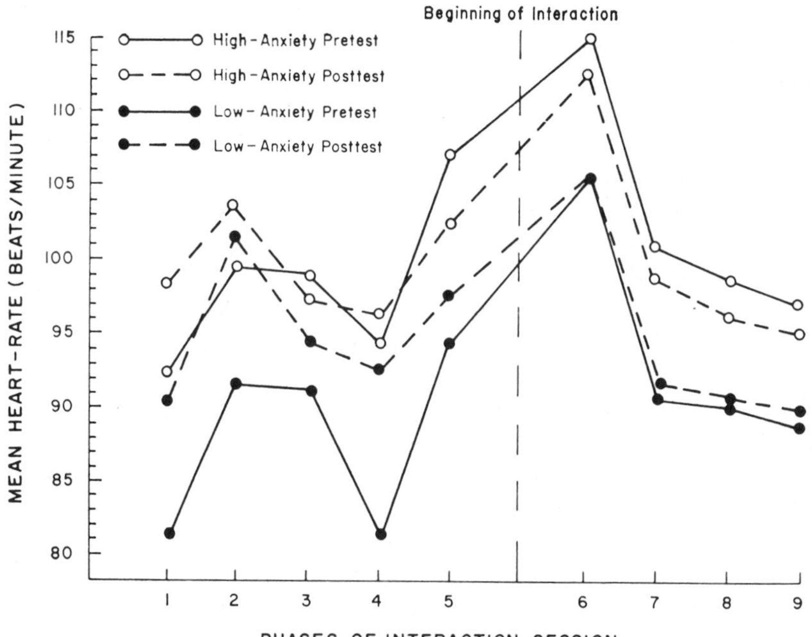

Figure 11–1. Pretest and posttest heart rate means for low- and high-anxiety groups during nine phases of the session. [From T. D. Borkovec, N. M. Stone, G. T. O'Brien, and D. G. Kaloupek, Evaluation of a clinically relevant target behavior for analog outcome research. *Behavior Therapy,* 1974, *5,* 503–513. Copyright (1975) by Academic Press. Reproduced by permission.]

Watson, Gaind, and Marks (1972) provide data on a series of case studies of specific phobics who were repeatedly administered fear stimuli both in vivo and in fantasy. Eight patients were presented floodings of anxiety provoking imagery scenes over three sessions followed by in vivo testing. Heart rate and skin conductance were continuously recorded. Prior to the flooding sessions, two phobic and two neutral scenes were imagined to provide for anxiety assessment. Heart rate, skin conductance level (SCL), skin conductance responses (SCRs), and subjective ratings of anxiety were all significantly greater for phobic versus neutral scenes at the beginning of treatment. Across flooding sessions, the difference was eliminated first for SCL, then SCRs, and finally for heart rate. Reports of subjective anxiety were diminished but never completely abolished. In contrast to this orderly progression during the repeated assessments, there was considerable individual variation in heart rate during the actual flooding periods. Two subjects displayed no change in heart rate in flooding; four responded greatest early in flooding sessions; and the remaining two responded specifically to individual flooding scenes. Some of the responding was large, reaching over 110 B/M during flooding fantasy, whereas others barely exceeded base rates.

The authors found that small heart rate responses during flooding were not necessarily associated with mild response to subsequent in vivo practice. One balloon phobic displayed little arousal during fantasy, but his heart rate exceeded 150 B/M for almost 15 minutes as balloons were repeatedly burst about him. In such circumstances the flooding treatment was continued in vivo until tachycardia and subjective anxiety subsided, and trials were repeated until the response habituated. In general, fantasy sessions produced lower heart rate arousal than real practice sessions.

All these results indicate that heart rate is fairly reliably found to be high, and sometimes extremely high, when subjects are directly presented with stimuli that from other considerations are known to provoke anxiety. The data from the Watson et al. (1972) study indicate that the same statement cannot be made as confidently for anxiety stimuli presented through visual imagining. Imagery is one of the most private of events and is frequently reported as being a vague, fleeting, and uncontrollable phenomenological experience (see Richardson, 1969, for a wide ranging historical view of the literature). Objective measurement of imagery has not been satisfactorily attained, and we are left to rely on verbal reports of vividness, which correlate mostly only with themselves (Rehm, 1973). The level of communication provided by these verbal reports is tenuous at best, and the aversive nature of the anxiety response may attenuate the imagery without doing great damage to the verbal report. Most studies of phobic reactions, both assessment and behavioral treatment, have employed imagined phobic scenes based on the assumption that responding to images parallels responding to real stimuli, albeit markedly reduced in magnitude. In the main this appears to be a valid assumption. Jacobson (1930a, b, c, d, 1931a, b) consistently reported precise specificity of muscle contractions associated with imagining particular motor acts. Totten (1935) and Brown (1968) found that eye movements occurring in imagery paralleled those present in actual visual inspection of the objects but were more variable and often smaller. Other somatic variables are found to be augmented by imagery scenes of anxiety. For example, Rimm and Bottrell (1969) report greater change in respiration rate during imagining scenes of fear compared to imagining neutral scenes.

Before reviewing the data on heart rate, several methodological problems must be attended to. Although responses to imagery can be very large (e.g., Watson et al., 1972), they are generally smaller and more variable compared to real administrations of the phobic object. Great measurement and procedural care must be taken to ensure that the phenomena of interest are not either inadvertently lost when they do exist. A number of stimulus dimensions must be equated when comparing anxiety to neutral scenes or high anxiety to low anxiety scenes. First, although descriptions of neutral scenes are often not even provided in method sections of published reports, these benign scenes usually picture very familiar and uncomplicated events, and thus they are relatively easy to visualize. The autonomic and somatic quiescence attending these visualizations may simply reflect ease of imagining, whereas the physiological arousal accompanying the fear scenes could signify only greater difficulty in imagining them. Second, just as with in vivo tasks, the motor acts described in fear scenes are likely to be more extensive than those in neutral scenes, and hence they arouse more somatic and autonomic responding.

Subjects with both high and low total scores on the Fear Survey Schedule imagined individually tailored scenes of high and low fear in a study by Grossberg and Wilson (1968). For the first presentation of the fear scene, heart rate increased from a base of 74 B/M during scene description to 82 B/M during imagination of the scene. Heart rate showed a comparable increase from base to reading for the first neutral scene, but then it dropped to 78 B/M during imagination. Although all absolute levels declined over repeated trials, the heart rate separation for imagining fear and neutral scenes continued. The results for SCL were comparable although not quite as large, and they showed a decline in size of imagining fear scenes and neutral scenes over trials. For both heart rate and SCL, it should also be noted that over trials maximum activity occurred at reading, not at imagining, indicating that these measures were more aroused by the processing of the information than by the actual imagining in later administrations. The groups scoring high and low on the FSS did not differ, and thus the autonomic differences found were specific to the quality of the scenes, irrespective of the general level of reported fears.

The Grossberg and Wilson (1968) experiment also contained a control group formed of subjects who reported low fear of both the neutral and fear scenes. These control subjects should have displayed equal responsiveness to both the neutral and fear scenes of their matched experimental subjects. However, when comparing reading to imagining, control subjects similarly displayed greater heart rate and SCL to fear versus neutral scenes. All the other differences, then, may have been due to some content difference in the fear scenes other than the threat component. A specific relationship between threat and heart rate (and SCL) was not shown by these data.

An experiment by Lang, Melamed, and Hart (1970) using an automated desensitization device provides data that support the relationship between imagery-generated anxiety and heart rate. Heart rate, SCRs, and respiration rate were compared for desensitization trials signaled as evoking anxiety versus one preceding and two succeeding nonsignaled trials. All three physiological responses were found to be higher on signaled trials, with heart rate showing the most dramatic differential. Unless the signaled trials of these snake phobic systematically differed in content from nonsignaled trials, these data provide a strong correlation between subjective anxiety and heart rate responses.

The Lang et al. (1970) study also provides a rare example of a careful parametric investigation of physiological responses to a graded series of anxiety scenes. Individualized hierarchies of scenes were created for groups of spider and public-speaking phobics, and all scenes, including neutral scenes, were visualized. The correspondence of the heart rate and verbal report across the graded series of phobic stimuli was remarkable. If control groups of nonphobic subjects visualizing the same scenes were to display no such heart rate gradient, this design would provide a fairly conclusive demonstration of the relationship between verbal and cardiac components of anxiety. Finally, it should be noted that the SCR responses and respiration rate showed a significant linear trend only for spider phobics, and these were not as graphically dramatic as those for heart rate.

Van Egeren, Feather, and Hein (1971) also examined autonomic responding to a hierarchy of threat scenes in public-speaking phobics. Heart rate, respiration rate, and SCR were significantly greater for the mean of all threat scenes compared to a neutral scene of a pleasant walk along the sidewalk, with digital vasoconstriction being greater for the highest threat scene. Visual inspection of the graph of three responses over the five hierarchy items revealed a roughly linear increase in all physiological responses with increasing threat, and the linear trend of the composite responses was statistically significant. However, although heart rate appeared to increase linearly, the linear trend was not statistically significant, in contrast to Lang et al. (1970). The same was true for respiration rate; SCRs and digital vasoconstriction appear to have carried the statistical burden of the significant composite linear trend.

These results taken together lead to the conclusion that heart rate acceleration is an integral part of the imagery-induced anxiety response ensemble. The addition of appropriate controls in the future should serve mostly to establish more precisely the magnitude and waveform of the threat component of the response. The data base related to pictorially administered fear stimuli is not nearly so large, leading to only provisional conclusions. In contrast to the general positive results for imagery in his lab, colleagues of Lang (Klorman, 1974; Melamed, Note 2) have not found similar heart rate response differences between pictorial presentations of fear and neutral stimuli. Klorman (1974) presented snake-phobic subjects with 10- to 13-second film strips of seascapes and snakes, using three levels of snake films with scaled fear intensity. Not only did high, medium, and low snake films fail to produce differential heart rate responses, but heart rate was similar for seascapes and snake films with snake films yielding slightly and insignificantly lower rates. In a previous study of similar material Melamed (Note 2) also failed to find heart rate differentiation of snake and seascape films.

Waters and McDonald (1973) report an experiment comparing three modes of fear evocation in snake phobics: verbal description of a snake slide, actual presentation of the snake slide, and imagining the snake slide, always presented in this order. The heart rate, skin resistance response (SRR), and skin potential response (SPR) were greater for imagery than for either verbal description or the slide itself. An opposite trend was shown for vasoconstriction, when the verbal description evoked the greatest response. Unfortunately, the consistent order of presentation of the three stimuli does not allow for a clear interpretation of these data.

Pictorial stimuli should powerfully activate attentional intake processes, including their associated heart rate deceleration as will be discussed below. The threatening nature of fear pictures could defensively prompt equally powerful perceptual-cognitive rejection processes. The dominance of these two conflicting activities may well depend on stimulus and subject variables not well delineated at this time. Parallel considerations are present in other methods of stimulus presentation, and major advances in the assessment of physiological anxiety may have to wait for the experimental unraveling of these perceptual-cognitive processes.

In summary, heart rate has consistently been the cardiovascular measurement of choice in the assessment of physiological anxiety. It is a continuous output parameter of heart action that often shows marked increases under threat conditions. However, it is also responsive to a number of perceptual, cognitive, and motor task requirements that may interact with the threat aspect of these stimuli; hence appropriate control procedures are crucial.

Electrodermal responses. A number of excellent reviews of the research that seeks relationships between psychological variables and electrodermal activity have recently appeared, including a chapter by Edelberg (1973) and an edited book of chapters by Prokasy and Raskin (1973). These reviews provide considerable insight into this highly active and complex response channel and are recommended reading for experimenters willing to brave this measurement venture.

Edelberg (1973) concludes that there are two separate effectors involved in electrodermal activity: sweat glands and an epidermal membrane. As sweat ducts fill, SPL becomes more negative and SCL increases. Fullness of the ducts appears to be the major determinant of these levels. The resistance response is produced in large part by a change in membrane permeability. Although the sweat glands may be partially involved, the membrane reabsorption reflex is the major source of SCR and positive SPRs.

The division of electrodermal responding into two separate elements appears to have profound implications for future anxiety research. When the reabsorption reflex is prominent, SCRs recover (return to base) very rapidly. Edelberg (1970) found that recovery rate was independent of the amplitude of SRR and SCR, and Edelberg (1972) found it to vary when SCR amplitude, frequency of SCRs, and SCL were invariant. In this later experiment, warning of shock and a cold pressor test produced slow recovery of SCRs. These and other data have led Edelberg (1973) to conclude, "Rapid recovery is apparently associated with mobilization for goal oriented behavior and is positively correlated with level of performance on simple tasks, but is not a measure of activation per se" (pp. 181-182). On the other hand, slow recovery appears to be evoked by threat. Future anxiety research may do well to focus on this relatively new electrodermal measure. Unfortunately, little other empirical data are available at this point.

Raskin (1973) has emphasized the attentional influences on phasic electrodermal responses, both evoked and spontaneous. Electrodermal responding is exquisitely sensitive to both novel and interesting stimuli, and SCR is clearly a component of the orienting response (Sokolov, 1963). An experiment by Zimny and Kienstra (1967) demonstrates this phenomenon. They interpolated a neutral tone in a series of electric shocks and found that the tone-evoked SCR was larger than that of the preceding shock; novelty overrode noxiousness. Repeated presentations of a stimulus, even a noxious stimulus, result in habituation (i.e., a decline) in electrodermal response amplitude. This occurs in all physiological response channels; experiments reported in the cardiovascular section have reported such data, but electrodermal activity is most dramatically effected.

The difference between physiological reactions to discrete noxious and neutral stimuli is sometimes in the waveform and magnitude of the initial response but more often in the rate of habituation. For example, the heart rate response to a neutral stimulus is one of deceleration, whereas a noxious stimulus provides an acceleration followed by a deceleration (Graham & Clifton, 1966). Over repeated presentations, the decelerative component habituates, but the accelerate component remains essentially unchanged. An experiment by Raskin, Kotses, and Bever (1969), using a range of intensities of white noise in a within-subjects design, demonstrated the effect on electrodermal measures. Over 15 trials the SCR to 120 db tones (near pain threshold) did not habituate; increasingly softer stimuli produced increasingly greater habituation, with little differences in the size of the initial response. Measures of SPL and SCL showed a similar result, although not quite as markedly. Using both within- and between-subjects designs, Jackson (1974) found a similar intensity effect on SCR habituation but with an apparently somewhat greater effect of intensity on initial SCR.

The phenomenon of habituation over repeated trials of presentation generally holds for clinically relevant phobic stimuli. Grossberg and Wilson (1968) found both heart rate and SCL to decline with repetition of both fear and neutral imagery scenes. Melamed (Note 2) and Klorman (1974) both found habituation of SCL and SCR over trials and sessions of presentations of snake slides. Although it has also generally held in these and other experiments that fear stimuli produce larger SCL and SCRs than neutral stimuli, the finding of decreasing habituation with increasing fear intensity has been difficult to achieve. Klorman (1974) suggests that general adaptation to the entire setting and type of stimuli may have an overriding effect in such experiments.

A new electrodermal anxiety assessment technique has recently been reported. Williams, Jones, and Williams (1975) and Williams, Jones, Workhoven, and Williams (1975) measured the time required for slow infusion of thiopental sodium to abolish spontaneous SCRs (SCAT technique) in patients anxiously awaiting surgical operations and abortion. This measure correlated well with IPAT scores of anxiety and was reduced with therapy intervention. Although the measure is not satisfactory for examination of SCRs evoked by brief fear stimuli, it may be useful for measurement of anxiety states of longer duration.

Electrodermal responses provide indirect measures of sweat secretion and reabsorption. Direct, but not continuous, measures of sweat secretion are also available and are recommended because of their simplicity of procedure. Paul's (1966) Palmar Sweat Index is an example of such a technique, but it is technically cumbersome. Sutarman and Thomson (1952) report a simple, cheap, and clear plastic ink technique for counting the number of active sweat glands. More recently, Strahan, Todd, and Inghs (1974) have reported a technique utilizing only a bottle of distilled water and a simple apparatus for measuring the conductivity of the sweat accumulated in the water. These techniques are amenable to naturalistic measurement, but the resultant data have not yet been examined in relation to anxiety.

In summary, electrodermal responses are extremely sensitive to novel and interesting stimuli, and hence large responses will occur to almost any stimulus when it is first presented. Fear stimuli elicit larger initial responses than do neutral stimuli, but more important, these responses habituate at a slower rate and individual responses recover more slowly than do responses to neutral stimuli. The recovery rate measure is relatively new and deserves close attention; another new technique, the SCAT, also holds promise and deserves further investigation.

Problems in Interpretation of Anxiety Measures

Although the foregoing discussion of measurement instruments included reference to their validity, substantive consideration of the validity issue has been postponed until now. The present section will explore the nature of interrelationships among the various measures of response components, problems that can preclude the acquisition of valid data for each response component, and general methods of improving the quality of the data obtained. The physiological domain will require particularly detailed comments.

Classical validity notions (cf. Cronbach, 1960) have been represented in the development of most of the anxiety measures described in this chapter. Thus, for example, Zuckerman (1960) began the evolution of his AACL with *face-valid* adjective scales (e.g., "afraid," "shaky"), whereas Walk (1956) compared FT scores with parachute-training performance (*concurrent validity*) and with ultimate success or failure in the training program (*predictive validity*). In addition, every therapy outcome study inherently contains a *construct validation* of its dependent measures; on the basis of anxiety theory, it is predicted that certain treatment conditions should effect decreases in anxiety scores whereas certain control conditions should not. However, there are three important problems associated with these validation approaches when they are applied to anxiety assessment. Failure to resolve these problems (conceptually in the case of all three and procedurally as well in the case of the third) negates whatever previously established validity is possessed by a given instrument in a given study.

Lack of Interrelationships Among Measures of Response Components

Investigators in the anxiety area have routinely been concerned about the general lack of concurrent validity in studies of therapy outcome. Specifically, measures of cognitive, behavioral, and physiological reactions in feared situations rarely correlate highly with one another. Table 11–2 is a summary of five anxiety studies that have reported intercorrelation matrices among and between multiple measures of the three components of the anxiety response. Target behaviors in these five studies include snake phobia (Borkovec & Craighead, 1971), speech anxiety (Paul, 1966; Woy & Efan, 1972), and social anxiety (Borkovec et al., 1974a; O'Brien, 1975). Representative measures include (1) self-report: FT, AD, APQ, PRCS, and the S–R Inventory; (2) overt behavioral: TBCL, speech disfluencies, percentage of speaking time, ratio of disfluencies to speaking time, and BAT distance; (3) physiological: pulse rate, heart rate, and palmar sweat print. Since comparisons of correlation coefficients among these studies would be meaningless, Table 11–2 presents a ratio of the number of significant correlations relative to the total number of correlations calculated within each of the three response component domains and between domains across all five studies. Multiple assessment in the physiological domain is virtually absent in the behavioral outcome literature; thus that cell has no entry.

Table 11–2. Ratio of significant correlations to total number of correlations within and between various self-report, behavioral, and physiological measures of anxiety

	Self-report		Behavioral		Physiological	
	Ratio	Percentage	Ratio	Percentage	Ratio	Percentage
Self-report	30/30	100.00	13/88	14.8	4/48	8.3
Behavioral			13/36	36.1	5/53	9.4

Two conclusions are obvious from inspection of Table 11–2. (1) Correlations within a domain are more frequently significant than correlations between domains; in the case of self-report measures, every correlation was significant in all five studies. (2) Correlations between domains are rarely significant, although the percentage is above chance. It is important to note that although these results are based on the number of significant correlations, the specific correlations are generally quite low. Although some evidence of concurrent validity is thus found within the self-report domain, it is clear that different instruments within and especially between response domains are measuring different aspects of behavior called "anxiety."

At this point it is important to recall our previous discussion of the anxiety construct itself. A social learning point of view rejects a unitary conceptualization of anxiety and suggests instead the notion of separate but interacting response components that differ in pattern from individual to individual. The data in Table 11–2 support such a view. Our concern in the assessment of anxiety is to identify the extent to which each response component contributes to the client's (or research subject's) presenting problem and to apply therapeutic interventions (or to formulate research conclusions) appropriate to the type of response characterizing the individual's reaction to the feared situation. A commitment to functional analysis of response components, whether in the clinic or the research laboratory, can thus live comfortably with these data.

Selective Use of Measures

Absence of strong relationships among measures in research on the outcome of therapy has not prevented use of selected data on which conclusions are based. All too often, the results of a therapy study indicate theoretically predicted changes in one or two measures and no changes in other measures, even within the same domain; the investigator may draw conclusions from the few predicted outcomes. In the absence of a more reasonable approach, there is nothing else the investigator can do, and the results are certainly worthy of public dissemination. The conceptualization of anxiety offered in this chapter does, however, provide two additional suggestions: (1) Most generally, broad and sweeping conclusions regarding the efficacy of a technique or its components cannot be made on the basis of one or only a few measured changes, and (2) the view of separate-but-interacting anxiety responses suggests that certain therapy techniques would be more effective for certain maladaptive response components. The finding that a particular technique routinely influences a particular response is valuable, but it should ultimately be incorporated into a theoretical framework relating technique variables and response functions. The clinical analogue of this issue is obvious: Failure to modify every relevant response component contributing to the client's problem must be viewed as incomplete treatment.

Influence of Factors Not Related to Anxiety

A measured anxiety score may represent the influence of a variety of factors in addition to level of anxiety, especially in the case of obtrusive procedures and face-valid instruments. This general problem was repeatedly seen during earlier discussions of each response channel. Great care must be taken to ensure that measurement procedures provide valid data uncontaminated by influences not related to anxiety and that interpretation of those data is based on a clear understanding of the nature of the responses being measured and their determinants.

The conceptual points made in the preceding two sections are predicated, of course, on the more basic statement reflected in the first paragraph of this section. The remainder of this section will discuss typical contaminating influences and possible methods of reducing their impact on anxiety assessment.

As noted earlier, each specific component of a total pattern of anxiety response is a joint function of not only proximal and distal anxiety-provoking stimuli but also of subject characteristics as well as social and situational cues and contingencies unrelated to those stimuli. This means that determination of a client's degree of anxiety for clinical or research purposes is a very complex undertaking.

Clinically, identification of both anxiety level and the factors contributing to its measured level is the clear goal of a functional analysis. Without valid measurement of response components and their conditions, successful treatment is unlikely. Thus, for example, a client may report intense anxiety but show no strong avoidance of or physiological reaction to the feared situation owing to a good deal of social reinforcement for such reports from relatives and friends. Although this "anxiety problem" is clearly in need of treatment, therapy would involve procedures quite different from those applied to a case of conditioned anxiety. Similarly, if inadequate assessment procedures result in an underestimation of the degree of physiological reaction, inappropriate or inefficient treatment procedures that ignore this variable unfortunately may be employed.

Oddly enough, the history of behavior therapy research has until recently reflected little concern with the subtleness of these issues. However, recognition of the role of individual differences and the complexity and multiple determinants of anxiety scores obtained in laboratory settings is producing a reanalysis of procedures for measuring anxiety.

Self-report and behavioral measures. Sundberg, Tyler, and Taplin (1973) note that when we are trying to learn about the behavior of another person, we can either "ask 'em'" or "watch 'em'." When we "ask 'em'" about anxiety in an interview or on questionnaries or other paper-and-pencil measures, the data generated are open to distortion by all the factors known to alter self-reports of other types (e.g., Azrin, Holz, & Goldiamond, 1961; Henry & Rotter, 1956; Holmes, 1974; Masling, 1960; Page & Yates, 1975). Thus although such data represent a relatively convenient means of data collection and are the most obvious and direct approach to the cognitive component of the anxiety construct, self-report anxiety measures are far from perfect indicators (Mischel, 1968; Paul & Bernstein, 1973; Sundberg & Tyler, 1962). The most serious concern is that the individual's verbal response may not be a valid report of experience or of other behaviors. Because it is a response system under direct voluntary control, a self-report may function instrumentally to achieve other anticipated consequences for the individual, leading to responses that are simply untrue and that depend on the individual's perception of the assessment situation. Lower degrees of anxiety than actually experienced may be reported if consequences for doing so are positive, whereas spuriously high levels of anxiety may be reported for similar reasons. In addition, habitual response styles, active or passive forgetting, arousal during testing, contrast effects, idiosyncratic cognitive labeling processes, temporal isolation from or lack of familiarity with relevant stimulus situations, and inexact or confusing test items may also contribute to the contamination of self-report data. Factors such as these may play a role in the usually low predictive validity of self-report measures of personality in general (Mischel, 1968; Peterson, 1968) and of anxiety scales in particular.

One approach to reducing response bias in self-report measures of anxiety was mentioned earlier: the use of a format that makes it difficult for the subject to determine the meaning of various responses. Thus Husek and Alexander (1963) employed a semantic differential form whose scales were not clearly related to anxiety. Scores on their Anxiety Differential apparently reflect subjects' subjectively experienced stress at a given time and are not as vulnerable to intentional faking as may be the case with more straightforward self-report tests.

Assessments of the direct or indirect effects of arousal on overt motor behavior are also plagued by potential problems. The most fundamental of the problems is establishing the reliability of one's observational system. Whether the behavior of interest is stammering while delivering a speech or making physical contact with a snake during a BAT, operational definitions must be used in such a way that independent observers can all agree whether various target behaviors did or did not occur. As already indicated, interrater reliabilities for observational systems such as the TBCL (Paul, 1966) can be quite high; this appears to be owing to the fact that they are designed to measure specific, highly objective behaviors whose presence or absence can be recorded without interpretation or inference by the observers. In the absence of such well-defined target behaviors, interjudge reliability tends to drop (e.g. Bijou, Peterson, & Ault, 1968), and the system's vulnerability to expectancy effects and other sources of bias increases (e.g. Kent, O'Leary, Diament, & Dietz, 1974). Nevertheless, as noted earlier, repeated (perhaps continuous or unobtrusive) reliability checks seem important to assure that observers do not gradually alter their scoring criteria. When possible, members of observer teams should be rotated so that a given pair does not "drift' (Patterson, 1969) away from established criteria; such drifting would reduce the overall reliability of the observation system but might not be reflected in the degree of interjudge agreement.

When observing the *direct* effects of physiological events (i.e., on performance adequacy or disruption) it is important to recognize that because of autonomic response stereotypy not every subject's performance will be affected in the same way. Some may display heavy breathing whereas others show perspiration, trembling, or facial flushing. The validity of direct data on behavioral anxiety would be reduced if only a few arousal indicants were targeted, and thus it is vital that instruments such as the TBCL include a wide range of scorable behaviors designed to reflect as many behavioral consequences of autonomic activity as possible.

The complexity of the task on which clients' performance is being assessed may influence anxiety scores; performance by certain subjects may be poor and/or appear disrupted partly as a function of their lack of familiarity with it. Although problems such as these may not be entirely controllable, they can be minimized by (1) including in observational coding systems categories that reflect obvious attempts to suppress overt signs of arousal (e.g., the "hands restrained" item on the TBCL) and (2) choosing performance tasks complex enough to be easily disrupted by clinically significant overarousal but not so intricate as to obstruct the smooth functioning of even moderately aroused individuals.

Another problem for both direct and indirect assessment of behavior involves the fact that, just as was the case in self-report measures, subjects may exert some voluntary control over specific overt behaviors indicative of anxiety. Furthermore, because both direct and indirect assessment involves observation of operants that are under control of a wide variety of proximal and distal stimuli, indirect behavioral measures (e.g., escape/avoidance) are particularly susceptible to influence by factors not related to anxiety. Consequently, the validity of such measures in the research context must be constantly scrutinized. As an example of the problem, consider an individual who has reported anxiety in association with a particular stimulus or situation (e.g., closed, dark places) and who is about to undergo an indirect behavioral assessment of the intensity of this anxiety by attempting to remain in a small, unlit chamber for as long as possible. Obviously, the length of time spent in the test situation will be a function of the chamber itself and the cognitive stimuli the subject produces while in it, but in addition various social contingencies may play a major role. How would it look for a person claiming to be claustrophobic to remain in the test chamber indefinitely? To some extent, an early exit from the test situation is probably expected (by both subject and experimenter) and is certainly legitimized. The result may be spuriously inflated anxiety scores.

A growing body of literature suggests that such social/situational cues, communicated by instructions and test procedures, can significantly alter behavioral anxiety scores in relation to targets as diverse as small animals (Bernstein, 1973; Bernstein, 1974; Bernstein & Nietzel, 1973; Bernstein & Nietzel, 1974; Borkovec, 1973; Feist & Rosenthal, 1973; Kazdin, 1973; Smith, Diener, & Beaman, 1974), closed places (Miller & Bernstein, 1972), giving speeches (Blom & Craighead, 1974), and interpersonal assertion (Nietzel & Bernstein, Note 3). In addition, manipulation of social cues across repeated assessments can produce intrasubject alterations in overt fearfulness sufficient to change an individual's classification from phobic to nonphobic or vice versa (e.g., Bernstein, 1974; Borkovec, 1973). The same effects are probably operative in self-report and even physiological channels. The data cited above highlight a serious threat to the validity of measures of anxiety and, although no final resolution of the problem has yet evolved, several viable alternatives have been suggested and investigated, principally in research settings, in an attempt to eliminate that threat.

One of the alternatives is to conduct behavioral assessments under social/situational conditions that place strong demands on the subjects to display *fearless* behavior (Bernstein, 1973; Bernstein & Paul, 1971). The assumption here is that anxious behavior that occurs during exposures with high demand is likely to be mainly a function of the target stimulus, not implicit social cues for anxiety. Use of such procedures may make the researcher's job more difficult because it will reduce the number of individuals who are identified as phobic (e.g., Bernstein, 1974; Evans, 1975) according to research criteria. On the other hand, those individuals identified as anxious by behavioral tests with high demand are likely to be more comparable to clinical population. Thus more stringent tests may increase the external validity (Campbell & Stanley, 1963) of data generated on treatment outcome. Tests having high demand may be a useful clinical assessment tool as well since they may help (1) to identify individuals whose reports of anxiety are merely operant verbal behavior that has been socially reinforced by family and friends, (2) to establish the client's level of skill in dealing with the feared stimulus or situation (this is less likely to happen in tests having low demand because the testee tends to terminate them rather quickly), and (3) to determine the degree to which arousal and avoidance are owing to a lack of familiarity with the feared target stimulus (sometimes a BAT with high demand provides the subject with his first experience with a stimulus or situation that had previously been consistently avoided, and results in a large decrement in discomfort).

Another way of dealing with the effects of social/situational cues operating on behavioral assessments in outcome research is to measure them rather than to attempt to eliminate them, a particularly useful strategy in cases when convenience and speed in screening subjects is important. Social/situational effects can be measured by adding a "demand-change" control group to the experimental design (Bernstein, 1973). Subjects in this condition receive the usual pretreatment behavioral test that has low demand, then no treatment, and then a posttest that contains as much or more demand for fearlessness as do tests that follow active treatment. The magnitude of improvement shown in the demand-change group can then be used to estimate the degree to which changes in treated groups can be attributed to social/situational factors.

A more satisfactory means of handling social/situational influences in research settings is simply to identify target problems that are (1) frequent and severe enough to be clinically relevant and (2) not significantly influenced by artifacts. Studies by Borkovec and his colleagues (Borkovec, Stone, O'Brien, & Kaloupek, 1974; Borkovec, Wall, & Stone, 1974) have indicated that anxiety associated with social interaction and public speaking appear to be treatment targets that meet these criteria and, in addition, are accompanied by substantial physiological arousal that is not susceptible to the effects of habituation. Behavioral assessment of these targets may be somewhat more complex than measuring avoidance of small animals, but the benefits in terms of less ambiguous data on treatment, treatment components, or other variables of interest make the added effort worthwhile.

A particularly troublesome subset of influences in research on therapy outcome has been the effects of client expectation, therapist suggestion, and therapeutic demand characteristics on anxiety measures. Measured improvement in self-report and behavioral (perhaps even physiological) indices may occur subsequent to therapy owing to these factors, either alone or in combination with active treatment effects. The usual control group for these variables has been the placebo condition that is theoretically inert with respect to changing the target behavior but presumably containing the nonspecific therapy factors common to all therapeutic relationships. The use of a placebo group assumes that the inert condition creates expectancy and social/situational cues for improvement equivalent to that generated by the active therapy procedure. Empirical data, however, indicate that this may not be the case (Borkovec & Nau, 1972; Nau, Caputo, & Borkovec, 1974). An alternative solution is to establish expectations and demands in opposition to a display of improvement. Under this counterdemand condition, any measured improvement will more likely be a function of active treatment effects than of situational variables. Barlow, Agras, Leitenberg, Callahan, and Moore (1972), for example, initially told a client receiving covert sensitization for homosexual behavior that the procedure would *increase* sexual arousal to homosexual stimuli. Measures of penile circumference in response to slides of homosexual stimuli indicated a reduction in arousal during treatment despite the negative instructions. Similarly, two outcome studies of sleep disturbance employed a counterdemand strategy to increase the validity of self-reported latency to sleep onset (Borkovec, Kaloupek, & Slama, 1975; Steinmark & Borkovec, 1974). In both investigations, subjects were told not to expect sleep improvement until after the fourth therapy session. Critical statistical comparisons between placebo groups and groups in active therapy were then conducted on sleep data reported before the fourth session. In both studies treatment produced significantly greater improvement in the active treatment group than in the placebo group during the counterdemand period, despite demand instructions in opposition to reports of improvement. Such a demonstration provides strong support for the efficacy of a therapy technique separate from expectancy or demand effects. The counterdemand method, successfully used with physiological and self-report data, is equally applicable to measures of behavior and offers a promising approach to the valid assessment of anxiety change.

Physiological measures. Assessment of the physiological component of anxiety requires selection and interpretation of measures based on considerations of response function, stimulus and situation demands, and individual differences. These considerations are routinely weighed in measurement of overt behavioral and verbal-cognitive systems and cannot be disregarded in determinations of physiological responding. Thus by definition assessment of avoidance responses takes into account the function of the responding as a means of averting contact with an aversive stimulus, and recognition is given both to the manner in which these overt avoidance acts are molded by situational variables and to the considerable variations found in individual response styles. In a parallel fashion, when measurement of physiological activity is undertaken, it must be kept in mind that heart rate is an output parameter of the cardiovascular pump, that electrodermal activity reflects sweat secretion and reabsorption processes occurring in the epidermis of particular skin sites, that electromyographic readings monitor the contractile state of specific muscle groups, and so forth, and that this responding is the physiological substrate of particular individuals' interactions with manifold aspects of the stimulus situation. When the known physiological functions of monitored organs are taken into account and these functions are considered with respect to stimulus and subject characteristics, obtained results become more interpretable and useful.

Different threatening stimuli prompt different patterns of physiological responding. It is well established that even simple, nonsignal stimuli, such as weak tones, lights, and touches, evoke physiological component profiles unique to the stimuli (Davis, Buchwald, & Frankman, 1955). Lacey (1959) has explained these pattern differences as the physiological aspect of interactions between the organism and the stimulus. That is, organisms neither passively take in nor simply become aroused by stress or neutral stimuli but rather engage in specific transactions with each stimulus in all response systems, including the physiological. The nature of the particular interaction depends on characteristics of the stimulus. Many of the transactions that take place do, of course, include vigorous overt motor responding, as Cannon's theory emphasizes, and such actions or anticipated actions involve numerous autonomic accommodations, such as increased pumping action of the heart. On the other hand, when fear stimuli are presented to subjects in situations that do not require or even allow overt responding (e.g., imagery of snakes in snake phobics) many autonomic channels, including heart rate, are found to increase in response to these stimuli as well. Although such autonomic accelerations are often assumed to be conditioned or vestigial in nature, Lacey (1959) has offered another interpretation that focuses on the perceptual-cognitive transactions taking place in stress situations. Some stressors (e.g., cold pressor task) call for a perceptual-cognitive rejection of the stimulus whereas others (e.g., rapid mental arithmetic) require an intense internal cognitive focus; heart rate acceleration specifically appears to be a concomitant of both these cognitive processes. The increases in heart rate elicited by snake slides then may at least partially represent the autonomic aspect of a stimulus rejection process or some other intense, and perhaps pathological, internally focused coping process, rather than being solely an isolated conditioned or vestigial autonomic response.

The influence of perceptual-cognitive requirements on autonomic functioning can be seen more dramatically in the reverse case, when the situation calls for increased attentiveness and perceptual intake. The heart rate responses accompany direct, imaginal, and vicariously induced stress reported by Craig (1968) provide an example of the effect of perceptual transactional differences. Subjects were required to :(1) immerse their hand in 2° C water for two minutes (cold pressor task), (2) imagine immersing their hand in painfully cold water, and (3) observe someone else going through the cold pressor task (vicarious stress). Heart rate was found to increase by two to three beats per minute in the direct and imagined conditions. In contrast, heart rate decelerated by two to three beats per minute during vicarious stress. The vicarious stress task obviously required subjects to attend to an external event, whereas the imaginal and direct experiences encouraged an internal focus and exclusion of external stimuli. Heart rate is often to be decelerative under conditions that invoke increased attention, and as the Craig (1968) data demonstrate, this deceleration may well occur even when stimuli are threatening. Somatic activity (respiration rate, muscle and ocular activity, etc.) has often been found to follow heart rate in situations involving variations in the perceptual intake/exclusion dimension, reinforcing the common notion of autonomic-somatic coupling (see Obrist, Howard, Lawler, Galosy, Myers, Gaebelein, 1974, for a discussion of this literature). However, cardiac-somatic concordance does not always occur, and the Craig (1968) experiment provides such an example. Respiration rate showed a decrease, whereas heart rate was accelerated in the direct condition. Respiration rate remained unchanged, whereas heart rate decelerated in the vicarious condition. Thus although attentional demands may drive heart pumping, other physiological responses will not necessarily be affected in a parallel fashion, demonstrating the specificity of the effects.

The variety and precision of physiological-stimulus transactions perhaps may best be seen in electrodermal responding. Electrodermal activity is chosen as an example because of all the bodily systems available for measurement, the skin's electrical properties have most often been elected as a convenient measure of the physiology of the anxiety state. There are a number of properties that argue for its election. First, the skin receives only sympathetic and not parasympathetic innervation in contrast to most other dually innervated autonomic organs, and thus the sympathetic action cannot be inhibited by an opposing neural influence. Second, electrode application procedures are relatively straightforward and painless, and the electrical circuitry required is not particularly complicated or expensive. Finally, polygraphic output clearly reveals abrupt, discrete responding that is intuitively appealing compared to the continuous responding of other physiological systems, such as heart rate and respiration. In short, the skin appears ideal for immediate assessment of sympathetic arousal.

That electrodermal responding cannot be considered a simple meter of sympathetic activity is apparent from Edelberg's (1973) review of the literature in which it is pointed out that the electrical activity of the skin often reflects adaptive processes appropriate to the stimulating situation in the same way as do other physiological responses. The nature of these processes must be considered in the interpretation of electrodermal measures. The skin does not simply serve as a casing for the body; more important, it is the point of interface between the organism and its environment. This is especially true for the surface of the hands and the feet, the sites of most electrodermal recording in psychology. These surfaces perform grasping and manipulating, locomotion, and sensory acuity functions, functions crucial for successful organism-environment interactions. When sweat gland activity is recruited from low levels, the resultant increased hydration of the skin produces a more frictional surface, which facilitates grasping, manipulation, and locomotion. In addition, tactile acuity improves, resistance to abrasion increases, and evaporative heat loss is facilitated. The palmar and plantar (sole of the foot) electrodermal responses commonly measured should be viewed as epiphenomena of sweat secretion and reabsorption processes at these surfaces. Components of the different electrodermal measures are now seen as reflecting different aspects of this hydration process, and an improved understanding of the relationship between these polygraphic indices and the underlying neurodermal events is accruing (see Edelberg, 1973).

From the above discussion it should be apparent that many relatively benign situations will provoke considerable electrodermal activity. This responding may even be quite specific to the body location being stimulated. Thus the relatively simple task of identifying a soft material was found to produce dramatically greater potential activity in the skin of the hand engaged in the task compared to that of the inactive hand (Edelberg, 1973). It should also be apparent that threatening stimuli will often elicit widespread increases in palmar and plantar electrodermal responding. Many danger-laden situations should appropriately call into play precisely those motor and sensory functions facilitated by increased neurodermal activity. It is not surprising to find substantial electrodermal responding present in these situations.

It must always be kept in mind that threat is not the only dimension that arouses increases or decreases in measures of physiological response. Hence, all assessments of physiological responding in the face of threat must be made relative to responding to stimuli equal to the threat stimuli on all dimensions except that of threat. The dimensions of attentional and motor demands appear to be particularly important, but the less obvious dimensions of stimulus complexity, stimulus novelty, and cognitive difficulty are also relevant. Creating neutral tasks equivalent on these dimensions to threat stimuli will clearly tax the ingenuity of the researcher and clinical assessor, but the benefits outweigh the costs. In practice this means that when the physiology that attends snake approach is assessed, it should be compared to approach to a neutral animal. When public-speaking physiology is measured, it must be interpreted relative to some other equally complex, but nonthreatening overtly verbal task. When threat imagery or pictures are employed, neutral items of comparable novelty, complexity, and physical action, not benign landscapes or familiar home situations, must be compared.

Up to this point discussion of physiological measurement has emphasized the specific nature of the functional relationships between environmental variables and physiological responses. It has been pointed out that the attentional demands of some threat situations may drive heart rate down and that the sensory-motor requirements of some nonstress situations may push electrodermal responding up. However, this focus on precise stimulus-response functional relationships misses several important and related considerations germane to the assessment of the physiology of anxiety. First, stimulus and response uncertainty is a hallmark of anxiety situations. The exact nature of the threat present in stress situations will often be vague and ambiguous, and the responses necessary for an appropriate and efficient transaction with the stressors are correspondingly unclear. This ambiguity not only intensifies the threat (see Weiss, 1971a, b, c for evidence on ulcerative effects of stress uncertainty), but it is also likely to produce a diffuse and fluctuating pattern of physiological responding because of the perceived wide range of possible threat components and useful coping responses. Even the seemingly straightforward threats commonly contrived for procedures for assessing anxiety, such as the BAT and public-speaking tasks, lack perceived stimulus and response clarity. Observation and interrogation of subjects in these situations reveals that many persons with snake and public-speaking phobias are unaware of even the fundamental characteristics of their phobic object and respond clumsily in its presence. The physiological component of this confusion can be expected to be variable and unreliable in single subjects and to manifest wide individual differences, rather than displaying tidy functional relationships.

A second source of variability and diffuseness in physiological responding originates from individual differences in emotional responses to stimulus situations. A group of classic studies in the mid-1950s (Ax, 1953; Funkenstein, 1955; Funkenstein, King, & Drolette, 1957; Schachter, 1957) convincingly demonstrated physiological pattern differences, especially cardiovascular differentiation, between fear and anger states. Martin's (1961) review of these studies concluded that fear and anxiety display an epinephrine-like profile of high heart rate, cardiac output, respiration rate, and SCL, whereas anger states showed more of a norepinephrine-like pattern of high diastolic blood pressure, peripheral resistance, and number of

SRRs. This line of research unfortunately appears to have been temporarily squelched by Schachter and Singer's (1962) seemingly well-buttressed contention that differentiation of emotional states rests primarily on cognitive labeling of the external situational events. Recent research on physiological differentiation of emotional states in Weerts' laboratory (Weerts & Roberts, Note 4) using individually tailored imagery scenes to induce emotional arousal, has obtained results that confirm the earlier findings. It is hoped that subsequent research will extend our knowledge of the nature of the physiological organization of these and other emotions.

Individuals clearly differ in their emotional responses to situations, perhaps because they focus on different aspects of any particular situation or because past history of learning leads them to perceive situations differently. Whatever the origin of these individual differences. they are found in physiological assessments as well as in behavioral and cognitive assessments. The findings reported from Funkenstein's (1955; Funkenstein, King, & Drolette, 1957) research program illustrate this point. In his paradigm all subjects were administered the same frustrating stress situation and were subsequently categorized on the basis of interview data as to their type of emotional response: anger directed outward or inward, or anxiety. Division of subjects on this basis revealed the physiological differences described above, with anger-inward responding resembling that of anxiety. These wide individual differences in emotional reactions mean that no particular stimulus can ever be considered anxiety provoking without also stipulating the characteristics of the person being administered the stimulus.

Besides producing basic scientific difficulties, these data also have important implications for assessment of anxiety in individuals. A single subject, for example, can display a shift in physiological pattern over repeated presentations of a stimulus, a phenomenon that may be reflecting a shift in the larger emotional reaction to the stimulus. For example, assessment of cardiovascular responding in hypertensive patients reveals high cardiac output early in the development of the disorder, which is in marked contrast to the normal cardiac output and high peripheral resistance found in the later stages (Forsyth, 1974). This change over time could be signaling an emotional transition from anxiety to anger or irritation or frustration, and although such an interpretation is speculative, shifts in pattern over time is a data problem that can be encountered. Emotional reaction changes could be involved.

An additional consideration, mentioned previously and related to this issue, is the blunt empirical finding of rigid response specificity in some subjects. Response specificity (or stereotypy) is Lacey's term for consistent individual patterns in physiological responses across stressors (Lacey, Bateman, & VanLehn, 1953; Lacey, 1959). Some subjects display much the same hierarchy of responses no matter what the precise characteristics of the stress. Response specificity, restated more simply, means that a fraction of the subjects encountered (as many as one third) have a strongly "preferred" physiological response channel or channels. Thus some people will respond with increased heart rate whereas others will present an electrodermal storm. At first glance this appears contrary to the rule of stimulus specificity. However, stimulus specificity refers to the patterns of average groups in reaction to stimuli whereas response specificity refers to the relative rank order of an individual's responses. There is enough quantitative range in each response rank and enough subjects not showing rigid response specificity for the two phenomena to co-exist substantially and peacefully.

The origins of the hyperresponsivity of particularized channels are unclear. It may reflect emotional, attitudinal, and cognitive sets toward the entire class of stress stimuli or may be more simply an inherent feature of individuals' autonomic nervous systems. Causal considerations aside, response specificity means that physiological assessment of individuals showing anxiety is not likely to reveal an epinephrine response profile. A solution to this problem may be found in appropriate data manipulation. Paul (1969a) describes a scoring procedure patterned after the statistical techniques recommended by Lacey (1959), which adjusts for individual response stereotypy. Lability scores were calculated for each of the four physiological systems monitored (heart rate, respiration rate, forearm flexor and extensor muscle tension, and plantar SCL) for each subject for the responses accompanying imagery-induced anxiety. A subject's composite lability score was then derived by averaging only lability scores that had shown greater reaction to the stress compared to a neutral score. Such a scoring procedure adjusts for response specificity, but it also represents a surrendering of the physiological channel as a response measurement vehicle for qualitative assessment of anxiety. That is, it relies on considerations of the stimulus and responses in other channels for tagging the response with an "anxiety" label.

A final problem in physiological measurement is that of noise. Physiological channels are inherently labile, even at rest, and the spontaneous activity seen is probably often a result of physical organ needs and psychological variable influences not apparent to the researcher. There are some obvious biological variations that must be controlled for, such as time of day, week and (for women) menstrual month. In addition, dietary deficiencies, overindulgences, fatigue, and exhaustion must be assessed before measurement is attempted. However, there are presumably many other variables that cannot be specified at this time and must be controlled for by design and statistics. Repeated measures are essential for averaging out noise; single presentation of items is not adequate. This holds even for habituation. One series of fear stimuli is not adequate to eliminate the influences of spontaneous activity. The signal is quite likely to be lost in the biological and psychological noise unless repeated measurements are made.

Comments relevant to all three response measures

Since the three components of anxiety response potentially interact, the investigator must keep in mind that change in one component may have implications for change in the other components. Knowing the extent to which the assessment situation itself influences one channel of measurement will therefore facilitate interpretation of data from other channels; failure to take such factors into consideration may result in invalid conclusions despite valid measurement. Two specific examples are relevant here. First, investigators of outcome have often obtained FT measures subsequent to pretest and posttest BATs. The level of self-reported fear does not always show significant improvement, despite significant increases in approach behavior. It has become clear that even though treatment is effective in bringing the subjects closer to the feared object than ever before, self-reports of distress have remained. A more appropriate verbal index of fear reduction due to treatment would therefore be the degree of posttest fear reported at the point of closest pretest approach (e.g., Farmer & Wright, 1971; Kazdin, 1974). Second, BATs in general allow the subject to make avoidance responses (e.g., terminate the test). Consequently, whatever measures of cognitive and physiological arousal are obtained, they are unlikely to reflect the degree of fear to a constant stimulus situation across all subjects. Ordinarily, subjects are matched on level of behavioral avoidance prior to assignment to a treatment group to preclude this problem. Although this procedure suffices for group research that focuses on behavioral avoidance, it is inadequate for obtaining valid clinical data in the case of a single subject and certainly less than desirable for studies interested in cognitive and physiological components of anxiety. The alternative is to employ test situations that provide no opportunity for overt avoidance (e.g., speech presentation, examinations, social interactions) or to bring all subjects to the same degree of pretest approach through the use of strong incentives. Notice that in either case the investigator purchases more valid multichannel measures with the loss of an avoidance measure. When all measures are desirable, assessments under each method may be conducted.

SUMMARY

The construct of anxiety has long played a prominent role in psychological theories of behavior. Unfortunately, decades of research have failed to provide an adequate approach to understanding the nature of anxiety and its determinants. Reviewing recent developments in anxiety assessment from a social learning perspective, this chapter has emphasized the operational definition of three separate but interacting components of anxiety response (overt behavioral, cognitive, and physiological), the functional analysis of each component in terms of antecedent and consequential conditions, and the development of valid and reliable measurement procedures for each response component. Thus far, assessment efforts using this approach have focused on the quantification of anxious behavior in response to laboratory and real-life exposures to specific anxiety-provoking stimuli.

Behavioral measures typically involve observational coding systems of the direct effects of physiological activity on behavioral performance and/or its indirect effects (escape/avoidance). Self-report measures provide information regarding the cognitive-phenomenological component of anxiety and usually involve either general survey questionnaires or specific rating forms assessing the degree discomfort experienced during exposures to feared stimuli. Although numerous autonomic systems have been monitored, heart rate and electrodermal activity are the most commonly reported physiological responses in the behavior therapy literature and appear to show the greatest promise for anxiety assessment.

Measures of the three components of the anxiety response rarely correlate highly with one another, reflecting the role of individual differences in patterns of anxiety response and the complexity and multidimensional character of the anxiety construct. Any attempt to measure anxiety must include an awareness of the nature of the specific responses being measured, and valid interpretation of obtained measures assumes proper control of numerous factors not related to anxiety that can influence behaviors assumed to be indicative of anxiety.

It is hoped that future research will focus on improving quantification under more carefully controlled conditions, on expanding assessment techniques to provide data relevant to functional-analytic questions in addition to response quantification, and on increasingly naturalistic assessment settings for the sake of ecological validity.

REFERENCE NOTES

1. Ullmann, L. P. *Abnormal psychology without anxiety*. Paper presented at the Western Psychological Association, San Francisco, May, 1967.

2. Melamed, B. G. *The role of habituation in systematic desensitization*. Paper presented at the American Psychological Association, Washington, D.C., September, 1971.
3. Nietzel, M. T., & Bernstein, D. A. *The effects of instructionally mediated demand upon the behavioral assessment of assertiveness*. Unpublished manuscript, University of Kentucky, 1975.
4. Weerts, T. C., & Roberts, R. J. *The physiological effects of imagining anger-provoking and fear-provoking scenes*. Paper presented at the Society for Psychophysiological Research, Toronto, October, 1975.

REFERENCES

Alexander, S., & Husek, T. R. The anxiety differential: Initial steps in the development of a measure of situational anxiety. *Educational and Psychological Measurement*, 1962, **22,** 325–348.

Allen, G. J. Effectiveness of study counseling and desensitization in alleviating test anxiety in college students. *Journal of Abnormal Psychology*, 1971, **77,** 282–289.

Allen, G. J. The behavioral treatment of test anxiety: Recent research and future trends. *Behavior Therapy*, 1972, **3,** 253–262.

Ax, A. F. The physiological differentiation between fear and anger in humans. *Psychosomatic Medicine*, 1953, **15,** 433–442.

Ayllon, T., & Azrin, N. *The token economy: A motivational system for therapy and rehabilitation*. New York: Appleton-Century-Crofts, 1968.

Azrin, N. H., Holz, W., & Goldiamond, I. Response bias in questionnaire reports. *Journal of Consulting Psychology*, 1961, **25,** 324–326.

Bailey, J., & Atchinson, T. The treatment of compulsive handwashing using reinforcement principles. *Behaviour Research and Therapy*, 1969, **7,** 327–329.

Bandura, A. *Principles of behavior modification*. New York: Holt, Rinehart, & Winston, 1969.

Bandura, A. Psychotherapy based upon modeling principles. In A. E. Bergin & S. L. Garfield (Eds.), *Handbook of psychotherapy and behavior change*. New York: Wiley, 1971.

Bandura, A., Blanchard, E. G., & Ritter, B. Relative efficacy of desensitization and modeling approaches for inducing behavioral, affective, and attitudinal changes. *Journal of Personality and Social Psychology*, 1969, **13,** 173–199.

Barlow, D. H., Agras, W. S., Leitenberg, H., Callahan, E. J., & Moore, R. C. The contribution of therapeutic instruction to covert sensitization. *Behaviour Research and Therapy*, 1972, **10,** 411–416.

Bates, H. D. Relevance of animal-avoidance analogue studies to the treatment of clinical phobias: A rejoinder to Cooper, Furst, and Bridger. *Journal of Abnormal Psychology*, 1970, **75,** 12–14.

Bergman, J. S., & Johnson, H. J. The effects of instructional set and autonomic perception on cardiac control. *Psychophysiology*, 1971, **8,** 180–190.

Bernstein, D. A. Behavioral fear assessment: Anxiety or artifact? In H. Adams & P. Unikel (Eds.), *Issues and trends in behavior therapy*. Springfield: Thomas, 1973.

Bernstein, D. A. Manipulation of avoidance behavior as a function of increased or decreased demand on repeated behavioral tests. *Journal of Consulting and Clinical Psychology*, 1974, **42,** 896–900.

Bernstein, D. A., & Nietzel, M. T. Procedural variation in behavioral avoidance tests. *Journal of Consulting and Clinical Psychology*, 1973, **41,** 165–174.

Bernstein, D. A., & Nietzel, M. T. Behavioral avoidance tests: The effects of demand characteristics and repeated measures of two types of subjects. *Behavior Therapy*, 1974, **5,** 183–192.

Bernstein, D. A., & Paul, G. L. Some comments on therapy analogue research with small animal "phobias." *Journal of Behavior Therapy and Experimental Psychiatry*, 1971, **2,** 225–237.

Bijou, S. W., Peterson, R. F., & Ault, M. H. A method to integrate descriptive and experimental field studies at the level of data and empirical concepts. *Journal of Applied Behavior Analysis*, 1968, **1,** 175–191.

Blanchard, E. G., Young, L. D., & McLeod, P. Awareness of heart activity and self-control of heart rate. *Psychophysiology*, 1972, **9,** 63–68.

Blom, B. E., & Craighead, W. E. The effects of situational and instructional demand on indices of speech anxiety. *Journal of Abnormal Psychology*, 1974, **83,** 667–674.

Borkovec, T. D. Effects of expectancy on the outcome of systematic desensitization and implosive treatments for analogue anxiety. *Behavior Therapy*, 1972, **3,** 29–40.

Borkovec, T. D. The effects of instructional suggestion and physiological cues on analogue fear. *Behavior Therapy*, 1973, **4,** 185–192.

Borkovec, T. D. Physiological and cognitive processes in the maintenance and reduction of fear. In G. E. Schwartz & D. Shapiro (Eds.), *Consciousness and self-regulation: Advances in research*. New York: Plenum, 1976.

Borkovec, T. D., & Craighead, W. E. The comparison of two methods of assessing fear and avoidance behavior. *Behaviour Research and Therapy*, 1971, **9,** 285–291.

Borkovec, T. D., Fleischmann, D. J., & Caputo, J. A. The measurement of anxiety in an analogue social situation. *Journal of Consulting and Clinical Psychology*, 1973, **41,** 157–161.

Borkovec, T. D., Kaloupek, D. G., & Slama, K. The facilitative effect of muscle tension-release in the relaxation treatment of sleep disturbance. *Behavior Therapy*, 1975, **6,** 301–309.

Borkovec, T. D., & Nau, S. D. Credibility of analogue therapy rationales. *Journal of Behavior Therapy and Experimental Psychiatry*, 1972, **3,** 257–260.

Borkovec, T. D., Stone, N. M., O'Brien, G. T., & Kaloupek, D. G. Evaluation of a clinically relevant target behavior for analogue outcome research. *Behavior Therapy*, 1974, **5,** 504–514. (a)

Borkovec, T. D., Wall, R. L., & Stone, N. M. False physiological feedback and the maintenance of speech anxiety. *Journal of Abnormal Psychology*, 1974, **83,** 164–168. (b)

Brown, B. B. Visual recall ability and eye movements. *Psychophysiology*, 1968, **4,** 300–306.

Brunswick, E. *Systematic and representative design of psychological experiments with results in physical and social perception*. Berkeley: University of California Press, 1947.

Butterfield, W. H. Instrumentation in behavior therapy. In E. J. Thomas (Ed.), *Behavior modification procedure: A sourcebook*. Chicago: Aldine, 1974.

Campbell, D. T., & Stanley, J. C. Experimental and quasi-experimental designs for research on teaching. In N. L. Gage (Ed.), *Handbook of research on teaching*. Chicago: Rand McNally, 1963.

Cannon, W. B. *Bodily changes in pain, hunger, fear, and rage*. New York: Appleton-Century-Crofts, 1915.

Cattell, R. B., & Scheier, I. H. *Neuroticism and anxiety*. New York: Ronald, 1961.

Cautela, J., Flannery, R., & Hanley, E. Covert modeling: An experimental test. *Behavior Therapy*, 1974, **5**, 494–502.

Clevenger, T., & King, T. R. A factor analysis of the visible symptoms of stage fright. *Speech Monographs*, 1961, **28**, 296–298.

Craig, K. D. Physiological arousal as a function of imagined, vicarious, and direct stress experiences. *Journal of Abnormal Psychology*, 1968, **73**, 513–520.

Craighead, W. E. The assessment of avoidance responses on the Levis Phobic Test Apparatus. *Behavior Therapy*, 1973, **4**, 235–240.

Cronbach, L. J. *Essentials of psychological testing*. New York: Harper & Row, 1960.

Davidson, P. O., & Hiebert, S. F. Relaxation training, relaxation instruction, and repeated exposure to a stressor film. *Journal of Abnormal Psychology*, 1971, **78**, 154–159.

Davis, R. C., Buchwald, A. M., & Frankman, R. W. Autonomic and muscular responses and their relation to simple stimuli. *Psychological Monographs*, 1955, **69**, Whole No. 405.

Dollard, J., & Mowrer, O. H. A method of measuring tension in written documents. *Journal of Abnormal Psychology*, 1947, **42**, 3–32.

Duffy, E. Activation. In N. S. Greenfield & R. A. Sternbach (Eds.), *Handbook of psychophysiology*. Chicago: Holt, Rinehart, & Winston, 1972.

Edelberg, R. The information content of the recovery limb of the electrodermal response. *Psychophysiology*, 1970, **6**, 527–539.

Edelberg, R. Electrodermal recovery rate, goal-orientation, and aversion. *Psychophysiology*, 1972, **9**, 512–520.

Edelberg, R. Mechanisms of electrodermal adaptations for locomotion, manipulation or defense. In E. Stellar & J. M. Sprague (Eds.), *Progress in physiological psychology*. Vol. 5. New York: Academic, 1973.

Edelman, R. I. Vicarious fear induction and avowed autonomic stereotypy. *Behaviour Research and Therapy*, 1972, **10**, 105–110.

Ellis, E. *Humanistic psychotherapy*. New York: McGraw–Hill, 1973.

Emmelkamp, P. M. G. Self-observation versus flooding in the treatment of agoraphobia. *Behaviour Research and Therapy*, 1974, **12**, 229–238.

Endler, N. S., Hunt, J. McV., & Rosenstein, A. J. An S–R inventory of anxiousness. *Psychological Monographs: General and Applied*, 1962, **76**, No. 536.

Ernst, F. Self-recording and counterconditioning of a self-mutilative compulsion. *Behavior Therapy*, 1973, **4**, 144–146.

Evans, M. B. Procedures for a high demand behavioral avoidance test and for a diagnosis/treatment subject expectancy manipulation: Brief note. *Behavior Therapy*, 1975, **6,** 72–77.

Everaerd, W., Rijken, H. M., & Emmelkamp, P. M. G. A comparison of "flooding" and "successive approximation" in the treatment of agoraphobia. *Behaviour Research and Therapy*, 1973, **11,** 105–118.

Farmer, R. G., & Wright, J. M. C. Muscular reactivity and systematic desensitization. *Behavior Therapy*, 1971, **2,** 1–10.

Fazio, A. F. Implosive therapy with semiclinical phobias. *Journal of Abnormal Psychology*, 1972, **80,** 183–188.

Feist, J. R., & Rosenthal, T. L. Serpent versus surrogate and other determinants of runway fear differences. *Behaviour Research and Therapy*, 1973, **11,** 483–489.

Forsyth, R. P. Mechanisms of the cardiovascular responses to environmental stressors. In P. A. Obrist, A. H. Black, J. Brener, & L. V. DiCara (Eds.), *Cardiovascular psychophysiology*. Chicago: Aldine, 1974.

Frankel, A. J. Beyond simple functional analysis—The chain: A conceptual framework for assessment with a case study example. *Behavior Therapy*, 1975, **6,** 254–260.

Funkenstein, D. H. The physiology of fear and anger. *Scientific American*, 1955, **192,** 74–80.

Funkenstein, D. H., King, S. H., & Drolette, M. E. *Mastery of stress*. Cambridge, Mass.: Harvard University Press, 1957.

Geer, G. H. The development of a scale to measure fear. *Behaviour Research and Therapy*, 1965, **3,** 45–53.

Gelder, M. G., & Marks, I. M. Severe agoraphobia: A controlled prospective trial of behavior therapy. *British Journal of Psychiatry*, 1966, **112,** 309–319.

Goldfried, M. R., & Trier, C. S. Effectiveness of relaxation as an active coping skill. *Journal of Abnormal Psychology*, 1974, **83,** 348–355.

Goldstein, M. L. Physiological theories of emotion: A critical historical review from the standpoint of behavior therapy. *Psychological Bulletin*, 1968, **69,** 23–40.

Goodenough, F. L. *Mental testing*. New York: Rinehart, 1949.

Graham, F. K., & Clifton, R. K. Heart rate change as a component of the orienting response. *Psychological Bulletin*, 1966, **65,** 305–320.

Grinker, R. R. The psychosomatic aspects of anxiety. In C. D. Spielberger (Ed.), *Anxiety and behavior*. New York: Academic, 1966.

Grossberg, J., & Wilson, H. K. Physiological changes accompanying the visualization of fearful and neutral situations. *Journal of Personality and Social Psychology*, 1968, **10,** 124–133.

Hawkins, R. P. Who decided that was the problem? Two stages of responsibility for applied behavior analysis. In W. S. Wood (Ed.), *Issues in evaluating behavior modification*. Champaign, Ill.: Research Press, 1975.

Hekmat, H. The role of imagination in semantic desensitization. *Behavior Therapy*, 1972, **3,** 223–231.

Henry, E. M., & Rotter, J. B. Situational influences on Rorschach responses. *Journal of Consulting Psychology*, 1956, **20,** 457–461.

Hersen, M. Self-assessment of fear. *Behavior Therapy*, 1973, **4,** 241–257.

Holmes, D. S. The conscious control of thematic projection. *Journal of Consulting and Clinical Psychology*, 1974, **42,** 323–329.

Husek, T. R., & Alexander, S. The effectiveness of the Anxiety Differential in examination stress situations. *Educational and Psychological Measurement*, 1963, **23,** 309–318.

Jackson, J. C. Amplitude and habituation of the orienting reflex as a function of stimulus intensity. *Psychophysiology*, 1974, **11,** 647–659.

Jacobson, E. Electrical measurements of neuromuscular states during mental activities. *American Journal of Physiology*, 1930, **92,** 567–608. (a)

Jacobson, E. Electrical measurements of neuromuscular states during mental activities. *American Journal of Phsyiology*, 1930, **94,** 22–34. (b)

Jacobson, E. Electrical measurements of neuromuscular states during mental activities. *American Journal of Physiology*, 1930, **95,** 694–702. (c)

Jacobson, E. Electrical measurements of neuromuscular states during mental activities. *American Journal of Physiology*, 1930, **95,** 703–712. (d)

Jacobson, E. Electrical measurements of neuromuscular states during mental activities. *American Journal of Physiology*, 1931, **96,** 115–121. (a)

Jacobson, E. Electrical measurements of neuromuscular states during mental activities. *American Journal of Physiology*, 1931, **96,** 122–125. (b)

Johnson, S. M., & Sechrest, L. B. Comparison of desensitization and progressive relaxation in treating test anxiety. *Journal of Consulting and Clinical Psychology*, 1968, **32,** 280–286.

Jones, R. R., Reid, J. B., & Patterson, G. R. Naturalistic observation in clinical assessment. In P. McReynolds (Ed.), *Advances in psychological assessment*. Vol. 3. San Francisco: Jossey-Bass, 1974.

Kazdin, A. The effect of suggestion and pretesting on avoidance reduction in fearful subjects. *Journal of Behavior Therapy and Experimental Psychiatry*, 1973, **4,** 213–222.

Kazdin, A. E. The effect of model identity and fear-relevant similarity on covert modeling. *Behavior Therapy*, 1974, **5,** 624–635.

Kent, R. N., O'Leary, K. D., Diament, C., & Dietz, A. Expectation biases in observational evaluation of therapeutic change. *Journal of Consulting and Clinical Psychology*, 1974, **42,** 774–780.

Klorman, R. Habituation of fear: Effects of intensity and stimulus order. *Psychophysiology*, 1974, **11,** 15–26.

Klorman, R., Weerts, T. C., Hastings, J. E., Melamed, B. G., & Lang, P. J. Psychometric description of some specific-fear questionnaires. *Behavior Therapy*, 1974, **5,** 401–409.

Krasner, L., & Ullmann, L. P. *Behavior influences and personality*. New York: Holt, Rinehart, & Winston, 1973.

Lacey, J. I. Psychophysiological approaches to the evaluation of psychotherapeutic process and outcome. In E. A. Rubenstein & M. B. Parloff (Eds.), *Research in psychotherapy*. Vol. 1. Washington, D.C.: American Psychological Association, 1959.

Lacey, J. I. Somatic response patterning and stress: Some revisions of activation theory. In M. H. Appley & R. Trumball (Eds.), *Psychological Stress*. New York: Appleton-Century-Crofts, 1967.

Lacey, J. I., Bateman, D. E., & VanLehn, R. Autonomic response specificity. *Psychosomatic Medicine*, 1953, **15,** 8–21.

Lang, P. J. Fear reduction and fear behavior: Problems in treating a construct. In J. M. Shlien (Ed.), *Research in psychotherapy*. Washington, D.C.: American Psychological Association, 1968.

Lang, P. J. The application of psychophysiological methods to the study of psychotherapy and behavior modification. In A. E. Bergin & S. L. Garfield (Eds.), *Handbook of psychotherapy and behavior change: An empirical analysis*. New York: Wiley, 1971.

Lang, P. J., & Lazovik, A. D. Experimental desensitization of a phobia. *Journal of Abnormal and Social Psychology*, 1963, **66,** 519–525.

Lang, P. J., Melamed, B. G., & Hart, J. A psychophysiological analysis of fear modification using an automated desensitization procedure. *Journal of Abnormal Psychology*, 1970, **76,** 220–234.

Lazarus, A. A. *Behavior therapy and beyond*. New York: McGraw-Hill, 1971.

Leitenberg, H., Agras, W. S., Butz, R., & Wincze, J. P. Relationships between heart rate and behavioral change during the treatment of phobias. *Journal of Abnormal Psychology*, 1971, **78,** 59–68.

Levis, D. J. The phobic test apparatus: An objective measure of human avoidance behavior to small objects. *Behaviour Research and Therapy*, 1969, **7,** 309–315.

Levis, D. J. The case for performing research on non-patient populations with fears of small animals: A reply to Cooper, Furst, and Bridger. *Journal of Abnormal Psychology*, 1970, **75,** 36–38.

Levitt, E. E. *The psychology of anxiety*. New York: Bobbs-Merrill, 1967.

Levitt, E. E., DenBreeijen, A., & Persky, H. The induction of clinical anxiety by means of a standardized hypnotic technique. *American Journal of Clinical Hypnosis*, 1960, **2,** 206–214.

Lindsley, D. B. Emotion. In S. S. Stevens (Ed.), *Handbook of experimental psychology*. New York: Wiley, 1951.

Mac, R., & Fazio, A. F. Self-report and overt behavioral measures of fear with changes in aversive stimuli. *Behaviour Research and Therapy*, 1972, **10,** 283–285.

Mahl, G. F. Disturbances and silences in patient's speech in psychotherapy. *Journal of Abnormal and Social Psychology*, 1956, **53,** 1–15.

Malmo, R. B. Studies of anxiety: Some clinical origins of the activation concept. In C. D. Spielberger (Ed.), *Anxiety and behavior*. New York: Academic, 1966.

Mandler, G. Helplessness: Theory and research in anxiety. In C. D. Spielberger (Ed.), *Anxiety: Current trends in theory and research*. New York: Academic, 1972.

Mandler, G., & Kremen, I. Autonomic feedback: A correlational study. *Journal of Personality*, 1958, **26,** 388–399.

Mandler, G., Mandler, J. M., & Uviller, E. T. Autonomic feedback: The perception of autonomic activity. *Journal of Abnormal and Social Psychology*, 1958, **56,** 367–373.

Marks, I. M. Patterns of meaning in psychiatric patients: Semantic differential responses on obsessives and psychopaths. *Maudsley Monograph* No. 13. Oxford University Press, 1965.

Martin, B. The assessment of anxiety by physiological and behavioral measures. *Psychological Bulletin*, 1961, **58,** 234–255.

Masling, J. The influence of situational and interpersonal variables in projective testing. *Psychological Bulletin*, 1960, **57,** 65–82.

Mathews, A. Psychophysiological approaches to the investigation of desensitization and related procedures. *Psychological Bulletin*, 1971, **76,** 73–91.

McFall, R. M., & Marston, A. R. An experimental investigation of behavior rehearsal in assertive training. *Journal of Abnormal Psychology*, 1970, **76,** 295–303.

McFall, R. M., & Twentyman, C. T. Four experiments on the relative contributions of rehearsal, modeling, and coaching to assertion training. *Journal of Abnormal Psychology*, 1973, **81,** 199–218.

McReynolds, W. T. Anxiety as a fear: A behavioral approach to one emotion. In M. Zuckerman & C. D. Spielberger (Eds.), *Emotions and anxiety: New concepts, methods, and applications.* Potomac, Md.: Lawrence Erlbaum, in press.

Meichenbaum, D. Self-instructional methods. In F. H. Kanfer & A. P. Goldstein (Eds.), *Helping people change.* New York: Pergamon, 1974.

Miklich, D. R. Radio telemetry in clinical psychology and related areas. *American Psychologist*, 1975, **30,** 419–425.

Miller, B. V., & Bernstein, D. A. Instructional demand in a behavioral avoidance test for claustrophobic fear. *Journal of Abnormal Psychology*, 1972, **80,** 206–210.

Miller, B. V., & Levis, D. J. The effects of varying short visual exposure times to a phobic test stimulus on subsequent avoidance behavior. *Behaviour Research and Therapy*, 1971, **9,** 17–21.

Mischel, W. *Personality and assessment.* New York: Wiley, 1968.

Mischel, W. *Introduction to personality.* New York: Holt, Rinehart, & Winston, 1971.

Murray, D. C. Talk, silence, and anxiety. *Psychological Bulletin*, 1971, **75,** 244–260.

Nau, S. D., Caputo, J. A., & Borkovec, T. D. The relationship between credibility of therapy rationale and the reduction of simulated anxiety. *Journal of Behavior Therapy and Experimental Psychaitry*, 1974, **5,** 129–133.

Nietzel, M. T. *The effects of assessment and treatment mediated demand characteristics in a psychotherapy analogue outcome study.* Unpublished doctoral dissertation, University of Illinois, 1973.

Nowlis, V., & Green, R. F. The experimental analysis of mood. *Acta Psychologica*, 1959, **15,** 426–427. (Abstract)

O'Brien, G. T. *The role of progressive muscular relaxation in the systematic desensitization of analogue social anxiety.* Unpublished master's thesis, University of Iowa, 1975.

Obrist, P. A., Howard, J. L., Lawler, J. E., Galosy, R. A., Meyers, K. A., & Gaebelein, C. J. The cardiac-somatic interaction. In P. A. Obrist, A. H. Black, J. Brener, & L. V. DiCara (Eds.), *Cardiovascular physiology.* Chicago: Aldine, 1974.

Orne, M. T. Demand characteristics and the concept of quasi-controls. In R. Rosenthal & R. L. Rosnow (Eds.), *Artifact in behavioral research.* New York: Academic, 1969.

Orne, M. T., & Holland, C. H. On the ecological validity of laboratory deception. *International Journal of Psychiatry*, 1968, **6,** 282–293.

Osgood, C. E., Suci, G. J., & Tannenbaum, P. H. *The measurement of meaning.* Urbana, Ill.: University of Illinois Press, 1957.

Page, S., & Yates, E. Effects of situational role demands on measurement of attitudes about mental illness. *Journal of Consulting and Clinical Psychology*, 1975, **43,** 115.

Patterson, G. R. A community mental health program for children. In L. A. Hamerlynck, P. O. Davidson, & L. E. Acker (Eds.), *Behavior modification and ideal mental health services.* Calgary, Alberta: University of Calgary Press, 1969.

Paul, G. L. *Insight vs. desensitization in psychotherapy.* Stanford, Calif: Stanford Univerity Press, 1966.

Paul, G. L. Inhibition of physiological response to stressful imagery by relaxation training and hypnotically suggested relaxation. *Behaviour Research and Therapy*, 1969, **7,** 249–256. (a)

Paul, G. L. Outcome of systematic desensitization I: Background, procedures, and uncontrolled reports of individual treatment. In C. M. Franks (Ed.), *Behavior therapy: Appraisal and status.* New York: McGraw-Hill, 1969. (b)

Paul, G. L., & Bernstein, D. A. *Anxiety and clinical problems: Systematic desensitization and related techniques.* New York: General Learning Press, 1973.

Persky, H., Maroc, J., Conrad, E., & DenBreeijen, A. Blood corticotropin and adrenal weight-maintenance factor levels of anxious patients and normal subjects. *Psychosomatic Medicine*, 1959, **21,** 379–386.

Peterson, D. R. *The clinical study of social behavior.* New York: Appleton-Century-Crofts, 1968.

Prokasy, W. R., & Raskin, D. C. (Eds.). *Electrodermal activity in psychological research.* New York: Academic, 1973.

Rachman, S., Hodgson, R., & Marks, I. M. Treatment of chronic obsessive compulsive neurosis. *Behaviour Research and Therapy*, 1971, **9,** 237–247.

Rachman, S., Hodgson, R., & Marzillier, J. Treatment of an obsessional-compulsive disorder by modeling. *Behaviour Research and Therapy*, 1970, **8,** 385–392.

Raskin, D. C. Attention and arousal. In W. F. Prokasy & D. C. Raskin (Eds.), *Electrodermal activity in psychological research.* New York: Academic, 1973.

Raskin, D. C., Kotses, H., & Bever, J. Autonomic indicators of orienting and defensive reflexes. *Journal of Experimental Psychology*, 1969, **80,** 423–433.

Rehm, L. P. Relationships among measures of visual imagery. *Behaviour Research and Therapy*, 1973, **11,** 265–270.

Richardson, A. *Mental imagery.* New York: Springer, 1969.

Rimm, D. C., & Bottrell, J. Four measures of visual imagination. *Behaviour Research and Therapy*, 1969, **7,** 63–69.

Rimm, D. C., & Masters, J. C. *Behavior therapy: Techniques and empirical findings.* New York: Academic, 1974.

Ritter, B. The use of contact desensitization, demonstration-plus-participation and demonstration-alone in the treatment of acrophobia. *Behaviour Research and Therapy*, 1970, **7,** 157–164.

Rutner, I. T., & Pear, J. J. An observational methodology for investigating phobic behavior: Preliminary report. *Behavior Therapy*, 1972, **3,** 437–440.

Sarason, S. B. The measurement of anxiety in children: Some questions and problems. In C. D. Spielberger (Ed.), *Anxiety and behavior*. New York: Academic, 1966.

Sarbin, T. R. Anxiety: Reification of a metaphor. *Archives of General Psychiatry*, 1964, **10,** 630–633.

Sarbin, T. R. Ontology recapitulates philology: The mythic nature of anxiety. *American Psychologist*, 1968, **23,** 411–418.

Schachter, J. Pain, fear, and anger in hypertensives and normotensives. *Psychosomatic Medicine*, 1957, **19,** 17–29.

Schachter, S. The interaction of cognitive and physiological determinants of emotional state. In L. Berkowitz (Ed.), *Advances in experimental social psychology*. Vol. 1. New York: Academic, 1964.

Schachter, S., & Singer, J. E. Cognitive, social and physiological determinants of emotional state. *Psychological Review*, 1962, **69,** 379–399.

Smith, G. P. Adrenal hormones and emotional behavior. In E. Stellar & J. Sprague (Eds.), *Progress in physiological psychology*. Vol. 5. New York: Academic, 1973.

Smith, R. E., Diener, E., & Beaman, A. Demand characteristics and the behavioral avoidance measures of fear in behavior therapy analogue research. *Behavior Therapy*, 1974, **5,** 172–182.

Sokolov, Ye. N. *Perception and the conditioned reflex*. New York: Pergamon, 1963.

Spielberger, C. D. Theory and research on anxiety. In C. D. Spielberger (Ed.), *Anxiety and behavior*. New York: Academic, 1966.

Staats, A. W. Language behavior therapy: A derivative of social behaviorism. *Behavior Therapy*, 1972, **3,** 165–192.

Staats, C. K., & Staats, A. W. Meaning established by classical conditioning. *Journal of Experimental Psychology*, 1957, **54,** 74–80.

Steinmark, S. W., & Borkovec, T. D. Active and placebo treatment effects on moderate insomnia under counterdemand and positive demand instructions. *Journal of Abnormal Psychology*, 1974, **83,** 157–163.

Stern, R. S., Lipsedge, M. S., & Marks, I. M. Obsessive ruminations: A controlled trial of thought-stopping technique. *Behaviour Research and Therapy*, 1973, **11,** 659–662.

Stone, N. M., & Borkovec, T. D. The paradoxical effect of brief CS exposure on anolgue phobic subjects. *Behaviour Research and Therapy*, 1975, **13,** 51–54.

Strahan, R. F., Todd, J. B., & Inghs, G. B. A palmar sweat measure particularly suited for naturalistic research. *Psychophysiology*, 1974, **11,** 715–720.

Suinn, R. M. The STABS, a measure of test anxiety for behavior therapy: Normative data. *Behaviour Research and Therapy*, 1969, **7,** 335–339.

Sundberg, N. D., & Tyler, L. E. *Clinical psychology*. New York: Appleton-Century-Crofts, 1962.

Sundberg, N. D., Tyler, L. E., & Taplin, J. R. *Clinical psychology* (2nd ed.). New York: Appleton-Century-Crofts, 1973.

Sutarman, M. L., & Thomson, M. L. A new technique for enumerating active sweat glands in man. *Journal of Physiology*, 1952, **117**, 52.

Totten, E. Eye movement during visual imagery. *Comparative Psychology Monographs*, 1935, **11**, 1–46.

Trexler, L. D., & Karst, T. O. Rational-emotive therapy, placebo, and no-treatment effects on public-speaking anxiety. *Journal of Abnormal Psychology*, 1972, **79**, 60–67.

Ullmann, L. P., & Krasner, L. *A psychological approach to abnormal behavior*. Englewood Cliffs, N.J.: Prentice-Hall, 1969.

Valins, S., & Nisbett, R. E. Attribution processes in the development and treatment of emotional disorder. In E. E. Jones, D. E. Kamouse, H. H. Kelley, R. E. Nisbett, S. Valins, & Weiner (Eds.), *Attribution: Perceiving the causes of behavior*. Morristown, N.J.: General Learning Press, 1971.

Van Egeren, L. F., Feather, B. W., & Hein, P. L. Desensitization of phobias: Some psychophysiological propositions. *Psychophysiology*, 1971, **8**, 213–228.

Walk, R. D. Self-ratings of fear in a fear-invoking situation. *Journal of Abnormal and Social Psychology*, 1956, **52**, 171–178.

Waters, W., & McDonald, D. G. Autonomic response to auditory, visual and imagined stimuli in a systematic desensitization context. *Behaviour Research and Therapy*, 1973, **11**, 577–585.

Watson, D., & Friend, R. Measurement of social-evaluative anxiety. *Journal of Consulting and Clinical Psychology*, 1969, **33**, 448–457.

Watson, J. P., Gaind, R., & Marks, I. M. Physiological habituation to continuous phobic stimulation. *Behaviour Research and Therapy*, 1972, **10**, 269–278.

Watson, J. P., & Marks, I. M. Relevant and irrelevant fear in flooding—A cross-over study of phobic patients. *Behavior Therapy*, 1971, **2**, 275–293.

Webb, E. J., Campbell, D. T., Schwartz, R. D., & Sechrest, L. *Unobtrusive measures: Nonreactive research in the social sciences*. Chicago: Rand McNally, 1966.

Weiss, J. M. Effects of coping behavior in different warning signal conditions on stress pathology in rats. *Journal of Comparative and Physiological Psychology*, 1971, **77**, 1–13. (a)

Weiss, J. M. Effects of punishing the coping response (conflict) on stress pathology in rats. *Journal of Comparative and Physiological Psychology*, 1971, **77**, 14–21. (b)

Weiss, J. M. Effects of coping behavior with and without a feedback signal on stress pathology in rats. *Journal of Comparative and Physiological Psychology*, 1971, **77**, 22–30. (c)

Williams, J. G. L., Jones, J. R., & Williams, B. The chemical control of preoperative anxiety. *Psychophysiology*, 1975, **12**, 46–49.

Williams, J. G. L., Jones, J. R., Workhoven, M. N., & Williams, B. The psychological control of preoperative anxiety. *Psychophysiology*, 1975, **12**, 50–54.

Wolpe, J., & Lang, P. A fear survey schedule for use in behavior therapy. *Behaviour Research and Therapy*, 1964, **2**, 27–30.

Woy, J. R., & Efran, J. S. Systematic desensitization and expectancy in the treatment of speaking anxiety. *Behaviour Research and Therapy*, 1972, **10,** 43–50.
Zimny, G. H., & Kienstra, R. A. Orienting and defensive responses to electric shock. *Psychophysiology*, 1967, **3,** 351–362.
Zuckerman, M. The development of an affective adjective checklist for the measurement of anxiety. *Journal of Consulting and Clinical Psychology*, 1960, **24,** 457–462.

CHAPTER 12

Assessment of Addictive Behaviors

PETER M. MILLER

One of the most essential yet frequently overlooked aspects of the treatment and research of substance abuse is objective behavioral assessment. It is ironic that this widespread social and health problem, which has received so much public attention and concern, has been subjected to possibly the least objective evaluation of any clinical syndrome. This deficit may account for the numerous public and professional myths regarding the etiology of addictions, together with the lack of efficacious treatment modalities to combat them.

Although in the broad sense any recurrent approach behavior toward a substance (food, tobacco, drugs, alcohol) that results in problems of living or health may constitute an addiction, this chapter will be limited to the abuse of alcohol and/or drugs. This includes the chronic use of these substances in such a way that psychological and/or physical addiction exists. The former condition (known as drug dependence) generally refers to a strong desire for a drug in lieu of a more satisfying life style. The alcohol or drug use significantly interferes with the individual's social, emotional, marital, vocational, or medical functioning. Thus abuse is not defined in terms of amount or frequency of use but rather by its effects on the individual. Variations in individual tolerance levels for alcohol and drugs make any other definition clinically unfeasible. An individual may also be physiologically addicted to alcohol or some drugs. Physical addiction refers to the presence of physiological withdrawal symptoms subsequent to termination of drug intake after a period of use. Although alcohol and many drugs can lead to physical addiction, some drugs, such as marijuana and cocaine, are not addicting in this sense.

The author wishes to thank Thomas R. Tondo for his assistance with a portion of this paper that was presented at the meeting of the Southeastern Psychological Association, Atlanta, 1975.

Assessment of alcohol and drug abuse is important for two separate types of studies. The first type includes investigations of etiology in which the relationship between specific social, psychological, or physiological variables and substance abuse is analyzed. For example, an investigator may be interested in the relationship between social pressure to "have a drink with the guys" and drinking behavior. To examine this relationship experimentally (as opposed to a retrospective clinical analysis), a specific method of assessing alcohol consumption per se would be needed. The second type of study includes evaluation of treatment when both the short- and long-term effects of clinical intervention are assessed. In these studies assessment occurs in various areas of functioning. Thus not only are the amount, frequency, and type of drug or alcohol evaluated but also other aspects of the individual's social, marital, vocational, and physiological functioning. Since this book is devoted to descriptions of detailed methods of assessment in many of these areas, this chapter will focus on the assessment of consumatory behavior. The analysis of behavior patterns that often occur concommitantly with or subsequent to abusive drug use has been discussed at length in other sources. These patterns include social interactions (Kanfer & Saslow, 1969), marital relationships (Hersen, Miller, & Eisler, 1973), motivational behaviors (Miller, 1976), emotional behaviors such as anxiety and depression (Hersen, 1973; Williams, Barlow, & Agras, 1972), and vocational behaviors (Hunt & Azrin, 1973). The fact that this chapter focuses on alcohol and/or drug ingestion does not mean to imply that an analysis of this single behavioral pattern is sufficient with regard to the evaluation of treatment strategies. However, it has been noticeably absent from such evaluations.

TRADITIONAL METHODS

Traditional methods of assessment in the alcohol and drug abuse fields have emphasized the categorization of individuals based on specific criteria associated with their addiction. An illustrative example is provided by the categories presented in the Diagnostic and Statistical Manual of Mental Disorders (1968) of the American Psychiatric Association. Alcoholism is divided into three categories: *episodic excessive drinking, habitual excessive drinking,* and *alcohol addiction.* These diagnoses are based on such criteria as the number of times a year an individual becomes intoxicated or the presence of physiological withdrawal symptoms. *Drug dependence* is divided into a number of categories based on the specific drug being abused. Definition of dependence is vaguely described as ". . . evidence of habitual use or a clear sense of need for the drug" (DSM II, 1968, p. 45).

A similar categorical system includes Jellinek's (1960) classification based on physical and psychological concomitants of alcohol abuse. His levels of alcoholism include (1) *alpha,* in which alcohol is used to cope with life, (2) *beta,* in which no dependency exists but various physiological concomitants of excessive drinking are apparent, (3) *gamma,* in which both physical dependence and loss of control exist, and (4) *delta,* in which the individual is unable to refrain from alcohol use even for short periods of time.

Other diagnostic systems rely more heavily on the presence or absence of a variety of "symptoms" associated with the addiction. For example, the National Council on Alcoholism (1972) has set forth criteria for the diagnosis of alcoholism. Major and minor criteria are presented, such as the presence of early morning drinking or the presence of liver disease. In a similar manner many investigators have attempted to evaluate addicts on the basis of personality categories derived from psychological testing.

The major disadvantage of these systems is that they add very little to our ability to accurately assess the behavior in question. Alcohol and drug abuse are excess behavior patterns that exist along a continuum of use. Labeling someone as either having or not having "alcoholism" or "drug abuse" does not allow for either precise or continuous monitoring of changes in consummatory behaviors that may occur as a function of treatment.

A more useful traditional measure of substance abuse includes self-report data and data obtained from "significant others." In many cases this information is limited since most researchers have failed to establish the reliability of self-reports. Researchers into drug abuse use periodic urine screening as a reliable assessment tool. Alcoholism researchers, however, have generally been blinded to the necessity for establishing such reliability.

Another traditional procedure of merit is the evaluation of events that are the consequences of alcohol or drug abuse. Thus number of arrests for alcohol- or drug-related offenses or number of hospitalizations may provide a useful index of abuse. However, such events frequently occur too long after substance abuse has been initiated to be precise indicators of behavior change.

BEHAVIORAL ASSESSMENT APPROACHES

Behavioral assessment procedures that have been used to evaluate alcohol and drug abuse include two general types: laboratory analogue measures and in vivo measures. The former include operant measures, taste rating tasks, physiological assessment, and ad lib substance use in laboratories or in simulated natural environments. For various practical reasons these measures have been developed and used more in the alcoholism field than in the drug abuse field. In vivo measures include indirect assessments of alcohol and drug abuse by means of urinalysis, blood samples, or breathalyzer tests.

Many of these methods consist of the *direct observation* of alcohol or drug ingestion. Although observational approaches to the study of addictions may appear rather obvious, it has not been until the last several years that clinical research utilizing such data was reported. Providing alcohol to alcoholics even under experimental conditions with informed consent is still a controversial issue. Such assessment procedures have been considered unethical by some who hold the opinion that any amount of alcohol is clinically harmful to alcoholics and exacerbates their problems. However, recent experimental evidence (Faillace, Flamer, Imber, & Ward, 1972; Gottheil, Murphy, Skoloda, & Corbett, 1972), refutes this notion by demonstrating that alcoholics who drink under these conditions are *not* more prone to initiate a drinking binge. Similar arguments could be used against allowing access to a drug. All these procedures are conducted under closely controlled and supervised hospital or laboratory environments that would allow for prompt intervention in the case of gross intoxication. However, access to alcohol or drugs is typically limited in these procedures so that such a condition does not occur.

Laboratory Analogue Procedures

Operant Systems

Operant systems have been used almost exclusively for the assessment of alcohol drinking (with the exclusion of animal experimentation). In an operant analysis alcohol is used as a reinforcer for a specific behavioral response. Alcohol can be made contingent on the performance of either a simple motor task (e.g., lever pressing) or a more complex set of self-help behaviors in a hospital or laboratory setting. Thus motivation for alcohol is measured quantitatively in terms of how much and how frequently subjects "work" for an alcohol "pay-off."

An apparatus used in this manner is the BRS-Lehigh Valley Modular test system. This apparatus consists of a slanted metal console on a small table. A small insert on the front of the console contains a 1½-ounce shot glass. A tube suspended inside the console directly above the glass is connected to a polyethylene bottle containing an alcohol and water mixture. A squirt of alcohol can be delivered into the shot glass contingent on a specified number or pattern of lever presses, depending on the schedule of reinforcement used. Subjects can be allowed either continuous or intermittent access to the console. This apparatus has proven to be useful in studies using either single or group experimental designs of a descriptive (Mello & Mendelson, 1971) or treatment-evaluation nature (Cohen, Liebson, & Faillace, 1971a).

Nathan, Titler, Lowenstein, Solomon, and Rossi (1970) and Nathan and O'Brien (1971) utilized an operant apparatus to investigate both social and drinking behaviors of Skid Row alcoholics. Rather than receiving alcohol reinforcements directly from the operant console, patients earned points for lever pressing that could be exchanged for either whiskey or escape from social isolation. Such use of this system provides a quantitative index of the relative reinforcing properties of a number of events. Davidson and Wallach (1972) used two levers so that the alcoholic could work on one lever to earn alcohol and on the other to obtain a nonalcoholic beverage.

In drug research studies points earned in an operant system can be spent on a variety of drugs whose point price could be set to be equivalent to their "street" value. This more naturalistic use of the operant assessment system has been used by Cohen, Liebson, and Faillace (1971a) with chronic alcoholics. Rather than lever pressing, their inpatient subjects were required to engage in a variety of social and vocational behaviors around the hospital to earn points with which to buy alcohol. This system has the advantage of providing a simulated version of the natural environment where patients must engage in vocational behaviors to earn money for alcohol or social behaviors necessary to "bum" a drink. Such a procedure also provides an opportunity to evaluate the range and pattern of social behaviors functionally related to alcohol consumption. Additionally, as far as treatment is concerned, modification in alcohol purchases in such an assessment environment might be more likely to generalize to the natural environment owing to the similarity of these conditions.

In a more clinical use of this procedure Miller, Hersen, Eisler, and Elkin (1974) examined the efficacy of an operant system in assessing motivation of alcoholics to participate in and benefit from a comprehensive treatment program. Retrospective operant data were gathered for 10 therapeutic successes and 10 therapeutic failures from an alcoholism treatment program. During the first two weeks of their hospitalization, each of these patients had received three separate ten-minute sessions during which operant drinking (FR50 schedule of reinforcement) was assessed. All patients subsequently participated in an eight-week behavioral alcoholism treatment program and were followed up for periods ranging from two to

Table 12–1. The mean number of operant drinking responses for therapeutic successes and failures.

	Age	Education	Length of Problem Drinking	Length of follow-up	Number of Operant Responses
Successes					
$\bar{X}$	45.9	11.2	11.2	4.7	1176.70
S.D.	3.84	3.65	7.85	1.4	486.78
Failures					
$\bar{X}$	49.7	12.2	11.8	4.3	2116.70
S.D.	5.03	2.61	7.55	2.58	544.98

Source: P. M. Miller, M. Hersen, R. M. Eisler, and T. E. Elkin, A retrospective analysis of alcohol consumption on laboratory tasks as related to therapeutic outcome. *Behaviour Research and Therapy*, 1974, *12*, 73–76. Copyright (1974) by Pergamon Press. Reprinted by permission.

12 months. Relationships between operant performance and later clinical success or failure (based on reports from others, and hospital, jail, and employment records) are illustrated in Table 12–1. Statistical analysis (*t* test) revealed that the failure group responded significantly more (mean = 2116.70) on the operant measure than the success group (mean = 1176.70). Thus this measure may have predictive significance in therapeutic settings.

Taste-Rating Task

One disadvantage of operant assessment is that *what* is being measured is often too obvious to the subject. Both Marlatt, Demming, and Reid, (1973) and Miller and Hersen (1972) separately developed a similar surreptitious drinking measure based on assessments used by Schachter (1971) in his studies of obesity.

The taste-rating measure is presented to the subject as being a "taste experiment." During the assessment, the subject is seated in front of a table on which are placed a number of glasses. Each glass contains exactly 100 cc of either an alcoholic or a nonalcoholic mixture. Glasses are opaque to avoid making the constant amount conspicuous. The subject is presented with a rating sheet and asked to rate the taste of each beverage on a number of dimensions (e.g., sweet-sour). Subjects are allowed 10 minutes to complete the task. After the subject leaves the room, the exact amount of each beverage consumed is calculated. The subject is not told that his consumption is being measured. Rating sheets are in the form of a semantic differential so that attitudes toward alcohol can be assessed by scoring the evaluative scale. In Marlatt's studies subects were also observed through a one-way window so that sip rate and amount consumed per sip could be calculated. The taste test can be used to evaluate treatment using either pretests of posttests or using continuous daily assessments throughout treatment.

Marlatt, Demming, and Reid (1973) recently utilized this assessment procedure to test the "loss of control" hypothesis inherent in the disease concept of alcoholism. This theory implies that once an alcoholic consumes even a small amount of alcohol, he will not be able to discontinue drinking voluntarily but will inevitably drink to the point of intoxication. Marlatt and his colleagues assessed the drinking behavior of alcoholics and social drinkers under two different sets of expectancy conditions. Half the subjects in each group were told that the beverages in the test contained alcohol, whereas the other half were told that the drinks were nonalcoholic. In actuality half the subjects in each instructional condition received alcoholic beverages and half received nonalcoholic ones. The results indicated that the total amount of beverage consumed by the alcoholics was highly related to instructional set and *not* to whether alcohol was actually being consumed. Thus an alcoholic who was told that he was drinking alcohol would drink more regardless of the content of the beverage. These findings were related to the importance of cognitive as opposed to physiological factors in determining loss of control over drinking.

In the drug abuse field Liberman (1968) has been one of the few to utilize a procedure similar to the alcohol taste test in evaluating an aversion conditioning procedure in the treatment of two chronic morphine addicts. Prior to treatment sessions the patients were periodically presented with a choice situation in which they could freely choose morphine, coffee, soft drinks, candy, or cigarettes. If the subject chose morphine, the conditioning session progressed as usual. If he chose any other substance, he spent the next 30 minutes simply conversing with the therapist. Unfortunately, this task was rather obvious, and it seems doubtful that patients would actually choose the drug with such contingencies in operation. Avoidance of the drug in this situation may be related more to an avoidance of the aversive treatment session together with a desire to demonstrate cooperation with the therapist than it is to any real change in the value of drugs to the individual. The technique probably has more value when used as a taste experiment with no contingencies attached to performance. With this method experimental demand to respond in a certain way (e.g., trying to please the therapist) should be minimized.

Physiological Measures

Physiological changes in an individual's responses to alcohol or drug stimuli can also serve as a useful assessment procedure. This procedure has not received a great deal of attention possibly because of the rather sophisticated equipment necessary to monitor physiological reactivity. An excellent example of this method is illustrated in a study by Hallam, Rachman, and Falkowski (1972). In addition to subjective and attitudinal ratings, these authors utilized physiological measures to assess the effects of both electrical aversion therapy and general psychiatric therapy on alcoholics. Heart rate and skin resistance were assessed by means of a polygraph before and after treatment. During the assessment sessions, subjects were seated in a sound-proof, dark room. Heart rate was recorded on a cardiotachometer, which was receiving data on pulse volume from a photoelectric transducer attached to the subject's ear. Skin resistance was measured by means of electrodes attached to the palmar surface of two adjacent fingers. As part of the assessment procedure, each subject was requested to obtain a clear image of each of eight fantasies (four were drinking situations and four were neutral situations) that were described. Photographic slides of bar scenes were also presented. Heart rate and skin resistance were recorded prior to, during, and after both the subject's signal (button press) indicating he was imagining the fantasy and the presentation of each slide.

Using a similar procedure Elkin, Williams, Barlow, and Stewart (Note 1) obtained pretreatment and posttreatment (chemical aversion therapy) physiological measurement with a heroin addict. Heart rate responses to videotaped scenes of the patient "shooting up" were obtained and provided a useful measure of change as a function of treatment.

It may be noted that a variety of physiological measures have been reported in the pharmacology literature in relation to alcohol. However, the present brief survey was limited to studies that used reactions to alcoholic stimuli as dependent variables to evaluate treatment.

Ad Lib Substance Use in Simulated Environments

The ideal method of assessing substance abuse behavior is to observe its occurrence in natural settings. Since this method is often not feasible, the next best approach consists of bringing a facsimile of the natural environment into the laboratory or treatment setting. With this purpose in mind Schaefer, Sobell, and Mills (1971) and Mills, Sobell, and Schaefer (1971) converted a hospital dayroom into a cocktail lounge complete with padded bar, dimmed lighting, and bartender. Subjects were allowed access to the bar and its supply of alcoholic beverages while observers (both in the bar and by closed-circuit television) recorded (1) number of drinks ordered, (2) kinds of drinks ordered, and (3) magnitude of sips. This drinking measure not only differentiates alcoholics from social drinkers but

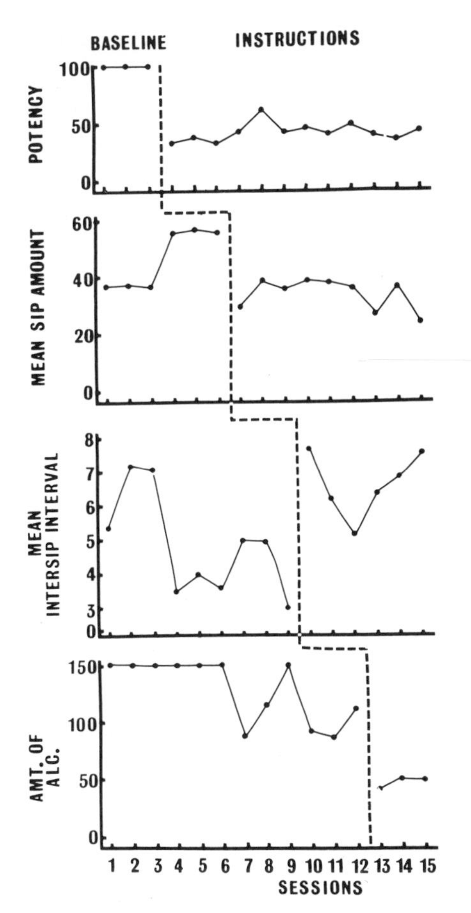

Figure 12–1. Ratings of sequential effects of instructions on components of drinking behavior. (From P. M. Miller, J. V. Becker, D. W. Foy, and L. S. Wooten, Instructional control of the components of alcoholic drinking behavior. *Behavior Therapy,* 1976, *7,* 472–480. Copyright by Academic Press. Reproduced by permission).

also effectively monitors changes in drinking patterns as a function of treatment.

Simulated home settings (e.g., living room, den) can also be used in this way. In analyzing components of drinking behavior Miller, Becker, Foy, and Wooten (1976) utilized a simulated living room in which an alcoholic subject was provided with his favorite alcoholic beverage and mixers and asked to drink while watching television or reading. The subject's behavior was videotaped from an adjacent room, and the components of drinking behavior were rated. Figure 12–1 illustrates the separate effects of instructions on these behavior patterns.

The subject was sequentially instructed to reduce the potency of his drink, to reduce the amount consumed with each sip, to increase the amount of time in between sips, and to decrease the absolute amount of alcohol consumed. This measurement system allowed for post hoc rating of the videotaped drinking on each of these components.

Results with this subject indicated that during baseline he was drinking 150 cc (5 ounces) of straight bourbon. Following instructions to reduce the potency of the drink, the ratio of alcohol to water stabilized at 50–50. Interestingly, as potency decreased the subject began taking larger sips and drinking at a faster rate. He appeared to be compensating for changes in one component by making changes in others, going in the direction of a more "alcoholic" drinking pattern. Instructions to decrease sip amount and to increase mean intersip interval resulted in changes in these measures in the appropriate direction. Finally, the subject was instructed to limit himself to one drink during the session.

The use of simulated environments is relatively new and has not as yet been used extensively in the field of drug abuse.

In Vivo Assessment

Direct Observations and Self-report

For practical reasons the self-report (direct self-observation) of the individual remains the most widely used measure of substance abuse. Because this information is usually anecdotal in nature and is subject to memory distortion, some investigators have provided their patients with special data sheets on which to record their behavior on a daily basis.

For example, as an adjunct to treatment Sobell and Sobell (1973) have developed an Alcohol Intake Sheet (AIS) to be used by patients for monitoring and recording their own daily alcohol consumption. The AIS provides space for the date, specific type of drink, percentage of alcohol content in the liquor, time the drink was ordered or prepared, number of sips per drink, total amount consumed, and the environment where the drinking occurred. A separate entry is required for each drink, and if the patient does not drink alcohol on a given day, he is instructed to record the date and write the word "None" under type of drink. Besides providing fresh, quantifiable data to the therapist or researcher, the AIS has additional therapeutic value in that it (1) helps to make the alcoholic aware of his drinking patterns, (2) promotes discussion of situations when drinking occurs, and (3) facilitates early treatment intervention.

Even when specific frequency counts are recorded by the patient on a daily basis, the data are subject to numerous sources of distortion (e.g., misperception or deliberate underestimates). Some investigators have attempted to deal with this problem by using reports of direct observations made by relatives, friends, or employers. Training these informants in behavioral observation techniques would be helpful in providing a system for obtaining such data.

Ultimately, the notion of having specially trained personnel directly observe a patient's abuse of a substance in the natural environment must be considered. Personnel could be sent to specific public places (e.g., bars, night clubs) to observe and record alcoholic drinking patterns, using either wrist counters or data sheets similar to the one developed by Sobell and Sobell (1973) for self-monitoring.

In a recent study along these lines, Kessler and Gomberg (1974) sent two observers into various bars in the community to record components of drinking behavior. Once established in a bar the observers were instructed to rate the behavior of the next male patron to sit in close proximity to them. Data were recorded on number of drinks ordered, the time the drink was served, type of drink, number of sips per drink, and total time to consume each drink. Records were also kept regarding each subject's age, height, weight and whether he was by himself or drinking with others. The percentage of interrater agreement was high for drinking measures. The number and type of drinks ordered demonstrated 100 and 99 percent agreement, respectively. Pearson product-moment correlations for time to consume a drink was 0.99 whereas the correlation for number of sips was slightly lower at 0.81.

The mean number of drinks ordered by the 53 males in the sample was 2.41. Most subjects finished their drinks in about 20 minutes, taking four to nine sips per drink. Most subjects drank beer. The most stable measure over time for each subject was number of sips. Thus although the rate at which an individual drank varied, the number of sips remained relatively constant. It is interesting to note that these data differ in many respects from the social drinking norms obtained in an *experimental* bar setting by Sobell, Schaefer, and Mills (1972). For example, in Sobell's study most of this subjects chose to drink mixed drinks with only a minority drinking beer. Also, social drinkers ordered a mean of 6.65 drinks each, considerably more than subjects in the Kessler and Gomberg (1974) study. The amount of time to consume a beer was also considerably longer in the Sobell study. Unfortunately, with so little normative data available, it is difficult to determine the source of these differences. Such discrepancies could be a function of numerous factors including the geographic location of the studies (California versus New England), age and socioeconomic status of the subjects, or differences in methods used. These differing results, however, must be accounted for to determine which of these two procedures for gathering drinking data is more valid. Certainly it would seem that Kessler and Gomberg (1974) found few practical difficulties in gathering their information and demonstrated significant reliabilities for their rating technique.

There is obviously less control over and knowledge about subjects using the in vivo procedure. For example, information regarding subjects' drinking behavior immediately prior to entering the bar may be of considerable importance. Such data would be important in establishing norms and in evaluating the effects of therapeutic intervention. In certain, more controlled environments (e.g., military or college campus bars and night clubs) direct observations could be made during continuous monitoring of these facilities by closed-circuit television. These data would be useful in assessing the effects of military or college stresses on drinking behavior and in identifying those individuals who are abusing alcohol so that early intervention is possible.

Obtaining naturalistic observations on drinking patterns is relatively simple since alcohol is a legal drug in our society and its use is public. Owing to legal restrictions on their use, other drugs are consumed or injected privately or with peers who are also engaging in this behavior. This necessarily precludes direct observations except by friends or relatives. Although it may be possible to train these individuals in behavioral rating techniques, it would probably be difficult to obtain reliabilities on these ratings. In addition, such observations of drug taking may lead to the drug user's becoming more surreptitious in his behavior. Use and/or abuse of prescribed drugs probably could be monitored through pharmacists or physicians, but such an endeavor would be a monumental task with numerous practical difficulties.

Blood/Alcohol Concentration

Analysis of blood/alcohol concentration is an excellent alternative to the use of in vivo direct observations. Various types of breathalyzers are available for this purpose. Breathalyzers range from the simple screening type that provides crude but immediate estimates to the more complex type that provides more precise estimates by means of gas chromatography.

For example, Miller, Hersen, Eisler, and Watts (1974) utilized breath samples to monitor the effects of reinforcement contingencies on the drinking of a chronic Skid Row alcoholic in the natural environment. The breath test used was a small portable device consisting of a glass tube connected to a balloon-like collection bag. The subject blew into the tube and filled the bag with a breath sample that was later analyzed by means of gas chromatography. These analyses are quite accurate with an average maximum deviation from actual blood tests of 0.003 percent (Huntington, 1972). Because the body generally oxidizes alcohol at the rate of approximately one ounce per hour, traces of a large amount of alcohol (e.g., a fifth of bourbon) can be detected as long as 24 hours after consumption.

In the Miller, Hersen, Eisler, and Watts (1974) study an *A-B-C-B* single case experimental design was used in which contingent reinforcement of a zero blood/alcohol concentration was systematically introduced, removed, and reintroduced. Throughout the experiment breath tests were administered to the subject in his natural environment biweekly on a random basis. The subject was called by telephone to determine his whereabouts and within an hour a research assistant was sent to the subjects home or place of employment to administer the breath test. Within less than an hour, and exact blood/alcohol concentration was determined, and the reinforcement contingencies were administered when appropriate.

Figure 12–2 illustrates the blood/alcohol concentrations for each phase of the study. As can be seen, contingent reinforcement led to decreases in blood/alcohol concentrations as measured by random breath tests. Thus analyses of blood/alcohol concentrations offer an objective and convenient means both for scheduling consequences of drinking and for assessing therapeutic results in the natural environment.

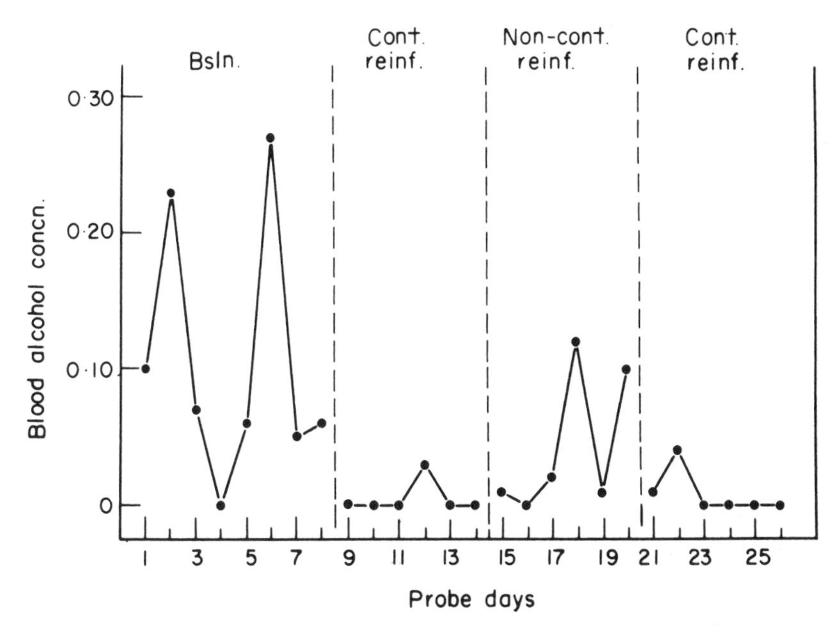

Figure 12–2. Bi-weekly blood/alcohol concentrations for each phase. [From P. M. Miller, M. Hersen, R. M. Eisler, and J. G. Watts, Contingent reinforcement of lowered blood/alcohol levels in an outpatient chronic alcoholic. *Behaviour Research and Therapy,* 1974, *12,* 261–263. Copyright (1974) by Pergamon Press. Reproduced by permission.]

Breath analyses have also been used to evaluate an individual's ability to judge his own blood/alcohol level. This skill is considered to be important both in developing controlled drinking skills in alcoholics and as it relates to strategies to prevent alcoholism. In developing this ability, subjects are requested to judge their blood/alcohol concentration while they are consuming specific amounts of alcoholic beverages. Breathalyzer or direct blood samples are then accumulated, and the accuracy of the objects' judgments is calculated. The subjects are instructed to focus on various emotional and physiological experiences (e.g., relaxation, numbness) associated with a wide range of blood/alcohol concentrations. After training is complete some investigators (Lovibond & Caddy, 1970), in an aversion-conditioning paradigm, repeatedly associate electric shock with blood/alcohol levels at or above a specified level (e.g., 0.065 percent).

In one of the most extensive analyses of blood/alcohol discrimination training, Silverstein, Nathan, and Taylor (1974) evaluated the relative efficacy of feedback, social reinforcement, and token reinforcement. Four male chronic alcoholics were initially exposed to a baseline condition during which they were to consume alcoholic beverages and periodically rate their level of intoxication on a 40-point scale. Breath tests were administered at least 10 times each day to each subject. Training was then instituted and consisted of three phases, each lasting two days. During the first phase, subjects were provided with feedback regarding their blood/alcohol level after each of their intoxication judgments. Emotional and physiological cues associated with various levels were discussed. The second phase consisted of a similar procedure with the exception that feedback was intermittent, occurring after 50 percent of the judgments. Finally, accurate estimations were reinforced by a token economy system. Through a shaping procedure, subjects were reinforced for maintaining blood/alcohol levels between 70 to 90 mg/100 cc.

Results indicated that these alcoholic subjects took many hours to learn to judge their intoxication levels accurately. Intermittent feedback was essential for judgments to remain accurate. Reinforcement seemed to add little to accuracy.

Urine Surveillance

Urine surveillance can be used on an outpatient or follow-up basis to detect the presence of drugs in a person's system. This assessment procedure has been used mostly to evaluate treatment strategies although it would seem to be a beneficial procedure in establishing norms for drug intake among certain population groups. In addition, periodic surveillance of this nature allows for an assessment of the reliability of reports from clients as to their drug use.

In relation to alcohol research, urinalysis allows for a determination of ethanol levels. However, the precise correlation of these levels with plasma levels remains to be determined. This procedure has been used by the Drug Dependence Unit at Yale University School of Medicine to determine the prevalence of alcohol problems among drug-dependent patients. Kleber (Note 2) reports a 76 percent correlation between ethanol levels in the urine and self-report data. Such assessments are typically administered on a random basis approximately two times a week.

Urine screening has been most often used in monitoring treatment of drug dependence. This is particularly true of methadone maintenance programs in which such surveillance is required by government regulation. The major importance of these assessments lies in the fact that they provide an objective evaluation of a client's progress and of the success of the treatment program as a whole. Urine specimens may be collected and analyzed on a daily basis (Dole & Nyswander, 1965) or randomly (Goldstein & Brown, 1970). Urine samples have the advantage of being easy to obtain and inexpensive to analyze (usually by thin layer chromatography).

In a recent report Trellis, Smith, Alston, and Siassi (1975) attempted to evaluate the accuracy of urine surveillance in a methadone maintenance clinic. To assess the accuracy of laboratory analyses, three type of urine samples were submitted over time for analysis. The first type included randomly obtained client samples, part of which were submitted in the client's name and part using an alias. Second, drugged samples were prepared by adding a prescribed amount of drug in stock solution to a "clean" urine. Third, samples of "clean" urine from donors not taking drugs were submitted. The investigators reported significant errors in analysis with false-positive reports (report of the presence of a drug in a urine specimen known to be free of drugs) being as high as 15 percent of the drug-free samples. Both false-positive reports and the percentage of failure to detect a drug in a known "dirty" urine decreased markedly when feedback on the accuracy of individual analyses were fed back to the toxicology lab. The authors concluded that periodic feedback of such information is necessary owing to the danger of lack of precision in analyses when so many are performed in a routine manner.

TREATMENT EVALUATION

One of the most important uses of strategies for behavioral assessment is the evaluation of the therapeutic efficacy of alcoholism and drug abuse intervention programs. Although these strategies are used only sporadically in these fields, they provide invaluable information on treatment effectiveness. For the most part, behavioral assessments have been used to evaluate behavior modification treatments because many were originally developed in that theoretical orientation. Those treatment procedures that have received the most extensive behavioral evaluations include the aversion therapies, operant conditioning approaches, training alternative behaviors, and comprehensive behavioral approaches.

Because objective assessment of alcohol and drug abuse behavioral treatment strategies is so recent, it would be premature to evaluate the current status or efficacy of these procedures based on minimal investigations. The studies presented below will thus serve simply to acquaint the reader with recent assessment research as it applies to various treatment procedures.

Aversion Therapies

Because the aversion therapies represent one of the first attempts to apply behavioral principles to alcoholism and drug abuse, they were among the first techniques to be evaluated. Unfortunately, aversion therapy did not fare well under close scrutiny.

Based on a counterconditioning model, aversion therapy, involves the repeated association between the thought, sight, smell, taste, or injection of drugs and/or alcohol and an unpleasant event of an electrical, chemical, or imaginal nature. Most reports of "success" with these methods are based on uncontrolled clinical case studies based on general reports from clients. Each of these studies reports precise details of the treatment procedure but provides very little information on the ways in which outcome data were collected.

In the field of alcoholism electrical aversion has been subjected to recent behavioral assessment, and chemical aversion and covert sensitization have yet to be closely examined. Although in some cases (Anant, 1967; Ashem & Donner, 1968; Clancy, Vanderhoff, & Campbell, 1967; Farrar, Powell, & Martin, 1968; Sanderson, Campbell, & Laverty, 1963) these treatments have been subjected to controlled experimental evaluation, only those few cases in which quantitative behavioral assessments were used will be described in this chapter.

One of the earliest attempts to quantify the effects of electrical aversion therapy was reported by Hallam et al. (1972). These authors compared 10 alcoholics who had received aversion therapy with eight who had received general psychiatric care. Behavioral assessments included physiological reactions (heart rate and skin resistance responses) to fantasies and photographic slides of stimuli related and not related to alcohol. Specifics of this procedure were described previously in this chapter. Surprisingly, increased physiological sensitivity to alcohol stimuli was not related to type of treatment administered. Rather, clinically successful patients in each group developed these reactions. The authors noted that these findings indicate that the success of aversion therapy appears to be more related to general therapeutic factors (e.g., instructions, therapeutic demand characteristics) than to counter-conditioning per se.

As a follow-up to this study, Miller, Hersen, Eisler, and Hemphill (1973) evaluated the effects of electrical aversion conditioning, a pseudo-conditioning procedure, and group therapy on the drinking behavior of 30 chronic alcoholics. Aversion therapy (escape paradigm) was administered over a 10-day period with a total of 500 conditioning trials in which alcohol intake was paired with faradic shock to the arm. The pseudoconditioning group received the same procedure with the omission of the unpleasant shock (shock intensities were kept to a minimal level that was barely perceptible). The remaining subjects received group therapy throughout this same period. Prior and subsequent to treatment, all patients were assessed by means of three daily taste-rating tests in which they were requested to judge the taste of a number of alcoholic and nonalcoholic beverages. The total amount of alcoholic beverage consumed served as the dependent variable. Comparing pretest-posttest changes, no significant differences were found in alcohol consumption among the three groups. Only about one third of the subjects in each treatment condition significantly reduced their consumption (by 50 percent or more). These findings question the efficacy of electrical aversion therapy for alcoholics and support the conclusions of Hallam et al. (1972) regarding the nature of aversion therapy.

Using a crossover experimental design with four inpatient alcoholics, Wilson, Leaf, and Nathan (1975) reported similar "negative" findings. Apparently, when the immediate shock contingencies are removed, patients resume their excessive alcohol consumption on a laboratory drinking task. Wilson et al. (1975) did present evidence, however, that this lack of generalization may be partly overcome by the use of self-administered contingent shocks.

These studies illustrate the use of objective procedures in evaluating a behavioral treatment strategy. Prior to these studies, investigations on the specific effects of aversion therapy on drinking behavior and physiological responses to alcohol were lacking.

The effects of aversion therapy in the treatment of drug addiction are still based almost exclusively on clinical reports. One exception involves a report by Thompson and Rathod (1968) in which the authors evaluated chemical aversion therapy with young heroin addicts. In their treatment procedure brief muscular and respiratory paralysis was paired with the self-administration of heroin injection. Follow-up assessment included ". . . urine analysis which was done frequently and without prior warning (and by parents when patients were on 48 hour weekend leaves). . . ." On the basis of this measure, eight out of 10 addicts treated remained drug free during the follow-up interval (the longest follow-up was five months).

Operant Conditioning

Fortunately, the nature of the process of operant conditioning necessitates the exact specification of behavioral events. Contingencies must be applied to specific behaviors in terms of either their occurrence or their frequency, duration, or intensity. Cohen, Liebson, and Faillace (1971b) have utilized an ad lib drinking situation to evaluate the effects of contingency management on alcoholics' drinking behavior. These authors provided a 39-year-old chronic alcoholic with access to 24 ounces of ethanol each day. The total amount of alcohol consumed during each session served as their dependent measure. When contingencies were in effect, the subject was placed in an enriched ward environment if he consumed less than five ounces of alcohol a day. Consumption of more than this amount resulted in a loss of privileges for the rest of the day. The daily drinking situation provided a continuous way of monitoring changes in drinking as a function of the contingencies. When these contingencies were in effect, the subject maintained a daily drinking level at or below five ounces. Using similar assessment procedures these investigators have also demonstrated the reinforcing effects of money (Cohen, Liebson, Faillace, & Speers, 1971) and visits to a girl friend (Bigelow, Liebson, & Griffiths, Note 3) on decreasing alcohol consumption.

As described earlier in this chaper, Miller, Hersen, Eisler, and Watts (1974) demonstrated the use of randomly administered breathalyzer assessments in evaluating the effects of operant conditioning in the natural environment. In an expansion of this procedure Miller (1975) utilized positive contingencies provided through community agencies to improve the adjustment of a group of Skid Row alcoholics who were frequently charged with public drunkeness. Specific goals of the project were to decrease alcohol consumption, increase work behavior, and decrease the number of arrests for public drunkenness. Twenty Skid Row alcoholics served as subjects, 10 receiving behavioral intervention and 10 serving as a control group. The total program was administered through various community agencies that regularly dealt with the Skid Row population. These agencies were all located in the central downtown area of the city.

The 10 subjects in the control group received goods and services (e.g., clothing, cigarettes, job counseling) regardless of their behavior. The behavioral treatment group received goods and services contingent on their sobriety. Drinking behavior was assessed by breathalyzer analyses collected on a random basis and administered approximately every five days. Evidence of intoxication on any of these breath tests resulted in a five-day suspension of eligibility for services. It may be noted that the Salvation Army customarily employs such contingencies with respect to their services.

Data on number of arrests for public drunkenness, number of hours worked per week, and blood/alcohol levels were compared for the two months before the initiation of the program and the two months after. The mean number of arrests decreased significantly from 1.70 to 0.30 for the behavioral group and remained approximately the same for the control group (1.40 to 1.30). The mean number of hours worked increased significantly from 3.2 to 12. Control subjects evidenced a slight decrease from 4.4 to 3.2 hours. Breathalyzer analyses for the behavioral subjects significantly decreased from a mean of 0.05 percent to 0.002 percent.

Thus both in controlled laboratory settings and in the natural environment rearrangement of contingencies can lead to significant decreases in alcohol consumption. Target measures to which consequences can be attached include either drinking or blood/alcohol levels.

Few operant programs with individuals addicted to drugs have been reported. Studies by Boudin (1972), Boudin and Valentine (Note 4), and Polakow and Doctor (1973) clearly describe the technology of contingency contracting with drug abusers but fail to present assessments of the consummatory behavior in question. Although these authors have attempted to quantify their results in terms of self-rating scales, periodic urine surveillance would have greatly strengthened the validity of their findings.

Training Alternative Behaviors

Although attempts to train more adaptive coping skills have been reported with drug addicts (Callner, Note 5), the evaluation of this treatment strategy in terms of consummatory behavior has been reported with alcoholic exclusively. In this treatment procedure alcohol and drug abusers are taught more appropriate alternatives to situations that typically precipitate substance abuse. Alternatives to such situations may include assertiveness, relaxation, or self-management responses.

Eisler, Miller, Hersen, and Alford (1974) evaluated the effects of assertion training on an alcoholic's marriage and on his drinking behavior. The subject was a 52-year-old male with a six-year history of sporadic, excessive drinking. Drinking episodes were frequently precipitated by disagreements in his marriage. His typical response to these arguments was one of passive avoidance. The goal of assertion training was to teach him to express his personal rights and feelings in an appropriate manner. Using instructions, modeling, videotape feedback, and behavioral rehearsal, the patient was trained to behave more assertively in role-played marital encounters. A female treatment assistant enacted the part of the patient's wife in these training scenes. To determine the extent to which this training generalized to the real-life situation, marital interaction was assessed by means of pretest-posttest ratings of a videotaped 20-minute interaction between the husband and wife. The tapes were rated on such variables as speech duration, looking duration, references to drinking, and requests for the spouse to change his/her behavior. This assessment procedure revealed that the assertion training generalized to the marital situation and resulted in the wife's becoming less domineering. Assessment of drinking behavior included breath samples collected weekly six weeks before and six weeks after training. The samples were later analyzed by gas chromatography to obtain exact blood/alcohol levels. Assertion training resulted in a marked decrease in mean blood/alcohol concentration from 0.08 percent (Range = 0.01 percent to 0.21 percent) to 0.02 percent (Range = 0.00 percent to 0.04 percent). Providing an alcoholic with a new response to problem situations appeared to decrease the likelihood of excessive alcohol consumption.

Along these same lines Martorano (1974) assessed the effects of assertion training on the drinking of four Skid Row alcoholics. In a controlled laboratory setting the alcoholics were given access to alcoholic beverages prior to and subsequent to six days of assertion training. Surprisingly, the subjects drank to higher blood/alcohol levels *after* assertion training. It is also interesting to note that the positive effects of assertiveness (feeling less tense and aggressive, more friendly and vigorous) were experienced only during sobriety with little generalization once drinking began. In relation to this study Miller (1976) noted that ". . . during the initial stages of assertion training the client's behavior often becomes disrupted and at times overly aggressive until he learns the subtleties of assertiveness and the judgment involved in how and when to use it appropriately." (p. 13). This may explain why drinking *increased* after the relatively short period of six days of training.

Although relaxation responses (Wolpe, 1958) have been used extensively as behavioral alternatives to problem behaviors, few investigations of the use of this procedure with alcoholics and drug addicts exist. Although procedures of muscle relaxation training and systematic desensitization have been used clinically with both alcoholics (Blake, 1967; Kraft &

Al-Issa, 1967) and drug addicts (Kraft, 1969, 1970; Spevack, Pihl, & Rowan, 1973), their effects on specific behavioral patterns with these populations have received little attention.

Steffen (Note 6) evaluated the differential effects of both electromyographically induced muscle relaxation training and an attention placebo treatment on four chronic alcoholics. Drinking was assessed through a 12-day free-access drinking period before treatment and a 4-day free-access drinking period after treatment. Pretest-posttest measures included blood/alcohol concentrations, electromyographic tension levels from the frontalis muscle, and self-reports of anxiety. Relaxation training resulted in lowered blood/alcohol levels, lowered levels of muscle tension, and reports of less anxiety. Increases in blood/alcohol levels over the initial drinking period were associated with increased muscle tension but, paradoxically, with decreased reports of anxiety. Thus although the alcoholic perceives himself as being more relaxed after alcohol consumption, he is actually more tense physiologically.

Although self-control or self-management skills have been used in the treatment of some addictive behaviors (i.e., obesity, cigarette smoking), their application to alcohol and drug abusers has been minimal. Self-management skills consist of responses that the addict can make that decrease the probability of excessive drug or alcohol use. These skills may include such behaviors as self-monitoring alcohol or drug intake, rearranging environmental stimuli that precipitate substance abuse (e.g., avoiding companions who abuse drugs), or rearranging the consequences of substance abuse (e.g., scheduling favorite activities contingently upon undergoing a specified period of time in a drug-free state).

In one of the few objective assessments of such procedures with alcoholics, Miller and Epstein (Note 7) evaluated the effects of self-monitoring and self-reinforcement on an alcoholic's drinking patterns. Two subjects were evaluated by means of a single-case experimental design. Each subject was separately seated in front of a table on which were placed four beverages containing 80 cc of a mixture of bourbon and water. This drinkink task was described to the subjects as a taste-rating task in which they were to consume and rate the taste of each beverage. In an adjoining room the subject could be observed through a two-way mirror. An observer counted the total number of sips taken from each beverage. Subjects were told to consume the total amount in each glass.

The study was divided into four phases for Subject 1. The purpose of the study was to determine the effects of verbal instructions and self-reinforcement on actual number of sips consumed and reliability of self-report of number of sips consumed. During each phase of the study, the subject was requested to count (on a manual counter) the total number of sips consumed from each glass and write it on an index card. The subject kept this card throughout the study, turning it in after the study was complete. Drinking sessions were scheduled every day for 12 consecutive days. The first three-day phase constituted a baseline condition during which the subject was observed, and the total number of sips for each beverage was recorded. During the next phase the subject was instructed to try to take more sips from each beverage. Since he was consuming the total of each beverage, more sips would result in a smaller sip amount (one of the components of appropriate social drinking). After three sessions baseline conditions were reinstated, and the subject was told to ignore the instructions to take more sips. During the final phase, the subject was again instructed to take more sips but also to reward himself with a canteen booklet (coupons exchangeable for cigarettes) contingent on complying with the instructions for each beverage. After this self-reinforcement phase, the experiment with this subject was terminated.

Mean number of sips for the four drinks during each phase are shown in Figure 12.3. During baseline the subject was taking a mean of only two sips per beverage. His self-report of number of sips was highly accurate during this phase. When instructions were introduced, the subject reported that his number of sips increased to a mean of 4.3. Behaviorally, however, the subject was not complying with the instructions since he was still taking about two sips per beverage. When baseline was reinstated, the subject's self-report came more in line with his actual behavior. Finally, during the self-reinforcement phase the subject's actual number of sips *and* his self-

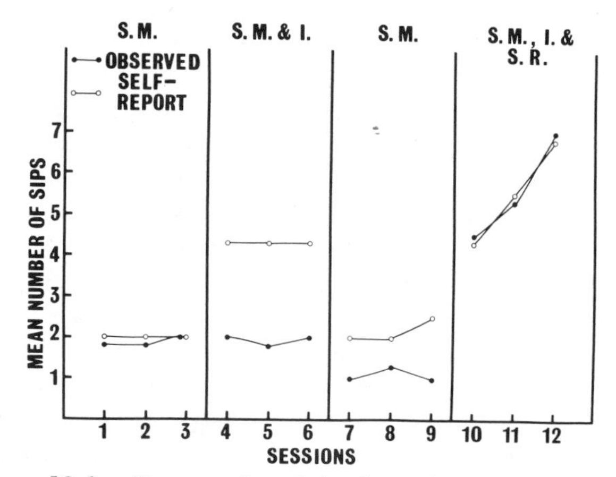

Figure 12-3. Mean number of sips for each experimental phase.

report of these sips increased with a high degree of reliability between these two measures. Thus instructions served only to change the reports of the subject whereas self-reinforcement changed the target behavior itself.

With Subject 2 instructions led to a slight decrease in the number of sips whereas self-reinforcement resulted in marked increases in this behavior. In contrast to Subject 1, Subject 2 demonstrated a high degree of reliability between self-reports and actual behavior throughout each phase. An additional phase with this subject also indicated that self-monitoring did not significantly change the number of sips taken.

Although the results of this study are highly tentative, they do indicate that some self-management procedures (i.e., self-reinforcement) may help the alcoholic to modify his drinking behavior. In addition, reliabilities between behavior and self-reports of behavior probably vary greatly from subject to subject.

Comprehensive Behavioral Programs

Comprehensive behavioral programs for treatment of drug addiction are relatively few. Those that are reported are generally case studies with limited assessment of drug use. This is unfortunate since urine surveillance is so easily arranged and is in regular use to evaluate the efficacy of methadone maintenance programs.

The combination of assessment procedures reported by O'Brien, Raynes, and Patch (1972) in their treatment of two heroin addicts bears mention. These authors used a combination of relaxation training, electrical aversion, and covert sensitization with their patients. On the basis of several measures, one patient remained drug free for 14 months and the other for six months. Although self-reports of drug use were used, these were confirmed by reports from employers. In addition, the patients were examined for track marks from injections during follow-up visits. A self-rating scale of the degree of subjective craving in response to drug-related stimuli also illustrated changes before and after treatment. Test-retest reliability on this scale was 0.97.

Sobell and Sobell (1973a) evaluated a comprehensive behavioral treatment program for chronic alcoholics. Treatment included self-management training, social skills training, videotape feedback of drunken and sober behaviors, a programmed failure experience, and aversive conditioning. Seventy alcoholics were assigned to either a treatment goal of complete abstinence or one of controlled social drinking. Subjects with each goal were then randomly assigned to either a behavioral treatment or a more traditional psychodynamic treatment.

A variety of assessment data were collected during treatment and at six-week, six-month, one-year, and two-year follow-up intervals. During treatment, components of drinking during probe sessions were rated to determine the effects of aversive conditioning procedures on teaching controlled social drinking. Treatment took place in a simulated bar setting in which subjects received electric shocks contingent on any of the following: ordering straight, nonmixed drinks, taking sips larger than one sixth of the glass's total volume, ordering a drink within 20 minutes of a previously ordered drink, or ordering a total of more than three drinks. Ratings of these components during conditioning sessions indicated that the subjects learned the correct drinking habits. However, during periodic probe sessions in which electrodes were removed and no contingencies were administered, subjects reverted to their alcoholic drinking patterns. It would appear that the conditioning was having very little effect. However, at longer term follow-up assessments, many of these subjects were drinking in a controlled manner. It may be that other procedures in the total treatment package were responsible for these changes. Unfortunately, the probe drinking measures during treatment did not reflect these changes. It may be that these drinking assessments were administered too early in the total treatment process for the beneficial influence of the behavioral strategies to be noted.

The Sobells' follow-up measures were unique in that they did not utilize the traditional categorical system equating success with one year's complete abstinence from alcohol. Rather, they made continuous assessment of number of days intoxicated (consumption of more than 10 ounces of alcohol), number of days of controlled drinking (consumption of six ounces or less), number of abstinent days, number of abstinent days resulting from hospital or jail incarceration, vocational status, use of therapeutic supports, and residential stability. All information of this type was verified by such varied collateral information sources as friends, relatives, employers, the California Department of Motor Vehicles, credit bureaus, telephone companies, Welfare Departments, courts, hospitals, and the Social Security Administration. The intensity with which patients were followed (some were tracked as far as Spain) and the manner in which information was verified are commendable. At times as many as 15 collateral sources were used to verify follow-up data. When discrepancies occurred in the information obtained from the patient and a collateral or in information between collaterals, the data supported by the most objective information was used. Possibly the only addition to this assessment procedure that may have improved its accuracy would have been the inclusion of periodic breathalyzer analyses to verify drinking information. This procedure would have controlled for occasions during which the patient was drinking alone with no collateral present to provide information.

The analysis of the follow-up data revealed that subjects receiving behavioral treatment—both abstainers and controlled, social drinkers—were functioning better than those receiving traditional treatment. Since the specific quantitative results are numerous, the reader is referred to Sobell and Sobell (1973b) for a detailed description of these findings. Unfortunately, it is difficult to compare these results to those found in other studies because the criteria for success are presented so differently. The Sobells, however, present a methodology that provides a more realistic and objective evaluation of treatment efficacy. The most important aspect of their assessment scheme lies in its emphasis on continuously gathered verifiable data.

Although not evaluating a behavioral treatment program, the assessment procedure utilized by Skoloda, Alterman, Cornelison, and Gottheil (1975) deserves mention. The authors utilized a Fixed Interval Drinking Decision program to evaluate an alcoholism inpatient program employing psychodynamically oriented individual and group psychotherapy. During the first week of treatment, no alcohol was available. However, during the next four weeks patients could choose to drink up to two ounces of 40 percent ethanol each hour from 9:00 A.M. to 9:00 P.M. Thus a total of 13 drinking decisions were made daily. Prior to leaving the hospital, the patients were again exposed to a week in which no alcohol was available. The authors compared drinking during hospitalization with drinking in the community after discharge. Although patients varied greatly in their drinking patterns, three distinct groups of patients emerged: heavy drinkers (those who consumed 250 ounces or more during the program), moderate drinkers (those who consumed 250 ounces or less), and nondrinkers (those who did not drink during the entire program). This latter group consisted of 44 percent of the entire 98 patients studied.

Results indicated that patients who did not drink at all during the program showed the greatest improvement during follow-up assessment at six months (based on self-reports and reports from significant others). Heavy and moderate drinkers did less well and did not differ from one another in their response to treatment. Probably the most important finding of this study lies in the fact that drinking on the program was found to be related to drinking during the follow-up period. As mentioned earlier, similar results have been obtained by Miller, Hersen, Eisler, and Elkin (1974) in regard to an operant drinking task and a taste-rating task. These measures, then, appear to have significant relevance to treatment programs in terms of predicting response to treatment. Continuous monitoring of drinking during the treatment process may indicate whether intervention should continue or whether the patient has received maximum benefits. In addition, the efficacy of specific treatment strategies could be evaluated in this manner using single-case experimental designs (Barlow & Hersen, 1973). In this type of experiment a treatment procedure is sequentially withheld, introduced, removed, and reintroduced with continuous assessment of drinking behavior. Decreases in drinking should be responsive to the most effective treatment strategy.

CONCLUSIONS

Further development and refinement of behavioral assessments—both the laboratory analogue and the in vivo procedures—is crucial for the advancement of research in substance abuse. Both types of procedures have their advantages and disadvantages, and possibly a combination of assessment techniques would be most beneficial at this stage of their development. Such combined use would also allow for a comparison of various assessment procedures in regard to their clinical feasibility and their relationships among one another.

Each of the analogue procedures (operant systems, taste-rating tests, physiological assessments, simulated environments) represents a standard system that objectively measures substance use and abuse. Although they are relatively free from subjective biases, their main value lies in the fact that they can be administered quickly and easily under controlled conditions. Thus they can be used in a hospital or laboratory setting for continuous or pretest-posttest evaluation of the effectiveness of a treatment technique. They are particularly useful in evaluating the efficacy of treatment strategies within a single-case design experiment since they are sensitive to relatively small changes in behavior owing to their quantitative nature. After the evaluation of numerous treatments within this framework, those that show the most promise could then be clinically evaluated with an experimental design using groups. At this point in vivo assessment procedures would appear to be useful in examining the long-term outpatient effects of a total treatment regime. One limitation of the analogue procedures (with the possible exception of physiological measurement) is related to the goal of treatment programs for substance abuse—namely, complete abstinence from alcohol and/or drugs. Since the analogue measures were designed to evaluate variations in consummatory behavior, they may not be useful for follow-up when abstinence is the goal. However, in the alcoholism field alternatives to abstinence in the form of controlled, social drinking are currently being pursued. Analogue drinking procedures would be ideal to evaluate the ability to drink in a controlled fashion.

Another possible liability of these procedures is that they are analogues and as such may be construed as being too artificial. Thus for these measures to be optimally useful, their validity in relation to drinking in the natural environment must be assessed. Although Skoloda et al. (1975) and Miller, Hersen, Eisler, and Elkin (1974) have demonstrated correspondence between in-hospital drinking and later drinking in the environment as reported by patients and their relatives, more quantitative correlational relationships are needed. Correlating responses on the analogue measures with blood/alcohol determinations in the natural environment would appear to be a practical and objective means of validating these measures.

Correlations between assessments collected in the natural environment are also needed. For example, the relationship between self-reports by alcoholics and their blood/alcohol levels has yet to be determined. These measures have an advantage over the analogue procedures in that they can provide data on substance abuse in natural settings. They must be administered randomly or often enough, however, so that the client does not learn to predict their occurrence and abuse drugs or alcohol during periods of nonassessment. Daily surveillance during weekdays only could lead to a pattern of binge drinking or drug taking over the weekend. Blood, breath or urine samples also have limitations in that they do not provide necessary data for an analysis of *patterns* of substance abuse. Important data regarding the time, place, circumstances, type of drugs or alcohol ingested, the manner in which the substances were injected, and precipitating events are omitted. Only verified self-reports or direct observation by others can generate these data. The use of direct observations in the natural environment by trained observers or significant others may present numerous practical and ethical problems. On ethical grounds the subject must provide informed consent for such observations to occur. Under such conditions, however, how much does the observation process itself influence the subject's behavior? This is basically an empirical question that must await experimentation to be answered.

REFERENCE NOTES

1. Elkin, T. E., Williams, J. J., Barlow, D. H., & Stewart, W. R. *Measurement and modification of I.V. drug abuse: A preliminary study using succinylcholine*. Unpublished manuscript, University of Mississippi Medical Center, 1974.
2. Kleber, H. Personal communication, January 15, 1975.
3. Bigelow, G., Liebson, I., & Griffiths, R. *Experimental analysis of alcohol drinking*. Paper presented at the American Psychological Association, Montreal, 1973.
4. Boudin, H. M., & Valentine, V. E. *Behavioral techniques as an alternative to methadone maintenance*. Unpublished manuscript, University of Florida, 1973.

5. Callner, D. A. *The assessment and training of assertive behavior in a drug addict population*. Paper presented at the meeting of the American Psychological Association, Montreal, 1973.
6. Steffen, J. J. *Tension-reducing effects of alcohol: Further evidence and some methodological corrections*. Unpublished manuscript, 1974.
7. Miller, P. M., & Epstein, L. H. *An experimental analysis of the effects of self-management procedures on the drinking behavior of chronic alcoholics*. Unpublished data, University of Mississippi Medical Center, 1975.

REFERENCES

American Psychiatric Association. *Diagnostic and statistical manual of mental disorders* (2nd ed.). Washington, D.C.: American Psychiatric Association, 1968.

Anant, S. S. A note on the treatment of alcoholics by a verbal aversion technique. *Canadian Psychologist*, 1967, **8,** 19–22.

Ashem, B., & Donner, L. Covert sensitization with alcoholics: A controlled replication. *Behaviour Research and Therapy*. 1968, **6,** 7–12.

Barlow, D. H., & Hersen, M. Single case experimental designs. *Achieves of General Psychiatry*, 1973, **29,** 319–325.

Blake, B. G. A follow-up of alcoholics treated by behavior therapy. *Behaviour Research and Therapy*, 1967, **5,** 89–94.

Boudin, H. M. Contingency contracting as a therapeutic tool in the deceleration of amphetamine use. *Behavior Therapy*, 1972, **3,** 604–608.

Clancy, J., Vanderhoff, E., & Campbell, P. Evaluation of an aversive technique as a treatment for alcoholism: Controlled trial with succinylcholine-induced apnea. *Quarterly Journal of Studies of Alcohol*, 1967, **28,** 476–485.

Cohen, M., Liebson, I., & Faillace, L. A. The modification of drinking in chronic alcoholics. In N. K. Mello and J. H. Mendelson (Eds.) *Recent advances in studies of alcoholism: An interdisciplinary symposium*. Washington, D.C.: U.S. Government Printing Office, 1971. (a)

Cohen, M., Liebson, I., & Faillace, L. A. The role of reinforcement contingencies in chronic alcoholism: An experimental analysis of one case. *Behaviour Research and Therapy*, 1971, **9,** 375–379. (b)

Cohen, M., Liebson, I., Faillace, L., & Speers, W. Alcoholism: Controlled drinking and incentives for abstinence. *Psychological Reports*, 1971, **28,** 575–580.

Davidson, R. S., & Wallach, E. S. Shock facilitation and suppression of alcohol- and coke-maintained behavior. *Psychological Reports*, 1972, **31,** 415–424.

Dole, V. P., & Nyswander, M. A medical treatment for heroin addiction. *Journal of the American Medical Association*, 1965, **193,** 648.

Eisler, R. M., Miller, P. M., Hersen, M., & Alford, H. Effects of assertive training on marital interaction. *Archives of General Psychiatry*, 1974, **30,** 643–649.

Faillace, L. A., Flamer, R. N., Imber, S. D., & Ward, R. F. Giving alcohol to alcoholics: An evaluation. *Quarterly Journal of Studies of Alcohol*, 1972, **33,** 85–90.

Farrar, C. H., Powell, B. J., & Martin, L. K. Punishment of alcohol consumption by apneic paralysis. *Behaviour Research and Therapy*, 1968, **6,** 13.

Goldstein, A., & Brown, B. W. Urine testing schedules in methadone maintenance treatment of heroin addiction. *Journal of the American Medical Association*, 1970, **214**, 311–315.

Gottheil, E., Murphy, B. F., Skoloda, T. E., & Corbett, L. O. Fixed interval drinking decisions. II. Drinking and discomfort in 25 alcoholics. *Quarterly Journal of Studies on Alcohol*, 1972, **33**, 325–340.

Hallam, R., Rachman, S., Falkowski, W. Subjective attitudinal and physiological effects of electrical aversion therapy. *Behaviour Research and Therapy*, 1972, **10**, 1–13.

Hersen, M., Self-assessment of fear. *Behavior Therapy*, 1973, **4**, 241–257.

Hersen, M., Miller, P. M., & Eisler, R. M. Interactions between alcoholics and their wives: A descriptive analysis of verbal and nonverbal behavior. *Quarterly Journal of Studies on Alcohol*, 1973, **34**, 516–52.

Hunt, G. A., & Azrin, N. H. A community reinforcement approach to alcoholism *Behaviour Research and Therapy*, 1973, **11**, 91–104.

Huntington, J. DWI arrests increase. *Treasure State Health* (Montana Department of Health and Environmental Sciences) July, 1972.

Jellinek, E. M. *The disease concept of alcoholism*. New Haven: College and University Press, 1960.

Kanfer, F. H., & Saslow, G. Behavioral diagnosis. In C. M. Franks (Ed.), *Behavior therapy: Appraisal and status*. New York: McGraw-Hill, 1969.

Kessler, M., & Gomberg, C. Observations of barroom drinking: Methodology and preliminary results. *Quarterly Journal of Studies on Alcohol*, 1974, **35**, 1392–1396.

Kraft, T. Treatment of Drinamyl addiction. *Journal of Nervous and Mental Disease*, 1970, **150**, 138–144.

Kraft, T. Successful treatment of a case of chronic barbiturate addiction. *British Journal of the Addictions*, 1969, **64**, 115–120.

Kraft, T., & Al-Issa, I. Alcoholism treated by desensitization: A case study. *Behaviour Research and Therapy*, 1967, **5**, 69–70.

Liberman, R. Aversive conditioning of drug addicts: A pilot study. *Behaviour Research and Therapy*, 1968, **6**, 229–231.

Lovibond, S. H., & Caddy, G. Discriminated aversive control in the moderation of alcoholics' drinking behavior. *Behavior Therapy*, 1970, **1**, 437–444.

Marlatt, G. A., Demming, B., & Reid, J. B. Loss of control drinking in alcoholics: An experimental analogue. *Journal of Abnormal Psychology*, 1973, **81**, 233–241.

Martorano, R. D. Mood and social perception in four alcoholics: Effects of drinking and assertion training. *Quarterly Journal of Studies on Alcohol*, 1974, **35**, 445–457.

Mello, N. K., & Mendelson, J. H. A quantitative analysis of drinking patterns in alcoholics. *Archives of General Psychiatry*, 1971, **6**, 527–539.

Miller, P. M. *Behavioral treatment of alcoholism*. New York: Pergamon, 1976.

Miller, P. M. A behavioral intervention program for chronic public drunkeness offenders. *Archives of General Psychiatry*, 1975, **32**, 915–922.

Miller, P. M., Becker, J. V., Foy, D. W., & Wooten, L. S. Instructional control of the components of alcoholic drinking behavior. *Behavior Therapy*, 1976, **7**, 472–480.

Miller, P. M., & Hersen, M. Quantitative changes in alcohol consumption as a function of electrical aversive conditioning. *Journal of Clinical Psychology*, 1972, **28**, 590–593.

Miller, P. M., Hersen, M., Eisler, R. M., & Elkin, T. E. A retrospective analysis of alcohol consumption on laboratory tasks as related to therapeutic outcome. *Behaviour Research and Therapy*, 1974, **12**, 73–76.

Miller, P. M., Hersen, M., Eisler, R. M., & Hemphill, D. P. Electrical aversion therapy with alcoholics: An analogue study. *Behaviour Research and Therapy*, 1973, **11**, 491–497.

Miller, P. M., Hersen, M., Eisler, R. M., & Watts, J. G. Contingent reinforcement of lowered blood/alcohol levels in an outpatient chronic alcoholic. *Behaviour Research and Therapy*, 1974, **12**, 261–263.

Mills, K. C., Sobell, M. B., & Schaefer, H. H. Training social drinking as an alternative to abstinence for alcoholics. *Behavior Therapy*, 1971, **2**, 18–27.

Nathan, P. E., & O'Brien, J. S. An experimental analysis of the behavior of alcoholics and non-alcoholics during prolonged experimental drinking. *Behavior Therapy*, 1971, **2**, 455–476

Nathan, P. E., Titler, N. A., Lowenstein, L. M., Solomon, P., & Rossi, A. M. Behavioral analysis of chronic alcoholism. *Archives of General Psychiatry*, 1970, **22**, 419–430.

National Council on Alcoholism. Criteria for the diagnosis of alcoholism. *American Journal of Psychiatry*, 1972, **2**, 127–135.

O'Brien, J. S., Raynes, A. E., & Patch, V. D. Treatment of heroin addiction with aversion therapy, relaxation training, and systematic desensitization. *Behaviour Research and Therapy*, 1972, **10**, 77–80.

Polakow, R. L., & Doctor, R. M. Treatment of marijuana and barbituate dependency by contingency contracting. *Journal of Behavior Therapy and Experimental Psychiatry*, 1973, **4**, 375–377.

Raymond, M. J. The treatment of addiction by aversion conditioning with apomorphine. *Behaviour Research and Therapy*, 1964, **1**, 287–291.

Sanderson, R. E., Campbell, D., & Laverty, S. G. An investigation of a new aversive conditioning treatment for alcoholism. *Quarterly Journal of Studies on Alcohol*, 1963, **24**, 261–275.

Schachter, S. Some extraordinary facts about obese humans and rats. *American Psychologist*, 1971, 26, **2**, 129–144.

Schaefer, H. H., Sobell, M. B., & Mills, K. C. Baseline drinking behaviors in alcoholics and social drinkers: Kinds of sips and sip magnitude. *Behaviour Research and Therapy*, 1971, **9**, 23–27.

Silverstein, S. J., Nathan, P. E., & Taylor, H. A. Blood alcohol level estimation and controlled drinking by chronic alcoholics. *Behavior Therapy*, 1974, **5**, 1–15.

Skoloda, T. E., Alterman, A. I., Cornelison, F. S., & Gottheil, E. Treatment outcome in a drinking decisions program. *Quarterly Journal of Studies on Alcohol*, 1975, **36**, 365–380.

Sobell, M. B., Schaefer, H. H., & Mills, K. C. Differences in baseline drinking behavior between alcoholics and normal drinkers. *Behaviour Research and Therapy*, 1972, **10**, 257–267.

Sobell, L. C., & Sobell, M. B. A self-feedback technique to monitor drinking behavior in alcoholics. *Behaviour Research and Therapy*, 1972, **11,** 237–238.

Sobell, M. B., & Sobell, L. C. Individualized behavior therapy for alcoholics. *Behavior Therapy*, 1973, **4,** 49–72. (a)

Sobell, M. B., & Sobell, L. C. Alcoholics treated by individualized behavior therapy: One year treatment outcome. *Behaviour Research and Therapy*, 1973, **11,** 599–618. (b)

Spevack, M., Pihl, R., & Rowan, T. Behavior therapies in the treatment of drug abuse: Some case studies. *Psychological Record*, 1973, **23,** 179–184.

Thompson, I. G., & Rathod, N. H. Aversion therapy for heroin dependence. *Lancet*, 1968, 382–384.

Trellis, E. S., Smith, F. F., Alston, D. C., & Siassi, I. The pitfalls of urine surveillance: The role of research in evaluation and remedy. *Addictive Behaviors*, 1975, **1,** 83–88.

Williams, J. G., Barlow, D. H., & Agras, W. S. Behavioral measurement of severe depression. *Archives of General Psychiatry*, 1972, **27,** 330–333.

Wilson, T., Leaf, R., & Nathan, P. E. The aversive control of excessive alcohol consumption by chronic alcoholics in the laboratory setting. *Journal of Applied Behavior Analysis*, 1975, **8,** 13–26.

Wolpe, J. *Psychotherapy by reciprocal inhibition.* Stanford, Calif.: Stanford University Press, 1958.

CHAPTER 13

Assessment of Sexual Behavior

DAVID H. BARLOW

Behavioral assessment is more important than behavior therapy. Anyone who has struggled with the application of behavioral techniques to complex behavioral problems is aware that the most difficult part of this endeavor is the development of adequate behavioral measures. Once adequate measures are developed, therapy is often a matter of applying the usual and standard techniques of selective, positive reinforcement or modeling, as even a cursory look at the literature of the last decade will illustrate (e.g., Agras, Leitenberg, & Barlow, 1968; Williams, Barlow, & Agras, 1972). The notion that assessment will determine the nature of therapy is not limited to the behavioral approach. Bergin and Strupp (1972) note that more accurate assessment of various problems comprising any diagnostic category will lead to the construction of specific treatments aimed at specific components of a problem.

Yet the development of the area of behavioral assessment has lagged behind the development of new behavior therapies. In our headlong rush to develop new treatment in the 1960s, assessment efforts by which we judged the adequacy of these treatments were often no better than an answer a patient would give to the question, "How are you feeling now?" In some cases actual behavioral measures were utilized, but more often than not these measures were tangential to the behavioral problems that brought the patient for treatment. Although this book begins to address the problem of the underdevelopment of behavioral assessment and the communication of recent developments in this area to practicing clinicians, it will come as no surprise that there are many more questions than answers concerning procedures and techniques used in behavioral assessment, particularly in clinical settings. Against this background, the behavioral assessment of sexual behavior is particularly interesting since many of the problems and issues confronting the field of assessment today are illustrated when one attempts to assess sexual behavior.

Major issues to be discussed in this chapter include the relationship of self-report to behavioral and physiological response systems in the assessment of sexual behavior. A second issue involves the use of contrived situations versus naturalistic observations in the assessment of all three components of sexual behavior. The necessity of assessing early components in the chain of sexual arousal will also be discussed. In addition, the complexity of sexual behavior, discovered in the last few years, has led to the conclusion that many of our labels for sexual behavior are inadequate. In sexual deviation, for example, no client is the same. Each has some combination of behavioral excesses and deficits, and each requires individual assessment. Data presented later in this chapter will illustrate that people supposedly falling in the category of one label used in sexual deviation, such as pedophilia, may actually be more different from one another than any two people who do not share this label. Similarly, it is not useful to talk about sexual inadequacy such as orgasmic dysfunction or impotence unless one is using these terms in a purely descriptive manner, because these terms do not carry the precision to lead to specific interventions. Finally, in deviations in gender role the categorization of males as "effeminate" or females as "masculine" grossly oversimplifies the enormous complexities of gender identity and deviations in gender role as well as their implications for treatment.

This chapter will first discuss the major issue of self-report and its relation to other response systems, as well as contrived versus natural observation in the assessment of sexual behavior. Following this discussion is a description of the three major components of sexual behavior: sexual arousal, heterosexual social skills(heterosocial skills), and gender identity or gender role deviations. A review of the three generally accepted response systems (verbal, behavioral, and physiological) as they apply to assessment of the three major components of sexual behavior and the measures used to assess each response system, will comprise the remainder of this chapter.

SELF-REPORT IN THE ASSESSMENT OF SEXUAL BEHAVIOR

The importance of assessing all three response systems (Lang, 1968; Leitenberg, Agras, Butz, & Wincze, 1971) is one of the more important developments in recent years and appears repeatedly throughout this book. The lack of relationship among the verbal (or self-report), the motororic (or behavioral), and the physiological response systems is well known by now (e.g., Leitenberg et al., 1971). In the assessment of most behavioral problems, however, differential importance is attributed to these response systems depending on one's general approach or orientation to the problems. Certainly the term *behavioral assessment* indicates a preference for assessment of the behavioral or motoric response system. Many behavioral clinicians assess self-report only if direct measurements of behavior are unobtainable. Until recent years, the difficulty in measuring sexual behavior directly forced a reliance on verbal or self-report measures.

The tendency to ignore self-report since the development of reliable physiological measures of sexual arousal is not consistent with the discovery of three independent response systems and could even be dangerous. This tendency in behavioral assessment of sexual behavior or other clinical problems ignores the fact that self-report *is* behavior and therefore is just as important as direct observation of physiological arousal or heterosexual social skills, or even direct observation of sexual interactions. This notion is at variance with the approach that categorizes self-report measures as indirect measures of behavior. Because self-report of sexual problems may or may not correlate with the other response systems, it is inaccurate to call these measures indirect.

The fact is that there are several different types of self-report measures used in the assessment or sexual problems or other clinical problems, some of which may correlate with behavioral or physiological response systems better than others. For example, self-monitoring of sexual behavior, such as reports of number of orgasms reached during sexual interactions, may correlate highly with directly observed behavior under certain conditions. Rating scale measures of subjective discomfort during sexual behavior may correlate poorly with physiological or behavioral measures of sexual behavior. For example, in a recent study, the sexual responding of six heterosexual and six homosexual males was assessed while they were watching several erotic movies, including a movie depicting homosexual interaction (Mavissakalian, Blanchard, Abel, & Barlow, 1975). Penile circumference, subjective reports of sexual arousal, and attitudinal ratings of "pleasantness" were measured. Heterosexual males reported the homosexual movie as distinctly unpleasant but demonstrated penile erection averaging 20 percent of a full erection and also reported being sexually aroused. The point of interest here is the split between two different self-report measures of sexual functioning.

In general, self-report correlates fairly well with objective measures of arousal, at least in nonpatient populations. In the study cited above, a self-report measure of arousal correlated 0.64 with measures of erection across all subjects and attitudinal reports of "pleasantness" correlated 0.55. Attitudinal measures and self-reports of arousal correlated 0.82. Geer (in press) notes that Heiman reports similar correlations for "normal" women between self-report of arousal and genital responding of 0.54 to 0.60. As Geer points out, this is a higher correlation than is found between self-report and other physiological responding.

In a patient population, however, Hoon, Wincze, and Hoon (in press) noted that sexually "normal" women and sexually dysfunctional women subjectively rated their arousal as similar during an erotic movie. But sexually dysfunctional women were not aroused compared to the normal group, suggesting a split between objective and subjective measures in this patient population. A more careful exploration of the different varieties of self-report of sexual behavior and their relationship to one another as well as to treatment outcome is an important area for future research.

Whatever the results of future research, one can make a strong case that in the assessment of sexual behavior in the clinic, self-report measures are at present more important than behavioral or physiological measures. This rather unusual statement is true because sexual problems that one confronts in the clinic occur almost entirely in adult populations. These patients are typically voluntary outpatients who report that they have a sexual problem such as a deviant arousal pattern or sexually dysfunctional behavior. Self-report of these problems, then, becomes the only necessary criterion for entry into treatment (Barlow, in press; Goldfried & Sprafkin, 1974). This differs markedly from the way in which institutionalized people or other patients in closed settings enter into treatment, a process that usually begins with direct observation of some unacceptable behavior. Similarly, self-assessment of progress is often the major criterion for terminating the intervention. Accurate depiction of patterns of sexual arousal that are reliably and independently measured and that demonstrate continued existence of a sexual problem will not keep a patient in treatment if he reports that he feels better and has recovered from the problem. When this happens, treatment is over. This fairly common occurrence in the clinic highlights the importance of understanding the relationship of self-report to other response systems and to outcome at follow-up. A further understanding of the variables controlling the reporting of different aspects of self-report is particularly important in cases when self-report diverges from behavioral or physiological measures. This is a common occurrence, as demonstrated in several cases described later.

Despite the relatively high correlation between self-report and physiological response in nonpatient populations, experience indicates that it is very common for divergences in the various response systems to occur during the assessment of sexual behavior in patient populations as in the Hoon et al. (in press) study described above. There seem to be at least two reasons for this. In our culture sexual behavior is still a rather sensitive subject, difficult for many people to describe. Second, recent findings from our laboratories indicate that even patients who seem very willing to report their sexual behavior as accurately as possible produce reports that diverge from objectively measured sexual arousal.

A patient who came to one of our outpatient clinics several years ago with complaints of anxiety and some depression provides an example of the difficulty in pinpointing sexual problems. Subsequent careful interviewing in a behavioral context revealed that the anxiety or feeling of uneasiness seemed to be correlated with specific people in his environment, but it was difficult to determine why. After some further discussion, it was decided there were some general social skill deficits, and a treatment program was begun to deal with these interpersonal problems. This patient came regularly for his appointments, weekly at first and then once every two weeks, for almost a year. Although some improvement was evident, the patient continued to report general feelings of unhappiness, anxiety, and depression at intensities that were unchanged since he had begun treatment, yet he continued to come, paying the standard fee each session. It was only by chance, during a routine reevaluation, that the patient finally blurted out that he had overwhelming homosexual attraction and arousal that was "the reason" for his difficulty in interpersonal situations. When asked why he had continued to come to treatment sessions all year long, paying $40.00 an hour, without mentioning what was really bothering him, he simply said that he had wanted to report these attractions all year but was unable to bring himself to do so.

Similar situations have arisen on several occasions in our clinics where presumably there is some expertise in identifying and interviewing sexual problems. This illustrates the scope of the problem and highlights the importance of the initial interview. In view of the fact that one cannot begin to assess sexual behavior in voluntary adult patients unless the patients first report the presence of a sexual problem, the manner in which one approaches sexual behavior in the initial interview is very important. In our view the problem in obtaining such information most often comes about when young clinicians communicate to patients in subtle ways that they are more uneasy gathering information in the sexual area than in other areas of the patient's life. If the clinician communicates that he is sensitive about sexual matters, it is very difficult for the patient. The best approach is a direct approach in which inquiries about sexual matters are treated much the same as inquiries about other aspects of the patient's behavior. If one suspects that the patient is having difficulty reporting sexual behavior, it is helpful to return to the subject later in the interview. At that time the clinician can remind the patient that some people have difficulty talking about sexual material but that accurate reporting of such behavior is necessary to determine how best to help the patient. One must often move from the clinical language of sexual functioning to colloquialisms peculiar to the patient's own cultural setting. Interviewing procedures will be discussed further in the section on self-report measures.

A second example of the discrepancy between verbal report and behavior occurs when the patient is perfectly willing to discuss his problem but seems unable to report the functional relationships accurately. It seems as though he really doesn't know what his problem is. In describing a patient with whom this problem occurred, I will also describe what I think is one of the more sophisticated approaches to assessment of sexual arousal. This approach uses direct measures of genital arousal, and I will illustrate its use in a typical, functionally analytic manner. The procedure was devised by Abel (Abel, Blanchard, Barlow, & Mavissakalian, 1975) and is one we have been using in our laboratory for several years. Essentially, the method involves presenting sexual cues by audiotapes, which are then played back to the patient. While he listens to the tape, the erection responses on the read-out are observed. New audio tapes are then made, enlarging on the content that was correlated with penile responses. The new tape, in turn, will occasion further erections, usually larger than those noted on the first tape. Finally, the content of the tape correlated with the larger erections is once again elaborated on after considerable discussion with the patient. What emerges is an audiotape that is highly erotic to the patient undergoing assessment. This approach will be described again in the section on assessing male sexual arousal. This method of establishing functional relationships between specific audio cues and erection responses can uncover patterns of arousal of which the subject is unaware. Such was the case with the patient who is described in the following paragraph.

The patient was a 22-year-old male who reported being very sexually aroused by white or brown, open-toed sandals. This pattern of arousal had been bothering him for approximately two years. In his detailed description he also reported fantasies of kissing the girl's feet and even smelling the girl's feet to see how sexy they were. He denied, however, that the woman's foot alone was erotic and noted that the open-toed sandal was the key ingredient. Using the audiotape method, the first tape described an interaction with such a sandal, based on his report of what was erotic:

"You are in a room, in a room with a girl, she's got some sandals on, you see her sandals there. She's very attractive, you see her sandals, the white kind. You see them on her feet there, see the strap between her toes. She's got very pretty feet. You are looking at the white sandals there, very pretty, see how they fit her feet, going in between her toes there, going

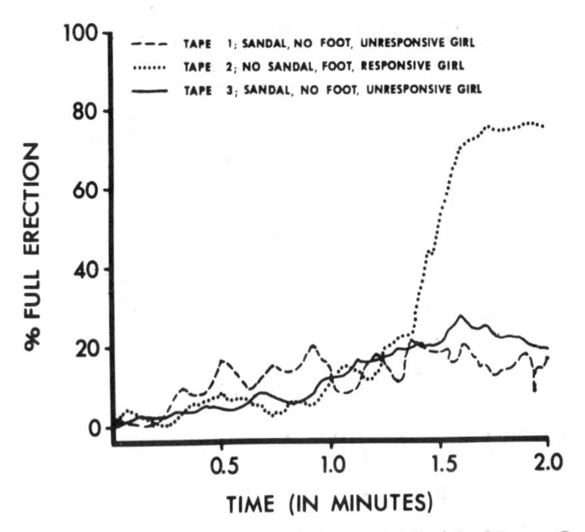

Figure 13-1. Erection responses of possible sandal fetish. [From G. G. Abel, E. B. Blanchard, D. H. Barlow, and M. Mavissakalian, Identifying specific erotic cues in sexual deviations by audio-taped descriptions. *Journal of Applied Behavior Analysis,* 1975, *8,* 247–260. Copyright (1975) by Society for the Experimental Analysis of Behavior, Inc. Reproduced by permission.]

in between her toes. See the leather there with the plastic in between her toes, very attractive, white, very attractive, white leather sandals, open-toed, very attractive and white. See them on her, on her feet there, very attractive, and you see the shoes, sandals, white sandals, as you are walking over, and you're feeing the sandal, very white, you can feel it in your hands, the sandal, very white, holding it, you can feel the material." (Abel et al., 1975, p. 252)

Surprisingly, this scene generated very little arousal, only on the order of 20 percent (see Figure 13–1). Another tape was developed, excluding mention of the sandal but describing in some detail the girl's foot.

"You are in a room with a girl and you are looking over at her, looking over at her, and you see her feet. She's really got beautiful feet, she's got sandals on, but you are looking at her feet, really beautiful feet, soft skin, very soft skin, very attractive feet, and you are starting to move over there towards her. She's just kind of playing with her sandals there, they drop to the ground. You come over and she's very willing to let you play with her feet, to hold her feet, caress them. You have your hands on her feet now, you are licking her feet, you can smell her feet, you are licking her feet. She wants you to do that, she wants you to feel her feet there, get a hold of her foot in your hands, you are licking her foot, kissing it, it's very, very sexy smelling. Really sexy smelling, she really wants you to hold her foot there. You feel it, you feel the smooth skin, very smooth, smooth skin on her foot, very attractive. You're just kind of holding her foot there, kissing her foot, holding it and kissing it. She's really turned on. Holding her foot, she's really turned on by it. She's really turned on, holding her foot. You're really, really enjoying it. Feeling the skin on her foot, holding her foot, feeling the skin there, very smooth, very smooth skin." (Abel et al., 1975, p. 252)

This description generated 75 percent of a full erection. These data suggested that the foot rather than the sandal was the erotic cue. To confirm this, the patient listened to subsequent tapes containing references only to sandals. The data also supported the supposition that the girl's foot was the erotic object rather than the sandal, as the patient had reported. The discrepancy here was between a physiological measure of arousal and reports of arousal. When this discrepancy was discussed with the patient, he changed his verbal report to agree with the physiological findings.

Differences between verbal report and physiological assessment of arousal in the assessment of sexual behavior can easily be produced in the laboratory. Several years ago we collected data during an experiment that examined the role of expectancy in an aversive procedure—covert sensitization (Barlow, Agras, Leitenberg, Callahan, & Moore, 1972). In covert sensitization the sexually arousing scene, as described by the therapist, is paired in imagination with noxious scenes such as nausea and vomiting or other aversive scenes taken directly from the patient's experiences. Both arousal, as measured by penile circumference changes, and self-report of arousal were assessed. During the first phase the sexually arousing scene was presented without the noxious scene. The subjects relaxed and imagined a sexually arousing scene, but the instructions indicated that this would make them better, that is, less aroused. They were told that relaxing would "counteract" the arousal. When covert sensitization was administered, the patients were told that this procedure would actually make them more aroused owing to an increase in general tension that would translate into an increase in sexual arousal. Figure 13–2 reports the average responding of four homosexual patients. As the data indicate, deviant sexual arousal as measured by penile circumference changes increased during the relaxation phase but dropped during covert sensitization. Subjective reports of arousal, however, actually dropped considerably during relaxation but rose during covert sensitization. Three patients said they were much better during the relaxation phase and were ready to stop treatment. At no time did anyone say he was worse despite the fact that deviant arousal was

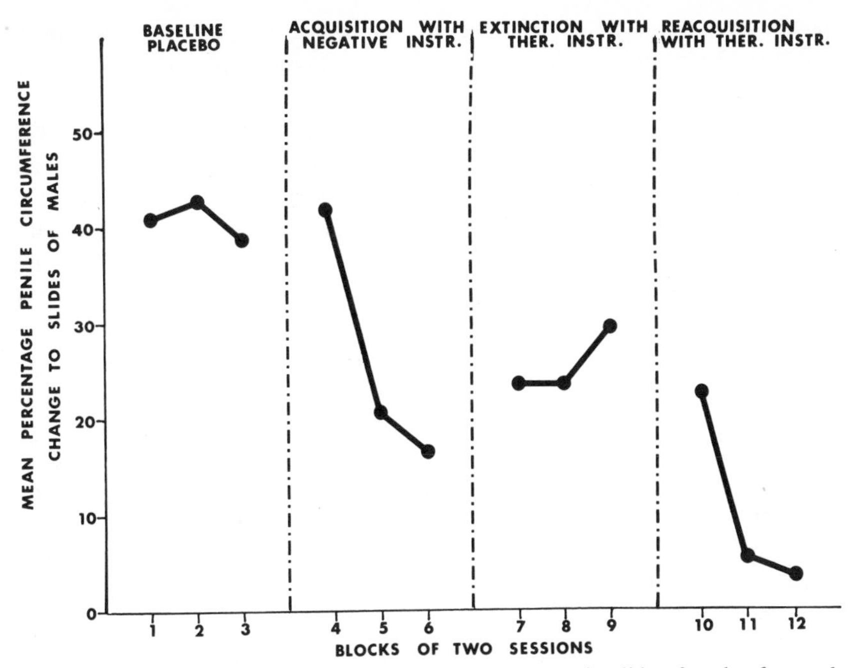

Figure 13–2. Mean penile circumference change to male slides for the four subjects, expressed as a percentage of full erection. In each phase, data from the first, middle, and last pair of sessions are shown. [From D. H. Barlow, W. S. Agras, H. Leitenberg, E. J. Callahan, and R. C. Moore, The contribution of therapeutic instructions to covert sensitization. *Behaviour Research and Therapy,* 1972, *10,* 411–415. Copyright (1972) by Pergamon Press. Reproduced by permission.]

increasing. Conversely, three patients said they were getting worse during covert sensitization although their deviant arousal was dropping daily. These data provide another example of splits among the various response systems comprising sexual behavior and the seeming ease with which these systems can be made to diverge.

Yet another situation that may produce marked splits in response systems is the presence of strong legal contingencies. If certain sexual arousal patterns or behaviors will result in imprisonment or other legal sanctions, report of them will obviously not occur (e.g., Quinsey, Steinman, Bergersen, & Holmes, 1975).

CONTRIVED SITUATIONS

The function of behavioral assessment in an ideal world would be the direct and continuous measurement of the three response systems comprising the behavioral problem in the setting where the behavior presents a problem. Usually the setting is home, work, school, or social situations, or perhaps all these. Whatever the setting or combination of settings, it has become known as the natural environment. Any procedure other than direct and continuous assessment of behavior in the natural environment is second best. Yet in applied work this principle is constantly compromised for practical or ethical reasons. Thus clinicians cannot or will not measure behavior in the natural environment if it occurs in settings remote from the therapeutic setting, nor will they measure behavior such as aggressive behavior that occurs at very low frequencies. For ethical reasons clinicians also will not observe some behaviors such as sexual interactions in the natural environment beyond the very beginnings of this chain of behavior (e.g., initial social approaches). To overcome these problems, contrived situations are devised to observe these behaviors at higher frequencies or in more convenient locations. In some cases the behaviors cannot be conveniently produced even in contrived situations. When this happens, as in the case of sexual behavior, clinicians move back down the behavioral chain and measure sexual arousal, presumably an earlier component in the chain of sexual behavior.

These are all necessary and helpful procedures, but it is easy to lose sight of the fact that these measures are only as good as their relationship to the behavior as it occurs in the natural environment. If these measures predict the occurrence or frequency of behavior in the natural environment, then they are useful. If not, they are useless. Nevertheless, although one may read journals or listen to presentations on therapeutic intervention in clean experimental designs that demonstrate highly effective therapeutic procedures, one seldom questions the relationship of the analogue measures so commonly used in these clinical trials to behavior in the natural environment. This observation is particularly applicable to studies of sexual behavior.

A Model of Sexual Behavior

Early in the chapter we noted that sexual behavior is more complex than the labels making up our well-known diagnostic categories would indicate. Glibly referring to certain behavioral patterns as "pedophilic" or "dysfunctional" may be useful from a descriptive point of view, but it vastly oversimplifies the components of sexual behavior elucidated by recent research. First outlined in 1974 (Barlow, 1974), these components cut across all sexual problems. This chapter is organized around a description of procedures used to assess the various components of sexual behavior. In the beginning of the chapter it was noted that there are three major components of sexual behavior—sexual arousal, heterosexual social skills (hereafter referred to as heterosocial skills), and gender role deviations. Sexual problems may be biochemically or genetically based (Money & Ehrhardt, 1972), and there are sophisticated procedures for assessing these biochemical and genetic factors. However, it would not be appropriate to consider them in a chapter on behavioral assessment. Nevertheless the behavioral assessment strategies described in the next section are frequently used as auxiliary measures in the assessment of biochemically and genetically based sexual disorders.

Sexual Arousal Behavior

The genital aspects of sexual behavior have received the most attention over the years in studies of sexual problems, and thus assessment procedures utilizing the genitals are the most advanced. The genital component of sexual behavior involves a chain of events beginning with the early aspects of sexual arousal through sexual contact of some kind and eventually orgasm. If two or more patterns of sexual arousal and/or behavior are present, they may or may not be related to one another in terms of frequency or strength. For instance, some patients may have frequent heterosexual arousal and behavior with a spouse and still often engage in alternative forms of sexual behavior. The "true" bisexual and some fetishistic patients are included in this group. However, deviant sexual arousal is often accompanied by diminished heterosexual arousal. Diminished heterosexual arousal and behavior do not, of course, necessarily imply the existence of alternative patterns of arousal.

Heterosocial Skills

Most cultures have developed elaborate social patterns of behavior surrounding the genital aspects of sexual behavior (e.g., Marshall & Suggs, 1971). In our culture many patients may have adequate arousal patterns as well as the necessary behavioral repertoire to engage in the genital aspects of sex. However, these patients may be unable to engage in the type of heterosocial behaviors necessary for meeting, dating, and relating to desired persons. Similarly, many patients have adequate social skills but lack the necessary arousal patterns to engage in sexual behavior.

Deviations in Gender Role

A percentage of patients, particularly those with certain patterns of deviant arousal, may have some degree of deviation in gender role. Behaviors appropriate to the opposite sex are present and some preference for the role of the opposite sex is verbalized. This is most common in homosexual or transvestite arousal patterns. When opposite sex behavior is completely adopted and the patient consistently thinks, feels, and behaves in the opposite sex role this mistaken gender identity is called *transsexualism* (Green & Money, 1969). Such clients usually request surgery to reassign their sex.

Schema for the Assessment of Sexual Behavior

To summarize, there are three major components of sexual deviation. Each of these components may be assessed in either the natural environment or in contrived situations. Because each component of sexual behavior can potentially be assessed in each of the three response systems (i.e., self-report, behavioral, physiological) and because these three response systems are relevant to both contrived and naturalistic settings, it is possible to construct a three-by-three-by-two grid along these dimensions that results in 18 cells (see Figure 13-3 after the manner of Cone, Note 1). The remainder of this chapter will review current assessment procedures. Each of the behavioral assessment procedures described will fit into one of the cells of the schema. For example, Twentyman and McFall (1975) have described a procedure to measure physiological responses (anxiety) in a contrived situation designed to assess heterosocial skills. The extent to which procedures are available to fill in the cells will make the current status of the assessment of sexual behavior readily observable.

SEXUAL AROUSAL BEHAVIOR

Introductory Comments

The direct assessment of the genital aspects of sexual behavior in all three response systems presents every possible roadblock to behavioral assessment. This behavior ordinarily occurs in places remote from the therapeutic setting. Because of the very nature of sexual behavior, these places are most often those that cannot be directly observed or monitored to allow the proper assessment. Indeed, the cultural sanctions against attempting any such assessment would ensure that, if they were carried out on a wide scale, the behavior would be so altered as to bear little resemblance to its normal and usual occurrence. Ordinarily, when behavior cannot be observed in the natural environment, contrived situations are constructed to assess the nature and strength of a given behavior in a more convenient setting. But the sensitivity of sexual behavior in our culture

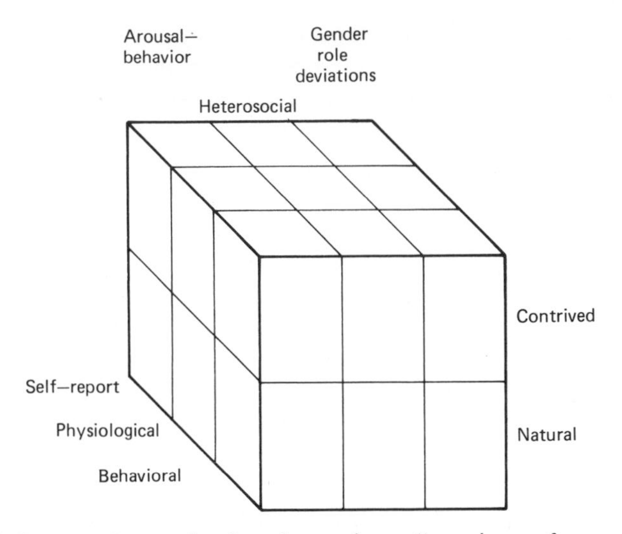

Figure 13–3. A schema showing the various dimensions of assessing sexual behavior.

makes assessment of the full range of sexual behavior, even in a contrived laboratory situation, extremely difficult. It is to the credit of Masters and Johnson (1966) that the cultural restrictions against the direct assessment of sexual responding in a laboratory situation were broken. Through this research the physiological mechanisms of the genital aspects of human sexual behavior were clarified, paving the way for a more careful and valid assessment of various aspects of the chain of behaviors making up the human sexual response. Since most investigators and clinicians lack the facilities and/or the administrative and community support to study the end points of genital sexual behavior, such as heterosexual intercourse, alternative procedures have been developed. These procedures have in common a movement back down the behavioral chain to a point where earlier aspects of sexual arousal are measured. The assumption has been that sexual arousal is a necessary step in the chain leading to the consummation of sexual behavior. As such, changes in the strength or patterns of sexual arousal will have a direct relation to the strength or patterns of later behaviors in the chain.

There are other reasons why assessment of early components of the chain are desirable (Barlow & Abel, 1976). For instance, in certain sexual deviations such as pedophilia, a patient may be able to engage in adult heterosexual intercourse on repeated occasions. A more careful examination of his behavioral chain, however, will reveal he is accomplishing this by engaging in those behaviors that ordinarily would lead to a pedophilic interchange. The most important of these behaviors will be intense pedophilic fantasies that will continue through intercourse. Some patients are able to carry on their behavior over a period of years although they report the act of intercourse itself to be aversive. If satisfying heterosexual relationships are the goal, then events that precede intercourse, such as interest in social behaviors and sexual features of the partner, as well as fantasies of heterosexual interactions, are important targets for assessment and treatment. In view of these relationships, assessment (and treatment) of early events in the chain of the genital aspects of sexual behavior may be more important to long-lasting sexual satisfaction than assessments of the end point of this chain.

A second reason for assessing early components in the chain is a practical one. Many patients with sexual problems do not have a partner with whom they can interact sexually. Measures requiring such interaction would then not be possible. These factors notwithstanding, one must be careful not to overinterpret data based on assessment of sexual arousal. The assumption has been made over the years that arousal is a necessary precursor to later genital behavior. The example of the married pedophiliac illustrates, however, that arousal patterns often are not absolutely necessary for later consummation behavior. Bancroft noted as early as 1971 that arousal itself bears an uncertain relationship to later sexual behavior. The large role played by cognitive representations of sexual stimuli and the effect of these representations on arousal patterns led Bancroft to suggest that both sexual behavior and arousal patterns should be assessed whenever possible.

More recently, Caird and Wincze (in press) observed that the correlation between sexual arousal and other aspects of sexual behavior in women may also be poor at times. In their clinical experience they have observed women complaining of deficiencies in sexual arousal who report orgasm rates as high as 75 percent during intercourse. They also report women who have normal levels of arousal and who even initiate sexual contacts at a high frequency, yet who rarely if ever experience orgasm.

Yet another problem with objective measures of sexual arousal is that they occur in contrived situations, and the relationship between sexual arousal measured in the laboratory and later sexual behavior outside the laboratory is uncertain. It is also true that the relationship between sexual arousal in a contrived laboratory situation and sexual arousal in the patient's natural environment is not clear. Even the relationship between sexual arousal in the laboratory and sexual behavior in a similar contrived laboratory situation is unknown. The popularity in clinical settings of assessing sexual arousal in contrived situations, then, is based on its high discriminate validity when compared to other psychophysiological measures of arousal (Zuckerman, 1971) and also on a high correlation with what reliable people report their sexual arousal patterns and behavior in the natural environment to be. One clear goal is the development of procedures to assess sexual behavior as well as sexual arousal in contrived situations. A first step might be the creation of situations in the laboratory when at least the initial stages of approach and contact can be recreated and observed. Forgione (Note 2) has recently used mannikins of children to assess approach behavior in pedophiliacs. He reports that while approaching and fondling the mannikins these patients engage in a variety of behaviors not reported in a detailed interview.

Similarly, Marks, Gelder, and Bancroft (1970) allowed transvestites to cross-dress in a contrived laboratory setting as part of treatment. However, there is no reason why this could not be a behavioral assessment procedure independent of treatment. In assessing heterosocial skills, this type of contrived situation is common.

A more remote but equally important goal would be the development of methods to observe approach behavior in the natural environment. The practical and ethical problems inherent in this type of assessment seem overwhelming at the present time, but in view of advances in naturalistic observation and the relaxation of attitudes toward sexual behavior in our society, something like this may be possible, assuming the ethical issues could be resolved. The increased use of female collaborators in clinical treatment of sexual problems could possibly be extended to naturalistic studies of sexual approach behavior in males and similar procedures could be used to assess behaviors leading up to genital interactions in females.

The early success in establishing certain types of validity for objective measures of early components in the chain of sexual behavior, such as sexual arousal, has led to an exaggerated idea of the usefulness of these measures, but used and interpreted properly, these measures are essential in a complete assessment of sexual behavior. Procedures most useful in the assessment of components of early sexual arousal measure both physiological and self-report aspects in both the male and female. Physiological measures of early male sexual arousal, specifically erections, have been available longer than measures of female arousal and have been subjected to wider experimentation and validation.

Objective Measurement of Male Sexual Arousal

A recent review article by Zuckerman (1971) was largely responsible for the upsurge in interest in measurement of male erections. Until the publication of this review, penile erection was but one of many physiological measures employed in the assessment of sexual arousal. Other measures, such as GRS, cardiac rate, respiration, and pupil size, were thought to be valid and reliable indicators of sexual arousal. Although changes in these responses do occur during sexual arousal, Zuckerman concluded from his review that other emotional states, such as fear, anger, and pain, could cause similar changes. The nonspecificity or lack of discriminate validity obviated the usefulness of these measures. Penile erections, however, were specific to sexual arousal with the exception of rare, pathological physical conditions (Barlow & Abel, 1976). These conclusions renewed interest in devices and procedures to measure erections and caused a flurry of activity devoted to investigating the relative merits of existing apparatus.

The increased interest in arousal and erections during the late 1960s and the 1970s in turn activated the psychohistorians (Mountjoy, 1974), who wondered if interest in erections was a modern phenomenon or something also of interest to our forefathers (foremothers?). In their search the historians once again discovered that very little is new in the world and that farmers at the turn of the century were concerned about excessive masturbation by their horses. In addition to being unsightly, and perhaps immoral, this practice resulted in a low sperm count and an inability to impregnate mares. To prevent it they built a large, cuff-like apparatus that enclosed the horse's penis and testicles. The beginnings of tumesence of the penis connected two points which then set off an alarm connected to the device. The inventor of the device noted that when the alarm rang, the horse needed some attention. Some modern-day theorists might say, however, that the alarm was effective because it interrupted the horse's sexual fantasies (Mahoney, 1974).

In Czechoslovakia in the late 1950s Kurt Freund developed an apparatus that would quantify erectile responses (Freund, 1957). He was also the first to use the apparatus in any serious manner in sex research. The development of this device, which is still in use, was a major advance in the measurement of male sexual behavior. Essentially, Freund's apparatus is a glass cylinder with a rubber cuff on one end into which the penis is inserted. As the penis enlarges, the amount of air displaced in the cylinder is measured. Thus this device measures penile volume changes. In reviewing various apparatuses to quantify penile erections, Abel and Blanchard (1976) have described a variety of such devices. Jovanovic (1971) had published a similar review earlier. At the present time, however, all devices can be classified into two categories—those that measure penile volume and those that quantify penile circumference changes.

Freund and his colleages described his device to measure penile volume in a technical article in 1965 (Freund, Sedlacek, & Knob, 1965). Freund has utilized his apparatus in numerous investigations over the years and continues to collect data important to the field of sex research (e.g., Freund, 1961, 1963, 1971). McConaghy (1967) has also developed a volumetric device that is somewhat simpler and less expensive.

More recently, two devices have been developed to measure penile circumference changes. The first utilizes mercury-filled tubing. Bancroft, Jones, and Pullan (1966) devised an apparatus that was similar to one described by Fisher, Gross, and Zuch (1965). Essentially this apparatus was a mercury-filled elastic tube that encircled the penis. As penile tumesence occurred, the elastic tube lengthened around the penis causing contraction of the inner diameter of the tubing. In Bancroft's device, which has been adopted by a number of researchers, the mercury-filled tubing forms one arm of a Wheatstone bridge circuit. As tumesence occurs and the diameter of the mercury in the tubing decreases, electrical resistance of the mercury column is increased. The electrical changes can then be recorded. Bancroft (1971, 1974) described the technology of this device in some detail.

A second widely used device to measure penile circumference was developed by Barlow, Becker, Leitenberg, and Agras (1970). It is a thin, metal, ring-like device open at one end that is placed around the penis, forming a semicircle around it. At the base of the ring are located one or more strain gauges. During erection, the "wings" of the ring separate, which causes a slight bending of the strain gauge and produces increased electrical output. The device is easily calibrated by fashioning a smooth wooden cone on which the full range of circumferences is indicated by a pencil. For calibration, one simply runs the ring up and down the cone noting the read-out at the penciled size indicators. This process demonstrates a remarkably linear output over the full range of circumference changes that is stable over time.

No formal comparison of the mercury tubing or strain gauge methods of measuring penile circumference has yet been undertaken, although informal comparisons in our laboratory indicate that the strain gauge produces a more linear output over a wider range of cylindrical sizes when calibrated on wooden cones. In addition, owing to its design, the strain gauge device is more rugged than the mercury tubing in that it is less susceptible to damage. Furthermore, the mercury gauge is expandable over only 10 percent of its resting length and tends to separate at the upper range of displacement regardless of the size of the tube's boring. The mercury gauge has also been reported as restrictive (Peterson, 1966). Because there is no restriction of expansion, the strain gauge requires six times less force than the mercury gauge to achieve the same amount of expansion. Further aspects of strain gauge technology can be found in Barlow et al. (1970). A disadvantage of the strain gauge device, when compared to the mercury tubing, is cost. The strain gauge currently costs in the neighborhood of $25.00 to $50.00 as compared to $5.00 to $10.00 for the mercury tubing, although the recent initiation of commercial production of the strain gauge device may lower the cost somewhat.

In reviewing the two devices Bancroft (1974) notes that the strain gauge devices may be more prone to movement artifacts. In our experience movement artifacts have not been a problem and when they do occur, they are easily identifiable on any read-out. Nevertheless, none of these comments represent data, and all subjective impressions are easily testable. When they are properly used, it would seem that the devices would be equally satisfactory, with the strain gauge possessing a slight advantage based on durability, ease of handling (e.g., Caird & Wincze, in press), and less restrictiveness.

Comparison of Volumetric and Circumferential Devices

Several investigators have recently directly compared circumferential devices with volumetric devices. In Freund's laboratory in Toronto the Barlow et al. strain gauge was compared with Freund's original volume device. Volunteer subjects wore both devices while exposed to erotic stimulation. Independently, McConaghy (1974) in Australia also compared volumetric versus circumferential devices, in this case the mercury tubing device. Although the data were complex, the general conclusion was that volumetric devices are more sensitive and pick up changes at smaller penile sizes than circumference devices. Although both devices are capable of picking up low levels of arousal of which the patient is often unaware, the volume devices are usually employed in studies where measurement of low levels of arousal are necessary. Circumferential devices, on the other hand, are more flexible and less cumbersome and are usually employed in studies measuring larger, more functional levels of arousal, in the range of 25 to 100 percent of a full erection.

The relative complexity of a device to measure volume versus circumference contributes to two other differences between the two approaches. Volumetric devices are considerably more expensive, and enclosing the entire penis as they do, they are more cumbersome and difficult to work with than the circumferential devices that are quite easily positioned by the subject himself. Nevertheless, these differences are probably not important because the trend in assessment of sexual arousal is to choose a specific measurement device, basing one's choice on the purpose of the study. Because volumetric devices are more sensitive and pick up smaller changes, the apparatus has often been used in theoretical studies of patterns of sexual arousal when large amounts of arousal are not necessary to test certain hypotheses. For example, Freund, Langevin, Cibiri, and Zajac (1973) demonstrated that homosexuals showed no more detumescence to heterosexual slides than heterosexuals to homosexual slides. The purpose of the experiment was to test the theory that homosexuals have a heterosexual phobia. Absolute amounts of arousal were not necessary to test this hypothesis. A second common use of volume devices is diagnosis or assessment of various arousal patterns in individuals or groups. The sensitivity of the volumetric device will allow the pin-pointing of patterns of arousal, even if individuals are instructed to mask or suppress the arousal (Freund, 1961, 1963, 1971).

Circumferential measures, on the other hand, being less cumbersome, more sturdy, and relatively less expensive, are effective in measuring the large, functionally relevant levels of sexual arousal useful in assessing changes in patterns or levels of arousal as a result of treatment. The goals here are quite different. Sexual arousal less than 20 percent of a full erection may have decided theoretical interest but be of little or no clinical value to the patient attempting to learn a new functional pattern of arousal. More arousal, in the area of 75 percent of a full erection, is necessary. This may account for the differential methods of reporting data obtained from volume versus circumferencial devices. Volumetric devices often report data in terms of z scores, rank order scores, or other methods to make the data more amenable to statistical analysis (e.g., McConaghy, 1969, 1970). The disadvantage of this method, of course, is that one is unable to determine the quantity or range of arousal with which the investigator is working. Circumferential measures, on the other hand, most often report data in terms of a percentage of full erection. Although this method is less sensitive to statistical comparisons, the clinical implications of the arousal with which one is working are readily apparent.

This discussion implies a growing specificity of function for volumetric and circumferential devices, but it would be premature to draw conclusions on the optimal uses of these devices at this time. Circumferential devices, although somewhat less sensitive, have been used successfully to study low levels of arousal (e.g., Abel, Blanchard, Barlow, & Becker, Note 3) and to assess diagnostic or more theoretical questions (Bancroft, 1971). Conversely, there is no obvious reason why volumetric devices could not be used to measure larger erections, as in the assessment of change during treatment. Considerably more data are needed in this important area of assessment.

Objective Measurement of Female Sexual Arousal

The study of female sexual arousal has lagged behind that of male sexual arousal as scientists in the field have awaited the development of the proper technology. Despite the demonstrated nonspecificity of general physiological measures, nothing else has been available, and some investigators (e.g., Hamrick, 1974) have conducted investigations using multiple physiological measures. The most exciting development in sex research in the past decade has been the development of a vaginal photoplethysmograph, which is a measure of female sexual arousal having the same discriminate validity as erection measures in males (Geer, Morokoff, & Greenwood, 1974; Sintchak & Geer, 1975). Based on the pioneering work of Masters and Johnson (1966), this device was constructed to take advantage of the massive, localized vasocongestive reaction that occurs in the vaginal wall early in sexual arousal. Geer et al. (1974) constructed a clear, acrylic probe approximately ½ inch in diameter and 1¾ inches in length. An incandescent light source was mounted on one end of the probe, and a selenium photocell detector was mounted on the side. Essentially, the probe measures the amount of light reflected from vaginal wall tissue. The less light reflected, the more vasocongestion and, hence, the more arousal. Geer et al. (1974) originally validated this device as a measure of sexual arousal.

More recently, Hoon, Wincze, and Hoon (1976) have developed and described what seems to be an improved probe device, which substitutes an infrared light source and a phototransistor detector cell that may eliminate artifacts in the original device. Although the improvements seem logical, they have yet to be demonstrated as being more efficient. More important, the two devices work on exactly the same principle, and some preliminary data on validity are available. In a model study Hoon, Wincze, and Hoon (1976) demonstrated that the infrared photoplethysmograph measures blood volume changes and not changes mediated by vaginal wall contractions or changes in lubrication. In a second important experiment, designed to determine whether the device discriminates sexual arousal from other arousal states, Hoon et al. illustrated clear differences between sexually arousing, dysphoric, and neutral emotional conditions in women. In a second paper Hoon, Wincze, & Hoon (in press) wrote that sexually "normal" women achieved greater levels of vasocongestion when compared to women seeking help for sexual problems. Systolic blood pressure discriminated normal from sexually dysfunctional women, but other physiological indicators, such as heart rate, did not. Hoon et al. are already beginning to employ this device to assess changes during treatment of sexual problems in women in the same way measures of erection are used in assessment of male sexual problems (Hoon, Wincze, & Hoon, Note 4).

In Geer's laboratory Heiman (Geer, in press) also found that arousal measured by the probe device was less for anorgasmic women viewing erotic films than for orgasmic women, and recently Geer and Quartararo (Geer, in press) have demonstrated that measurement of changes in vaginal blood volume provides in some women an unambiguous indication of orgasm.

Although the probe device is in use in only a few laboratories at this time, the early data are extremely promising. In addition, the ease of handling and use should ensure a rapid expansion of research on female sexual arousal.

Stimulus Modalities, Content, and Methods in the Objective Measurement of Sexual Arousal

With the advent of valid devices for the assessment of sexual arousal, investigators have worked on refining their procedures so as to assess a variety of arousal patterns under optimal conditions. One of the first questions that occurred to various investigators when they were measuring male sexual arousal was: What is the optimal stimulus modality that will set the occasion for the greatest amounts of arousal? Investigators and clinicians have used movies, videotapes, slides, and free fantasies, as well as the audiotape method mentioned earlier. In one recent experiment modalities of stimuli were compared in people with different patterns of arousal. A group of 20 voluntary homosexual subjects were presented with a two-minute clip of videotapes depicting homosexual interactions, the audiotapes describing the same homosexual interactions, or slides. These three stimuli were presented twice in each of three successive sessions, for a total of six stimuli per session, in random order. During the first session, subjects were told to become involved with the person described or depicted. In the second session they were also told to become involved but to suppress their erection response by any mental means. In the third session they were once again told to involve themselves with the person in the situation. The results (Figure 13-4) indicated that the videotape produced the largest amount of arousal, even when subjects were attempting to suppress this arousal. Slides produced an intermediate level of arousal. Some suppression of arousal occurred during both movies and slides. It is interesting to note that audiotapes produced the least arousal; however, subjects seemed unable to suppress this arousal when asked to do so. Other studies indicate that the general pattern in which movies or videotapes produce maximal arousal is also true for heterosexuals (e.g., Freund, Langevin, & Zajac, 1974; McConaghy, 1974; Sandford, 1974) and exhibitionists (Kolarsky

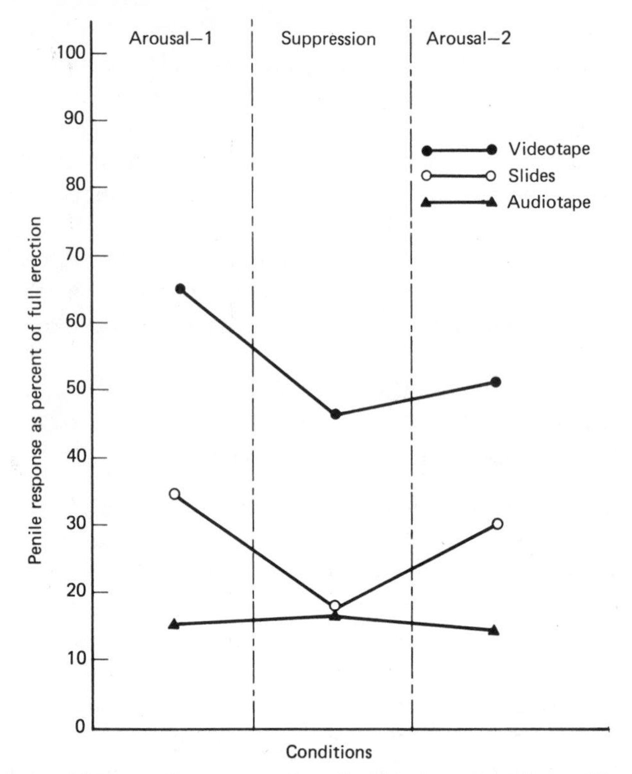

Figure 13–4. Mean penile response for all subjects under all conditions as a percentage of full erection. [From G. G. Abel, D. H. Barlow, E. B. Blanchard, and M. Mavissakalian, Measurement of sexual arousal in male homosexuals: The effects of instructions and stimulus modality. *Archives of Sexual Behavior,* 1975, *4,* 623–629. Copyright (1975) by Plenum Publishing Corp. Reproduced by permission.]

& Madlafousek, 1972). However, for more idiosyncratic patterns of arousal, or patterns that are more difficult to represent on film, such as pedophilia, audiotapes would seem the preferred method (Abel et al., 1975). Movies, audiotapes, and fantasies have also been used with success to occasion sexual arousal in females (e.g., Hoon, Wincze, & Hoon, in press; Heiman, Note 5), but no comparison of these modalities has been reported.

Yet another question concerns the structure of heterosexual arousal. In behavioral assessment there are often criterion behaviors decided on by the patient and the therapist that then become the goal of behavioral intervention. It is difficult to determine the criterion behaviors, however, if one is not aware of the population norms for a given set of behaviors. In assessment of sexual arousal it was assumed for a period that an explicit film depicting heterosexual intercourse, which elicited arousal in heterosexuals, would not elicit arousal in people with other patterns of arousal. This proved not to be true. For instance, homosexuals look at this complex stimuli, focus on the male in the scene, and become quite aroused. Transexuals look at the same stimuli and become aroused for quite a different reason; they identify with the female in the scene and fantasize that they are making love to the male. Thus it is important in assessment to develop content that discriminates one group from another so as to provide meaningful and valid assessment of changes during any intervention.

To determine the stimulus content that discriminates heterosexuals from people with other patterns of arousal, six volunteer exclusive heterosexuals and six volunteer exclusive homosexuals were shown four videotapes with different content in the study by Mavissakalian et al. (1975). One videotape depicted a nude woman assuming various sexual postures. A second depicted a lesbian couple engaged in lovemaking. A third depicted a heterosexual couple engaged in sexual intercourse. The fourth depicted a male homosexual couple engaged in lovemaking. Over the course of two sessions, each subject saw examples of each content area four times, for a total of sixteen video clips that were counterbalanced for content. Penile circumference changes were measured along with subjective reports of arousal and reports on a pleasantness-unpleasantness continuum for each film clip. The data are presented in Table 13–1.

It is clear from these data, which are presented in terms of average penile circumference change based on percentage of full erection as well as average rate of arousal and on a zero to 100 scale, that the heterosexual film clip did not discriminate between homosexual and heterosexual subjects. Even the single girl did not discriminate these groups although there was a trend in that direction. The two film clips that clearly discriminated the two groups were the lesbian couple and the male homosexual couple. Heterosexuals responded with significantly more arousal to the lesbian couple than did homosexuals, and the reverse was true for the homosexual film clip. These data indicate that arousal to lesbian films should be the criterion when one is attempting to instigate heterosexual arousal.

Sandford (1974) has also analyzed the structure of heterosexual arousal. He measured erection responses to films of women engaging in various sexually oriented behaviors as well as to films of couples engaging in sexual behaviors. A woman alone, either stripping or naked, produced less arousal than depictions of intercourse in various positions. Geer (in press) has begun a major research project whose purpose is to determine culturally prescribed modal patterns of sexual arousal, based on Gagnon's social scripting theory of sexuality (Gagnon & Simon, 1973). If

Table 13–1. Mean values of percentage of full erection, percentage of subjective arousal, and subjective ratings of pleasantness in six homosexuals and six heterosexual males under four erotic stimulus conditions. [From M. Mavissakalian, E. B. Blanchard, G. G. Abel, and D. H. Barlow, Reponses to complex erotic stimuli in homosexual and heterosexual males. *British Journal of Psychiatry*, 1975, *126*, 252–257. Copyright (1975) by Headly Brothers, LTD. Reproduced by permission.]

Group	Erotic stimuli: Single girl	Lesbian	Heterosexual couple	Homosexual couple
	x̄ Per cent full penile erection			
Heterosexual	42·83 a[1]	60·17 a	51·00 a	18·17 b
Homosexual	22·33 a	28·50 a	44·67 b	54·67 b
Level of significance between group comparison	·10	·05	n.s.	·01
	x̄ Per cent subjective arousal			
Heterosexual	57·67 a	68·67 a	68·17 a	10·33 b
Homosexual	30·33 a	33·67 a	72·33 b	78·17 b
Level of significance of between group comparison	·10	·05	n.s.	·001
	x̄ Subjective rating of pleasantness			
Heterosexual	1·92 a	2·00 a	1·96 a	−1·33 b
Homosexual	0·25 a	0·54 a	2·47 b	2·46 b
Level of significance of between group comparison	·05	·05	n.s.	·001

Note: Within any row, cell means that do not share subscripts are different at least the ·05 level.

these investigators can determine a sequence of sexual behavior to which arousal increased in a linear fashion, these patterns will then become "criterion" patterns for use in individual assessment. Preliminary efforts with audiotapes indicate that this is feasible and, furthermore, that male and female sexual arousal correlate highly to an audiotaped sequence of sexually related events or behaviors.

In one of the more sophisticated and detailed investigations on the structure of sexual arousal, Freund, McKnight, Langevin, and Cibiri (1972) investigated sexual arousal patterns of adult heterosexual males along several continuua. Stimulus slides and moving pictures of males and females of various ages, some as young as six to eight years old, were shown to 40 adult males. In addition, different parts of the anatomy in each of the various age groups were selected to determine the specificity of sexual arousal. The results indicated that heterosexual adults respond not only to adult women but also to girls as young as eight years old, with the pubic and chest areas being the most erotic. Freund et al. (1972) conclude that pedophiliac arousal patterns may be only quantitatively rather than qualitatively different from normal heterosexual arousal patterns.

One valid method of investigating sexual arousal patterns therefore, is to show erotic material in various stimulus modalities for brief periods to large groups of people. Average responses are calculated to determine modal response patterns. A second equally valid approach uses variations of withdrawal designs in single-case methodology (Barlow & Hersen, 1973; Hersen & Barlow, 1976). In this approach sexual arousal is measured repeatedly as erotic stimuli in various modalities are introduced and withdrawn. This method is illustrated by procedures used in the assessment of a foot fetish described earlier (pp. 466–468) (Abel et al., 1975). This method is also illustrated in some interesting recent attempts to assess the sexual arousal of rapists (Abel, Barlow, Blanchard, & Mavissakalian, Note 6; Abel, Blanchard, Barlow, & Flanagan, Note 7). The use of the repeated presentation of erotic stimuli to assess changes during treatment for sexual arousal patterns has been in use for some time (Barlow & Agras, 1973). These assessment methods share the strengths and weaknesses of single-case versus group-comparison designs used in more general experimental inquiry (Hersen & Barlow, 1976).

The Relation of Cognitive Factors to Sexual Arousal

In 1971 Zuckerman, in a presentation at the American Psychological Association, posed the question, "Does the penis lie?" His conclusion was, yes, the penis can lie if the mind distracts or deludes its owner. Zuckerman's paper was a statement on the relation of cognitive activity to patterns of sexual arousal. This aspect of the physiological assessment of sexual arousal patterns, is one that most sex researchers would like to ignore. The fact is that subjects can suppress erections during periods of sexual arousal. Geer (Note 8) has confirmed Zuckerman's supposition that "distraction" may lead to suppression. In a clever experiment Geer demonstrated through the use of a dichotic listening paradigm that erotic descriptions presented in one ear of the subject were highly arousing but produced erections only when a cognitive task presented in the other ear, to which the subject was required to attend, was not complex. As the cognitive task became more complex, erections diminished.

In analogue laboratory experiments using heterosexual volunteers Laws and Rubin (1969) and Henson and Rubin (1971) investigated subjects' ability to suppress erections while watching erotic films. Even while subjects were describing the particular film they were viewing, they could suppress their erections if instructed to do so. Abel et al. (Note 3) demonstrated that a group of subjects with homosexual arousal patterns could also suppress erections. The mechanism by which subjects can suppress erections is presumably the distraction or shift in attention required in the Geer (Note 8) paradigm. However, the ability of subjects in the Henson and Rubin (1971) experiment to suppress erections while watching and verbalizing the content of the film, suggests that further experimental analysis is necessary to isolate the factors involved. These experiments do illustrate, however, the importance of cognitive activity in patterns of sexual arousal and sexual behavior.

The implication of this work is that assessment of arousal patterns may have little relation to the measurement of arousal or sexual behavior beyond the limitations to external validity. Using clinical populations, Freund examined this issue by asking both homosexuals and heterosexuals to attempt to hide their arousal patterns and fake alternative arousal patterns (Freund, 1961, 1963). Only a few subjects were actually able to fake their arousal patterns, using Freund's sensitive assessment of volume. Under slightly different conditions, only five out of 42 heterosexuals and six out of 24 homosexuals were successful at faking their arousal patterns. In a later study (Freund, 1967) only one out of 27 pedophiliacs was able to represent himself as exclusively heterosexual for adult women. Although several more were able to fake a heterosexual arousal pattern, only one was able to hide his pedophiliac pattern of arousal completely. In line with these more encouraging findings, it should be noted that subjects in the Henson and Rubin (1971) study still averaged measurable arousal even under instructions to suppress arousal. Similarly, homosexual subjects in the Abel et al. (Note 3) study did not suppress below 20 percent of a full erection on the average. This is certainly enough for adequate assessment, particularly if one is using the more sensitive volumetric devices. Whether one would attempt to assess patterns of arousal against the subject's wishes is, of course, an ethical issues.

Nevertheless, the fact is that subjects or patients can suppress sexual arousal, and this fact must be taken into consideration during any assessment of patterns of sexual arousal. To facilitate arousal and circumvent suppression for whatever reasons, one should use the strongest erotic stimuli possible and arrange the laboratory situation to facilitate attention to the erotic stimulus. These studies illustrate the importance of cognitive activity and demonstrate again the importance of collecting attitudinal and self-report measures in a comprehensive assessment of sexual arousal behavior. The next section reviews and discusses the variety of assessment techniques and procedures subsumed under the category of self-report.

Assessment of Sexual Arousal Behavior by Self-Report

The preceding section described procedures for the physiological assessment of sexual arousal. With the few exceptions cited, there has been no important work on the development of direct behavioral observations of sexual arousal or behavior. However, as one might expect, the third response system, self-report, has undergone considerable development because it was the only method available to sex researchers for several years.

We noted earlier that self-report measures of sexual arousal and behavior can be broken down into several distinct entities. Unfortunately, there is little agreement in the field of psychological assessment on the nature or content of these entities. Following the categories of Whalen (1966), Bancroft (1974) mentions at least four categories: (1) sexual preferences and other sexual attitudes; (2) sexual gratification (i.e., the mutuality and intensity of sexual pleasure); (3) sexual arousability (i.e., the capacity to respond to sexual stimulation with increased sexual arousal); and (4) sexual activity, fantasized or real. Quinn, Graham, Harbison, and McAllister (1975) suggest three categories: (1) sexual orientation that attempts to describe the direction of preference toward male or female sexual objects; (2) sexual interest, describing the intensity of attraction toward either object; and (3) sexual evaluation, describing the level of esteem placed on any sexual behavior or interest.

We recognize that any such categories are arbitrary; those given above are described simply as alternatives for the reader. For the purposes of this chapter, however, three categories will be used: (1) self-reports of sexual experience or behavior records; (2) self-reports of sexual arousal; (3) self-reports of sexual attitudes. In the latter category, one may evaluate various aspects of sexual experience or arousal. Techniques used in each of these categories are most usually paper-and-pencil assessments in the form of a brief "test" or a behavior record sheet to be filled in daily.

The most important assessment procedure used to collect self-report data on sexual behavior is not a paper-and-pencil test and runs across all three categories. It is the interview to assess sexual functioning, outlines for which have been suggested by many sex researchers. Masters and Johnson (1970) outline specific questions to be asked during an interview and a specific sequence for asking the questions. They note that the tone of the interview, however, should be left to the clinical judgment of the therapist. The structured interview sets the occasion for more objective means of assessing sexual behavior with the introduction of questions that can be asked repeatedly as therapy progresses. Since so many clinicians continue to rely on the interview to assess progress, developments in this area must be taken seriously. Birk, Huddleston, Miller, and Cohler (1971) and Bancroft (1970, 1974) also discuss the interview as a means of assessing sexual behavior. In addition, numerous case history outlines have been constructed and are in common use in sex clinics around the country.

One of the best discussions of sex interviewing occurs in a recent book by Caird and Wincze (in press). Although the book is directed primarily toward sexual dysfunction rather than sexual deviation or deviation of gender role, the interview techniques described would be similar. Caird and Wincze discuss interviewing the male and interviewing the female in separate chapters and touch on such issues as the behavior of the therapist in the interview, the type of language a therapist should use (i.e., clinical language or "street" language), and the effect of the sex of the interviewer on the patient. The necessity to be accepting and at ease with sexual material as well as the ability to use both clinical and street langauge greatly enhances the quality and quantity of data one may gather from these interviews, according to Caird and Wincze. Sample interviews provided in their book are useful to the beginning interviewer.

Self-Report of Sexual Experiences and Behavior Records

Podell and Perkins (1957) constructed a scale of 15 heterosexual activities ranging from "embrace" to "oral contact with female genitalia." Their hypothesis that subjects would not experience behaviors higher on the scale until they had first experienced lower items was confirmed by a sample of 100 male college students. Similar scales were conducted by Brady and Levitt (1965), Zuckerman (1973), and Bentler (1968a, 1968b). Bentler's scales, constructed for both males and females, were subjected to a sophisticated statistical analysis that demonstrated internal consistency. A cross-validation sample supported the generality of the scale. Essentially all these scales attempt to represent a normal progression of sexual experience. Treatment of those patients who are deficient in sexual behavior should bring about a change in the score derived from such a scale. The data on self-report response modes are similar to those Geer and his associates are attempting to develop in the physiological response mode (Geer, in press). These measures can be valuable for gathering information on changes in sexual experience, but they are rather insensitive to the range and variety of sexual experience and are not entirely suited to repeated use over the course of treatment. LoPiccolo and Steger (1974) have developed a similar scale for the assessment of sexual dysfunction in heterosexual couples. However, LoPiccolo and Steger add an evaluative component to their questionnaire so that patients will rate the various behavioral items on a continuum of pleasantness or unpleasantness. Thus this inventory is also a device for assessing sexual attitudes under the categorization used in this chapter.

In our own research (i.e., Herman, Barlow, & Agras, 1974) patients keep detailed behavior records of several aspects of their sexual functioning. Simple forms are constructed on which the patient can record all instances of sexual experience, all instances of masturbation and the fantasies accompanying masturbation, and all sexual fantasies occurring independently of sexual behavior or masturbation. These records are constructed so that they are convenient to carry on one's person and are coded to the patient's usual sexual experience. In most instances the patient must simply make a mark in the appropriate column. Since these records are individualized, the psychometric qualities of this type of record keeping cannot be determined. However, the purpose is not to compare the records with other patients' records but to examine changes over time in a given patient.

Self-Report Measures of Sexual Arousal

Included in self-reports of sexual arousal are questionnaries that attempt to assess patterns of sexual arousal, often called sexual orientation or sexual interest. One of the best known methods of measuring patterns of sexual arousal is the sexual orientation method devised by Feldman, MacCulloch, Mellor, and Pinschoff (1966). This scale was designed to measure changes in homosexual and heterosexual arousal patterns during treatment of males. The method has since prompted a fair amount of research on its psychometric qualities. Feldman and MacCulloch (1971) stated that the scale was internally consistent and that test/retest reliability was satisfactory. One difficulty with this scale was an early inclination by the authors to arbitrarily assign the label of "improved" or "cured" to a patient after a small amount of change on the scale. Although the scale does have end points in exclusive heterosexuality or exclusive homosexuality (within the limitation of self-report of arousal patterns) change within those boundaries is relative. Another difficulty is that the method is somewhat hard to score. Nevertheless, this instrument is used in our laboratories and is a helpful addition to our overall assessment program. Sambrooks and MacCulloch (1974) describe its use in a clinical setting in some detail. The Belfast group (Harbison, Graham, Quinn, McAllister, & Woodward, 1974) have modified the sexual orientation somewhat to include scales indicating anxiety as well as interest in different aspects of sexual behavior. The revised versions have also been subjected to the usual psychometric procedures.

More recently, Hoon, Hoon, and Wincze (1976) have developed an inventory to measure female sexual arousal that is called the SAI (Sexual Arousal Inventory). The inventory consists of 28 items describing erotic experiences which a respondent rates along a seven-point Likert-like scale of arousal, and it is as much an attitudinal scale as a method of reporting arousal. The advantage of this scale, according to its originators, is that it is easy to administer and score, has had good test/retest reliability, and may be used for single, married, and lesbian women. Concurrent and discriminate validity have also been established. At present, this seems to be the only scale applicable to single women.

Self-Report of Sexual Attitudes

The LoPiccolo and Steger (1974) scale and the Hoon, Hoon, and Wincze (1976) inventory both qualify as attitudinal measures of sexual behavior in the categorization adopted for this chapter, since they share an evaluative component. The Hoon, Hoon, and Wincze inventory is used exclusively with women, whereas the LoPiccolo and Steger is applicable only to heterosexual couples. Marks and Sartorius (1968) have published a sexual attitude scale based on the semantic differential technique. This scale has been used primarily with sexual deviates and contains both sexual and nonsexual concepts that are rated on 13 bipolar scales. Marks and Sartorius (1968) report that the sexual concepts are useful for assessing changes in the evaluation of deviant sexual attitudes, and they give examples of its use with transvestites and fetishists.

Other scales have been developed to evaluate anxiety associated with various sexual behaviors exclusively rather than as part of a larger scale. Although scales such as this do not assess sexual behavior directly, they may be useful in a comprehensive assessment. A good example is a scale constructed by Obler (1973).

In our own laboratories a card sort method has been devised that, like the behavior record used by Herman et al. (1974), is highly individualized and therefore has not been subjected to psychometric evaluation. In the card sort method (e.g., Barlow, Leitenberg, & Agras, 1969; Barlow, Reynolds, & Agras, 1973) a series of sexual "scenes" is constructed. These scenes usually reflect the patient's experience, real or fantasized, with the sexual objects or situations in question. For example, in one experiment (Barlow et al., 1969) the patient was a 25-year-old, married pedophiliac. One scene in his card sort read, "You are alone in a room with a very sexy looking 10-year-old girl with long blond hair." For the transsexual in the Barlow, Reynolds, and Agras (1973) article where propensity toward mistaken gender identity was the goal of assessment, one scene card read, "I want to have female genitals." As many scenes as are relevant may be constructed and typed on three-by-five-inch cards. A similar set of scenes reflecting heterosexual arousal, masculine gender identity, or any other concept one wishes to assess can also be constructed. Every day, or as often as desired, the patient takes the cards and sorts them into five envelopes marked 0 to 4. He is instructed, "The numbers on these envelopes represent the amount of sexual arousal you experience" (in the case of assessment of patterns of sexual arousal) or "how much you desire this situation or set of circumstances at this time" (in the case of gender identity concepts). Zero equals none at all, one equals a little, two a fair amount, three much, and four very much. If he then puts one card in the No. 4 envelope and one in No. 3, his score to that point would be 7, and so on. Caird and Wincze (in press) have adopted this procedure for individual assessment of sexual dysfunction. The obvious advantage of this procedure is its flexibility in that one can assess the strength of idiosyncratic attitudes concerning sexual concepts over time.

Thus far this chapter has reviewed the assessment of sexual arousal and behavior in both contrived and natural situations in all three response modalities—the verbal, the motoric, and the physiological. The length of the first part of this chapter reflects the amount of data collected in this area, particularly in recent years. Figure 13–3 shows two more major components of sexual behavior, heterosocial skills and deviations in gender role. The potential exists for assessing each of these components in all three response modalities in both contrived and natural situations, but the actual development of procedures to assess them has lagged behind the assessment of sexual arousal behavior.

HETEROSOCIAL SKILLS

That heterosocial skills are a major component of sexual behavior is not a new idea. Basing their procedures on the idea that sexual deviation, particularly homosexuality, is a result of fear or avoidance of the opposite sex (e.g., Rado, 1949), therapists of many persuasions have encouraged and taught appropriate social behaviors in a heterosexual context. Many have reported this strategy to be successful (Ellis, 1956; Ovesey, Gaylin, & Hendin, 1953; Stevenson & Wolpe, 1960). Other therapists and clinical researchers working with procedures to change patterns of sexual arousal have noted the insufficiency of such efforts alone in establishing functional heterosexual behavior in many cases. Even if successful sexual behavior is established, many patients are still unable to meet, date, or successfully relate to persons of the opposite sex (Barlow, 1972, 1974). Many of the therapists working on this problem have concluded that deficits in social skills in heterosexual situations are responsible for these failures and that there is a necessity of assessing heterosocial skills. In a general review of the literature concerned with training in social skills, Hersen and Eisler (in press) point out that many forms of treatment have implicitly acknowledged the existence of poor interpersonal adjustment but have focused their treatment efforts for the most part on relatively unstructured attempts to improve socializing through therapeutic milieus or group therapy. The behavioral approach to treatment, as applied to training in social skill, has emphasized a more precise analysis of the verbal and nonverbal components of adequate social skills in treatment, but this emphasis requires a more precise assessment of behaviors comprising social skills than was heretofore available. Moreover, Eisler, Hersen, Miller, and Blanchard (1975) have noted that effective and necessary social skills may differ depending on the situation or circumstance. Thus skills necessary for heterosocial situations may differ from social skills necessary in work-related situations.

There are at least three facets of heterosocial skills: (1) a set of social behaviors is necessary to initiate relationships with the opposite sex; (2) a chain of social and interpersonal behaviors precedes sexual behavior; (3) the maintenance of heterosocial relationships may require behaviors different from the first two facets.

The assessment of heterosocial behavior has not progressed far. Current assessment procedures are directed at only the first step in the chain of heterosocial behavior—initiating a relationship. Almost all these assessment procedures have been developed in contrived situations, usually involving some sort of role playing. The emphasis thus far has been on direct behavioral assessment in a contrived situation although self-report and, in one instance, physiological assessment of heterosocial skills have also occurred. Behavioral assessment in the natural environment has occurred infrequently although one interesting example will be cited later. Self-report or behavior records similar to those used in assessing sexual arousal behavior in the natural environment have also been used to assess social skills. Physiological assessment has not occurred in the natural environment.

To date the bulk of the work on development of assessment procedures for heterosocial skills has come from analogue studies on college students with dating problems, rather than patients. Borkovec, Stone, O'Brien, and Kaloupek (1974) have suggested that deficits in dating skill are an appropriate vehicle for clinical analogue research. However, in attempting to determine behaviors that differentiate people with adequate social skills from those with inadequate skills, most studies have been unable to identify specific behaviors. These studies (e.g., Arkowitz, Lichtenstein, McGovern, & Hines, 1975; Borkovec et al., 1974; Glasgow & Arkowitz, 1975) have found that overall ratings of heterosocial skills discriminate high-frequency daters from low-frequency daters, but the identification of specific behaviors has proved elusive. In these and other studies (e.g., McDonald, Lindquist, Kramer, McGrath, & Rhyne, 1975; Rehm & Marston, 1968) the only valid assessment of heterosocial skills seemed to be trained raters' judgment of overall social skills while observing interactions in contrived situations.

In these contrived situations self-reports of social skills and other aspects of heterosocial functioning such as "confidence" were often collected in addition to direct behavioral observation (e.g., Glasgow & Arkowitz, 1975). Twentyman and McFall (1975) carried this one step farther and had male subjects record frequency and duration of contacts with women outside the contrived situation in the natural environment. They also demonstrated that physiological assessments of anxiety in social situations, in this case simple pulse rate, showed improvement after training in social skills, indicating that assessment of this response modality may be useful. Most of this research investigated the social behavior of male subjects only, although Glasgow and Arkowitz (1975) have recently begun investigating heterosocial behavior in females.

In a clinical setting Barlow, Abel, Blanchard, Bristow, and Young (in press) have constructed a behavioral checklist that differentiates competent heterosocial males from socially incompetent male patients with sexual problems. To develop this scale, high school and college males judged socially attractive by a panel of popular females in their schools were videotaped interacting with female research assistants. Ten patients with sexually deviant behaviors who reported and were judged to be heterosocially inadequate were also videotaped interacting with a female. Behaviors in three categories—form of conversation, affect, and voice—significantly discriminated the adequate from the inadequate males. *Voice* quality was rated on loudness, pitch, and inflection whereas *affect* was rated on the basis of facial expression, eye contact, and laughter. Judgment of the appropriate *form* of conversation was based on whether the male initiated conversation, responded to the females' vocalization, prevented uncomfortably long silences in the conversation, and showed interest in his partner. Responses as defined in the behavior checklist could be reliably scored by trained raters. For purposes of the original validation, patients entered a room and were instructed to engage the female confederate in conversation with the ultimate purpose of asking for a date. The interaction lasted approximately four to five minutes and was divided into 30-second blocks. If any inappropriate behavior occurred within a 30-second block, the block was rated inappropriate. For further information on the use of this behavioral checklist, see Barlow et al. (in press).

Like other investigations using nonpatient populations, this scale was constructed around a contrived situation and is appropriate for males only. Direct behavioral assessment in the natural environment, using this checklist should present no technical problems, since the transference of the raters into the natural environment would be the only change required. Such an assessment in the natural environment would be necessary only if the initiation of heterosocial relationships occurred in a public setting. By posing as a bar patron, Maletzky (Note 9) surreptitiously observed homosexuals initiating relationships in a gay bar. In this case the observations were used as an assessment of the effectiveness of treatment. This type of assessment presents obvious ethical problems, however, which is most likely why it has been utilized infrequently. A proper assessment can only be done surreptitiously, since the presence of known raters would make the measures extremely obtrusive. Current-day ethical standards in either research or clinical settings preclude this type of observation without the informed consent of the patient. Hersen and Eisler (1976) have suggested that it might be possible to circumvent this ethical barrier by obtaining the subjects' permission to make these types of observation without telling them the specific time. Investigations along these lines are sorely needed, if only to determine the validity of assessment in contrived situations.

Similarly, assessment procedures to investigate social behavior related to the initiation of genital contact are lacking despite the frequent clinical observation of deficits in this area. Even married couples often report "shyness," that is, deficits in the types of behaviors necessary to initiate sexual relationships.

DEVIATION IN GENDER ROLE

The final component of sexual behavior is confused gender identity or deviation in gender role, which refers to some degree of incongruence between one's biological and genetic sex and the behavior accompanying that sex as defined by a given culture.

Society is more familiar with the concepts of masculinity and femininity than with the other aspects of sexual behavior mentioned in this chapter, and yet these concepts are among the most difficult to measure or assess. The familiarity and pervasiveness of maleness and femaleness ensured an early interest in these concepts from the psychological point of view. Still, the ease with which people identify and discuss male and female behavior may be responsible for the lack of development of precise definitions. The growth of interest in gender identity and gender role behavior is owing to two recent developments. The phenomenon of transsexualism, in which a biologically and genetically normal person thinks, feels, and behaves as if he or she were a member of the opposite sex and often requests sex reassignment surgery, has rearoused interest in the development of gender identity. Second, the emergence of women's role in our society as a political issue has aroused interest in sex role stereotypes that can be broken down into gender-specific behaviors and attitudes, or the more common terms, "masculinity" and "femininity."

The discovery that transsexualism is a clinical entity and not merely a defense mechanism (Green & Money, 1969) highlighted gender role behavior and raised some intriguing questions on the relation of gender role behavior to sexual problems, particularly sexual deviations. Why are gender role deviations associated with some sexual arousal patterns, such as homosexuality and transvestism, and not with others? Why are some homosexuals effeminate and others not? Is femininity in females the same as femininity in males? Is femininity in males related to pedophilia (e.g., Freund, Langevin, Laws, & Serber, 1974)? Does society tolerate masculine women more than feminine men? These and other questions require precise assessments of the degree of gender role deviations.

The discovery that gender role deviation is related to outcome in the treatment of some sexual deviations has aroused even more interest. Bieber, Bieber, Dain, Dince, Drellich, Grand, Grundlach, Kremer, Wilbur, and Bieber (1963), in reporting that up to 50 percent of certain subgroups of homosexuals achieved some heterosexual orientation after psychoanalysis, observed that no subjects responded positively to psychoanalysis if there was evidence of gender role deviation in their background. Marks, Gelder, and Bancroft (1970) reported encouraging success in treating a group of transvestites who had no gender role deviations, but among those transvestites who had some degree of gender role deviation, there was no recovery. These studies, from quite different approaches, suggest the importance of gender role deviations as a factor in sexual deviations.

Early attempts to measure gender identity are of some historical interest. They consisted mostly of questionnaires requiring the subject to state interests or preferred activities. One of the best known tests was the M–F test of Terman and Miles (1936), which consisted of a number of different questions and exercises, including inkblot associations. Variations on this test have included the well-known scale on the MMPI and the femininity scale of the California Psychological Inventory (Gough, 1952). Scales of this type have proved useless in assessing gender identity or gender role deviations. Major problems with these scales were their vagueness and the cultural/temporal relativity of the questions. For instance, on the California Personality Inventory scale a question, "I would like to be a soldier" must be answered in the affirmative to score as masculine.

Some investigators (e.g., Freund et al., 1974) have suggested that the assessment of gender role deviations such as femininity in males requires a different instrument from the usual M–F test since some items would be unique to feminine males. Thus extremely effeminate males or transexuals, rather than women, should be the referrent group. Although the scale constructed by Freund et al. (1974) (described in the next section) is very useful, the similarities and differences (other than the obvious ones) between effeminate males and females or masculine females and males have yet to be identified. The development of reliable and valid measuring instruments is required. To date, instruments to assess gender role have been developed in both the self-report and behavioral response systems. The physiological response system does not seem relevant to this component of sexual behavior. However, there is recent evidence of the possible biochemical nature of gender role deviation. This evidence is important and requires assessment (e.g., Yalom, Green, & Fisk, 1973). Unlike other components, behavioral measures of gender role can occur in the natural environment as well as in contrived situations.

Self-Report Measures

One of the more interesting developments in recent years in the assessment of gender identity in males is a questionnaire developed by Freund, Nagler, Langevin, Zajac, and Steiner (1974). This scale consists of 19 items, of which 12 are applicable to all males and an additional seven apply only to homosexual or transsexual males. A sample of the items follows:

> Between the ages of 6 and 12, did you
> (a) prefer boys' games and toys (soldiers, football, etc.)
> (b) prefer girls' games and toys (dolls, cooking, sewing, etc.)
> (c) like or dislike both about equally
>
> Between the ages of 13 and 16, did you wish you had been born a girl instead of a boy

(a) often
(b) occasionally
(c) never

Since the age of 17, have you put on womens' underwear or clothing
(a) once a month or more, for at least a year
(b) (less often, but) several times a year for at least a year
(c) very seldom did this since age 17
(d) never did this since age 17

Norms are provided to illustrate the scores of different groups on the masculinity-femininity continuum. The scale is psychometrically satisfactory and has already been used in several research reports (e.g., Freund, Langevin, Laws, & Serber, 1974; Freund, Langevin, Zajac, Steiner, & Zajac, 1974). For instance, Freund, Langevin, Laws, & Serber (1974) found that the degree of femininity in ephebophilic, androphilic, homosexual, and heterosexual pedophiliac groups were approximately equal and all greater than in a normal group of males. The findings that heterosexual pedophiliacs were more feminine than heterosexuals is particularly interesting. This scale is widely used in our laboratories.

A body-image scale for evaluating transsexuals has been reported by Lindgren and Pauly (1975). This scale measures a person's satisfaction with the physical appearance of his different body parts. Transsexuals are typically very dissatisfied with their actual physical appearance, particularly in the genital area, and thus an assessment of this factor is useful whether one is treating transsexuals by surgical means or by modifying gender role behaviors (Barlow, Reynolds, & Agras, 1973). However, the scale has not as yet been widely used. In our laboratory the card sort measure, described in the section above on self-report of sexual arousal, is also used to assess transsexual attitudes.

A second recent approach to measure deviation in gender role grows out of the developing interest in sex-role stereotypes and attempts to measure a person's affinity for one sex role or the other in nonpatient populations. Perhaps the best example of this type of questionnaire is a sex role inventory developed by Bem (1974). Her inventory treats masculinity and feminity as two independent dimensions so that it is possible to characterize a person as either masculine, feminine, or androgynous, which represents the positive aspects of both sex roles. Typical masculine personality items the subject may choose in this sex role inventory are "aggressive" and "ambitious." Typical feminine items are "affectionate" and "cheerful." This scale is satisfactory on most psychometric dimensions, but it was not designed to assess the degree of gender role deviations. However, it has been applied in our laboratories to transsexuals and other patients with gender role deviations and provides interesting information on sex role preference.

Behavioral Measures

Assessment of gender-specific behavior presents fewer technical problems than other sexual behavior. Gender-specific behaviors tend to occur in any setting where behavior is occurring at all, including sitting, standing, or walking. Two distinct methods for developing behavioral checklists for masculine and feminine behavior are emerging, one for children and the other for adults. For children, the typical checklist for gender role behavior is used in a contrived situation, usually a room set up with specific types of toys or other play activities previously determined to be feminine or masculine. This type of assessment has been in use for some time, beginning with Terman and Miles (1936), and has occasionally been updated and revalidated by other investigators (e.g., Rosenberg & Sutton-Smith, 1959, 1964). In recent years Green, Fuller, Rutley, and Hendler (1972) have conducted the most sophisticated analysis of toy preference and have reported high discriminant validity when testing masculine and feminine boys. Green and others (e.g., Rekers & Lovaas, 1974) are using this measure in a variety of studies to assess the effects of treating gender role deviations in effeminate boys.

The ready availability of observers, usually parents or teachers, should ensure an easy extension of assessment of gender role behavior into the natural environment. Such assessment will be facilitated by the development of a variety of behavior checkists that go beyond play activities in children. For instance, Hanaway (Note 10) isolated a specific behavior the way in which one carries books and discovered that it accurately discriminated high school and college students. He then followed this behavior down through progressively younger age groups and found that the behavior discriminated males and females very well through the fourth grade but broke down in the third grade and below. These data indicate that assessments of 9- and 10-year-old children for gender-specific behavior could include the book-carrying task.

Attempts to develop behavior checklists or rating scales of gender-specific behavior in adults are limited, despite the fact that "clinical impressions" are in abundance. Some work in identifying gender-specific behaviors in adults has begun recently. This work has emerged from two sources although the goals of pinpointing sex differences or gender-specific behaviors are similar. The first area of work originated in the investigations of Birdwhistell (1970) and Argyle (1969). A good example of this line of research is a study reported by Weitz (Note 11). As a social psychologist, Weitz approaches the problem of sex role stereotypes and normal sex role development in the manner of Bem (1974). For example, Weitz noted, while studying nonverbal behavior associated with interactions, that women elicit more nonverbal warmth than men and that women in general are more responsive and attentive to the other interactant. Weitz's working assumption is that the microprocesses of interaction reveal the macrostructure of sex roles. Although this type of investigation is not intended to have any direct relevance on the assessment or treatment of sexual problems, alterations of deviations in gender role must eventually consider the full full range of range of gender-specific behavior, including social behavior, to assess adequately deviation in gender role.

Approaching the assessment of gender-specific behaviors from the viewpoint of sexual problems, Schatzberg, Westfall, Blumetti, and Birk (1975) devised a quantitative rating of effeminacy for use with males. Noting that deviations in gender role were an important component of many sexual deviations, they constructed a comprehensive list of 67 items scored on a simple yes/no basis. The items were assumed to break down effeminate behavior in males into discrete behavioral fragments so that the presence or absence of the behavior could be easily scored. The checklist was then tested on a nonpatient population of heterosexual and homosexual males. Items in the area of speech (Does he speak with soft tones?), gait (Does he move sinuously?), mouth movements (Does he purse his lips when he speaks?), and the like were examples of items on the checklist. Seventeen of the 67 items were not scored for any of the 32 subjects in the initial study. Subjects were interviewed during a 15-minute, semistructured interview. After the interview two raters completed the scale. Although the correlation of the total scores of the raters was high (0.94), the interrater agreement was low at chance level (total number of items agreed on/total number of items endorsed 0.54). This interrater agreement is not surprising because raters could not score behaviors until after the interview was over. The homosexual group scored somewhat more effeminate with a mean of 7.0 on this scale, which compared to approximately 3.5 for the heterosexual group of males. The fact that one is more likely to find gender role deviations in homosexuals than in heterosexuals suggests that the scale has some discriminate validity, although given the low interrater agreement, the nature of the discriminating factors are not clear. It is probable that an overall impression of femininity was being rated. In addition, the scale seems to have a very small range of effectiveness. Out of 67 items (17 of which were never endorsed for any subject), the authors scored a total of five through nine as being mildly effeminate. Nevertheless, the scale is a breakthrough of sorts in that it is the first of its kind and deserves further investigation. An advantage of this scale is that it need not be administered in the contrived situation of a semistructured interview but can theoretically be administered in any setting, including surreptitious settings in the natural environment. The investigators (Westfall, Schatzberg, Blumetti, & Birk, 1975) tested the scale in a variety of social contexts that occurred in four encounter groups. They found a wide variability in ratings of effeminacy, which they correlated with emotional responses such as anxiety or anger.

For the past several years a checklist of masculine-feminine motoric behavior has been in use in our laboratories, particularly for the assessment of deviations in gender role (e.g., Barlow, Reynolds, & Agras, 1973). This checklist pinpoints gender-specific aspects of sitting, standing, and walking. For instance, males tend to sit with the lower back and buttocks away from the back of a hard-backed chair and cross their legs with the ankle resting on the opposite knee. Females, on the other hand, sit with their lower back and buttocks close to the back of the chair and cross their legs with one knee resting on the other. Interrater agreement is 92.5 percent for walking, 100 percent for sitting, 97.45 percent for standing.

The Barlow et al. (1973) checklist demonstrates that females have a much greater variety of behaviors while sitting, standing, and walking than males, who tend to fall in a very narrow range of characteristically masculine behaviors. However, when transsexual males were assessed, they scored consistently more feminine than our female sample, raising once again the interesting question of the difference (if any) between effeminate males and women. The scale is currently undergoing cross-validation, in preparation for publication.

Like the Schatzberg et al. (1975) scale, the Barlow et al. (1973) behavior checklist is readily adaptable to assessment in the patients natural environment since raters are relatively easily trained and the total observation time of a trained rater is under 30 seconds. Nevertheless, it is limited in that it deals only with gender specific motoric or postural behavior. Behavioral checklists assessing interactional components of sexual behavior, such as the type of scale proposed by Weitz (Note 11), are needed to complement the Barlow et al. checklist. There is also strong evidence from some of our earlier work on the masculine-feminine checklist of motoric behavior that "masculine" behavior is not a unitary concept and varies at least with race. Black and white males, judged "masculine" by their peers, stood and walked somewhat differently. Further specifications of racial differences awaits cross-validation.

CONCLUDING COMMENTS

This chapter has been structured around a new model of sexual behavior first proposed in 1974 (Barlow, 1974). A growing concensus on the importance of the method of behavioral assessment based on the three response systems has further influenced the organization of this chapter. Finally, the recognition that assessment of sexual behavior can occur in both contrived and natural situations has provided the third factor necessary to construct the schema (Figure 13–3) for the assessment of sexual behavior. However, all three components of this grid, the model of sexual behavior, the three response systems, and the contrived versus natural issue, represent advances in thinking that have taken place in the last five years, and the usefulness of assessing sexual behavior along these radically different conceptual lines has yet to be demonstrated. Furthermore, there is no easy or established method of demonstrating their usefulness as there is when one wishes to test a new "treatment" variable that can be subjected to the usual scientific procedure. This model (or paradigm?) would be successful only if a majority of scientists and clinicians working in this area become convinced that this approach opens the door to the development of more effective procedures to relieve human suffering and enhance human functioning.

By examining the degree to which each cell in the grid contains useful assessment procedures, the current, rather primitive state of assessment of sexual behavior becomes apparent. Even the cell representing self-report of sexual arousal in either contrived or natural situations, which did not depend on the development of new technology, is relatively empty of useful procedures. Only in the last few years have reliable and valid techniques for assessing this important area been developed (e.g., Caird & Wincze, in press). Final acceptance of this new way of conceptualizing the assessment of sexual behavior will ultimately depend on filling the cells in the proposed scheme with reliable, valid, and useful assessment procedures.

REFERENCE NOTES

1. Cone, J. D. *What's relevant about reliability and validity for behavioral assessment?* Paper presented at the meeting of the American Psychological Association, Chicago, September, 1975.
2. Forgione, A. G. *The use of mannequins in the behavioral treatment of "child molesters."* Paper presented at the meeting of the Association for Advancement of Behavior Therapy, Chicago, November, 1974.
3. Abel, G. G., Blanchard, E. B., Barlow, D. H., & Becker, J. B. *The objective assessment*

of patterns of sexual arousal in rapists and other sexual aggressives. Paper presented at the meeting of the Association for Advancement of Behavior Therapy, San Francisco, December, 1975.

4. Hoon, P. W., Wincze, J. P., & Hoon, E. F. *Enhancing female sexual arousal: The efficacy of vaginal blood volume biofeedback and erotic fantasy*. Unpublished manuscript.
5. Heiman, J. *Facilitating erotic arousal: Toward sex-positive sex research*. Paper presented at the meeting of the American Psychological Association, New Orleans, September, 1975.
6. Abel, G. G., Barlow, D. H., Blanchard, E. B., & Mavissakalian, M. *The relationship of aggressive cues to the sexual arousal of rapists*. Paper presented at the meeting of the American Psychological Association, New Orleans, September, 1975.
7. Abel, G. G., Blanchard, E. B., Barlow, D. H., & Flanagan, B. *A controlled behavioral treatment of a sadistic rapist*. Paper presented at the meeting of the Association for Advancement of Behavior Therapy, San Francisco, December, 1975.
8. Geer, J. H. *Cognitive factors in sexual arousal—Toward an amalgam of research strategies*. Paper presented at the meeting of the American Psychological Association, New Orleans, September, 1975.
9. Maletzky, B. M. *"Assisted" covert sensitization: A preliminary report*. Unpublished manuscript.
10. Hanaway, T. P. *The development of sexually dimorphic book-carrying behavior*. Unpublished doctoral dissertation, The University of Tennessee, 1974.
11. Weitz, S. *Sex differences in nonverbal communication*. Paper presented at the meeting of the American Sociological Association, San Francisco, August, 1975.

REFERENCES

Abel, G. G., & Blanchard, E. B. The measurement and generation of sexual arousal in male sexual deviates. In M. Hersen, R. M. Eisler, & P. M. Miller (Eds.), *Progress in behavior modification*. Vol. 2. New York: Academic, 1976.

Abel, G. G., Blanchard, E. B., Barlow, D. H., & Mavissakalian, M. Identifying specific erotic cues in sexual deviations by audiotaped descriptions. *Journal of Applied Behavior Analysis*, 1975, **8,** 247–260.

Agras, W. S., Leitenberg, H., & Barlow, D. H. Social reinforcement in the modification of agoraphobia. *Archives in General Psychiatry*, 1968, **19,** 423–427.

Argyle, M. *Social interaction*. London: Methuen, 1969.

Arkowitz, H., Lichtenstein, E., McGovern, K., & Hines, P. The behavioral assessment of social competence in males. *Behavior Therapy*, 1975, **6,** 3–14.

Bancroft, J. A comparative study of aversion and desensitization in the treatment of homosexuality. In L. E. Burns & J. L. Worsley, (Ed.), *Behavior therapy in the 1970s*. Bristol: Wright, 1970.

Bancroft, J. The application of psychophysiological measures to the assessment and modification of sexual behavior. *Behaviour Research and Therapy*, 1971, **9,** 119–130.

Bancroft, K. *Deviant sexual behavior: Modification and assessment*. Oxford: Clarendon Press, 1974.

Bancroft, J., Jones, H., & Pullan, B. A simple transducer for measuring penile erection, with comments on its use in the treatment of sexual disorders. *Behaviour Research and Therapy*, 1966, **4,** 239–241.

Barlow, D. H. Aversive procedures. In W. S. Agras (Ed.) *Behavior modification: Principles and clinical applications.* Boston: Little, Brown, 1972.

Barlow, D. H. The treatment of sexual deviation: Towards a comprehensive behavioral approach. In K. S. Calhoun, H. E. Adams, & K. M. Mitchell (Eds.), *Innovative treatment methods in psychopathology.* New York: John Wiley, 1974.

Barlow, D. H. An overview of behavioral assessment in clinical settings. In J. D. Cone & R. P. Hawkins (Eds.), *Behavioral assessment: New directions in clinical psychology.* New York: Brunner-Mazel, in press.

Barlow, D. H. & Abel, G. G. Sexual deviation. In W. E. Craighead, A. E. Kazdin, & M. J. Mahoney (Eds.), *Behavior modification: Principles, issues, and applications.* Boston: Houghton Mifflin, 1976.

Barlow, D. H., Abel, G. G., Blanchard, E. B., Bristow, A. R., & Young, L. D. A heterosocial skills behavior checklist for males. *Behavior Therapy*, in press.

Barlow, D. H., & Agras, W. S. Fading to increase heterosexual responsiveness in homosexuals. *Journal of Applied Behavior Analysis*, 1973, **6,** 355–367.

Barlow, D. H., Agras, W. S., Leitenberg, H., Callahan, E. J., & Moore, R. C. The contribution of therapeutic instructions to covert sensitization. *Behaviour Research and Therapy*, 1972, **10,** 411–415.

Barlow, D. H., Becker, R., Leitenberg, H., & Agras, W. S. A mechanical strain gauge for recording penile circumference change. *Journal of Applied Behavior Analysis*, 1970, **3,** 73–76.

Barlow, D. H., & Hersen, M. Single case experimental designs: Uses in applied clinical research. *Archives of General Psychiatry*, 1973, **29,** 319–325.

Barlow, D. H., Leitenberg, H., & Agras, W. S. The experimental control of sexual deviation through manipulation of the noxious scene in covert sensitization. *Journal of Abnormal Psychology*, 1969, **74,** 596–601.

Barlow, D. H., Reynolds, E. H., & Agras, W. S. Gender identity change in a transsexual. *Archives of General Psychiatry*, 1973, **28,** 569–579.

Bem, S. L. The measurement of psychological androgyny. *Journal of Consulting and Clinical Psychology*, 1974, **42,** 155–162.

Bentler, P. M. Heterosexual behavior assessment—I. Males. *Behaviour Research and Therapy*, 1968, **6,** 21–25. (a)

Bentler, P. M. Heterosexual behavior assessment—II. Females. *Behaviour Research and Therapy*, 1968, **6,** 27–30. (*b*)

Bergin, A., & Strupp, H. *Changing frontiers in the science of psychotherapy.* Chicago: Aldine-Atherton, 1972.

Bieber, B., Bieber, I., Dain, H. J., Dince, P. R., Drellich, M. G., Grand, H. G., Grundlach, R. H., Kremer, M. W. Wilbur, C. B., & Bieber, T. D. *Homosexuality.* New York; Basic Books, 1963.

Birdwhistell, R. *Kinesics and context.* Philadelphia: University of Pennsylvania Press, 1970.

Birk, L., Huddleston, W., Miller, E., & Cohler, B. Avoidance conditioning for homosexuality. *Archives of General Psychiatry*, 1971, **25,** 314–323.

Borkovec, T. D., Stone, N. M., O'Brien, G. T., & Kaloupek, D. G. Evaluation of a clinically relevant target behavior for analog outcome research. *Behavior Therapy*, 1974, **5,** 503–513.

Brady, J. P., & Levitt, E. E. The scalability of sexual experiences. *Psychological Record*, 1965, **15,** 275–279.

Caird, W., & Wincze, J. *Treatment of sexual dysfunction: A behavioral approach.* New York: Harper & Row, in press.

Eisler, R. M., Hersen, M., Miller, P. M., & Blanchard, E. B. Situational determinants of assertive behavior. *Journal of Consulting and Clinical Psychology*, 1975, **43,** 330–341.

Ellis, A. The effectiveness of psychotherapy with individuals who have severe homosexual problems. *Journal of Consulting Psychology*, 1956, **20,** 58–60.

Feldman, M. P., & MacCulloch, M. J. *Homosexual behavior: Theory and assessment.* Oxford: Pergamon, 1971.

Feldman, M., MacCulloch, M., Mellor, V., & Pinschoff, J. The application of anticipatory avoidance learning to the treatment of homosexuality: III: The sexual orientation method. *Behaviour Research and Therapy*, 1966, **4,** 289–299.

Fisher, C., Gross, J., & Zuch, J. Cycle of penile erection synchronous with dreaming (REM) sleep. *Archives of General Psychiatry*, 1965, **12,** 29–45.

Freund, K. Diagnostika homosexuality u muzu. *Ceskoslovenska Psychiatrie*, 1957, **53,** 382–393.

Freund, K. Laboratory differential diagnosis of homo- and heterosexuality—An experiment with faking. *Review of Czechoslovak Medicine*, 1961, **7,** 20–31.

Freund, K. A laboratory method for diagnosing predominance of homo- or hetero-erotic interest in the male. *Behaviour Research and Therapy*, 1963, **1,** 85–93.

Freund, K. Diagnosing homo- or heterosexuality and erotic age preference by means of a psychophysiological test. *Behaviour Research and Therapy*, 1967, **5,** 209–228.

Freund, K. A note on the use of the phallometric method of measuring mild sexual arousal in the male. *Behavior Therapy*, 1971, **2,** 223–228.

Freund, K., Langevin, R., Cibiri, S., & Zajac, Y. Heterosexual aversion in homosexual males. *British Journal of Psychiatry*, 1973, **122,** 163–169.

Freund, K., Langevin, R., Laws, R., & Serber, M. Femininity and preferred partner age in homosexual and heterosexual males. *British Journal of Psychiatry*, 1974, **125,** 442–446.

Freund, K., Langevin, R., Zajac, Y., Steiner, B., & Zajac, A. The trans-sexual syndrome in homosexual males. *The Journal of Nervous and Mental Disease*, 1974, **158,** 145–153.

Freund, K., McKnight, C. K., Langevin, R., & Cibiri, S. The female child as a surrogate object. *Archives of Sexual Behavior*, 1972, **2,** 119–133.

Freund, K., Nagler, E., Langevin, R., Zajac, A., & Steiner, B. Measuring feminine gender identity in homosexual males. *Archives of Sexual Behavior*, 1974, **3,** 249–261.

Freund, K., Sedlacek, J., & Knob, K. A simple transducer for mechanical plethysmography of the male genital. *Journal of Experimental Analysis of Behavior*, 1965, **8,** 169–170.

Gagnon, J. H., & Simon, W. *The social sources of human sexuality*. Chicago: Aldine, 1973.

Geer, J. H. Sexual functioning: Some data and speculations of psychophysiological assessment. In J. D. Cone & R. P. Hawkins (Eds.), *Behavioral assessment: New directions in clinical psychology*. New York: Brunner-Mazel, in press.

Geer, J., Morokoff, P., & Greenwood, P. Sexual arousal in women: The development of a measurement device for vaginal blood volume. *Archives of Sexual Behavior*, 1974, **3**, 559–564.

Glasgow, R., & Arkowitz, H. The behavioral assessment of male and female social competence in dyadic heterosexual interactions. *Behavior Therapy*, 1975, **4**, 488–499.

Goldfried, M. R., & Sprafkin, J. N. *Behavioral personality assessment*. Morristown, N.J.: General Learning Press, 1974.

Gough, H. G. Identifying psychological femininity. *Educational and Psychological Measurement*, 1952, **12**, 427–439.

Green, R., Fuller, M., Rutley, B. R., & Hendler, J. Playroom toy preferences of fifteen masculine and fifteen feminine boys. *Behavior Therapy*, 1972, **3**, 425–429.

Green, R., & Money, J. *Transsexualism and sex reassignment*. Baltimore, Md.: Johns Hopkins Press, 1969.

Hamrick, N. D. Physiological and verbal responses to erotic visual stimuli in a female population. *Behavioral Engineering*, 1974, **2**, 9–16.

Harbison, J. J., Graham, P. J., Quinn, J. T., McAllister, H., & Woodward, R. A questionnaire measure of sexual interest. *Archives of Sexual Behavior*, 1974, **3**, 357–366.

Henson, D. E., & Rubin, H. B. Voluntary control of eroticism. *Journal of Applied Behavior Analysis*, 1971, **4**, 37–44.

Herman, S. H., Barlow, D. H., & Agras, W. S. An experimental analysis of classical conditioning as a method of increasing heterosexual arousal in homosexuals. *Behavior Therapy*, 1974, **5**, 33–47.

Hersen, M., & Barlow, D. H. *Single case experimental designs: Strategies for studying behavior change*. New York: Pergamon, 1976.

Hersen, M., & Eisler, R. M. Social skills training. In W. E. Craighead, A. E. Kazdin, & M. J. Mahoney (Eds.), *Behavior modification: Principles, issues, and applications:* Boston: Houghton Mifflin, 1976.

Hoon, E. F., Hoon, P. W., & Wincze, J. P. An inventory for the measurement of female sexual arousability: The SAI. *Archives of Sexual Behavior*, 1976, **5**, 291–300.

Hoon, P., Wincze, J., & Hoon, E. Physiological assessment of sexual arousal in women. *Psychophysiology*, 1976, **13**, 196–204.

Hoon, P. W., Wincze, J. P., & Hoon, E. F. A comparison of the physiological responsivity of normal and sexually dysfunctional women during exposure to an erotic stimulus. *Journal of Psychosomatic Medicine*, in press.

Jovanovic, U. J. The recording of physiological evidence of genital arousal in human males and females. *Archives of Sexual Behavior*, 1971, **1**, 309–320.

Kolarsky, A., & Madlafousek, J. Female behavior and sexual arousal in heterosexual male deviant offenders. *Journal of Nervous and Mental Disease*, 1972, **155,** 110–118.

Lang, P. J. Fear reduction and fear behavior: Problems in treating a construct. In J. M. Shlien (Ed.), *Research in psychotherapy*. Vol. 3. Washington, D.C.: American Psychological Association, 1968.

Laws, D., & Rubin, H. Instructional control of an autonomic sexual response. *Journal of Applied Behavior Analysis*, 1969, **2,** 93–100.

Leitenberg, H., Agras, W., Butz, R., & Wincze, J. Relationship between heart rate and behavioral change during the treatment of phobias. *Journal of Abnormal Psychology*, 1971, **78,** 59–68.

Lindgren, T. N., & Pauly, I. B. A body image scale for evaluating transsexuals. *Archives of Sexual Behavior*, 1975, **4,** 639–656.

LoPiccolo, J., & Steger, J. C. The sexual interaction inventory: A new instrument for assessment of sexual dysfunction. *Archives of Sexual Behavior*, 1974, **3,** 585–596.

MacDonald, M. L., Lindquist, C. U., Kramer, J. A., McGrath, R. A., & Rhyne, L. L. Social skills training: The effects of behavior rehearsal in groups on dating skills. *Journal of Counseling Psychology*, 1975, **22,** 224–230.

Mahoney, M. J. *Cognition and behavior modification*. Cambridge, Mass.: Ballinger, 1974.

Marks, I., Gelder, M., & Bancroft, J. Sexual deviants two years after electric aversion. *British Journal of Psychiatry*, 1970, **117,** 173–185.

Marks, I. M., & Sartorius, N. H. A contribution to the measurement of sexual attitude. *Journal of Nervous and Mental Disease*, 1968, **145,** 441–451.

Marshall, D. S., & Suggs, R. C. (Eds.). *Human sexual behavior: Variations in the ethnographic spectrum*. Englewood Cliffs, N.J.: Prentice-Hall, 1971.

Masters, W., & Johnson, V. *Human sexual response*. Boston: Little, Brown, 1966.

Masters, W., & Johnson, V. *Human sexual inadequacy*. Boston: Little, Brown, 1970.

Mavissakalian, M., Blanchard, E. B., Abel, G. G., & Barlow, D. H. Responses to complex erotic stimuli in homosexual and heterosexual males. *British Journal of Psychiatry*, 1975, **126,** 252–257.

McConaghy, N. Penile volume change to moving pictures of male and female nudes in heterosexual and homosexual males. *Behaviour Research and Therapy*, 1967, **5,** 43–48.

McConaghy, N. Subjective and penile plethysmograph responses following aversion-relief and apomorphine aversion therapy for homosexual impulses. *British Journal of Psychiatry*, 1969, **115,** 723–730.

McConaghy, N. Penile response conditioning and its relationship to aversion therapy in homosexuals. *Behavior Therapy*, 1970, **1,** 213–221.

McConaghy, N. Measurements of change in penile dimensions. *Archives of Sexual Behavior*, 1974, **3,** 381–388.

Money, J., & Ehrhardt, A. A. *Man & Woman, Boy & Girl*. Baltimore, Md.: Johns Hopkins Press, 1972.

Mountjoy, P. T. Some early attempts to modify penile erection in horse and human: An historical analysis. *Psychological Record*, 1974, **24,** 291–308.

Obler, M. Systematic desensitisation in sexual disorders. *Journal of Behavior Therapy and Experimental Psychiatry*, 1973, **4**, 93–101.

Ovesey, L., Gaylin, W., & Hendin, H. Psychotherapy of male homosexuality. *Archives of General Psychiatry*, 1963, **9**, 19–31.

Peterson, L. H. General types of dimensional transducers. In R. F. Rusher (Ed.), *Methods in medical research*. Vol. 11. Chicago: Year Book Medical Publishers, 1966.

Podell, L., & Perkins, J. C. A Guttman scale for sexual experience—A methodological note. *Journal of Abnormal and Social Psychology*, 1957, **54**, 420–422.

Quinn, J. T., Graham, P. J., Harbison, J. J. M., & McAllister, H. The assessment of sexual function. In T. Thompson & W. S. Dockens (Eds.), *Application of behavior modification*. New York: Academic, 1975.

Quinsey, V. L., Steinman, C. M., Bergersen, S. G., & Holmes, T. F. Penile circumference skin conductance and ranking responses of child molesters and "normals" to sexual and nonsexual visual stimuli, *Behavior Therapy*, 1975, **6**, 213–219.

Rado, S. An adaptational view of sexual behavior. In P. Hoch & J. Zubin (Eds.), *Psychosexual development in healthy and disease*. New York: Grune and Stratton, 1949.

Rehm, L. P., & Marston, A. R. Reduction of social anxiety through modification of self-reinforcement. *Journal of Consulting and Clinical Psychology*, 1968, **32**, 565–574.

Rekers, G. A., & Lovaas, O. I. Behavioral treatment of deviant sex-role behaviors in a male child. *Journal of Applied Behavior Analysis*, 1974, **7**, 173–190.

Rosenberg, B. G., & Sutton-Smith, B. The measurement of masculinity and femininity in children. *Child Development*, 1959, **30**, 373–380.

Rosenberg, B. G., & Sutton-Smith, B. The measurement of masculinity and femininity in children: An extension and revalidation. *The Journal of Genetic Psychology*, 1964, **104**, 259–264.

Sambrooks, J. E., & MacCulloch, M. J. Sexual orientation method questionnaire and its use in the assessment and management of cases of sexual dysfunction. *Behavioral Engineering*, 1974, **2**, 1–6.

Sandford, D. Patterns of sexual arousal in heterosexual males. *Journal of Sex Research*, 1974, **10**, 150–155.

Schatzberg, A. F., Westfall, M. P., Blumetti, A. B., & Birk, C. L. Effeminacy. I. A quantitative rating scale. *Archives of Sexual Behavior*, 1975, **4**, 31–41.

Sintchak, G., & Geer, J. A vaginal plethysmograph system. *Psychophysiology*, 1975, **12**, 113–115.

Stevenson, I., & Wolpe, J. Recovery from sexual deviations through overcoming nonsexual neurotic responses. *American Journal of Psychiatry*, 1960, **116**, 739–742.

Terman, L. M., & Miles, C. *Sex and personality: Studies in masculinity and femininity*. New York: London, 1936.

Twentyman, C. T., & McFall, R. M. Behavioral training of social skills in shy males. *Journal of Consulting and Clinical Psychology*, 1975, **43**, 394–395.

Westfall, M. P., Schatzberg, A. F., Blumetti, A. B., & Birk, C. L. Effeminacy. II. Variation with social context. *Archives of Sexual Behavior*, 1975, **4,** 43–51.

Whalen, R. E. Sexual motivation. *Psychological Review*, 1966, **73,** 151–163.

Williams, J. G., Barlow, D. H., & Agras, W. S. Behavioral measurement of severe depression. *Archives of General Psychiatry*, 1972, **27,** 330–334.

Yalom, I., Green, R., & Fisk, N. Prenatal exposure to female hormones: Effect on psychosexual development in boys. *Archives of General Psychiatry*, 1973, **28,** 554–561.

Zuckerman, M. Physiological measures of sexual arousal in the human. *Psychological bulletin*, 1971, **75,** 297–329.

Zuckerman, M. Scales for sex experience for males and females. *Journal of Consulting and Clinical Psychology*, 1973, **41,** 27–29.

CHAPTER 14

Assessment of Social Skills

MICHEL HERSEN and ALAN S. BELLACK

The contribution of deficits in social skill to behavior pathology has recently been documented in the behavior modification literature (Argyle, Trower, & Bryant, 1974; Goldsmith & McFall, 1975; Hersen & Bellack, 1976; Hersen & Eisler, 1976; Hersen, Turner, Edelstein, & Pinkston, 1975; Percell, Berwick, & Beigel, 1974). Deficits in social skill seen in clients and psychiatric patients are generally attributed to (1) a deficient learning history wherein the necessary responses never became a viable part of the individual's repertoire, (2) the disruptive effects of anxiety that inhibit behavior (e.g., Wolpe, 1969), or (3) the pervasive effects of institutionalization in the case of chronic psychiatric patients whereby disuse of social responses resulted in an inability to reproduce what may have once been an integral part of the patients' repertoires (Hersen & Bellack, 1976). Irrespective of the origin of a particular social skill deficit, the general consensus is that an individual with such a deficit requires a period of reeducation or training, during which time adaptive responses to interpersonal situations must be taught (Hersen & Eisler, 1976). In the instances when anxiety has been especially disruptive, greater attention to anxiety-reducing techniques may be warranted (Wolpe, 1958, 1969). However, a recent study (Percell, Berwick, & Beigel, 1974) interestingly shows that instigation of a social skill therapy (i.e., assertion training) not only led to improved ratings of overall assertiveness in psychiatric outpatients but resulted in significant decreases in anxiety concurrent with improvement in "self-concept." No anxiety-reducing techniques were employed in this study.

Traditional Approach

Prior to the behaviorists' current interest in the social skill deficits of their patients, nonbehaviorists recognized the importance of social skill deficiencies as concomitants of psychiatric disorder. For example, Gladwin (1967) pointed out ". . . that in order to become effective the psychologically inadequate person not only needs to relieve his anxieties and correct his maladaptive behavior but also to learn alternative success-oriented ways of behaving in society" (p. 87). More recently, Frank (1974), in the 25-year report of the psychotherapy project conducted in the Psychiatry Department of Johns Hopkins University, noted that improvement in social skill was one of the two beneficial aspects of short-term psychotherapy. Also, for a period of more than 15 years, Zigler and his colleagues (e.g., Levine & Zigler, 1973; Phillips & Zigler, 1961, 1964; Zigler & Levine, 1973; Zigler & Phillips, 1960, 1961, 1962) have carefully examined the relationship between social competence and psychiatric disorder, social competence and the process-reactive distinction in schizophrenia, social competence and alcoholism, and social competence as it relates to prognosis in psychiatric disorders. Although many complicated statistical analyses between and among the aforementioned variables were conducted, there is a major finding that underscores most of Zigler's work: the better a patient's level of social competence (i.e., social skill) prior to being hospitalized, the more likely (on a statistical basis) is his ability to succeed in terms of posthospital adjustment.

In assessing premorbid social competence, Zigler and his colleagues have grouped case history data into clusters, developed specific indices, and designed various scales that classify patients into levels of social competence. With the advent of psychotherapy outcome research in the 1950s, and extending into the 1960s and 1970s when pharmacological treatments were also evaluated, additional measures of social adjustment and social competence appeared. In a recent review of the literature Weissman (1975) reported on the characteristics of 15 currently available measuring instruments that she concluded to be sufficiently reliable and valid for use in outcome research concerned with social adjustment. Measurement instruments examined in this review article included the patient as informant, significant others as informants, the use of case history data to obtain and codify information, and the use of psychiatric ratings regarding current social functioning.

Behavioral and Traditional Approaches Compared

Thus the behaviorists' recent excursions into the areas of social skill, social competence, and social adjustment have been precluded by a lengthy history of study in the same areas by their nonbehavioral colleagues. What, then, constitutes the primary difference between the approaches of the traditionalists and the behaviorists in this important area? As has been carefully documented elsewhere (Hersen & Barlow, 1976. Chapter 4; Mischel, 1968, 1972), the most outstanding feature of the behavioral analysis, in general, is its one-to-one relationship between assessment and treatment. Whereas in the traditional approach there frequently exists a vague and undefined relationship between the diagnostic process and the ensuing therapy (particularly when there is an attempt to identify "presumed dynamics underlying the problem"), in the behavioral approach the specific behaviors measured during assessment (be they motoric, self-report, or physiological) are the very ones targeted for modification. This is especially highlighted in the experimental single case approach in which rates of behaviors measured during baseline assessment (Barlow & Hersen, 1973; Hersen & Barlow, 1976) are then modified during treatment phases of the withdrawal, reversal, and multiple baseline analyses. Examples of assessment and modification of social skill deficits using the single case strategy have periodically appeared in the psychological and psychiatric literatures (see Eisler, Hersen, & Miller, 1974; Foy, Eisler, & Pinkston, 1975; Hersen, Turner, Edelstein, & Pinkston, 1975). Similarly, the one-to-one relationship between assessment and modification holds when such modification of skill deficits is evaluated in controlled group comparison research (e.g., Hersen, Eisler, & Miller, 1974; Hersen, Eisler, Miller, Johnson, & Pinkston, 1973). Naturally, during the clinical course of skill training (i.e., in consulting room practice) the same close relationship between diagnosis and treatment follows (see Wolpe, 1969; Hersen & Miller, Note 1).

Social Skill Deficit

Although specific component behaviors comprising overall judgments of social skill and assertiveness can be identified (e.g., Eisler, Hersen, Miller, & Blanchard, 1975; Eisler, Miller, & Hersen, 1973) and precisely defined, a good generic definition of social skill has implications both from the theoretical and clinical frameworks, and may indeed lead to testable hypotheses. A number of definitions of social skill have been proposed in the literature. Argyris (1965, 1968, 1969) refers to social skill as those interpersonal behaviors that contribute to the individual's effectiveness as part of a larger group of individuals. Libet and Lewinsohn (1973), working in the area of depression, consider social skill ". . . as the complex ability both to emit behaviors which are positively or negatively reinforced and not to emit behaviors which are punished or extinguished by others" (p. 304). Weiss (1968) had previously defined social skill in terms of communication, understanding, interest, and rapport between the speaker and listener.

Rather than providing a single, global definition of social *skill,* we prefer a situation-specific conception of social *skills.* The overriding factor is effectiveness of behavior in social interactions. However, determination of effectiveness depends on the context of the interaction (e.g., returning a faulty appliance, introducing oneself to a prospective date, expressing appreciation to a friend) and, given any context, the parameters of the specific situation (e.g., expression of anger to a spouse, to an employer, or to a stranger). Although recognizing that no single definition of skill can be universally functional, we feel that some semispecific conceptualization is necessary for those working in the area.

Our own views are heavily influenced by the research interests we pursue (i.e., assertion training with psychiatric patients). We therefore emphasize an individual's ability to express both positive and negative feelings in the interpersonal context without suffering consequent loss of social reinforcement. Such skill is demonstrated in a large variety of interpersonal contexts (ranging from family to employer-employee relationships), and it involves the coordinated delivery of appropriate verbal and nonverbal responses. In addition, the socially skilled individual is attuned to the realities of the situation and is aware when he is likely to be reinforced for his efforts. Thus at times the socially skilled individual may have to forgo the expression of "hostile" assertiveness if such expression is likely to result in punishment or social censure.

Behavioral Approaches to Assessment

Behavioral interest in social skills training has developed along two parallel pathways. The primary emphasis has been on assertion training with both college student and psychiatric populations. Recently, an increasing amount of effort has been devoted to the development of heterosexual-interpersonal skills to increase dating behavior in shy and withdrawn college students. Assessment strategies have been similar in both contexts. It has become almost a maxim that to be effective, assessment must include a set of measures that tap multiple response channels (e.g., motoric, physiologic, verbal-cognitive) (Hersen, 1973; Lang, 1971). No single measure can provide a comprehensive picture of the multiple parameters of any targeted behavior. This admonition is as applicable to assessment of social skills as it is to other behaviors. The social skills literature has emphasized measurement of the cognitive and motoric aspects of the social skills complex.

Numerous self-report inventories have been developed explicitly to secure data on the self-evaluation of assertive skill, including the Wolpe-Lazarus Assertiveness Scale (Wolpe & Lazarus, 1966), the College Self-expression Scale (Galassi, DeLo, Galassi, & Bastien, 1974), and the Rathus Assertiveness Schedule (Rathus, 1973a). Twentyman and McFall (1975) developed the Survey of Heterosexual Interactions as a self-report measure of heterosexual skill. There has been considerable controversy over the relative importance of anxiety and skill deficits in the (poor) performance of targeted responses. Several inventories have been developed to assess anxiety in interpersonal situations. Arkowitz, Lichtenstein, McGovern, and Hines (1975) have used a modified form of the S–R Inventory of Anxiousness. Watson and Friend (1969) developed the Social Anxiety and Distress Scale and the Fear of Negative Evaluation Scale. Numerous traditional self-report scales of fear and anxiety not specific to social skills have also been utilized, including the Taylor (1956) Manifest Anxiety Scale, the Fear Survey Schedule (Wolpe & Lang, 1964), and the Zuckerman Affect Adjective Checklist (Zuckerman, 1960).

Overt behavioral-motoric assessment has involved two strategies. One approach has been to have subjects role play in a series of situation-specific scenes (e.g., dating or assertion relevant situations). The most notable examples are the Behavioral Assertiveness Test (Eisler, Hersen, & Miller, 1973) and the Situation Test (Rehm & Marston, 1968). The second approach has subjects interacting with experimenter-confederates in various in vivo situations such as calling a prospective date, resisting a salesperson on the telephone, or conversing with a prospective date for a brief period. In all these approaches the subject's response is rated on a variety of dimensions such as eye contact, speech duration, anxiety, compliance, and affect. Only a handful of studies have incorporated physiological assessment procedures. Those studies have measured cardiovascular activity (heart rate or pulse rate) during role-played interactions. Specific procedures for assessment of assertion and heterosexual skill will be discussed separately.

MINIMAL DATING

An increasing amount of interest has recently been devoted to the evaluation and remediation of deficits in heterosexual-interpersonal functioning in college students. Variously categorized as withdrawn, shy, socially anxious, and socially unskilled, the students who are low-frequency daters have several characteristics that make them attractive for both process research and clinical intervention. The problem has clinical significance: It involves considerable felt distress and is a potential forerunner of other more severe pathology (Twentyman & McFall, 1975). It is a dysfunction that is encountered frequently in college populations (Martinson & Zerface, 1970). It is not readily modified by experimental demand characteristics or incidental environmental experiences (Borkovec, Stone, O'Brien, & Kaloupek, 1974). Finally, the problem appears to be responsive to a variety of behavioral interventions (Christensen & Arkowitz, 1974; Curran, 1975; Rehm & Marston, 1968; Twentyman & McFall, 1975).

The literature on minimal dating has been marked by somewhat of a controversy over the nature of the dysfunction. One group of researchers has explained the dating deficit on the basis of high levels of social and evaluative anxiety (e.g., Arkowitz, Note 2). A second group has concluded that the critical factor is a lack of appropriate social skills (Twentyman & McFall, 1975). Assessment strategies have, therefore, emphasized measurement of both social anxiety *and* social skills. Self-report devices and overt behavioral techniques have been utilized with varying degrees of success. Very few studies have incorporated physiological assessment.

Before proceeding to describe and evaluate specific assessment techniques, some general issues must be considered. Effective validation of a device for assessment of social skills or social anxiety would require two steps: first, the *independent* rating of the degree of dysfunction by some existing criterion (e.g., dating frequency, self- or peer report), and second, determination of the ability of the new device to predict (replicate) that rating. This could be accomplished by calculating the correlation between criterion and test scores or by comparing the test scores of groups high and low on the criterion. Few studies have been conducted with such evaluation of assessment techniques as a primary consideration (Arkowitz et al., 1975; Borkovec et al., 1974; Rehm & Marston, 1968; Twentyman & McFall, 1975). The results of those studies have been inconsistent. Most research on dating deficits has focused on the evaluation of treatment techniques. Assessment procedures in these studies have been incorporated as dependent variables with presumed validity. Little consideration has been given to the fact that most measurement procedures have been developed in the context of treatment studies and without adequate psychometric control. The evaluation of both the assessment devices and the treatment procedures is therefore quite difficult as they must serve as criteria for one another. If pretreatment to posttreatment changes are not found, either the treatment could be ineffective *or* (and) the assessment device could be invalid. If significant pretreatment to posttreatment changes are found, one possible conclusion is that the treatment is effective *and* the assessment device is valid. However, without independent information as to the reliability and validity of the assessment device, that conclusion cannot be safely drawn. Those "positive" results can, at best, contribute to the nomological validity network surrounding the device. Much of the evaluative material discussed below will, by necessity, be based on such validational networks rather than on concrete psychometric procedures.

Self-Report Techniques

The primary focus of self-report measures has been on the measurement of anxiety. Several inventories have been developed explicitly to measure social anxiety. Another approach has been to form mini-scales by abstracting interpersonal items from broad-based anxiety and fear inventories. These general scales have been used infrequently in their entirety and will not be discussed. Characteristics of scales used for assessing heterosexual skill and anxiety are presented in Table 14–1.

Social Anxiety and Distress Scale (SAD). The SAD was developed by Watson and Friend (1969) to measure the tendency to avoid and experience negative affect (fear, anxiety, etc.) in interpersonal situations. The scale contains 28 items to be answered true or false. Scoring is in the direction of high anxiety. Representative items (with score) are: "I feel relaxed even in unfamiliar situations (F)," "I try to avoid talking to people unless I know them well (T)." As can be seen from these examples, items are not confined to heterosexual anxiety but, rather, deal with interpersonal anxiety per se. The scale was standardized with a population of male and female undergraduates at the University of Toronto. Test-retest reliability (one month) was 0.68 and the KR–20 index of homogeneity was 0.94, indicating adequate reliability and consistency. The correlation between the SAD and the Crowne-Marlowe Social Desirability Scale was low and negative, indicating that responses to the SAD are not heavily influenced by the social desirability of items. The mean score for the standardization sample was 9.11 and the S.D. was 8.01. The modal score was zero, and the distribution was not normal. Caution is therefore necessary in the use of parametric statistics to analyze SAD data.

Watson and Friend (1969) reported the results of a number of studies that supported both the convergent and divergent validity of the social anxiety construct and the validity of the SAD for measuring this construct. Although these results are suggestive, they do not bear directly on the utility of the SAD for measuring heterosexual anxiety and/or heterosexual skill. The SAD has been a frequently used inventory in both treatment and assessment studies, thereby providing some basis for its evaluation. Arkowitz et al. (1975) conducted an extensive validation study in which they examined a number of measures, including the SAD. College students were recruited as subjects and classified as high-or low-frequency daters on the basis of self-report of dating history. SAD scores for the two groups were significantly different. The mean SAD score for low-frequency daters was 14.94, whereas the mean for the high daters was 4.25. Further support for the utility of the SAD comes from several treatment studies. Christensen and Arkowitz (1974) and Curran, Gilbert, and Little (1976) found

Table 14.1 Characteristics of Scales for Heterosexual Skill and Anxiety

References	Scale	No. of Items	Format	Normative Population
Arkowitz et al. (1975)	S–R Inventory of Anxiousness	5	14 response modes rated for each situation on a 1–5 point scale	Male undergraduates
Curran (1975)	Fear Survey Schedule (interpersonal items)		1–5 point scale	None
McGovern et al. (1975)	Self-rating Form	15	True-false	None
Rehm & Marston (1968)	Situation Questionnaire	30	1–7 point ratings	Male undergraduates
Twentyman & McFall (1975)	Survey of Heterosexual Interactions	20	1–7 point ratings	Male undergraduates
Watson & Friend (1969)	Fear of Negative Evaluation Scale	30	True-false	Male & female undergraduates
Watson & Friend (1969)	Social Anxiety & Distress Scale	28	True-false	Male & female undergraduates

significant decreases in SAD scores after treatment was administered. Bander, Steinke, Allen, and Mosher (1975), using a variant of the SAD, reported a similar finding. Less positive results were reported by McGovern, Arkowitz, and Gilmore (1975). They did not find any consistent, significant decreases on SAD scores after treatment. Their negative findings cannot be entirely attributed to ineffectiveness of treatment procedures, as significant changes were found on other measures.

The SAD appears to be a promising measure. There is, however, some question about the reliability of scores. The reliability figures for the standardization sample were quite modest (0.68). Bander et al. (1975) reported a reliability coefficient of only 0.47 for their variation of the SAD. Future use (and evaluation) of the SAD should consider this issue and calculate test-retest correlations for untreated groups and for pseudotherapy groups.

Fear of Negative Evaluation Scale (FNE). Watson and Friend (1969) conceptualized social-evaluative anxiety as having two components: (1) negative affect and discomfort in social situations, and (2) fear of receiving negative evaluations from others. The FNE is a 30-item true-false inventory developed by Watson and Friend to assess the fear of evaluation component of social anxiety. Two representative items are: "I react very little when other people disapprove of me (F)." "I am usually worried about what kind of impression I make (T)." The FNE was developed in conjunction with the SAD, using the same standardization sample. Both the test-retest reliability (0.78) and the KR–20 index of homogeneity (0.94) were quite satisfactory. The correlation of the FNE and the SAD was 0.51, suggesting that the two tests have a moderate amount of common variance. The correlation with the Crowne-Marlowe scale was low and negative. The mean score and standard deviation for the standardization sample were 15.47 and 8.62, respectively. As was the case for the SAD, FNE scores were *not* normally distributed.

Arkowitz et al. (1975) found that low-frequency daters had significantly higher FNE scores (e.g., greater fear) than high-frequency daters. Curran et al. (1976) reported that FNE scores decreased significantly after treatment. In contrast, Christensen and Arkowitz (1974) and McGovern et al. (1975) found nonsignificant pretreatment to posttreatment changes in FNE scores. In both of those studies treatment resulted in significant changes in other measures. As discussed above, there are two alternative interpretations of these negative findings: They could be a function of the treatment procedures applied (e.g., treatment did not reduce evaluation anxiety), *or* they could be a function of the FNE (e.g., there were real changes to which the FNE was not sensitive). The first alternative seems more viable for two reasons. First, there is some other support for the validity of the FNE (Arkowitz et al., 1975; Watson & Friend, 1969). Second, the treatment procedures in these studies did not explicitly focus on remediation of evaluation anxiety. Further use (and evaluation) of the FNE seems warranted, especially if social-evaluative anxiety is a focus of interest.

Situation Questionnaire (SQ). The SQ was developed by Rehm and Marston (1968). It consists of 30 items that were originally contained in a desensitization hierarchy for heterosexual social anxiety. Each item consists of a description of an interpersonal situation presented with a 7-point rating scale. Subjects are instructed to indicate the degree of anxiety they would experience in each situation from none (score of 1) to extreme (score of 7). The SQ was developed for use with males. Sample items include calling a girl just to talk and dancing with a girl on a date. Rehm and Marston (1968) do not present explicit data on the standardization, reliability, or validity of the SQ. However, they reported that a sample of low-frequency daters had significantly higher ($\bar{X} = 121.3$) SQ scores than an otherwise matched sample of high-frequency daters ($\bar{X} = 71.8$). They also found significantly greater decreases in SQ scores for subjects exposed to treatment than for those in a no-treatment control condition.

The original SQ or variations of it have been employed in a number of studies. Curran and Gilbert (1975) and Curran et al. (1976) found significant changes in SQ scores for subjects exposed to treatment procedures that were also found to be affective by other measures. Curran (1975) also used the SQ as a dependent variable in a treatment study. He reported finding a significant overall F ratio for Time (e.g., across measurement phases), which included treatment *and* control groups. The interaction was not significant, suggesting that scores of both treated and control subjects changed. These results raise some question about the reliability of the SQ. Bander et al. (1975) used a variant of the SQ. Although they found significant changes for treatment groups alone, they reported that the test-retest reliability of their SQ was only 0.58. More extensive evaluation of th SQ seems warranted. Further psychometric evaluation is needed if it is to be used effectively. It would also be desirable to develop a form for use with women.

S–R Inventory of Anxiousness. Arkowitz et al. (1975) have used a modified version of the S–R Inventory developed by Endler. The Arkowitz form includes five interpersonal situations along with the original 14 response modes (e.g., experience nausea, heart beats faster) employed by Endler, Hunt, and Rosenstein (1962). Situations are of the form: "You are going to pick up a new date." The subject is required to rate (on a

5-point scale) the degree to which he would typically experience each of the 14 responses in each situation. The higher the total score, the greater the degree of self-reported distress. No standardized data have been presented. Arkowitz et al. (1975) found significant differences between the S–R scores of high- and low-frequency daters. Christensen and Arkowitz (1974) reported that S–R scores decreased after treatment, and McGovern et al. (1975) found an inconsistent pattern of changes. MacDonald, Lindquist, Kramer, McGrath, and Rhyne (1975) reported that the revised S–R Inventory did not reflect posttreatment changes in dating skill.

Fear Survey Schedule (FSS). Curran and his colleagues have developed a mini-FSS by abstracting the interpersonal items from the full scale. The results of several studies (Curran, 1975; Curran & Gilbert, 1975; Curran et al., 1976) have provided only moderate support for the continued use of this device.

Survey of Heterosexual Interactions (SHI). The SHI was developed by Twentyman and McFall (1975) as a self-report measure of heterosexual avoidance. It contains 20 items pertaining to the ability to interact effectively in social situations. Each item is scored on a 7-point scale. The SHI was developed for use with college males. The mean score for an unselected standardization sample was 88.21 (S.D. = 18.45). Twentyman and McFall (1975) administered a variety of behavioral, physiological, and self-report measures to groups of subjects classified as shy or confident on the basis of SHI scores and dating frequency. Shyness was ascribed to students scoring 70 or less on the SHI (one S.D. below the mean) and reporting having no more than one date per month. Significant differences were found between shy and confident subjects on measures on all three response channels, providing some validational support for the SHI. Interestingly, correlations between the SHI and measures other than self-report were generally low. The low relationship of measures in different response modalities has been frequently reported (Arkowitz et al., 1975; Borkovec et al., 1974), and will be further discussed later.

The SHI has been used as a dependent variable in two treatment studies. McGovern et al. (1975) and Twentyman and McFall (1975) both found significant increases in SHI scores (decrease in shyness) after treatment. The SHI appears to be a promising assessment device. As with other measures discussed above, the scale should be subjected to psychometric analyses and standardized for both male and female populations. Reliability and susceptibility to experimental demand and expectancy factors should be carefully scrutinized.

Self-rating Form (SRF). The SRF is a 15-item true-false scale that measures self-evaluation of anxiety and skill in heterosexual situations.

Developed by McGovern et al. (1975), the SRF was modeled after a scale originally used by Arkowitz et al. (1975) to secure peer ratings of skill and anxiety (see reference to Peer Ratings on page 527). McGovern et al. found that the SRF significantly differentiated treated subjects from those in a control condition.

Anxiety and Skill Thermometers. In a number of studies, subjects have been requested to make single, global evaluations of their anxiety and skill or effectiveness in role-playing situations. These ratings have characteristically been scored on 5- or 7-point scales similar to the Fear Thermometer (Lang & Lazovik, 1963). Borkovec et al. (1974), Glasgow and Arkowitz (1975), and Twentyman and McFall (1975) all found that such measures differentiated subjects with high (confident) and low (shy) skill. Curran and Gilbert (1975) reported that self-ratings of fear were significantly lower for treated subjects than for controls after treatment. Despite this *apparent* validity, the reliability of these measures is suspect. Borkovec et al. (1974) administered an assessment battery twice (three weeks apart) and found significant increases in self-ratings of effectiveness over trials. Twentyman and McFall (1975) reported that the reliabilities of such anxiety ratings ranged from 0.10 to 0.28. The results of those two studies cast major doubt on the usefulness of these measures. The validity of a test is severely limited by its reliability (Cronbach, 1960, p. 132), and reliabilities as questionable as those reported above preclude acceptable levels of validity.

General Comments. Several issues must be considered in the evaluation of self-report measures. The first issue pertains to the process of scale construction. The consistent emphasis has been on the development of situation-specific measures. General or broad-based anxiety scales or measures of traditional psychopathology have been infrequently used. Although the rejection of traditional and general measures is appropriate, it has resulted in a demand for the quick development of new, specific measures. For the most part, these measures have been constructed (or adapted) primarily on the basis of face validity. If items *appear* to be relevant to the target behavior, they are included. Scales thus constructed have frequently been used in a few (for the most part treatment-oriented) studies, modified to suit individual investigators' needs, and quickly retired if they do not yield significant differences between groups (or pretreatment to posttreatment). This approach to assessment is not apt to result in the development of sound instruments, and it precludes meaningful evaluation of much of the existing treatment research. As stated previously, greater attention must be paid to fundamental psychometric requirements in the development of new scales or the further evaluation of existing scales.

A second consideration relates to what Campbell and Fiske (1959) refer to as method variance. Different measurement devices that use the same response modality (e.g., self-report) for the assessment of the same attribute (e.g., social anxiety) have shared modality variance. The results of such measures are likely to be intercorrelated to some extent *regardless* of the specific content of the scales or their validity. Extreme care must therefore be taken in drawing conclusions from measures within single measurement domains. Arkowitz et al. (1975), Borkovec et al. (1974), and Twentyman and McFall (1975) all reported finding high correlations between devices within domains and low correlations between domains. This phenomenon has special relevance for the use and validation of self-report measures, because *subject recruitment* is itself based on self-report. Subjects volunteering for treatment are self-reporting low skill and/or high anxiety by the fact of volunteering. It is not surprising, therefore, that they *also* self-report low skill and/or high anxiety on questionnaires or inventories. Validating such inventories against self-report screening criteria, therefore, has limited implications. Unless they are validated against measures from other domains, they can be justifiably used only to indicate status or change in status (as after treatment) of self-evaluation. Assessment of self-evaluation is an appropriate and necessary process. However, the results of such assessment should not be confused with other aspects of subjects' behavior or used independently to explain other behavior.

Behavioral Measures

The skills conception of heterosexual deficits ascribes a central role to behavioral functioning. As would be expected, there has been considerable emphasis placed on the assessment of overt behavior. Almost every behavioral study of heterosexual skill has incorporated some measurement of actual performance in heterosexual situations. In most cases a battery of such measures has been employed. Two aspects of the behavior assessment process have been extensively varied. One aspect involves specific behaviors that have been presumed to comprise heterosexual skill and have therefore been considered relevant as targets (e.g., response latency, voice quality, dating frequency). The second aspect involves the circumstances or situations in which target behaviors have been observed. Three general types of situations have been employed: role playing, standardized in vivo interactions, and actual dating interactions (See Table 14–2). We will organize our presentation around those situations.

Table 14.2 Characteristics of Behavioral Tasks for Heterosexual Skills

Reference	Task	Number of Items
Arkowitz et al. (1975)	In vivo interaction	Ten-minute role-played interaction "on a date"
Arkowitz et al. (1975)	Taped Situation Test	Responses to 10 audiotaped situations
Curran (1975)	In vivo interaction	Five-minute role-played interaction to "try to secure a date"
Glasgow & Arkowitz (1975)	In vivo interaction	Ten-minute interaction with an opposite-sex subject
MacDonald et al. (1975)	Role-Played Dating Interaction	Three four-minute role-played interactions
Rehm & Marston (1968)	Situation Test	Responses to 10 audiotaped situations (2 forms available)
Twentyman & McFall (1975)	Forced Interaction Test	Five-minute role-played interaction with "girl you just met"
Twentyman & McFall (1975)	Social Behavior Situations	Responses to 6 role-played situations

Role-Played Techniques

Situation Test (*ST*). The ST was developed by Rehm and Marston (1968) and is the prototype for a number of role-played batteries currently in use. It consists of 10 situations requiring some form of heterosexual interaction. (An alternate form is also available.) Each situation is described to the subject over an intercom (by tape recording) after which a female confederate reads a line of dialogue appropriate to the situation. The subject is then required to respond aloud as if he were actually in the situation. A representative example is: You are on a date and have just come out of a theater after seeing a movie. You ask your date what she would like to do since it is early, and she replies, "Oh, I don't know. It's up to you." The subject's response is audiotaped for subsequent behavioral rating. Arkowitz et al. (1975) used a modification of the ST called the Taped Situation Test (TST). The procedure for the TST is identical to that of the ST, but it contains slightly different items. Melnick (1973) presented ST situations on videotape rather than audiotape.

The procedure for evaluating responses to the ST and most other role-played tests has been fairly consistent across studies. Target behaviors are identified on an a priori basis by the experimenter. Undergraduate or graduate student raters are trained to a criterion level of reliability (typically 0.70 to 0.90). Behavior ratings are made surreptitiously on live performance or retrospectively from tapes by pairs of raters. Scores used for data analysis are derived from the means of each pair of ratings, summed and averaged across all situations. A number of different behaviors have been measured. Rehm and Marston (1968) examined the validity of the ST by comparing groups of anxious and nonanxious males. Significant differences were found for ratings of general anxiety, latency of response (from the end of the role model's prompting), and specific anxiety indices (such as speech disfluencies). There were no differences between the groups on ratings of adequacy of response or number of words spoken. The high-anxious subjects had significantly higher ratings on appropriateness of verbal content and overall social skill after treatment. Arkowitz et al. (1975) rated high- and low-frequency daters on response latency and number of words spoken. High-frequency daters had a shorter latency and, in contrast to Rehm and Marston's findings, also spoke significantly more words. Melnick (1973) and Rehm and Marston (1968) used the ST as a dependent variable in treatment evaluation studies. The results were inconsistent and do not bear directly on the validity of the ST.

Social Behavior Situations (SBS). Role play on the ST requires a single response from the subject, and there is no ongoing interaction with the role model. The SBS (Twentyman & McFall, 1975) allows for a responsive interaction. As with the ST, the subject is requested to role play a response in a set of six situations. However, a live female confederate in an adjoining room responds to the subject's response. The interaction continues until the subject stops responding, or for a maximum of three minutes. Confederates are trained to respond in a pleasant, standardized manner. Twentyman and McFall (1975) compared the performance of shy and confident subjects on a number of behaviors. Shy subjects were rated higher on global ratings of anxiety and specific anxiety indicators. They were rated lower on skill and time spent in the situations. They also failed to respond at all to significantly more situations than confident subjects. A similar pattern of differences was found in a comparison of shy subjects exposed to treatment and those in a control group.

In Vivo Interactions

The most frequently used behavioral assessment procedure has been to require subjects to interact with a live confederate in a face-to-face situation. These techniques have frequently been referred to as being in vivo although they are role-played situations in the clinic or laboratory. The subject is given a preparatory set (e.g., "You are on a date") and instructed to respond as if the interaction were real. Confederates are trained to respond in a standardized neutral manner, to avoid making excessively facilitating responses and to prevent long silences.

Arkowitz et al. (1975) employed a 10-minute interaction in which subjects were told to act as if they had just met a female and wanted to get to know her further. The performance of high- and low-frequency daters was compared to talk time, number of silences lasting 10 seconds or longer, verbal reinforcement of the partner, head nods, smiles, time spent gazing at partner, and content of response (verbal disclosures, substantive comments, and responsive comments). The only significant difference was on the number of silences (low daters had more silences). In addition, seven untrained female undergraduates rated subjects on social skill (low, moderate, or high). High daters were rated as significantly more skillful. Borkovec et al. (1974) compared high-anxious and low-anxious males on a three-minute interaction during which the subject was to attempt to create a favorable impression. The confederate in this interaction did *not* respond. The groups did not differ in anxiety ratings, speech disfluencies, or percentage of the session spent speaking. The confederates rated the performance of the low-anxious subjects as more effective (7-point scale).

Rather than employing a confederate, Glasgow and Arkowitz (1975) had male and female subjects interact with each other. Pairs of unacquainted subjects were observed for 10 minutes, during which time they were requested to try to get to know each other. Ratings were made on seven behaviors and interaction patterns. Results of comparisons between high- and low-frequency daters were primarily non-significant. Interestingly, both male and female low-frequency daters were rated less physically attractive than high-frequency daters. This finding raises a question about the effect of physical appearance on other ratings.

In contrast to the studies described above, Twentyman and McFall (1975) found a pattern of consistent differences between groups on an in vivo test (Forced Interaction Test). Their subjects were told to respond as if they had just met a girl in a classroom. The interaction continued for five minutes or until the subject stopped responding. Shy subjects were rated significantly lower than confident subjects in skill and higher in specific anxiety indices and overall anxiety. Subsequent application of this procedure in a treatment study yielded reliability measures for these behaviors ranging from 0.40 to 0.68. MacDonald et al. (1975) developed the Role-Played Dating Inventory (RPDI), which combined elements of role play and in vivo interactions. They found differences in overall skill level between high- and low-frequency daters and from pretreatment to posttreatment for low-frequency daters.

The results for in vivo tests in treatment-oriented studies have been similarly mixed. Curran has consistently found significant changes in skill and anxiety ratings after treatment (Curran, 1975; Curran & Gilbert, 1975; Curran et al., 1976). Melnick (1973) found significant posttreatment changes in masculine assertiveness, anxiety, overall pleasantness and appropriateness. Bander et al. (1975) reported negative results for number of silences, smiles, head nods, and instances of eye contact. Twentyman and McFall (1975) found changes only in anxiety ratings.

One variation of role-played techniques that has not been discussed is mock telephone calls. Arkowitz et al. (1975) had subjects engage in a five-minute call with a confederate under the set of trying to obtain a date. Twentyman and McFall (1975) examined the response of subjects in anticipation of making such a call. No differences between high- and low-frequency daters were found in either study.

General Comments. Few firm conclusions can be drawn about the two forms of role-played techniques. Most investigators have found differences between high and low dating groups in overall ratings of interpersonal skill and anxiety. The raters are reliably detecting some differences between the groups. However, attempts at identifying the source or nature of those differences have not been successful. No consistent pattern has been detected either for specific behaviors or types of interaction (e.g., situations).

There are several factors that might contribute to the disappointing results achieved thus far. First, as Arkowitz has suggested, low-frequency dating may be a function of anxiety rather than of behavioral skill deficits. If that is the case, assessment of discrete behavior components is not a viable endeavor. The lower skill ratings generally reported for subjects with low-frequency dating may result primarily from raters' incidental attention to anxiety indicators or the physical attractiveness of subjects. This possible explanation pertains to the nature of the dysfunction rather than to assessment factors per se. There are a number of issues relating directly to the assessment procedure that suggest restraint in drawing conclusions.

As with the self-report techniques, most behavioral procedures have been conducted on an a priori basis. The apparent primary consideration for the selection of situations and behaviors has been face validity. There has not been any consistent attempt to base selection empirically on external criteria. Eisler, Miller, and Hersen (1973) and Eisler et al. (1975) have shown that social skill deficits of chronic psychiatric patients are situation specific. Any skill deficits in otherwise well-functioning college students should be at least as specific. These students would not be expected to manifest gross dysfunction in *all heterosexual interactions.* Calculating summative skill scores across a set of nonvalidated situations is likely to mask group-wide deficits in any particular situation as well as any individualized pattern of deficits. This latter issue does not pertain to the open-ended in vivo interactions. Nevertheless, both the reliability and validity of that technique are undetermined.

A number of problems exist in relation to the particular behaviors that have been assessed, independent of the situations in which the behaviors were observed. Raters have consistently found overall skill differences between high- and low-frequency daters. An intensive analysis of the rating process should be conducted in an effort to identify the determinants of the ratings. Independent ratings should be made of audio and video portions of responses as well as components of each in an effort to isolate pertinent factors.

Just as situational patterns can be statistically masked by summing scores across situations, specific behavioral deficits can be masked by summing scores across individuals. If lower-frequency daters do have behavioral deficits, it is unlikely that they all have the same deficits. By grouping data, individual skill patterns are masked. Individual behavioral analyses must be conducted before it can be safely concluded that skill deficits do not exist. A third issue exists in regard to the rating procedure itself. Although the reliability of rating has typically been satisfactory, reliability does not guarantee validity. In most studies definitional criteria for specific behaviors are not provided. It is therefore not clear that raters in different studies are in fact rating the same behaviors, despite the labels (e.g., skill) provided.

A final caution should be considered in regard to the subjects recruited for both assessment and treatment research. Selection criteria used thus far have varied widely in stringency and kind. Borkovec et al. (1974) selected subjects on the basis of two FSS items. Melnick (1973) accepted subjects with self-reported dating frequencies of up to two dates a month. Glasgow and Arkowitz (1975) required low-dating males to have had no more than three dates in the previous six months, but low-dating females could have had up to six dates in that period. It is unlikely that subjects selected under these diverse criteria are a homogeneous group. Furthermore, it is not at all clear that "low-frequency dating" is a unitary nosological category. It might well be that some low-frequency daters suffer primarily from interpersonal fear and anxiety, whereas others have significant skill deficits (with or without high levels of anxiety). If that were the case, recruitment of high-anxious subjects could result in a different sample than recruitment of low-frequency daters or subjects with low skill. It would also mean that grouping data across individuals, situations, or behaviors would each tend to mask patterns of skill deficit.

Dating Records

A number of investigators have attempted to examine the actual dating behavior or real-life interpersonal interaction patterns of subjects. Curran and Gilbert (1975) secured retrospective descriptions of dating experiences from subjects. Clark and Arkowitz (Note 3), Christensen et al. (1975), Rehm and Marston (1968), and Twentyman and McFall (1975) all used self-monitoring procedures to assess ongoing behavior immediately before, during, and after treatment. No reliability data are available for these techniques. The accuracy of self-monitoring in general is, however, somewhat suspect (Lipinski & Nelson, 1974). Most studies have reported increases in interactions after treatment. Arkowitz et al. (1975) required subjects to provide the names of peers who could evaluate their dating behavior and skill (Peer Rating Inventory). Peer ratings corroborated self-report ratings. High-frequency daters were viewed as more skilled and comfortable in social situations and were reported to date more frequently than self-identified low-frequency daters.

Curran and Gilbert (1975) provide a lucid discussion of a number of problems inherent in the use of dating frequency as a dependent variable. One issue they raise is that there is no commonly accepted definition of a "date," which tends to decrease comparability of reports within and across studies. Another issue of paramount importance is that dating frequency is *not* a direct parallel of heterosexual skill. Frequent dating does not guarantee high skill (or low anxiety). Individuals of low skill may maintain relationships with partners of equally low skill. They might also lack skills necessary to sustain relationships, while having sufficient skills (or resources) to secure initial dates with new partners. Caution is therefore advised in the use of dating rates as either a dependent variable or criterion variable.

Physiological Measures

In two studies of social anxiety physiological recordings have been made during role-played interactions. Borkovec et al. (1974) measured heart rate (HR) during nine 10-second intervals before and during a three-minute in vivo interaction. Physiological arousal increased prior to the interaction, reached a peak shortly after the interaction began, and then steadily decreased for both high-anxious and low-anxious subjects. However, the high-anxious subjects evidenced higher arousal at every measurement point.

Twentyman and McFall (1975) recorded pulse rate in intervals before, during, and after the simulated phone call, the Social Behavior Situations, and the Forced Interaction Test. Both shy and confident subjects manifested higher arousal when listening to instructions and interacting with confederates than they did during baseline (resting) periods. Shy subjects had significantly higher pulse rates than confident subjects during the SBS, but there were no differences for either the phone call or forced interaction. The differences in results for the forced interaction are impossible to interpret at this point. Differences in the subjects' set, the confederate, the nature of the subject samples (different recruitment criteria were used), and scoring procedures could all have contributed to the differences. The results and response patterns were otherwise similar. Further use of physiological assessment does seem warranted. In both studies correlations of measures in different response modalities were low. Lack of correspondence of measurement systems confounds interpretation of results and restricts the strength of conclusions that can be drawn from any one system. Further research is needed to help clarify this complex issue.

MEASURING ASSERTIVENESS AND SOCIAL SKILL

In the following sections we will examine the self-report inventories, behavioral tasks, rating scales, and physiological measures that have been used to assess assertiveness and social skill in college students and psychiatric patients. Questions of reliability and validity will be discussed. For both the college and psychiatric populations the relationship between and among self-report, motoric, and physiological measures will be surveyed separately. In addition, the behavioral tasks (primarily of a surreptitious nature) used to assess generalization effects of treatment will be critically examined.

College Students (Self-Report Inventories)

The Wolpe-Lazarus Assertiveness Scale (Wolpe & Lazarus, 1966), originally designed for administration in clinical situations, has been used to measure assertiveness in college students (e.g., Kazdin, 1974; McFall & Marston, 1970; Young, Rimm, & Kennedy, 1973). Several other self-report inventories have also been used. Some of the identifying characteristics of these latter measures are presented in Table 14–3.

Because most of these scales have been developed in independent laboratories, considerable overlap in items is typically found between scales. For example, consider item 15 from the Galassi et al. (1974) College Self-Expression Scale ("If food which is not to your satisfaction is served in a restaurant, would you complain about it to the waiter?") and item 25

Table 14–3. Characteristics of Assertiveness Scales for College Populations

Reference	Scale	No. of Items	Format	Population[a]
Bates & Zimmerman (1971)	Constriction Scale 1	43	yes-no	M & F, U
	Constriction Scale 2	29	yes-no	M & F, U
Bryant & Trower (1974)	Social Situations Questionnaire	30	0–4 point ratings	M & F, U
Friedman (1968)	Action Situation Inventory	10	5–6 alternatives	M & F, U
Galassi et al. (1974)	College Self Expression Scale	50	0–4 point ratinrs	M & F, G & U
Lawrence (1970)	Assertive Inventory	69	several alternatives	F, U
McFall & Lillesand (1971)	Conflict Resolution Inventory	8-item face sheet; 35 refusal items	several alternatives per item; 5 alternatives	M & F, U
Rathus (1973a)	Assertiveness Schedule	30	−3 to +3	M & F, U
	Short Form	19	−3 to +3	

[a] M – male, F – female; G – graduate students, U – undergraduates

from Rathus' (1973a) Assertiveness Schedule ("I complain about poor service in a restaurant and elsewhere"). Although most of the scales are concerned with expression of both positive and negative feelings, the items predominantly reflect the expression of "hostile assertion" rather than "commendatory assertion" (Wolpe, 1969). Reliability and validity data are available in some cases, although cross-validation is the exception rather than the rule. Several of the scales (e.g., Friedman, 1968; Lawrence, 1970) were developed primarily for specific research projects and have not had much clinical application. There are a number of studies in which at least two or more of the scales have been used concurrently in evaluating treatment efficacy (Kazdin, 1974; Young, Rimm, & Kennedy, 1973), but actual correlations between and among scales have not been presented. Two of the scales have been factor analyzed (Bates & Zimmerman, 1971; Bryant & Trower, 1974). There follow brief descriptions of published scales and inventories used to assess assertiveness in college students.

Constriction Scales. The Bates and Zimmerman (1971) Constriction Scales (CS1, CS2) are empirically derived but surprisingly have not been used by researchers or clinicians in the social skills area. Constriction Scales 1 and 2 were derived from an initial pool of items administered to some 600 male and female undergraduates. The items in the scale vary along a number of continua including familiarity, individual-group, and status. The items are scored so that a high constriction score is comparable to a low score on an assertiveness schedule. Following a principal components factor analysis with CS1 (43 items), 13 factors were identified for males and 14 for females. Fourteen overlapping items were then dropped from the CS1 to form the abbreviated CS2. Correlations between CS1 and CS2 are 0.93 and 0.95 respectively for males and females. Internal reliability (homogeneity) for the CS2 ranges from 0.78 to 0.80, and test-retest reliability ranges from 0.79 to 0.91 for one-month intervals. For both males and females, the CS2 (i.e., level of constriction) correlates positively at low levels (0.26 to 0.34) with the EPI Neuroticism and MMPI fear scales, but negatively with extraversion and affiliation (−0.28 to −0.55). In addition to concurrent validity, Bates and Zimmerman presented some evidence for the predictive value of the CS scales. They reasoned that students highly constricted on the CS1 would be more compliant than low CS1 students, thus being more likely to obtain higher grade point averages (GPA). A comparison of high and low CS1 students confirmed that the high group obtained significantly better GPAs than the low CS1 group. However, the relationship of the CS scales to behavioral tasks requiring assertiveness and behavioral ratings made by significant others in the student's environment have not been obtained.

Social Situations Questionnaire. Bryant and Trower (1974) obtained normative data for the Social Situations Questionnaire from a mailing sent to some 223 male and female undergraduates (71 percent responded) attending Oxford University. The items in this questionnaire involve interpersonal situations ranging from the casual (e.g., "Going into shops") to the more intimate (e.g., "Getting to know someone in depth"). Data were subjected to a principal components factor analysis, with the primary component accounting for 25.5 percent of the variance. This component is related to social difficulty and involves ". . . actually seeking out relative strangers, particularly of the opposite sex" (Bryant & Trower, 1974, p. 18). Respondents to this questionnaire who loaded high on the social difficulty factor were compared with their low counterparts. The resulting analyses indicated that respondents who loaded low on social difficulty had significantly greater numbers from Socioeconomic Classes I and II, whereas respondents with high social difficulty came from significantly smaller families (i.e., only child or one sibling). Reliability and validity data are not provided for the questionnaire.

Action Situation Inventory (ASI). Friedman (1968) developed this inventory, which contains a brief description of 10 interpersonal situations, with five to six response alternatives provided for the subject. In Friedman's (1971) validation study, the first 100 subjects who filled out the ASI reported that they asserted themselves in only five of the 10 situations depicted. Thirty-six percent of the males and 42 percent of the females obtained scores of less than 4. The ASI was also administered to a random sample of male and female undergraduates during separate semesters of the academic year. In addition, they participated in a behavioral task requiring overt expression of assertive responses (this task yields a Sum Assertion measure). The ASI correlated 0.12 and 0.00 for males and 0.49 and 0.34 for females with the Sum Assertion score. Reliability data for the ASI are not given by Friedman (1971).

College Self-Expression Scale (CSES). Developed by Galassi et al. (1974), the CSES contains 50 items (21 worded positively, 29 worded negatively) designed to measure three aspects of assertiveness (positive, negative, self-denial) in a number of interpersonal contexts for college students. Items in this scale were derived from Lazarus (1971), Wolpe (1969), and Wolpe and Lazarus (1966). Test-retest reliability coefficients obtained for two samples were 0.89 and 0.90 (Galassi et al., 1974). Males obtained higher scores than females for all samples tested. Construct validity was assessed by correlating the CSES with the Adjective Check List Scales. Significant positive correlations were obtained with the following scales: Defensiveness, Favorable, Self-confidence, Achievement, Dominance, Intraception, Heterosexuality, Exhibition, Autonomy, and Change. Significant negative correlations were obtained with the following scales: Unfavorable, Succorance, Abasement, Deference, and Counseling Readiness. Positive correlations were found with scales that typify the assertive individual; by contrast, negative correlations were found with scales that typify the unassertive and socially insecure individual. Concurrent validity was evaluated by correlating self-ratings on the CSES for 121 student teachers with ratings of assertiveness made by their supervisors. A low but significant correlation ($r = 0.19$, $p < 0.04$) resulted. In an additional attempt to assess construct validity of the scale, Galassi and Galassi (1974) found a correlation of 0.33 ($p < 0.005$) between CSES ratings made by male and female undergraduate dormitory residents and ratings made by residence hall counselors.

Conflict Resolution Inventory (CRI). The CRI (McFall & Lillesand, 1971) is an empirically derived self-report measure of assertiveness. Eighty-two items were selected from an exhaustive list of items relating to unreasonable requests that college students identified as difficult to refuse. These 82 items were then administered to a sample of 60 students. An additional item ("How much of a problem do you feel you have when it comes to saying 'no' to people regarding things you don't want to do?") was presented in the format of a 100-point scale. Students scoring below 35 on this item comprised the low assertiveness group; students scoring above 65 comprised the high assertiveness group. Highs and lows were compared on the original 82 items. Thirty-five items that discriminated between the two groups were retained in the final form of the CRI. Although specific test-retest reliability data are not provided by McFall and Lillesand (1971), significant positive correlations were obtained between the CRI and ratings of students' assertiveness in an actual behavioral task (pretest $r = 0.69$, posttest $r = 0.63$). The CRI has been used in subsequent studies as a dependent measure by McFall and Twentyman (1973) and Kazdin (1974).

Rathus Assertiveness Schedule (RAS). The RAS (Rathus, 1973a) contains 30 items based on those found in the Allport (1928) and Guilford and Zimmerman (1956) scales, Wolpe (1969), Wolpe and Lazarus (1966), and on diary notes maintained by college juniors and seniors. Test-retest reliability for a group of male and female undergraduates was 0.78 over a two-month period. Split-half reliability based on odd-even item scores was 0.77. The RAS was evaluated in several ways. In one study RAS scores of 67 students were compared with ratings of assertiveness made by 18 additional students who knew the RAS respondents well. Ratings were made by these 18 students on a 17-item semantic differential inventory that was factor analyzed using a principal components technique. RAS ratings correlated positively and significantly with five of the items contributing to the assertiveness factor (boldness, outspokeness, assertiveness, aggression, confidence). An additional measure of validity was obtained by correlating responses of 47 female undergraduates on the RAS with ratings of their audiotaped responses to five situations requiring assertiveness. Audiotaped responses to the five questions were rated independently by two judges (interrater reliability achieved was $r = 0.94$). The correlation between RAS scores and judges' ratings of responses was 0.70. An item analysis was also performed, indicating that 27 of the 30 items correlated significantly with the total RAS score. The RAS has been used to assess the effects of assertion training in college students (Rathus, 1972; Rathus, 1973b).

College Students (Behavioral Tasks)

A number of behavioral tasks requiring subjects to role play various interpersonal situations have been used as dependent measures during the course of assertion training investigations (see Kazdin, 1974; McFall & Lillesand, 1971; McFall & Marston, 1970; McFall & Twentyman, 1973; Rathus, 1972, 1973b; Young, Rimm, & Kennedy, 1973). Subjects' responses to these role-played encounters are either audiotaped or videotaped and subsequently rated by independent judges. Ratings are usually made for overall assertiveness. More specific component measures (e.g., response latency, response duration, and speech disfluencies) have also been rated at times. Ratings are typically made on 5-point or 7-point Likert scales.

The prototype of the behavioral tasks is the one developed by McFall and Marston (1970), which is known as the Behavioral Role Playing Test. The items that comprise the test were empirically selected from an initial pool of over 2000 situations. This list was then decreased to 80 situations and administered to 60 undergraduates. Resulting data were factor analyzed, and items with the highest factor loadings and rated most difficult were cross-validated in an additional sample of 45 undergraduates. Sixteen situations were retained on the basis of the cross-validation study. Each scene is presented with narration, an antagonist's prompting, and then the student is expected to respond following a given cue (e.g., bell, buzzer). An illustration is presented below:

NARRATOR: In this scene, picture yourself standing in a ticket line outside of a theatre. You've been in line now for at least ten minutes, and it's getting pretty close to show time. You're still pretty far from the beginning of the line, and you're starting to wonder if there will be enough tickets left. There you are, waiting patiently, when two people walk up to the person in front of you and they begin talking. They're obviously all friends, and they're going to the same movie. You look quickly at your watch and notice that the show starts in just two minutes. Just then, one of the newcomers says to his friend in line:

NEWCOMER: Hey, the line's a mile long. How 'bout if we cut in here with you?

PERSON IN LINE: Sure, come on. A couple more won't make any difference. (McFall & Marston, 1970, p. 297)

Although the behavioral situations used from one study to the next vary to some extent, such differences are not considerable. Interjudge reliability ratings for most of the components of assertiveness are generally high. For example, Kazdin (1974) reports percentage agreements between raters of 90.4 percent and 88.5 percent for latency and response duration and an *r* of 0.98 for disfluency ratings. Similarly, overall ratings of assertiveness range from 0.73 to 0.93 in the McFall and Twentyman (1973) study and 0.86 and 0.94 in studies conducted by Rathus (1972, 1973b).

A somewhat different behavioral task, which yields a Sum Assertion score, was developed by Friedman (1971). This task consists of the subject's putting together a 12-piece puzzle during which time the experimenter's accomplice enters the laboratory and disrupts the subject's performance (i.e., talking loudly, playing the radio, insulting the subject). Ratings of subjects' audiotaped reactions to the accomplice are made on the basis of 24 behavioral units. Scores range from 0 to 24. Some of the units included are threat, demand, insult, strong disagreement, request to stop. Interrater reliabilities for this task are somewhat lower than those previously reported for the other behavioral tasks, ranging from 0.56 to 0.86. This task has not gained general acceptance as a viable dependent measure and has been used only by Friedman (1971).

College Students (Physiological Measurement)

McFall and Marston (1970) have conducted the only study in the area of social skills in which physiological measurements have been used. Following recommendations made by Paul (1966), pulse rate was employed as the index of autonomic arousal prior to and after the administration of the Behavioral Role Playing Test (on a pretreatment and posttreatment basis). Pulse rate appeared to be the least sensitive of the measures used by McFall and Marston (1970). Significant differences between experimental and control conditions were obtained for pulse rates taken after the Behavioral Role Playing Test *only* when the experimental groups were *combined* and compared with the *combined* control groups. The specific relationships between pulse rate and self-report measures and pulse rate and overt behavioral measures were not presented.

College Students (Assessing Generalization of Training)

A survey of the literature indicates that three types of behavioral measures have been used to assess generalization of the effects of skill training. The first simply involves pretest-posttest evaluations of "untrained" items of the Behavioral Role Playing Test (see Kazdin, 1974; McFall & Lillesand, 1971; McFall & Marston, 1970; McFall & Twentyman, 1973; Young, Rimm, & Kennedy, 1973). That is, pretreatment measures are taken on all items of the Behavioral Role Playing Test selected for study, and training is applied to half of the items, but posttreatment measures are taken on all items. Thus when comparing different treatment strategies, an assessment of both training and generalization is possible.

A second strategy for assessing generalization was used by McFall and Lillesand (1971) and is labeled the Extended Interaction Test.

"Following the behavioral test, each *S* was confronted with one additional role-played situation: . . . A prerecorded antagonist made an unreasonable request, if *S* refused, the antagonist pleaded; if he refused again, the antagonist became more insistent; and so on, until *S* either acquiesced or refused five times. This extended interaction differed from the behavioral assessment task and rehearsal training in that it required *S*s to persevere beyond one response in order to refuse successfully." (McFall & Lillesand, 1971, p. 316)

A third method for evaluating generalization effects is an extralaboratory measure of a surreptitious nature conducted in the subject's natural environment (see Kazdin, 1974; McFall & Lillesand, 1971; McFall & Marston, 1970; McFall & Twentyman, 1973). This measure was first utilized by McFall and Marston (1970) following a brief course of assertion training. All subjects in the study were contacted by telephone two weeks after their posttreatment assessment. An experimenter, naive as to the subject's experimental condition, called and posed as a magazine salesman. He followed a carefully designed "sales pitch" using a "hard sell" approach in trying to convince subjects to purchase a subscription to two of the magazines offered. The telephone call was terminated if the subject agreed to buy or hung up, or if five minutes had elapsed during which time the "salesman" was unable to sell to his prospective customer. Following completion of all aspects of the study, subjects were recontacted and debriefed. Each of the calls was tape-recorded for subsequent rating purposes. A number of measures were obtained including total time of the call, time until the subject's first expression of refusal, verbal activity level, and social skill in dealing with the situation. Average interrater reliability agreements for resistance, activity and social skill were 0.85, 0.70, and 0.30, respectively.

Although this measure proved to be viable in McFall and Marston's (1970) first study, subsequent work (Kazdin, 1974; McFall & Lillesand, 1971; McFall & Twentyman, 1973) using similar measures has resulted in somewhat disappointing findings. Therefore, in the fourth of a series of experiments reported in a paper by McFall and Twentyman (1973), a telephone follow-up situation more germane to subjects' particular interests (related to specific classes and course work) was introduced. The measure consists essentially of a graded series of seven unreasonable requests terminated only when the subject first refuses. This is the actual script that was followed:

"(Answers phone). Hi, may I speak to (subject's name). (Subject)? You're taking Introductory Psychology, aren't you? I'm Tom Blake. I don't think you know me, but I'm in (Professor)'s lecture, too. I don't know anyone in the class, so I got your name off the registration list they have in the psych office. (Request 1:) I really hate to bother you, but I have some questions on some of the lecture material. Do you think you could help me for a few minutes? (Request 2:) I think all I need is to take a look at your notes. Could that be arranged? (Request 3:) I haven't made it to all the lectures, so I'll need to borrow your notes for awhile to fill in what I've missed, okay? (Request 4:) Well, actually, (subject), the truth of the matter is, I haven't been in to class since the 12-weeks exam, so I'll probably need your notes for two days. Would that be all right? (Request 5:) Let's see now. I have a paper due on Wednesday (5 days before the subject's exam), so I won't be able to get them before that. Could I get them sometime on Thursday? (Request 6:) Oh, wait a minute! I've got a chemistry exam on Friday. Could I get them after that? That would be three days before the psych exam (Request 7:) Now that I think about it, I'll probably need a night to recover from the chem exam, so is it all right if I get them Saturday instead, for the two days before the exam?" (McFall & Twentyman, 1973, p. 212)

The telephone follow-up measure using unreasonable requests is considered to be superior to the all-or-none telephone follow-up technique previously used to assess generalization effects. However, as in most of the contrived generalization measures there are some serious ethical reservations in the use of deception. McFall and Twentyman (1973) propose a solution that warrants investigation. "If subjects were informed following treatment that their in vivo behavior was going to be assessed unobtrusively, this might serve to facilitate the extension of treatment effects to real-life behaviors" (p. 215).

College Students (Critical Commentary). Our critical commentary will be tempered by the fact that behavioral assessment in the area of social skills is of relatively recent origin (i.e., the last five to 10 years). Indeed, the more carefully designed assessment strategies have been developed in the last three to four years. A major problem is that most of the strategies were designed for specific research projects and generally have not been cross-validated in other laboratories with both similar and different subject populations.

When examining the tripartite division (i.e., self-report, motoric, physiological), it is of some interest that the self-report inventories have received the most careful attention with respect to the critical measurement considerations of reliability and validity. However, here too the range of precision varies depending on the particular study. As was the case in the self-assessment of fear (see Hersen, 1973) and dating skills, there are a number of gaps in the literature. Thus future study might be directed toward filling in these gaps along the following lines of inquiry.

1. Through factor analytic techniques, the primary factors accounting for social skill in the separate schedules should be ascertained, with a goal of diminishing duplication in items between and among schedules. The use of factor-derived scores instead of total scale scores might then result in more homogeneous populations when one is conducting comparative research.
2. Although there is some evidence for split-half reliability and test-retest reliability, longer-term reliability studies are needed to assess naturally occurring increments or decrements as a function of time. Such data would have obvious implications in terms of controlled group comparisons in which treatment requires several month's duration.
3. Although concurrent validity and predictive validity have been examined for some of the scales, in most instances the resulting correlation coefficients are quite low (e.g., Galassi & Galassi, 1974), accounting for small portions of the response variance even when statistically significant. It is quite probable that if validation studies focused more on factor scores rather than total scale scores, such coefficients would be higher. However, one must recognize that although high correlations between verbal and motoric indices are desirable in terms of predictive validity, large verbal

and motoric discrepancies are frequently found in behavioral research. As noted by Begelman and Hersen (1973) in another context (the verbal-motor discrepancy in schizophrenia with respect to fear), ". . . the verbal response is a criterion of a different psychological variable. It is a criterion of a *S*'s belief that he has a fearful attitude. Whether he does or not will be clarified for him as well as others in light of how he behaves motorically" (p. 179). It does not follow that once the motoric behavior is modified the verbal response (i.e., attitude) will automatically change. Frequently it will, but at other times the verbal response must also undergo direct modification.

4. More data are needed with respect to sex differences on these schedules. This is critical with respect to treatment inasmuch as norms may and undoubtedly will vary between the sexes.

5. As has been pointed out in several other publications (e.g., Hersen & Bellack, 1976; Hersen, Eisler, & Miller, 1973; Lazarus, 1971; Wolpe, 1969), considerably greater attention needs to be directed toward assessing the expression of positive feelings. Many of the schedules incorporate items that involve positive expression, but the accent is on the negative and on refusing unreasonable requests (e.g., McFall & Lillesand, 1971). Not only should such schedules tap the subject's ability to engage in positive social interactions, but separate reliability and validity data need to be presented for each form ("hostile" and "commendatory") of assertive response. Given assertiveness schedules that evaluate positive responding, more attention might be paid to increasing positive responses in treatment paradigms.

Some of the above criticisms apply equally well to the contrived behavioral tasks that have been designed to evaluate assertive behavior. The primary gap here is that the emphasis has also been on refusal and expression of negative feelings. The situations in the Behavioral Role Playing Test need to be expanded, as they were in the case of the Revised Behavioral Assertiveness Test (see Eisler, Hersen, Miller, & Blanchard, 1975). Aspects that should be added include situations requiring the expression of positive and negative assertiveness with variations in situational context and sex of the protagonist. Additional research is needed to determine the specific relationship between self-reports of positive and negative assertiveness and actual behavior in role-played situations requiring such expression. Similarly, the relationship of positive and negative responding in role-playing tasks to physiological responding would add to our knowledge of what constitutes social skill. With the exception of the original McFall and Marston (1970) investigation, the absence of attention to physiological measurement in the area of social skills is striking. The existence of the sophisticated physiological measurement devices that have recently appeared (some of which record at long range through telemetry) makes this gap in the literature surprising. Absence of data concerning the impact of physiological responding with respect to social skill is of major import, given Hersen's (1973) and Lang's (1968) contention that successful behavioral treatment must involve the modification of all three response systems to obtain maximum results.

The measurement area that requires the most attention at this time is the one concerned with assessing generalization of treatment effects. Although the method of comparatively evaluating changes in trained and untrained items in role-playing tasks is straightforward, Kazdin (1974) cogently argues, "A better test of generalization is assessment by a measure methodologically distant from previous measures" (p. 248). In this connection McFall and his colleagues (McFall & Lillesand, 1971; McFall & Marston, 1970; McFall & Twentyman, 1973) developed extralaboratory measures (telephone follow-ups) to detect generalization. However, in addition to the ethical issue of deception involved in such measures, Kazdin (1974) questions whether these telephone follow-ups are adequate measures of generalization. Perhaps the all-or-none quality of such measures and their vague relationship to the specific targets actually modified during treatment mitigate against obtaining evidence for generalization. An intriguing possibility that presents itself is to specifically evaluate those targets modified during treatment (e.g., eye contact, duration of speech, making requests, etc.) in extratreatment settings under naturalistic conditions (see Hersen, Turner, Edelstein, & Pinkston, 1975, for an example of such generalization in a single case analysis). Once again, however, the issue of deception must be tackled, and McFall and Twentyman's (1973) recommendation that subjects be apprised that they will be monitored unobtrusively following treatment appears relevant. Not only does this seem like the most ethical solution to the problem, but from a treatment viewpoint, it is likely that generalization effects would be enhanced.

It is clear that much research is needed to identify the most relevant measures for assessing generalization in addition to determining the relationship between measures of generalization and within-treatment role-playing tasks.

Psychiatric Patients (Self-Report Inventories)

Fewer self-report instruments have been developed for use with psychiatric patients than with college students. The characteristics of three such instruments to measure assertiveness are presented in Table 14–4. As noted there, Lazarus' (1971) Assertive Questionnaire is primarily a clinical tool,

Table 14–4. Characteristics of Assertive Scales for Psychiatric Populations

References	Scale	No. of Items	Format	Normative Population
Goldsmith & McFall (1975)	Interpersonal Situation Inventory	55	1–5 point ratings	Male psychiatric patients.
Lazarus (1971)	Assertive Questionnaire	20	yes–no	None originally reported but used clinically with psychiatric patients.
Wolpe & Lazarus (1966)	Assertiveness Scale	30	yes–no	None originally reported but used clinically with psychiatric patients.

and no reliability or validity data are presented. Similarly, the Wolpe and Lazarus (1966) Assertiveness Scale was developed for use in clinical situations. Although no normative data were originally presented, male inpatient subjects who rated high and low in overall assertiveness on the Behavioral Assertiveness Test (Eisler, Miller, & Hersen, 1973) and on the Behavioral Assertiveness Test—Revised Male (Eisler, Hersen, Miller, & Blanchard, 1975) were significantly differentiated on the Wolpe-Lazarus Assertiveness Scale. The Wolpe-Lazarus scale was used as an outcome measure in an analogue treatment study with psychiatric patients (Hersen, Eisler, Miller, Johnson, & Pinkston, 1973) but failed to differentiate among the groups.

In contrast to the clinical development of the aforementioned scales, Goldsmith and McFall (1975) derived their 55-item Interpersonal Situation Inventory (ISI) empirically. On the basis of detailed interviews with eight male and eight female psychiatric patients, a list of 55 problematic interpersonal situations was devised. These 55 situations were then submitted to a second group of 20 male inpatients through audiotape. Patients were asked to respond to each situation with one of five alternatives, ranging from being able to handle a situation and feeling comfortable in it at one extreme, to not being able to handle that situation and feeling uncomfortable in it at the other extreme. An additional response alternative was included to indicate that a situation described was not personally relevant to the subject. Examination of resulting data indicated that more than 80 percent of the subjects reported some difficulty in these situations. Reliability and validity data for this inventory are not available at this time.

Psychiatric Patients (Behavioral Tasks)

As in the case of the behavioral tasks used to assess social skill in college students, many of the specific strategies used with psychiatric populations were developed primarily for use in one or two specific studies. Therefore, reliability and validity data (particularly cross-validation) are frequently not available. Furthermore, correlations between these measures and self-report indices are generally not reported despite the fact that they are often used concurrently in outcome studies.

As we describe the several measures that have been developed (see Table 14–5), we will attempt to highlight particular strengths and weaknesses of each measure.

Videotaped Conversation. Argyle, Bryant, and Trower, 1974) reported this measure that simply involves having the patient talk informally to male and female interpersonal partners separately in a semistructured interview. The length of the interview and the specific format employed are not indicated. Behavior is rated retrospectively by videotape (e.g., content, sequence, posture, gaze, clarity, pitch, etc.). Ratings are made on 17 scales using a series of 5-point scales anchored by 0 (denoting normal appropriate behavior) and 4 (denoting severe impairment). Interrater reliability studies yield correlations ranging from 0.71 to 0.91 on total scores. Intrarater reliability by one rater at a 19-week test-retest interval resulted in a 0.87 correlation for total score. A two-year test-retest study for intrarater reliability yielded coefficients ranging from 0.38 to 0.74. A validity study in which subjects were dichotomized into high and low skill groups indicated that the lesser skilled were rated as "more anxious, less rewarding, less poised, less happy, and more lacking in warmth than the others" (Argyle, Bryant, & Trower, 1974, p. 439). Separate norms are not presented for male and female subjects in relation to their interactions with male and female interpersonal partners. In addition, responses on this task are not correlated with self-report measures of social and interpersonal skill or comfort in such situations.

Behavioral Assertiveness Test (BAT). The BAT involves a series of 14 standard interpersonal situations, each of which requires an assertive response on the subject's part following a prompting by a female role model (Eisler, Miller, & Hersen, 1973). In their initial study Eisler, Miller, and Hersen (1973) administered this test to an unselected (diagnostically) group of 30 male psychiatric patients. Because of the interactive nature of situations on this task, subjects were either married, separated, or divorced. Patients' videotaped responses were rated on the basis of overall assertiveness, and subjects were dichotomized at the median into high and low assertiveness groups. Specific components of assertiveness (e.g., latency of response, compliance content, requests for new behavior) were rated. Subjects with high and low assertiveness were differentiated on five of the nine components measured. In addition, subjects with high and low assertiveness were significantly differentiated on the Wolpe-Lazarus Assertiveness Scale but not on the Willoughby Personality Inventory. Interrater percentages of agreement ranged from 99.3 percent to 100 percent, and interrater reliabilities ranged from 0.96 to 0.99 on the component measures. The BAT and its variants have frequently been used as outcome measures in single case and controlled group comparison studies (Eisler, Hersen, & Miller, 1973; Foy, Eisler, & Pinkston, 1975; Hersen, Eisler, & Miller, 1974; Hersen, Eisler, Miller, Johnson, & Pinkston, 1973; Hersen, Turner, Edelstein, & Pinkston, 1975).

Although the BAT is empirically derived, it is somewhat limited inasmuch as it focuses on "hostile" assertiveness, with responses directed only

Table 14–5. Characteristics of Behavioral Tasks for Psychiatric Populations

Reference	Task	Number of Items	Ratings
Argyle, Bryant, & Trower (1974)	Videotaped Conversations	Informal conversation with male and female	17 verbal and non-verbal measures
Eisler, Miller, & Hersen (1973)	Behavioral Assertiveness Test	Responses to 14 role played situations	10 verbal and non-verbal measures
Eisler et al. (1975)	Behavioral Assertiveness Test-Revised	Responses to 32 role played situations	12 verbal and non-verbal measures
Goldsmith & McFall (1975)	Interpersonal Behavior Role-Playing Test	Responses to 25 role played situations	0–2 point ratings per situation on competence
Goldstein et al. (1973)	Tape Recorded Interpersonal Situations	Responses to 50 audio-taped situations	5 point rating scale for independence-dependence
Gutride, Goldstein, & Hunter (1973)	Interaction with Experimental "Accomplice"	Responses to 6 questions posed by experimental confederate	20 ratings on a social interaction checklist
Weinman et al. (1972)	Behavior in Critical Situations	Responses to four contrived situations	2–5 point rating scales on the 4 critical situations

toward female role models. Test-retest reliability has not been evaluated to date.

Behavioral Assertiveness Test—Revised Male (*BAT–RM*). Eisler et al. (1975) described the BAT–RM which consists of 32 situations, half of which involve expression of positive assertiveness while the other half involve expression of negative assertiveness. Situational context is varied in that the scenes are divided along a familiarity-unfamiliarity dimension. In half the protagonist is unfamiliar to the subject; in the remaining half the protagonist is familiar to the subject. The scenes are further subdivided along the male-female dichotomy with respect to sex of the role model used to prompt subjects' responses. Eisler et al. (1975) administered the BAT–RM to 60 unselected male psychiatric patients who were married, divorced, or separated. Subjects' responses were videotaped and rated retrospectively by two independent raters on 12 verbal and nonverbal measures. Percentages of agreement and correlation coefficients between raters were in the mid 90s. A second set of independent judges made ratings of overall assertiveness. High-assertive (top third) and low-assertive (bottom third) subjects were differentiated on nine of the 12 measures and on the Wolpe-Lazarus Assertiveness Scale. In addition, data with respect to sex of the protagonist, familiarity or unfamiliarity of the protagonist, and positive versus negative assertion clearly indicate the stimulus specificity of assertive responding in terms of the 12 verbal and nonverbal indices. Comparable data for female psychiatric patients are now being collected by the authors of this chapter.

Interpersonal Behavior Role-Playing Test (*IBRT*). The IBRT (Goldsmith & McFall, 1975) consists of 25 tape-recorded interpersonal situations used as stimulus materials for patients' role-played responses. Patients' responses to each situation are scored on a 0- to 2-point scale of competence, with two points allotted if all criteria for competence are met for that situation. "Blind" raters achieved 95 percent agreement on total scores of all responses.

Scenes for the IRBT were taken from Goldsmith and McFall's (1975) 55-item ISI, previously described on page 541. Responses to the 55-item ISI by eight staff members of a psychiatric institute were rated on a competence dimension. Criteria for competence were identified from these ratings. For a response to be labeled as competent, four of five raters were required to judge it as such with no rater labeling it incompetent. The 25 items comprising the final IBRT were those deemed most relevant to the particular inpatient population under study.

Tape-Recorded Interpersonal Situations. Tape-recorded interpersonal situations were used by Goldstein et al. (1973) in three experiments designed to assess the effects of modeling on independent behavior in psychiatric patients. Fifty audiotaped situations involving a stimulus person and a target person are presented to patients. Two choices representing an independent and a dependent response are available, and the subject is asked to select the one most representative of his "projected" response in that situation. An example is presented below for illustration:

E_1: A friend asks you to go downtown to buy a special present for her mother. However, you buy a different present because the one she wanted is sold out. She says to you:

E_2: I think it's rubbish!

Independent response alternative: Then you should have gone yourself.

Dependent response alternative: I'll change it for you. (Goldstein et al., 1973, p. 33)

Interaction Task with an Experimental "Accomplice." Gutride, Goldstein, and Hunter (1973) reported how the interaction with an experimental accomplice is unobtrusively observed through a one-way mirror while the patient is seated in a waiting room. The accomplice (actually another patient taught to role-play a part) asks questions at 30-second, 60-second, 90-second, two-minute, three-minute, and four-minute intervals. Responses to queries are rated by a trained observer on a number of verbal and nonverbal indices (e.g., eye contact, responds to conversation, leaning forward, etc.). Reliability data for this task are not presented, but similar observations made on the ward yielded an average interrater agreement of 85 percent.

Behavior in Critical Situations. Critical situations were developed by Weinman et al. (1972) to assess the effects of assertion training and other behavioral techniques in chronic schizophrenics. Subjects' responses to four contrived situations labeled *affiliation, failure, disagreement,* and *default* were observed behind a one-way mirror. In each of the situations some deception was involved in accordance with actions perpetrated by the experimenter's confederate. Scales for each situation were rated on a 2- to 5-point basis, with scores for each situation transformed to a total of 25 points. Test-retest data for a two-week period resulted in a rank difference correlation of 0.72. Interrater agreement reached a 98 percent level. Ratings on this behavioral task correlation 0.31 ($p < 0.025$) with scores on the Brief Psychiatric Rating Scales.

Psychiatric Patients (Assessing Generalization of Training)

Examination of the currently available literature indicates that several methods have been employed to examine generalization of treatment effects. As in the case of such assessment with college students, the first method involves pretest-posttest assessments of "untrained" items on BAT and BAT-like situations (Edelstein & Eisler, 1976; Frederiksen, Jenkins, Foy, & Eisler, 1976; Goldsmith & McFall, 1975; Hersen, Eisler, & Miller, 1974; Hersen, Turner, Edelstein, & Pinkston, 1975).

A second method involves generalization across stimulus persons and was used by Edelstein and Eisler (1976) and Frederiksen et al. (1976). Specifically, a second role model (with whom the subject has had no previous interactive experience) is substituted for the original role model during the generalization phase of a BAT presentation.

A third strategy consists of making unobtrusive naturalistic observations of behaviors independent of skills training. Behaviors on the ward (e.g., Frederiksen et al., 1976; Gutride, et al., 1973) and in group psychotherapy settings (e.g., Hersen et al., 1975) have been monitored.

Still a fourth strategy was developed by Goldsmith and McFall (1975) in which a confederate, blind to research conditions, engages the psychiatric patients in several interpersonal situations.

A fifth strategy, in which the patients' responses to being "short-changed" are videotaped and rated retrospectively on several target behaviors, was developed by Hersen, Eisler, and Miller (1974). Unfortunately, both the fourth and fifth strategies described use deception, and it appears to us that observations in naturalistic settings are to be preferred for at least two reasons: (1) The ethical issues are minimized, particularly if the patient, at the beginning of experimentation, consents to being unobtrusively observed in a variety of settings, and (2) obviously the naturalistic setting has greater face validity as a measure of generalization inasmuch as it is frequently identical to or at least very closely resembles actual situations the psychiatric patient will encounter after discharge.

Target behaviors measured in these generalization situations have yielded consistently high interobserver agreements. With one exception (Hersen, Eisler, & Miller, 1974) the particular relationships of these measures to changes in self-report and other behavioral measures of social skill are not identified. Hersen, Eisler, and Miller (1974) reported a negative relationship ($r = -0.64$, $p < 0.05$) between latency on the "short-change" situation with overall ratings of assertiveness on the 10 posttest BAT scenes. However, this significant relationship was obtained for only one of the three experimental conditions.

Psychiatric Patients (Critical Commentary). Our critical comments directed toward the work with college students apply equally to the studies made with psychiatric patients. In fact, the work in this area is of still more recent origin and even less coordinated from one laboratory to the next. Again, with the exception of the studies conducted by Eisler, Miller, and Hersen (1973), Eisler et al. (1975), and Goldsmith and McFall (1975), the approach to measuring social skills in psychiatric patients has generally been carried out on an "as needed" basis instead of on a planned, systematic program, as was earlier suggested by Goldfried and D'Zurilla (1969). There can be no doubt that from considerations of pure measurement Goldfried and D'Zurilla's recommendations for developing assessment strategies are critical in terms of achieving suitable reliability and validity.

To avoid needless duplication, we will focus here on the most glaring omissions in the current literature. The first involves the total absence of data on physiological responding in psychiatric subjects. Physiological responding is obviously a critical element in the triadic approach to measuring skill behavior, or for that matter any designated behavior. The relationships between and among verbal, motoric, and physiological response systems are not only of interest for academic reasons but are important in terms of treatment. Following the arguments presented by Lang (1968) and Hersen (1973) with respect to the study of fear, it may be necessary to modify all three response systems (motoric, attitudinal, physiological) separately to obtain maximum treatment benefits.

Two other deficiencies in current studies are concerned with sex role differences in responding and measuring generalization effects of treatment. The second most glaring omission has greatest relevance to the systematic approach recommended herein and has many treatment ramifications. Without good normative data for female psychiatric subjects, the direction and degree of modification would be judgmentally based rather than empirically based. Studies obtaining such normative data that also compare male and female responses to behavioral tasks are warranted. The third omission has been discussed in the previous section, but we will repeat it for emphasis. Indeed, the importance of generalization in most behavioral research has been acknowledged more in print than in actual practice. In spite of the fact that behavior change techniques are neither fully developed nor as potent as might eventually be possible, their application is of greater *academic interest* than of *clinical utility* if only within-treatment modification can be obtained. In the social skills area in particular, the fostering of generalization must be done in such a way that the environment reinforces the individual's newly developing response repertoire (Hersen & Bellack, 1976; Hersen & Eisler, 1976; Hersen, Eisler, & Miller, 1973). Measurement of transfer from the clinical setting to the natural environment is difficult and is presently hampered by inadequate technology as well as by serious ethical limitations. Our stated preference is to use naturalistic rather than contrived situations, with the subject cognizant (i.e,, having given full informed consent) of what observations will be made and how they will be engineered. If, as a result of such strategy, the subject were to err in the direction of expected change in target responding, then so much the better for the treatment. As repeatedly emphasized by Kelman (1967, 1975), deception in social psychological research may not be needed and is not desirable from a methodological or ethical standpoint.

ASSESSMENT AS RELATED TO TREATMENT

As previously noted, there is an extremely close relationship between assessment and treatment in behavior modification in general and assessment and treatment in the social skills area in particular. Consistent with the "skill deficit" hypothesis proposed in a number of papers (e.g., Goldsmith & McFall, 1975; Hersen & Bellack, 1976; Hersen & Eisler, 1976; Hersen, Eisler, & Miller, 1973), it becomes apparent that the primary goal of treatment is one of education and/or re-education. Following a careful behavioral analysis in which all three response systems (i.e., motoric, physiological, self-report) are considered, specific techniques for instituting or reinstituting given responses are then applied. As research in this area accumulates, the most effective behavioral technique for a given deficit will have been identified, thus permitting its "automatic" application, given the particular restrictions or contraindications of the case. For example, Hersen et al. (1973) found that a simple instructional technique was effective in reinstating appropriate rates of eye contact in unassertive psychiatric patients. Data suggested that the addition of modeling in this case did not lead to further enhancement. On the other hand, it was found that for the more complex components of assertive behavior (e.g., refusing to be compliant, making an appropriate request from an interpersonal partner) a mere instructional set was not effective. Instead, the combination of modeling plus instructions resulted in the most pronounced behavioral change.

Unfortunately, techniques for treating minimal dating are less advanced. Although packages for treating skills appear to be effective in bringing about changes in self-reports and observer ratings of global skill and anxiety (e.g., Curran, 1975; Twentyman & McFall, 1975), the particular treatments that will yield changes in specified component behaviors have not been isolated. This can be attributed to (1) the newness of the area, (2) the absence of a careful assessment of the specific components comprising dating skill, and (3) the examination of treatment strategies prior to establishing a methodological approach to assessment. Goldfried and D'Zurilla's (1969) empirical approach to developing assessment techniques needs to be adhered to with greater consistency. If this approach were to be followed, the needed rapport between assessment and treatment of minimal dating would be achieved.

In general, the most consistent relationship between assessment and treatment is made possible by using the single case strategy. The reader is referred to Barlow and Hersen (1973) and Hersen and Barlow (1976) for more complete analysis of this relationship. In brief, however, the single case strategy not only permits an initial assessment of the patient's skills and weaknesses during the baseline period, but, as a function of consistent monitoring (i.e., repeated measurements), it allows for a continual reassessment of the particular efficacy of a given behavioral technique. Thus the relation of treatment to the original diagnosis is portrayed graphically on an ongoing basis, permitting a flexible therapeutic approach (i.e., changing and/or adding techniques) as dictated by the requirements of the case. This is particularly useful when one is dealing with deficit behaviors.

SUMMARY AND CONCLUSION

Behavior modifiers have only recently become interested in deficits in social skills and their remediation. As with other new areas, the initial focus has been on treatment. Assessment has been carried along almost reluctantly, like a poor cousin, and more questions have been raised about assessment than have been answered. Lack of clear assessment has retarded understanding of the nature of social skills as well as the planning and evaluation of treatment.

The only issue that *appears* to have been resolved pertains to response modalities. Self-report, overt behavioral, and physiological response measures have had consistently low relationships with one another. There is no indication that any one modality is sufficient to adequately represent the social skill complex. Therefore, the use of a multi-channel measurement battery appears to be a necessity. The question as to which devices should be included in such a battery is still unanswered. Our opinions about the most promising devices have been provided in the preceding sections. However, no single device has yet been clearly and thoroughly validated. Reliability (stability and homogeneity) has been an especially neglected issue. In conclusion we recommend that future research take one of two directions: *psychometric evaluation* of existing devices or *psychometric construction* of new devices.

REFERENCE NOTES

1. Hersen, M., & Miller, P. M. *Social skills training for neurotically depressed clients.* Unpublished manuscript.
2. Arkowitz, H. *College dating inhibitions: Assessment and treatment.* Paper presented at the American Psychological Association, Montreal, Canada, 1973.
3. Clark, J. V., & Arkowitz, H. *The behavioral treatment of social inhibition: A case report.* Unpublished manuscript.

REFERENCES

Allport, G. *A-S reaction study.* Boston: Houghton Mifflin, 1928.

Argyle, M., Bryant, B., & Trower, P. Social skills training and psychotherapy. *Psychological Medicine*, 1974, **4,** 435–443.

Argyle, M., Trower, P., & Bryant, B. Explorations in the treatment of personality disorders and neuroses by social skills training. *British Journal of Medical Psychology*, 1974, **47,** 63–72.

Argyris, C. Explorations in interpersonal competence—I. *Journal of Applied Behavioral Science*, 1965, **1,** 58–83.

Argyris, C. Conditions for competence acquisition and therapy. *Journal of Applied Behavioral Science*, 1968, **4,** 147–177.

Argyris, C. The incompleteness of social-psychological theory: Examples from small group, cognitive consistency, and attribution research. *American Psychologist*, 1969, **24,** 893–908.

Arkowitz, H., Lichtenstein, B., McGovern, K., & Hines, P. The behavioral assessment of social competence in males. *Behavior Therapy*, 1975, **6,** 3–13.

Bander, K. W., Steinke, G. V., Allen, G. J., & Mosher, D. L. Evaluation of three dating-specific treatment approaches for heterosexual dating anxiety. *Journal of Consulting and Clinical Psychology*, 1975, **43,** 259–265.

Barlow, D. H., & Hersen, M. Single-case experimental designs: Use in applied clinical research. *Archives of General Psychiatry*, 1973, **29,** 319–325.

Bates, H. D., & Zimmerman, S. F. Toward the development of a screening scale for assertive training. *Psychological Reports*, 1971, **28,** 99–107.

Begelman, D. A., & Hersen, M. An experimental analysis of the verbal-motor discrepancy in schizophrenia. *Journal of Clinical Psychology*, 1973, **29,** 175–179.

Borkoveck T. D., Stone, N. M., O'Brien, G. T., & Kaloupek, D. G. Evaluation of a clinically relevant target behavior for analog outcome research. *Behaviour Therapy*, 1974, **5,** 503–513.

Bryant, B. M., & Trower, P. E. Social difficulty in a student sample, *British Journal of Educational Psychology*, 1974, **44,** 13–21.

Campbell, D. T., & Fiske, D. W. Convergent and discriminant validation by the multitrait-multimethod matrix. *Psychological Bulletin*, 1959, **56,** 81–105.

Christensen, A., & Arkowitz, H. Preliminary report on practice dating and feedback as treatment for college dating problems. *Journal of Counseling Psychology*, 1974, **21,** 92–95.

Christensen, A., Arkowitz, H., & Anderson, J. Practice dating as treatment for college dating inhibitions. *Behaviour Research and Therapy*, 1976, **13,** 321–331.

Cronbach, L. J. *Essentials of psychological testing* (2nd ed.). New York: Harper & Row, 1960.

Curran, J. P. Social skills training and systematic desensitization in reducing dating anxiety. *Behaviour Research and Therapy*, 1975, **13,** 65–68.

Curran, J. P., & Gilbert, F. S. A test of the relative eflectiveness of a systematic desensitization program and an interpersonal skills training program with date anxious subjects. *Behavior Therapy*, 1975, **6,** 510–521.

Curran, J. P., Gilbert, F. S., & Little, L. M. A comparison between behavioral replication training and sensitivity training approaches to heterosexual dating anxiety. *Journal of Counseling Psychology*, 1976, **23,** 190–196.

Detre, T. P., & Jarecki, H. G. *Modern psychiatric treatment.* Philadelphia: J. B. Lippincott, 1971.

Edelstein, B. A., & Eisler, R. M. Effects of modeling and modeling with instructions and feedback on the behavioral components of social skills. *Behavior Therapy*, 1976, **7,** 382–389.

Eisler, R. M., Hersen, M., & Miller, P. M. Effects of modeling on components of assertive behavior. *Journal of Behavior Therapy and Experimental Psychiatry*, 1973, **4,** 1–6.

Eisler, R. M., Hersen, M., & Miller, P. M. Shaping components of assertiveness with instructions and feedback. *American Journal of Psychiatry*, 1974, **131,** 1344–1347.

Eisler, R. M., Hersen, M., Miller, P. M., & Blanchard, E. B. Situational determinants of assertive behaviors. *Journal of Consulting and Clinical Psychology*, 1975, **43,** 330–340.

Eisler, R. M., Miller, P. M., & Hersen, M. Components of assertive behavior. *Journal of Clinical Psychology*, 1973, **29,** 295–299.

Endler, N. S., Hunt, J. M. & Rosenstein, A. J. An S–R inventory of anxiousness. *Psychological Monographs.* 1962, **76,** (17, Whole No. 536).

Foy, D. W. Eisler, R. M., & Pinkston, S. G. Modeled assertion in a case of explosive rage. *Journal of Behavior Therapy and Experimental Psychiatry*, 1975, **6,** 135–138.

Frank, J. D. Therapeutic components of psychotherapy: A 25 year-progress report of research. *Journal of Nervous and Mental Disease*, 1974, **159,** 325–342.

Fredericksen, L. W., Jenikns, J. O., Fox, D. W., & Eisler, R. M. Social skills training in the modifications of abusive verbal outbursts in adults. *Journal of Applied Behavior Analysis*, 1976, **9,** 117–125.

Friedman, P. H. The effects of modeling and role-playing on assertive behavior. Unpublished doctoral dissertation, University of Wisconsin, 1968.

Friedman, P. H. The effects of modeling and role-playing on assertive behavior. In R. D. Rubin, H. Fensterheim, A. A. Lazarus, & C. M. Franks (Eds.), *Advances in behavior therapy*. New York: Academic, 1971.

Galassi, J. P., & Galassi, M. D. Validity of a measure of assertiveness. *Journal of Counseling Psychology*, 1974, **21,** 248–250.

Galassi, J. P., DeLo, J. S., Galassi, M. D., & Bastien, S. The collete self-expression scale: A measure of assertiveness. *Behavior Therapy*, 1974, **5,** 165–171.

Gladwin, T. Social competence and clinical practice. *Psychiatry*, 1967, **30,** 30–43.

Glasgow, R., & Arkowitz, H. The behavioral assessment of male and female social competence in dyadic heterosexual interactions. *Behavior Therapy*, 1975, **6,** 488–498.

Goldfried, M. R., & D'Zurilla, T. J. A behavior-analytic model for assessing competence. In C. D. Spielberger (Ed.), *Current topics in clinical and community psychology. Vol. 1.* New York: Academic, 1969.

Goldsmith, J. B., & McFall, R. M. Development and evaluation of an interpersonal skill-training program for psychiatric inpatients. *Journal of Abnormal Psychology*, 1975, **84,** 51–58.

Goldstein, A. P., Martens, J., Hubben, J., van Belle, H. A., Schaaf, W., Wiersman, H., & Goedhart, A. The use of modeling to increase independent behaviour. *Behaviour Research and Therapy*, 1973, **11,** 31–42.

Guilford, J. P., & Zimmerman, W. S. *The Guilford-Zimmerman temperament survey.* Beverly Hills, Calif.: Sheridan Psychological Services, 1956.

Gutride, M. E., Goldstein, A. P., & Hunter, G. F. The use of modeling and role playing to increase social interaction among asocial psychiatric patients. *Journal of Consulting and Clinical Psychology*, 1973, **40,** 408–415.

Hersen, M. Self-assessment of fear. *Behavior Therapy*, 1973, **4,** 241–257.

Hersen, M., & Barlow, D. H. *Single case experimental designs: Strategies for studying behavior change.* New York: Pergamon, 1976.

Hersen, M., & Bellack, A. S. Social skills training for chronic psychiatric patients: Rationale, research findings, and future directions. *Comprehensive Psychiatry*, 1976, **17,** 559–580.

Hersen, M., & Eisler, R. M. Social skills training. In W. E. Craighead, A. E. Kazdin, & M. J. Mahoney (Eds.), *Behavior modification: Principles, issues, and applications.* Boston: Houghton Mifflin, 1976.

Hersen, M. Eisler, R. M., & Miller, P. M. Development of assertive responses: Clinical, measurement, and research considerations. *Behaviour Research and Therapy*, 1973, **11,** 505–521.

Hersen, M., Eisler, R. M., & Miller, P. M. An experimental analysis of generalization in assertive training. *Behaviour Research and Therapy*, 1974, **12,** 295–310.

Hersen, M., Eisler, R. M., Miller, P. M., Johnson, M. B., & Pinkston, S. G. Effects of practice, instructions, and modeling on components of assertive behavior. *Behaviour Research and Therapy*, 1973, **11,** 443–451.

Hersen, M., Turner, S. M., Edelstein, B. A., & Pinkston, S. G. Effects of phenothiazines and social skills training in a withdrawn schizophrenic. *Journal of Clinical Psychology*, 1975, **31,** 588–594.

Kazdin, A. E. Effects of covert modeling and model reinforcement on assertive behavior. *Journal of Abnormal Psychology*, 1974, **83,** 240–252.

Kelman, H. C. Human use of human subjects: The problem of deception in social psychological experiments. *Psychological Bulletin*, 1967, **67,** 1–11.

Kelman, H. C. Was deception justified—And was it necessary? Comments on "Self-control techniques as alternative to pain medication." *Journal of Abnormal Psychology*, 1975, **84,** 172–174.

Lang, P. J. Fear reduction and fear behavior: Problems in treating a construct.

In J. M. Shlien (Ed.), *Research in psychotherapy*. Vol. 3. Washington, D.C.: American Psychological Association, 1968.

Lang, P. J. The application of psychological methods to the study of psychotherapy and behavior modification. In A. E. Bergin & S. L. Garfield (Eds.), *Handbook of psychotherapy and behavior change*. New York: Wiley, 1971.

Lang, P. J., & Lazovik, A. D. Experimental desensitization of a phobia. *Journal of Abnormal and Social Psychology*, 1963, **66**, 519–525.

Lawrence, P. S. The assessment and modification of assertive behavior. Unpublished doctoral dissertation, Arizona State University, 1970.

Lazarus, A. A. *Behavior therapy and beyond*. New York: McGraw-Hill, 1971.

Levine, J., & Zigler, E. The essential-reactive distinction in alcoholism: A developmental approach. *Journal of Abnormal Psychology*, 1973, **81**, 242–249.

Libet, J., & Lewinsohn, P. M. Concept of social skill with special reference to the behavior of depressed persons. *Journal of Consulting and Clinical Psychology*, 1973, **40**, 304–312.

Lipinski, D., & Nelson, R. The reactivity and unreliability of self-recording. *Journal of Consulting and Clinical Psychology*, 1974, **42**, 118–123.

MacDonald, M. L., Lindquist, C. U., Kramer, J. A., McGrath, R. A., & Rhyne, L. L. Social skills training: The effects of behavior rehearsal in groups on dating skills. *Journal of Counseling Psychology*, 1975, **22**, 224–230.

Martinson, W. D., & Zerface, J. P. Comparison of individual counseling and a social program with nondaters. *Journal of Counseling Psychology*, 1970, **17**, 36–40.

McFall, R. M., & Lillesand, D. B. Behavior rehearsal with modeling and coaching in assertion training. *Journal of Abnormal Psychology*, 1971, **77**, 313–323.

McFall, R. M., & Marston, A. R. An experimental investigation of behavior rehearsal in assertive training. *Journal of Abnormal Psychology*, 1970, **76**, 295–303.

McFall, R. M., & Twentyman, C. T. Four experiments on the relative contributions of rehearsal, modeling, and coaching to assertion training. *Journal of Abnormal Psychology*, 1973, **81**, 199–218.

McGovern, K. B., Arkowitz, H., & Gilmore, S. K. Evaluations of social skills training programs for college dating inhibitions. *Journal of Counseling Psychology*, 1975, **22**, 505–512.

Melnick, J. A comparison of replication techniques in the modification of minimal dating behavior. *Journal of Abnormal Psychology*, 1973, **81**, 51–59.

Mischel, W. *Personality and assessment*. New York: Wiley, 1968.

Mischel, W. Direct versus indirect personality assessment: Evidence and implications. *Journal of Consulting and Clinical Psychology*, 1972, **38**, 319–324.

Paul, G. L. *Insight versus desensitization in psychotherapy*. Stanford, Calif.: Stanford University Press, 1966.

Percell, L. P., Berwick, P. T., & Beigel, A. The effects of assertive training on self-concept and anxiety. *Archives of General Psychiatry*, 1974, **31**, 502–504.

Phillips, L., & Zigler, E. Social competence: The action-thought parameter and vicariousness in normal and pathological behaviors. *Journal of Abnormal and Social Psychology*, 1961, **63**, 137–146.

Phillips, L., & Zigler, E. Role orientation, the action-thought dimension, and outcome in psychiatric disorder. *Journal of Abnormal and Social Psychology*, 1964, **68,** 381–389.

Rathus, S. A. An experimental investigation of assertive training in a group setting. *Journal of Behavior Therapy and Experimental Psychiatry*, 1972, **3,** 81–86.

Rathus, S. A. A 30-item schedule for assessing assertive behavior. *Behavior Therapy*, 1973, **4,** 398–406. (a)

Rathus, S. A. Instigation of assertive behavior through videotaped-mediated assertive models and directed practice. *Behaviour Research and Therapy*, 1973, **11,** 57–65. (b)

Rehm, L. P., & Marston, A. R. Reduction of social anxiety through modification of self-reinforcement: An instigation therapy technique. *Journal of Consulting and Clinical Psychology*, 1968, **32,** 565–574.

Taylor, J. A. Drive theory and manifest anxiety. *Psychological Bulletin*, 1956, **53,** 303–320.

Twentyman, G. T., & McFall, R. M. Behavioral training of social skills in shy males. *Journal of Consulting and Clinical Psychology*, 1975, **43,** 384–395.

Watson, D., & Friend, R. Measurement of social-evaluative anxiety. *Journal of Consulting and Clinical Psychology*, 1969, **33,** 448–457.

Weinman, B., Gelbart, P., Wallace, M., & Post, M. Inducing assertive behavior in chronic schizophrenics: A comparison of socio-environmental, desensitization, and relaxation therapies. *Journal of Consulting and Clinical Psychology*, 1972, **39,** 246–252.

Weiss, R. L. Operant conditioning techniques in psychological assessment. In P. McReynolds (Ed.), *Advances in psychological assessment*. Palo Alto, Calif.: Science & Behavior, 1968.

Weissman, M. M. The assessment of social adjustment. *Archives of General Psychiatry*, 1975, **32,** 357–365.

Wolpe, J. *Psychotherapy by reciprocal inhibition*. Stanford, Calif.: Stanford University Press, 1958.

Wolpe, J. *The practice of behavior therapy*. New York: Pergamon, 1969.

Wolpe, J., & Lang, P. J. A fear survey schedule for use in behavior therapy. *Behaviour Research and Therapy*, 1964, **2,** 27–30.

Wolpe, J., & Lazarus, A. A. *Behavior therapy techniques*. New York: Pergamon, 1966.

Young, E. R., Rimm, D. C., & Kennedy T. D. An experimental investigation of modeling and verbal reinforcement in the modification of assertive behavior. *Behaviour Research and Therapy*, 1973, **11,** 317–319.

Zigler, E., & Levine, J. Premorbid adjustment and paranoid-nonparanoid status in schizophrenia. *Journal of Abnormal Psychology*, 1973, **82,** 189–199.

Zigler, E., & Phillips, L. Social effectiveness and symptomatic behaviors. *Journal of Abnormal and Social Psychology*, 1960, **61,** 231–238.

Zigler, E., & Phillips, L. Social competence and outcome in psychiatric disorder. *Journal of Abnormal and Social Psychology*, 1961, **63,** 264–271.

Zigler, E., Phillips, L. Social competence and the process-reactive distinction in psychopathology. *Journal of Abnormal and Social Psychology*. 1962, **65,** 215–222.

Zuckerman, M. The development of an affect adjective check list for the measurement. *Journal of Consulting and Clinical Psychology*, 1960, **24,** 456–462.

CHAPTER 15

Assessment of Marital Conflict and Accord

ROBERT L. WEISS and GAYLA MARGOLIN

The behavioral assessment of marital conflict and accord is much like a Möbius strip: Assessment and intervention flow imperceptibly into each other. Unlike traditional forms of assessment, there is little concern with enduring dispositional constructs of the dynamic or metaphoric variety. Behavioral assessment focuses on functional outcomes, relationship skills, capabilities for actions, and the results of intervention. In its broadest scope behavioral assessment has four objectives: (1) Sample description—who are the individuals being observed and/or treated? (2) Behavioral targets—what behaviors are targeted for change? (c) Treatment options × persons—who is being treated with which intervention methods? (d) Effectiveness—have target behaviors changed; has there been generalization of treatment effects; and is change maintained over time? Such an atheoretical stance is taken to be one of the strengths of behavioral assessment and indeed, this may be the case when client variables, criterion behaviors, and treatment options are fairly well defined. The analysis of social competence in defined settings provided an example of the utility of this approach (Goldfried & D'Zurilla, 1969).

However, the same atheoretical stance is frustrating to the clinician-counselor working with intimate adult relationships. To describe samples of marital clients presupposes a definition of criterion behaviors relevant to the marriage relationship. Certainly choice of intervention option rests on a conception of desired outcomes. Yet what are the criterion behaviors for marriage relationships? One way of defining these would be to select samples of "happily" married couples and match them with "unhappily" married couples. Although behavioral differences would be evident (cf. Birchler, Weiss, & Vincent, 1975; Vincent, Weiss, & Birchler, 1975), the temptation is strong to impute causality when only correlation may exist. Not only are we limited to the particular definition of "happiness," but to demonstrate causality it would be necessary first to train the subjects in the "missing behaviors" and then demonstrate desired change in outcome measures. In this sense "unhappiness" is equated with the absence of certain behaviors.

Problems in marital relationships are usually defined as *the presence of conflict and discord.* What little systematic information we have about intimate adult relationships is probably based more on what is wrong than on what is right with such relationships. Although focus on maladaptive behaviors (symptoms) has been a typical strategy in other areas of clinical endeavor, it is not necessarily a fruitful one. One would find little pollution, crime, disease, or big government spending on the moon, but their absence does not improve the compatability of that environment for human life. Although behavioral assessment of marital relationships still may be far from offering the World Health Organization a listing of criteria of successful, enjoyable, mutually beneficial marriages, perhaps this approach will some day contribute. Until that time we must make educated guesses as to which current target behaviors define "successful" marital skills.

In a related discussion Patterson, Weiss, and Hops (1976) considered five reasons why marital assessment and intervention is a most complex and difficult area: (1) Simultaneous change is required in the reinforcing contingencies for two persons, not one. (2) Behaviors thought to be of major importance to a marriage relationship are often low baseline operants, inaccessible to direct observation and control. (3) Marital complaints are presented in the language of value and emotion, not in the focused terms of behavioral engineering. (4) Experimental control, as in reversible ABA designs, may be neither possible nor ethically justified. (5) The vast body of published work in the marriage area is, by current standards, of such poor quality as to be of little utility (cf. Gurman, 1973; Hicks & Platt, 1970; Laws, 1971; Olson, 1970, for support of this editorial view).

The assessment of marital conflict and accord is further compounded by the fact that those criteria used to define a problem as marital, rather than sexual, parent-child, or even an individual problem are currently not well defined. Setting aside sample description *within* the area of marital problems, multiple *area* baseline assessment has not yet been considered. Clinical workers usually follow the lead of clients in that persons applying for marriage therapy probably do receive some form of professional intervention focused on the marriage. What this treatment entails, however, differs vastly across therapists. The focus need not even be on the relationship because some marriage therapists prefer to meet the couple individually rather than together (cf. Gurman's 1973 review of outcome studies). Some combination of client self-selection, therapist expertise and interest determines how a problem is defined for intervention. The therapist specializing in sexual dysfunction would be understandably reluctant to develop a parent-child module; a parent-child expert may be less inclined to delay intervention on that relationship while the marriage is worked on. Although advocates of a systems point of view (Olson, 1970; Note 1) argue for viewing presenting problems at a "transactional" or family level, we can only speculate at this time how a couple's problems with children interact with what could be defined as their marital problems, and vice versa. Not until all family-related cases are assessed simultaneously on marital, sexual, and parent-child dimensions will the choice of intervention be completely rational nor will much needed generalization data become available.

In one sense a chapter on behavioral approaches to assessment of marital interaction is premature in terms of available procedures for assessing important aspects of marital relationships. There are very few assessment options that facilitate behavioral intervention (cf. Bodin, 1968; Straus, 1969). There are, however, definite indications in the field that argue in favor of such an undertaking at this time.

The burgeoning interest in the role of cognitive factors in behavioral applications (e.g., self-regulation) indicates on the part of some a willingness to tackle more complex behavioral systems (Thoresen & Mahoney, 1974). The reputed complexity of marital interactions should challenge this willingness. We have become much more sophisticated about situation versus trait determination of behavior (e.g., Bem & Allen, 1974; Goldfried & Kent, 1972). Technological advances now have made possible far greater potential for analyzing interactional behaviors as opposed to the stultifying reliance on assessment of need patterns. But it is also true that although behavior technology has greatly expanded the catalogue of behaviors that can be assessed, it does not follow that the best behaviors are always selected for assessment (cf. Olson 1972). Adult intimacy has received little formal attention from psychology, and it may be a propitious time to inventory what has been done and to develop some points of view as we survey the assessment picture in this early stage of its development.

The chapter is divided into four major sections. The first, Conceptual Issues, views marital satisfaction concepts as represented in traditional and behavioral approaches, with particular attention to their shared methodology, namely, self-report. The second section provides a comprehensive survey of the behaviorally relevant literature on assessment of marital relationship behaviors within a multiple assessment model. Not only do we consider marital assessment procedures; we consider those that could be applied to this area as well. The third section raises the issue of which treatment for which persons, given the current status of marital assessment and intervention. Both as a stimulus for dealing conceptually with this problem and as a caution, we detail some of the methodological concerns common to such an undertaking. The final section provides a summary and a look toward newer possibilities.

CONCEPTUAL ISSUES

Marital conflict and accord traditionally are viewed in terms of "happiness" or "satisfaction." As a means of developing behavioral approaches to marital assessment, we first consider some of the conceptual issues defined in the traditional approach, what relevance "satisfaction" has for a behavioral view, and the problems presented by relying on self-report technology.

Traditional View of Marital Satisfaction

Hicks and Platt (1970) reviewed a decade of research on marital happiness and stability, the two norms by which marriages in our society are judged. Much of the traditional assessment literature pertains to either of two conceptions of marriage—*institutional* or *companionship* marriage (cf. also Tharp, 1963b). The former refers to traditional role specifications that emphasize mores, customs, and role fulfillments. Husbands are seen as playing instrumental roles and wives as playing expressive and integrative (accommodating) roles. Meeting role expectations is the basis for defining happiness and stability. In companionship marriages the emphasis is on affective factors. The expression of love, sexual enjoyment, communication, and affection are presumed to be the basis for marital happiness. Various assessment approaches have been reported that emphasize: (1) perception of role-behavior discrepancies (e.g., Hurvitz, 1965; Tharp, 1963a); (2) ability to communicate (e.g., Kahn, 1970; Navran, 1967); and (3) cognitive and personality variables (e.g., person perception, self-acceptance) (e.g., Murstein & Beck, 1972).

The literature on marital satisfaction measured by self-report indicates that verbal behavior, or attitudes concerning marital relationships, are fairly consistent in the psychometric sense of being reproducible. Measures such as the Locke-Wallace Marital Adjustment Scale (Locke-Wallace, 1959; Kimmel & van der Veen, 1974) show high test-retest reliability. Whatever it is that married couples talk about in responding to these tests, they seem to be able to do so reliably. The problem, of course, is the interface between the empirical data base of everyday experience and the cognitions that are evolved to describe one's satisfaction in a relationship.

Self-report measures of marital satisfaction have been scrutinized for evidence of trait-like propensities such as social desirability (e.g., Cone, 1967, 1971) and conventionalization (e.g., Edmonds, Withers, & Dibatista, 1972). On the assumption that measures of satisfaction (such as the Locke-Wallace) provide marital adjustment information, individuals may demonstrate a plus-getting tendency by agreeing with exaggerated unrealistic "truths" about marital bliss. As Murstein and Beck observed, it is likewise an assumption that happily married persons will perceive their spouses objectively; one might also assume that happily married persons will tend to exaggerate the "sterling quality of their mates" (1972, p. 399). Reported correlations between marital adjustment and various social desirability measures indicate that as much as 64 percent of the variance between the two is shared. In the absence of behavioral criteria, however, it is not possible to say whether this overlap reflects a serious limitation of such measures. Perhaps verbal indications of adjustment (satisfaction) necessarily entail acceptance of the current ethos (cf. Laws, 1971 for a feminist consideration of this broader issue).

Almost without exception studies of marital satisfaction have relied on retrospective self-report and survey data. The common practice of correlating verbal reports within subjects raises serious questions about the consistencies that result. As Mischel (1968) and others have noted, such consistencies may reflect the "implicit personality theory" of the respondents or, more simply, a consistency reflecting our linguistic conventions. In a similar vein, discrepancy measures (such as measured discrepancies between the self and the ideal self) may be far more indicative of mood or affective state than constructs presumed to underlie such measures (cf. Kornreich, Straka, & Kane, 1968).

All approaches that emphasize self-reported or derived measures of marital satisfaction assume that these are indicants of adjustment. (The same is true of marital stability and success.) To be sure, attempts to be more specific about sources of satisfaction have been made, for example, role fulfillment (Tharp, 1963a) and rated satisfaction with communication (Kahn, 1970). Using measures of adjustment that employ self-reported satisfaction essentially reduces to observation of a singular dimension—that of relationship satisfaction. To be dissatisfied is an indication of nonadjustment.

Given this view, it follows that the goal of intervention is to increase reported satisfaction. Not only does such a goal sidestep the question, "Adjustment to what type of relationship?" (cf. Laws, 1971), it also effectively ignores the basic therapeutic issue, which is to provide training that generalizes across situations. Behaviorally oriented treatments that do attempt to generalize therapeutic effects (Weiss, Hops, & Patterson, 1973; Rappaport & Harrell, 1972) provide couples with the skills to change behavior that they may apply through intervention and then continue to use beyond the end of treatment.

Behavioral View of Satisfaction

Assessment of marital satisfaction begins with the interface between relationship behaviors (empirical data base) and the cognitions held about relationship satisfaction. The issue is not whether to take seriously the reported satisfaction of married adults but to determine what needs to be done about it. The strategic error of the traditional approach has been to assume only the most general form of stimulus control: Various theoretical conditions are postulated as being necessary to satisfaction, and then inquiries are made of individuals to see whether these conditions have been met. The questionnaire emphasis on role enactments, for example, assumes that even if behaviors descriptive of such role enactments occur at a particular frequency, respondents will report satisfactions concomitant with these frequencies. Underlying this assumption is the expectation that clients, as untrained observers, track relevant behaviors and relate these to cognitions. A less optimistic possibility is that they start with a cognition and fit "relevant" events to that cognition.

The issue for behaviorists is to specify those behaviors and conditions necessary to maintain other targeted behaviors. What behaviors are associated with the cognition or the verbal report "I am satisfied with my marital relationship at level X"? A preliminary attempt to answer this type of question has been provided by Wills, Weiss, and Patterson (1974). Their purpose was to determine the extent to which five classes of daily events were systematically related to daily reports of relationship satisfaction. Exchanges of affectional and instrumental pleasures and displeasures and the quality of nonrelationship events were recorded by spouses for a two-week period. Pleasures (displeasures) were defined as any behavior emitted by a spouse that functioned as a pleasing (displeasing) event regardless of the intent. Affectional behaviors were defined as small expressions of closeness, regard, warmth, and so on. Instrumental behaviors were defined as those having to do with the accomplishments of the relationship, for example, services, parenting, and the like. Rated quality of outside events was defined as a rating of satisfaction with the nonmarital day up to the time of the rating. Work experiences, interactions with friends and so forth, were all contributors to this rating. Daily ratings were also made for relationship satisfaction, and these served as the dependent variable in a multiple regression analysis.

The five predictors combined to produce a multiple $R = 0.51$, which indicated that in a limited way it was possible to define daily events associated with variations in relationship satisfaction. The individual beta weights for each predictor were used to determine whether pleasures and displeasures contributed differently to satisfaction ratings. (Outside ratings were of minimal importance in this analysis.) Displeasures proved to function more potently than pleasures in terms of changes in relationship satisfaction.

This form of analysis could presumably be used to isolate relationship behaviors systematically associated with reported satisfaction. The major advantage over the traditional approaches discussed above is that for any given couple one can determine the empirical data basis for reported satisfaction. Then, by building these behavioral occurrences into their relationship repertoires, therapists could gain some degree of control over client satisfaction.

What of the alternative approach that uses extensive observation to inventory those contingencies which function to reinforce relationship behaviors? Why bother with assessing marital satisfaction at all? In addition to the difficulties associated with gaining access to representative settings, such naturalistic observation may be conceptually unwise during early stages of intervention.

Distressed couples rely on aversive control to bring about relationship changes. Patterson and Reid (1970) describe the coercion process as involving use of aversive consequences. Through the tandem occurrence of negative reinforcement and punishment it is possible to maintain, if not escalate, marital conflict. Conflict has been defined as a demand for immediate change (Patterson & Hops, 1972). Those responses that terminate the demanding behaviors of spouse ("Stop it, Goddammit!" or "Yeah, yeah, I'll take care of it later") are strengthened by negative reinforcement. High-amplitude aversive responses that follow demanding behaviors suppress such behaviors (i.e., serve as effective punishers). Since no new positive behaviors are shaped under these conditions, the couple can be expected to repeat this negative cycle without gaining the benefits of actual problem solving. It is not unusual, therefore, that couples define behavior deceleration as the goal of intervention, for example, "I just want him to stop yelling at the kids." Interaction has proven to be aversive, any reduction of the aversiveness seems like the goal of intervention! This coupled with a usually truncated repertoire of shared recreational events (cf. Birchler, Weiss, & Vincent, 1975) provides little in the way of natural reinforcers for the therapist to rely on. Although suppression of relationship adversity is an important immediate subgoal, developing a repertoire of reinforcing relationship behaviors is the long-term goal. It is these that will maintain newly acquired relationship skills.

Concern with marital satisfaction within an action-oriented framework has been cogently represented by those emphasizing *strategic interventions* (e.g., Haley, 1963, 1973). Based on the assumption that natural reinforcing contingencies will become operative once dysfunctional (e.g., stereotypical) relationship patterns are eliminated, intervention consists of quickly unbalancing or otherwise disrupting the negative patterns. For example, the therapist arranges events so that to avoid therapist control, clients actually engage in those behaviors intended by the therapist to be most therapeutic. Outcome satisfaction is derived from the execution of the behaviors themselves, for example, sexual gratification. Skill training, in the sense of increasing the strength of repertoire behaviors, is not undertaken in this conception. The requisite skills are either assumed to be present or the intervention strategy itself is sufficient to allow necessary behaviors to occur de novo.

Self-Report Methodology

Self-report methodology refers to those operations by which clients observe and keep records on their own behaviors. Lipinski and Nelson (1974) and Thoresen and Mahoney (1974, Chapter 3) have provided extensive treatment of the reliability issues involved in self-observation. Because this form of obtaining marital data on clients is common to both traditional and behavioral approaches, self-report methodology will be considered briefly.

An early study of Kenkel (1963) demonstrated that only 34 percent of a sample of married individuals were able to accurately predict the distribution of time spent in talk between themselves and their partners on a family decision-making task. Over half of the participants were inaccurate in their post-session judgment of the distribution of time spent in talk. The percentage of accurate presession or postsession judgments fell sharply when the target behavior was "social-emotional actions" or generally facilitative supportive behaviors. The Bales interaction codes were used in this study. Couples were unpracticed in making such observations even though the behavior and judgments were temporally close.

Olson (1969) supported, in terms of the construct of "power," this lack of agreement between self-report and behavioral measures in family decision-making situations. Furthermore, he found that empathy (an individual's ability to predict the decision of a spouse) was a necessary condition for congruence between self-report and behavior. This finding suggests that distressed couples could be expected to be least able to portray their situations accurately through self-report. (Cf. also Olson & Rabunsky, 1972, for validity of various "power" measures.) Using a situation-specific communication task, Kahn (1970) has shown this to be the case for nonverbal communication.

The reactivity of continuous self-observation has been discussed at length in the literature. Lipinski and Nelson (1974) found that face touching decreased markedly (from rates obtained by unobtrusive observers) when subjects were instructed to self-record. Rates returned to baseline levels after self-observation instructions were removed. Similar findings regarding interrater reliability have been reported for coding systems involving behaviors of others (e.g., Reid, 1970). The known presence of a reliability coder increased reliability over values obtained when an unobtrusive reliability check was made. Reliabilities of measures of face touching between observations made by others and self-observations were 0.86 when the observer was known to be checking and 0.52 when subjects did not know that reliability was being checked.

For some behaviors (e.g., smoking) self-observation may be associated with a decrease in rate relative to baseline (e.g., McFall, 1970). In the Wills, Weiss, and Patterson (1974) study individuals recorded daily occurrences of pleasures and displeasures received from their spouse, providing an example of the untrained or participant observer method. Two gross estimates of reactivity and reliability were made. No systematic change in pleasure-displeasure rates were found over trials for a 12-day period (Fs less than 1.00). Yet following surreptitious instructions to husbands on Day 12 to double their output of affectional pleasures, wives reported a significant increase in these behaviors. None of the other response classes reported by wives showed a significant increase over the previous mean rates.

It is fairly well agreed that self-report data may also suffer from lack of agreement between external and subjective definitions of a response; the "screen" used by the self-observer may be too fine, resulting in greatly lowered estimates of the behavior in question. Finally, establishing appropriate stimulus or reinforcing control for self-observation requires far more attention than seems to have been reported thus far.

A promising lead for establishing parameters of self-observation data has been taken by Weber, Wegman, Younger, and Mallue (Note 2). Although not directly concerned with marital interaction phenomena, their empirical analysis deserves consideration from those concerned with marital assessment. Weber et al. define a two-by-two classification of public versus private settings for behavioral occurrences, and objective versus subjective observation. In principle some estimate of interobserver reliability is possible for all but the private-subjective cell. Included in this cell are such cognitive events as thoughts, feelings, urges, and the like. The thesis of Weber et al. is that such events comprise a legitimate area of scientific study whenever a pattern or regularity can be demonstrated in their reporting.

In the Weber et al. study student subjects were instructed to provide estimates of frequency of occurrence data for *insights* and *bites,* two responses having very different topographies. (Insights were defined as a sudden inspiration or "aha" experience, whereas bites were defined as "one cyclical movement of the hand to the mouth and then back to the dish, table, and so on") Both daily estimates of frequency as well as real-time counts were obtained (golf counters were used). Finally, the same subjects provided anonymous ratings of percentage of data "fudged."

Both the distributions of estimate and the real-count data were similar, but only for insights did the correlation between estimate and count reach a reasonable magnitude ($r = 0.60$); for bites, $r = 0.30$. Weber found that 80 percent of his sample anonymously admitted to fudging from only 0 to 10 percent of the data. Since the distribution of estimates is known and the mean for estimates is lower than actual counts, it is possible to assess the effect of falsified data. In this instance the reported "real counts" would underestimate actual counts since the reported values would come from the estimate distribution. The finding of highly uniform distributions and being able to estimate the amount of falsified data are steps in the right direction.

In Weber et al's. study the importance of data collection and compliance with the observation tasks were emphasized to the subjects; the tasks were part of an experimental psychology course and counters were provided. In studies where the addition of an outsider increases interobserver reliability, the element of social control is probably of greatest importance. Therapists can ensure that self-observation procedures are brought under social control by having spouses check each other. At minimum, therapists have the responsibility of making use of such data themselves very soon after they have been collected by clients.

Self-report of ongoing behaviors is also likely to be affected by the fact that couples untrained in behavioral psychology may have little skill in counting small behavioral events and in record keeping. Even more likely, we suspect, is their less-than-total conviction that behavior is lawfully related to consequences, and that tracking antecedent consequent relationships has considerable pay-off. Instead of accepting a behaviorist's manifesto, couples are more inclined to explain behavior in terms of motives, traits, or the ultimate caprice, dumb luck. Language, and particularly the availability of cognitive labels, favors seeing consistency rather than perturbation in behaviors. Social psychological data (Bem & Allen, 1974; Jones & Nisbett, 1971) suggest that individuals utilize trait theory when explaining the behavior of others (seeing far greater behavioral consistency across situations than is warranted) but that they utilize state theory when their own behavior is at issue (seeing far greater situational dependence in their own behavior). "The other person is predictable, but I am uniquely complicated."

One advantage in working with couples is that mutual social control can be brought to bear on self-observations. When relationship behaviors are being tracked, husbands and wives can provide reliability data on each other's observations. The use of pleasures and displeasures in marital assessment, to be discussed in the next section, allows for this possibility.

REVIEW OF ASSESSMENT OPTIONS

In this section we will review currently available technologies for marital assessment. Once again the focus will be twofold: We will discuss procedures already existing and those being developed that hold promise.

As other chapters in this volume amply show, there is considerable interest in specifying how settings control behavior (e.g., Goldfried & Kent, 1972; Moos, 1969; Mischel, 1968; Weiss, 1968) and in utilizing multimethod-multitrait strategies (e.g., Campbell & Fiske, 1959). The reign of the single variable may well be ended. The necessity for multiple criteria in defining and assessing marital problems derives from the complexity of such relationships and, as noted earlier, the numerous options for levels of intervention (Olson, Note 1). Nonetheless, the most popular strategy has been to focus on one, or at most two, aspects of intervention. It is doubtful whether a singularly adequate outcome variable has been identified in marital research. As a first approximation to multilevel assessment of marital interaction, we have prepared Table 15–1, which focuses attention on observer and setting variables.

Observers (individuals, spouses, etc.) occupy observational settings (laboratory, home, social environment). Furthermore, a distinction can be drawn between observation as perception up to this point versus observation as perception of the ongoing behavior. The latter involves tracking or process recording of ongoing behavior(s). Settings vary from structured laboratory situations to naturalistic settings that are not typically monitored.

Sources of observation—from individual self-reports to observation by trained coders—range from private (objective or subjective) responses to public (objective) behaviors. The "sign" versus "sample" distinction is also relevant here. Samples maximize the similarity between test response and criterion measure, whereas the sign approach utilizes test responses as a basis for drawing numerous inferences about underlying constructs. Behavioral assessment favors the sample approach, but it also tends to assume that behavioral samples (taken in the laboratory, for example) are representative of other settings and other methods. A more detailed consideration of these assumptions will be deferred to the next major section.

Table 15–1 lists references from the literature as well as providing a rough heuristic device for those source by setting interactions as yet unreported. Some advantages and disadvantages of sampling from various cells of the matrix, and issues of generalization, are apparent from the table. For example, most marital research has made only limited use of assess-

Table 15–1. A matrix of observer sources by observational settings: Systematic ordering of assessment procedures

Observer and Type of data:	Observational Settings		
	Laboratory	Home	Social Environment
Individual observation			
Perception of self	Mood Checklist	Interpersonal Check List (e.g., Luckey, 1961) Marital Status Inventory (Weiss & Cerreto, Note 5) Marital Happiness (Azrin et al., 1973) Stuart Precounseling Inventory (Stuart & Stuart, 1972) Marriage Inventory (Knox, 1972)	No data
Self-Tracking	On-line signalling (Katz, 1974) Self-Video Tracking (Margolin & Weiss, Note 3) (Eisler et al., 1973)	Behavioral Diary Pleasant Thoughts (Patterson & Hops, 1972) Marital Activities Inventory (Weiss et al., 1973)	Marital Activities Inventory (Weiss et al., 1973) Behavioral Diary
Spouse observation	Communication Inventory (Murphy & Mendelson, 1973)	Adjective Check List (e.g., Leary, 1957; Gough & Heilburn, 1965)	

Perception of Spouse	Nonverbal Communication (Kahn, 1970)	Areas of Change Inventory (Weiss et al., 1973)	No data
Spouse Tracking	Signalling Devices (Thomas et al., 1971; Carter & Thomas, 1973; Katz, 1974) Video Tracking (Margolin & Weiss, Note 3)	Please-Displese Events (Weiss et al., 1973; Stuart, 1969; Rappaport & Harrell, 1972) Marital Activities Inventory (Weiss et al., 1973)	Marital Activities Inventory (Weiss et al., 1973)
Untrained other (e.g. peer or relative)			
Perception	No data	No data	No data
Tracking	No data	No data	No data
Trained other			
Analogue	Revealed difierences (Strodbeck, 1951; Kenkel, 1963, Olson, 1969; Goodrich & Boomer, (1963) SIMFAM (Olson & Straus, 1972)	No data	No data
Tracking	Tracking problematic behavior (Carter & Thomas, 1973; Eisler et al., 1973a) Standardized decision-making (Olson & Ryder, 1970); Vincent et al., 1975) Behavioral samples (Hops et al., 1972)	Couple &/or family interactions (Patterson et al., 1969)	No data

ment options, as seen by the number of studies listed in only one cell. Studies seem to assume that analogue tasks or communication skill training in the laboratory are representative samples of home behaviors, and furthermore, that these behaviors are stable over time and across observers. Assumptions may be more plentiful than empirical generalizations.

Laboratory Assessment

Laboratory or "in session" measures provide a wide variety of accessible, standardized techniques. Moving down this column of the table, we see that observers range from individuals to trained others, along a dimension of increasingly objectified, behaviorally desirable assessment options. The responses being examined tend to narrow from general (cognitive) labels to discrete behaviors.

Individual Observation

Relatively little use has been made of self-reports of in-session behavior (e.g., fluctuations of mood indicating on-going changes in private or subjective states). Mood checklists, although frequently used with individuals, have been absent in marital research. The behavioral counterpart of such self-reporting is the use of on-line signaling devices. Although such devices have been designed, there seems to be no application to marital research. Katz (1974) has developed an electromechanical system for gathering self-report data during a dyadic interaction. Subjects signal choices on a 5-point rating scale for "good-bad" or "helpful-unhelpful" dimensions. Thus far the system has been used for therapist training, but it is readily applicable to marital interactions in the laboratory as a means of integrating self-report with other concurrent behavioral data. Specific gains in communication training could be assessed (in a pretest posttest design) with such a system as Katz describes. Similarly, the technology described by Eisler, Hersen, and Agras (1973a), which allows couples to track specific behaviors from videotapes, could be applied in this cell.

The case demonstration by Margolin and Weiss (Note 3), described in the section on spouse tracking, can fit in this cell as well. Because spouse tracking emphasizes congruence of reporting by more than one observer, it is described later rather than here.

Spouse Observation

We may distinguish between *perception of spouse* and *spouse tracking* when the spouse is the source of observation.

Two studies have been reported in which perception of spouse was the response. Murphy and Mendelson (1973) sought to determine whether a self-report measure of communication process agreed with in vivo couple communication. The Marital Communication Inventory (MCI) (Bienvenu, 1970) and codes derived from Leary's (1957) Interpersonal Check List (ICL) (Level I, observed behaviors) were used as the covariates. The MCI contains items such as, "Does your spouse have a tendency to say things that would be better left unsaid?" and "Do you find your spouse's tone of voice irritating?" The 20-item inventory has a Spearman-Brown corrected reliability of 0.90, and it discriminated significantly between couples in counseling and those "not reporting marital difficulties." The ICL codes focus on status (dominant-submissive) and affective tone (positive-negative) in the context of ongoing dyadic verbal interactions. Rank order correlations between the MCI (self-report) and coded ICL behaviors were found to be significant ($r_s = 0.548$ and 0.415, for dominant and submissive scorings, respectively). Limited by methodological problems and the use of extreme groups in marital satisfaction, perception of spouse was found to be related to an analogue sample of spouses' communication.

In a study more compatible with the behavioral viewpoint, Kahn (1970) reported on his Marital Communication Scale (MCS), which can be compared to a structured charade or role-play task requiring use of nonverbal cues to communicate intent. For each of 16 situations (e.g., being served a chicken dinner four days in a row), there are three attitudes or intentions that reasonably could be communicated (e.g., irritation with the same meal again, curiosity whether your memory is correct, or elation and delight in getting a favorite dish and a favor). Simply by tone of voice (and presumably gesture) the sender communicated to the receiver the predetermined intention in each item. "Since the content is fixed and can imply all three of the intentions, the expressor's only means of providing the receiver with the necessary discriminations is through the use of nonverbal cues" (p. 451). The 16 items, half of which are played out by each spouse, have a reported reliability of 0.87 (corrected) and a test-retest reliability of 0.92 over a seven-week period. Although only six couples were involved in the test-retest determination, a larger sample of 97 college couples produced a split-half reliability of 0.70. Using the number of correct answers (agreement between what was sent and what was identified by the receiver), Kahn was able to discriminate between matched groups differing on the Locke-Wallace. Out of a possible score of 16, maritally satisfied couples scored a mean of 9.05 correct answers whereas less satisfied couples scored 7.33 correct answers. Chance was defined as 5.33 correct answers.

These attempts at defining behavioral correlates for perception-of-spouse reports represent a major improvement in self-report assessment methodology. However, our enthusiasm is tempered by the seeming lack of relationship between ongoing behavior and self-report (Kenkel, 1963; Olson, 1969). Although the relative economy of these self-report instruments make them attractive, a behavioral description of how a couple communicates is still necessary before making intervention decisions. The section to follow considers methodologies for observation of spouses that provide ongoing behavioral data.

Spouse Tracking

Spouses' tracking of each other's behavior has been used extensively by behavioral researchers. The gain in objectivity—the target is not also the observer—is offset somewhat by the fact that the observer is very much an interested party. When spouses track reciprocally (both track each other), the therapist may unintentionally affect a situation approximating dyadic training. The method is reactive because it provides discrimination training to spouses, as well as bringing observed responses under social control. Therapists gain information about the observer as well as the behavior observed.

Spouse tracking in the laboratory has been restricted largely to communication skills. The innovators in the field of automated signaling systems, Thomas, Carter, and Gambrill (1971) and Carter and Thomas (1973), introduced a signaling system for corrective feedback and instructions that is known as SAM. The system is flexible in design, permitting diverse combinations for sending and receiving signals (e.g., client to client, client to therapist, therapist to client, and therapist monitoring of client to client) in addition to providing a means of acknowledging behavior (e.g., spouse indicates the occurrence of a predetermined response such as "positive statement"). As a training device, SAM may be used to signal when a change is desired in the behavior of the other person, for example, gaining access to talk time. As an assessment device, SAM is still a youngster, but it is potentially useful for controlling precise response events either in a data-recording or a stimulus-controlling capacity. Opportunities for objectifying skill training are numerous.

An assessment-intervention alternative to in vivo coding has been described by Margolin and Weiss (Note 3). Couples were asked to track from a videotape playback of their interaction behaviors, which by spouses' own definitions represent facilitating responses during dyadic communication. (An electromechanical recording device, activated by button presses, records their responses singly and in temporal proximity.) Focusing on only one spouse at a time, both husband and wife indicate when the target did something that was helpful. In this way a measure of self-report and spouse report is obtained for the occurrence of helpful responses in each spouse's ongoing behavior when each spouse is the focus of the observation. Congruence, or joint agreements, indicate simply that *both* parties recognize an event as helpful to *one* of them. During the intervention phase, the spouses identify ongoing communication behaviors *they* deem important to their relationship (creating a repertoire of such behaviors) and then proceed to increase these behaviors in subsequent training discussion. Training is accomplished by introducing a cuing system that provides rewarding or aversive (pleasant chime tones or raucous buzzing) sounds. After a criterion response is emitted and then acknowledged by *both* spouses (simultaneous button presses), the couple is rewarded positively. Failure by the target person to emit the criterion response or lack of a joint acknowledgement produces the aversive sound. Subjects are held accountable for the behaviors being responded to in order to avoid simply conditioning the button presses. During preintervention and postintervention testing the cuing device was inoperative.

Preintervention and postintervention comparisons indicate that spouses simultaneously identified and tracked helpful behaviors at a higher rate after intervention and that trained coders [using the Marital Interaction Coding System (MICS), see page 573 coded an increase in problem solving codes. Although only a beginning, this study examined generalizability of behavior assessed across sources and across levels of observations, that is, the same behavior tracked by individual, spouse, and trained observer, and generalized from one domain to another.

Untrained Others (peers, relatives, and so on)

The cells for untrained others are empty, indicating that our search of the literature has failed to uncover instances in which assessment data have been provided by these observational sources. There are obvious problems of having one's friends reporting on couple behaviors, but the potential utility has not been sufficiently analyzed. With the increased popularity of couples' treatment groups and resulting friendships that may extend beyond the groups' sessions, such an observational system may find acceptance.

Observation By Trained Others

Laboratory assessment by trained others (coders) falls into three different but somewhat overlapping types: (1) decision-making tasks using actual or therapist-determined differences to assess power structure; (2) "game-like" situations based on exchange theory; and (3) behavioral samples of problem-solving situations examined through coding systems built on social learning theory.

The introduction to marital assessment of small group theory concerning conflict resolution was an innovative step away from standard questionnaires. The revealed difference technique (Strodbeck, 1951; Kenkel, 1963; Olson, 1969) consists of having marital partners discuss differences after having made individual evaluations or decisions on a predetermined topic. Goodrich and Boomer (1963) and Olson and Ryder (1970) modified this procedure and had couples resolve concealed differences (spouses were unaware that they had been given conflicting information). Goodrich and Boomer (1963) found that couples become surprisingly involved and demonstrate a good deal of their conflict behavior even when faced with a trivial task such as matching small colored paper squares.

With the development of the Inventory of Marital Conflicts (IMC), Olson and Ryder (1970) integrated two variants into the original revealed differences method: (1) similarity of source of conflict across couples and (2) relevant content of the conflict. Couples were instructed to resolve conflicts that had been created by giving spouses explanations of a marital problem that were slightly at variance. The experimenters looked not only at the outcome of these discussions, or "win scores," but also sequentially coded the couple's behaviors utilizing 29 categories having to do with information, opinions, suggestions, positive and negative support, and structural phenomena. Utilizing a somewhat different coding system from the Oregon Project, Vincent, Weiss, and Birchler (1975) also examined couples resolving differences elicited by the IMC. They successfully discriminated a priori distressed and nondistressed couples along the dimension of their frequency of problem-solving behaviors. The more inferential coding system proposed by Olson was unable to make this discrimination with the same subjects.

The primary contribution of the game-like tests used in marital assessment is the emphasis on evaluating the dyad as a unit (e.g., spouses either can work as a team to maximize rewards from the experimenter, or they can assume a competitive stance vis-à-vis each other). As assessment devices, the game-like tests arouse relatively little anxiety (Ravich, 1969; Liebowitz & Black, 1974; Schoenger & Wood, 1969).

The SIMFAM techniques developed by Olson and Strauss (1972) is among the observation systems less like analogues. Spouses and/or other family members play a game similar to shuffleboard in which reward contingencies are entirely controlled by the experimenter, that is, there is a noncontingent pay-off. Advantages of this procedure include (1) minimal opportunity to present interaction in a particularly positive or negative light; (2) minimal reliance on verbal skills; (3) no emotional history for the family with this experience; (4) provision of data that are different from what therapists typically identify. However, the adequacy of the assumptions drawn from this task is limited by its being unrelated to real-life situations. Meaningful contingencies are lacking, and families play under the supposition that they are in competition with other families, neither of which typifies actual family interactions.

Before introducing a highly complex coding system, it should be noted that several marital researchers have begun to use tape-recorded data to examine the specific behaviors intended for change during intervention. A recent study by Carter and Thomas (1973) has identified 27 disruptive communication behaviors as a step to more systematic assessment of audiotapes prior to corrective use of the SAM. Similarly, Eisler, Hersen, and Agras (1973b) coded videotapes before, during, and after intervention to assess looking and smiling responses. They found that observers were as reliable when coding two discrete nonverbal behaviors from a videotape as when observing the interactions live.

The Marital Interaction Coding System (MICS) developed by the Oregon Project (Hops, Wills, Patterson, & Weiss, 1972) differs from other forms of laboratory observation in that the observational codes were designed to examine specific behavioral exchange events and interchanges in the ongoing patterns in which they occur. Like Patterson's family interaction coding system (Patterson et al., 1969), this coding system can be applied to different types of behavior samples (e.g., either preplanned conflicts à la Olson and Ryder or attempted resolution of clients' own conflicts). The Oregon group primarily uses the MICS as a preintervention and postintervention comparison measure to examine "negotiation" sessions, 10-minute talk sessions during which the spouses engage in problem solving in regard to a major or minor conflict area identified from their precounseling information.

Extensive use of the MICS in recording interactions of married couples has demonstrated that the 29 codes provide an adequate accounting of most responses found in dyadic problem solving situations (Patterson, Hops, & Weiss, 1975). To enhance manageability of the data, the 29 original categories are often condensed into three summary scores: positive social reinforcement, negative social reinforcement, and problem-solving behaviors. The first two summary scores encompass both verbal (e.g., content of the speaker's statements) and nonverbal responses (e.g., facial expressions, attending). Problem-solving statements are coded strictly on verbal content, not on the value of the suggestions.

Trained observers record data sequentially in 30-second intervals from the videotapes of the couple's interaction. Reliability of coding, reported for each session, is scored by two pairs of observers. To maintain minimum reliability of at least 70 percent, coders undergo weekly calibration checks, with coders alternating as "coder" and "reader." Reliability is calculated with total frequency of agreement between "coder" and "reader" used as the numerator and total frequency of codes recorded by the "reader" as the denominator.

Validation of the MICS comes from both analogue and intervention studies. Birchler et al. (1975) and Vincent et al. (1975) analyzed interactions of couples responding to the Olson and Ryder (1970) vignettes. MICS coding of interactions of 12 distressed and 12 nondistressed couples showed that distressed couples display higher rates of aversive behaviors than nondistressed couples (Birchler et al., 1975) and display fewer problem-solving behaviors and reinforcement (Vincent et al., 1975).

A more recent validation of the MICS from the Oregon laboratory comes from a study by Lerner (Note 4), which sought to compare self-report and behavioral differences of ad hoc dyads in a task involving mild conflict resolution. Dyads were judged to be compatible or incompatible on the basis of dominance-submissive pairings. Compatibility was defined as the pairing of subjects rated for dominant and submissive behaviors, whereas the pairing of dominant-dominant partners defined incompatibility. Behavioral ratings were made in a prior group setting used to identify "dominant" and "submissive" subjects. A MICS coding of the interactions indicated that compatible subjects were significantly higher on positive categories (agreement, attention, compromise, humor, etc.) and significantly lower on negative or aversive categories (criticism, putting down, ignoring, no response, etc.). Furthermore, there was agreement between the verbal report of rated attraction to the partner and the behavioral measures as reported by MICS coding.

Further validation comes from a study of Royce and Weiss (1975) in which undergraduate judges first rated level of marital satisfaction in videotaped interactions of married couples and then generated lists of the behavioral cues used in making their judgments. Five of the codes found useful in predicting satisfaction overlapped with codes contained in the MICS. Thus the MICS includes variables that nonprofessionals deemed important in the evaluation of marital interaction between distressed and nondistressed couples; these were similar to cues the researchers considered important. The weightings were different, however.

As Patterson, Weiss, and Hops (1976) suggested, the MICS has shown to be moderately sensitive as a preintervention and postintervention measure on a clinic population. On a sample of 10 husbands and 10 wives (Patterson, Hops, & Weiss, 1975), an examination of all categories demonstrated that constructive problem-solving behaviors increased significantly (particularly compromise statements) whereas counterproductive behaviors significantly decreased (particularly putting down, disagreeing, and problem description statements). Compared to other observational systems described, the utility of the MICS lies in the fact that it enables the researcher to examine generalized changes in interaction patterns rather than focusing on the one or two behaviors targeted for intervention.

Assessment Measures in the Home

Individual Reporting—Perceptions of Self, Spouse, and Relationship

Individual and spouse reporting often takes on the dual function of being (1) before and after comparison measures and (2) ongoing assessment during intervention. For example, Azrin et al. (1973) requested daily ratings by each spouse of "current happiness" on a 10-point scale for nine potential problem areas (e.g., household responsibilities, sex, spouse independence, etc.). That inventory, plus others, actually span our categories of self-report and spouse reporting. Knox (1972) presented an inventory ranging from a symptom checklist to open-ended questions about specific spouse behaviors that the respondent found acceptable or annoying. Similarly, the Stuarts' Pre-Counseling Inventory (Stuart & Stuart, 1972) elicits ratings on a sampling of questions about the happiness of one's self and spouse (using a 5-point scale) as well as gathering information pertinent to treatment planning (e.g., "List three things you would like your spouse to do more often.").

The Oregon Project uses three assessment devices in the home setting that provide individual report data. The first, which is noteworthy for its appeal to clients rather than for its potential for treatment planning, is an Adjective Checklist (e.g., Gough & Heilbrun, 1965), used by spouses to describe each other. Comparisons of frequencies of favorable and unfavorable descriptions are examined before and after intervention. The purpose of this device is to explore whether desired changes in frequencies of spouse behaviors are accompanied by changes in perception of spouses.

Weiss and Cerreto (Note 5) demonstrated through the Marital Status Inventory that cognitive and behavioral examples of marital dissatisfaction could be ordered in a Guttman-like scaling. The 14-item scale ranges from preliminary thoughts of separation to taking concrete steps toward divorce proceedings (e.g., "Thoughts of divorce occur to me fairly frequently, about once a week or more," "I have set up an independent bank account," or "I have contacted a lawyer"). Preliminary analyses on approximately 125 married respondents, including university students and clients applying for marital therapy, indicated a coefficient of reproducibility of 0.90 for the 14-item scale. The main benefit of this scale at this point is sample description. Using fairly specific step indicators, it provides a means of indicating how close a respondent says he has come to divorce.

The Areas of Change (A–C) questionnaire (Weiss et al., 1973) is a 34-item inventory of specific relationship behaviors that asks each respondent to indicate on a 7-point scale ranging from −3 (Very Much Less) to +3 (Very Much More) the answers to such items as whether he desires spouse to change ("I want my partner to help with finances"), and whether it would please his partner if the respondent were to change as indicated ("It would please my partner if I helped with finances"). The same item content is responded to in each of the two modes. By comparing the congruence between "I want my partner to (change) . . . " and "It would please my partner if I (changed) . . . " between husband-wife and wife-husband combinations of these two modes, conflict agreement-disagreement scores are obtained. Agreements are scored when both spouses indicate a desired change in the same direction, whereas disagreements are scored when spouses indicate directional differences for change. The total conflict score is expressed as the sum of agreements and disagreements (out of a possible total score of 68).

The alpha internal consistency of the A–C, based on a total of 86 husbands and wives, was 0.89. For each of two samples of 43 husbands and 43 wives the product-moment *r*s with the Locke-Wallace were −0.70 and −0.70. Furthermore, as expected, couple scores decreased significantly following intervention (cf. Weiss et al., 1973). Birchler and Webb (Note 6) have developed norms based on 100 couples and have found A–C means for distressed and nondistressed dyads to be 28.0 and 6.9 points, respectively. (These data support the initial validation of the A–C in the original Birchler and Vincent studies on smaller groups.) Although these data support the A–C's ability to discriminate marital distress, such self-reporting instruments are readily distorted by the level of overall satisfaction. Observational techniques having a more solid grounding as criterion measures are discussed in the next three sections.

Self-Tracking

Self-observation, or tracking, of one's own behavior, cognitions, and so on has been neglected in the home as well as in the laboratory setting. Examination of cognitive events, which is virtually an untapped resource in marital behavior literature, was introduced as a dependent measure by Patterson and Hops (1972) through the instruction to clients to track pleasant thoughts about their spouses. Patterson and Hops found that an increase in pleasant thoughts corresponded to data on observed changes in rates of aversive behaviors in the home. In a more recent case study (Margolin & Weiss, Note 3) pleasant thoughts corresponded to an increase in spouses' rewardingness, as demonstrated through frequency of affectional events.

Another potential assessment resource is use of a daily diary to help spouses keep behavioral records of complex events (e.g., conflicts, particularly pleasing interactions, etc.). The diary has the advantage of moving self-reporting away from more general statements about marital satisfaction, and it is useful as a shaping device for more laborious recording of pinpointed behaviors.

Spouse Observation (Tracking Spousal Behavior)

Spouse observation is probably the most common extralaboratory assessment in the behavioral literature on marital interaction. This measure involves having spouses keep records on the frequencies of targeted behaviors. The behaviors may be counted continuously through the use of wrist-counters or tracking cards (cf. Wills et al., 1974), or they may be tracked at the end of a specified period (cf. Stuart, 1969, for use of kitchen timers; Weiss et al., 1973, for daily use of the spouse observation checklist).

As mentioned earlier, assessment and intervention are often indistinguishable. As participant observers, spouses function in both training and data collection roles. Stuart's (1969) use of token exchanges between spouses (as acknowledgment of the desired behaviors) in conjunction with simply tracking the behavior is an example of this interdependency. A similar format of reciprocal observation between spouses was used by Rappaport and Harrell (1972) who asked spouses to track targeted desirable and undesirable behavior. These studies are only beginnings in assessing the complex network of marital interactions.

As part of the assessment approach at Oregon, the Spouse Observation Checklist, or the pleasing (P) and displeasing (D) measures, is a unique instrument for the use of spouses as participant observers (Weiss et al., 1973). The list, which evolved from interviews with couples, consists of approximately 400 discrete behaviors that have been categorized a priori as pleasing or displeasing. These are behaviors either engaged in by one spouse and having value to the other (e.g., "Spouse gave me a massage; spouse left his clothes around the house") or engaged in together (e.g., "We went for a ride in the country'). Any of the behaviors on the list have the potential for being rewarding (Ps) or annoying (Ds) to the observer. The behaviors were originally considered to be representative of either affectional or instrumental behaviors. Since affectional behaviors are usually short in duration and frequent in number, they are recorded on mechanical counters or tracking cards. Recently, the list has been revised by recategorizing the behaviors into 12 areas of marital interaction (e.g., companionship, communication, sex, services, etc.) with the expectation of profiling the comparative strengths and weaknesses among areas for each couple.

Previous data on the P and D list illustrate approaches to questions of validity and reliability on assessment instruments of this nature. Weiss et al. (1973) obtained a P/D ratio of 4:3 for distressed couples—a significant contrast to the 29:7 ratio for nondistressed couples. Comparing a derived P/D ratio score to self-report yielded a correlation of 0.54 with the Locke-Wallace and 0.56 with intake interviewers' ratings of distress. In an attempt to analyze reported marital satisfaction into behavioral data components, Wills et al. (1974) found that displeasing behaviors accounted for greater variance than pleasing behaviors. Furthermore, as noted earlier in discussing this study, a sex difference was found in that for males, instrumental Ps, and for females, affectional Ps contributed more to satisfaction. A reliability check on the accuracy of reporting Ps and Ds was provided by asking husbands to double their rates of affectional Ps given to wives, without disclosing the aim. The data clearly demonstrated a significant increase in affectional Ps, approximating the targeted 100 percent; other P and D subtotals did not show significant changes.

An additional home assessment technology that deserves mention (cf. Stuart, 1970) has not been used with marital couples but has been used with a delinquent teenager and her family. Stuart developed a device whereby one person codes the ongoing responses (e.g., positive communication behaviors) of another person or persons. During intervention, a buzzer sounds at a predetermined interval to cue the observed person that the targeted behavior has not been coded. One of the most exciting aspects of this apparatus is that it can be used in the home—for example, during the dinner hour. Cassette tapes were made of the interaction and were later coded by the participants and by outside observers, thus providing a generalizability measure between those two cells in our matrix. Stuart (1970) found that the family recognized only 73 percent of the positive behaviors attributed to the girl by an observer.

Observation by Trained Others

Trained observers collecting data from the home setting is a technique more familiar to those involved in family intervention strategies (Patterson et al., 1969). However, the Patterson et al. coding system for home observation has been used to measure changes in family interactional patterns for four marital intervention cases (Patterson et al., 1975). Data from these cases indicated that treatment had the effect of increasing fathers' activities in the families but not necessarily their social skills. Overall approximately two thirds of both fathers and mothers showed gains in positively reinforcing behaviors. Unfortunately, use of trained observers is somewhat limited in getting accurate measures of many of the important behaviors that are exchanged in intimate adult relationships. Unlike the situation with parent-child interactions, adult interactions tend to be more private and thus more affected by the presence of an observer. Total involvement with a couple or family for a lengthy period, as illustrated by the nationally aired televised documentary *American Family,* is perhaps the only way to observe a multitude of behaviors unique to adult relationships.

Assessment of Social Environment Variables

As is clear from even a cursory glance at our matrix in Table 15–1, the area of assessment of the social environment is relatively untouched by marital researchers. Certainly observations in this setting could be accomplished (e.g., diary, tracking spouse behavior at a social engagement, audiotapes of spouse interactions with others, etc.). In a case study Margolin, Christensen, and Weiss (1975) instructed the wife to observe the husband's behavior in social settings, focusing on how frequently he brought her into a conversation or praised her in front of others.

The Marital Activities Inventory (MAITAI) (Weiss et al., 1973) is the only behaviorally oriented instrument known to us by which spouses make recordings of their contacts with the social world. The MAITAI, which presents a list of 84 recreational events (e.g., watching TV, going out to dinner, playing frisbee, etc.), is used to derive frequencies of these events as either solitary occurrences, occurrences with spouse, or occurrences with other persons. The diversity of events across situations and persons accounts for its appearance in a number of the matrix cells of Table 15–1. The Birchler and Vincent studies (Birchler et al., 1975; Vincent et al., 1975) found that spouses of distressed couples engaged in significantly fewer shared recreational events than did nondistressed couples. This can be interpreted as a demonstration of avoidance of spouse, which would be predicted from a social learning formulation of marital conflict (Weiss et al., 1973).

PERSONS-BY-TREATMENT OPTIONS

In this section we will briefly consider conditions under which person-by-treatment options may be specified. The issue of which treatments for which persons actually assumes an assessment technology far more sophisticated than any available at this time. It may prove helpful to offer an appraisal of where our present day technology is in relationship to the goal.

Marital Assessment-Intervention Packages

We noted earlier the basic atheoretical stance of behavioral assessment as a strength and weakness. Asking which couples for which treatment raises that issue again because marital intervention is multifaceted and by design attempts to effect changes on many fronts. In a review of outcome literature up to 1972, Gurman (1973) found an improvement rate of 66 percent across a variety of treatments, therapist orientations, outcome criteria, types of clients, and so on. Before considering which persons for which treatment, the baseline rate we are striving to exceed under the most general (perhaps even chaotic) conditions is a figure of 66 percent rated at least "somewhat improved." Similarly, whereas a deterioration effect of 10 percent has been reported for individual therapy, Gurman found three out of 15 studies reporting such an effect, for an individual rate of 2 percent (over all *individuals* seen in these marital studies). Thus setting aside considerations of best treatments for selected clients by well-trained therapists, the limits are 2 percent likely to be harmed by intervention and 66 percent likely to report some benefit. (As Gurman notes, the quality of these data are much less than what is required for decision making.)

Three assessment-intervention approaches have been reported in sufficient detail with some empirical support to qualify for the "package" designation (cf. Olson, 1970, for numerous other approaches). Two of the three approaches (Azrin et al., 1973 and Weiss et al., 1973) were not included in Gurman's 1973 review. Our working hypothesis is that the more difficult assessment question—which persons for which treatments?—will be more readily answered by knowing what currently available assessment-intervention packages provide. We will briefly sketch the assumptions underlying each approach as well as the stated treatment objectives.

Stuart's Operant-Interpersonal Theory (1969, 1975) draws asumptions from systems, social exchange, and operant reinforcement theories. Stuart suggests that any attempt to modify marital behavior must take into account the relationship between the spouses, between the individuals and society (nonmarital forces), and between the couple as a unit within society. From exchange theory, the concept of comparison levels for alternatives is necessary for defining adult relationship reinforcers. The reinforcing control partners exert over each other is in part a function of that exerted by outside agents. Finally, the work of communications analysts (e.g., Watzlawick, Beavin, & Jackson, 1967) is useful in formulating intervention procedures aimed at improving communication skills.

Stuart defines five hierarchically ordered objectives of intervention (analogous to the modules described by Weiss et al., 1973). These are (1) shaping a behaviorally specific interpersonal vocabulary; (2) acquiring behavior change skills based on shaping and on positive (rather than aversive) control; (3) increasing skills in giving and utilizing feedback about one's behavior and desires; (4) reallocating power to avoid coercion as the means of decision making; and (5) developing natural and efficient procedures for cuing and maintaining interaction changes.

Although the lucidity of Stuart's expository writing cannot be captured in so brief a summary, the above list does indicate the importance he places on a systematic (hierarchical) approach to intervention. He requires a treatment contract from couples, which specifies their agreement to carry out assignments and provide data in exchange for counsel or ministrations. Failure to sign the contract is the only condition for which he excludes couples from treatment. All other contingencies (e.g., difficulty in specifying spouse-rewarding behaviors, identifying acceleration targets, etc.) are dealt with in the treatment system. An important feature of Stuart's system is the use of a precounseling form that provides important assessment information as well as serving as an initial pretreatment socializing procedure, that is, clients become accustomed to circumscribed description of problems. Given Stuart's basic operating principle that decisions to terminate relationships cannot be made rationally until the couple has had an opportunity to experience the relationship at its best, Stuart asks his couples to act as if the relationship were a success for an initial three-to-five-week period. If during that time benefits are not realized, the couple is at least in a better position to decide that benefits from the relationship are unlikely.

Although Stuart provides no direct statement about which treatment for which couples, he does build into his system two checkpoints at which couples can be deselected: (1) the failure to agree with the treatment contract, and (2) continued dissatisfaction after a relatively short time in treatment. Particularly positive features of his program include: (1) The system requires full operation of dyadic exchange of reinforcing behaviors. The focus is on increasing such exchanges and carefully cuing mutual dependence on each other. (2) Treatment is extremely directive, problem oriented, and most important, outcome oriented. All changes are geared toward producing benefits. (3) Communication training, based largely on the work of the systems people, focuses on providing positive feedback in both verbal and nonverbal channels, and negative feedback in the verbal channel only. Since clients previously learn a behavioral exchange vocabulary that focuses on outcomes, the communication training relates directly to gaining benefits. Couples develop the expectations that communication will lead to obtaining their desired goals. It is important to emphasize that techniques that have become identified with Stuart's approach all follow from his model's objectives. Thus the use of cuing devices, and token exchanges are devices for highlighting mutual reinforcement, increasing discriminative stimulus control of interactions, and maintaining relationship changes. Because of the hierarchical arrangement of intervention, assessment, although not specified in great detail, is assumed to be ongoing.

In sum Stuart's approach pays considerable attention to precounseling determination of a couple's strengths and weaknesses. Outside of two rather early exit points, it is assumed that couples follow through on intervention, experiencing successive gains as they proceed.

The second assessment-intervention package is that described by Azrin et al. (1973), which is based totally on a reinforcing reciprocity model. Since no marriage contract can assure future satisfactions, it is necessary to build into marriage a system for ongoing adjustment of relationship satisfactions that fluctuates with new demands made on the relationship. The modus operandi of such a system is to ensure that reinforcing behavior is *itself* reinforced and thereby kept at a high rate. Obviously, by pleasing Wife, Husband stands to be reinforced by Wife, thereby producing a greater relationship benefit. Technical language, extensive self-recording, and communication skills training are all absent in this system.

The qualities that qualify this otherwise "hedonistic simplex" as a package, in the present sense, is the sequential use of structured predesigned sessions, routine assessment, and a carefully developed rationale for marital discord. To paraphrase briefly, the causes of discord include (1) too few marital reinforcers, limited to too few areas of interaction (e.g., sex, finances) with failure to acknowledge spouse-originated reinforcers; (2) loss of valence of previous reinforcers, failure to label current reinforcers, and failure to reinforce the reinforcing other; (3) inadequate (inhibited) communication about sources of satisfaction (e.g., sex); (4) insufficient personal independence; and (5) reliance on aversive rather than positive reinforcing control (Azrin et al., 1973, pp. 3–4).

The single outcome measure employed throughout is a daily rating of relationship satisfaction (happiness) completed by each spouse. The Marital Happiness Scale (a 10-point rating from completely unhappy to completely happy) covers nine well-defined areas of daily (marital) living (household responsibilities, rearing of children, sex, etc.) and a global measure (general happiness). Although good verbal descriptors are provided in the nine specific areas, assessment is limited to self-reports of satisfaction using a single method. The Azrin et al. system has the advantages of simplicity of focus and emphasis on reinforcing exchanges, but it is considerably lacking in how well it tracks other areas of functioning in the relationship.

Another limitation is the use of aversive control to keep mutual reinforcing exchanges at a high level. During intervention, direct contingency control is applied to keeping rates high: failure to provide for Wife (contractually) allows her to withdraw all reinforcers for one day from Husband. As suggested by Weiss et al. (1974) quid pro quo arrangements such as these are powerful, but they may be inappropriate for couples who have not yet established a basis for positive expectancies about outcomes. The kind of quid pro quo control often suggested by therapists simply continues the use of the aversive control that is already a highly developed skill with most distressed couples.

The third assessment-intervention package to be summarized here is that described by the Oregon group (e.g., Patterson & Hops, 1972; Weiss et al., 1973; Margolin, Christensen, & Weiss, 1975). It has much in common with the previously discussed two approaches in terms of objectives, but it differs most in terms of offering a much more systematic approach to assessment at just about every stage of intervention. (Many of the assessment procedures have already been described in the preceding section on assessment technologies.) Some of the unique features of the Oregon package germane to the issue of person-by-treatment options will be considered here.

In the Oregon package the domains of marital relationship behaviors may be greatly oversimplified by defining three areas in which partners must demonstrate ability: (1) the exchange of affectional behaviors; (2) problem solving over a wide range of issues both internal and external to the dyad; and, (3) attempts to bring about change in the relationship. The emphasis on behavior change is perhaps greater in this system than either of the others. A major objective is to equip couples with behavior change capabilities that will function even after supports provided by treatment are removed. As are the other two approaches, this system is a modular sequential approach to relationship skills training. Starting with pinpointing, spouse observation methods, communication training, conflict resolution programs, the treatment progresses to the formation of utility matrices, which is preparatory to actual training in contracting and negotiating skills (cf. Weiss et al., 1973; Weiss et al., 1974; Margolin, Christensen, & Weiss, 1975).

In view of the heavy commitment to ongoing assessment, it will perhaps be most illuminating to consider first the organization of the assessment elements before seeking an answer to, Which persons for which treatment?

Overall the assessment approach is multileveled, with assessment and intervention being closely interwoven. A precounseling package, embodying much of the rationale offered by Stuart, contains the following self-report devices: Locke-Wallace, Areas of Change Questionnaire, the Marital Activities Inventory (Alone, Together), the Marital Status Inventory (Steps toward Divorce). In addition, couples are instructed to select from a 28-item problem checklist three major areas of concern in their relationship and to indicate for each area three strengths and three weaknesses in their spouses' behaviors. This is analogous to a presession pinpoint exercise, in contrast to the more usual "What brings you people here?" opener. The first intake contact is made contingent upon return of the precounseling information.

During each of the two intake sessions over the initial two-week baseline period, couples provide two samples of their problem-solving behavior by attempting to resolve conflicts drawn from their precounseling materials. These 10-minute sessions are videotaped for scoring by the MICS coders. Also during these intake sessions, instructions in using the Pleasing and Displeasing Spouse Observation Checklists are given, and assistance is provided in defining relevant Ps and Ds. The rationale for frequent telephone contact is explained.

The entire intervention package is predicated on success in completing the baseline or assessment phase. Full explanations are given for every procedure, and assurances are offered that all data will be used to devise a tailor-made treatment program. The first intervention session begins with a summary statement based on all data obtained to that point. The treatment contract is discussed in terms of the previous two weeks' activity, so that couples are fully informed as to what will be required.

Needless to say, these measures are reactive. Couples report engaging in activities for the first time in years, and they often lament the fact that once-favorite activities are no longer utilized. Daily recording, however, does become old hat, and records begin to stabilize. Least susceptible to method effects are the in-session samples. In fact, keeping the intensity of the interactions contained in order to move on to other issues is sometimes a problem.

During intervention, couples provide daily 10-point satisfaction ratings along with P and D counts. Numerous behavioral samples are obtained by recording events practiced at home (e.g., communication training exercises). All homework products can be assessed for quality (e.g., how well the couple drew up a list of recreational events that could be potentially shared, etc.), "Love days," those days on which Husband is instructed to double his rate of affectional Ps to Wife and vice versa, are carefully tracked by telephone calls. Since therapists have these data sources available at the beginning of each session, they are in a powerful position to specify what that previous week was like for the couple.

On termination, a final sample of problem-solving sessions is videotaped, and the majority of the precounseling tests are readministered. Clients produce contracts on their own at this stage, and these unassisted contracts are used to assess further the progress in conflict control and bringing about change. Behaviors targeted for change through contracts are reported on through the P and D data.

One of the advantages of the almost continual assessment requirement is that therapists and clients can detect when procedures are not being effective. Inability to produce a utility matrix (those special events that are rewards from spouse, outside environment, etc.) focuses the problem immediately on the broader issue of relationship benefits. Contracting cannot logically proceed unless both spouses can define what the other does that is rewarding to them! Failure or unwillingness to complete precounseling forms, especially the inability to categorize one's hurts, are signs that the couple would not benefit from the program at this stage of its development. The accomplishment of assessment in this form is a continuous testing of readiness to take the next step in treatment.

In sum it seems appropriate to suggest that all three approaches state optimistically that any couple will benefit from the mélange of training offered. Both Stuart's and the present approach have numerous test conditions that make further offerings contingent upon past successes. To date none of the approaches has reported on couples whose interest is predominantly a traditional role-oriented marriage. The considerable egalitarian emphasis in these approaches (e.g., contracting) may well run into difficulty with such clients.

We turn next to a less optimistic consideration in terms of current accomplishment. This is the problem of whether our assessment enthusiasm is running ahead of our methodological sophistication.

SOME UNRESOLVED TECHNICAL ISSUES

Behavioral clinicians are prone to announce that "the evidence is in the data." Committed to the sample approach, this means that the data will be representative of behaviors in naturalistic settings, that is, interactions in the everyday world. Marital assessment cautions us to be wary of what may otherwise become an uncritical and enthusiastic embrace of "behavioral data," without full appreciation of the limitations inherent in the collection process. Such limitations will be examined here, especially with regard to the procedures of our own group, which naturally seem most "correct" and "appropriate" to us.

Observational Coding Systems in the Laboratory

Trained coders, using a multicode data collection system to provide antecedent-consequent analyses of family interactions in the home setting, are said to be observing the kinds of behaviors that would also be evident in a laboratory setting. Jones, Reid, and Patterson (1974) offer a cogent discussion on the theoretical and psychometeric issues encountered in conjunction with one such coding system, the Behavioral Coding System (BCS). Their discussion also has implications for such coding systems when they are used for couples.

Sequential analysis of videotaped interactions from the laboratory setting are equally as complex as those obtained by naturalistic observation, but those from the laboratory setting allow greater control over several confounding influences that affect reliability and validity. The use of videotape eliminates the problems caused by the conspicuous observer, the influence the observer's expectancies may have on subjects, and similarly, the information revealed to observers that may bias them. Other problems are not that easily eliminated, however.

In the use of the MICS, as an example of a laboratory coding system, particular attention is paid to the issues of observer bias and decay of instrumentation (cf. Johnson & Bolstad, 1973, p. 18). To reduce observer bias, coders are unaware of client assignment to either experimental or control conditions, and coders function during only one phase of treatment to avoid obvious pretreatment and posttreatment changes. The changes between experimental and control groups could be further masked by adding new observers in the last phase of the study (e.g., Bolstad & Johnson, 1972). In an unpublished study from our laboratory, Kathryn Engel (Note 7) undertook a series of quality control analyses of the MICS coding system and showed that with all dyadic pairings of four trained coders (over six videotaped problem-solving samples) the mean reliability ranged from 0.85 to 0.90. The data allowed her to conclude that interrater agreement was the result of the coding rules (or some other indoctrination) and was clearly not related to intrapair shaping. This, plus analyses of individual codes that are "confused" disproportionately with specific other codes, allow the researcher to better pinpoint ways in which problems have been removed from the system.

Reid's (1970) important work on the decay of observer accuracy (e.g., effects of fatigue, new learning, forgetting, and carelessness) demonstrated dramatic reductions in observer agreement after observers had completed training and assumed they no longer were being monitored. However, further work (Reid & DeMaster, 1972) showed that observer accuracy remained at satisfactory levels with the continuance of regular training sessions. Even after reaching criterion accuracy, MICS coders continue in weekly training sessions. In addition, on a weekly basis one of the trainer coders tests each standard coding pair for reliability.

The potential confounds in marital assessment due to observed reactivity (Webb, Campbell, Schwartz, & Secrest, 1966) remain virtually unexplored. Behavior highly reactive to specific situational variables (e.g., camera and microphones, observation window, time limits, etc.) is limited in its generalizability to other settings. Johnson and Lobitz (1976) found that adults, by changing their own behavior, are capable of influencing children to appear relatively deviant or normal. The relevant question for marital researchers is whether adults are able to control each other in a similar manner. A possibility to be considered is whether spouses' in-session behavior is under the control of an implicit prior agreement they have made (e.g., to look particularly distressed).

Similar confounds may arise when the therapists play the major role in an assessment session. It is highly likely that the therapists, who typically give instructions for the assessment procedures, inadvertently set up demand characteristics that affect the couple's performance. As termination becomes a reality for a couple, both therapists and clients have a great investment in a demonstration of improvement, particularly because of the greater social cue control when four persons are involved.

Spouses as Participant Observers in the Laboratory

The majority of the problems inherent in participant observation are dealt with in the next section on home observation. However, two issues unique to the laboratory setting are (1) subjects' ability to do two tasks at once (e.g., put out behavior while tracking spouse's behavior) and (2) reactive effects of knowing what behaviors are being tracked. Spouses' tracking of each other's behavior can be an on-line signaling process or a sample from videotapes. A pilot study by Bruhn (Note 8) is currently being done to examine the differential effects of tracking behavior in these two modalities. Her preliminary finding thus far is that accurate tracking is impeded by the complexity of tracking while interacting. Tracking the frequency of a given behavior from videotaped recordings has the advantage of getting an initial uncontaminated sample of behavior (i.e., subjects are unaware of what behavior is to be observed). However, after the first experience at tracking behavior, the subjects are no longer naive to expectations of the task. Situations of this type present problems if the researcher purports to generalize beyond a pinpointed behavior assessed with specific assessment procedures in a narrowly defined assessment situation. Simply stated, the cues inherent in the testing context may support the behavior to a far greater extent than would be the case if those cues were not present.

Spouses as Participant Observers in the Home

When spouses are participant observers, the problems of observer bias or expectancy effects are insurmountable. As participant observers, spouses directly communicate their expectations to each other. Since the observer is not a neutral figure but someone to be pleased, this communication itself may have vast consequences on the behavior under observation.

As observers of each other, spouses set the criteria for evaluating each other's performance. The observer's standards change with naturally occurring contingencies in the relationship. But the inherent danger is that the natural tracking threshold of spouse-generated behaviors may vary on a daily basis (e.g., if the wife is angry with her husband, she may "overlook" his compliments on dinner). Similarly, a behavior's valence changes with events not themselves recorded (e.g., a hug while watching TV is different from a hug while one is flipping Sunday morning's omelette).

Often the standards for a behavior meeting the criterion level are left up to the spouse (e.g., "a good kiss," "enough conversation"; Stuart, 1969). Thus the observer may, when feeling loving toward the spouse under observation, be a particularly accurate tracker of positive events in an effort to be more rewarding himself. Similarly, when angry at the spouse, the observer may be unusually cognizant of aversive behaviors, perhaps even collecting data to justify the foul mood.

Further complications in this type of data collection are the demand characteristics of the situation. Spouse data are typically available for inspection by the other member of the dyad. Moreover, both spouses, as observers, are aware of the time schedule of treatment. As termination approaches, it is punishing to the other spouse, as well as to the therapist, to present data that do not meet expectations. Thus the very strengths of participant observer assessment (e.g., clients become consultants to their treatment as well as evaluators of their therapeutic progress) become liabilities in terms of the quality of the data collected.

Since behaviors targeted for intervention are discussed in treatment sessions, each spouse knows which of his behaviors are being observed. Even using the P and D lists (Weiss et al., 1973), in which spouses track a multitude of behaviors, both spouses may work from the same lists. Unfortunately from the assessment point of view, the initial reaction to the P and D list is one of excitement over the potential of engaging in new behaviors, thus marking the beginning of an unintended intervention.

The other reaction to be noted is what happens when the newness of using the Spouse Observation Checklist, wrist counters, timers, and so on wears off. Participant observers are subject to effects of habituation and a concomitant lessening of interest just as are trained coders in the laboratory. When recording data becomes a task done before bedtime, or a task interrupted by a crying child, data accuracy is under the stimulus control of a number of irrelevant variables. The only control that therapists have is their ability to convey their own view of the importance of the data. To ensure the continuance of data collection efforts throughout the week, researchers of the Oregon project found it useful to monitor data collection efforts on a daily basis.

A further qualification has been suggested by the work of Reid (Note 9) on behavioral complexity and observer reliability, as reflected in the BCS. As complexity (defined as some measure of the number of discriminations required during a data collection session) increases, there is a moderately strong tendency for reliability to drop. Generalizing these results to participant observers, who have even more task demands, it can be assumed that as activity shared by spouses increases, their data may become less reliable. One may conclude from this that as interactions get more complicated (e.g., during a conflict or a particularly full day), the therapist gets less reliable information. Data reflecting low-key, maintenance levels of activity are probably the most reliably collected.

Cost-Benefit Analysis of Various Assessment Procedures

A cost-benefit analysis provides an illustration of those dimensions to be considered in making decisions about marital assessment procedures. At this stage of knowledge about assessment procedures for marital relationships, recommendations are based on a restricted sample of available procedures and limited evidence about the utility of those procedures. Referring to the matrix presented in Table 15–1, it is apparent that by moving either horizontally (in the direction of increased generalizability) or vertically (in the direction of increased behavioral specificity) there is a concomitant increase in the cost of assessment instruments. Although theoretically ideal, these more expensive devices are not readily available to many clinicians nor are they necessarily the practical choice. For example, home observations are limited in their likelihood of capturing the low-frequency, often private behaviors that play a large part in satisfaction derived from adult relationships. However, there do exist comparatively more accessible alternatives as suggested by Patterson, Weiss, and Hops (1976). One alternative is the innovative use of tape recorders, either equipped with a timer, activated when interactions reach certain decibel levels, or activated by the clients themselves.

Before it is automatically accepted that observations by a trained observer are more accurate than self-report or observations made by a spouse, there should be further comparisons along this dimension. A major outcome of utilizing technological advances to achieve greater purity of observation is the effect of bringing observations under stimulus control of the researcher, thereby eliminating variance in the ability and motivation of couples to track behavior. What is unclear in the process is what is lost in terms of clients' subjective reflections of their own interactions, their tracking of idiosyncratically significant events.

What are the Generalization Objectives?

The approach to generalizability suggested by Cronbach et al. (1972) suggests that the essential ingredient to be considered is the extent to which an obtained score is generalizable to the universe to which the researcher wants the score to apply. Our matrix (Table 15–1) looks at how data may be generalized across (1) observers and (2) observational settings. The eventual goal is generalization across both these variables as exemplified by the Patterson et al. (1975) finding. Wives who were rated by their husbands as giving more pleasures in the home were also coded as demonstrating higher rates of facilitation behaviors on the MICS. The rank order correlation of 0.85 ($p < 0.01$) was highly significant.

Overall, however, the question of *convergent validity* (measuring the same trait through maximally different methods) is just beginning to be meaningfully examined by marital researchers. Preliminary analyses are needed to determine whether there is congruence across observers in the same setting and across setting and/or modalities within settings for one observer.

Examining congruence across measures provided by the same observer, Wills et al. (1974) found that daily ratings of Ps and Ds significantly correlated with more global daily ratings of marital satisfaction. A promising direction for generalizability between observers is spouses' monitoring of their own behaviors as well as tracking those of the other spouse. The Oregon project is currently examining the level of congruence between self-report and spouse tracking of the same behaviors in the laboratory and home setting. It is expected that this will prove useful in ferreting out whether reported increases in frequency reflect actual changes in behavioral frequencies or simply more accurate tracking of them. The extent to which the spouses' reports are discrepant may even prove to be a sensitive indicator of relationship distress.

Only a few clinicians (Stuart, 1970; Weiss et al., 1973) have capitalized on the generalizability of their techniques across settings. Stuart had a family practice with a cuing device in the laboratory to make sure that they had mastered the mechanics of it. Rather than continuing to practice in the laboratory, they utilized the cuing device in their home setting, which provided the greatest potential for conflict. In a similar vein Weiss et al. worked with couples in the laboratory to achieve a criterion level in the use of communication skills (e.g., reflection, paraphrase, etc.). They then sent the couples home with a tape recorder to continue practicing.

The tape recorder served a dual purpose: (1) as a data collection device and (2) as an instrument that provided an increment of stimulus control to the couples' arguments (e.g., they were instructed to turn off the tape recorder and terminate the discussion when they began to escalate aversive behaviors).

The core of the determination of criteria for generalization is related to questions of *construct validity*. Construct validity should be evidenced by increased marital satisfaction following treatment. It also should be evidenced by comparisons between samples of distressed and nondistressed couples. The MICS (Vincent et al., 1975), the A–C (Birchler et al., 1975), and Please-Displease List (Weiss et al., 1973) all provide significantly discriminating measures between distressed and nondistressed marital populations.

The brevity of this section attests to the fact that many marital assessment techniques are useful only in a limited sense. There has been inadequate attention to established norms of reliability and validity. It is recommended that in the development of a more standardized approach to marital assessment greater consideration be given to these issues.

SUMMARY AND OVERVIEW

Given the veritable infancy of the assessment of marital conflict and accord, what purpose has been served by an in-depth review and critique of the available literature? Even a cursory sampling of the marriage literature suggests that there are very few valid generalizations. The preoccupations of the past were expressed by postulating need patterns, role fulfillments, and various measures of adjustment dealing with discrepancies of the self, the ideal self, and the ideal spouse. For the most part adjustment and satisfaction have been equated. The major research strategem has been reliance on self-report measures of marital satisfaction, or happiness. High scores on such measures are more likely to be obtained from persons who also indicate agreement with highly exaggerated claims about marriage, such as, "I have never been dissatisfied with anything my spouse has done."

Satisfaction is not to be derided as an inadequate measure in its own right. A behavioral approach to measuring satisfaction was discussed that focuses on the interface between daily relationship events (exchanges of pleasures and displeasures) and rated satisfaction with the relationship. Asking which behavioral events give rise to reported satisfaction is a very different enterprise from retrospective global attitude surveys about satisfaction.

A considerable amount of measurement related to satisfaction relies on self-report data. We have therefore treated self-report technology as a major area of concern to marital researchers and therapists, not in a sweeping denunciation of such a crude approach to "data" but in hopes of developing ways for estimating the limits of our self-report data. Research findings from other areas of clinical interest suggest that only with considerable social control—"You are being checked by another observer"—does self-observation begin to approximate the rates publicly recorded. Other studies have suggested that it is possible to determine the amount and effects of falsified data by actually generating distributions of subjects' estimates of defined behavioral events.

The behavioral approach, with its empirical and methodological commitment for reliable information, could be highly useful in defining criteria for evaluating relationships as complex as marriages. Although the strength of this approach may well be its atheoretical stance—which eschews constructs and trait structures—acceptance of multiple assessment procedures is necessary. Marital behaviors will not lend themselves to single target definitions, which are then generalized into something called "marriage success."

All available literature bearing even the remotest associations with behavioral assessment objectives was surveyed using a classification schema that varied source of observation by type of observational setting. A distinction was also made between observation of behavior preserved in time—percepts—and observation as tracking of ongoing behaviors. When we consider that behavioral assessment is committed to sample rather than sign strategies, observations must be increasingly representative of behaviors in naturalistic settings, that is, they must have maximal generalizability to those situations. Analogue observations are not likely to meet this criterion. A considerable number of procedures have been reported that lend themselves nicely to controlled observation of specific kinds of interactional skills. Some of these can be used in training to define when criteria have been met and whether clients are prepared to carry out the new skills in other less controlled settings.

A wide range of cuing possibilities can be utilized in laboratory settings to strengthen positive communication skills. Most exciting are those that train joint discrimination of helpful responding, that is, both husband and wife can discriminate when either is being helpful.

Behavioral coding of ongoing interactions also holds considerable promise for assessing deficits in problem solving and communication skill. The use of videotapes and trained coders still presents a problem for widespread utilization of these assessment procedures, but it is conceivable that tapes could be scored in central coding centers in a fashion analogous to specialized scoring of other assessment instruments.

Among the newer spouse observation procedures, those emphasizing ongoing tracking of spouse behaviors are probably most noteworthy. Since the majority of treatment models emphasize reciprocity, or some variant of social exchange, the use of an assessment technique that embodies such an obvious treatment element is to be recommended.

The clinician currently has available several techniques for content problems or specific skill deficits: communication skills, reinforcing ambience, conflict resolution skills, and specific behavior change pinpoints, such as with contracting. The total array of instruments is impressive.

Conspicuously lacking is any major effort to conduct multiple level assessment. With the exception of the Oregon group, and in spite of frequent admonishments from the systems people, the focus has been on single outcome variables. The multiple variable approach needs considerable development. Our review also indicated that use of nontrained others as observers is absent at this time. Although friends, peers, and associates all pose considerable difficulty as sources of couple observation, their utility in this enterprise has not yet been given serious consideration.

Have we progressed to the stage where it is meaningful to ask, Which treatment for which couples? (Postponing the additional question, By which therapists?) Such a question assumes a higher order of assessment wisdom than is now available. To explicate what may be relevant to answering that question, three assessment intervention packages available at this time were noted. Our assumption was that the entire package had to be viewed for its potential to clients, not isolated techniques drawn from one or another currently popular approach.

Both Stuart's and the Oregon packages seem to have most in common in that both stress ongoing assessment of hierarchical (nested) treatment options. The approach described by Azrin's group can be likened to a vitamin C blitz on a cold, whereas the other approaches adopt a more conservative multiple vitamin broadside. Azrin's package stresses massed practice of reinforcement to the extent of writing coercive contracts to ensure positive exchanges. The "multiple vitamin" approach provides a broad spectrum of skill training, including learning a behavioral vocabulary.

The survey outcome data for all forms of marital intervention, with all forms of clients, treated by all forms of therapists, yielded a familiar 66 percent rated at least "somewhat improved." The answer to the treatment-by-couple (by therapist?) question must beat the 66 percent figure to justify the effort. On the loss side, 2 percent of individuals (not couples) are reported as having gotten worse (deterioration effect) from therapy. But here too, as reviewer Gurman points out, the quality of these data leaves something to be desired.

The most promising procedures are not without methodological difficulties, which are painfully and candidly described for the coding systems we now use, spouse observations, and the entire issue of participant observation, spouses and therapists! From a cost-benefit determination, the best multileveled approaches are currently too expensive for general use.

Suggestions and Recommendations

We desperately need sample descriptions that are more systematic. Clinicians should make an effort to report fully on the marital status of their couples, including such information as likelihood of divorce, various self-report assessments of dissatisfaction, ability to pinpoint areas of desired change, and so on. All too frequently there is inadequate attention paid to activities of women in the samples. Males may be students, engineers, and the like, but wives also function in environments outside the household. With the increase in second marriages we suspect that many clinicians will be working with these kinds of samples as well; early preparation for systematically reporting actuarial information about these people would be wise.

Although not stressed among our other concerns, a few clinical observations follow that may be useful to the assessment-minded therapist.

Compliance

The extent of client compliance with our treatment suggestions, assignments, and instructions is noteworthy. In our experience clients show very early signs of noncompliance. If these signs are not assessed early enough, therapists can find themselves being shaped into generating more elaborate and (for them) creative efforts that fall on ears, if not totally deaf, certainly nearing impairment. Compliance, or more properly, noncompliance, may signal nothing more than profound skill deficit, which is then elaborately "explained" by motivational anomalies, middle age, or constitutional deficiencies. Too frequently client explanations, with all plausibility, sidetrack what might otherwise be a simple and effective intervention if it were only followed.

Adult Reinforcers

Therapists must be on constant watch for evidence of adult reinforcers. Generating menus of pleasures, shared recreational events, pleasuring sessions, and so on is very much needed during intervention, and couples—by the time they seek assistance—often have very limited repertoires. Early attempts to sample such reinforcers may prove disappointing. However, as therapy moves along, a good indication that behaviors are changing is the increased rate in suggesting events that would be reinforcers. The P and D lists provide this information, but it is well to stay vigilant on this issue.

Maintenance Indicators

Prior to termination of intervention, therapists may find it useful to identify from previous couple data which few pleasing events seemed best to covary with relationship satisfaction. After intervention, when maintenance is at stake, couples might track an abbreviated P and D list containing the critical items. When frequency (rate) of these drop below levels established prior to termination, the couple would be well advised to recharge their batteries, either by employing a therapist-designed program given to take away with them, or by seeking a "booster shot" from the therapist. In any event, tying relationship satisfaction to countable daily relationship behaviors is a relatively unexplored but very appealing possibility.

Newer Research Directions

In this section we will mention briefly some possibilities for further research, illustrating them with some of our own ongoing work in this area.

Pretraining or Modeling Client Roles

With the exception of Turner (Note 10), no one has presented data-based answers to basic questions, such as whether to use one versus two therapists, whether reading materials help in their own right, whether the emphasis should be on pleasures alone or pleasures and displeasures. Nor has the question of preparing clients for intervention been addressed empirically. We need to know whether it is possible to take advantage of the socializing effect of membership in a small group, and whether by presenting audio or video materials prior to treatment we can greatly facilitate intervention. Many of the modules of the Oregon system lend themselves to use of training tapes and can be presented in that format. If situational control of marital behavior operates as we assume, couples should have numerous common experiences. The normalizing effects of seeing others with the same complaints may be worth evaluating.

Pleasures and Displeasures Technology

Work is currently underway toward developing a more comprehensive and sensitive assessment of spouse observations, namely the Pleases and Displeases inventory. Our aim is to develop exemplars for the kinds of categories clients use in describing their relationships. Thus for the category "consideration-regard" there would be a listing of Ps and Ds, which like items of a subscale, give statistical coherence to that category. In addition to answering the interesting conceptual question of whether quality of the event interacts with category location—whether "companionship" Ps count more heavily than "personal habits" Ds in incrementing or decrementing satisfaction—the clinical utility of having a profile of relationship strengths and weaknesses is promising. Clients are often given "production" targets to achieve or rates of Ps to be accomplished. The use of a scaling device would be helpful in this regard.

The use of a deficiency indicator for postintervention maintenance is similar. We are currently working on a procedure for using client-generated daily data to predict to rated satisfaction by defining the most predictive components of the P and D inventory. The analysis requires taking the quality of event as well as its frequency into consideration, but the aim is to pinpoint critical exchange events whose rate of occurrence is closely associated with satisfaction.

Augmenting Frequencies with Cognitions

In a study underway in our laboratory Margolin is comparing the effectiveness of an attribution manipulation as a means of defocusing the blame assignment spouses so often employ. The attributions focus on (1) rational techniques to negate the destructive feelings one spouse holds for the other and (2) definition and evaluation of all outcomes in mutual dyadic rather than individual gain-loss terminology. The aim of the attributions is to encourage spouses to view behavior change as a step toward a mutually acceptable end product and not as a matter of one spouse giving in to the other. Thus two groups receive the same type of experience with frequency of Ps and Ds and their exchanges, but for one group the focus is on a "team score" and mutuality of outcome. Likewise, the mutuality attribution is further established by communication training involving identification of joint occurrences of "helpful" behaviors. The contrast is with couples given training on either sending or receiving helpful responses but not on the joint recognition. The overall aim is to assess whether simple frequency manipulations can be augmented by selected cognitive attributions that will thereby circumvent many of the problems encountered—usually early in treatment—with forced feeding of Pleasures.

Multiple Area Assessment

In multiple area assessment we are concerned with systematically taking data on untreated behaviors in areas germane to but not included in the marital intervention. Although it can obviously be said that numerous aspects of social living influence marital functioning, it is more difficult to suggest a beginning analysis. However, it seems worth mentioning that one could bring together some of the best assessment techniques now available for areas of sexual functioning, parent-child interactions, and together with the previously described techniques for marital assessment, provide a multiple area sampling before and after intervention for marital problems. We may still require more carefully controlled studies with multiple baseline designs *within* the dyadic relationship itself, but the prospect of multiple area assessment is not that distant. Generalization studies of this sort are possible (if costly) using home observation techniques described by Patterson. LoPiccolo and others have devised sexual functioning measures. So the beginnings of such an undertaking are at hand.

Last we will mention the possibilities for studying stimulus control in marital interaction sequences. Here again the work of Patterson is of note, suggesting that precise specification of antecedents to marital conflict may be investigated by means of sequential analyses. Our current approach has been to develop procedures for assessing fairly gross changes and, once having established the reliability of these, to seek finer sources of stimulus control.

The area of marital conflict and accord has enormous practical significance, and behavioral technology has much to offer. The thrust of this chapter has been to light, however dimly, the way down a very complex but promising tunnel of love.

REFERENCE NOTES

1. Olson, D. H. *Review and critique of behavior modification with couples and families: Or are frequency counts all that really count?* Association for the Advancement of Behavior Therapy, New York, October, 1972.
2. Weber, R. J., Wegman, M., Younger, K., & Mallue, M. *Self-knowledge and self-monitoring of bites, insights, and laughs: A cognitive ethology*. Unpublished manuscript, 1975.
3. Margolin, G., & Weiss, R. L. Communication training and assessment: A case of behavioral marital enrichment. Unpublished manuscript, 1976.
4. Lerner, L. F. *Actual versus expected compatibility in the problem-solving dyad*. Unpublished doctoral dissertation, University of Oregon, 1973.
5. Weiss, R. L., & Cerreto, M. *Marital Status Inventory: Steps to Divorce*. In preparation, 1975.
6. Birchler, G. R., & Webb, L. *Discriminant self-reported measures of happy and unhappy marriages: A social learning formulation*. Unpublished manuscript, University of California Medical School, San Diego, 1975.
7. Engel, K. *Improving the effectiveness of the Marital Interaction Coding System*. Unpublished manuscript, University of Oregon, Eugene, Oregon, 1975.
8. Bruhn, C. Personal communication, 1975.
9. Reid, J. B. *The relationship between complexity of observer protocols and observer agreement for 25 reliability assessment sessions*. Unpublished technical note, 1973.
10. Turner, A. J. *Couple and group treatment of marital discord: An experiment*. Paper presented at the Fifth Annual Meeting of the Association for the Advancement of Behavior Therapy, New York, 1972.

REFERENCES

Azrin, N., Naster, B., & Jones, R. Reciprocity counseling: A rapid learning-based procedure for marital counseling. *Behaviour Research and Therapy*, 1973, **11,** 365–382.

Bem, D. J., & Allen, A. On predicting some of the people some of the time: The search for cross situational consistencies in behavior. *Psychological Review*, 1974, **81,** 506–520.

Bienvenu, M. Measurement of marital communication. *The Family Coordinator*, 1970, **19,** 26–31.

Birchler, G. R., Weiss, R. L., & Vincent, J. P. A multimethod analysis of social reinforcement exchange between maritally distressed and nondistressed spouse and stranger dyads. *Journal of Personality and Social Psychology*, 1975, **31,** 349–360.

Bodin, A. M. Conjoint family assessment: An evolving field. In P. W. McReynolds (Ed.), *Advances in psychological assessment*. Vol. 1. Palo Alto, Calif.: Science & Behavior, 1968.

Bolstad, O. D., & Johnson, S. M. Self-regulation in the modification of disruptive classroom behavior. *Journal of Applied Behavior Analysis*, 1972, **5,** 443–454.

Campbell, D. T., & Fiske, D. W. Convergent and discriminant validation by the multitrait-multimethod matrix. *Psychological Bulletin*, 1959, **56,** 81–105.

Carter, R. D., & Thomas, E. J. A case application of a signaling system (SAM) to the assessment and modification of selected problems of marital communication. *Behavior Therapy*, 1973, **4,** 629–645.

Cone, J. D. Social desirability and marital happiness. *Psychological Reports*, 1967, **21,** 770–772.

Cone, J. D. Social desirability, marital satisfaction, and concomitant perceptions of self and spouse. *Psychological Reports*, 1971, **28,** 173–174.

Cronbach, L. J., Glaser, G. C., Nanda, H., & Rajaratnam, N. *The dependability of behavioral measurements: Theory of generalizability for scores and profiles.* New York: Wiley, 1972.

Edmonds, V. M., Withers, G., & Dibatista, B. Adjustment, conservatism, and marital conventionalization. *Journal of Marriage and the Family*, 1972, **34,** 96–103.

Eisler, R. M., Hersen, M., & Agras, W. S. Effects of videotape and instructional feedback on nonverbal material interaction: An analogue study. *Behavior Therapy*, 1973, **4,** 551–558 (a)

Eisler, R. M., Hersen, M., & Agras, W. S. Videotape: A method for the controlled observation of nonverbal interpersonal behavior. *Behavior Therapy*, 1973, **4,** 420–425. (b)

Goldfried, M. R., & Kent, R. N. Traditional versus behavioral personality assessment: A comparison of methodological and theoretical assumptions. *Psychological Bulletin*, 1972, **77,** & 409-420.

Goldfried, M. R., & D'Zurilla, T. J. A behavioral analytic model for assessing competence. In C. D. Spielberger (Ed.), *Current topics in clinical and community psychology*. Vol. I. New York: Academic, 1969.

Goodrich, E., & Boomer, D. S. Experimental assessment of modes of conflict resolution. *Family Process*, 1963, **2,** 15–24.

Gough, H. G., & Heilburn, A. B., Jr. *The adjective checklist manual.* Palo Alto, Calif.: Consulting Psychologists' Press, 1965.

Gurman, A. The effects and effectiveness of marital therapy: A review of outcome research. *Family Process*, 1973, **12,** 145–170.

Haley, J. *Strategies of psychotherapy.* New York: Grune and Stratton, 1963.

Haley, J. *Uncommon therapy.* New York: Ballantine, 1973.

Hicks, M. W., & Platt, M. Marital happiness and stability: A review of the research in the sixties. *Journal of Marriage and the Family*, 1970, **32,** 553–574.

Hops, H., Wills, T. A., Patterson, G. R., & Weiss, R. L. Marital interaction coding system. Unpublished manuscript, University of Oregon and Oregon Research Institute, 1972. See NAPS Document #02077 for 29 pages of supplementary material. Order from ASIS/NAPS, c/o Microfiche Publications, 305 E. 46th Street, New York, N.Y., 10017. Remit in advance for each NAPS accession number, $1.50 for microfiche or $5.00 for photo copies. Make checks payable to Microfiche Publications.

Hurvitz, N. The marital roles inventory as a counseling instrument. *Journal of Marriage and the Family*, 1965, **27,** 492–501.

Johnson, S. M., & Bolstad, O. D. Methodological issues in naturalistic observation: Some problems and solutions for field research. In F. W. Clark and L. A. Hamerlynck (Eds.), *Critical issues in research and practice: proceedings of the fourth Banff International Conference on behavior modification.* Champaign, Ill.: Research Press, 1973.

Johnson, S. M., & Lobitz, G. Parental manipulation of child behavior in home observations: A methodological concern. *Journal of Applied Behavior Analysis*, 1974, **7,** 23–31.

Jones, E. E. & Nisbett, R. E. *The actor and observer: Divergent perceptions of the causes of behavior.* New York: General Learning Press, 1971.

Jones, R. R., Reid, J. B., & Patterson, G. R. Naturalistic observation in clinical assessment. In P. McReynolds (Ed.), *Advances in psychological assessment.* Vol. 3. San Francisco: Jossey-Bass, 1974.

Kahn, M. Non-verbal communication and marital satisfaction. *Family Process*, 1970, **9,** 449–456.

Katz, D. An automated system for eliciting and recording self-observations during dyadic communication. *Behavior Therapy*, 1974, **5,** 689–697.

Kenkel, W. F. Observational studies of husband-wife interaction in decision-making. In M. Sussman (Ed.), *Sourcebook in marriage and the family*, Boston: Houghton Mifflin, 1963.

Kimmel, D., & van der Veen, F. Factors of marital adjustment in Locke's marital adjustment test. *Journal of Marriage and the Family*, 1974, **36,** 57–63.

Knox, D. *Marriage happiness: A behavioral approach to counseling.* Champaign, Ill.: Research Press, 1972.

Kornreich, L. B., Straka, J., J., & Kane, A. Meaning of self-image disparity as measured by the Q sort. *Journal of Consulting and Clinical Psychology*, 1968, **32,** 728–730.

Laws, J. L. A feminist review of marital adjustment literature: The rape of the Locke. *Journal of Marriage and the Family*, 1971, **33,** 483–515.

Leary, T. *Interpersonal Diagnosis of Personality*. New York: Ronald, 1957.

Leibowitz, B., & Black, M. The structure of the Ravich interpersonal game/test. *Family Process*, 1974, **13,** 169–183.

Lipinski, D., & Nelson, R. The reactivity and unreliability of self-recording. *Journal of Consulting and Clinical Psychology*, 1974, **42,** 118–123.

Locke, H. J., & Wallace, K. M. Short marital adjustment and prediction tests: Their reliability and validity. *Marriage and Family Living*, 1959, **21,** 251–255.

Luckey, E. B. Marital satisfaction and congruent self-spouse concepts. *Social Forces*. 1960, **39,** 153–157.

Margolin, G., Christensen, A., & Weiss, R. L. Contracts, cognition, and change: A behavioral approach to marriage therapy. *The Counseling Psychologist*, 1975, **5,** 15–26.

McFall, R. M. Effects of self-monitoring in normal smoking behavior. *Journal of Consulting and Clinical Psychology*, 1970, **35,** 135–142.

Mischel, W. *Personality and assessment* New York: Wiley, 1968.

Moos, R. H. Sources of variance in response to questionnaires and in behavior. *Journal of Abnormal Psychology*, 1969, **74,** 405–412.

Murphy, D. C., & Mendelson, L. A. Use of the observational method in the study of live marital communication. *Journal of Marriage and the Family*, 1973, **35,** 256–263.

Murstein, B. I., & Beck, G. D. Person perception, marriage adjustment, and social desirability. *Journal of Consulting and Clinical Psychology*, 1972, **39,** 396–403.

Navran. L. Communication and adjustment in marriage. *Family Process*, 1967, **6,** 173–184.

Olson, D. H. Marital and family therapy: Integrative review and critique. *Journal of Marriage and the Family*, 1970, **32,** 501–538.

Olson, D. H. The measurement of family power by self-report and behavioral methods. *Journal of Marriage and the Family*, 1969, **31,** 545–550.

Olson, D. H., & Rabunsky, C. Validity of four measures of family power. *Journal of Marriage and the Family*, 1972, **34,** 224–234.

Olson, D. H., & Ryder, R. G. Inventory of marital conflicts (IMC): An experimental interaction procedure. *Journal of Marriage and the Family*, 1970, **32,** 443–448.

Olson, D. H., & Straus, M. A. A diagnostic tool for marital and family therapy: The SIMFAM technique. *The Family Coordinator*, 1972, **21,** 251–258.

Patterson, G. R., & Hops, H. Coercion, a game for two: Intervention techniques for marital conflict. In R. E. Ulrich and P. Mountjoy (Eds.), *The experimental analysis of social behavior*. New York: Appleton-Century-Crofts, 1972.

Patterson, G. R., Hops, H., & Weiss, R. L. A social learning approach to reducing rates of marital conflict. In R. Stuart, R. Liberman, and S. Wilder (Eds.), *Advances in behavior therapy*. New York: Academic, 1974.

Patterson, G. R., Hops, H., & Weiss, R. L. Interpersonal skills training for couples in early stages of conflict. *Journal of Marriage and the Family*, 1975, **37,** 295–304.

Patterson, G. R., Ray, R. S., Shaw, D. A., & Cobb, J. A. Manual for coding of family interactions, 1969 revision. See NAPS Document #01234 for 33 pages of material. Order from ASIS/NAPS, c/o Microfiche Publications, 305 East 46th Street, New York, N.Y., 10017. Remit in advance $5.45 for photocopies or $1.50 for microfiche. Make checks payable to Microfiche Publications.

Patterson, G. R., & Reid, J. B. Reciprocity and coercion: Two facets of social systems. In C. Neuringer and J. Michael (Eds.), *Behavior modification in clinical psychology*. New York: Appleton-Century-Crofts, 1970.

Patterson, G. R., Weiss, R. L., & Hops, H. Training of marital skills: Some problems and concepts. In H. Leitenberg (Ed.), *Handbook of Behavior Modification*. New York: Appleton-Century-Crofts, 1976.

Rappaport, A. F., & Harrell, J. A behavioral-exchange model for marital counseling. *The Family Coordinator*, 1972, **21,** 203–212.

Ravich, R. A. The use of an interpersonal game-test in conjoint marital psychotherapy. *American Journal of Psychotherapy*, 1969, **23,** 217–229.

Reid, J. B. Reliability assessment of observation data: A possible methodological problem. *Child Development*, 1970, **41,** 1143–1150.

Reid, J. B., & DeMaster, B. The efficacy of the spot-check procedure in maintaining the reliability of data collected by observers in quasinatural settings: Two pilot studies. *Oregon Research Institute Bulletin*, 1972, **12,** No. 8.

Royce, W. S. & Weiss, R. L. Behavioral cues in the judgment of marital satisfaction: A linear regression analysis. *Journal of Consulting and Clinical Psychology*, 1975, **43,** 816–824.

Schoenger, D. W., & Wood, W. D. Comparison of married and ad hoc mixed-sex dyads negotiating division of a reward. *Journal of Experimental Social Psychology*, 1969, **5,** 483–499.

Straus, M. A. *Family Measurement Techniques: Abstracts of Published Instruments* 1935–1965. Minneapolis: University of Minnesota Press, 1969.

Strodbeck, F. L. Husband-wife interaction over revealed differences. *American Sociological Review*, 1951, **16,** 468–473.

Stuart, R. B. A cueing device for the acceleration of the rate of positive interaction. *Journal of Applied Behavior Analysis*, 1970, **4,** 257–260.

Stuart, R. B. Operant interpersonal treatment for marital discord. *Journal of Consulting and Clinical Psychology*, 1969, **33,** 675–682.

Stuart, R. B. Behavioral remedies for marital ills: A guide to the use of operant interpersonal techniques. In A. S. Gurman and D. G. Rice (Eds.), *Couples in Conflict*. New York: Jason Aronson, 1975.

Stuart, R. B., & Stuart, F. *Marital Pre-Counseling Inventory*. Champaign, Ill.: Research Press, 1972.

Tharp, R. G. Dimensions of marriage roles. *Marriage and Family Living*, 1963, **25, 4,** 389–404. (a)

Tharp, R. G. Psychological patterning in marriage. *Psychological Bulletin*, 1963, **60,** 97–117. (b)

Thomas, E. J., Carter, R. D., & Gambrill, E. D. Some possibilities of behavioral modification with marital problems using 'SAM' (signal system for the assessment and modification of behavior). In R. D. Rubin, H. Fensterheim, A. A.

Lazarus, and C. M. Franks (Eds.), *Advances in Behavior Therapy*, New York: Academic, 1971.

Thoresen, C. E., & Mahoney, M. J. *Behavioral Self Control*. New York: Holt, Rinehart, & Winston, 1974.

Vincent, J. P., Weiss, R. L., & Birchler, G. R. A behavior analysis of problem solving in distressed and nondistressed married and stranger dyads. *Behavior Therapy*, 1975, **6,** 475–487.

Watzlawick, P., Beavin, J. H., & Jackson, D. D. *Pragmatics of human communication: A study of interactional patterns, pathologies, and paradoxes*. New York: Norton, 1967.

Webb, E. J., Campbell, D. T., Schwartz, R. D., & Secrest, L. *Unobtrusive measures: A survey of non-reactive research in the social sciences*. Chicago: Rand McNally, 1966.

Weiss, R. L. Operant conditioning techniques in psychological assessment. In P. W. McReynolds (Ed.), *Advances in psychological assessment*. Palo Alto, Calif.: Science & Behavior, 1968.

Weiss, R. L., Birchler, G. R., & Vincent, J. P. Contractual models for negotiation training in marital dyads. *Journal of Marriage and the Family*, 1974, **36,** 321–330.

Weiss, R. L., Hops, H., & Patterson, G. R. A framework for conceptualizing marital conflict, a technology for altering it, some data for evaluating it. In F. W. Clark and L. A. Hamerlynck (Eds.), *Critical issues in research and practice: proceedings of the fourth Banff International Conference on behavior modification*. Champaign, Ill.: Research Press, 1973.

Wills, T. A., Weiss, R. L., & Patterson, G. R. A behavioral analysis of the determinants of marital satisfaction. *Journal of Consulting and Clinical Psychology*, 1974, **42,** 802–811.

CHAPTER 16

Assessment of Child Behavior Problems

IAN M. EVANS and ROSEMERY O. NELSON

It is obvious that children can exhibit all the behavioral disturbances being considered in Part Three of this book, with the exception of marital discord where a child may be the victim, or even the *cassus belli,* but not a protagonist. In this chapter, therefore, we will of necessity be examining general issues of child assessment but will choose as specific examples those behavior problems that are essentially limited to childhood or that represent common childhood assessment concerns, such as cognitive difficulties. We will also give some consideration to behavior problems for which the state of childhood constitutes a unique assessment challenge—for example, the influence of developmental changes or the impact of such exclusively childhood environments as the school and the family.

Special Features of Child Behavior Assessment

There are a number of features of child behavior assessment, common to a wide variety of specific clinical problems, that define the boundaries of this chapter. The first of these is that prepubertal problem behavior will usually have been identified and presented by an adult, whether parent, teacher, family physician, or some other concerned individual, so that referral may bear little relationship to the child's own subjective feelings of distress. Adult referral practices depend on the available resources, and revealing data on these practices are available. Harris (1974) has shown that wealthier parents tend to bring their children to clinics sooner and for less serious problems than do poor parents. Comparing low-income black mothers' reports of their children's behavior, the only differences between those children who had been brought for treatment and a control group were the presence of disobedience, fighting, and poor schoolwork, but many more behaviors distinguished a white clinic-referred group from a matched control (Shechtman, 1971). It has frequently been observed that it is the middle class that uses community child-guidance clinics (e.g., Roach, Gursslin, & Hunt, 1958), and that aggressive behavior is a dominant parental complaint (Anderson & Dean, 1956; Roach et al., 1958; Stevens, 1954). When an easily accessible mental health project was available for primary grade children, 27 percent of teacher referrals were for acting-out, aggressive problems, 25 percent were for learning difficulties, and 18 percent were for shy-anxious problems (the remainder had mixed difficulties) (Lorion, Cowen, & Caldwell, 1974). In contrast, half the referrals by teachers to school psychologists have been for academic difficulties and only 10 percent for behavior problems (Nicholson, 1967). With the increased availability of early detection procedures for "high risk" children, parental or teacher referrals may soon constitute a smaller percentage of all case finding. In the "high risk" screening programs either deviation from developmental norms or the presence of established organic symptoms are the identifying criteria. Thus although child assessment should recognize the biases that may temper adult judgments of problem behavior, the common behavioral claim (e.g., Nathan & Harris, 1975, p. 443; Ullmann & Krasner, 1975, p. 475) that abnormal child behavior can be defined by what bothers adults seems to be more an expression of philosophical idealism than substantiated fact.

Two other features characterizing child behavior assessment are related to this first difference between child and adult assessment. One is that the young child is typically under much stronger and more obvious sources of social control than the adult client, so that adequate assessment invariably requires consideration of the child's social environment, even when the exact organic etiology of his problem might be quite apparent. A corollary of this situation is the third characteristic of child assessment: Children with behavior problems are very frequently already involved in some attempt to alter their behavior. Put another way, the distinction between behavioral psychotherapy and education, or remedial education, or parental rearing practices, is a very fine one. In behavior therapy with adults the planned treatment strategies are already difficult to separate from other deliberate or accidental sources of social influence (Wilson & Evans, in press); in behavior therapy with children the separation is still less obvious. Child behavior therapy is either itself educational, or is concerned with the redirection of other teaching influences, as is so tellingly illustrated by Tharp and Wetzel's (1969) triadic model of behavioral intervention. Here the therapist's direct contact with the target child may be negligible, and the manipulation of mediating social influences may be all important. It is hardly surprising that, in their honest evaluation of the Mount Sinai School Project, Marmorale and Brown (1974) found that school experience alone was effective in the socialization and intellectual development of children with problem behaviors and that access to a comprehensive mental health program was of no additional benefit.

The fourth characteristic of child assessment is that behavior assessment is inexorably linked with cognitive, or intellectual, assessment. This state of affairs is related partly to the fact that children's behavior problems are frequently a secondary function of physical defects or cognitive deficits, and partly to the belief—not yet fully documented—that cognitive deficits, if properly assessed, are truly modifiable in young children. It would be most uncommon to consider a child's disruptive behavior in the home or classroom without assessing physical problems, such as hearing loss, or cognitive functions, such as auditory comprehension. Similarly, much more serious and concerted efforts are made to remedy the *cognitive* defects of the more severely handicapped, retarded, or psychotic child than would be made were he an adult, for whom the focus would rightly shift to a more compensatory model emphasizing independent living, general social functioning, or institutional adjustment.

Although our ability to alter significant cognitive deficits is not as well documented as professional zeal suggests, plasticity and change are the undeniable characteristics of the young, developing child. Developmental variables are intricately involved in assessing child behavior. The younger the child the more must deviation from developmental norm be the measure of abnormality. Developmental measurement constitutes a particularly major part of child behavior assessment when similar behaviors depend on the age of the child for their definition as problematic. Prognostic estimates and treatment outcome evaluations—two major aspects of behavior assessment—are particularly complicated by age variables. It has been reported, for instance, that the prognosis is poor for autistic children who have not developed speech by the age of five (Rutter, Greenfeld, & Lockyer, 1967), and the outlook for school-phobic children 10 years of age or under is dramatically better than for the older child (Miller, Barrett, & Hampe, 1974). Outcome studies must take into account the high rate of "spontaneous" improvement in behavior problems typically referred to the child guidance clinic (Levitt, 1971); according to Shechtman (1970), some problems (attention demanding, poor concentration, restlessness, temper tantrums, enuresis, and phobia) show a more pronounced decrease with age than others (disobedience, poor schoolwork). The social significance of the behavior problem alters according to the age of the child, and there are qualitative changes with age in a variety of syndromes (e.g., autistic children may become extroverted in adolescence; hyperactive children become slow moving).

Behavior Assessment and Traditional Child Assessment Methods

There have been several excellent discussions of the differences between behavior assessment and traditional assessment (e.g., Goldfried & Kent, 1972; Goldfried & Sprafkin, 1974; Kanfer & Saslow, 1969; Mischel, 1968). Most of the descriptions of child behavior assessment, however, are *basically* concerned with the identification and manipulation of specific target behaviors in the time-honored operant conditioning fashion (Bijou & Grimm, 1975; Bijou & Peterson, 1971; Browning & Stover, 1971; Gelfand & Hartmann, 1975). The strict operant approach, however, is unnecessarily narrow and limited in application. Our own preference is to be constructionist, not dismissing the psychometric testing tradition, but showing how a functional analysis of behavior uses and improves these methods (Evans & Nelson, 1974). Thus we are in sympathy with the spirit of a recent rapprochement between traditional psychometrics and social learning theory called "social behavioral psychometrics" by Staats (1975). Another contemporary publication of major significance is the report of the Project on Classification of Exceptional Children (Hobbs, 1975a, 1975b), which contains much material referred to later in this chapter; the final summary findings of the project (Hobbs, 1975c) are invaluable for anyone involved in child assessment. The project reflects the very desirable impact on child assessment of a broadly empirical approach to the analysis of childhood disorders.

Child behavior assessment represents not a break from "traditional" assessment methods but a logical development long overdue. It is apparent that clinical child psychology began as applied psychometrics but was not originally limited thereto. Lightner Witmer founded the first American "psychological clinic" (which was primarily for backward children) in the same year that Binet and Henri published their first major paper on tests—1896. Witmer had inherited the psychological laboratory at the University of Pennsylvania from James McKeen Cattell when the latter's enthusiasm for mental tests (his own term) was at its height; even so, Witmer mostly relied on observations of the child in a teaching situation—an approach he called "diagnostic teaching." In Britain, too, the original impetus to "child study" was the clear educational significance of Galton's anthropometric measures, which in Galton's words could provide "timely warnings of remedial faults" in children's development. (Galton charged parents fourpence for this timely warning.) However, Sully, who pioneered the first British psychological laboratory to provide teachers and parents with systematic reports on difficult children (University College, London, 1896), favored a detailed assessment of the child's adjustment to his environment, criticized the premature classification of children as mentally defective, argued against the medical predilection to discover pathology, and proposed that child psychologists apply to the individual child the principles of general psychology and the use of the scientific method. The involvement of psychiatrists in child guidance was a later development. Healy began his study of delinquent youth only in 1909, and the majority of the cases were recidivists over school age. But as the medical pressures that physicians should direct child guidance clinics grew, the province of the psychologist became increasingly restricted to intellectual development and the role limited to that of mental tester.

The child psychologist's role was still further defined by the advent of social workers when children's outpatient clinics opened at the Boston Psychopathic Hospital (1912) and the Phipps Clinic in Baltimore (1913)—thereby completing the prototypic clinical team that Kanner (1959) once referred to as the Holy Trinity. With the dramatic impact of Freudian theory on clinical practice, psychologists—the testers—were called on more and more frequently to assess the child patient's personality dynamics in addition to his cognitive capacity. By then somewhat isolated from experimental work in child development and learning, they were constrained to adopt the unstandardized and subjective "projective" devices that had evolved in psychoanalytic work with adults, so that between 1935 and 1946 projective techniques began to replace intellectual tests in frequency of use, and in the last 40 years or so child assessment techniques have shown little change. There have, of course, been challenges, protests and revolts—for example, Rotter's (1960) theory emphasizing the situational specificity of test behavior, and, in Britain particularly, Shapiro's (1951) inspired experimental-clinical model. Yet the traditional role of the applied child psychologist as tester, the expectations of other professionals, and the extraordinary faith in projective techniques have been hard to shrug off. As Clarke and Clarke (1973) caustically remark: "[Assessment] has been classically regarded as the main contribution of psychologists. As currently employed it appears more often as an epiphenomenon keeping them busy, stimulating often unprofitable research and leading to a perpetual quest for the philosopher's stone (better and better tests) which will ensure more and more accurate prediction" (p. 24).

Dependence on intuitive and invalid projective devices, lack of contact with the methods of experimental psychology and child development, and an overreliance on the routinely administered test battery are all real criticisms of the stereotyped assessment that has characterized child clinical psychology too long. This should not imply, however, that psychometric methods and diagnostic testing must be abandoned. It is true that in assessment the prescriptive (describing behavioral deficits and assets as the starting point for a treatment program) and evaluative (providing an objective measure of the child's progress) functions of assessment are much more significant than the diagnostic (describing the child with reference to some comparison population) or predictive (estimating the child's probable status at a later time. But the latter two functions are not without their uses and the assignment of diagnostic labels helps to summarize observations, assists in communication with other professionals, guides treatment strategies in a global fashion, and puts the behavior therapist in touch with a preexisting body of more detailed experimental and clinical data of relevance to him.

It is worth pointing out that the current nosology of childhood disorders is in many ways an improvement over that for adults because child psychiatry is a recent specialty (the term being first used in the 1930s), and there was little carry-over from the sparse nineteenth century nomenclature. Indeed, the classification of the behavior disorders of childhood is one of the few sections of the *Diagnostic and Statistical Manual* actually derived from empirical studies (Jenkins, 1969). Perhaps as a consequence of the relatively empirical orientation in child psychiatry, classification has been less rigid than some behavioral critics seem willing to believe. Cameron, a doyen of British child psychiatrists, wrote in 1955: "In attempting classification, it has appeared to me essential to focus on . . . a detailed description of the child, his behavior and symptoms, in a circumstantial description of his development and changing setting" (p. 68). A report written in 1957 by the Group for the Advancement of Psychiatry (1957) advocated detailed observation of the child and caution in classification, stating further: "Diagnosis in child psychiatry is directed at an understanding of past and present interactions with parents and at the strengths and weaknesses of the major persons in the cihld's constellation . . . siblings, other key relatives, and the personnel of schools and other institutions who may influence his maturing personality" (p. 315).

It is hoped that a happy medium can be found between rejection of all categories and the discovery of disorder lurking behind every action of the child. A concept such as *normal variation* is included in most nosologies, yet clinicians can be overly prone to observe "illness." In a random cross-section of over 1000 children from New York households, psychiatrists judged only 5.9 percent of them as being "well or minimally impaired" (Langner, Gersten, Greene, Eisenberg, Herson, & McCarthy, 1974), the absurdity of which was quickly pointed out by Conger and Coie (1975). Assessment of children requires a modicum of common sense as well as knowledge of the normal child's abnormalities. At the other extreme is the common behavior modification viewpoint, expressed accurately by Kessler (1971) (in what is, incidentally, an extremely thorough review of nosology in child psychopathology): "Each case is viewed as a unique example of a particular history of past experiences so that the grouping or classification is meaningless" (p. 114). There is a ring here uncomfortably similar to Kanner's (1959) observation that psychoanalysts, viewing all child problems as having a common cause in the disturbances of the mother-child relationship, refute distinction between, say, an anxious chlid and an autistic child, and therefore apply therapy in a "more or less stereotyped way to all comers" (p. 591).

It hardly seems necessary to point out that behavior therapists *do* rely on diagnostic categories: The behavior modifier who teaches speech sounds to a child wants no congratulation because the child was afraid of dogs—he wants it understood that this was an autistic child for whom we are expected to know that the prognosis is poor, correct treatments uncertain, and response acquisition often slow and laborious. Why then is there a general mistrust, and in some cases ridicule, of diagnostic labels in behavior modification? Of the many complex reasons one seems particularly worth examining here, if only briefly. This is the widespread idea that the use of labels for behavior invariably influences the child negatively. The sociological concept of interactionism (or societal reaction) has been readily adopted in behavior modification (e.g., Ullmann & Krasner, 1975), but it is a very large step from the concept of deviance as the infraction of societal rules to the proposition that society reacts to the label in a characteristic way and thereby creates or enlarges the problem. The most frequently cited childhood example of this is Rosenthal and Jacobson's *Pygmalion in The Classroom* (1968), describing studies of teachers who purportedly responded in a prophecy-fulfilling manner when normal children in their classroom were labeled as intellectually gifted. The methodology of this work has been severely criticized (see Elashoff & Snow, 1971), however, and the findings have not been replicated (Clairborn, 1969; Wilkins, 1975). Even if these findings were reliable, the phenomenon would be the relatively trivial one of showing response to a verbal label in the absence of other more compelling evidence.

The damage that can be done by diagnostic labeling arises from the possible failure thereafter to develop an adequate functional analysis of the child's behavior, but this failure is not a direct consequence of the labeling as such and can possibly be combated by training teachers and other professionals not to respond to labels as though they encompassed homogeneous behavior (Filler, Robinson, Smith, Vincent-Smith, Bricker, & Bricker, 1975). Langer and Abelson (1974) have already demonstrated that behavior therapists are less easily biased by labels. Another danger is that a child, having no physical, cognitive, or emotional anomalies and considered "normal" in his own social setting, is stigmatized in school or clinic with a label such as mental retardation on the basis of one intelligence testing session. For an excellent, salutary review of such occurrences the reader is referred to Mercer (1973). However, such occurrences represent professional incompetence rather than the intrinsic evils of labels, and a Luddite reaction to these abuses—smash classification—is no solution to the problem. After a measured review of the literature on labeling from the child's perspective, Guskin, Bartel, and MacMillan (1975) concluded: "There is no simple predictable consequence of labeling for the individual. If the label is a negative one, the labeled person will try to deny it and avoid its consequences. But he may prefer the label to any alternative labels and the associated treatment may protect him from other negative consequences. If the treatment has no demonstrable advantages, and is itself only a labeling device, certainly both the label and the treatment should be discontinued" (p. 209).

Behavior assessment of children can best be considered an exploratory strategy rather than a routine application of specific procedures. The elements of the strategy are complex, but they include an emphasis on the psychology of child development and an extension of the experimental method, although in practice the latter is often more reminiscent of Piaget's *méthode clinique* than a controlled experiment in the formal sense. It should be self-evident that child assessment must be prescriptive, but classification is not necessarily antagonistic to this function: A diagnostic system provides a shorthand notation, and those using it do not consider that the label tells one everything about the child's behavior. The purpose of the remainder of this chapter is to illustrate these contentions by sketching out the strategy of child assessment rather than providing a full portfolio of alternatives to traditional methods. Some of what follows is culled from sources other than clinical applications and in certain cases may be idealistic or practical only in limited settings. However, by presenting the strategy on a broad canvas we would hope to foster an attitude of objective inquiry, reducing thereby reliance on any formalized assessment procedure in the fascinating but demanding task of assessing the child for maximally beneficial behavior change.

BEHAVIORAL APPROACHES TO THE ASSESSMENT OF CHILDREN

This section is about assessment devices, that is to say, the instruments or procedures used in gathering the information mandated for child behavior therapy. The organization will reflect some of the assertions made in the introduction: Children are referred by adults and it is often necessary to obtain from the adults details regarding the problem behavior as well as the social and medical history of the child. Sometimes verbal information must be obtained from the child, so this first subsection will consider the issue of interviewing children as well. Second, there are various inventories and checklists that elicit verbal information about the child in a more structured, repeatable manner. As there are distinct limits to verbal information, it is usually necessary to conduct behavioral observations either in the natural setting—discussed in the third subsection—or in some contrived or simulated situation—the fourth topic to be considered. In either natural or contrived settings the choice of behavioral categories is a central problem, so that, in the fifth subsection, some attention will be given to the possibly more neutral ethological and ecological perspectives. Finally, standardized psychometric instruments tap aspects of behavior not otherwise amenable to observation, as do a variety of other specialized measures, including developmental scales and physiological indices. These will be considered in the sixth subsection.

Behavioral Interviews with Parent and Child

Interviewing the Parent or Other Potential Mediators

The characteristics of a good interview with parents or other adult informants are not fundamentally different from any other behavioral interview (see Meyer, Liddell, & Lyons, this volume), so only certain special issues will be considered here. The parental interview has a number of purposes, primarily the identification of the problem behavior or discovery of the reason for referral (to be mentioned again at the end of this chapter), but also the assessment of the parents' role in the present maintenance and future alleviation of the problem behavior. Regarding this second point, although it is quite in order to observe a parent's general style, characteristic handling of questions, and so forth, unsubstantiated inferences should be avoided. A useful *general* principle for reducing overhasty and meaningless judgments is not to write anything in the report on the child that you would be unwilling to share with the parents (Gorham, Des Jardins, Page, Pettis, & Scheiber, 1975).

Anyone acknowledging the situational specificity of most behavior will be alert to the stress parents experience in being interviewed about their child's handicaps or behavior problems; the parents' behavior, whether good or bad from the interviewer's point of view, cannot be thought of as characteristic. One of the classic studies in this regard is Schopler and Loftin's (1969) report that the parents of autistic children showed impaired thinking only when the focus was on their psychotic child and not when it was on their normal children. In a sensitive essay Schopler (1974) suggests some reasons why clinicians attempt to use parents as scapegoats: their own professional frustration with vaguely defined behavior disorders like childhood autism, the realization that they are making slow progress, conformity pressures from other professionals who automatically assume parents are to blame, and as an attempt to simplify the usually complex array of diagnostic factors.

Whatever one's impression of the parents, casually judged personality attributes are likely to be of little relevance to the child's problem and may not in any event be amenable to change. It would, therefore, be much more useful to try to establish the parents' potential for being a direct and specific help to the child. Would they make good mediators? How responsive are they to behavioral concepts and ideas? What would be the logistical problems at home in the parents' carrying out elements of the treatment program? Because a very substantial percentage of behavior therapy with children is conducted by the parents as mediators, either formally or informally, it is vital that the parents' strengths for this endeavor be ascertained and the problems anticipated. There are, unfortunately, not enough descriptions by parents of their experiences as "paraprofessional behavior modifiers," but such reports as have appeared to show some of the problems. Greenfeld (1972), describing the behavior modification received by his autistic son Noah at Lovaas's program, wrote: "In this home-care program, somehow the UCLA kids seem to expect us to devote days and nights to Noah, to ignore our lives to the point of self-sacrifice" (p. 162). Elsewhere in the book he describes graphically other parental problems with behavior modification: his conflict over the attempt to institute a severe food deprivation schedule, his reactions to the use of aversive stimuli, and his feelings that he was being "operantly conditioned" when he was praised for successes with Noah.

There is a fascinating echo of Greenfeld's diary in a paper by Lovaas, Koegel, Simmons, and Stevens-Long (1973) in which they reported anecdotal evidence that the most successful parent mediators with autistic children were those willing to use harsh contingencies and able to place responsibilities on the child with expectations of appropriate behavior. It is not known how far the failure was due to practical limitations of time and effort, or how far the less effective parents could be assisted to improve. Perhaps other types of programs have to be developed for the more passive and permissive parents. One senses, for example, that they might do better in the less strict program described by Schopler and Reichler (1971a, 1971b). Most discussions of training parents as behavior modifiers ignore individual differences; in LeBow's bibliography (1973) none of the 222 books, articles, and papers on the use of parents as therapists address technical difficulties in detail. Some difficulties turn out to be skill problems. Staats, Minke, Goodwin, and Landeen (1967) described one reading program aide who could not be taught the specified manner of reinforcement, and Wahler, Sperling, Thomas, Teeter, and Luper (1970) found it difficult to teach parents to respond differentially to fluent and stuttered speech. It has been frequently reported that a major reason for failure of the bell-and-pad treatment of enuresis is lack of parental cooperation (e.g., Freyman, 1963; Young, 1965a), so that checking on the parents' mechanical aptitudes might be a good idea. When difficulties are basically motivational, a little encouragement seems to work wonders. Numerous projects have resolved such problems through monetary reinforcement (Loeber & Weisman, 1975). Eyberg and Johnson's (1974) contract with patients—contingent fee return and therapist time—significantly improved their data collection and general cooperation. Tharp and Wetzel (1969) provide good clinical examples of more subtle attitudinal problems that they encountered in parents: (1) philosophical resistances such as rejection of determinism, and equating reinforcement with bribery and (2) personal difficulties such as being themselves disturbed or having extremely negative opinions of the child. Attitudes such as these should be identified and dealt with early in assessment.

Because the choice of mediators largely depends on who controls the child's reinforcers (Tharp & Wetzel, 1969), special attention should be paid to the selection of suitable peer mediators, for peers are especially reinforcing and have proved to be extremely helpful as mediators and models in behavior therapy. Peers are also a source of useful information. In life-history research, Roff (1970) noted that an excellent predictor of adult maladjustment is a reputation as a child for being disliked by one's peers. What is perhaps most interesting is the early detection program in Monroe County, New York, where there is also available a psychiatric register maintaining records of virtually all contacts with psychiatrists in the county. In comparing those adults appearing on the register with matched controls, it was possible to learn which of a large battery of tests and measures given these individuals when they were in the third grade could have predicted later problems. The measures included standardized intelligence and achievement tests as well as personality measures and teacher ratings, but the only measure that discriminated the psychiatric groups from the controls was peer selection of these children to fill *negative* roles in a hypothetical class play. "Children, more sensitively than test data, teacher judgment, etc., 'know the score' " (Cowen, Pederson, Babigian, Izzo, & Trost, 1973).

Reliability and Validity of Parental Report

In addition to learning the current behavior problems of the child, a major reason for interviewing parents is to obtain a developmental and social history for use in assessment. This anamnesis can be critical for planning behavioral interventions, and no really careful assessment of the child is possible without it. Furthermore, someone is likely to collect this information anyway and the developmental/social history becomes the background lore of the child against which diagnosis and treatment plans are often formulated. It is just as well, then, that psychologists have some idea of what it is they are dealing with. Dependence on retrospective parental reports has long been a serious shortcoming of developmental psychology (e.g., Pyles, Stolz, & MacFarlane, 1935), so that criticisms from this source tend to be harsh. The best and most comprehensive discussion of parental recollections as a research tool is the monograph by Yarrow, Campbell, and Burton (1970). The objective baseline data in their study were contemporary nursery school records, pediatric reports, and psychological test findings. The retrospectively gathered information came from open-ended interviews with the mothers anywhere from three to 30 years later. The mothers tended to paint a more satisfactory picture of the nursery school years than was revealed in the baseline and to modify their recall according to social stereotypes of sex-appropriate behavior. "The strongest and most consistent influences on recall were the respondent's perceptions of the subject's current personality" (p. 68). Further analyses of these same data showed that accuracy on easily definable variables such as height, weight, and health were recalled more accurately than personality assessments of the child (see also Haggard, Brekstad, & Skard, 1960). As one might expect, low validity tends to result from attempts to reduce the unpleasantness of events. Mednick and Shaffer's (1963) study showed that mothers tended to be accurate with respect to duration of breast feeding, but reported toilet training successfully completed six to nine months *earlier* than had actually been the case. Distortions in timing of the behavior problems reported by parents have been found (Chess, Thomas, & Birch, 1966) to be in line with popular theoretical causes of behavior disorder such as sibling rivalry (problems erroneously reported to have begun at birth of the next child) or loss of maternal security (problem erroneously reported to have begun when mother returned to work).

Clinicians and researchers who argue that the objective facts are less important than the parents' *perception* of events should bear in mind that error in this area of research refers to both low validity (mothers' recollections fail to accord with the known facts) and low reliability (information from one interview fails to agree with another). Attitudes, often considered important in clinical interviews, can obviously be evaluated only in terms of reliability, which, in the case of attitudes toward pregnancy, whether the child was planned, and anxiety over the new baby, proves to be low (Brekstad, 1966). Robbins (1963) demonstrated that discrepancies between two reports were in the direction of the dominant cultural attitudes toward child rearing: mothers shifted their recall in the direction of Dr. Spock's recommendations—late weaning and toilet training, self-demand feeding, and permissive attitudes toward thumbsucking.

Further evidence that social desirability influences the accuracy of interview data has been provided by McCord and McCord (1961), in which direct observation data in one group were contrasted with interview-gathered data in an otherwise matched group. The interview group apparently differed from the observed group by revealing less parental rejection of the child and more clearly differentiated family roles. "It would appear, therefore, that the validity of the interview was marred by the parents' tendency to make their picture of family life conform to cultural stereotypes" (McCord & McCord, 1961, p. 185). From interviews with the mothers of clinic-referred children, Wenar and Coulter (1962) concluded that reliability was least with events of highly emotional significance—for instance, the most unreliable item was the parents' attitude toward the problem behavior that had brought them to the clinic three to six years earlier. In an epidemiological study of behavior problems in normal children Lapouse and Monk (1958) found little reliability on the more ill-defined problems when reinterviewing mothers: 52 percent agreement on "overactivity," 65 percent agreement on "temper loss," 83 percent on nightmares, but 98 percent agreement on stuttering. Agreements on these same items between mother and child were, respectively, 52 percent (overactivity denied by the child); 69 percent (temper loss tended to be denied by mothers); 54 percent (child reported nightmares more than mother); and 76 percent (stuttering denied by mothers).

Although this long catalog of errors inherent in the anamnesis is intended to make the reader skeptical of children's clinical case histories, its purpose is not entirely destructive. By knowing some of the known sources of bias and error in these reports it is possible to reduce distortions in material often obtainable no other way. To this end, a few simple generalizations have been culled from the available data. Factual events in the child's developmental history are much more likely to be accurately reported than parental attitudes, feeling states, and child-rearing practices. Accuracy does not seem to be increased by repeated questioning, but it can be improved by diagrams and by precise statements of the information required (McGraw & Molloy, 1941). There tends to be poor recall of information related to (1) neonatal injuries or complications, (2) childhood illnesses (Mednick & Shaffer, 1963), (3) early attitudes regarding the arrival of the baby (Brekstad, 1966), and (4) clinic-referred behavior problems. Length of time from the event to the interview does not influence accuracy as much as the emotional significance of the event at the time and the current level of anxiety shown by the informant. Distortions are likely to be in the direction of social desirability: placing the informant in a positive light, showing precocity in development, or tending to be in line with socially accepted child-rearing practices.

Mothers are more reliable informants than fathers. However, when independent reports from mothers and fathers agree, the information is likely to be valid. Parents accurate in one area may be inaccurate in another, but individual differences in overall reliability also exist. The characteristics of accurate informants have not been identified; however, garrulous informants are less accurate, particularly if they provide information rapidly without much pondering. Conversely, if a parent states overtly that it is difficult to remember certain information, the probability is that the information *will* be misremembered. There is no evidence for social class or intellectual differences in reliability of retrospective reports. In general, if parental reports are being used as evidence of the efficacy of a treatment program or to support some other scientific conclusion, objective corroboration is urgently required (e.g., Allen & Goodman, 1966).

Interviewing the Child

Although there are good technical guides to interviewing children (L. J. Yarrow, 1960), it goes without saying that the value of the clinical interview will depend to some extent on the behavior therapist's knowledge of children and his skill in relating to children of all ages in an easy and natural manner—the child behavior therapist must be a "Kinderkenner," if we may adjust Kanfer and Phillips' (1966) apt term. There are two major types of information one wishes to obtain from an interview with a child: (1) information that only the child can give regarding his perception of the problem and of himself and (2) indications of how well the child can handle himself in a social situation with an adult. As is the case with parents, making global personality statements based on one or two brief interviews is a grievous error, and psychological reports heavy with psychoanalytic jargon and clinicese are instantly suspect. Anthony (1970), in his magisterial review of child psychopathology, although regretting the jargon, noted that the psychoanalytic language was still the *lingua franca* of clinical practice. Patois might have been a better-chosen term for these verbal substitutes for careful observation. Unless he is a provocateur whose parents have done the rounds of the local clinics, the chances are that the child client will have a limited behavioral repertoire for the interview situation. It is particularly important to know the conditions under which the child was brought into the clinic, his expectations, and his general understanding of the situation.

An interesting issue is whether the child and the parents should be interviewed together or apart. Separate interviews often leave the child on the outside of an apparent adult conspiracy, after which it may be harder to develop a close, trusting relationship with him. The effect of having to interview the parents and child together can be salutary; it provides everyone with a model of frank, open discussion and a possible strategy for future family problem solving, as well as forcing both sides to give a reasonably fair and balanced version of the problem. The complexities arise when the parents find it simply impossible to discuss certain issues in front of their child, and the child, in turn, is unable or too sacred to discuss his feelings toward the parents, so that the first time either are alone after a family interview there is an outpouring of new information.

In planning for behavior change, questions regarding the child's reinforcers soon crop up: who currently controls them and the degree to which he has regular or easy access to them. There is a useful reinforcement survey for children available (Clement & Richard, Note 1), which is usually completed by casual questioning of the child interwoven with other activities. If the child will comprehend, the questioning can be structured for him by explaining why the information is needed and how it will be used. In an institutional setting for delinquent teenage girls aged 11 to 15, Nay (1974) elicited possible reinforcers from a small group of the children in an open discussion. These were then listed on a questionnaire completed by all the girls. From the most highly valued items, Nay selected those that would *also* promote social behavior—for example, outings to public places, dances, and cultural events—and argued that the treatment value of a reinforcer should be an important selection criterion. Even simple questions regarding choice of reinforcers are not immune from demand characteristics: Weiss and Gallimore (1973) argued that a Hawaiian-American group of children showed preference for a small but immediate candy bar as a consequence of etiquette training. And one of the questions in the Reinforcement Survey—What would you do with a certain sum of money?—is very similar to the "windfall" question used to study differences in cultural values. The question, "What would you do with a windfall of $1500?" is answered quite differently by Japanese-American children ("save it for educational expenses") and Hawaiian-American children ("share it with friends") according to Gallimore, Weiss, and Finney (1974). It is possible, thinking along these lines, that if cultural differences in motivation can be well established, a priori guesses could be made as to the types of reinforcers likely to be effective. There is some modest evidence that Hawaiian-Americans favor group rewards, or rewards that can be shared; this kind of information might make or break a classroom behavior modification program (Gallimore, Boggs, & Jordan, 1974; MacDonald, 1971; Sloggett, 1971).

In addition to obtaining information on reinforcement, it is useful to discover how the child views himself, his parents, his peers, and his behavior problem. Behavior modifiers who try to focus exclusively on overt motor behavior seem to forget that the way children label events partially, at least, determines how they respond to them (Staats, 1975)—essentially what is being talked about here is the assessment of symbolic eliciting or controlling stimuli for the target behavior from the child's own perspective. Whereas attitudes are undoubtedly modified by changes in behavior, the reverse can be true and occasionally easier to bring about (Staats, 1972). A child who perceives his teacher or parent as unfair is not likely to be greatly influenced by that individual as a mediator. Aggressive behavior against peers or siblings may require modification of the child's negative attitude toward them. Handicapped children are mostly aware of their disabilities and of being different from other people. It might be difficult to understand the social behavior of mentally retarded persons unless it was realized that much of it is geared toward making their inadequacies inconspicuous—what Edgerton (1967), in his remarkable "ethnography" of the mentally retarded in the community, labeled "the cloak of competence."

It must be noted, however, that children's descriptions of their own unacceptable behavior are no more accurate than adults' in like circumstances, as Hartshorne and May (1928) showed in relation to honesty, and Fixsen, Phillips, and Wolf (1972) showed in relation to room cleaning. Furthermore, children cannot always verbally identify determinants of their own behavior. A useful tactic in such cases was described by Smith and Sharpe (1970), working with a 13-year-old school-phobic child. The child was unable to specify the sources of his anxiety although he claimed to be trying. So he was asked to recount and visualize a typical school day in minute detail. While doing so he was carefully watched for signs of anxiety. Tears, flushing, muscle tension, and voice tremor were noticed at certain parts of the narrative, and this gave the therapists rather precise information regarding the school situations that provoked anxiety.

Structured Verbal Information Gathering: Checklists and Inventories

Behavior Checklists

Behavior checklists have come to be popular in child behavior assessment, often as an addendum to the clinical interview. Novick, Rosenfeld,

Bloch, and Dawson (1966) found that the interview (with mother and child) provided only 17 percent of all aspects of psychopathology that could be derived from five different informants completing checklists. Checklists can be completed by telephone for convenient tracking of problem behavior before, during, and after treatment (Jones, Note 2). Lists of adaptive behaviors can also be used by institutional staff to help define the range of deficits needing attention (e.g., Balthazar, 1972, 1973; Cain, Levine, & Elzey, 1963; Doll, 1953), as well as to provide a convenient outcome measure for a broad remedial or therapeutic program (e.g., Walker, 1970). The problem behavior checklist for outpatient use usually contains numerous items such as "too few friends," "always late," "never chosen as a leader," "cruel to animals," "sleepwalks," "smokes," "watches TV all the time." After the parents make a first appointment, they are requested to underline all the listed items that they think apply to their child. Some checklists relate to but one problem area—Werry (1968) described an activity scale for hyperkinetic children, containing such items as "wriggles while watching TV," and Miller, Barrett, Hampe, and Noble (1972) described a fear scale for children. Like any other measuring device, a checklist has its limitations and restrictions, considered below, but it has also assumed an important place in child psychopathology research and reveals issues important to behavior assessment that will be discussed.

One of the central concerns for behavior modification is from whence cometh the list of items. The behaviors listed in the previous paragraph are clearly not equal in degree of specificity, objectivity, and complexity. Deciding whether a child smokes is easier than deciding how many friends is "too few"; one would expect close relationship between number of friends and being chosen as a leader; similarly both of these characteristics could be a function of watching TV all the time, or vice versa. The items in the earliest checklists were derived in a number of ways: (1) a retrospective analysis by Ackerson (1931) of children's case records; (2) the extraction of "symptoms" from clinic case histories by Hewitt and Jenkins (1946); (3) a tally of all referral problems coming to a child-guidance clinic (Gilbert, 1957); (4) MacFarlane, Allen and Honzik's (1954) description of behavioral problems in normal children. Naturally these studies depended on the reliability and validity of the informants' responses, the range of behaviors originally identified, the inclusion of children with known organic or psychotic syndromes, the type of factor analyses carried out, and decisions regarding age and sex. Despite their diversity on these variables, the studies all generated a rather similar finding: that common childhood behavior problems cluster into at least two large groups—the *conduct problems* related to aggression and acting-out, and the *personality problems* related to anxiety and withdrawal.

Of the more recent research, one of the best known studies is Peterson's (1961) factor analysis of teacher-identified behavior problems in normal school children from kindergarten to the sixth grade. In both boys and girls of all ages sampled, Peterson identified the two factors of conduct problems (e.g., disobedience, fighting, disruptiveness, attention-seeking, negativism, destructiveness) and personality problems (e.g., feelings of inferiority, social withdrawal, shyness, anxiety, lethargy, reticence). Peterson's list of behavior problems was then extensively used by Quay in studies of delinquent children (e.g., Quay, 1964) and emotionally disturbed children (Quay, Morse, & Cutler, 1966). In addition to Peterson's two factors, a third dimension emerged involving such attributes as laziness, daydreaming, lack of interest, and preoccupation. This cluster, labeled *inadequacy-immaturity,* accounted for a large percentage of the variance in children in classes for the emotionally disturbed. In using the list with delinquent children, a fourth factor emerged—*subcultural* (*socialized*) *delinquency* (Quay & Peterson, 1967), which had appeared, like the other three, in the early Hewitt and Jenkins (1946) study as involving loyalty to a delinquent gang, cooperative stealing, school truancy, and rebellion against authority. These ubiquitous four factors have appeared consistently across cultures: Japan (Kobayashi, Mizushima, & Shinohara, 1967), rural Illinois (Schultz, Salvia, & Feinn, 1973), clinic-referred children in Scotland (Wolff, 1971) and England (Collins, Maxwell, & Cameron, 1962), and Hawaii (Gordon & Gallimore, 1972). Schultz (Note 3), however, showed that in the Peterson-Quay Behavior Problem Checklist administered to delinquent youths in Honolulu the factor *structure* (items making up each factor) differed from those reported elsewhere.

There has been a logical interest in attempting to identify more specific behavior patterns as an empirical approach to classification of syndromes. Dielman, Cattell, and Lepper (1971), for instance, found that in normal school children the first-order factors of disciplinary problems, acting-out, and antisocial tendencies made up the second-order factor, sociopathic behavior (conduct disorder). Hyperactivity, sluggishness, and paranoiac tendencies made up neuroticism (personality disorder). And social withdrawal, speech problems, and antisocial tendency (negatively) made up autism (inadequacy-immaturity). Similarly the Children's Behavioral Classification Project (e.g., Dreger, 1964) has attempted to identify broad clinical syndromes, including, for instance, "organicism"—items pertaining to having convulsions. Three rather obvious problems are attendant on this strategy. One is that the items making up a "syndrome" show considerable overlap. For example, "sadistic aggressiveness" contains the items "hurts other children" *and* "pulls other children's hair, punches, steps on toes." Second, the range of items in the inventory, as well as the variety of behavior problems in the experimental sample, greatly affects the syndrome clusters that will emerge. For instance, Green (1974) has carefully documented a pattern of sissy, gender-inappropriate behavior, and cross-dressing in small boys. This appears in Dreger's classification project for preschool children (Baker & Dreger, 1973), but only as two items, presumably because few children display such behavior. Third, the more specific the problem the less the reliability: Schaeffer and Millman (1973) found the original 17 first-order factors of the Devereux Behavior Rating Scales (Spivack & Levine, 1964; Spivack & Swift, 1966) to be too unreliable and best reduced to three higher-order factors of conduct disorder, personality disorder, and inadequacy-immaturity. Miller (1967) came to a similar conclusion with respect to the Louisville Behavior Checklist.

Three other approaches could be particularly interesting for behavior modification in that they include positive behavioral items relating to competence. The Pittsburgh Adjustment Survey Scales (Ross, Lacey, & Parton, 1965) revealed a prosocial factor because items related to positive school adjustment were included. This inclusion was based on Ross's notion that good school adjustment is something more than absence of maladjustment (Ross, 1963). Items relating to the well-adjusted, prosocial child are, for example, "interested in school work," "volunteers to recite in class," "works well by himself," "popular with his classmates." Closely related is the longitudinal work of Digman (Note 4), suggesting that school success (academic achievement) is dependent on two factors: intellectual ability and the trait of *industriousness*. Industriousness is composed of such behaviors as systematic and independent work habits, persistence on tasks, and responsibility in carrying out assignments. Digman's data suggest that emotional variables correlating with low achievement, for instance hostility and insecurity, are concurrent correlates of low achievement, not determiners, so that attempts to deal with such problems directly are likely to be less useful than teaching the necessary skills of planning, persistent effort, and the like. Third, Browning and Stover (1971) have noted that most problems referred for treatment are those of commission rather than omission. They remark that clinicians need additional guidelines by which to select areas of deficiency and propose a variety of instruments that may help delineate missing behaviors: checklists, staff notes, developmental surveys, and records of critical incidents.

Despite their usefulness, checklists are subject to much the same sources of error as parental report of their children's developmental histories, and a tendency to give an optimistic report is particularly likely. Many studies in behavior modification with children have relied on parental report on follow-up as their measure of treatment effectiveness, which is of limited value. Schnelle (1974) collected follow-up questionnaire data on forms similar to those used by Tharp and Wetzel (1969), from parents whose children had been seen in a behaviorally oriented counseling center. The category focused on was school attendance, because that could be independently validated. Thirty-seven percent of the parents reported their children's school attendance as very improved even though their attendance had *dropped* following counseling; the overall correlation between ratings of improvement and actual school attendance was −0.20. In a strongly worded caution, Novick, Rosenfeld, Bloch, and Dawson (1966), who had gone to considerable lengths to reduce errors, concluded that "the use of symptom list endorsements by mothers *as a measure of change* may be misleading and erroneous" (p. 237, our italics). On the other hand, checklists relating to, for example, school adjustment, could be used as an *adjunct,* follow-up measure of clinical improvement when the target behavior has been a school phobia (Hersen, 1971) or academic failure.

What may be concluded from this brief excursion into behavior problem checklists? For one thing they represent a major tactic in child psychopathology research, particularly in the important endeavor of empirical classification, although in assessment they are primarily used as a quick screening device (Cowen, Dorr, Clarfield, Kreling, McWilliams, Pokracki, Pratt, Terrell, & Wilson, 1973), or for jogging informants' memories. Second, they are limited by the same errors of reliability and validity that affect any second-hand report on children's behavior. Despite limitations, certain consistencies seem to emerge in the research regarding the clustering of common childhood behavior problems. It is also quite likely that these empirically derived clusters, or response classes in operant terminology, will indicate to the behavior therapist how problem behaviors may interrelate and what their prognoses may be, thus guiding the selection of target behaviors for modification (Nelson, 1974). Behavioral clusters may also interact differentially with different treatment strategies; examples will be presented in the next section.

Personality Inventories for Children and Mediators

Although a start has been made in relating observed behavioral clusters to personality dimensions measured by standardized personality inventories—particularly the shy-anxious/acting-out dichotomy (Eysenck & Rachman, 1965)—there is little evidence that such self-report questionnaires have much clinical utility as far as devising optimal treatment plans for individual children goes. It has been pointed out (Eysenck, Note 5) that this belief stops behavior therapists from using such devices, thereby decreasing the probability that utility will ever be demonstrated. In fact we would encourage the systematic use of theoretically relevant personality inventories in large-scale research studies in behavior therapy and feel it would be amply rewarded, bringing closer together the multivariate and experimental traditions in clinical work, as has long been advocated in general psychology (e.g., Cronbach, 1957; Eysenck, 1967).

As even this general statement of the value of personality inventories may be challenged by many behavior therapists, it is worth noting the kind of work we feel already suggests the value of detente. Young (1965b) found that the relapse rate in enuretic children treated by the Mowrers' bell-and-pad method was related to high extroversion scores on the Junior Maudsley Personality Inventory. Although this finding can be readily predicted from Eysenck's theory, the formal evidence that extroverted children condition poorly and extinguish rapidly, or that the bell-and-pad involves classical conditioning at all, is slender. Another promising area, reviewed recently by Hogg (1973), is the growing investigation of retarded children's motivational orientation, discovering whether the children work harder to gain reward or avoid punishment and matching training conditions accordingly. Major interactions between student traits and teaching styles are readily observable in the normal classroom (Cronbach, 1975a; McKeachie, 1974).

As long as mediators are primarily involved in the treatment, one can expect that there will be an interaction between personality characteristics of the mediators and of the targets. One such interaction has been reported by O'Donnell and Fo (in press) in a community intervention program for delinquent youths in which adult companions were trained as mediators—the buddy system. They found that there was less behavior change in pairs where the mediating buddy was considerably more external in perceived locus of control than the target youth. If this finding were replicated, it would certainly serve as an empirical guide to matching target-mediator pairs, but there are still a large number of unknowns in the relationship. We do not know how perceived locus of control relates to actual responsiveness to reinforcement, although there is some indication that external children will respond relatively more favorably to external and direct social rewards (Switzky & Haywood, 1974). Nor do we know what kind of rewards external mediators are likely to deliver, although they will tend to be simply coercive. A major problem with the locus of control measure in children—and indeed any verbal measure of personality—is that the reliability of the scale fluctuates according to the children's language abilities, with less verbal children apparently responding randomly (Gorsuch, Henighan, & Barnard, 1972).

To understand how individual differences in child and mediator affect their interaction, it is important to know rather precisely how their respective behavioral patterns actually differ. A reasonable attempt at this specificity has been made in a longitudinal study started in 1956 by Thomas,

Chess, Birch and others, in which the "temperament" of infants has been related to parental child-rearing styles (e.g., Thomas, Chess, & Birch, 1968). Infant temperament refers to reliable categories of very early differences observed in young children: activity level, rhythmic sense, approach/withdrawal (nature of response to any new stimulus), and quality of mood, among others. Certain constellations of these characteristics appear likely to lead to later childhood behavior disorders if there is an inappropriate parental response. The "difficult child" who shows intense withdrawal to new stimuli, nonadaptibility to change, and frequent negative moods can be most effectively dealt with by patience during negative moods, treating some difficult behavior good humoredly, and setting firm limits but not having too many rules (being "permissive"). Similarly, if children show a quiet withdrawal to new situations—the "slow-to-warm-up" child—opportunities to reexperience new situations without pressure enhances the child's eventual interest and involvement; whereas if the behavior is viewed as oppositional and dealt with coercively, still greater withdrawal is likely to result. The outcome of guiding parents in these different strategies of interaction with the children seems rather good (the problems were eliminated or markedly improved in 33 out of 42 children), but the clinical ratings were not blind and the reliability was unknown (Chess & Thomas, 1972). A related finding has been reported by Leon and Morrow (1972). In direct observation of mother-son interactions it was shown that mothers of children with personality (shy-anxious) problems tended to be very directive and to use much positive reinforcement and verbal criticism. The mothers of the conduct (acting-out) problem children used few direct commands and less reinforcement. The authors argued that this represents an important assessment strategy as one would advise the two groups of mothers rather differently—for example, the mothers of the shy-anxious children would not require further instruction in contingency management. Interestingly, nonprofessional child aides, selected for their "warm, mothering characteristics," have been found to be more effective with shy-anxious children than with those revealing acting-out or learning problems (Lorion, Cowen, & Caldwell, 1974).

The personality perspective emphasizes the striking individual differences possible in mediators and the consequent diversity of treatment, whereas behavior modification is often erroneously presented as a uniform procedure. Patterson, Littman, and Hinsey (1964) rated parental reinforcement style (flat versus excited), and although rater agreement was low, they found exaggerated, emphatic reinforcement to be *detrimental*. The warmth and permissiveness of the home was a more significant factor in the efficacy of social reinforcement. Striking qualitative differences in the frequency with which teachers attended to cued and uncued appropriate and inappropriate behavior have been demonstrated (Sloggett, 1972). Only one personality variable predicted the teachers' actual classroom behavior: Teachers who rated themselves as "permissive" attended to more appropriate behavior, ignored more inappropriate behavior, and gave more positive social reinforcers and were, in essence, better behavior modifiers than teachers rating themselves as "strict."

Unless one can begin to analyze the qualitative nature of the contingencies, the label "behavior modification" is hardly more descriptive than "progressive," "structured," or "Montessori." This has been nicely illustrated by Bartak and Rutter (1971) in a study of three different schools for autistic children—the most ostensibly permissive school used the most physical restraint. Miezitis (1971) found that a Montessori preschool program and a structured preschool program (among others) did not produce different academic achievement in middle class children (except that the Montessori program produced most "self-reliance"), but did in lower class children, with the structured program showing the greatest gains. Insofar as the structured program meant highly specific behavioral goals and response consequences, it can be thought of as being characteristic of many "behavior modification" programs, so that we again have an individual difference effect—not all children will maximally benefit from the same program. Although Montessori programs appear antithetical to behavior modification and eschew explicit contingencies, they are probably best characterized not by the absence of contingencies but by the type of goal behaviors socially reinforced: exploratory responses, originality, self-direction. As will be seen in the section on observation of mother-child interactions, parents may be taught principles of contingency management, but they will retain wide latitude in the specific contingencies, rules, and standards that they introduce in the home. If behavior modification is seen as a descriptive language for social influences on behavior (Wilson & Evans, in press), then it will be easier to specify the qualitative outcomes of any learning situation, be it token economy or free school.

Although standardized personality inventories lack the specificity of description of the individual case necessary for behavior change, there is increasing evidence of major trait-treatment interactions that have been largely ignored in child behavior assessment. Greater concern with this area of research should significantly aid the gross choice of therapy or mediator. In addition, personality inventories (trait or aptitude measures) allow description of a client population on dimensions easily reproduced elsewhere. This is important for the evaluation and comparisons of treatment strategies. Similarly, for individual treatment evaluation, personality dimensions can be used with advantage as pretreatment and postreatment measures of change, particularly to measure changes in related dimensions of behavior not a direct target of treatment—depression and self-concept in obese teenagers, for example. The strategy of pre-post measurement can be extended, by many more repeated administrations, in a fashion analogous to the traditional behavioral baseline. Repeated administration of the same inventory to the child client, in the manner of Shapiro's Personal Questionnaire (Shapiro, 1966) or Cattell's P-technique (Cattell & Cross, 1952) could allow one to test hypotheses about the child by observing the efficacy of different therapeutic procedures. So far as we know, this has not yet been done in behavior therapy with children.

Direct Behavioral Observation

Although behavioral observation cannot be thought of as an alternative to the interview, there are occasions on which descriptive information about the child and his situation can best be obtained by seeing for oneself rather than asking someone (Wahler, 1969; Zeilberger, Sampen, & Sloane, 1968). As will be seen presently in the discussion of the ethological perspective, and elaborated further in the final section, there is a distinct difference in tactic between the descriptive function of observation and its analytic function. In this subsection it will be assumed that the behavior of interest has already been determined and that the concern is with its functional relationship to environmental events. The continued observation of an identified behavior is the major assessment strategy in child behavior modification because so few inferences have to be made (Goldfried & Kent, 1972) and the stimulus specificity of individual behavioral units (Mischel, 1973) is less of a problem when observations are made in the natural setting. So popular has the strategy become that in many child modification studies the sole dependent measure is the observational data collected on the occurrence of the target behavior. Prime considerations, then, are the choice of a dimension or behavioral unit that will be maximally sensitive to changes produced by the treatment manipulation, and an understanding of the problems and drawbacks to the use of direct observation.

Observational Procedures

There are a great many observational procedures and recording devices, elaborated in another chapter of this book by Ciminero, Nelson, and Lipinski with reference to self-observation. Similar procedures and devices are available to other types of observers. These procedures include frequency counts, percentages (of the occurrence of discriminated operants, or of completed elements in finite response classes), duration, time sampling, and spot checking.

Two time-sampling codes that merit special attention because of their frequent use in observing children are those devised by O'Leary for classroom observation and by Patterson for home observation. O'Leary's code (O'Leary, Romanczyk, Kass, Dietz, & Santagrossi, Note 6) consists of nine categories of disruptive child behavior (Romanczyk, Kent, Diament, & O'Leary, 1973) and eleven categories of teacher behavior. Precoded data sheets are provided the trained observers so that they can circle the symbol for each child or teacher behavior that occurs within a 20-second interval. At the present time, the O'Leary code does not permit the recording of behavioral interactions between students and teacher.

Whereas the O'Leary code was devised for classroom observations, the Patterson code (Patterson, Ray, Shaw, & Cobb, 1969) was designed for trained observers to use while observing behaviors in the home setting. The code consists of 29 behavioral categories that typify family interactions. Each category is represented by a symbol. The observer is provided with a clipboard and an interval timing device. The observer focuses on each family member for a period of five minutes, broken into 30-second intervals. During each 30 seconds, the observer writes the symbols that represent the behaviors as they occur, both the behaviors of the target person and those of other family members interacting with the target person. The members of the family are designated by a numerical code. Observations are conducted in the home during the hour prior to dinner. The family is requested to remain in two adjoining rooms and not to watch television. Each family member is observed for two 5-minute intervals. The use of this procedure is described by Patterson, Cobb, and Ray (1973) and by Patterson and Reid (1970). Jones, Reid, and Patterson (1975) present an outstanding analysis of the reliability and validity of their code. Regarding reliability, the code is shown to have temporal stability (test-retest reliability) and to produce (at least under some conditions) high interobserver agreement. Regarding validity, the code is shown to identify behaviors that mothers judge to be noxious or aversive (content validity), to produce scores that agree with parents' perceptions of their children's behavior (concurrent validity), to discriminate between socially aggressive and normal samples of children (construct validity), and to reveal significant changes in deviant behavior after socially aggressive boys undergo treatment (construct validity).

Types of Observers

The observer used to collect data in naturalistic settings in most behavioral research projects has been the nonparticipant, trained, or independent observer. The O'Leary code described above can be used in the classroom setting to record the behavior of selected target students, as was done by

O'Leary, Becker, Evans, and Saudargas (1969). The teacher selected seven children to be observed, and the trained observers recorded their behavior daily for 20 minutes per child. In contrast to studies in which only the behavior of particular children is observed, trained observers may also record the behavior of many children. An entire nursery school class has been observed by trained observers (Bushell, Wrobel, & Michaelis, 1968). At the beginning of each 5 minute period each of four observers noted the behavior of the first child on his list, then went on to note the behavior of the second child, and so on. Each observer thus observed each child 14 times daily. Thomas, Becker, and Armstrong (1968) also recorded the behavior of an entire class, but they did so by randomly selecting each day 10 children who were then observed for two minutes each. Similarly, trained observers can go into the home; Patterson's code has been used extensively this way. Zeilberger et al. (1968) relied on a trained observer to enter the home and, by use of time sampling, to record instances of child physical aggression, yelling, bossing, and any instructions the child received from his mother.

In contrast to these examples people already present in the classroom or home have been used to advantage as data collectors. In the classroom teachers have reliably recorded student data. Osborne (1969), for example, had a teacher record the frequency of her students' out-of-seat behavior; the teacher's data agreed 100 percent with the experimenter and a supervising teacher who served as reliability assessors. Hall, Fox, Willard, Goldsmith, Emerson, Owen, Davis, and Porcia (1971) described several examples when teachers made frequency counts by means of paper-and-pencil tallies or by mechanical counters; interobserver agreement was assessed by various outside sources and found to be very good. Foster, Keilitz, and Thomas (Note 7) have demonstrated that data collection by teachers interferes neither with the teaching process nor the acquisition of student skills, particularly if a spot-checking procedure is used (Kubany & Sloggett, 1973), but this may be more of a problem when the students themselves are used as observers (e.g., Surratt, Ulrich, & Hawkins, 1969). Another valuable procedure is to ask teachers to record their own positive and negative verbalizations in the classroom (Nelson, Hay, Hay, & Carstens, in press). In other studies students have self-monitored their studying and inappropriate talking (Broden, Hall, & Mitts, 1971; Clement, 1974).

Similar to the use of participant observers in the classroom, parents or others in the home setting have also been pressed into observational service. As the mother collected data in one study, reliability was assessed by either her spouse, a neighbor, a sibling, or an aunt. Interobserver agreement was found to be high (Hall, Axelrod, Tyler, Grief, Jones, & Robertson, 1972). Christophersen, Arnold, Hill, and Quilitch (1972) had parents serve as the primary observers in their own homes with an occasional reliability check performed by one of the experimenters. Depending on the method of calculation used, interobserver agreement was 84 to 91 percent. In addition to observing their children, parents have also self-monitored their own behavior. Herbert and Baer (1972) had two mothers self-record on wrist counters the frequency of their attention to appropriate child behaviors.

Problems in Observations of Children

The great many research studies that elaborate the problems found when trained observers are used to collect data are summarized by Johnson and Bolstad (1973), Lipinski and Nelson (1974), and Kent and Foster (this volume). The main problems have been maintaining high interobserver agreement particularly when the observer's reliability is not being monitored (Reid, 1970), preventing knowledge of experimental hypotheses from influencing data collection, and minimizing the effects of the observer as a novel stimulus in altering the observed behaviors. The reactive effect of home observation has been so striking that students of mother-child behavior now call the effect the girdle on/girdle off phenomenon, from the observation that mothers tend to smarten themselves up when they know an observer is due to visit.

It has been suggested that one way to minimize the reactive effects of a trained observer is to have a person already in the environment serve as data collector. As yet there has been little research into the methodological problems related to the use of parents or teachers as observers. Data that do exist suggest that similar methodological problems may exist when parents or teachers are used as when trained observers are used. Using trained observers, Kent, O'Leary, Diament, and Dietz (1974) showed that knowledge of experimental hypotheses altered global evaluations of treatment effects but not behavioral recordings. Walter and Gilmore (1973) confirmed that parents' global reports of treatment effects were inaccurate, yet, as was found with trained observers, behavioral recordings were unbiased.

Despite suggestions that the use of participant observers in the classroom may reduce reactivity, it seems that the very process of observing may be a sufficiently novel stimulus to produce behavioral alterations. In Surratt et al.'s study (1969) improvements in the studying of first graders were only partially maintained when the fifth-grade observer was not present, indicating that the fifth grader may have become a discriminative stimulus for appropriate studying. In addition, reports of "baseline cures," or decreases in the frequency of target behaviors that occur during baseline observation prior to the initiation of the treatment procedures (Forehand,

1973), suggest that observations made by the teacher may be reactive, owing at least partially to changes in the teacher's behavior, that is, observer-mediator reactivity. Both student reactivity and observer-mediator reactivity were found by Hay, Nelson, and Hay (in press). In their experimental design, data on student and teacher behaviors were collected for two weeks by trained observers; the trained observers continued to record for an additional two weeks while the teachers simultaneously recorded student behavior. The process of teacher observation was shown to alter both student and teacher behaviors as compared with controls. Furthermore, having parents, teachers, or children self-record their own behaviors is no simple solution to the methodological problems engendered by naturalistic observation; self-monitoring procedures also produce reactive and unreliable results (Nelson, Lipinski, & Black, 1975). Lewis and Lee-Painter (Note 8) emphasize that reactivity is a fact of life and that the degree of the observation effect on a given behavior must be determined by manipulating types of observer—black or white, male or female, friend or stranger.

Behavioral Observations in Simulated or Contrived Situations

Advantages and Disadvantages of Simulated Situations

During the behavioral observations in naturalistic situations described in the preceding section, very few limits were placed on the observation situation. In general, except for Patterson's procedure, the subjects were in their usual settings of a classroom or a home with no additional requirements placed on their activities. Although unstructured observations allow one to witness behaviors as they naturally occur, they have the obvious disadvantage that responses of interest may simply not occur during observation periods. Because any one observation period samples only a limited number of stimulus events, behaviors generated by these stimuli may occur with great frequency, and other behaviors may not occur at all. Bell (1964) describes this phenomenon as behaviors "piling up" in a small number of observational categories, with other categories represented by a few or no behavioral occurrences.

In simulated or contrived situations, conversely, specific stimuli are deliberately presented in order to maximize the probability that certain categories of behavior will appear. Sloggett (1972) taught four children to behave in a simulated classroom in both desirable and undesirable ways. This allowed her to observe the behavior of all the teachers who had been through a training program in behavior management to see how well they were able to respond to both good and bad behavior. Perhaps the most obvious situation in which stimuli are presented in a controlled fashion is the direct behavior avoidance test that has been used with children a number of times—Bandura, Grusec, and Menlove (1967) used a sequence of 14 steps toward friendship with a dog; Ritter (1968) felt that 29 items were needed to interact with a long snake. Particularly ingenious were Jersild and Holmes's (1935) tasks, in which, for example, the child was asked to retrieve a ball from a dark room where it had been "inadvertently" thrown. The special advantage of these simulated situations is their standardized nature (Santostefano, 1968). Because the same stimuli are presented, behavioral comparisons may be made between as well as within subjects. Zegiob and Forehand (1975), for example, used a standardized situation in which the mother was told to give three commands one at a time in a specified order to her child to compare maternal interactions as a function of race, socioeconomic class, and sex of child.

There are, however, some drawbacks to simulated situations. One of these difficulties is determining the stimulus situation likely to produce behaviors of significance. Bell (1964) has noted that since the heaviest use of structured parent-child interactions has been made by students of child development, stimulus situations have usually been selected on the basis of various child development theories as likely to produce, for example, aggression or achievement attempts. A second disadvantage of simulated situations is the possible lack of generalization from the behaviors observed in the simulated situation to behaviors that occur in the natural environment. One reason for this might be Rotter's (1960) proposal that the reinforcers in the simulated situation are perceived as being different from those in the natural setting. Chapanis (1967) has pinpointed other difficulties in generalizing from any laboratory study to the natural environment. The problems he mentions—for example, the limited number of stimuli available in the laboratory as compared with the plethora of stimuli in the natural environment—also restrict the generalization from simulated situations to the natural environment.

Research results have frequently confirmed this generalization difficulty. Moustakas, Sigel, and Schalock (1956) compared therapist-child interactions in a laboratory free-play situation with mother-child interactions in the same setting and in the natural home setting. Using an observational coding system, they concluded that both adult and child behavior differed from one situation to another, but that there was greater similarity in the behavior of mother and child in the playroom and in the home than in either of these situations as compared with that of the therapist and child in the playroom. O'Rourke (1963) similarly found that family problem-solving behavior differed depending on whether the discussion occurred in the laboratory or in the home. Although the above two studies found poor generalization from the laboratory to the home, Hatfield, Ferguson, and

Alpert (1967) reported poor generalization within different simulated situations in the laboratory setting. Specifically, they found low correlations between mother and child behaviors manifested during two sessions, one involving a role-playing telephone game (Sears, Rau, & Alpert, 1965) and the other a fishing game.

Imaginative Play as an Assessment Procedure for Children

A great deal of traditional child assessment takes place in the context of fantasy, and it is partly as a consequence of this that behavior therapists have shied away from exploration of the child's imagination. This is a pity because imagination has played a venerable role in behavior therapy, and the application of systematic desensitization and related techniques involving "covert" stimuli to children requires some knowledge of their interests and abilities in this area. With the exception of Lazarus and Abramovitz (1962), behavior therapists have been slow to capitalize on this powerful element in the influence of children's behavior. Another good reason for using imaginary situations in assessment is that children "lack sufficient verbal skills to describe the various components of their problems and observations at crucial moments may be impossible, [so that] role playing [can be] used to facilitate data gathering" (Rose, 1972, p. 44). This suggestion echoes M. R. Yarrow's (1960) recommendation that role playing be used in the assessment of children's problems, with the clinician taking on the role of a significant person and the child responding. Gittelman (1965) called role playing "behavior rehearsal" and used the procedure successfully to assess and modify children's aggressive responses evoked in various instigative situations.

Play with dolls has previously been used a great deal in clinical work with children to assess aggression, sibling rivalry, sex knowledge, and so on, but with little attempt to validate the observations by comparison with the child's actual performance in a natural setting. Essentially, the basic problem with role playing, "let's pretend" games, or imaginative play with doll-houses, family figurines, or whatever, is whether the observations can be accepted as veridical. It is our impression—and it is supported by the experimental literature (Singer, 1973)—that children from the age of three or so onward see clearly that a make-believe game involves fantasy, that is, things that are not real. Thus the invitation to a child to play a make-believe game provides an almost certain guarantee that the information obtained does not reflect reality. These cautionary comments do not apply to those situations where play is the target behavior and is, therefore, described and evaluated without any subsequent inference being made. This is typically of interest with autistic children, whose play is usually very limited, or children showing extreme cross-gender identity problems that are especially evident in play situations (Rekers & Lovaas, 1974). Lovaas, Freitag, Gold, and Kassorla (1965) described a useful multichannel event recorder for recording children's behavior in a free-play situation.

Structured Parent-Child Interactions

The major purpose of observing children and their parents together in the clinic is to clarify the problem behavior and observe its relationship to parental reactions. Some experimenters have brought parent-child dyads into laboratory free-play settings and have given them virtually no instructions regarding expected behaviors (e.g., Baumrind, 1967; Bishop, 1946). Bell (1964) notes that such unstructured interactions have the same problem as found in naturalistic observation, namely, the behaviors of interest may not occur. An example of this was presented by Wahler, Winkel, Peterson, and Morrison (1965) who requested that mothers play with their children in the laboratory playroom. These instructions had to be modified for one of the dyads because no deviant behavior occurred in the free-play context.

To maximize the probability that behaviors of interest will occur, other investigators have devised a variety of structured situations for parent-child interactions (reviewed by Bell, 1964; Lytton, 1971). For example, Bishop (1946) told an experimental group of mothers that their children had not acted up to their true capacities in order to assess the effects of these instructions on maternal dominance. Rosen and D'Andrade (1959) staged situations to make the children relatively dependent on their parents' help: The child was blindfolded and asked to build a tower out of irregularly shaped blocks with only one hand. To produce expressions of a wide variety of motives, Santostefano (1968) created what he labeled "miniature situations" in which the mother-child dyad were presented two games simultaneously and in which their interactions with the games and with each other were observed. Smith (1958) gave mothers a long questionnaire to fill out while in a playroom together with their children as a means of ascertaining how they handled bids for attention. As a before-and-after measure of behaviorally oriented family therapy, Parsons and Alexander (1973) had parents and children discuss family problems together. However, highly complex categories are required to describe family communication and metacommunication patterns (Tsoi-Hoshmand, Note 9).

In clinical studies of change in child behavior the observational categories tend to be focused on the immediate problem behavior and the accompanying social reinforcement. Wahler et al. (1965) identified a deviant behavior and a replacement behavior for each of three child subjects. Parent and child behaviors were coded in a laboratory setting during baseline periods and also during parent training periods when the mother was coached in extinction and reinforcement procedures. A 15-minute command situation was used by Mash, Lazare, Terdal, and Garner (1973) as a dependent measure of the efficacy of parent training in groups. The training increased rate of compliance with maternal requests to take off shoes, string beads, and other tasks. Forehand, King, Peed, and Yoder (1975) showed that a structured situation did produce examples of the noncompliance problems for which the children had been referred to the clinic. The mothers of the noncomplaint children differed from the mothers of the normal children not in using less reinforcement but in using more criticism and a greater number of commands—which suggests possible dimensions for modification by parent training.

It can be seen that child behavior therapists are prone to concentrate on social reinforcement contingencies, but, as was discussed in the context of mediator personalities, such contingencies reflect only a limited and possibly minor proportion of the differences in significant parental behaviors. White and Watts (1973) present a delightful description of the child-rearing practices they observed in their most effective parents. Also interested in cognitive enrichment, Hess and Shipman (1965) argued that in a stimulating intellectual environment mothers give the children verbal cues to look ahead and weigh decisions. They observed "deprived" environments, conversely, unrelated to physical attributes, in which the children related to authority rather than rationale, and although compliant, were not reflective. Bee (1967) observed the parents of distractible children and nondistractible children engaged in various games and puzzles. The parents of the distractible children gave more specific suggestions and left little decision making to the child—a type of dependency training. Of course, one cannot infer that the maternal teaching style was causally related to the child's distractibility, as the effects of children's behavior on adult mediators are well known (e.g., Osofsky, 1970; Sherman & Cormier, 1974). On the other hand, in a fine longitudinal study of mother-child interactions, Clarke-Stewart (1973) observed that although a mother's behavior tends to be influenced by her child's behavior in terms of social interactions, the child's intellectual development is greatly influenced by the responsiveness of the mother. Child behavior therapists would do well to explore mother-child relationships beyond elementary contingencies of praise and punishment.

Naturalistic Observation of Children: The Ethological Perspective

It can be seen from the two preceding topics that an impressive observational technology has developed as the central assessment technique of child behavior modification, with continuing concern for reliability and validity, as well as the clinical viability of the many procedures. But the topic that has not yet been adequately addressed is how the clinician divides the "stream of behavior" (Barker, 1963) into usable categories. This problem of category selection diminishes only when the focus of observation is on a behavior whose appearance and undesirability can be readily agreed on by all concerned, for example, thumb sucking. Even in these simple cases, however, responses preceding or following the category of interest sometimes fail to receive attention (Wahler & Cormier, 1970).

Ethological Observation

The problem of behavioral sequences and category selection can possibly be approached in child behavior assessment from the ethological perspective. Because ethology requires codifying long sequences of naturally occurring behavior with the least inferential categories possible, it provides an interesting model for clinical assessment and a valuable clinical exercise. Incidentally, use of the term "naturalistic" in this section should be interpreted broadly, not only in its ethological sense of behavior occurring in the settings where it evolved (Blurton Jones, 1974), but as referring to descriptions of observed behavior unconstrained by highly specific environmental conditions and uninterrupted by manipulations of known variables (as in the formal experiment) or interventions (as in clinical treatment). The ethological approach to the study of children is itself in a primitive stage of evolution, despite the early start given by Barker (Barker, 1963; Barker & Wright, 1951), but there is enough material to suggest the morphological benefits of a little outbreeding between behavior modification and child ethology (see, e.g., the collection of papers in Blurton Jones, 1974, and Freedman's monograph on infancy, 1974).

Currie and Brannigan (1970), to give one example, used ethological descriptions of social behavior to select the initial target behavior for behavior modification with an autistic child. Hutt and Hutt (1968) made an ethological analysis of stereotypic behaviors in autistic children (hand flapping, rocking, etc.) and found them to be related to increases in stimulus complexity, the presence of strangers, and the introduction of novel objects into the environment. In view of the important relationship between attempts to increase appropriate behavior in autistic children and these stereotypes (Koegel & Covert, 1972), this kind of functional analysis is useful and important. Various behavior modification studies have attempted to increase eye-contact in autisic children by simply reinforcing its occurrence. Ethological studies have provided a functional analysis of autistic gaze avoidance, suggesting it is related to such variables as distance of the child from the adult, resemblance of the stimulus to a human face, and level of arousal (Hutt & Ounsted, 1966). Hutt and Ounsted were also able to show that the total amount of time spent in physical contact with an adult in a free situation did not significantly distinguish autistic from nonautistic children, so that it is avoidance of eye contact (which was very different), not "social withdrawal," that is a significant diagnostic sign for childhood autism. A number of the papers on the relevance of these ethological studies for clinical practice are collected in the volume edited by Hutt and Hutt (1970).

One other feature of the ethological approach can be mentioned here. Because animal behavior studies involve lengthy spans of time, ethological studies of children have typically continued long enough to reveal marked periodicity in numerous behaviors, that is to say, consistent fluctuations in rate as a function of time of day or time of week (McGrew, 1972). Such fluctuations could well interfere with the validity of behavioral baselines as assessment and evaluative procedures. Of course, these periodic fluctuations are not random, and they presumably relate to consistent alterations in environmental events. In the younger child, perhaps, periodicity can be related to such biological factors as fatigue (sleeping and waking cycles), hunger, and so forth. Older children, although somewhat released from these determinants of behavior, are nevertheless influenced by environmental factors that may persist for some time. Evans (1971) demonstrated that echolalia in one autistic girl was related to the conditions immediately preceding the behavior modification session. "Mood" effects on behavior have not been given much attention in behavior modification, despite the obvious, long-term consequences of environmental incidents on children. Disappointments, punishments, promised treats, anticipation of parties, incipient illnesses, chronic pain, deaths in the family, and other events can all have general and in some cases profound effects on a child's behavior—as any parent knows. It is usually difficult, however, to relate these incidents to behavioral changes in a systematic and convincing way, so that they all too often remain at the speculative level of the descriptive field study (Bijou, Peterson, & Ault, 1968).

Ecological Assessment

The same point may be made with respect to many attempts at "ecological assessment" in which the child's behavior is related to general environmental conditions, such as space, crowding, noise, temperature, and so forth. Researchers who study different geographical areas rather than looking at the correlations within areas (Robinson, 1950) often emerge with spuriously inflated correlations between such variables and behavior. Only when these environmental factors can be manipulated do their functional relationships with the behavior become clear. Demonstrations that children with reading deficits tend to live in noisy apartments nearer the ground (Cohen, Glass, & Singer, 1973) or come from large families (Berger, Yule, & Rutter, 1975) are correlations too gross and inexplicable to be of much immediate value. Nevertheless, the astute behavioral clinician will be observant of simple environmental factors that influence behavior—an apt example is the child who was wetting his bed because the passageway to the bathroom was dark and frightening. It is also encouraging to see major ecological studies relating child behavior disorders quite precisely to marital disruption, parental psychiatric disorder, and poor social circumstances (Rutter, Yule, Quinton, Rowlands, Yule, & Berger, 1975).

It is from ecological studies of the classroom that information most immediately relevant to techniques of behavior change has emerged. With preschool children Horton (Note 10) found that a larger room produced more disruptive behavior than a smaller room, but wall color did not significantly affect behavior! Axelrod, Hall, and Tams (Note 11) found that a classroom seating arrangement of "clusters" produced more disruptive behavior than a seating arrangement of rows. Winett, Battersby, and Edwards (1975), conversely, demonstrated that clusters of children with homogeneous abilities produced small improvements in appropriate behaviors. Schwebel (1969) reported that children assigned by teachers to the front row were more attentive to classroom activities than their classmates seated in the middle and back rows. Of course, teachers have always utilized common-sense notions to alter classroom antecedents to modify inappropriate behavior: The class clown's seat is isolated from his peers, and the talkative student is in front of the teacher's desk. More systematic research is needed to identify antecedent conditions that may effectively modify disruptive behavior and to compare the effectiveness of standard classroom practices with modifying reinforcement conditions or with combining antecedent and consequent strategies.

Standardized, Developmental, and Objective Tests

Intelligence, developmental, and other normative task-related tests have played the major role in the traditional psychological evaluation of children, and our purpose in this section is to show how such tests interrelate with other tactics of behavioral assessment to guide the treatment program. The previous categories of information gathering are quantifiable to a degree and thus have the potential for yielding normative data. Quantification and procedural standardization, however, are the essentials of the measures to be considered here. Also, the focus is on aspects of behavior that require some sort of specialized instrument in order to obtain an adequate measure. This is why seemingly disparate topics—IQ tests and psychophysiological measures—can be presented together. As with other material in this chapter, we will try to steer a balanced course between the misty rock of the extreme behavioral Scylla, rejecting all testing, and the sucking whirlpool of the psychometric Charybdis, administering routine test batteries to all unsuspecting comers. This is concordant with our belief that behavior modification represents the empirical ethic and not the metatheoretical assumption of any particular tradition or school.

The Behavioral Perspective on Children's IQ Tests

The major limitation of IQ tests for the clinician interested in modifying behavior is that the developers of these scales are really concerned with large group prediction. Behavior modification is concerned with confounding these predictions by altering the child's course of development. Every psychologist knows that Binet developed the mental test as a screening device so that feeble-minded children could receive special education in the Parisian schools. What is significant is that no one seems to know how successful they were. That is, did those children end up better off than just sitting it out at the bottom of the regular classes? Even today research comparing the academic achievement of children in special education classes versus regular classes has yielded equivocal results (Blatt, 1958; Cassidy & Stanton, 1959; Goldstein, Moss, & Jordan, 1965). Using tests to make skilled placement decisions—channeling children into the special programs that are proven to be beneficial—is one thing; removing children from the mainstream of education because they are thought to be constitutionally incapable of learning is quite another matter and has led to the countless abuses of IQ testing that have now been documented (e.g., Hobbs, 1975b; Hunt, 1961, 1969).

It is the subtle shift from prediction to potential that has obscured the disadvantaged, race, intelligence, compensatory education debate (Cronbach, 1975b). In everyday clinical practice the allure of the IQ score as a measure of "intellectual potential" is very strong despite the fact that the predictive validity of the IQ score for most special populations is largely unknown. On the other hand, the gross indications are that the higher the child's IQ score, the better his chances. What, for example, would be anticipated when an eight-year-old autistic child has an IQ score of 110? Obviously we do not expect him to outperform 70 percent of his peers in the third grade of the local elementary school, but we might be grateful on the grounds of reports that the long-term outcome of autistic children with good IQ scores was somewhat better than those with lower scores (DeMyer, Barton, DeMyer, Norton, Allen, & Steele, 1973; Rutter et al., 1967). For most clinical groups this sort of information is lacking or extremely crude and has to be modified by other factors, particularly the nature of the remedial (treatment) program.

Given the existing predictive limitations of the IQ score, why shouldn't a behavior modifier (who is, in any case, out to confound the predictions) ignore IQ testing and concentrate instead on direct observation, as Bersoff (1973) recommends, or daily measurements, as proposed by Eaton and Lovitt (1972)? One reason is the standardization feature. Behavioral observations in natural settings can, of course, be standardized too (Bijou & Peterson, 1971; Nelson & Bowles, 1975), and a standardized observation system allows interesting comparisons between, for instance, different teachers (MacDonald, 1971, pp. 4–8). However, the "norms" usually have to be limited to local conditions, which lowers their predictive power. The standardization feature of tests allows definition of one's target population relative to others, which is very important in evaluating the outcome of behavior therapy programs. Reporting standardized test data also permits evaluation of the *substantive* significance of a behavior modification program (Nelson, 1974). The majority of behavioral studies currently report outcome data in the form of changes on some idiosyncratic and arbitrary scale, the meaningfulness of which is unknown. It has further been suggested that standardized test scores provide an additional source of data against which to evaluate statistically the success of a behavior modification program (Staats, 1971, 1973), the standardization sample being analogous to a large control group. The statistical problems inherent in this strategy are considerable (Payne & Jones, 1957) and would require knowledge of the reliability of the test for the population from which the treated children were drawn, since test-retest reliabilities typically are low for the kinds of special children usually treated by behavior modification (Zigler & Butterfield, 1968). There seems to be no substitute for the good old-fashioned control group.

The second advantage of the test with well-constructed age norms is that within one child it reveals areas of deficit and thus helps set up academic goals for remediation by behavioral methods (Bijou, 1971). There are essentially two problems with this apparently reasonable notion. One is to ascertain by how much a score on one subtest has to deviate before the child can be thought to have a serious deficiency in that area. Again, the answer is partly tied to a statistical issue regarding the measurement error of the individual subtests and the scatter of all the scores obtained. Even supposing that one decided a particular score showed a deficit of some kind, its remediation is not usually obvious from the test item—this is the second problem. A child who does poorly on mazes, for instance, would not be referred for extra instruction in mazes but for remedial "visual-spatial" work, or something along those lines. But the content of the test items is highly complex and not representative of basic cognitive processes. Despite major advances in understanding child learning, many IQ tests still contain items devised by Binet. To someone concerned with prediction, of course, item content is not terribly important, and test constructors continue to insist that IQ tests should not be used as tests of cognitive abilities (Wechsler, 1975).

A third use of standardized IQ tests emerges from their being designed to include knowledge of items not learned exclusively at school. This allows one to compare what the child has learned generally (IQ score) with what he has learned specifically at school (score on some school achievement test). A statistically significant difference between the two, with the scholastic achievement score being lower, would suggest remediation of rather general classroom learning and studying skills. A similar case could be made for comparing scores on one IQ test with those obtained from a more "culture fair" test, to estimate the degree of deficiency in skills specific to the dominant culture. A test, for instance, given in both standard and nonstandard English could yield a discrepancy that would allow the clinician to determine if the minority group child had a cognitive deficiency or simply a limited knowledge of standard English (Quay, 1971). Day, Boggs, Gallimore, Speidel, and Tharp (Note 12) have described such a strategy for a sentence repetition test available in both standard English and Hawaiian creole. Much of the current interest in cultural differences in cognitive skills has relevance for the behavioral clinician. For instance, showing that a child from a different culture fails a test presented in one way (the typical Western European fashion) but passes a similar test presented in another way (using more familiar stimuli) is an assessment of the importance of those stimulus variables for a given task (Cole, Gay, Glick, & Sharp, 1971; Price-Williams, 1966). This strategy could be most usefully adapted for the handicapped child.

It has often been argued, following this same line of reasoning, that the *context* of testing is different from culture to culture. That is to say, the child has developed a repertoire of behaviors for the test situation that may or may not be conducive to success on the tasks. What can be a major problem for the comparison of test scores across cultures, subcultures, ethnic groups, or social classes can be most useful to the clinical psychologist because the testing situation now represents an opportunity to observe the child's style of behavior on cognitive tasks. This is the fourth major use of IQ tests in behavior modification, but like the others it is not without its drawbacks. One is that the observational categories are subjective and there is no opportunity for reliability checking, yet clinicians will often make much of the child's test behavior in a psychological report. Another drawback is that the tasks themselves are not well designed to reveal the child's problem-solving strategy. To give one simple example, it is usually difficult to tell how a child is completing a standard form-board task. But when a child is asked to insert the shapes into a Tupperware ball, he will turn it over and over if he is finding the correct hole by a search strategy, rather than by a matching of outlines or by trial-and-error pushing. Furthermore, there is a confounding between problem-solving strategy and the broader class of social, emotional, and motivational deficits that a child may reveal during testing. It has been observed, for instance, that some children respond randomly in a testing situation (Kubany, 1971; Staats et al., 1967)—it would be important to know if this is owing to anxiety, lack of test-taking skill, or motivational deficiency. To illustrate the difficulty of finding the answer, we will look at studies of one common variable: the reinforcement of test performance.

The Reinforcement of Standardized Test Performance

It is a truism that motivation affects performance in any situation, yet although in IQ testing the examiner is admonished to ensure continued interest from the child, one must assume that the use of reinforcement to fulfill a manual's requirement of "maximum effort" (Wechsler, 1967) is a violation of the standardization procedure, thereby reducing the predictive validity of the test. Behavioral clinicians, not being much interested in predictive validity, have advocated the use of tangible reinforcement in order to reduce motivational artifacts. However, the *addition* of tangible reinforcement does not affect test scores in a consistent fashion. Klugman (1944) found no difference in the delivery of praise or of money on Stanford-Binet scores for white children. Clingman and Fowler (1975) carried out a pretest/posttest (forms L and M of the Stanford-Binet) study with three groups: reinforcement contingent on correct response, yoked noncontingent reinforcement, and no additional reinforcement. The reinforcement was M&M candies. The three groups of above average IQ, normal children showed *no* significant differences in their pretest-posttest change scores. From this one could conclude either that contingent M&Ms are not effective rewards (there was no independent evaluation of this), or that the non-M&M group was already motivated and performing at maximum capacity. Perhaps testing a special population, such as low socioeconomic status (SES) or handicapped children, would show rather different results, for although Tiber and Kennedy (1964) found no effect of candy reward on Stanford-Binet performances of different SES children, the reward was presented *noncontingently* only at the end of each subtest.

Smeets and Striefel (1975) did find a marked effect of immediate contingent reinforcement (token points) on deaf children's progressive matrices scores. The control comparison groups were end-of-session, noncontigent, and contingent but delayed, reinforcement. The authors point out that the contingent reward had marked feedback effects, in that if the children failed to receive a point, they revised their choice. Deaf children may be unusually dependent on external feedback. Kubany (1971, Experiment III) showed that delinquent boys were considerably influenced by a monetary reward for a mathematics achievement test. Using low SES subjects, Edlund (1972) also reported improved test performance when correct responses were reinforced (candy). Ayllon and Kelly (1972) observed the effect in trainable retarded children, although in that study (Experiment I of the report) the reinforcement variable was confounded with retest variables because no control group was used. In an incisive critique of these latter two studies, O'Connor and Weiss (1974) pointed out that the significance of the findings could not be determined unless one were able to show a *differential* effect between two groups of children. If studies such as those already described of normal or middle class children do consistently show them to be uninfluenced by additional reinforcement, then one would have the necessary comparison group with which to reveal the differential effects. However, the literature does not show much consistency—for example, Ayllon and Kelly's (1972) normal group showed *improvement* with reinforcement.

The topic of reinforcing test performance of the handicapped child is intimately bound up with the common argument that children from ethnic minorities or low SES groups tend to have poor scores on IQ tests because of motivational differences in the test situation. Zigler, Abelson, and Seitz (1973) observed a greater relative increase in Peabody Picture Vocabulary test scores on simple *retest* for a group of nondisadvantaged children. Zigler has been for some time arguing the motivational deficiency hypothesis (e.g., Zigler & deLabry, 1962), specifically that disadvantaged and handicapped children approach the test situation with greater "wariness." In a second study in the 1973 report, he and his associates found that a period of play with the examiner prior to testing had more influence on the disadvantaged than the nondisadvantaged children, which seemed to support his argument. However, the data reveal a statistical regression effect, with low scorers (the disadvantaged children) being the ones more likely to improve their score on retest. If one were really interested just in *class* (SES) differences, groups should be matched for initial IQ. Along rather similar lines, Spence (1971) has suggested that the effects of material rewards may be unique to those situations in which the low SES children have previously experienced failure and thus withdrawal, so that the reward simply helps to "keep them in the situation." In her own study to test this assumption, however, she generally found that material reinforcement was *less* effective than praise regardless of previous training on the task. Two careful studies by Quay (1971, 1975) both failed to reveal an effect of candy and money reinforcers on Stanford-Binet scores in low SES children. On the other hand, Kubany (1971) *did* observe a differential persistence effect of money reinforcement for correct responses on a mathematics achievement test: Hawaiian children spent relatively more time working on the test under reinforcement conditions.

Unless there is an attempt to break down a global improvement in test score into components—such as accuracy and persistence—the precise effects of reinforcement on test scores are likely to remain unknown. Perhaps the reinforcement simply has very general drive value, in which case contingent and noncontingent reinforcement would be equally effective. Perhaps the reinforcement gives more accurate "feedback" regarding adequacy of the performance, which will be particularly important if correction is allowed or the nonreinforced presentation provides no feedback. Perhaps the introduction of reinforcement actually interferes with performance either as a distraction (Spence, 1970) or by enhancing the child's frustration following no reward—children have been shown to be very sensitive to the pattern of success and failure experienced in the course of testing (Zigler & Butterfield, 1968). Perhaps the reinforcement has the effect of making the child solve the problem more adaptively—this is Osler's (1973) suggestion following her demonstration that reinforcement reduced perseveration of position preferences in a concept learning task.

The reinforcement of test performance was introduced as a means of reducing error variance in test scores, but the discussion has led to a more fundamental assessment issue: What should one do with a child, such as the one reported by Kubany and Sloggett (1971), whose test performance is markedly improved by reinforcement? Should one recommend the use of specific reinforcements in the classroom, or should an attempt be made to increase the child's "intrinsic motivation"? This latter term was first used, we think, by Hunt (1969) in describing the reinforcing value of stimulus change, novelty, and information. He implied that, although they require nurturing, active curiosity and responsiveness to information are *fundamental* in young children, a concept dominating current thinking in infant cognitive development (Stone, Smith, & Murphy, 1973). Haywood (1971) has expanded the distinction between the two different types of motivation: "task-extrinsic" factors such as comfort, security, material reward, and "task-intrinsic" factors such as satisfaction of completing the task itself, responsibility, challenge, opportunity to learn. Children differ, Haywood has argued, in the degree to which they are intrinsically or extrinsically motivated, and their performance is a function of the match between the type of reward (task intrinsic or extrinsic) and their own motivational orientation. Recently, Switzky and Haywood (1974) have related intrinsic motivation to self-reinforcement, which is useful, if this relationship can be confirmed, because self-reinforcement can perhaps be enhanced by training (Bandura, 1969). Staats, on the other hand, has identified intrinsic reinforcement as the secondary reinforcement of the activity itself, generated when the "skilled verbal and motor behaviors we call knowledge are . . . paired with strong positive A–R–D stimuli (money, social approval, material possessions, and so on" (Staats, 1975, p. 102). He further argues that activities—reading in particular—do not acquire intrinsic motivational value until a certain facility of performance has been achieved. Prior to that time a rather high level of extrinsic reinforcement may be required. This could be a very important area of research because Piaget and Montessori educational models suggest a very different strategy for fostering intrinsic motivation in children, one in which children can choose their own activity and persist at it for long periods of time (Elkind, 1967, 1969). As Bruner (1974) has expressed it, the child "should be encouraged to venture (or at least not discouraged), rewarded for venturing his own acts, and sustained against distraction or premature interferences in carrying them out" (p. 179).

Developmental Assessment

Because developmental scales (e.g., Bayley, 1969) are similar to intelligence scales in design, the above discussion is applicable to developmental measures, with some additional provisos. Being designed primarily for infants and having detailed age norms, developmental scales can be usefully employed in the evaluation of intervention and enrichment programs for young or handicapped children, although, as with IQ tests, the availability of norms does not obviate the use of control groups. Probably the most serious criticism of the developmental quotient (DQ) used in this way is the assumption that raising children's DQs is important. It has now been rather clearly established that DQ does not correlate well with later measures of IQ or school achievement (Bayley, 1970; Lewis, 1973; McCall, Hogarty, & Hurlburt, 1972).

If increasing children's DQs cannot be thought of as raising their future intellectual potential, so failing to increase DQs cannot be taken as a criticism of the intervention program (Zigler, 1974). Perhaps concerned that the latter finding will prove to be the more common, interactionalist writers have argued that intervention must be evaluated by specific improvements in the skill taught (Gewirtz, 1971; Lewis, 1973). This ethic is clearly embraced in child behavior modification, with the emphasis on concurrently monitored observable changes in behavior, but the ultimate *social* significance of the observed changes must nevertheless be evaluated. The issue will be touched on again in a later section on the selection of target behaviors.

Criticisms regarding the predictive validity of developmental scales apply somewhat less to a second use for these measures—as screening devices for the early detection of neurological abnormalities, specific syndromes of mental retardation, or organic problems with complex social etiologies such as malnourishment and failure to thrive. The classic text describing this strategy is Gesell and Amatruda's *Developmental Diagnosis,* and in the most recent edition (Knobloch & Pasamanick, 1974) behavior modification is frequently mentioned as part of the overall pediatric management of young children with developmental disorders (mental retardation, cerebral palsy, epilepsy, autism). The developmental diagnosis is similar to naturalistic observation except that the categories are predetermined on the basis of developmental norms, and interest is focused on appearance or nonappearance of a behavior rather than its frequency. This qualitative feature aids the assessment of autistic or deaf-blind children (e.g., Alpern, 1967) who, like infants, are impossible to test in a verbal context, and it guides behavioral intervention by distinguishing between the necessity for teaching a new skill or increasing one already in the child's repertoire.

Although developmental scales may usefully select children in need of early behavioral intervention, it does not follow that they provide a completely satisfactory descriptive mapping of the young child's handicaps. One of the reasons why developmental scales fail to predict later progress is that if the very deviant minority (most of whom will be truly disabled) is excluded, the range of remaining scores is not very substantial, and the behaviors measured may not be the ones critical for continued social and intellectual attainment. White (1971), therefore, has suggested a new appraisal of what constitutes "competence" in the preschool child. Starting with an ethological description of just how children under two spend their days, White and his associates have devised detailed developmental scales covering what they consider to be the important social and cognitive abilities. These categories have precise behavioral definition and established observer reliabilities (White & Watts, 1973) but have not yet had any major impact on assessment practices in behavior modification.

Physiological Indices

The strategy proposed in this chapter is to extend the measures commonly relied on in experimental research with children into the assessment arena, both because child clinical psychology should be a spin-off from advances in child development and because clinical work has to be experimental in nature given our current limitations. It is for this reason that the role of physiological measurement in behavior assessment is mentioned here, but only briefly, in view of the highly specialized nature of the field. The procedures used are technically complicated by the fact that children rarely sit around for recordings to be made, so that most indices have to be obtained by telemetry. What little standardization there is takes place within the context of such rites as proper electrode placement, type of electrolyte, control of movement artifacts, and methods of transforming the raw data. There are no standardized procedures, although there are common paradigms that can probably yield results comparable in different laboratories or clinics, such as rate of habituation of an orienting reflex which could be considered a test with standardization possibilities.

Work along these lines is being done on Mauritius on the prevention of psychosis in children. It has been shown that children of schizophrenic mothers, who later themselves developed severe psychiatric disorders, have overly reactive autonomic nervous systems showing little habituation and excessive response to stimulation (Mednick, 1970). Using this as a measure of risk, 1800 three-year-old Mauritian children have been screened, and standardized measures of tonic as well as phasic levels of electrodermal activity and heart rate obtained (Mednick, Schulsinger, & Garfinkel, 1975). This fascinating project is in a preliminary stage, and it is hoped further details will soon appear. Other investigations of psychophysiological monitoring for the early detection of physical or behavioral anomalies in infants are under way. There are scattered reports of the GSR and evoked cortical potentials used in the assessment of hearing loss in children. Rourke (1975) has begun to relate learning disability to the habituation of the cortical arousal response evoked by a complex auditory stimulus. Using such GSR measures as rate of habituation and number of spontaneous fluctuations, Spring, Greenberg, Scott, and Hopwood (1974) showed that at least some hyperkinetic children responsive to Ritalin are less "aroused" than normal children. If it may be called physiological, Schulman, Kaspar, and Throne's (1965) activity measure is a classic because it clearly showed brain-damaged children not to be generally more active but more distractible than normal children. To add to this chop suey, mention may be made of the use of peak expiratory flow rate to monitor the effects of progressive muscle relaxation training on asthmatic children (Alexander, Miklich, & Hershkoff, 1972). Like chop suey, the proof is in the eating. So far, child behavior therapists have not sampled the possibilities of psychophysiological techniques for the choice and guidance of treatment, with one notable exception—Lang and Melamed's (1969) virtuoso EMG assessment of a nine-month-old infant with chronic ruminations.

ASSESSMENT FOR TREATMENT

In the previous section the focus was on procedures for systematically gathering information about a child and his environment, but there was no avoiding discussion of their clinical application. In this third section we will attempt to examine more directly how assessment information relates to the planning, execution, and evaluation of children's intervention programs. As is shown in other chapters of this book, there exist in adult behavior therapy a certain number of refined treatment "packages" as well as certain indications and contraindications for their use with individual clients. There is no such precision in child behavior therapy. The nearest analogy, which we have already alluded to, is the value that individual differences might have for dictating the optimal *parameters* of the treatment program. Because this is still a distinctly futuristic hope, the present relationship between assessment and treatment of children is a confused one. An understanding of this relationship, it is hoped, will materially enhance the efficacy of child treatment. In attempting to clarify it, we will begin by examining the biasing influence of the behavioral model on assessment practice. Then we will consider the functional analysis, illustrated by reference to social withdrawal problems. We will then turn to organic deficits to reveal other issues in the selection of treatment strategies. We will finally consider the selection of target responses.

Preassessment Bias

The term *bias* is not used in a derogatory sense but to underscore the fact that both the common treatment strategies—such as the manipulation of reinforcement contingencies—and the metatheoretical assumptions implicit in behavior modification greatly influence assessment. This has advantages and disadvantages. An advantage is that throughout the assessment procedure the clinician has available a coherent model of behavior from which to formulate and test basic hypotheses. In interviewing a parent, for example, information is not simply absorbed like a sponge, but questions are posed that will allow the interviewer to test out certain ideas and possibilities as he goes along. The assessment task is much like an experiment—formulating hypotheses and testing them objectively—but that analogy does not make clear where the hypotheses come from initially. To some extent these ideas come from the current clinical knowledge about the child's disorder, hence the importance of diagnosis. To some extent the hypotheses derive from knowledge of child development, which is why experimental child psychology is advocated as the discipline basic to adequate applied work with children. And to some extent the hypotheses derive from the assumptions of the learning model, vindicated by the relative success of child behavior therapy.

Herein, however, lie some of the disadvantages. Commonly held assumptions about behavior can reduce the range of hypotheses that are entertained in behavioral assessment. Although not incompatible with an operant analysis of behavior, manipulation of antecedent stimulus events in the classroom (such as improving the match between the troublesome child and the curriculum materials given him) has been used much less than arranging positive consequences for appropriate academic and social behaviors, a tactic which, as already intimated, may have long-term detriments (Lepper & Greene, 1975). Consider the child who refuses to go to school: The psychoanalyst thinks of separation anxiety, the classical learning theorist thinks of traumatic aversive conditioning in the classroom, the operant conditioner thinks of the reinforcement for staying away from school. All three possibilities are plausible and perfectly compatible with a general behavioral model and would have to be considered in any careful assessment. Despite individual treatment preferences, no child clinician can afford to make rigid a priori judgments about the causes of behavior or, as has often been recommended, commence by teaching the client to speak the behavioral language. Behavior therapists have to be particularly on their guard against automatically assuming environmental influences on problem behavior, rather than such "organismic" variables as hearing loss, convergence difficulties, allergy reactions, malnutrition, toothache, and so forth.

It is common to think the appropriate treatment so obvious that assessment is instituted only for that plan. For example, in planning to treat an enuretic child by means of the bell and pad, the measure of interest would automatically be frequency of nocturnal accidents to serve as the baseline data and from which to monitor progress. One might perhaps go so far as to ascertain the duration of the problem, on the grounds that recent onset after a history of dry nights (secondary enuresis) could be indicative of some traumatic event or recent environmental change. But according to Yates's (1975) most recent analysis, the crucial assessment measure is frequency of urination during the day, based on pediatric findings that enuretic children void less urine more frequently than normal children. Treatment can then be designed to increase duration of voluntary retention during the day (somewhat like Kimmel & Kimmel, 1970), and to induce sphincter *contraction* by inhibition of detrusor muscle activity. Here, then, is an example of an unusual relationship between assessment and treatment in which a new measure leads to the design of a new treatment—a source of joy to those of us who believe assessment to be important.

The Socially Withdrawn Child in the Classroom: An Illustration of the SORC Model

We have labeled the issue treated in the preceding paragraph as "preassessment" bias in order to distinguish it from the much more readily recognized problem of unreliability and distortion in the measures themselves. Most recent writers on behavior assessment have tacitly acknowledged this source of bias by outlining the classes of variables to be considered in any individual case of assessment. Goldfried and Sprafkin (1974) presented these as stimulus antecedents to the behavior (S), organismic variables (O), descriptions of the behavior currently in the child's repertoire (R), and analysis of the consequences (C). To illustrate the extension of this model to childhood assessment, we will look at the problem of social isolation in young children (recently reviewed by Wildman, Note 13).

Although social isolation and withdrawal in an adult can be the result of deliberate choice after evaluation of the reinforcement available from differing lifestyles, in a child such behavior is detrimental to learning and development. To estimate the severity of the child's social withdrawal, obtaining normative comparative data for other children of similar age, setting, and socioeconomic background is crucial. O'Connor (1969) followed this procedure to confirm teachers' ratings that particular children were unusually socially isolated. Observers coded the interaction behavior of 45 children rated as withdrawn and 26 nonwithdrawn children. Of 32 observation intervals, the latter group engaged in a mean of 9.1 social interactions. By comparison with this norm, a child was considered withdrawn if he exhibited five or fewer interactions.

Such normative data may be used not only to identify withdrawn children but also to evaluate the effects of intervention programs. Thus O'Connor's symbolic modeling procedure increased the isolated children's rate of interaction to a mean of about 11 interactions per 32 observation intervals. Ross, Ross, and Evans (1971) used a similar procedure involving normative data. During baseline observations, the socially isolated subject earned a Peer Interaction Score of 1.06, the maximum possible being 20. By comparison, the mean score for five normal peers was 11.05. Following intervention, which consisted of modeling and guided participation, the subject's score was 9.67.

In assessing stimulus antecedent variables, an important question is whether the social withdrawal occurs in all situations (suggesting a possible skill deficiency) or in one particular setting that would then merit further analysis of actual or expected aversive elements. If the child is isolated because of lack of opportunities for social interaction, these opportunities may be provided by the parents' inviting other children over, driving the child to other children's homes, playground, or club meetings. The play materials provided for children have been demonstrated to control rates of social interaction (Quilitch & Risley, 1973); "social" toys could be provided the isolated child when peers are present. Buell, Stoddard, Harris, and Baer (1968) found that reinforcement that increased a preschool girl's use of outdoor play equipment produced collateral increases in her interactions with other children. Another example of altering the antecedent conditions would be to change the child's desk, classroom, or school, if the social withdrawal were a result of unalterable rejection by particular children.

If the child is low in reinforcement value, as assessed by a sociogram or by class and neighborhood interaction patterns, the child's reinforcement value may be increased. Retish (1973) found that teacher praise addressed to specific second and fifth grade students increased their social status. Kirby and Toler (1970) demonstrated that having a preschool boy pass out candy to his nursery school classmates increased his rate of interaction with them during a free-play period. This procedure may have been effective because pairing the child with candy increased his reinforcement value, or because passing out candy increased the opportunities for social interaction.

The reinforcement value of a child to others might be considered an organism, or subject, variable, and can usefully be thought of in terms of Staats's A–R–D theory (1975). The child may evoke negative emotion (attitude, or A) in other children because of physical appearance (such as obesity, which would then become the treatment target), excessive academic skill (the despised teacher's pet situation), unconventional behaviors because of ethnic or class differences, or deficiencies in athletic, linguistic, and other skills. If the history of isolation has been long-term and not of sudden onset, social skill deficiencies become a plausible focus of treatment because although these deficiencies are rarely originally causal, they are strongly implicated in what Staats (1971) has called the "downward spiral of hierarchical learning." Skill deficiencies can be assessed by observation, role playing, and the other methods of information gathering already described. O'Connor (1969, 1972) successfully increased social interaction in isolated preschoolers by showing them a film depicting positive interaction among children. An alternative strategy is to combine modeling, behavior rehearsal, and opportunities for social interaction, as in the group therapy sessions proposed by Rose (1972). The procedure employed by Ross et al. (1971) used, in addition, a "buddy" who participated in graduated social activities with the isolated child. In the Ross procedure the buddy was a male undergraduate student, but a peer buddy also has possibilities.

Finally, reinforcement contingencies may be altered to increase social interactions. Material reinforcers contingent on interactions have been shown to increase the latter's frequency and quality (O'Leary, O'Leary, & Becker, 1967; Reynolds & Risley, 1968; Whitman, Mercurio, & Caponigri, 1970; Wiesen, Hartley, Richardson, & Roske, 1967). Social reinforcement from teachers contingent on positive interactions has also been demonstrated to increase interaction frequency (Brison, 1966; Harris, Wolf, & Baer, 1964; Hart, Reynolds, Baer, Brawley, & Harris, 1968). Last, peer contingencies may be modified so that peer social reinforcement is available following approach behaviors (Wahler, 1967) or peer aversive contingencies are reduced.

The social withdrawal example illustrates quite fully the logical relationship between assessment and intervention, revealing at the same time the range of tactics that may be open, depending on the circumstances of the child's problem. It can also be seen that the detailed clinical assessment of an isolated child should pursue all these classes of variables because the child client will typically have a conglomeration of problems. Another question, which has received minimal attention, is what would happen if the assessment revealed, for example, a lack of social skills, but it was decided to dramatically increase the child's positive attitudinal value to his peers? How crucial is it to hit on one treatment target rather than another, and what are the long-term implications? Does the child who dishes out candies really become more popular, or is he just approached more often because his peers hope he may still be under behavioral treatment? How, in any case, does one measure genuine affection as opposed to cupboard love? Perhaps an A–B–A–B reversal design can be used: If the reversal effect is found, the treatment has failed!

Assessment of Deficits: The Example of the Brain-Damaged Child

Somewhat similar issues arise if we switch our attention from deviant social behavior to cognitive and intellectual deficits, particularly those involving organic brain disorders, when the child seems to have failed to learn from the spontaneous environmental conditions. The basic behavioral strategy has simply been to attempt to optimize learning parameters—for instance, Sidman and Stoddard's (1967) work on teaching fine discriminations to severely retarded children by an errorless training procedure, or the countless instances of teaching complex new skills by shaping and chaining. For these tactics assessment usually consists of a broad, global analysis of where the child currently stands with respect to basic skills (Balthazar, 1972, 1973). However, there are two additional strategies relating closely to assessment issues. One is to remedy the child's cognitive deficits by teaching some more basic, underlying responses; the other is to teach the child responses that will in turn improve his learning ability for other, more complex tasks.

The first of these strategies can best be illustrated by reference to the brain-damaged child, or, when the hard neurological evidence is lacking, the "minimally brain-damaged" child. Everyone in behavior modification recognizes the futility of that latter label, but it is sobering to recall that interest in the possible organic basis of the soft signs displayed by children with severe learning difficulties was partly a reaction to the "overwhelming tendency [in child-guidance clinics] to weave a complete causative fabric out of the fragile threads of stereotypes such as sibling rivalry, rejecting parents, repressed hostility" (Clements & Peters, 1962, p. 185). In behavior modification authors have been a trifle overhasty in dismissing the possible treatment implications of brain damage. For example, in one of the earlier behavior therapy studies of children with neurological disorders (hydrocephaly, encephalitis induced seizures, spastic hemiplegia) it was shown that *play* could be increased by systematic social reinforcement. From this was drawn the extraordinary conclusion that "there is no evidence indicating that the brain-injured child conforms to a basically different set of principles than that which has been shown to apply to other organisms" (Hall & Broden, 1967).

It is true, of course, that psychologists' ability to pick out children with known brain disorder by means of psychological tests is extremely limited—see Herbert's (1964) excellent review and more recent discussion in Mittler (1970). In marked contrast to the failure of tests to identify children with organic problems, all the hypothesized manifestations of brain damage have been successfully ameliorated in children by behavioral methods (e.g., hyperactivity, impulsivity, response perseveration, and reading delays), but that does not mean that organic damage is a meaningless issue in behavior assessment. For one thing, even obvious organic conditions are not without their environmental influences. Zlutnick, Mayville, and Moffat (1975) analyzed the events regularly leading up to epileptic seizures in children and were able to influence seizure frequency by modifying the preseizure response chains. For another, behavioral measurement is ideally suited to the assessment of drug and other treatments likely to be prescribed for neurologically disordered children. A good description of this strategy was recently furnished by Stableford, Butz, Hasazi, Leitenberg, and Peyser (Note 14). These investigators used systematic observation of classroom behavior to monitor the effects of gradually switching two hyperactive children from amphetamines to a placebo. Finally, as has been noted before, knowledge or suspicion of brain damage can alert the clinician to a range of more basic response dimensions he might otherwise have overlooked if focusing simply on the parents' or teacher's complaints.

We cannot yet say how far the strategy of identifying more basic responses can be taken. Consider the problem of specific reading disability, or dyslexia, usually thought to be a soft neurological sign. Children with reading problems are often found to have concomitant visual perceptual difficulties (spatial disorientation and figure-ground confusion), auditory perceptual difficulties, and limited attention. A great deal of time is spent attempting to "diagnose" these underlying deficits and to "prescribe" remedial programs, which would seem a very logical procedure were it not for the meager supporting evidence. Having children creep and crawl according to the Dolman-Delacato method has no effect on poor readers (Kershner, 1968; Robbins, 1967). Silver and Hagin's attack on visual perceptual deficits prior to teaching reading proved to have no differential benefit (Silver & Hagin, 1967). Training children on the Frostig programs for developing visual perception improves performance on Frostig's diagnostic tests, but it has no significant impact on reading (e.g., Rosen, 1966).

An informative study relevant to these remedial teaching strategies was recently completed at the Universtiy of Hawaii (Collette-Harris & Minke, Note 15). First, they demonstrated that the token-based Staats Motivation Activating Reading Technique (SMART) (see, e.g., Staats et al., 1967) was superior to individualized tutoring in reading by a commercial agency. However, the SMART was equally effective (a 17-month improvement in reading age after 40 hours of instruction) with poor readers diagnosed as either dyslexic or nondyslexic. The diagnosis of dyslexia was based on perceptual development scores being one year below mental age (MA), as well as on various soft neurological signs. The nondyslexics were matched for severity of reading retardation and IQ score, but they did not have the additional perceptual, motor, and lateral dominance problems. What is especially interesting was that following successful reading remediation by the token program, both dyslexic and nondyslexic children showed significant improvement in the original *assessment* measures of perceptual and attentional deficit, as measured by the Detroit Tests of Learning Aptitude (Baker & Leland, 1959). In general, their report suggests the best way to teach moderately dyslexic children to read is to teach them to read and not to spend time assessing "underlying" perceptual problems. But since they excluded children unable to read at least 20 words, it is possible that the more severely brain-damaged the child or the more severe the reading delay, the more pretraining on cognitive skills will be needed. Unfortunately, the cognitive skills essential for complex learning such as reading are not yet fully known (Maliphant, Supramaniam, & Saraga, 1974).

The Assessment-for-Learning Strategy with Retarded Children

There has developed, in the past 10 or so years, a revolutionary set of concepts relating to the treatment of mentally retarded children, although the concepts are still in a rather formative theoretical-experimental stage. Like any other novel development, the roots go back a long way, to such pioneers as Itard, Sullivan, and, more recently, Skeels, the Clarkes, Tizard,

Zeaman, and House—in fact, all those individuals who demonstrated, well before the advent of formal behavior modification, that retarded children could learn more than was generally realized if the conditions were optimal. The decrements observed in retarded children were owing in some measure, therefore, to the failure of the environment to provide those idealized conditions. Behavior modification has further endorsed this argument by describing very precisely the familiar environmental modifications of shaping, chaining, stimulus control, prompting, and reward necessary to produce quite dramatic alterations in behavior. The novel trend, however, is to teach the retarded child those skills or strategies necessary to benefit from the less-than-optimal conditions of the real world—in Harlow's oft-repeated phrase, "learning to learn."

It is not possible in the space available to say much about this strategy, and the reader is referred to other major sources, particularly Estes (1970) and Clarke and Clarke (1973), but certain examples will be given to whet the appetite. It is a fairly obvious development in human learning that the individual in new situations learns to inhibit overt responding and to covertly examine the available possibilities. Mentally retarded children, however, seem less likely to use these covert scanning strategies and are often described as impulsive or distractible. In a well known study Meichenbaum and Goodman (1971) taught impulsive children to do this covert scanning by self-instructions to "go slow," "let's see now, I must be careful" and similar verbal mediators. Unfortunately, there was no control group simply taught to proceed more slowly on these tasks, and a conceptual replication of the study by Higa (1973) failed to show any difference between direct training to go more slowly and the teaching of the mediating verbal strategy. There was also little carry-over to other tasks. Despite these disappointing findings, the strategy appears to be a good one in principle, as revealed by a number of earlier studies showing that retarded subjects could learn to use verbal mediators with specific training and that this improved their performance on a variety of learning tasks (see Estes, 1970).

To take another example, it seems that retarded subjects fail to rehearse verbal material on serial learning tasks (Ellis, 1970) or to label nonverbal stimuli (Sprague & Binder, 1966). Jensen and Rohwer (1963), attempting to remedy these mediational deficiencies, produced increases in the acquisition rate of paired associates when the retarded subjects were taught to form sentences containing the items to be associated. Rohwer and Ammon (1971) compared simple practice on paired associates to the teaching of an "elaborative learning technique," namely, envisioning objects when presented with their names, making up sentences involving these objects, and further envisioning the episodes depicted in the sentences. The subjects were low SES black children and high SES white children. The high SES children benefited both from practice and from learning the strategy, whereas the low SES children benefited no more from simple practice than an untaught control group but did benefit from learning the strategy. Rohwer (1971) concluded that "children can be trained to learn more effectively, and that a *test of learning proficiency* is useful in evaluating the efficiency of the training" (p. 208, our italics). Gallimore, Lam, Speidel, and Tharp (Note 16) have made an informative extension of Rohwer's elaborative learning technique. In this study low SES Hawaiian-American children were taught shape names either by elaboration strategy (in this case associating the shape name and a common object in a familiar story) or by overt rehearsal. The interesting finding was that the benefit of the elaboration strategy was not immediately revealed—only on longer-term retention tests did elaboration training prove its value.

Assuming that these strategies have validity and future potential, the implications for assessment are rather interesting. The most obvious procedure would be to discover how the retarded or learning-disabled child tackles learning problems by devising exercises for new learning that clearly reveal mediation deficiencies, a term popularized by Flavell, Beach, and Chinsky (1966) when they argued that minority group children have difficulty in the *production* of mediators. A more precise *S–R* analysis has recently been made by Kendler (1972), in which she distinguishes between production deficiencies—the failure of an environmental stimulus to elicit a hypothetical mediating response (*r*)—and control deficiencies—the failure of the *r*, even though it occurs and has appropriate feedback (*s*) to control the final overt desired response. Kendler describes a learning task that is sensitive to developmental changes in both production and control deficiencies (the latter decline more rapidly with age) and that could be adapted for individual assessment.

Coming from a slightly different position, Clarke and Clarke (1973) have recently made a strong case for the importance of observing new learning, not previously acquired responses as in the usual IQ test, for assessing mental retardation. Years ago Clarke and his colleagues showed that when given a new task, as might be encountered in a rehabilitation workshop, the retarded clients' performances on the first trial did not predict later ability on the task after some practice. Gold (1972) described how highly experienced supervisors in sheltered workshops predicted that none of their moderately and severely retarded adolescent clients would be able to learn a complex 24-piece assembly task. All but one of the 64 subjects learned the assembly task in the 55 trials allowed. The instructors were untrained volunteers. The children retained their ability without further practice for more than a year. A mini-learning situation not only confounds expectancies but also allows comparison between different ways of presenting the task, grouping the materials, and so forth, to discover which is the most effective. As Bortner and Birch (1970) have expressed it: "Glaring differences occur in the estimates of potential when meaningful alterations are made in the conditions for performance. It is clear that we have but begun to explore the universe of conditions for learning and performance which will facilitate most effectively the expression of the potentialities for adaptation which exist in mentally subnormal children" (p. 742). Any moderately competent person can learn to administer and score standardized IQ tests or record incidents of behavior, but it is difficult to devise assessment tasks that reveal deficiencies in strategies of selective attention, distinctiveness of cues, coding, rehearsal, seeking relevant information, and motivation, and then deduce specific procedures that will result in generalized improvement on new and different learning tasks. However, these are the skills of a true scientist-professional, and it is hoped they can be proved worth using.

The Selection of Treatment Goals and the Evaluation of Child Assessment

It is ironic that although the reliability of diagnostic categories has been derided by behavior therapists, there has been no consideration of agreement that might be found in choice of target behaviors (Mash & Terdal, 1974)—or, as Hawkins (1975) expressed it so neatly in the title of his paper, "Who decided *that* was the problem?" Since a large part of the discussion up to this point has been concerned with the selection of the behavior to be changed, a succinct statement on this complex issue is hardly possible at this stage. Yet in many ways it is the crucial assessment problem, with wide ramifications. At a relatively simple level is the conflict, alluded to earlier, between children's, parents', teachers', and professionals' perceptions of appropriate behavior. For this there are some potential empirical solutions. One is to determine local standards. For example, since disagreements frequently occurred between parents and young teenagers, Nelson (1974) gathered normative data to determine an appropriate age to begin wearing eye make-up and the usual time to return home from evenings out. Another empirical approach is anthropological observation. Examples of the clash between family-appropriate and school-appropriate behavior in Hawaii have been described by Gallimore, Boggs, and Jordan (1974). Hammond (1973) had groups of Hawaiian-American parents and predominantly Japanese-American school teachers view videotapes of classroom scenes and signal each time they saw inappropriate behavior. Another empirical strategy is to take into account the natural history of different behavior problems. It has frequently been observed that psychologists tend to emphasize the significance of social withdrawal and anxiety in children, whereas teachers focus on aggression and lack of respect for authority (e.g., Griffiths, 1952). If ultimate outcome is used as the criterion of seriousness, it is the aggressive, not the withdrawn children, that have the poorest prognosis—a highly reliable finding for both treated and untreated children (Levitt, 1971; Morris, Escoll, & Wexler, 1956; Morris, Soroker, & Burruss, 1954; O'Neal & Robins, 1958).

When the child has a number of parallel difficulties in need of modification the choice of order is, superficially, not too difficult—pragmatists have recommended starting with the most irritating one (Tharp & Wetzel, 1969) or the easiest one (O'Leary, 1972b), but these recommendations neglect the important issues of the interrelationships among behaviors and their adaptive value in society. At one level interrelationships are based on simple compatibility of responding. For example, Winett and Winkler (1972) criticized some behavioral studies for teaching children to "be still, be quiet, be docile" in the classroom. Behavior modification has succeeded in increasing academic achievement directly (as O'Leary, 1972a, pointed out in his rejoinder), but achievement is not necessarily enhanced by improvements in attention (Ferritor, Buckholdt, Hamblin, & Smith, 1972), on-task behavior (Hay, Hay, & Nelson, in press), on school attendance (MacDonald, Gallimore, & MacDonald, 1970). Multivariate studies already described (e.g., Digman, Note 4), however, have pinpointed classroom skills, more centrally related to scholastic achievement, that could be the focus of treatment. The success of such a strategy was demonstrated by Cobb and Hops (1973; Hops & Cobb, 1974) who taught first-grade children "survival skills" such as attending to the teacher, following teacher instructions, and volunteering to answer questions that improved, collaterally, their academic performance. Behavior therapists are just beginning to realize the potential of teaching behaviors that will in turn enhance the child's environment (Gelfand & Hartmann, 1975; Gewirtz, 1968).

Generally speaking, the interrelationships that have been recognized in child behavior therapy are those based on common functional relationships with the environment; they require multiple response measurement and careful ecological description. Reid and Hendricks (1973), to give an outstanding example, showed that aggressive children who also stole responded less well to a home-based intervention program than simply aggressive children, although the latter's behavior was more deviant. This may have been because the stealers' antisocial behaviors occurred predominantly outside the home, and because their family environments seemed socially unresponsive in ways not redressed by the treatment program. Wahler (1969, 1975) must be credited with emphasizing repeatedly the functional covariance of different clinically significant responses.

A rather different level of behavioral interdependence can be seen from the developmental perspective, which has been underrepresented in child behavior therapy—possibly because developmental descriptions have traditionally implied fixed stages and automatic growth through maturation. There are descriptions of "developmental therapy" in which learning principles have been combined with developmental principles in the treatment program. This combination has been strongly advocated for psychotic and multiply handicapped children (Hewett, 1968; Schopler, 1974). Although developmental concepts are incorporated in these programs for the selection and ordering of teaching goals, their unique contribution has not been independently assessed. Nevertheless, examples of teaching one behavior preparatory to the attempted acquisition of another have been scattered throughout this chapter. Staats (1971) in particular has reasoned that behavior is hierarchically organized and that responses should be considered as independent, not simply dependent, variables in planned behavior change.

The developmental perspective reveals some unusual difficulties in evaluating assessment that have not yet been adequately addressed. In the first place it would be sensible to choose target behaviors that will not be taught much more easily at a slightly later point in time. Behavior therapists have rightly eschewed an extreme "readiness" viewpoint, but they have neglected the fact that many behaviors in the developing child have a very low ceiling for practice effects. More important, the developmental perspective indicates the need for two or more treatment goals—the immediate target response and the long-term goals—which should be measured as broadly as possible. Further demonstrations of the efficacy of behavior modification with children are now needed much less than comparative assessment studies showing that the selection of one immediate target response is more economical or has broader long-term benefits for the child than some other response. Individual baseline studies do not show whether the optimal response category has been selected for manipulation. In addition, we do not know the long-term side effects of introducing highly explicit, extrinsic reinforcement contingencies to developing children, but certain studies touched on in this chapter at least suggest that they may not be entirely desirable for the development of the competent child. Finally, without group comparisons, identifying an area of cognitive deficit indicates little about the selection of the best remedy. Even in one of the classic studies of the experimental-clinical model for assessment (Bartlet & Shapiro, 1956) the design of the remedial program bore a rather slender relationship to what had been learned about the boy's cognitive difficulties and was not strikingly different from any of countless remedial reading programs available. The user of this exacting experimental strategy may spend some time assessing very precisely the specific nature of the child's difficulty and still wind up designing a fairly general remedial program. We do not yet have much precision in the interfacing of assessment and treatment.

SUMMARY

The assessment of childhood problems is a particularly fascinating task because of the very broad network of variables implicated, and it is difficult to single out one approach as being especially promising. However, the most common theme of this chapter is the need to consider the interdependence of children's responses selected for assessment and the implications for the choice of treatment. The most obvious level of interdependence is the observation that similar behavioral tendencies are likely to occur together in different children—a syndrome in nosological terms, or response class in operant parlance. Assigning a descriptive label to a given cluster of responses does not tell one a great deal about the individual child, as behavior therapists have emphasized. At the same time observed regularities in response clusters do seem to offer a useful research framework for child psychopathology, providing the practicing child therapist with some guidelines regarding the types of controlling variables worth considering, with estimates of the severity of the behavior pattern for long-term future adjustment, the degree of persistence expected (prognosis), and insights into etiology and future prevention.

It is because labeled clusters sometimes set up negative expectancies and stigmatize children that the abuses of diagnosis can rightly be decried. At the same time, too, the planning of programs, the organization of services, the distribution of private and government funds, and the determination of administrative and professional accountability are all dependent on some classification of children's behavior, and this is a reality that must be faced in behavior modification. Hobbs (1975c) has urged that the advantages and disadvantages of classification be respectively increased and decreased "through the development of a classification system that takes into account (for *individual children in particular settings*) assets and liabilities, strengths and weaknesses, linked to *specified* services required to increase the former and decrease the latter (p. 281, our italics). Assessment strategies in child behavior modification must stretch from selection of the most reinforcing candy to the determination of social policy.

Behavior therapists have added a major methodological dimension to the problem of behavioral classification and description that has not yet been fully exploited. Much current classification is dependent on a combination of (1) static tests, which, although beautifully standardized, may discriminate between children on criteria unrelated to the design of better education (particularly for the intellectually subnormal) and (2) subjective judgmental rating scales that are not standardized at all. When a teacher or parent rates a child as "very socially withdrawn," we have no quantified basis for comparison with other children similarly rated by other individuals. Direct observation techniques, however, with very precise specification of behavioral categories, established reliabilities, and recognition of such determining factors as opportunity for the behavior being rated to occur, *can* provide normative data that are comparable across settings. Examples of this normative observation, both theoretical and practical, were provided in this chapter. One could almost say that behavior assessment favors standardizing the descriptive behavioral measures and destandardizing or using more descriptively the formal tests, but since the latter are mostly samples of *cognitive* behavior, a basis for cross-setting (clinic, school, or experimental program) comparison is vital here as well. The clinical significance of much of the outcome data in child behavior therapy cannot be determined because of the still unstandardized, unquantified, and unrepeatable form in which it is reported.

To better understand the long-term significance of behavioral treatments, then, it is recommended that data be presented along dimensions common to a number of different treatment settings. Some outcome measures—number of dry nights or minutes playing happily with a dog, for instance—are sufficiently exact that one treatment program can be compared with another, but even so it is necessary to know how well the child clients fared on other related dimensions. Broad behavioral measurement quickly confirms the clinical expectation that problems like enuresis or dog phobia rarely occur in isolation in children. Multiple measures of success and adjustment in other aspects of the child's life become crucial in treatment evaluation. The work of Patterson and his associates at the Oregon Research Institute is exemplary in this regard. To compare the *relative* value of different treatment strategies, we also need normative measures that fully describe the problem child and the severity of his handicap.

If a central function of assessment is the evaluation of treatment, how then can one evaluate assessment for treatment? In terms of selection of treatment goals, it has been pointed out that studies of agreement between different assessing clinicians would be valuable. Furthermore, continuous appraisal is needed of the reliabilities of the chief measuring devices—structured and unstructured interviews, direct behavioral observation, standardized tests, and physiological measurement. As for validity, the more direct the measures of child behavior become, the less one has to worry about validity (in the psychometric sense). The measures described in this chapter tend to be samples of the behavior of concern (i.e., criterion-referenced measures), not indirect or inferential estimates. However, there has not been much attention paid to the sampling tactic itself so that the behavioral categories selected for measurement tend to represent the metatheoretical biases of behaviorism. A particular problem with children is that the categories selected are often those considered most undesirable by adults not always able or willing to consider the best interests of the child. It is here that the more neutral, descriptive ethological perspective has some value for childhood assessment, and research attempts to integrate the two approaches might be rewarding. Developmental descriptions of behavior should also help the clinician to select his categories, and it is unfortunate that behavioral work with children has had little truck with developmental descriptions on account of the latter's equation, by no means required, with maturation, fixed growth, and sequential stage assumptions. In general, it seems that the problem of sampling the behavior stream of childhood is likely to continue as a major concern for some time.

Ultimately, therefore, it is the utility of the measures that counts, but utility is not readily evaluated. We have argued in this chapter that ecological appraisal of the child is useful, that GSR habituation is useful, that developmental analysis is useful—but utility *is* what the behavior therapist *does,* and the true value of the various procedures discussed here cannot be argued by fiat, depending instead on systematic demonstration that by their use more potent treatment strategies result. There is little or no work in the literature of behavior therapy with children showing that a treatment has failed because of inadequate assessment, or that far better results accrue following more precise or thorough functional analysis. In fact, when it comes to children's cognitive development, the behavioral literature shows, if anything, that intensive teaching programs (admittedly self-paced, closely monitored and motivating, but not individually tailored) are effective and that detailed assessment is superfluous.

We have argued in this chapter that behavior therapists, in reacting against the excessive interest of clinical child psychologists in psychometrics to the exclusion of treatment, swung themselves too far in the opposite direction. However, it is going to take some rather single-minded research to demonstrate convincingly the real utility of detailed assessment in the design of comprehensive behavioral programs. Perhaps the difference will be seen not at the level of immediate results—which have been impressive in child behavior therapy—but at the level of long-term outcome and the successful maintenance of treatment effects, for which there is very little evidence. Until quite recently the major strategies for ensuring maintenance have been (1) to alter permanently the supportive structure of mediator behavior (by training staff and parents), (2) to institute elaborate reinforcement "economies," (3) to shift to natural contingencies, and (4) to employ tactics derived from animal operant studies such as partial reinforcement during acquisition.

In the experimental study of child learning, however, new strategies for maintenance of behavior have evolved, such as the development of self-reinforcement and intrinsic motivational systems, the teaching of coping skills, the teaching of effective personal management of classroom and study behaviors, the teaching of mediating responses that will alter the child's learning potential—teaching children to *be* competent, not just to wear the cloak of competence. These interesting possibilities have only just begun to be explored in child behavior therapy, although they are beginning to influence compensatory education. We predict that the acquisition of mediating strategies will be the predominant focus of the next decade of child behavior therapy. This is why understanding the interrelationship of behaviors, alluded to frequently in this chapter, becomes so important. It appears possible to modify some fundamental aspect of behavior (the target response) to effect a more general change in desired behavior (the treatment goal). We are on the verge of a second-generation behavior therapy in which principles of behavior change, child development, and child psychopathology can be finally integrated.

REFERENCE NOTES

1. Clement, P. W., & Richard, R. C. *Children's reinforcement survey*. Unpublished manuscript, 1971. (Available from Graduate School of Psychology, Fuller Theological Seminary, Pasadena, Calif.)
2. Jones, R. R., *"Observations" by telephone: An economical behavior sampling technique* (ORI Tech. Rep., 1974, Vol. 14, No. 1). Eugene: Oregon Research Institute, 1009 Patterson Street, Eugene, Ore. 97403.
3. Shultz, T. *Dimensions underlying the use of the Peterson-Quay Behavior Problem Checklist with delinquent youth in Hawaii*. Unpublished paper, University of Hawaii, 1974.
4. Digman, J. M. *High school academic achievement as seen in the context of a longitudinal study of personality characteristics*. Paper presented at the meeting of the American Psychological Association, Honolulu, September, 1972.
5. Eysenck, H. J. Personal communication, March, 1974.
6. O'Leary, K. D., Romanczyk, R. G., Kass, R. E., Dietz, A., & Santagrossi, D. *Procedures for classroom observation of teachers and children*. Unpublished manuscript, 1971. (Available from Point-of-Woods Laboratory School, State University of New York at Stony Brook, Stony Brook, N.Y. 11790.)
7. Foster, C., Keilitz, I., & Thomas, D. *Data collection by the teacher: Interference or stimulus control*. Paper presented at the meeting of the American Psychological Association, New Orleans, September 1974.

8. Lewis, M., & Lee-Painter, S. *An infant's interaction with its social world: The origin of meaning*. Paper presented at a conference on Issues in Developmental and Historical Structuralism, Ann Arbor, Mich, August 1972.
9. Tsoi-Hoshmand, L. *The analysis of human verbal communication with the observation method: An argument for rational behavior assessment*. Unpublished manuscript, University of Maryland, 1974.
10. Horton, P. *The effects of wall color and room size on the classroom social behavior of nursery school children*. Unpublished Master's thesis, University of North Carolina at Greensboro, 1973.
11. Axelrod, S., Hall, R. V., & Tams, A. *A comparison of common seating arrangements in classroom settings*. Unpublished manuscript, Temple University, 1973.
12. Day, R. R., Boggs, S. T., Speidel, G. E., Gallimore, R., & Tharp, R. G. *The Standard English Repetition Test (SERT): A measure of standard English performance for Hawaii creole English-speaking children* (Technical Report No. 15). Honolulu: The Kamehameha Early Education Project, 1850 Makuakane Street, Honolulu, HI, 96817.
13. Wildman, H. *The assessment of socially withdrawn children*. Unpublished manuscript, University of North Carolina at Greensboro, 1974.
14. Stableford, W., Butz, R., Hasazi, J., Leitenberg, H., & Peyser, J. *Sequential withdrawal of stimulant drugs and behavior therapy with two hyperactive boys*. Paper presented at the annual meeting of the Association for the Advancement of Behavior Therapy, Chicago, November 1974.
15. Collette-Harris, M. A., & Minke, K. A. *A behavioral experimental analysis of dyslexia*. Paper presented at the second Annual International Federation of Learning Disabilities, Rotterdam, January 1975.
16. Gallimore, R., Lam, D. J., Speidel, G. E., & Tharp, R. G. *The effects of elaboration and rehearsal on long-term retention of shape names by kindergarteners* (Technical Report No. 31). Honolulu: The Kamehameha Early Education Project, 1850 Makuakane Street, Honolulu, HI, 96817.

REFERENCES

Ackerson, L. *Children's behavior problems*. Chicago: University of Chicago Press, 1931.

Alexander, A. B., Miklich, D. R., & Hershkoff, H. The immediate effects of systematic relaxation training on peak expiratory flow rates in asthmatic children. *Psychomatic Medicine*, 1972, **34,** 388–394.

Allen, T. E., & Goodman, J. D. Home movies in child psychodiagnostics: The unobserved observer. *Archives of General Psychiatry*, 1966, **15,** 649–653.

Alpern, G. D. Measurement of "untestable" autistic children. *Journal of Abnormal Psychology*, 1967, **72,** 478–486.

Anderson, F. N., & Dean, H. C. Some aspects of child guidance clinic intake policy and practice. *Public Health Monographs*, 1956 (Whole No. 42).

Anthony, E. J. The behavior disorders of childhood. In P. H. Mussen (Ed.), *Carmichael's manual of child psychology*. Vol. 2. New York: Wiley, 1970.

Ayllon, T., & Kelly, K. Effects of reinforcement on standardized test performance. *Journal of Applied Behavior Analysis*, 1972, **5,** 477–484.

Baker, H., & Leland, B. *Detroit tests of learning aptitude* (rev. ed.). Indianapolis, Ind.: Bobbs-Merrill, 1959.

Baker, R. P., & Dreger, R. M. The preschool behavioral classification project: An initial report. *Journal of Abnormal Child Psychology*, 1973, **1**, 88–120.

Balthazar, E. E. *Balthazar scales of adaptive behavior. I: The scales of functional independence*. Palo Alto, Calif.: Consulting Psychologists Press, 1972.

Balthazar, E. E. *Balthazar scales of adaptive behavior. II: Scales of social adaptation.* Palo Alto, Calif.: Consulting Psychologists Press, 1973.

Bandura, A. *Principles of behavior modification.* New York: Holt, Rinehart, & Winston, 1969.

Bandura, A., Grusec, J. E., & Menlove, F. L. Vicarious extinction of avoidance behavior. *Journal of Personality and Social Psychology*, 1967, **5**, 16–23.

Barker, R. G. (Ed.). *The stream of behavior.* New York: Appleton-Century-Crofts, 1963.

Barker, R. G., & Wright, H. F. *One boy's day.* New York: Harper & Row, 1951.

Bartak, L., & Rutter, M. Educational treatment of autistic children. In M. Rutter (Ed.), *Infantile autism: Concepts, characteristics and treatment.* Edinburgh: Churchill Livingstone, 1971.

Bartlet, D., & Shapiro, M. B. Investigation and treatment of a reading disability in a dull child with severe psychiatric disturbances. *British Journal of Educational Psychology*, 1956, **26**, 180–190.

Baumrind, D. Child care practices anteceding three patterns of preschool behavior. *Genetic Psychology Monographs*, 1967, **75**, 43–88.

Bayley, N. *The Bayley scales of infant development.* New York: Psychological Corporation, 1969.

Bayley, N. Development of mental abilities. In P. H. Mussen (Ed.), *Carmichael's manual of child psychology.* Vol. 1. New York: Wiley, 1970.

Bee, H. L. Parent-child interaction and distractibility in 9-year-old children. *Merrill-Palmer Quarterly*, 1967, **13**, 175–190.

Bell, R. Q. Structuring parent-child interaction situations for direct observation. *Child Development*, 1964, **35**, 1009–1020.

Berger, M., Yule, W., & Rutter, M. Attainment and adjustment in two geographical areas: II. The prevalence of specific reading retardation. *British Journal of Psychiatry*, 1975, **125**, 510–519.

Bersoff, D. N. Silk purses into sows' ears: The decline of psychological testing and a suggestion for its redemption. *American Psychologist*, 1973, **28**, 892–899.

Bijou, S. W. Environment and intelligence: A behavioral analysis. In R. Cancro (Ed.), *Intelligence: Genetic and environmental influences.* New York: Grune and Stratton, 1971.

Bijou, S. W., & Grimm, J. A. Behavioral diagnosis and assessment in teaching young handicapped children. In T. Thompson & W. S. Dockens, III (Eds.), *Applications of behavior modification.* New York: Academic, 1975.

Bijou, S. W., & Peterson, R. F. The psychological assessment of children: A functional analysis. In P. McReynolds (Ed.), *Advances in psychological assessment.* Vol. 2. Palo Alto, Calif.: Science and Behavior, 1971.

Bijou, S. W., Peterson, R. F., & Ault, M. H. A method to integrate descriptive and experimental field studies at the level of data and empirical concepts. *Journal of Applied Behavior Analysis*, 1968, **1,** 175–191.

Bishop, B. M. A measurement of mother-child interaction. *Journal of Abnormal and Social Psychology*, 1946, **41,** 37–49.

Blatt, B. The physical personality and academic status of children who are mentally retarded attending special classes as compared to children who are mentally retarded attending regular classes. *American Journal of Mental Deficiency*, 1958, **62,** 810–818.

Blurton Jones, N. G. Ethology and early socialization. In M. P. M. Richards (Ed.), *The integration of a child into a social world.* London: Cambridge University Press, 1974.

Bortner, M., & Birch, H. G. Cognitive capacity and cognitive competence. *American Journal of Mental Deficiency*, 1970, **74,** 735–744.

Brekstad, A. Factors influencing the reliability of anamnestic recall. *Child Development*, 1966, **37,** 603–612.

Brison, D. W. A nontalking child in kindergarten. *Journal of School Psychology*, 1966, **4,** 65–69.

Broden, M., Hall, R. V., & Mitts, B. The effect of self-recording on the classroom behavior of two eighth-grade students. *Journal of Applied Behavior Analysis*, 1971, **4,** 191–199.

Browning, R. M., & Stover, D. O. *Behavior modification in child treatment.* Chicago: Aldine-Atherton, 1971.

Bruner, J. S. The organisation of early skilled action. In M. P. M. Richards (Ed.), *The integration of a child into a social world.* London: Cambridge University Press, 1974.

Buell, J., Stoddard, P., Harris, F. R., & Baer, D. M. Collateral social development accompanying reinforcement of outdoor play in a preschool child. *Journal of Applied Behavior Analysis*, 1968, **1,** 167–173.

Bushell, D., Wrobel, P. A., & Michaelis, M. L. Applying "group" contingencies to the classroom study behavior of preschool children. *Journal of Applied Behavior Analysis*, 1968, **1,** 55–61.

Cain, L. F., Levine, S., & Elzey, F. F. *Cain-Levine Social Competency Scale.* Palo Alto, Calif.: Consulting Psychologists press, 1963.

Cameron, K. Diagnostic categories in child psychiatry. *British Journal of Medical Psychology*, 1955, **28,** 67–71.

Cassidy, V. M., & Stanton, J. E. *An investigation of factors involved in educational placement of mentally retarded children* (Cooperative Research Project 043). Washington, D.C.: U.S. Office of Education, 1959.

Cattell, R. B., & Cross, K. P. Comparison of the ergic and self-sentiment structures found in dynamic traits by R- and P-techniques. *Journal of Personality*, 1952, **21,** 250–271.

Chapanis, A. The relevance of laboratory studies to practical situations. *Ergonomics*, 1967, **10,** 557–577.

Chess, S., & Thomas, A. Differences in outcome with early intervention in children with behavior disorders. In M. Roff, L. N. Robins, & M. Pollock (Eds.), *Life history research in psychopathology*. Vol. 2. Minneapolis: University of Minnesota Press, 1972.

Chess, S., Thomas, A., & Birch, H. G. Distortions in developmental reporting made by parents of behaviorally disturbed children. *Journal of the American Academy of Child Psychiatry*, 1966, **5,** 226–231.

Christophersen, E. R., Arnold, C. M., Hill, D. W., & Quilitch, H. R. The home point system: Token reinforcement procedures for application by parents of children with behavior problems. *Journal of Applied Behavior Analysis*, 1972, **5,** 485–497.

Clairborn, W. L. Expectancy effects in the classroom: A failure to replicate. *Journal of Educational Psychology*, 1969, **60,** 377–383.

Clarke, A. D. B., & Clarke, A. M. Assessment and prediction. In P. Mittler (Ed.), *Assessment for learning in the mentally handicapped.* Edinburgh: Churchill Livingstone, 1973.

Clarke-Stewart, K. A. Interactions between mothers and their young children: Characteristics and consequences. *Monographs of the Society for Research* in *Child Development*, 1973, **38,** (6–7, Serial No. 153).

Clement, P. W. Parents, peers, and child patients make the best therapists. In G. J. Williams & S. Gordon (Eds.), *Clinical child psychology: Current practices and failure perspectives.* New York: Behavioral Publications, 1974.

Clements, S. D., & Peters, J. E. Minimal brain dysfunctions in the school-age child. *Archives of General Psychiatry*, 1962, **6,** 185–197.

Clingman, J., & Fowler, R. L. The effects of contingent and noncontingent rewards on IQ scores of children of above-average intelligence. *Journal of Applied Behavior Analysis*, 1975, **8,** 90.

Cobb, J. A., & Hops, H. Effects of academic survival skill training on low achieving first graders. *Journal of Educational Research*, 1973, **67,** 108–113.

Cohen, S., Glass, D. C., & Singer, J. E. Apartment noise, auditory discrimination, and reading ability in children. *Journal of Experimental Social Psychology*, 1973, **9,** 407–422.

Cole, M., Gay, J., Glick, J. A., & Sharp, D. W. *The cultural context of learning and thinking*. New York: Basic Books, 1971.

Collins, L. F., Maxwell, A. E., & Cameron, K. A factor analysis of some child psychiatric clinic data. *Journal of Mental Science*, 1962, **108,** 274–285.

Conger, A. J., & Coie, J. D. Who's crazy in Manhattan: A reexamination of "Treatment of psychological disorders among urban children." *Journal of Consulting and Clinical Psychology*, 1975, **43,** 179–182.

Cowen, E. L. Dorr, D., Clarfield, S. P., Kreling, B., McWilliams, S. A., Pokracki, F., Pratt, D. M., Terrell, D. L., & Wilson, A. The AML: A quick screening device for early detection of school maladaptation. *American Journal of Community Psychology*, 1973, **1,** 12–35.

Cowen, E. L., Pederson, A., Babigian, H., Izzo, L. D., & Trost, M. A. Long-term follow-up of early detected vulnerable children. *Journal of Consulting and Clinical Psychology*, 1973, **41,** 438–446.

Cronbach, L. J. The two disciplines of scientific psychology. *American Psychologist*, 1957, **12,** 671–684.

Cronbach, L. J. Beyond the two disciplines of scientific psychology. *American Psychologist*, 1975, **30,** 116–127. (a)

Cronbach, L. J. Five decades of public controversy over mental testing. *American Psychologist*, 1975, **30,** 1–14. (b)

Currie, K. H., & Brannigan, C. R. Behavioural analysis and modification with an autistic child. In S. J. Hutt & C. Hutt (Eds.), *Behaviour studies in psychiatry*. Oxford: Pergamon, 1970.

DeMyer, M. K., Barton, S., DeMyer, W. E., Norton, J. A., Allen, J., & Steele, R. Prognosis in autism: A follow-up study. *Journal of Autism and Childhood Schizophrenia*, 1973, **3,** 199–246.

Dielman, T. E., Cattell, R. B., Lepper, C. Dimensions of problem behavior in the early grades. *Journal of Consulting and Clinical Psychology*, 1971, **37,** 243–249.

Doll, E. A. *The measurement of social competence*. Minneapolis, Minn.: Educational Publishers, 1953.

Dreger, R. M. A progress report on a factor analytic approach to classification in child psychiatry. *Psychiatric Research Reports* (Report 18), 1964, **22,** 22–74.

Eaton, M. D., & Lovitt, T. C. Achievement tests versus direct and daily measurement. In G. Semb (Ed.), *Behavior analysis and education*—1972. Lawrence: University of Kansas Press, 1972.

Edgerton, R. B. *The cloak of competence: Stigma in the lives of the mentally retarded*. Berkeley: University of California Press, 1967.

Edlund, C. V. The effect on the behavior of children, as reflected in the IQ scores, when reinforced after each correct response. *Journal of Applied Behavior Analysis*, 1972, **5,** 317–319.

Elashoff, J. D., & Snow, R. E. (Eds.). *Pygmalion reconsidered*. Worthington, Ohio: Charles A. Jones, 1971.

Elkind, D. Piaget and Montessori. *Harvard Educational Review*, 1967, **37,** 535–545.

Elkind, D. Piagetian and psychometric conceptions of intelligence. *Harvard Educational Review*, 1969, **39,** 319–337.

Ellis, N. R. Memory processes in retardates and normals: Theoretical and empirical considerations. In N. R. Ellis (Ed.), *International review of research in mental retardation*. Vol. 4. New York: Academic, 1970.

Estes, W. K. *Learning theory and mental development*. New York: Academic, 1970.

Evans, I. M. Theoretical and experimental aspects of the behaviour modification approach to autistic children. In M. Rutter (Ed.), *Infantile autism: Concepts, characteristics and treatment*. Edinburgh: Churchill Livingstone, 1971.

Evans, I. M., & Nelson, R. O. A curriculum for the teaching of behavior assessment. *American Psychologist*, 1974, **29,** 598–606.

Eyberg, S. M., & Johnson, S. M. Multiple assessment of behavior modification with families: Effects of contingency contracting and order of treated problems. *Journal of Consulting and Clinical Psychology*, 1974, **42,** 594–606.

Eysenck, H. J. *The biological basis of personality*. Springfield, Ill.: Thomas, 1967.

Eysenck, H. J., & Rachman, S. *The causes and cures of neurosis*. London: Routledge & Kegan Paul, 1965.

Ferritor, D. E., Buckholdt, D., Hamblin, R. L., & Smith, L. The non-effects of contingent reinforcement for attending behavior on work accomplished. *Journal of Applied Behavior Analysis*, 1972, **5,** 7–17.

Filler, J. W., Robinson, C. C., Smith, R. A., Vincent-Smith, L. J., Bricker, D. D., & Bricker, W. A. Mental retardation. In N. Hobbs (Ed.), *Issues in the classification of children*. Vol. 1. San Francisco: Jossey-Bass, 1975.

Fixsen, D. L., Phillips, E. L., & Wolf, M. M. Achievement place: The reliability of self-reporting and peer-reporting and their effects on behavior. *Journal of Applied Behavior Analysis*, 1972, **5,** 19–30.

Flavell, J. H., Beach, D. R., & Chinsky, J. M. Spontaneous verbal rehearsal in a memory task as a function of age. *Child Development*, 1966, **37,** 283–299.

Forehand, R. Teacher recording of deviant behavior: A stimulus for behavior change. *Journal of Behavior Therapy and Experimental Psychiatry*, 1973, **4,** 39–40.

Forehand, R., King, H. E., Peed, S., & Yoder, P. Mother-child interactions: Comparison of a non-compliant clinic group and a non-clinic group. *Behaviour Research and Therapy*, 1975, **13,** 79–84.

Freedman, D. G. *Human infancy: An evolutionary perspective*. Hillsdale, N.J.: Erlbaum, 1974.

Freyman, R. Follow-up study of enuresis treated with a bell apparatus. *Journal of Child Psychology and Psychiatry*, 1963, **4,** 199–206.

Gallimore, R., Boggs, J. W., & Jordan, C. *Culture, behavior and education: A study of Hawaiian-Americans*. Beverly Hills, Calif.: Sage Publications, 1974.

Gallimore, R., Weiss, L. B., & Finney, R. Cultural differences in delay of gratification: A problem of behavior classification. *Journal of Personality and Social Psychology*, 1974, **30,** 72–80.

Gelfand, D. M., & Hartmann, D. P. *Child behavior analysis and therapy*. New York: Pergamon, 1975.

Gewirtz, J. L. On designing the functional environment of the child to facilitate behavioral development. In L. L. Dittmann (Ed.), *Early child care: The new perspectives*. Chicago: Aldine-Atherton, 1968.

Gewirtz, J. L. Stimulation, learning, and motivation principles for day-care settings. In E. H. Grotberg (Ed.), *Day care: Resources for decisions*. Washington, D.C.: U.S. Government Printing Office, 1971.

Gilbert, G. M. A survey of referral problems in metropolitan child guidance centers. *Journal of Clinical Psychology*, 1957, **13,** 37–42.

Gittelman, M. Behavior rehearsal as a technique in child treatment. *Journal of Child Psychology and Psychiatry*, 1965, **6,** 251–255.

Gold, M. W. Stimulus factors in skill training of the retarded on a complex assembly task: Acquisition, transfer and retention. *American Journal of Mental Deficiency*, 1972, **76,** 517–526.

Goldfried, M. R., & Kent, R. N. Traditional versus behavioral assessment: A comparison of methodological and theoretical assumptions. *Psychological Bulletin*, 1972, **77,** 409–420.

Goldfried, M. R., & Sprafkin, J. N. *Behavioral personality assessment*. Morristown, N.J.: General Learning Press, 1974.

Goldstein, H., Moss, J. W., & Jordan, L. J. *The efficacy of special class training on the development of mentally retarded children* (Cooperative Research Project 619). Washington, D.C.: U.S. Office of Education, 1965.

Gordon, C. P., & Gallimore, R. Teacher ratings of behavior problems of Hawaiian-American adolescents. *Journal of Cross Cultural Psychology*, 1972, **3**, 209–213.

Gorham, K. A., Des Jardins, C., Page, R., Pettis, E., & Scheiber, B. Effect on parents. In N. Hobbs (Ed.), *Issues in the classification of children*. Vol. 2. San Francisco: Jossey-Bass, 1975.

Gorsuch, R. L., Henighan, R. P., & Barnard, C. Locus of control: An example of dangers in using children's scales with children. *Child Development*, 1972, **43**, 579–590.

Green, R. *Sexual identity conflict in children and adults*. New York: Basic Books, 1974.

Greenfeld, J. *A child called Noah: A family journey*. New York: Holt, Rinehart, & Winston, 1972.

Griffiths, W. *Behavioral difficulties of children as perceived and judged by parents, teachers, and children themselves*. Minneapolis: University of Minnesota Press, 1952.

Group for the Advancement of Psychiatry. *The diagnostic process in child psychiatry* (GAP Report No. 38). New York: Group for the Advancement of Psychiatry, 1957.

Guskin, S. L., Bartel, N. R., & MacMillan, D. L. Perspective of the labeled child. In N. Hobbs (Ed.), *Issues in the classification of children*. Vol. 2. San Francisco: Jossey-Bass, 1975.

Haggard, E. A., Brekstad, A., & Skard, A. G. On the reliability of the anamnestic interview. *Journal of Abnormal and Social Psychology*, 1966, **61**, 311–313.

Hall, R. V., Axelrod, S., Tyler, L., Grief, E., Jones, F. C., & Robertson, R. Modification of behavior problems in the home with a parent as observer and experimenter. *Journal of Applied Behavior Analysis*, 1972, **5**, 53–64.

Hall, R. V., & Broden, M. Behavior changes in brain-injured children through social reinforcement. *Journal of Experimental child Psychology*, 1967, **5**, 463–479.

Hall, R. V., Fox, R., Willard, D., Goldsmith, L., Emerson, M., Owen, M., Davis, F., Porcia, E. The teacher as observer and experimenter in the modification of disputing and talking-out behaviors. *Journal of Applied Behavior Analysis*, 1971, **4**, 141–149.

Hammond, O. W. *Cultural learning and complex behavioral stimuli*. Unpublished doctoral dissertation, University of Hawaii, 1973.

Harris, F. R., Wolf, M. M., & Baer, D. M. Effects of adult social reinforcement on child behavior. *Young Children*, 1964, **30**, 8–17.

Harris, S. L. The relationship between family income and number of parent-perceived problems. *International Journal of Social Psychiatry*, 1974, **20**, 109–112.

Hart, B. M., Reynolds, N. J., Baer, D. M., Brawley, E. R., & Harris, F. R. Effect of contingent and non-contingent social reinforcement on the cooperative play of a preschool child. *Journal of Applied Behavior Analysis*, 1968, **1**, 73–76.

Hartshorne, H., & May, M. A. *Studies in the nature of character. I: Studies in deceit*. New York: Macmillan, 1928.

Hatfield, J. S., Ferguson, L. R., & Alpert, R. Mother-child interaction and the socialization process. *Child Development*, 1967, **38**, 356–414.

Hawkins, R. P. Who decided that was the problem? Two stages of responsibility for applied behavior analysts. In W. S. Wood (Ed.), *Issues in evaluating behavior modification.* Champaign, Ill.: Research Press, 1975.

Hay, W. M., Hay, L. R., & Nelson, R. O. Direct and collateral changes in on-task and academic behavior resulting from on-task versus academic contingencies. *Behavior Therapy*, in press.

Hay, L. R., Nelson, R. O., & Hay, W. M. A brief report on the use of teachers as behavioral observers. *Journal of Applied Behavior Analysis*, in press.

Haywood, H. C. Individual differences in motivational orientation: A trait approach. In H. Day, D. E. Berlyne, & D. E. Hunt (Eds.), *Intrinsic motivation: A new direction in education.* Toronto, Canada: Holt, Rinehart, & Winston, 1971.

Herbert, E. W., & Baer, D. M. Training parents as behavior modifiers: Self-recording of contingent attention. *Journal of Applied Behavior Analysis*, 1972, **5,** 139–149.

Herbert, M. The concept and testing of brain-damage in children: A review. *Journal of Child Psychology and Psychiatry*, 1964, **5,** 197–216.

Hersen, M. The behavioral treatment of school phobia. *The Journal of Nervous and Mental Disease*, 1971, **153,** 99–107.

Hess, R. D., & Shipman, V. C. Early experience and the socialization of cognitive modes in children. *Child Development*, 1965, **36,** 869–886.

Hewett, F. M. *The emotionally disturbed child in the classroom: A developmental strategy for educating children with maladaptive behavior.* Boston, Mass.: Allyn and Bacon, 1968.

Hewitt, L. E., & Jenkins, R. L. *Fundamental patterns of maladjustment: The dynamics of their origin.* Springfield, Ill.: State of Illinois, 1946.

Higa, W. R. *Self-instructional versus direct training in modifying children's impulsive behavior.* Unpublished doctoral dissertation, University of Hawaii, 1973.

Hobbs, N. (Ed.). *Issues in the classification of children* Vol. 1. San Franciso: Jossey-Bass, 1975. (a).

Hobbs, N. (Ed.). *Issues in the classification of children* Vol. 2. San Francisco: Jossey-Bass, 1975. (b)

Hobbs, N. *The futures of children: Categories, labels, and their consequences.* San Francisco: Jossey-Bass, 1975. (c)

Hogg, J. Personality assessment as the study of learning processes. In P. Mittler (Ed.), *Assessment for learning in the mentally handicapped.* Edinburgh: Churchill Livingstone, 1973.

Hops, H., & Cobb, J. A. Initial investigations into academic survival-skill training, direct instruction, and first-grade achievement. *Journal of Educational Psychology*, 1974, **66,** 548–553.

Hunt, J. McV. *Intelligence and experience.* New York: Ronald, 1961.

Hunt, J. McV. *The challenge of incompetence of poverty.* Urbana, Ill., University of Illinois Press, 1969.

Hutt, C., & Hutt, S. J. Stereotypy, arousal and autism. *Human Development*, 1968, **11,** 277–286.

Hutt, C., & Ounsted, C. The biological significance of gaze aversion with particular reference to the syndrome of infantile autism. *Behavioral Science*, 1966, **11,** 346–356.

Hutt, S. J., & Hutt, C. (Eds.). *Behaviour studies in psychiatry*. Oxford: Pergamon, 1970.

Jenkins, R. L. Classification of behavior problems of children. *American Journal of Psychiatry*, 1969, **125,** 1032–1039.

Jensen, A. R., & Rohwer, W. D., Jr. The effect of verbal mediation on the learning and retention of paired associates by retarded adults. *American Journal of Mental Deficiency*, 1963, **68,** 80–84.

Jersild, A. T., & Holmes, F. B. Children's fears. *Child Development Monographs*, 1935 (Whole No. 20).

Johnson, S. M., & Bolstad, O. D. Methodological issues in naturalistic observation: Some problems and solutions for field research. In L. A. Hamerlynck, L. C. Handy, & E. J. Mash (Eds.), *Behavior change: Methodology, concepts, and practice*. Champaign, Ill.: Research Press, 1973.

Jones, R. R., Reid, J. B., & Patterson, G. R. Naturalistic observation in clinical assessment. In P. McReynolds (Ed.), *Advances in psychological assessment*. Vol. 3. San Francisco: Jossey-Bass, 1975.

Kanfer, F. H., & Phillips, J. S. Behavior therapy: A panacea for all ills or a passing fancy? *Archives of General Psychiatry*, 1966, **15,** 114–128.

Kanfer, F. H., & Saslow, G. Behavioral diagnosis. In C. M. Franks (Ed.), *Behavior therapy: Appraisal and status*. New York: McGraw-Hill, 1969.

Kanner, L. Trends in child psychiatry. *Journal of Mental Science*, 1959, **105,** 581–593.

Kendler, T. S. An ontogeny of mediational deficiency. *Child Development*, 1972, **43,** 1–18.

Kent, R. N., O'Leary, K. D., Diament, C., & Dietz, A. Expectation biases in observational evaluation of therapeutic change. *Journal of Consulting and Clinical Psychology*, 1974, **42,** 774–780.

Kershner, J. R. Doman-Delacato's theory of neurological organization applied with retarded children. *Exceptional Children*, 1968, **34,** 441–450.

Kessler, J. W. Nosology in child psychopathology. In H. E. Rie (Ed.), *Perspectives in child psychopathology*. Chicago: Aldine-Atherton, 1971.

Kimmel, H. D., & Kimmel, E. An instrumental conditioning method for the treatment of enuresis. *Journal of Behavior Therapy and Experimental Psychiatry*, 1970, **1,** 121–123.

Kirby, F. D., & Toler, H. C. Modification of preschool isolate behavior: A case study. *Journal of Applied Behavior Analysis*, 1970, **3,** 309–314.

Klugman, S. F. The effect of money incentive versus praise upon the reliability and obtained scores of the revised Standord-Binet Test. *Journal of Genetic Psychology*, 1944, **30,** 255–269.

Knobloch, H., & Pasamanick, B. (Eds.). *Gesell and Amatruda's developmental diagnosis: The evaluation and management of normal and abnormal neuropsychologic development in infancy and early childhood*. New York: Harper & Row, 1974.

Kobayashi, S., Mizushima, K., & Shinohara, M. Clinical groupings of children based on symptoms and behavior. *International Journal of Social Psychiatry*, 1967, **13,** 206–215.

Koegel, R. L., & Covert, A. The relationship of self-stimulation to learning in autistic children. *Journal of Applied Behavior Analysis*, 1972, **5,** 381–387.

Kubany, E. S. The effects of incentives on the test performance of Hawaiians and Caucasians. Doctoral dissertation, University of Hawaii, 1971. *Dissertation Abstracts International*, 1972, **32,** 5446B. (University Microfilms No. 72-10,165)

Kubany, E. S., & Sloggett, B. B. The role of motivation in test performance and remediation. *Journal of Learning Disabilities*, 1971, **4,** 24–26.

Kubany, E. S., & Sloggett, B. B. A coding procedure for teachers. *Journal of Applied Behavior Analysis*, 1973, **6,** 339–344.

Lang, P. J., & Melamed, B. G. Case report: Avoidance conditioning therapy of an infant with chronic ruminative vomiting. *Journal of Abnormal Psychology*, 1969, **74,** 1–8.

Langer, E. J., & Abelson, R. P. A patient by any other name . . . : Clinician group difference in labeling bias. *Journal of Consulting and Clinical Psychology*, 1974, **42,** 4–9.

Langner, T. S., Gersten, J. C., Greene, E. L., Eisenberg, J. G., Herson, J. H., & McCarthy, E. D. Treatment of psychological disorders among urban children. *Journal of Consulting and Clinical Psychology*, 1974, **42,** 170–179.

Lapouse, R., & Monk, M. A. An epidemiologic study of behavior characteristics in children. *American Journal of Public Health*, 1958, **48,** 1134–1144.

Lazarus, A. A., & Abramovitz, A. The use of "emotive imagery" in the treatment of children's phobias. *Journal of Mental Science*, 1962, **108,** 191–195.

Leach, G. M. A comparison of the social behaviour of some normal and problem children. In N. Blurton Jones (Ed.), *Ethological studies of child behaviour*. London: Cambridge University Press, 1972.

LeBow, M. D. Behavior modification in parent-child therapy: A bibliography. JSAS *Catalog of Selected Documents in Psychology*, 1973, **3,** 12.

Leon, G. R., & Morrow, V. Differing patterns or maternal behavioral control and their association with child behavior problems of an active or passive interpersonal nature. JSAS *Catalog of Selected Documents in Psychology*, 1972, **2,** 136.

Lepper, M. R., & Greene, D. Turning play into work: Effects of adult surveillance and extrinsic rewards on children's intrinsic motivation. *Journal of Personality and Social Psychology*, 1975, **31,** 479–485.

Levitt, E. E. Research on psychotherapy with children. In A. E. Bergin & S. L. Garfield (Eds.), *Handbook of psychotherapy and behavior change: An empirical analysis*. New York: Wiley, 1971.

Lewis, M. Infant intelligence tests: Their use and misuse. *Human Development*, 1973, **16,** 108–118.

Lipinski, D. P., & Nelson, R. O. Problems in the use of naturalistic observation as a means of behavioral assessment. *Behavior Therapy*, 1974, **5,** 341–351.

Loeber, R., & Weisman, R. G. Contingencies of therapist and trainer performance: A review. *Psychological Bulletin*, 1975, **82,** 660–688.

Lorion, R. P., Cowen, E. L., & Caldwell, R. A. Problem types of children referred to a school-based mental health program: Identification and outcome. *Journal of Consulting and Clinical Psychology*, 1974, **42,** 491–496.

Lovaas, O. I., Freitag, G., Gold, V. J., & Kassorla, I. C. Recording apparatus and procedure for observation of behaviors of children in free play settings. *Journal of Experimental Child Psychology*, 1965, **2,** 108–120.

Lovaas, O. I., Koegel, R., Simmon, J. Q., & Stevens-Long, J. Some generalization and follow-up measures on autistic children in behavior therapy. *Journal of Applied Behavior Analysis*, 1973, **6,** 131–166.

Lytton, H. Observation studies of parent-child interaction: A methodological review. *Child Development*, 1971, **42,** 651–684.

MacDonald, W. S. *Battle in the classroom: Innovations in classroom techniques.* Scranton, Pa.: Intext Educational Publishers, 1971.

MacDonald, W. S., Gallimore, R., & MacDonald, G. Contingency counseling by school personnel: An economical model of intervention. *Journal of Applied Behavior Analysis*, 1970, **3,** 175–182.

MacFarlane, J. W., Allen, L., & Honzik, M. P. *A developmental study of the behavior problems of normal children between twenty-one months and fourteen years.* Berkeley: University of California Press, 1954.

Maliphant, R., Supramaniam, S., & Saraga, E. Acquiring skill in reading: A review of experimental research. *Journal of Child Psychology and Psychiatry*, 1974, **15,** 175–185.

Marmorale, A. M., & Brown, F. *Mental health intervention in the primary grades* (Community Mental Health Journal Monograph Series, No. 7). New York: Behavioral Publications, 1974.

Mash, E. J., Lazare, R., Terdal, L., & Garner, A. Modification of mother-child interactions: A modeling approach for groups. *Child Study Journal*, 1973, **3,** 131–143.

Mash, E. J., & Terdal, L. G. Behavior therapy assessment: Diagnosis, design, and evaluation. *Psychological Reports*, 1974, **35,** 587–601.

McCall, R. B., Hogarty, P. S., & Hurlburt, N. Transitions in infant sensoriomotor development and the prediction of childhood IQ. *American Psychologist*, 1972, **27,** 728–748.

McCord, J., & McCord, W. Cultural stereotypes and the validity of interviews for research in child development. *Child Development*, 1961, **32,** 171–185.

McGraw, M. B., & Molloy, L. B. The pediatric anamnesis: Inaccuracies in eliciting developmental data. *Child Development*, 1941, **12,** 255–265.

McGrew, W. C. *An ethological study of children's behavior.* New York: Academic, 1972.

McKeachie, W. J. The decline and fall of the laws of learning. *Educational Researcher*, 1974, **3,** 7–11.

Mednick, S. A. Breakdown in children at high risk for schizophrenia: Behavioral and autonomic characteristics and possible role of perinatal complications. *Mental Hygiene*, 1970, **54,** 50–63.

Mednick, S. A., Schulsinger, F., & Garfinkel, R. Children at high risk for schizophrenia: Predisposing factors and intervention. In M. L. Kietzman, S. Sutton, & J. Zubin (Eds.), *Experimental approaches to psychopathology.* New York: Academic, 1975.

Mednick, S. A., & Shaffer, J. B. P. Mothers' retrospective reports in child-rearing research. *American Journal of Orthopsychiatry*, 1963, **33,** 457–461.

Meichenbaum, D. H., & Goodman, J. Training impulsive children to talk to themselves: A means of developing self-control. *Journal of Abnormal Psychology*, 1971, **77,** 115–126.

Mercer, J. R. *Labeling the mentally retarded.* Berkeley: University of California Press, 1973.

Miezitis, S. The Montessori method: Some recent research. *Interchange*, 1971, **2,** 41–59.

Miller, L. C. Louisville Behavior Check List for males 6–12 years of age. *Psychological Reports*, 1967, **21,** 885–896.

Miller, L. C., Barrett, C. L., & Hampe, E. Phobias of childhood in a prescientific era. In A. Davids (Ed.), *Child personality and psychopathology: Current topics.* Vol. 1. New York: Wiley, 1974.

Miller, L. C., Barrett, C. L., Hampe, E., & Noble, H. Factor structure of childhood fears. *Journal of Consulting and Clinical Psychology*, 1972, **39,** 264–268.

Mischel, W. *Personality and assessment*. New York: Wiley, 1968.

Mischel, W. Toward a cognitive social learning reconceptualization of personality. *Psychological Review*, 1973, **80,** 252–283.

Mittler, P. (Ed.), *The psychological assessment of mental and physical handicaps.* London: Methuen, 1970.

Morris, D. P., Soroker, E., & Burruss, G. Follow-up studies of shy, withdrawn children. I. Evaluation of later adjustment. *American Journal of Orthopsychiatry*, 1954, **24,** 743–754.

Morris, H. H., Escoll, P. J., & Wexler, R. Aggressive behavior disorders of childhood: A follow-up study. *American Journal of Psychiatry*, 1956, **112,** 991–997.

Moustakas, C. E., Sigel, I. E., & Schalock, H. D. An objective method for the measurement and analysis of child-adult interaction. *Child Development*, 1956, **27,** 109–134.

Nathan, P. E., & Harris, S. L. *Psychopathology and society*. New York: McGraw-Hill, 1975.

Nay, W. R. Comprehensive behavioral treatment in a training school for delinquents. In K. S. Calhoun, H. E. Adams, & K. M. Mitchell (Eds.), *Innovative treatment methods in psychopathology*. New York: Wiley, 1974.

Nelson, R. O. An expanded scope for behavior modification in school settings. *Journal of School Psychology*, 1974, **12,** 276–287.

Nelson, R. O., & Bowles, P. E. The best of two worlds—observations with norms. *Journal of School Psychology*, 1975, **13,** 3–9.

Nelson, R. O., Hay, L. R., Hay, W. M., & Carstens, C. B. The reactivity and accuracy of teachers' self-monitoring of positive and negative classroom verbalizations. *Behavior Therapy*, in press.

Nelson, R. O., Lipinski, D. P., & Black, J. L. The effects of expectancy on the reactivity of self-recording. *Behavior Therapy*, 1975, **6,** 337–349.

Nicholson, C. A. A survey of referral problems in 59 Ohio School Districts. *Journal of School Psychology*, 1967, **5,** 280–286.

Novick, J., Rosenfeld, E., Bloch, D. A., & Dawson, D. Ascertaining deviant behavior in children. *Journal of Consulting Psychology*, 1966, **30,** 230–238.

O'Connor, J. J., & Weiss, F. L. A brief discussion of the efficacy of raising standardized test scores by contingent reinforcement. *Journal of Applied Behavior Analysis*, 1974, **7**, 351–352.

O'Connor, R. D. Modification of social withdrawal through symbolic modeling. *Journal of Applied Behavior Analysis*, 1969, **2**, 15–22.

O'Connor, R. D. Relative efficacy of modeling, shaping, and the combined procedures for modification of social withdrawal. *Journal of Abnormal Psychology*, 1972, **79**, 327–334.

O'Donnell, C. R., & Fo, W. S. O. The buddy system: Mediator-target locus of control and behavioral outcome. *American Journal of Community Psychology*, in press.

O'Leary, K. D. Behavior modification in the classroom: A rejoinder to Winett and and Winkler. *Journal of Applied Behavior Analysis*, 1972, **5**, 505–511. (a)

O'Leary, K. D. The assessment of psychopathology in children. In H. C. Quay & J. S. Werry (Eds.), *Psychopathological disorders of childhood.* New York: Wiley, 1972. (b)

O'Leary, K. D., Becker, W. C., Evans, M. B., & Saudargas, R. A. A token reinforcement program in a public school: A replication and systematic analysis. *Journal of Applied Behavior Analysis*, 1969, **2**, 3–13.

O'Leary, K. D., O'Leary, S. G., & Becker, W. C. Modification of a deviant sibling interaction pattern in the home. *Behaviour Research and Therapy*, 1967, **5**, 113–120.

O'Neal, P., & Robins, L. N. The relation of childhood behavior problems to adult psychiatric status: A 30-year follow-up study of 150 subjects. *American Journal of Psychiatry*, 1958, **114**, 961–969.

O'Rourke, J. F. Field and laboratory: The decision-making behavior of family groups in two experimental conditions. *Sociometry*, 1963, **26**, 422–435.

Osborne, J. G. Free-time as a reinforcer in the management of a classroom behavior. *Journal of Applied Behavior Analysis*, 1969, **2**, 113–118.

Osler, S. F. Early strategies in concept learning. In F. Richardson (Ed.), *Brain and intelligence: The ecology of child development*. Hyattsville, Md.: National Educational Press, 1973.

Osofsky, J. D. The shaping of mother's behavior by children. *Journal of Marriage and the Family*, 1970, **32**, 400–405.

Parsons, B. V., & Alexander, J. F. Short-term family intervention: A therapy outcome study. *Journal of Consulting and Clinical Psychology*, 1973, **41**, 195–201.

Patterson, G. R., Cobb, J. A., & Ray, R. S. A social engineering technology for retaining the families of aggressive boys. In H. E. Adams & I. P. Unikel (Eds.), *Issues and trends in behavior therapy*. Springfield, Ill.,: Thomas, 1973.

Patterson, G. R., Littman, R. A., & Hinsey, W. C. Parental effectiveness as rienforcers in the laboratory and its relation to child rearing practices and child adjustment in the classroom. *Journal of Personality*, 1964, **32**, 180–199.

Patterson, G. R., Ray, R. S., Shaw, D. A., & Cobb, J. A. *Manual for coding of family interactions*, 1969 (Document No. 01234). Available from ASIS/NAPS, c/o Microfiche Publications, 305 East 46th Street, New York, N.Y., 10017.

Patterson, G. R., & Reid, J. B. Reciprocity and coercion: Two facets of social systems. In C. Neuringer & J. L. Michael (Eds.), *Behavior modification in clinical psychology*. New York: Appleton-Century-Crofts, 1970.

Payne, E. W., & Jones, H. G. Statistics for the investigation of individual cases. *Journal of Clinical Psychology*, 1957, **13,** 115–121.

Peterson, D. R. Behavior problems of middle childhood. *Journal of Consulting Psychology*, 1961, **25,** 205–209.

Price-Williams, D. R. Cross cultural studies. In B. M. Foss (Ed.), *New horizons in psychology*. London: Penguin, 1966.

Pyles, M. K., Stolz, H. R., & MacFarlane, J. W. The accuracy of mothers' reports on birth and developmental data. *Child Development*, 1935, **6,** 165–176.

Quay, H. C. Personality dimensions in delinquent males as inferred from the factor analysis of behavior ratings. *Journal of Research in Crime and Delinquency*, 1964, **1,** 33–37.

Quay, H. C., Morse, W. C., & Cutler, R. L. Personality patterns of pupils in special classes for the emotionally disturbed. *Exceptional Children*, 1966, **32,** 297–301.

Quay, H. C., & Peterson, D. R. *Manual for the behavior problem checklist*. Champaign: University of Illinois, Children's Research Center, 1967.

Quay, L. C. Language dialect, reinforcement, and the intelligence-test performance of Negro children. *Child Development*, 1971, **42,** 5–15.

Quay, L. C. Reinforcement and Binet performance in disadvantaged children. *Journal of Educational Psychology*, 1975, **67,** 132–135.

Quilitch, H. R., & Risley, T. R. The effects of play materials on social play. *Journal of Applied Behavior Analysis*, 1973, **6,** 573–578.

Reid, J. B. Reliability assessment of observation data: A possible methodological problem. *Child Development*, 1970, **41,** 1143–1150.

Reid, J. B., & Hendricks, A. F. C. J. Preliminary analysis of the effectiveness of direct home intervention for the treatment of predelinquent boys who steal. In L. A. Hamerlynck, L. S. Handy, & E. J. Mash (Eds.), *Behavior change: Methodology, concepts, and practice*. Champaign, Ill.: Research Press, 1973.

Rekers, G. A., & Lovaas, O. I. Behavioral treatment of deviant sex-role behaviors in a male child. *Journal of Applied Behavior Analysis*, 1974, **7,** 173–190.

Retish, P. M. Changing the status of poorly esteemed students through teacher reinforcement. *Journal of Applied Behavioral Science*, 1973, **9,** 44–50.

Reynolds, N. J., & Risley, T. R. The role of social and material reinforcers in increasing talking of a disadvantaged preschool child. *Journal of Applied Behavior Analysis*, 1968, **1,** 253–262.

Ritter, B. The group desensitization of children's snake phobias using vicarious and contact desensitization procedures. *Behaviour Research and Therapy*, 1968, **6,** 1–6.

Roach, J. L., Gursslin, O., & Hunt, R. G. Some social-psychological characteristics of a child guidance clinic caseload. *Journal of Consulting Psychology*, 1958, **22,** 183–186.

Robbins, L. C. The accuracy of parental recall of aspects of child development and of child rearing practices. *Journal of Abnormal and Social Psychology*, 1963, **66,** 261–270.

Robbins, M. P. Test of the Doman-Delacato rationale with retarded readers. *Journal of the American Medical Association*, 1967, **202,** 389–393.

Robinson, W. S. Ecological correlations and the behavior of individuals. *American Sociology Review*, 1950, **15,** 351–357.

Roff, M. Some life history factors in relation to various types of adult maladjustment. In M. Roff & D. F. Ricks (Eds.), *Life history research in psychopathology*. Vol. 1. Minneapolis: University of Minnesota Press, 1970.

Rohwer, W. D., Jr. Learning, race and school success. *Review of Educational Research*, 1971, **41,** 191–210.

Rohwer, W. D., Jr., & Ammon, M. S. Elaboration training and paired-associate learning efficiency in children. *Journal of Educational Psychology*, 1971, **62,** 376–383.

Romanczyk, R. G., Kent, R. N., Diament, C., & O'Leary, K. D. Measuring the reliability of observational data: A reactive process. *Journal of Applied Behavior Analysis*, 1973, **6,** 175–184.

Rose, S. D. *Treating children in groups*. San Francisco: Jossey-Bass, 1972.

Rosen, B. C., & D'Andrade, R. The psychological origins of achievement motivation. *Sociometry*, 1959, **22,** 185–218.

Rosen, L. C. An experimental study of visual perceptual training and reading achievement in first grade. *Perceptual and Motor Skills*, 1966, **22,** 979–986.

Rosenthal, R., & Jacobson, L. *Pygmalion in the classroom: Teacher expectation and pupils' intellectual development*. New York: Holt, Rinehart, & Winston, 1968.

Ross, A. O. The issue of normality in clinical child psychology. *Mental Hygiene*, 1963, **47,** 267–272.

Ross, A. O., Lacey, H. M., & Parton, D. A. The development of a behavior checklist for boys. *Child Development*, 1965, **36,** 1013–1027.

Ross, D. M., Ross, S. A., & Evans, T. A. The modification of extreme social withdrawal by modeling with guided participation. *Journal of Behavior Therapy and Experimental Psychiatry*, 1971, **2,** 273–279.

Rotter, J. B. Some implications of a social learning theory for the prediction of goal directed behavior from testing procedures. *Psychological Review*, 1960, **67,** 301–316.

Rourke, B. P. Brain-behavior relationships in children with learning disabilities: A research program. *American Psychologist*, 1975, **30,** 911–920.

Rutter, M., Greenfeld, D., & Lockyer, L. A five- to fifteen-year follow-up study of infantile psychosis. II: Social and behavioural outcome. *British Journal of Psychiatry*, 1967, **113,** 1183–1199.

Rutter, M., Yule, B., Quinton, D., Rowlands, O., Yule, W., & Berger, M. Attainment and adjustment in two geographical areas. III: Some factors accounting for area differences. *British Journal of Psychiatry*, 1975, **125,** 520–533.

Santostefano, S. Miniature situations and methodological problems in parent-child interaction research. *Merrill-Palmer Quarterly*, 1968, **14,** 285–312.

Schaeffer, C. E., & Millman, H. L. A factor analytic and reliability study of the Devereux Child Behavior Rating Scale. *Journal of Abnormal Child Psychology*, 1973, **1,** 241–247.

Schnelle, J. F. A brief report on invalidity of parent evaluations of behavior change. *Journal of Applied Behavior Analysis*, 1974, **7,** 341–343.

Schopler, E. Changes of direction with psychotic children. In A. Davids (Ed.), *Child personality and psychopathology: Current topics*. Vol. 1. New York: Wiley, 1974.

Schopler, E., & Loftin, J. Thought disorders in parents of psychotic children: A function of test anxiety. *Archives of General Psychiatry*, 1969, **20,** 174.

Schopler, E., & Reichler, R. J. Developmental therapy by parents with their own psychotic child. In M. Rutter (Ed.), *Infantile autism: Concepts, characteristics and treatment*. Edinburgh: Churchill Livingstone, 1971. (a)

Schopler, E., & Reichler, R. J. Parents as cotherapists in the treatment of psychotic children. *Journal of Autism and Childhood Schizophrenia*, 1971, **1,** 87–102. (b)

Schulman, J. L., Kaspar, J. C., & Throne, F. M. *Brain damage and behavior: A clinical-experimental study*. Springfield, Ill.: Thomas, 1965.

Schultz, E. W., Salvia, J., & Feinn, J. Deviant behaviors in rural elementary school-children. *Journal of Abnormal Child Psychology*, 1973, **1,** 378–389.

Schwebel, A. *Physical and social distancing in teacher-pupil relationships*. Unpublished doctoral dissertation, Yale University, 1969.

Sears, R. R., Rau, L., & Alpert, R. *Identification and child rearing*. Palo Alto, Calif.: Stanford University Press, 1965.

Shapiro, M. B. An experimental approach to diagnostic psychological testing. *Journal of Mental Science*, 1951, **97,** 748–764.

Shapiro, M. B. The single case in clinical-psychological research. *Journal of General Psychology*, 1966, **74,** 3–23.

Shechtman, A. Age patterns in children's psychiatric symptoms. *Child Development*, 1970, **41,** 683–693.

Shechtman, A. Psychiatric symptoms observed in normal and disturbed black children. *Journal of Clinical Psychology*, 1971, **27,** 445–447.

Sherman, T. M., & Cormier, W. H. An investigation of the influence of student behavior on teacher behavior. *Journal of Applied Behavior Analysis*, 1974, **7,** 11–21.

Sidman, M., & Stoddard, L. T. The effectiveness of fading in programming a simultaneous form discrimination for retarded children. *Journal of the Experimental Analysis of Behavior*, 1967, **10,** 3–15.

Silver, A. A., & Hagin, R. A. Specific reading disability: An approach to diagnosis and treatment. *Journal of Special Education*, 1967, **1,** 109–118.

Singer, J. L. *The child's world of make-believe: Experimental studies of imaginative play*. New York: Academic, 1973.

Sloggett, B. B. Use of group activities and team rewards to increase individual classroom productivity. *Teaching Exceptional Children*, 1971, **3,** 54–66.

Sloggett, B. B. The comparative effects of verbal information, passive observation, and active observation on the acquisition of classroom management skills, Doctoral dissertation, University of Hawaii, 1972. *Dissertation Abstracts International*, 1973, **34,** 426B–427B. (University Microfilms No. 73-15,948).

Smeets, P. M., & Striefel, S. The effects of different reinforcement conditions on the test performance of multihandicapped deaf children. *Journal of Applied Behavior Analysis*, 1975, **8,** 83–89.

Smith, H. A comparison of interview and observation measures of mother behavior. *Journal of Abnormal and Social Psychology*, 1958, **57,** 278–282.

Smith, R. E., & Sharpe, T. M. Treatment of a school phobia with implosive therapy. *Journal of Consulting and Clinical Psychology*, 1970, **35,** 239–243.

Spence, J. T. The distracting effects of material reinforcers in the discrimination learning of middle- and lower-class children. *Child Development*, 1970, **41,** 103–111.

Spence, J. T. Do material rewards enhance the performance of lower-class children? *Child Development*, 1971, **42,** 1461–1470.

Spivack, G., & Levine, M. The Devereux child behavior rating scales: A study of symptom behaviors in latency age atypical children. *American Journal of Mental Deficiency*, 1964, **68,** 700–717.

Spivack, G., & Swift, M. The Devereux elementary school behavior rating scales: A study of the nature and organization of achievement-related disturbed classroom behavior. *The Journal of Special Education*, 1966, **1,** 71–90.

Sprague, R. L., & Binder, A. Verbal and motor perceptual responses of the retarded to ambiguous stimuli. *American Journal of Mental Deficiency*, 1966, **71,** 48–54.

Spring, C., Greenberg, L., Scott, J., & Hopwood, J. Electrodermal activity in hyperactive boys who are methylphenidate responders. *Psychophysiology*, 1974, **11,** 456–462.

Staats, A. W. *Child learning, intelligence, and personality*. New York: Harper & Row, 1971.

Staats, A. W. Language behavior therapy: A derivative of social behaviorism. *Behavior Therapy*, 1972, **3,** 165–192.

Staats, A. W. Behavior analysis and token reinforcement in educational behavior modification and curriculum research. In C. E. Thoreson (Ed.), *Behavior modification in education*. Chicago: University of Chicago Press, 1973.

Staats, A. W. *Social behaviorism*. Homewood, Ill.: Dorsey, 1975.

Staats, A. W., Minke, K. A., Goodwin, W., & Landeen, J. Cognitive behavior modification: "Motivated learning" reading treatment with sub-professional therapy-technicians. *Behaviour Research and Therapy*, 1967, **5,** 283–299.

Stevens, S. An ecological study of a child guidance clinic intake. *Smith College Studies in Social Work*, 1954, **25,** 73–84.

Stone, L. J., Smith, H. T., & Murphy, L. B. (Eds.). *The competent infant*. New York: Basic Books, 1973.

Surratt, P. P., Ulrich, R. E., & Hawkins, R. P. An elementary student as a behavioral engineer. *Journal of Applied Behavior Analysis*, 1969, **2,** 85–92.

Switzky, H. N., & Haywood, H. C. Motivational orientation and the relative efficacy of self-monitored and externally imposed reinforcement systems in children. *Journal of Personality and Social Psychology*, 1974, **30,** 360–366.

Tharp, R. G., & Wetzel, R. J. *Behavior modification in the natural environment*. New York: Academic, 1969.

Thomas, A., Chess, S., & Birch, H. G. *Temperament and behavior disorders in children*. New York: New York University Press, 1968.

Thomas, D. R., Becker, W. C., & Armstrong, M. Production and elimination of disruptive classroom behavior by systematically varying teacher's behavior. *Journal of Applied Behavior Analysis*, 1968, **1,** 35–45.

Tiber, N., & Kennedy, W. A. The effects of incentives on the intelligence test performance of different social groups. *Journal of Consulting Psychology*, 1964, **28**, 187.

Ullmann, L. P., & Krasner, L. *A psychological approach to abnormal behavior*. Englewood Cliffs, N.J.: Prentice-Hall, 1975.

Wahler, R. G. Child-child interactions in free field settings: Some experimental analyses. *Journal of Experimental Child Psychology*, 1967, **5**, 278–293.

Wahler, R. G. Setting generality: Some specific and general effects of child behavior therapy. *Journal of Applied Behavior Analysis*, 1969, **3**, 239–246.

Wahler, R., & Cormier, W. H. The ecological interview: A first step in outpatient child behavior therapy. *Journal of Behavior Therapy and Experimental Psychiatry*, 1970, **1**, 279–289.

Wahler, R. G. Some structural aspects of deviant child behavior. *Journal of Applied Behavior Analysis*, 1975, **8**, 27–42.

Wahler, R. G., Sperling, K. A., Thomas, M. R., Teeter, N. C., & Luper, H. L. The modification of childhood stuttering: Some response-response relationships. *Journal of Experimental Child Psychology*, 1970, **9**, 411–428.

Wahler, R. G., Winkel, G. H., Peterson, R. F., & Morrison, D. C. Mothers as behavior therapists for their own children. *Behaviour Research and Therapy*, 1965, **3**, 113–134.

Walker, H. M. *Walker problem behavior identification checklist*. Los Angeles: Western Psychological Services, 1970.

Walter, H. I., & Gilmore, S. K. Placebo versus social learning effects in parent Training procedures designed to alter the behavior of aggressive boys. *Behavior Therapy*, 1973, **4**, 361–377.

Wechsler, D. *Manual for the Wechsler Preschool and Primary Scale of Intelligence*. New York: The Psychological Corporation, 1967.

Wechsler, D. Intelligence defined and undefined: A relativistic appraisal. *American Psychologist*, 1975, **30**, 135–139.

Weiss, L. B., & Gallimore, R. Some problems of behavioral classification in cross cultural research. In S. MacDonald & G. Tanabe (Eds.), *Focus on classroom behavior: Theory and research*. Springfield, Ill.: Thomas, 1973.

Wenar, C., & Coulter, J. B. A reliability study of developmental histories. *Child Development*, 1962, **33**, 453–462.

Werry, J. S. Developmental hyperactivity. *Pediatric Clinics of North America*, 1968, **15**, 581–599.

White, B. L. *Human infants: Experience and psychological development*. Englewood Cliffs, N.J.: Prentice-Hall, 1971.

White, B. L., & Watts, J. C. (Eds.). *Experience and environment: Major influences on the development of the young child*. Vol. 1. Englewood Cliffs, N. J.: Prentice-Hall, 1973.

Whitman, T. L., Mercurio, J. R., & Caponigri, V. Development of social responses in two severely retarded children. *Journal of Applied Behavior Analysis*, 1970, **3**, 133–138.

Wiesen, A. E., Hartley, G., Richardson, C., & Roske, A. The retarded child as a reinforcing agent. *Journal of Experimental Child Psychology*, 1967, **5**, 109–113.

Wilkins, W. E. Teacher expectations and classroom behaviors: A test of the Rosenthal and Jacobson model. JSAS *Catalog of Selected Documents in Psychology*, 1975, **5,** 246.

Wilson, G. T., & Evans, I. M. The therapist-client relationship in behavior therapy. In A. S. Gurman & A. M. Razin (Eds.), *The therapist's contribution to effectivene psychotherapy: An empirical approach.* New York: Pergamon, in press.

Winett, R. A., Battersby, C. D., & Edwards, S. M. The effects of architectural change, individualized instruction, and group contingencies on the academic performance and social behavior of sixth graders. *Journal of School Psychology*, 1975, **13,** 28–40.

Winett, R. A., & Winkler, R. C. Current behavior modification in the classroom: Be still, be quiet, be docile. *Journal of Applied Behavior Analysis.* 1972, **5,** 499–504.

Wolff, S. Dimensions and clusters of symptoms in disturbed children. *British Journal of Psychiatry*, 1971, **118,** 421–427.

Yarrow, L. J. Interviewing children. In P. H. Mussen (Ed.), *Handbook of research methods in child development.* New York: Wiley, 1960.

Yarrow, M. R. The measurement of children's attitudes and values. In P. H. Mussen (Ed.), *Handbook of research methods in child development.* New York: Wiley, 1960.

Yarrow, M. R., Campbell, J. D., & Burton, R. V. Recollections of childhood: A study of the retrospective method. *Monographs of the Society for Research in Child Development*, 1970, **35,** (5, Serial No. 138).

Yates, A. J. *Theory and practice in behavior therapy.* New York: Wiley, 1975.

Young, G. C. Conditioning treatment of enuresis. *Developmental Medicine and Child Neurology*, 1965, **7,** 559–562. (a)

Young, G. C. Personality factors and the treatment of enuresis. *Behaviour Research and Therapy*, 1965, **3,** 103–105. (b)

Zegiob, L. E., & Forehand, R. Maternal interactive behavior as a function of race, scoioeconomic status, and sex of the child. *Child Development*, 1975, **46,** 564–568.

Zeilberger, J., Sampen, S. E., & Sloane, H. N. Modification of a child's problem behaviors in the home with the mother as therapist. *Journal of Applied Behavior Analysis*, 1968, **1,** 47–53.

Zigler, E. F. Children's needs in the seventies: A federal perspective. In G. J. Williams & S. Gordon (Eds.), *Clinical child psychology: Current practices and future perspectives.* New York: Behavioral Publications, 1974.

Zigler, E., Abelson, W. E., & Seitz, V. Motivational factors in the performance of economically disadvantaged children on the Peabody Picture Vocabulary Test. *Child Development*, 1973, **44,** 294–303.

Zigler, E., & Butterfield, E. C. Motivational aspects of changes in IQ test performance of culturally deprived nursery school children. *Child Development*, 1968, **39,** 1–14.

Zigler, E., & deLabry, J. Concept-switching in middle-class, lower-class, and retarded children. *Journal of Abnormal and Social Psychology*, 1962, **65,** 267–273.

Zlutnick, S., Mayville, W. J., & Moffat, S. Modification of seizure disorders: The interruption of behavioral chains. *Journal of Applied Behavior Analysis*, 1975, **8,** 1–12.

CHAPTER 17

Assessment of Psychotic Behavior

PETER N. ALEVIZOS and EDWARD J. CALLAHAN

Psychosis is defined in the Diagnostic and Statistical Manual II (American Psychiatric Association, 1968) as a disorder involving problems in thought or language processes, distorted affect, or a perceptual distortion in the individual's relationship to reality. Few of these psychotic symptoms are directly observable, and thus the traditional assessment of these variables has usually involved the subjective impression of a clinician.

Although assessment for the presence or absence of psychosis shows acceptable reliability, there are two disturbing aspects of the traditional diagnosis. One is that it implies the presence or absence of the disorder as a whole (Kiesler, 1971); the other is that, once labeled psychotic, a person can be assured of continued diagnosis as either psychotic or psychotic in remission for much of his life (cf. Rosenhan, 1973). Selecting and observing behavior defined as psychotic can offer an alternative to this diagnostic trap. Behavioral assessment allows the clinician to measure the frequency or duration of disturbing behavior rather than the presence or absence of a vaguely defined illness.

Traditional psychiatric diagnoses, resting on a medical model, imply that the problems assessed occur only in the individual. Psychosocial formulations indicate that one's milieu must also be taken into account. Family members and social milieu are considered to have a critical impact on the behavior of individuals within that constellation. In a psychosocial model, assessment of psychosis must consider where and under what conditions

---

The writing of this chapter was supported in part by a National Institute of Mental Health Research Grant MH-R20. The opinions stated are those of the authors and do not necessarily reflect the views of the Regents of the University of California or the California Department of Health. The authors wish to thank Philip L. Berck, Michael D. Campbell, Denise Lafey, Sandranne Lenhardt, Melinda R. Maggiani, Linda Sherman, James Teigen, David D. Wood and especially Drs. Donald P. Hartmann and Robert P. Liberman for their contributions to research cited here.

the psychotic behaviors occur. This imples the importance of assessing the social milieu of the psychotic and not only the psychotic himself.

Although there is no widespread consensus as to what behaviors constitute psychosis, there are several points of agreement. Paul (1969) outlined four major areas of chronic patient behaviors associated with psychosis: (1) social interaction, (2) instrumental role performance (work behavior), (3) symptomatology such as hallucinations and delusions, and (4) self-care. Each of these areas can be assessed by clinicians or treatment staff using direct observation and measurement of behaviors. In fact, such informally conducted observations already provide much of the basis for the global ratings that traditionally make up the clinical assessment of psychotics.

There are two related approaches that can be used in the behavioral assessment of psychosis. The first of these is the direct observation and recording of behaviors. The second is ratings of behaviors based on naturalistic interactions. Although the first method of assessment offers great accuracy of recording, it does not guarantee reliability across observers and can be difficult and expensive to implement. The second methodology, indirect global evaluation using behavioral cues, offers more economical assessment but may not be as accurate or as sensitive to change.

This chapter will begin by covering what ought to provide the most reliable measurements related to *chronic psychosis in adult populations*—the observation and recording of specific behaviors of individuals labeled psychotic. A second section will cover specific observation techniques that gauge the social ecology of living situations of groups of psychotics (hospital wards and community resident care facilities), while a later section will cover observation-based rating scales for individual behavior and for the social milieu. Finally, this chapter will summarize the development of a specific instrument designed to assess several areas of the individual psychotic's behavior in a residential treatment setting—The Behavioral Performance Tests.

ASSESSING SPECIFIC PSYCHOTIC BEHAVIORS

Nonverbal Motor Behavior

Much of the behavior of individuals diagnosed as psychotic consists of motor behaviors that are not so much unusual or bizarre as they are discrepant with normative levels of occurrence and situational appropriateness (see Ullmann & Krasner, 1969). These behaviors can be measured by the same recording techniques used to assess any nonverbal behavior.

Extremely high or low levels of activity are examples of distortion in the frequency of certain behaviors of psychiatric residents. Salzinger and Portnoy (1964) conclude that chronic psychotics can more accurately be described as exhibiting a low overall rate of behavior rather than as displaying "flat affect." Providing confirmation of this normatively low activity level of groups of psychiatric residents are reports by Alevizos, DeRisi, Callahan, Eckman and Liberman (Note 1), Harmatz, Mendelsohn and Glassman (Note 2), and Hunter, Schooler, and Spohn (1962).

In two case studies measuring activity level McFarlain and Hersen (1974) assessed the effects of drug treatment and token reinforcement in a manic psychotic and in a depressed inpatient resident. A modified wristwatch or "actometer" (Schulman & Reisman, 1959) was attached to the leg to measure changes in cumulative daily activity levels. Reliable changes in cumulative movement were shown to be related to phenothiazine reduction and token reinforcement. In individual cases increased movement may be a reliable index of lessened pathology. Another type of activity measure has been related to adjustment in schizophrenic residents. The frequency of high school activities joined during late adolescence and young adulthood was shown to differentiate between active and withdrawn schizophrenics (Depue & Dubicki, 1974). Frequency of high school activities was also related to length of hospitalization and other outcome variables.

Other nonverbal behaviors in psychotic residents have also been measured by counting their frequencies, including annoying or pesty behavior (e.g., Ayllon & Michael, 1959), incontinence (e.g., Wagner & Paul, 1970), excessive crying (Reisinger, 1972), aggressive and physically assaulting acts (e.g., Liberman, Wallace, Teigen, & Davis, 1974; Ludwig, Marx, Hill, & Browning, 1969), fire setting (Royer, Flynn, & Osadea, 1971), extreme noncompliance and provocative, high frequency, and situationally inappropriate sexual and excretory behaviors (e.g., Liberman et al., 1974). Although screaming is actually verbal behavior, it shares the measurement characteristics of nonverbal behaviors and can be measured by recording its frequency or duration. For example, during one-hour DRO treatment sessions, Bostow and Bailey (1969) initiated a time-out procedure when loud, disruptive verbalizations activated a portable tape recorder generating a 2-second discriminative signal. The sessions were tape recorded to provide a means of independent measurement of response frequencies. Unfortunately, the inexpensive signal equipment used was poorly calibrated, precluding precise measurement or replication of the auditory threshold. In a reversal (A-B-A) design, O'Brien and Azrin (1972) compared contingent and noncontingent token reinforcement for positive and incompatible behaviors to reduce screaming (not defined in the report) in chronic mental patients. Screaming was assessed during treatment sessions using an interval recording format in which the frequency of 30-second intervals during which the behavior occurred was tabulated.

Delusional Speech

By far the greatest amount of behavioral research in individual psychotic behaviors has been in the measurement and modification of speech and language behaviors. This is appropriate since delusional or bizarre speech is a major contributor to labeling individuals as schizophrenic or functionally psychotic. Epidemiological studies indicate that the verbalization of delusional or bizarre ideation is the most frequent behavior reported to lead to readmission of previously hospitalized schizophrenics (Hoenig & Hamilton, 1966; Wing, Monck, Brown, & Carstairs, 1964). Bizarre speech (often termed "sick" or "crazy" talk by both clinicians and researchers) attracts considerable social attention across many settings, especially when grandiose or persecution themes are evident. Laboratory research in verbal conditioning has been instrumental in demonstrating that appropriate and non–delusional speech can be increased by the social responses of an interviewer (e.g., Sommer, Witney, & Osmond, 1962; Ullmann, Krasner, & Edinger, 1964). Such studies laid groundwork for the clinical application of extinction and punishment to decrease delusional speech and the application of positive reinforcement to increase "rational" verbal responses.

Rickard, Dignam and Horner (1960) used a social extinction procedure to decrease delusional speech and social reinforcement to increase rational speech in a 60-year-old chronic hospital resident. Delusional speech was defined and measured as the frequency of specific phrases or sentences: "I have a fractured head and a broken nose because of spinal pressure," or "Stars have metal bottoms and exert a magnetic pressure on the earth." Ayllon and Haughton (1964) used extinction and reinforcement (attention and intermittently offering or sharing candy and cigarettes) to modify "neutral," "psychotic," and high-frequency "hypochondriacal" verbalizations in three hospitalized subjects reinforcing first, nondelusional behavior, next delusional behavior, and finally nondelusional behavior again. The cumulative frequency of psychotic responses was measured from 180 to 500 days in naturally initiated interactions by nurses who limited their conversations with residents to three minutes. Psychotic verbalizations were specifically defined for one resident as references to "queen," "king," and "the royal family." High frequncy somatic references, such as "I can't hear," "I'm going to die," and "I've got gas in my stomach," were measured in two other residents. Results were consistent with earlier findings by Lindsley (1956; 1959) indicating that psychotic verbal behavior can be influenced by controlling its consequences.

Using broader response categories, Ullmann, Forsman, Kenny, McInnis, Unikel, & Zeisset (1965) measured the percentage of "sick" talk (% ST) or "healthy" talk (% HT) during semistructured 20-minute interviews with schizophrenic inpatients. The first and last five minutes of each 20-minute interview were independently rated by the examiner and two raters; one of the raters conducted separate interviews with the subjects. Interrater reliability coefficients (product-moment correlations) ranged between 0.62 and 0.70 for composite % ST scores; differences between raters failed to reach statistical significance. Thus the measure appeared quite useful. Later studies by Meichenbaum (1966, 1969) utilized Ullmann et al.'s broad definition of ST to study the effects of prolonged training with social and token reinforcement on abstract thinking and language behavior in schizophrenics. Meichenbaum and Cameron (1973) trained schizophrenic subjects to talk to themselves first overtly, then covertly, to develop attentional controls and appropriate thinking, speech, and language as measured by a variety of tasks. These tasks included proverb interpretation, word association, and digit-span performance tests as pre-post dependent measures of attentional control and "healthy" thinking and language behavior. Interestingly, both Ullmann et al. and Meichenbaum and Cameron sought to concurrently validate direct behavioral measures with indirect performance measures.

Other researchers using experimental single-subject interventions have by-passed indirect measures and used relatively naturalistic methods to define and assess delusional and nondelusional verbal behavior. Wincze, Leitenberg, and Agras (1972) investigated the effects of feedback and token reinforcement on the delusional responses of 10 chronic paranoid schizophrenics using a series of single-subject designs. Inpatients' verbal behavior was measured in three situations. In the first situation (training sessions with a therapist) each subject was asked a series of 15 questions designed to evoke delusional responses. These questions were randomly drawn each day from a pool of 105 questions that dealt specifically with that subject's "known" delusional verbalizations. Each response was judged either "delusional" or "nondelusional" by the therapist and later by an independent rater, using audiotape recordings of 25 percent of the sessions. In the second assessment situation each subject's verbal behavior was recorded on the ward by nursing staff in 20 randomly scheduled three-minute time samples each day. In the third assessment situation interviews were conducted by fourth-year psychiatric residents unfamiliar with the experiment. These interviews were recorded after each phase of the study. Token reinforcement showed more consistency than feedback in reducing the percentage of delusional verbal behavior in the schizophrenic population studies. However, the independent interview ratings did not reliably detect changes in overall mental status or in delusional speech that could be specifically correlated with changes evidenced in the training sessions.

Thus the effects of training did not appear to generalize beyond the ward to other situations.

In a multiple baseline design Liberman, Teigen, Patterson, and Baker (1973) found that the duration to onset of delusional speech in four chronic paranoid schizophrenics could be increased by contingent termination of conversation as soon as delusional speech occurred. Four 10-minute interviews were conducted each day to train increases in rational conversation. Delusional topics and statements were predetermined for each subject; unstructured conversations with a nurse focused on questions of demographic fact or attitudes concerning hospital and home living situations. To test for generalization, Liberman et al. (1973) measured the frequency of delusional speech expressed to nurses, and the duration of rational, delusional, and silence behavior during evening chats with a favorite nurse over coffee and "goodies." No generalization of treatment effects was detected between interviews and ward speech or evening chats. One of the subjects from this study subsequently received further training in the hospital, and following discharge, in a community care home (Patterson & Teigen, 1973). Some generalization was found, but the authors concluded that the subject had learned to give evasive answers in place of her previous bizarre responses to factual questions. This implies that the absence of generalization in verbal behavior may present a major problem for clinicians attempting to change delusional speech directly.

Hallucinatory Behavior

Determining what delusional speech is has presented many problems for behavioral assessment. In comparison the measurement of hallucinatory responses is even more challenging, encompassing problems in the reliability and validity of self-report measures. Hallucinatory behaviors include a range of auditory and visual experiences that are primarily observable by the client. However, in an exploratory study Lindsley (1960) found that in a lever-pulling task the performance of chronic psychotic subjects was incompatible with hallucinatory behaviors. In this study hallucinations were defined as nonverbal and verbal responses to stimuli ("things" or "voices") not actually present. Whenever the subjects experienced a hallucinatory psychotic episode, they exhibited considerable latency (a pause) in their reinforced motor responses. Lindsley found that contingent mild punishment (social disapproval by a nurse) produced a decrease in the pauses and a considerable increase in operant lever pulling.

A series of uncontrolled case studies have sought to decrease self-monitored hallucinatory behavior. Butcher and Fabricatore (1970) treated a subject with self-administered punishment, using a portable shock device to reduce his disturbing hallucinatory voices. The successful elimination of the voices did not generalize to extratherapeutic settings. In a case study by Slade (1972) hallucinatory behaviors were sampled on 53 occasions across three weeks by an 18-year-old outpatient using an auditory hallucinations record form. Assessment included an attempt to relate patient mood rating and environmental variables to auditory hallucinatory behavior. From these records tension and situationally elicited anxiety were found to occur at times when hallucinations were present. Treatment then consisted of systematic desensitization for specific situations encountered in his family and home life. Other uncontrolled studies have used self-monitored frequency records of daily hallucinations to assess the efficacy of social reinforcement (Rutner & Bugle, 1969), covert punishment (Moser, 1974), and assertive training combined with social reinforcement (Nydegger, 1972) for reducing the frequency of hallucinations. Haynes and Geddy (1973) used interval recording of 10-minute staff and resident conversation sessions, divided into 60 10-second periods, to assess the suppressive effect of a time-out procedure for hallucinations. They focused on observable characteristics, defining hallucinations as any verbal behavior that was not in response to or directed toward identifiable environmental stimuli.

In a case study using multiple measures Anderson and Alpert (1974) collected both self-report and indirect measures of hallucinatory behavior. Self-reported frequency and "density," a measure of the duration of hallucinations, was recorded by the subject during a series of one-hour interviews with the experimenter using a switch to deflect the pen on a polygraph. The indirect measures consisted of (1) observers rating the "density" of hallucinations on a 1 to 10 scale with hallucinations defined by the occurrence of concomitant breathing and facial mannerisms or rituals and (2) the duration required for completion of morning activities, presumably because of the interference of compulsive rituals related to hallucinations.

The difficulty clinical researchers have experienced in reaching common definitions of complex hallucinatory and delusional behavior may well be related to the reliability and validity of measuring a behavioral-psychological "construct." Large-scale studies suggest that the practice of viewing delusions or hallucinations as discrete phenomena that are either present or absent in a given patient may be invalid (Mosher & Feinsilver, 1973). With these complex phenomena it may be necessary to seek convergent indices in hypothetically related measures as suggested in studies of stress and fear (e.g., Lacey, 1967; Lang, 1968). Delusional and hallucinatory behaviors may thus be conceptualized and assessed by concurrent measurements of three interrelated but independent response systems: (1) verbal-cognitive (e.g., cognitive performance and self-report measures), (2) behavioral-motoric, (3) and physiological-autonomic. A few investigators have measured both verbal-cognitive and motoric behaviors (e.g., Anderson & Alpert, 1974; Meichenbaum, 1969), but researchers have generally ignored the validity of their measures and failed to observe multiple responses in assessing or modifying hallucinatory or delusional behavior. The analysis of interrelationships among these measures can utilize the methodology of multimethod convergent validation (Campbell & Fiske, 1959). Multimethod analysis, however, does not obviate the need for a behavioral assessment of response generalization across time, situation, and setting.

Assessing Conversation and Social Interaction

Reinstating Speech

Mutism or the apparent refusal to talk is frequently characteristic of some psychotic individuals. Behavioral attempts to increase verbalizations have largely been confined to case studies (e.g., Isaacs, Thomas, & Goldiamond, 1960; Sabatasso & Jacobson, 1970; Sherman, 1963, 1965) and studies (e.g., Baker, 1971; Wilson & Walters, 1966) using a small number of subjects. These investigators have simply measured the cumulative frequency of words spoken in response to controlled and naturalistic stimuli or the percentage of questions answered in structured groups or interviews. Event records of the amount of speech in mute or near mute schizophrenics are relatively easy to obtain with a tape recorder under controlled conditions. The measurement of speech in the natural environment is more difficult, and most studies fail to report data for assessing generalization.

Increasing Verbal and Conversational Response Classes

Low frequencies of verbal and social interaction characteristic of many hospital residents has generally been measured by recording discrete or globally defined classes of verbal and nonverbal social behavior. Hauserman, Zweback, and Plotkin (1972) and Liberman (1972), for example, simply measured the frequency of speech initiation, regardless of content, in patient conversation groups.

The content of a patient's speech, representing a generally defined class of verbal behavior, has been studied by many behavioral researchers. Davison (1969) has reviewed much of the earlier work in modifying verbal behavior of institutionalized individuals, and the reader is referred to his review. Recent studies indicate that investigators tailor their measures to the purposes of their specific interventions. For example, some researchers have sought to alter discrete words or classes of verbalization with limited response possibilities. Kale, Kaye, Whelan, and Hopkins (1968) measured the rate of "prompted" and "spontaneous" greeting responses (e.g., "hi" or "hello") in 30-second staff and resident contacts spaced at least 10 minutes apart. Greetings were reinforced with cigarettes and social praise. Later, promptings and reinforcement were experimentally faded to simulate normal interaction. O'Brien, Azrin, and Henson (1969) sought to increase the number of direct suggestions and reports made by residents for feasible improvements in their ward treatment program. During individual and group sessions with professionals, the residents' suggestions and requests were reiterated by a staff member, affirmed by the resident, and recorded by an independent transcribing secretary. Three ward attendants independently scored the secretarial transcripts. Kale et al. found that the number of suggestions made was a direct function of the number of prior suggestions reinforced (followed) by ward staff. In an uncontrolled study Page and Copeland (1972) sought to increase clients' statements of opinion with implied prefaces of 'I think," "I feel," (e.g., "The ward is a really nice place") or informative statements of fact or rumor. Following an earlier study by Centers (1963), each of 38 psychiatric subjects had a brief informal chat with the experimenter. The first 10 minutes of this chat served as baseline and was followed by 20 minutes of nonspecific social reinforcement for target behavior. Tape recordings of the interview were independently scored by two listeners who tallied the three variables: the frequencies of information and opinon statements and their combined total.

In an attempt to assess the generalization of verbal conditioning to extratherapeutic conversation and activity, Tracey, Briddell, and Wilson (1974) manipulated positive statements about optional activities and about people by 12 chronic inpatients. During 45-minute group meetings held twice weekly, a group leader and an independent rater continuously recorded the subject speaking, the time interval (the first, second or third 15-minute segment of the 45 minutes), class of response (positive statements about people or about activities) and whether these verbalizations were spontaneous or prompted. Whereas both response classes increased with combined social and token reinforcement, positive statements about activities actually generalized to increased participation in ongoing ward activities. Positive statements about people failed to generalize to extragroup interactions. In these interactions verbatim transcripts were scored for positive, negative, or neutral responses to a single question: "How do you feel about the other people on the ward?" Positive responses included "any statement expressing affection, approval or liking" of others.

Wallace and Davis (1974) used an auditory signal following 10 consecutive seconds of conversation to reinforce verbal interchanges between two chronic patient dyads. The tone signaled the earning of one token, which could be accumulated toward purchasing candy, beer, or grounds privileges. Criticizing the asocial or nonfunctional focus of prior studies, Wallace and Davis measured the duration of eye contact and talk on directed topics (cars, current events, or sports) to assess the effects on residents' conversations of providing information, instructions, and reinforcement. Information consisted of providing three to four minutes for reading topic-related materials taken from that day's newspaper; this information was tested by a three-question multiple-choice exam on the material given immediately before the dyadic conversations. Reinforcement alone appeared to sustain conversation, measured by recording the total seconds of conversation across more than 50 sessions for each of the two dyads.

Social Interaction Skills

As suggested by Wallace and Davis (1974), conversations are part of the social repertoire needed to sustain chronic patients outside the institutional setting. A few researchers have combined verbal and nonverbal measurement and treatment procedures for "deinstitutionalizing" or "renormalizing" the interactions of chronic psychotics. Some of these interventions have focused on increasing the amount of social interaction in withdrawn and apathetic residents. Milby (1970) measured the percentage of daily two-minute time samples during which extremely withdrawn subjects were talking to, working with, or playing with residents or staff. Staff were successfully trained to use verbal and nonverbal social reinforcement to increase residents' social behavior. A recent study by Stahl, Thomson, Leitenberg, and Hasazi (1974) utilized individualized definitions of social behavior to establish praise as a conditioned reinforcer in three socially unresponsive psychiatric patients. The investigators measured the number of words uttered by the first patient in conversations with the experimenter, the percentage of his eye contact, and ratings of his personal appearance. Appropriate conversation, eye contact, and personal appearance were targeted in the second subject, and positively oriented statements (sampled from tape recordings divided into 10-second intervals), work performance, and latency of responding served as social measures of the third subject. The investigators found that social praise acquired reinforcing properties after continuous pairing with token reinforcers. Using similar measures, Bennett and Maley (1973) modified interactive behavior by making reinforcement contingent on one patient's responding appropriately to another patient. One patient dyad and a pair of control subjects attended 10 30-minute treatment sessions in which signaled reinforcement was tied to the duration of talking to another, paying attention, asking questions, and answering questions. Each of the response classes was observable to the target subject through the use of four signal lights on a control panel.

Bennett and Maley utilized a duration and interval recording system in which the duration of signal illumination tied to subject behavior was recorded by an observer in consecutive 5-minute segments. The results indicated a strong contingent reinforcement effect on the performance of target behaviors during treatment sessions. Bennett and Maley also presented evidence for generalization using three levels of measurement: direct observation, permanent products, and global ratings (staff perceptions) of change. Observers sampled for the presence or absence of audible patient to patient verbalizations on the ward in 20 daily one-minute observations throughout the study and found that only subjects reinforced contingently increased their daily interactions. Similar changes were evidenced in records of job earnings, activity earnings, and total token earnings. Selected rating scales from the Ellsworth MACC Behavioral Adjustment Scale and Psychotic Reaction Profile indicated that the treatment staffs' perceptions agreed with the other measures showing positive changes in the two experimental subjects.

The studies thus far reviewed derive from a laboratory conditioning model that uses instruction and contingent reinforcement to manipulate discrete classes of social interaction. Social skill training (e.g., Goldsmith & McFall, 1975; Gutride, Goldstein, & Hunter, 1973) represents a more naturalistic evaluation and treatment strategy for psychotic behavior. Social skill training is based on the technology of behavior rehearsal and role playing, modeling, social reinforcement, and instructional coaching and feedback. The problems and procedures characteristic of this model are reviewed by Hersen and Bellack (this volume). Three studies have focused on skill training in hospitalized schizophrenics. Gutride, Goldstein, and Hunter (1973) used modeling and role playing with instructions to increase social interaction among 133 acute and chronic asocial psychiatric inpatients in a state mental hospital. They used three kinds of measures to assess skill training: (1) "standard observations," consisting of unobtrusive ratings by an observer from behind a one-way mirror of eye contact, leaning toward and physical contact, initiating or responding to conversation, and 10 consecutive minutes of talk in a semistructured interaction with an experimental accomplice, (2) naturalistic observations, consisting of essentially the same rating measures made from a single 10-minute ward observation, and (3) staff and self-report rating instruments. Similar measures were used by Gutride, Goldstein, Hunter, Carrol, Clark, Furia, and Lower (1974) for assessing the social behaviors of chronic hospital residents at meal time.

The standard and naturalistic observations are methodologically identical to the verbal and conversations measures previously reviewed; they are grouped to afford an operational definition of a multiple response phenomenon—social interaction skills. However, when the focus in measurement changes from measuring discrete responses to measuring a multiple response phenomenon, problems in convergent and content validity are encountered (Johnson & Bolstad, 1973; Alevizos et al., Note 1). Gutride et al. (1973, 1974) approach this issue by collecting multilevel measures (semistructured interviews, naturalistic time-sampled observation, and both staff impression and subject self-report rating measures.) The authors report data from 65 ANOVAs comparing specific subscales on these four measures.

Goldsmith and McFall (1975) empirically developed their measures to assess interpersonal skill training in 36 male inpatients, including 18 schizophrenics. Although reliability and validity data were not yet available, the authors presented two related scales, the Interpersonal Situation Inventory (ISI) and the Interpersonal Behavior Role–Playing Test (IBRT). The first instrument, an empirically derived self-report measure, asks the subject to respond to 55 questions about social interactions by choosing one of five written responses that best characterizes his comfort and handling of that situation. Using items from the ISI, Goldsmith and McFall then devised the IBRT, in which items from the self-report instrument are used to create 25 simulated interpersonal situations that can be tape recorded. In pretests and posttests the IBRT tape provided stimulus situations for residents' role playing their responses; they were instructed to use the words they might use if they were in the actual situation. Role-played responses were rated on a 0- to 2-point scale of competence on which two points were scored if all the criteria of competence were manifest in the test situation. To these behavior rating scales they added a series of seven interaction tasks to assess generalization; these included a permanent product (number of performance tasks completed) and experimenter and subject self-ratings of comfort and competence in handling the tasks.

In the Gutride et al. (1973, 1974) and Goldsmith and McFall (1975) studies, the relationships among the multilevel measures are not explored. A current multimethod validation procedure using a behavior rating scale as its focus (cf. Mariotto & Paul, 1974) provides a more rigorous analysis of skill measurement. Despite these methodological issues, social or interpersonal skill measurement seems to be one of the more naturalistic, underdeveloped, and promising approaches to empirically assessing psychotic individuals.

MULTIDIMENSIONAL BEHAVIORAL ASSESSMENT

Although specific measures have been shown to be useful for the experimental analysis of psychotic behaviors, there is currently a need to expand the methodology of behavioral analysis to include multidimensional measures to assess living groups and educational or treatment programs for psychotic individuals. A multidimensional measure refers here to a direct or indirect recording system that incorporates a broad range of subject behavior into a finite number of categories. Direct multidimensional measures have been designed to study behavior in a variety of social settings including families (e.g., Jones, Reid, & Patterson, 1975), daycare centers (Cataldo & Risley, 1974; Doke & Risley, 1972), playrooms (e.g., Boer, 1968), and psychiatric wards (Hargreaves, 1969; Ittleson, Rivlin, & Proshansky, 1970; Paul, McInnis, & Mariotto, 1973; Schaefer & Martin, 1966, 1969).

The basis and impetus for developing multidimensional measures derive from three emerging forces. First, behavioral ecologists suggest two needs for multidimensional behavioral measures: (1) to detect unintended positive or negative changes in the behavioral repertoire of individuals receiving treatment to alter a specific target behavior and (2) to assess the effects of experimental-therapeutic interventions on the individual's social or environmental network (Willems, 1974). A second force emerges from the current social, political, and economic demand for accountability in treatment services, a demand that has necessitated a rapid development of program evaluation methodology. Presumably this methodology should include direct behavioral measurement at some point in its development or application. A third and more subtle impetus for expanded measures derives from the kind of methodological analysis needed to evaluate either service- or research-based treatment interventions. Behavior analysts have suggested that in using direct observational measures to assess interventions in natural settings we must demonstrate the accuracy, reliability, and validity of our measures (Johnson & Bolstad, 1973). Methodologically this is best done when a range of behaviors and settings are used to assess behavior change (see Cronbach, Gleser, Nanda, & Rajaratnam, 1973).

Behavioral-Ecological Assessment

The behavioral-ecological assessment of psychotic inpatients has usually consisted of recording multiple categories of behavior in relation to locations or treatment settings. Hunter et al. (1962) devised the Location-Activity Inventory (LAI) to measure the behaviors of 100 chronic schizophrenic males in relation to their environment (two wards of a large neuropsychiatric hospital.) The LAI was used to record four dimensions of patient ward behaviors: (1) geographical location, (2) position in relation to the wall, (3) posture or body disposition, and (4) activity or response to ward stimuli. Patients were observed in 14 successive locations specially mapped for two wards. Position codes noted body orientation:

against or facing walls, corners, or windows. Posture codes included sitting, standing, and walking. Activity codes consisted of 11 detailed classes of motor, verbal, nonverbal, and social related activities. Patient behavior was time sampled during 15 minutes each hour of a 12-hour day across each day for six months; each patient was observed for 10 seconds in unplanned order corresponding to the location observed. The authors report summary data as an objective means of assessing schizophrenic behavior. These data were found to correlate with Rorschach responses but were not correlated with phases of the moon ("lunacy") or prevailing meteorological conditions. Interrater agreement was assessed by contingency coefficients averaging over 0.78 for position, posture, and activity dimensions. Instrument reliability (0.91) was assessed by an odd-even correlation across observational sessions, corrected for attenuation. No attempt was made to determine the validity of the instrument for assessing behavioral or programmatic changes.

Schaefer and Martin (1966) subsequently devised a simpler format, the Behavioral Study Form (BSF), to study apathy in institutionalized schizophrenic inpatients. Behavior was coded into three general categories: (1) *mutually exclusive behaviors,* including sitting, standing, walking, and lying down; (2) *concomitant behaviors,* consisting of 13 specific behavior classes that could occur simultaneously (e.g., eating, rocking, talking to others), and (3) *location,* consisting of notations for five living areas. Apathy was operationally defined as the occurrence of one of five mutually exclusive behaviors with no concurrent (concomitant) behaviors. Schaefer and Martin (1969) later described the use of the BSF as a baseline measure and record-keeping system at Patton State Hospital, California. Nurses time sampled 140 ward patients every half hour, 30 times a day across two years. The data from mutually exclusive and concomitant categories served as a basis for identifying and evaluating treatment plans on a variety of inpatient behaviors. Although formal validity studies were not reported, the prior study (Schaefer & Martin, 1966) indicated that a behavioral-ecological scale could be sensitive to specific programmatic interventions. Using 40 patients randomly assigned to experimental and control groups, Schafer and Martin were able to show a reliable decrease in apathy in the experimental group by differential reinforcement (tokens) of three classes of behaviors—personal hygiene, work behaviors, and social interaction. Controls received a fixed amount of tokens noncontingently.

More recently, Harmatz et al. (Note 2) gathered objective naturalistic data on schizophrenic inpatients using an interval recording scale. These investigators devised the Behavior Observation System (BOS) to code the frequency and duration of 12 behavior categories using an electric 20-pen

(Esterline-Angus) event recorder. Two observers watched each of 77 patients for 10-minute intervals, randomly distributed across time of day and day of week. Results were reported in terms of the percentage of total time a given behavior was observed: (1) Null behaviors (50.8 percent) including "non-involvement" and "self-stimulatory" codes; (2) functional behaviors (28.5 percent), consisting of "passive" and "active entertainment"; (3) social behavior (8.1 percent) combining two verbal and one nonverbal interpersonal behavior categories, and (4) pathological behavior (2.3 percent) including 'bizarre" and "atavistic" behavior codes.

Behavioral-ecological measures have also been used by environmental psychologists interested in the effects of the physical setting on resident behavior. Ittleson, Rivlin, and Proshansky (1970) have studied the differing behavioral ecologies of three psychiatric hospitals. Ittleson et al. devised their instrument by first making narrative recordings of patient behavior and collapsing their observations into 18 categories of activity involving social and isolate behaviors. Using a time-sampling method, observers recorded six classes of behavior and the locations in which they were performed. The categories included the number of patients interacting with other people (social), interacting with their physical environment (active), or not interacting at all. The observations were used to provide an environmental map of the effects of different physical settings in hospitals on residents' behavior. For example, changes in behavior were measured in a city hospital solarium as a function of altering the furniture. Before the addition of new furniture, only 15 percent of social behavior and 33 percent of active behavior took place in the solarium. These figures rose to 27 percent and 55 percent, respectively, after the change. Act-by-act reliability figures are not given; instead, reliability figures are given by patient, by physical area, and across analytical categories. Agreement between observers is given for these as 83 percent, 84 percent, and 99 percent respectively. Holahan (1972) also used a coded observation format to study the behavioral effects of furniture arrangement in the day hall of a psychiatric hospital. Holahan and Saegert (1973) found that remodeling a treatment ward altered general classes of observed social and nonsocial behavior as well as attitudinal responses recorded in interviews with the experimenter.

Although direct observation made with a responsive instrument can detect changes in behavior resulting from changes in environment, it is evident that the wards studied did not emphasize learning of social, task-oriented behaviors. Social interactions in the Ittleson et al. (1970) investigation ranged from 12.2 percent to 27.9 percent in contrast to nonsocial activities, which range from 36.3 percent to 55.0 percent.

Programmatic Assessments

Most of the behavioral-ecological measures reviewed above ignore the methodological basis of time-sampled observational records. Behavior analysts of child-family interaction (e.g., Jones et al., 1975) and ward inpatient behavior (e.g., Alevizos et al., Note 1) have demonstrated the reliability of instruments that sample specific behaviors.

Behavioral-Ecological Procedures

Two behavioral-ecological instruments with demonstrated reliability and validity have very recently been derived from Schaefer and Martin (1966, 1969) to assess programmatic interventions. The Behavior Observation Instrument or BOI (Alevizos et al., Note 1) and the Time Sample Behavior Checklist or TSBC (Paul & Lentz, Note 3) were each designed to allow gathering of systematic information about the impact of programmatic changes on the behavior of residents in psychiatric living environments. Like the BSF, the BOI divides coded observations into three categories: (1) mutually exclusive behaviors (lying, sitting, standing, walking, running), (2) concomitant behaviors, including over 15 activities that can occur with mutually exclusive behaviors (e.g., smoking, conversation with staff), and (3) location, the physical location in which the resident is observed. The representativeness of BOI sampling schedules was determined in two ways. First, the optimal length of an observational interval was parametrically determined by comparing 1-, 5-, and 15-second observation intervals with a 30-second criterion. The optimal sampling frequency within and across days was also determined using 12 to 15 observations on each of 60 inpatients across 12 hours a day for two weeks (Alevizos & Callahan, Note 4). They found that two 5-second observations on a random single day each week could yield data consistent with longer intervals and with daily observations. Reactive effects of observation were also examined in another study by Callahan and Alevizos (Note 5). The frequency with which residents were observed with their eyes closed was the only behavior that demonstrated statistically significant increases with increased frequency of observations. Alevizos et al. (Note 1) used the BOI to evaluate the behavioral effects of service program changes. The day treatment center (DTC) programs of two community mental health centers were evaluated using a modified reversal and control group design. A change to an educational workshop format for treatment patients at one DTC was evaluated by assessing three behavior classes that combined certain concomitant categories of the BOI: social participation, nonsocial isolation, and work and task involvement. A significant increase in social participation and a concomitant decrease in nonsocial isolate behavior was demonstrated in comparison with the maintained milieu of the DTC. Although the workshop format showed the greatest magnitude of change, both programs improved. It was hypothesized that this was a "John Henry" reactive effect resulting from the control DTC staff's being aware that the two programs were being compared. The BOI was also used to assess a chemotherapeutic program change in a state hospital ward (Callahan, Alevizos, Teigen, Neuman, & Campbell, 1975). The behavioral effects of reducing the daily frequency of phenothiazine administration, with dosage held constant, were studied in a two-group multiple baseline design. Multivariate analyses of variance showed only that patients were more alert with changes in administration schedule. Alertness was operationally defined as the percentage of patients coded with their eyes open. The results of these two studies were interpreted as evidence that direct observation of the behavior ecology of patients in clinical treatment settings is a systematic and efficient means of evaluating change in institutional treatment programs.

The second instrument, the Time Sample Behavior Checklist (TSBC) (Paul & Lentz, Note 3), is currently being validated across patients and multiple treatment settings. Described in Mariotto and Paul (1974), the TSBC is used to sample inpatient behavior with a 2-second observation made each hour on each patient. The categories coded include, (1) location, (2) position, including lying or sitting on floor, bed, or on chair, (3) wake or asleep (eyes open or closed), (4) facial expression (smiling, laughing, frowning, or none of these), (5) social orientation (alone or with specific others), and (6) over different activities. The instrument is being used as part of an extensive evaluation of the comparative treatment effects of milieu and social learning treatment programs for chronic psychotic individuals.

Behavioral-ecological assessments of inpatient settings are also useful in assessing behaviors that cause people to be hospitalized and diagnosed as psychotic. These behaviors fall into a limited number of categories. Social interaction, the presence or absence of bizarre behaviors, and instrumental role performance are instrumental in determining whether a person is labeled and responded to as deviant or normal (Paul, 1969). The later studies reviewed indicate that these behaviors can be measured reliably and over extended periods to determine the effects of environmental treatment programs.

Other Observational Programmatic Assessments

Behavior analysts in nonpsychiatric settings have devised sampling procedures that deserve to be tested in assessing psychotic behavior treatment programs. Risley (Note 6) developed the Placheck as a behavioral assessment technique to evaluate programs in community and institutional settings. Observers using the Placheck made periodic recordings of the number of persons who were participating in the activity planned for a particular time. By manipulating program elements in a daycare center for children, such as posted schedules, furniture, and floor space arrangement, the authors demonstrated a decrease in inappropriate and nonproductive use of time by both children and staff. By designing and posting feeding time schedules, the researchers were also able to reduce crying time from 80 percent to 30 percent. Similarly, the researchers increased the amount of child-staff social interaction from 45 to 82 percent by making individual staff responsible for carrying out a series of planned, scheduled activities during the day. The Placheck system was thus able to show that high levels of participation were maintained by the proper sequencing of activities and by providing sufficient materials for those involved in the activities.

Cataldo and Risley (1974) describe the Resident Activity Manifest which contains measures of activity, interaction, and stimulation between individuals and elements in their therapeutic or living environments. The type of measure used, as well as the level of ongoing behavior, provide an index of the quality of a developmentally disabled treatment environment. The Resident Activity Manifest was shown to be sensitive to even small changes in the therapeutic environment and to be suitable for program evaluation purposes.

Permanent Products in Programmatic Assessment

Since their inception, token economies have received wide application in managing institutionalized psychotic behavior (cf. Atthowe & Krasner, 1968; Ayllon & Azrin, 1968). Many features and issues surrounding their use have been recently reviewed (e.g., Carlson, Hersen, & Eisler, 1972; Gripp & Magaro, 1974; Kazdin & Bootzin, 1972). Of brief interest here is that token economy records serve as permanent products of a broad range of behavior that can be utilized in programmatic assessments of resident psychotic behavior.

Although many experimental and economic variables in token systems are usually complex and difficult to control (see Gripp & Magaro, 1974; Kazdin, 1975; Winkler, 1971a, 1971b), token exchange patterns can be viable assessment tools in both individual and programmatic assessment. For example, the differential rate across time of token spending and token fines are important dependent variables in evaluating many aspects of a token economy (Winkler, 1972). Doty, McInnis, and Paul (1974) have used response cost records (recorded fines) on a token system to evaluate the utilization of reinforcers. Although a few clinical investigators report permanent product measures, the development of program evaluation in token economies seems to be overshadowed by the need to overcome problems in response maintenance and the transfer of training to less controlled settings (see Kazdin, 1975; Kazdin & Bootzin, 1972).

A variety of other permanent product measures may serve as indices of patient change and programmatic effectiveness. The proportion of eligible resident patients utilizing off-unit facilities was a primary measure reported by Curran, Lentz, and Paul (1973). Olson and Greenberg (1972) used the percentage of scheduled activities attended, passes for days on town, and days out of the program to compare milieu, milieu plus group therapy, and token reinforcement programs with chronic institutionalized mental patients. Birky, Chambliss, and Wasden (1971) assessed discharge rates and length of prior hospitalization in comparing a token economy and traditional ward care. Pomerleau, Bobrove, and Harris (1972) studied the impact of providing cash incentives to psychiatric aides for the improvement of pairs of refractory psychiatric inpatients over eight months. They made before and after assessments comparing the number and median length of stay of those residents still present, transferred, discharged, and eloped (changed to discharge after two weeks) to a weekly ward behavior rating scale. However, their study was uncontrolled and subject to methodological confounding as discussed by Kazdin (1975). Recently, Palmer and McGuire (1973) studied the relationship between 50 unobtrusive measures (including various behaviors) and four criteria of treatment effectiveness across 15 state hospital wards: (1) rate of readmission, (2) rate of discharge, (3) median days of hospitalization, and (4) administrator's ranking of treatment effectiveness for the 15 wards. Correlations of at least 0.50 ($p < 0.10$) were found between the four criteria and such unobtrusive measures as available daily showers, pieces of resident mail, number of residents on home visits, hours spent by family in group therapy, number of special incidents (fights), and number of residents wearing their own clothes.

Despite their face validity and simplicity, permanent product measures are influenced and confounded by many practical and methodological difficulties. The duration of current or previous hospitalization, for instance, can be misleading because it is affected by such variables as hospital administrative needs, treatment orientation of hospital staff, social class of the resident, the distance resident lives from the hospital, familial support, and the resident's instrumental role in the family (Strauss & Carpenter, 1972). Economic variables such as the price, accumulation rate, and spending rates of tokens may be related to satiation, modeling influences, or the availability of purchasable goods, privileges, and services. Furthermore, when "key" permanent products such as length of hospitalization are used to match research subjects in contrasting chronic patient groups, such variables do not necessarily relate to subjects' test performance or to ward behavior criteria (Rappaport, Chinsky, & Mace, 1972). However, permanent products can provide indices of critical outcome criteria such as work and social relations. When practical and methodological variables are controlled, permanent products may be used to help establish a multi-method convergent validation (Campbell & Fiske, 1959; Jackson, 1969) of change in psychotic resident behavior and of treatment program effectiveness. There is, therefore, a need to evaluate empirically the reliability and validity of permanent (behavioral) product measures in assessing psychiatric residents.

Indirect Behavior Measures

Psychotic Behavior Rating and Interview Scales

A number of indirect measures such as interviews and rating scales have frequently been used to assess the ward behavior of psychotic residents (e.g., Hargreaves, 1969; Honigfield, 1966; Lorr & Klett, 1966; Wittenborn, 1955). Behavioral researchers have generally characterized indirect measures as methodologically weak, inadequate, and vulnerable to major interpretative difficulties. Indirect assessments are also thought to be less accurate than direct observational procedures (Goldfried & Kent, 1972; Mischel, 1972).

Recently, it has been shown that when individuals are asked to record targeted behaviors, the validity of their concomitant general ratings increases when compared to criterion observational records (Wahler & Leske, 1973). Given the expense entailed in collecting most observational data and the interest of administrators and clinicians in the self-report of both staff and residents, researchers have begun to reevaluate the use of specified indirect measures. Rappaport and Chinsky (1970) reported that behavior ratings of psychiatric residents on the Ellsworth MACC Behavioral Adjustment Scale (Ellsworth, 1962) showed significant cross-situational and cross-rater agreement; they concluded that the scale tapped relatively stable components of resident behavior. Their pre-post design was not controlled, and no attempt was made to assess the generalizability of treatment across time. In a controlled study Mariotto and Paul (1974) found that another common rating scale, the Inpatient Multidimensional Psychiatric Scale or IMPS (Lorr & Klett ,1966) was reliable but not valid for assessing change when compared to a structured interview and a direct behavior measure, the TSBC.

Certain multidimensional rating and interview scales may nevertheless serve as convergent indices of behavior outcome and treatment effectiveness. Lentz, Paul, and Calhoun (1971) demonstrated that reliable and valid measures could be obtained from three such indirect measures. They analyzed the behavior of 137 chronic psychotic inpatients using (1) the Nurses Observational Scale of Inpatient Evaluation (NOSIE-30) (Honigfeld, 1966) in which two nurses are asked to rate specific patient behaviors over the prior three days, (2) the Social Breakdown Syndrome Gradient Index (SBSGI) (Gruenberg, Brandon, & Kasius, 1966), a questionnaire in which staff rate the frequency of occurrence of specific behaviors in an institutional setting during the prior week, and (3) the Minimal Social Behavior Scale (MSBS), modified from Farina, Arenberg, and Guskin (1957). The modified MSBS is an interesting structured behavioral interview in which the rater's verbal and nonverbal behavior during the interview is designed to elicit easily ratable verbal and performance responses from the client. Lentz et al. (1971) found high interrater reliabilities for all three instruments. Intercorrelations among the three measures evidenced a common factor, supporting their validity and indicating that additional information was added by each instrument. Lentz et al. concluded that in combination the three indirect measures provided an efficient, reliable, and valid battery for assessing "global level of functioning" in hard core chronically hospitalized patient groups. Lentz and Paul (1971) then used the NOSIE-30 and the SBSGI to compare the effects of interinstitutional transfer in three groups of chronic mental patients. Paul, Tobias, and Hally (1972) also used the SBSGI, the NOSIE-30, and the MSBS to assess the effects of maintenance psychotropic drugs, abrupt withdrawal, and placebo medication on 52 hard core mental patients. In a "triple blind" controlled study they found that except in the early stages of treatment, where drugs interfered with treatment, continued low-dosage maintenance chemotherapy failed to produce direct effects or to contribute to responsiveness to environmental treatment programs.

The utility of these selected indirect measures for behavioral analysis was more carefully demonstrated in Mariotto and Paul (1974), who found that the raw score totals from the NOSIE-30, the SBSGI, and the MSBS correlated between 0.54 and 0.75 with the total scores on a direct observational measure, the TSBC, sampled on each of 80 inpatients for 10 seconds each waking hour. We are inclined to agree with Paul and his colleagues that the advantages and efficiency of selected indirect instruments can more readily be appreciated when they have been rigorously compared to direct behavior measures.

Assessing the Treatment Environment

The importance of situational and environmental influences on psychotic behavior and the utility of certain indirect measures in programmatic evaluations are demonstrated in two recent scales, the Ward Atmosphere Scale (WAS) and the Community Oriented Programs Environment Scale (COPES).

The WAS (Moos & Houts, 1968) is a 100-item true-false instrument developed to assess a psychiatric ward's social environment as perceived by patients and by staff on 10 dimensions reflecting (1) *relationship variables* (e.g., involvement in the program, support from staff, encouragement of spontaneous action and affect, and expression of anger and aggression), (2) *treatment program variables* (e.g., autonomy and self-direction, practical orientation and release preparation, and focus on understanding personal problems), and (3) *administrative structure variables* (e.g., activity planning and organization, program clarity, and staff control). Moos (1972) found that the WAS differentiated between psychiatric wards with high profile stability over several months. The instrument was standardized on a national sample of 160 psychiatric wards, and a variety of extensive outcome studies have been reported (see Moos, 1974). Wiggins (Note 7) recently demonstrated that the WAS could be used as an independent predictor of ward behavior apart from other self-report or rating scales.

Moos (1972) revised the WAS, renamed it the COPES, and used it to assess community treatment programs such as halfway houses, residential care homes, rehabilitation centers, and daycare programs. The COPES-Form C is a 102-item true-false measure with 10 subscales labeled identically to the WAS. Its effectiveness was reported by Moos (1972, 1974). Milby, Pendergrass, and Clarke (1975) have also demonstrated its utility in evaluating staff and patient attitudes toward ward environment on token economy and control wards. Both the WAS and COPES have been carefully developed and standardized; each possesses considerable promise for interpreting and extending data from direct behavioral measures in evaluating behavioral treatment programs.

The Behavioral Performance Test

The bulk of research involving behavioral measures for psychosis has selected individual behaviors for measurement and ignored the issue of whether the resident individual changes on some range of psychotic behaviors. Measures of these specific behaviors have shown that they do respond to behavioral intervention. However, this line of research has not produced a single behavioral assessment instrument to assess the global performance of individuals.

For these reasons the Behavioral Performance Tests were designed by us and initially tested by our co-workers and ourselves at Camarillo State Hospital between 1973 and 1975. The Behavioral Performance Tests

(BPT) are a series of *observation based* tests that can be conducted by staff members and professionals. They cover a variety of critical patient behaviors, including six major areas of functioning:

1. Unusual behavioral incidents (low-frequency unusual behavior).
2. Aggressive behavioral incidents.
3. Self-care assessments.
4. Work behaviors.
5. High-frequency unusual behaviors.
6. Verbal interaction.

These selected areas of patient behavior match Paul's (1969) list of critical behaviors of residents labeled as chronic psychotic and also include behaviors most frequently cited in nursing notes, patient progress summaries, and observations on hospital units. The BPT assesses the functioning of each patient along these variables and can be used as (1) a baseline to determine the severity of the psychotic problem of the individual at the point of institutionalization, (2) any change in behavior of the individual with the introduction of a particular treatment, and (3) the effectiveness of a given program, given the amount of change across individuals within that program. This chapter will describe how six subareas of the BPT were developed and implemented with clients at the Hospital Improvement Project at Camarillo State Hospital.

Description of the Instrument

Aggression and unusual behavior. The first two BPT scales—Aggression and Low-Frequency Unusual (LFU) Incidents—are recorded in a nursing log or daybook (event) recording every observed occurrence of the target behaviors. Both aggression and low-frequency unusual behavioral incidents occur infrequently, which makes it necessary and economical to record each observed occurrence of the behavior for the purpose of greater accuracy.

Low-frequency unusual incidents include any type of psychotic behavior that does not occur on a regular basis with the client (i.e., episodes of inappropriate sexual behavior, delusional speech, hallucinations, pseudo-epileptic seizures, etc.) Low-frequency unusual behaviors are generally defined as any infrequent behavior that may cause problems outside the hospital setting or that appear abnormal for the individual or resident group in the hospital setting.

In standardizing the behaviors listed, common incidents were culled from daybooks of hospital units in two patient programs (Psychiatric Rehabilitation and Research). Others have factor analyzed incident reports and have found similar categories (see Evenson, Sletten, Altman, & Brown,

1974). Narrative observations of aggressive and unusual behaviors were also conducted to help establish observation categories. The use of predefined categories such as incontinence, pacing, rocking, overactivity, and the like allows on-line staff to record and tabulate incidences rapidly. Along with checking a category the staff can record time and place and can write a brief note of the observed antecedents and consequences of the recorded behavior(s). *Aggressive Behavioral Incidents,* including physical or verbal assaults on others or on oneself, are recorded on the other half of the daybook form. Information related to each aggressive incident is entered in the same way that unusual behavioral incidents are recorded. In this procedure an observer writes in the date and time of day, checks off the appropriate box describing the aggressive behavioral incident, and finally records the antecedents and consequences of the acting-out behavior. In this way both aggressive incidents and unusual incidents can be used to create a behavioral program to manage these problems. These behaviors are summarized once a month in the client's chart. A frequency count in each category is then available so that the staff can evaluate the program's effectiveness for the individual.

Self-Care Assessment. Four behaviors were selected as critical indices of the level of skill of residents in caring for themselves: toileting, eating, bathing, and grooming. These behaviors are directly observed by staff members and rated on a four-point scale. The four rating points are: 0—no help required; 1—verbal prompting required; 2—physical or both verbal and physical help required; and 3—complete care required. Each of these behaviors, except bathing, is observed three times over a five-day interval. For bathing, residents are observed on the first two scheduled showers of the month. At the end of the rating period, results are summed and placed in the residents' charts.

Assessment procedures vary slightly across specific self-care behaviors. For example, in dressing, the staff member records how much help the client required *after* the resident dresses in the morning or at night. If the staff member reminds the resident to start or to finish dressing, or tells him which articles of clothing to wear, verbal prompting is checked. If the resident must be helped in some limited fashion with dressing (i.e., tying shoes, laying out clothes, fastening buttons, etc.), a staff member checks the item "verbal prompting and some physical assistance." "Complete care" indicates that physical assistance was required with each article of clothing as the person dressed.

Eating, on the other hand, is observed three times a day—once at each scheduled mealtime for three nonconsecutive days. Staff members rate the client's grooming, however, on alternate days over the first five days of the month. Each self-care behavior has its own master data sheet. Data are recorded every month on a regular data sheet and then transferred to the master data sheet. Later, average weights are assigned to the amount of care that each client required during observation for each self-care behavior. Thus the client can be rated from 0 to a total of 16 points, indicating the degree of care required. This total score can then be compared from one month to the next across a client's stay in an institution. Comments on the observation sheets are available for incorporation into nursing or progress notes for potential use in treatment programming.

Psychosis is often defined in terms of an individual's relatedness to reality; in other terms, relatedness to reality is measurable by the amount and quality of social interaction and the amount of distracting and interfering behavior. The next section of the BPT is concerned with the measurement of the amount of interaction and distracting behaviors; a later section taps quality of interaction through the assessment of verbal behavior.

Work Behavior. If the resident is engaged in a remunerated or therapeutic work assignment, work behaviors can be assessed by a direct supervisor using one of two instruments. The Work Behavior Questionnaire (WBQ) (Tarlow, Alevizos, & Lafey, Note 8), a 26-item instrument on which staff are asked to circle "true" sentences describing behavioral characteristics of the resident individual's work performance as observed on a particular day. The WBQ is used for at least five consecutive work days each month. The Work Behavior Coding System (WBCS) (Tarlow & Alevizos, Note 9), is a multicategory direct observation coding instrument that records verbal interaction, aggression, unusual behavior, and task behavior.

In a study of the concurrent validity of the WBQ, the work behavior of 14 female and 10 male residents was assessed for a single work day in five hospital settings: (1) waiting on counters at the hospital canteen, (2) assembling goods in a hospital workshop, (3) mending and sewing clothing articles in the sewing room, and (4) cleaning up and landscaping with the grounds crew. Two observers recorded the behavior of two residents using the WBCS for a full workday. At the end of a work day the direct supervisor of each observed resident was asked to complete two instruments, the WBQ and the Occupational Therapy Trait Rating Scale (OTTRS) (Clark, Koch, & Nichols, 1965). The latter instrument is a standardized and behavioral trait rating scale using factor analysis. Intercorrelations using product moment coefficients were 0.85 (df $= 16, p < 0.01$) with the WBQ and 0.53 ($df = 16, p < 0.05$) with the OTTRS (Tarlow & Alevizos, Note 9). Further studies of the interrelation between these instruments are indicated before the work assessment scale of the BPT can be recommended for further use.

High-Frequency Behaviors. In the case of high-frequency behaviors staff members record the amount of social interaction, solitary activity, task behavior and "self-stimulation" a resident engages in in the hospital ward environment. Ten brief observations are conducted on each resident by a staff member on two nonconsecutive days. This sampling was found to provide a statistically accurate record of client behavior in comparison to 50 samples spread over a one-week period (Campbell, Wallace, & Maggiani, Note 10). In each of these observations the staff member is instructed to watch the resident for a 10-second period and then to code the behavior of the resident for the presence of the following behaviors:

SC—Social Activity. Conversation or participation in a structured or unstructured recreational or work activity with one or more persons (essentially interaction with others).

SI—Solitary Activity. Resident is observed to be independently involved in a functional activity such as reading, writing, watching TV, working on crafts projects, studying, playing an instrument, and the like.

T—Instrumental Task. Resident is engaged in behaviors that contribute to the resident's personal maintenance or to that of the ward. Grooming, dressing, bed making, bathing, sweeping, folding laundry, and so on are behaviors included in this category, provided that the resident is performing these tasks—rather than observing their occurrence. If the resident is being bathed, dressed, or the like, this is not recorded as performance of instrumental tasks but is recorded as non-functional behavior.

P—Unusual Posture. Any unusual bodily contortions held for three seconds or more involving arms, legs, and/or shoulder or trunk body parts. For example, holding arms over head, leaning far to one side, slumping far over, and so on.

M—Repetitive Motor Activity. Any unusual or repetitive body movements of the face (grimacing), arms (such as waving hands in front of face), or legs. Also included in this category are gross motor activity of larger parts of the body or the entire body (rocking, swaying, walking in circles). Pacing is coded as repetitive motor activity if a complete turn is made during the 10-second observation. Repetitive motor activity must have no observable effects on the patient's environment.

V—Unusual verbal behavior. Audible verbalizations (noise, words, sentences) that are not conversation with another resident. (Conversation would define "social activity.") Examples are repetitive and nondirected verbal activity.

NA—Not available for observation. Resident was not on the unit at designated time for observation.

Prior to each observation, a list of residents is randomly arranged. One staff member then observes each resident on the list in order. During the observations, the staff member is instructed to remain as inconspicuous as possible.

One or more of the above codes is then listed on the individual resident's data sheet. Staff members are instructed not to record behavior that does not fall into the 10-second observation interval. However, any behavior that occurs for any duration during the 10-second interval is recorded.

After two days of observation, data are combined and placed on a master data sheet in each individual's chart by summing the number of coded observations on each particular resident and entering that number in the master data sheet. Then the frequency of individual codes per total number of observations is registered as the critical data.

Verbal Interaction. The *Verbal Report Form* is designed to assess disorders in a person's verbal interactions. The resident is interviewed informally for two minutes by one nursing staff member and one professional staff member. Each then rates the interaction independently.

Prior to going through the interview with the client, the staff member reviews the categories that will describe the verbal interaction. Following the completion of the interaction, the staff member then codes each aspect of the person's speech into one of three categories: (1) appropriate, (2) questionable, or (3) inappropriate.

Speech is rated appropriate if, in the opinion of the rater, it would not cause the person any problem in adjustment to the community at large. The questionable category, on the other hand, is used when the rater is unsure whether this speech pattern would cause the person a problem in the community. Inappropriate is used if the rater is *sure* this speech characteristic would cause the person a problem in community adjustment. Staff members are warned not to rate the person any more or less severely because of the amount of medication he is taking. In this way, the actual verbal behavior of the client in the interview is what is critical in the rating—not how the client should be expected to speak.

Rated aspects of speech include speech patterns, content, and nonverbal interaction; each is scored for the amount of pathology found. A sum is found for each of these subareas, and these are summed to provide a score for the entire verbal report form. The greater the pathology for the individual, the higher the sum of this score. The two sets of verbal report form ratings (by the staff and professional person) are then summed on the patient's master data sheet. The recording is done in subareas of speech content, nonverbal and other problems, and a total verbal report form score. From month to month it is possible to check to see whether any of the subareas has changed in its overall rating or whether the total verbal report form score has changed significantly with treatment.

The verbal report form has been assessed in several ways (Tarlow, Alevizos, & Callahan, in press). Three major questions addressed were: (1) What length of interview is necessary for the reliable and valid assessment of verbal speech patterns? (2) What is the accuracy of trained raters? and (3) What is the contribution of the training of observers and the type of client observed?

For the first question, three different interview lengths were tested using videotape samples of clients' behaviors: 30 seconds, two minutes, and five minutes. The amount of information on speech pathology found with each of these rating intervals was then compared. It was found that the two-minute rating interval provided the most reliable and valid description of the verbal detraction pattern of the client.

The second question involved determining the accuracy of raters. Eight raters (one psychologist, one social worker and six B.A.-level research assistants) were shown a series of videotapes that had been preprogrammed to include speech pathology. There were fifteen "bits" of pathology that a panel of three clinicians agreed were present in these videotape recordings. The accuracy of the raters was then tested by showing speech segments and determining how frequently each rater reported the pathology that was programmed into the particular tapes. A high level of accuracy was found for the eight raters, ranging from 85 to 95 percent across raters, with a mean percentage over 90 percent. Thus the scale shows sensitivity to pathology in speech.

Finally, Tarlow et al. compared three types of raters: trained clinicians, professional level staff members (i.e., nursing staff), and laypersons. The amount of pathology rated by each of these groups was then tested. It was found that the trained clinicians reported less pathology than any other group, followed by the laypeople, followed by the nursing staff personnel. This may relate to role expectations placed on clinicians and on nursing staff members. In this same study the ratings of these three groups of raters were compared across three populations as well: (1) normal (nonhospitalized laypersons), (2) persons living in a board-and-care facility, and (3) hospitalized schizophrenics. It was found that the amount of pathology found in each of these populations increased according to the state of diagnosis. That is, community persons were found to have little or no speech pathology, board-and-care facility individuals were found to have an intermediate level of speech pathology, and hospitalized psychotics had the greatest reported pathology in their speech. Thus the verbal report form apparently is a valid and accurate descriptor of speech pathology. It remains to be shown whether the VRF is capable of picking up changes in the speech pathology of an individual across time. If it is not, the problem may lie with the raters, or it may be a problem with the sensitivity of an instrument.

CONCLUSION

As has been apparent throughout this review, behavioral assessment of psychosis now rests at a relatively primitive level of development and application. To date, behavioral assessment of psychotics has most often been conducted to provide dependent measures in research designs testing the effects of treatment variables. Little work has actually been directed toward the development and validation of behavioral assessment techniques for widespread clinical use.

An immediate concern in the behavior assessment of psychosis is the need to establish a sound methodological base for clinical evaluation. Johnson and Bolstad (1973) have clearly shown that applied behavior analysts need to examine the reliability, validity, and accuracy of their measures for clinical populations in the natural environment. The *reliability* of a few behavioral assessment instruments has been assessed only in inpatient (e.g., Alevizos et al., Note 1) and family settings. (e.g., Johnson & Bolstad, 1973). These studies assess the stability of behavior measures using intraclass correlations between odd and even days of observation. *Sampling frequency* should also be empirically determined by choosing a sampling schedule and observation interval (e.g., once a day for one hour) and assessing the schedule's direct influence on stability reliability coefficients (e.g., Patterson, Cobb, & Ray, 1973) or by correlating brief behavior samples (e.g., 10-second observations made twice weekly) with more extensive (e.g., daily 8-hour) observations (e.g., Alevizos & Callahan, Note 4). Alternatively, reliability and sampling considerations can be analyzed with reference to generalizability theory (Cronbach et al., 1970). The generalizability of observational data refers to the use of statistical analyses of variance to determine the representativeness of the data across different observers, settings, response classes, and other potentially confounding variables (see Wiggins, 1973). The *validity* of a behavioral measure of psychosis must also be considered in clinical and programmatic assessment. With multidimensional measures the choice of which behaviors are to be observed generally requires some content validation. If decisions are to be made regarding treatment or discharge, multidimensional and specific behavioral measures should also demonstrate some ability to predict behavior with reference to particular settings. The few published studies demonstrating validity in behavioral assessment have been those of Paul and his colleagues and those done in Oregon (e.g., Johnson & Bolstad, 1973; Jones et al., 1975). These studies have primarily involved concurrent or convergent validation (Campbell & Fisk, 1959) using behavior ratings and questionnaires to evaluate treatment outcome. Finally, the accuracy of behavior observations consists of the many variables related to the presence and performance of human observers. These variables are reviewed in part elsewhere (see Johnson & Bolstad, 1973).

Other major problems in psychotic behavior assessment relate to the diagnosis of psychosis and the diversity of behaviors exhibited in the disorder. Psychosis consists of not one but many different behaviors such that no simple description or assessment is adequate to the diversity of the problems presented. The psychotic behaviors of an individual are often accompanied by and are sometimes indistinguishable from several behaviors resulting from institutionalization. Assessment is further complicated as it becomes apparent that these behaviors occur under different stimulus conditions (such as home versus hospital, interacting with friends versus interacting with a coinhabitant). Ideally, clinical assessment of psychotic individuals should include not only a topography of specific behaviors but also a detailed description of the times, places, and conditions under which these behaviors occur. This goal exceeds the current capabilities of clinicians and institutions, although it is possible in terms of small-scale demonstration. The broad range of behaviors selected for assessment and change by behavioral reseachers suggests that we are currently assessing skills and excesses or deficits of individuals much more than we are assessing "psychosis" per se. If psychosis is analyzed in terms of the social acceptability of behavior it may be possible to help patients normalize their behavior and ultimately to reduce the stigma of the label "psychotic." Such a therapeutic goal would necessitate further development of a methodology for assessing the functional behaviors and social interaction skills of psychotic individuals. Functional and social behavior assessments can also be useful in analyzing the therapeutic effectiveness of psychotropic medication in treatment and residential care settings. There is also scant research that clearly defines the relative and exclusive contributions of drugs and learning experiences to psychotic behavior change (see as exceptions, Liberman & Davis, 1975; Paul et al., 1972). Such behavioral and pharmacological investigations require common dependent measures of specific and functional or social behaviors as are potentially provided in psychometrically base applied behavior analyses.

Our own attempt to develop a behavioral assessment scale for chronic psychotics yielded limited but interesting results. First, it was shown that a variety of methods can be used to functionally assess the behavior of individual residents. Second, despite some problems, methodological studies yielded some promising results. Third, the development and testing of the BPT has shown microcosmic evidence of the difficulty of persuading institutions (or even wards) to implement broad-scale behavior assessment. In this area lie most of the obstacles to full-scale testing of behavioral assessment.

Fortunately, more success has been found with other scales that rest directly or indirectly on a foundation of direct observation. These scales have shown their usefulness in the assessment of ward-wide behavior (the BOI and TSBC) and in ward atmosphere (the WAS). It seems likely that these and similar scales may provide more utility in the long-range development of applied program analysis. These assessment procedures provide low-cost and reliable data for program analysis, but they cannot fulfill the need for intensive analysis of the skills and deficits of the individual psychotic. In these cases behavioral clinicians must continue to improvise specific behavioral measures for individuals or devise multidimensional tests such as the BPT.

The greatest single need in this developing field is a comparison of behavioral and traditional assessment of individuals and the programs that comprise their treatment in terms of utility, cost, reliability, validity, and accuracy. Such an undertaking will be most difficult, but only such a test can establish the need for behavioral assessment in this field.

REFERENCE NOTES

1. Alevizos, P., DeRisi, W., Callahan, E., Eckman, T., & Liberman, R. P. *The Behavior Observation Instrument: A behavior assessment methodology for program evaluation.* Unpublished manuscript, 1975.
2. Harmatz, M. G., Mendelsohn, R., & Glassman, M. L. *Behavioral observations in the study of schizophrenia.* Paper presented to the 81st Annual Meeting of the American Psychological Association, Montreal, Quebec, Canada, August, 1973.
3. Paul, G. L., and Lentz, R. J. (Eds.) *Observational assessment instrumentation for institutional research and treatment.* In preparation.
4. Alevizos, P. N., & Callahan, E. J. *Observation instruments and the reliability of data sampling in direct patient observation.* Symposium paper presented to the 81st Annual Meeting of the American Psychological Association, Montreal, Quebec, Canada, August, 1973.
5. Callahan, E. J. & Alevizos, P. N. *Reactive effects of direct observation of patient behaviors.* Symposium paper presented to the 81st Annual Meeting of the American Psychological Association, Montreal, Quebec, Canada. August, 1973.
6. Risley, T. R. *Environmental organization: The impersonal control of behavior.* Paper presented at 4th Annual Meeting of the Southern California Conference on Behavior Modification, Los Angeles, 1972.

7. Wiggins, L. A. *The Ward Atmosphere Scale as a predictor of ward behavior*. Paper presented to the Western Psychological Association, Sacramento, April, 1975.
8. Tarlow, G., Alevizos, P. N., & Lafey, D. *The work behavior questionnaire: Concurrent validity*. Unpublished manuscript, 1975.
9. Tarlow, G., & Alevizos, P. N. *The work behavior coding system for psychiatric patients*. Unpublished manuscript, 1975.
10. Campbell, M. D., Wallace, C., & Maggiani, M. *A statistical analysis of sampling strategies for behavioral observations*. Manuscript in preparation.

REFERENCES

American Psychiatric Association, *Diagnostic and statistical manual of mental disorders*, 2nd ed., Washington, D.C.: American Psychiatric Association, 1968.

Anderson, L. T., Alpert, M. Operant analysis of hallucination frequency in a hospitalized schizophrenic. *Journal of Behavior Therapy and Experimental Psychiatry*, 1974, **5,** 13–18.

Atthowe, J. M., & Krasner, L. Preliminary report on the application of contingent reinforcement procedures (token economy) on a "chronic" psychiatric ward. *Journal of Abnormal Psychology*, 1968, **73,** 37–43.

Ayllon, T., & Azrin, N. *The token economy: A motivational system for therapy and rehabilitation*. New York: Appleton-Century-Crofts, 1968.

Ayllon, T., & Haughton, E. Modification of symptomatic verbal behavior or mental patients. *Behaviour Research and Therapy*, 1964, **2,** 87–97.

Ayllon, T., & Michael, J. The psychiatric nurse as a behavioral engineer. *Journal of the Experimental Analysis of Behavior*, 1959, **2,** 323–334.

Baker, R. The use of operant conditioning to reinstate speech in mute schizophrenics. *Behaviour Research and Therapy*, 1971, **9,** 329–336.

Bennett, P., & Maley, R. Modification of interaction behaviors in chronic mental patients. *Journal of Applied Behavior Analysis*, 1973, **6,** 609–620.

Birky, H. J., Chambliss, J. E., & Wasden, R. A comparison of residents discharged from a token economy and two traditional psychiatric programs. *Behavior Therapy*, 1971, **2,** 46–51.

Boer, A. P. Application of simple recording system to the analysis of free play in autistic children. *Journal of Applied Behavior Analysis*, 1968, **1,** 335–340.

Bostow, D. E., & Bailey, J. B. Modification of severe disruptive and aggressive behavior using brief time-out and reinforcement procedures. *Journal of Applied Behavior Analysis*, 1969, **2,** 31–37.

Butcher, B., & Fabricatore, J. Use of patient administered shock to suppress hallucinations. *Behavior Therapy*, 1970, **1,** 382–385.

Callahan, E. J., Alevizos, P. N., Teigen, T. T., Neuman, H., & Campbell, M. D. Behavioral effects of reducing the daily frequency of phenothiazine administration. *Archives of General Psychiatry*, in press.

Campbell, D. T., & Fiske, D. W. Convergent and discriminant validation by the multitrait-multimethod matrix. *Psychological Bulletin*, 1959, **56,** 81–105.

Carlson, C. G., Hersen, M., & Eisler, R. M. Token economy programs in the treatment of hospitalized adult psychiatric patients. *Journal of Nervous and Mental Disease*, 1972, **155,** 192–204.

Cataldo, M. F., & Risley, T. R. Evaluation of living environments: The MANIFEST description of ward activities. In P. O. Davidson, F. W. Clark, L. A. Hamerlynck (Eds.), *Evaluation of behavioral programs in community residential & school settings*. Champaign, Ill.: Research Press, 1974.

Centers, R. A laboratory adaptation of the conversational procedure for the conditioning of verbal operants. *Journal of Abnormal and Social Psychology*, 1963, **67,** 334–339.

Clark, J. R., Koch, B. A., & Nichols, R. C. A factor-analytically derived scale for rating psychiatric patients in occupational therapy. Part I., development. *American Journal of Occupational Therapy*, 1965, **19,** 14–18.

Cronbach, L. J., Gleser, G. C., Nanda, H., & Rajaratham, N. *The dependability of behavioral measurements*. New York: Wiley, 1970.

Curran, J. P., Lentz, R. J., & Paul, G. L. Effectiveness of sampling-exposure procedures on facilities utilization by psychiatric hardcore chronic patients. *Journal of Behavior Therapy and Experimental Psychiatry*, 1973, **4,** 201–207.

Davison, G. C. Appraisal of behavior modification techniques with adults in institutional settings. In C. M. Franks (Ed.), *Behavior therapy: Appraisal and status*, 1969, 220–278.

Depue, R. A., & Dubicki, M. D. Hospitalization and premorbid characteristics in withdrawn and active schizophrenics. *Journal of Consulting and Clinical Psychology*, 1974, **42,** 628–632.

Doke, L. A., & Risley, T. The organization of day care environments: Required vs. optional activities, *Journal of Applied Behavior Analysis*, 1972, **5,** 405–421.

Doty, D., McInnis, T., & Paul, G. L. Remediation of negative side-effects of an ongoing response-cost system with chronic mental patients. *Journal of Applied Behavior Analysis*, 1974, **7,** 191–198.

Ellsworth, R. *The MACC II behavioral adjustment scale*, Beverly Hills, Calif.: Western Psychological Services, 1962.

Evenson, R. C., Sletten, I. W., Altman, H., & Brown, M. L. Disturbing Behavior: A study of incident reports. *The Psychiatric Quarterly*, 1974, **48,** 1–10.

Farina, A., Arenberg, D., & Guskin, S. A scale for measuring minimal social behavior. *Journal of Consulting Psychology*, 1957, **21,** 265–268.

Goldfried, M. R., & Kent, R. N. Traditional versus behavioral personality assessment: A comparison of methodological and theoretical assumptions. *Psychological Bulletin*, 1972, **77,** 409–420.

Goldsmith, J. B., & McFall, R. M. Development and evaluation of an interpersonal skill training program for psychiatric inpatients. *Journal of Abnormal Psychology*, 1975, **84,** 51–58.

Gripp, R. F., & Magaro, P. A. The token economy program in the psychiatric hospital: A review and analysis. *Behaviour Research and Therapy*, 1974, **12,** 205–228.

Gruenberg, E. M., Brandon, S., & Kasius, R. D. Identifying cases of the social breakdown syndrome. In E. M. Gruenberg (Ed.), *Evaluating the effectiveness of community mental health services*. New York: Milbank, 1966.

Gutride, M. E., Goldstein, A. P., & Hunter, G. F. The use of modeling and role playing to increase social interaction among asocial psychiatric patients. *Journal of Consulting and Clinical Psychology*, 1973, **40,** 408–415.

Gutride, M. E., Goldstein, A. P., & Hunter, G. F., Carrol, S., Clark, L., Furia, R., & Lower, W. Structured learning therapy with transfer training for chronic inpatients. *Journal of Clinical Psychology*, 1974, **30,** 277–279.

Hargreaves, W. Rate of interaction between nursing staff and psychiatric patients. *Nursing Research*, 1969, **18,** 418–425.

Hauserman, N., Zweback, S., & Plotkin, A. Use of concrete reinforcement to facilitate verbal initiations in adolescent group therapy. *Journal of Consulting and Clinical Psychology*, 1972, **38,** 90–96.

Haynes, S., & Geddy, P. Suppression of psychotic hallucinations through time-out. *Behavior Therapy*, 1973, **4,** 123–127.

Hoenig, J., & Hamilton, M. W. The schizophrenic patient in the community and his effect on the household. *International Journal of Social Psychiatry*, 1966, **12,** 165–176.

Holahan, C. Seating patterns and patient behavior in an experimental dayroom. *Journal of Abnormal Psychology*, 1972, **80,** 115–124.

Holahan, C. J., & Saegert, S. Behavioral and attitudinal effects of large-scale variation in the physical environment of psychiatric wards. *Journal of Abnormal Psychology*, 1973, **82,** 454–462.

Honigfeld, G. *Nurses' observation scale for inpatient evaluation (NOSIE-30)*. Glen Oaks, Ill.: Honigfeld, 1966.

Hunter, M., Schooler, C., & Spohn, H. E. The measurement of characteristic patterns of ward behavior in chronic schizophrenics. *Journal of Consulting Psychology*, 1962, **26,** 69–73.

Isaacs, W., Thomas, J., & Goldiamond, I. Application of operant conditioning to reinstate verbal behavior in psychotics. *Journal of Speech and Hearing Disorders*, 1960, **25,** 8–12.

Ittleson, W., Proshansky, H. M., & Rivlin, L. The environmental psychology of the psychiatric ward. In H. M. Proshansky, W. Ittleson, & L. Rivlin (Eds.), *Environmental psychology: Man and his physical setting*. New York: Holt, Rinehart, & Winston, 1970.

Ittleson, W., Rivlin, L., & Proshansky, H. M. The use of behavioral maps in environmental psychology. In H. Proshansky, W. Ittleson & L. Rivlin (Eds.), *Environmental psychology: Man and his physical setting*. New York: Holt, Rinehart, & Winston, 1970.

Jackson, D. N. Multimethod factor analysis in the evaluation of convergent and discriminant validity. *Psychological Bulletin*, 1969, **72,** 30–49.

Johnson, S. M., & Bolstad, O. D. Methodological issues in naturalistic observation: Some problems and solutions for field research. In L. A. Hamerlynck, L. C. Handy, & E. J. Mash (Eds.), *Behavior change Methodology, concepts and practice*. Chamapign, Ill.: Research Press, 1973.

Jones, R. R., Reid, J. B., & Patterson, R. G. Naturalistic observation in clinical assessment. In P. McReynolds (Ed.), *Advances in psychological assessment*. Vol. 3. San Francisco: Jossey-Bass, Inc., 1975.

Kale, R. J., Kaye, J. H., Whelan, P. A., & Hopkins, B. L. The effects of reinforcement on the modification, maintenance, and generalization of social responses of mental patients. *Journal of Applied Behavior Analysis*, 1968, **1**, 307–314.

Kazdin, A. E. Recent advances in token economy research. In M. Hersen, R. M. Eisler, & P. M. Miller (Eds.), *Progress in behavior modification*. New York: Academic, 1975.

Kazdin, A. E., & Bootzin, R. R. The token economy: An evaluative review. *Journal of Applied Behavior Analysis*, 1972, **5**, 343–372.

Kiesler, D. J. Experimental designs in psychotherapy research. In A. E. Bergin and S. L. Garfield (Eds.), *Handbook of psychotherapy and behavior change: An empirical analysis*. New York: Wiley, 1971.

Lacy, J. I. Somatic response patterning and stress: Some revisions of activation theory. In M. H. Appley & R. Trumbull (Eds.), *Psychological Stress: Issues in research*, New York: Appleton-Century-Crofts, 1967.

Lang, P. J. Fear reduction and fear behavior: Problems in treating a construct. In J. M. Shlien (Ed.), *Research in psychotherapy*. Vol. III. Washington, D.C.: American Psychological Association, 1968.

Lentz, R. J. & Paul, G. L. "Routine" vs "therapeutic" transfer of chronic mental patients. *Archives of General Psychiatry*, 1971, **25**, 187–191.

Lentz, R. J., Paul, G. L., & Calhoun, J. F. Reliability and validity of three measures of functioning with "hard core" chronic mental patients. *Journal of Abnormal Psychology*, 1971, **78**, 69–76.

Liberman, R. P. Reinforcement of social interaction in a group of chronic mental patients. In R. Rubin, H. Fensterheim, J. D. Henderson, & L. P. Ullmann (Eds.), *Advances in behavior theory*. Vol. 3. New York: Academic, 1972.

Liberman, R. P., & Davis, J. Drugs and behavior analysis. In M. Hersen, R. Eisler & P. Miller (Eds.), *Progress in behavior modification*. New York: Academic, 1975.

Liberman, R. P., Teigen, J., Patterson, R., & Baker, V. Reducing delusional speech in chronic paranoid schizophrenics. *Journal of Applied Behavior Analysis*, 1973, **6**, 57–64.

Liberman, R. P., Wallace, C., Teigen, J., & Davis, J. Interventions with psychotic behaviors. In K. S. Calhoun, H. E. Adams, & K. M. Mitchell (Eds.), *Innovative treatment methods on psychopathology*, New York: Wiley, 1974.

Lindsley, O. R. Operant conditioning methods applied to research in chronic schizophrenia. *Psychiatric Research Reports*, 1956, **5**, 118–139.

Lindsley, O. R. Reduction in rate of vocal psychotic symptoms by differential positive reinforcement. *Journal of the Experimental Analysis of Behavior*, 1958, **2**, 269.

Lindsley, O. R. Characteristics of the behavior of chronic psychotics as revealed by free operant conditioning methods. *Diseases of the Nervous System Monograph supplement*, 1960, **21**, 66–78.

Lorr, M., & Klett, C. J. *Impatient multidimensional psychiatric scale*. Manual. Palo Alto, Calif.: Consulting Psychologists Press, 1966.

Ludwig, A. M., Marx, A. J., Hill, P. A., & Browning, R. M. The control of violent behavior through faradic shock. *Journal of Nervous and Mental Diseases*, 1969, **148**, 624–637.

Mariotto, M. J., & Paul, G. L. A multimethod validation of the inpatient multidimensional psychiatric scale with chronically institutionalized patients. *Journal of Consulting and Clinical Psychology*, 1974, **42,** 497–508.

McFarlain, R. A., & Hersen, M. Continuous measurement of activity level in psychiatric patients. *Journal of Clinical Psychology*, 1974, **30,** 37–39.

Meichenbaum, D. H. Effects of social reinforcement on the level of abstraction in schizophrenics. *Journal of Abnormal and Social Psychology*, 1966, **71,** 354–362.

Meichenbaum, D. H. The effects of instructions and reinforcement on thinking and language behavior of schizophrenics. *Behaviour Research and Therapy*, 1969, **7,** 101–114.

Meichenbaum, D. H., & Cameron, R. Training schizophrenics to talk to themselves: A means of developing attentional controls. *Behavior Therapy*, 1973, **4,** 515–534.

Milby, J. B. Modification of extreme social isolation by contingent social reinforcement. *Journal of Applied Behavior Analysis*, 1970, **3,** 149–152.

Milby, J., Pendergrass, P. D., & Clarke, C. Token economy versus controlled ward: A comparison of staff and patient attitudes toward ward environment. *Behavior Therapy*, 1975, **6,** 22–29.

Mischel, W. Direct versus indirect personality assessment: Evidence and implications. *Journal of Consulting and Clinical Psychology*, 1972, **38,** 319–324.

Moos, R. Assessment of the psychosocial environments of community-oriented psychiatric treatment programs. *Journal of Abnormal Psychology*, 1972, **79,** 9–18.

Moos, R. *Evaluating treatment environments: A social ecological approach.* New York: Wiley, 1974.

Moos, R., & Houts, P. The assessment of the social atmospheres of psychiatric wards. *Journal of Abnormal Psychology*, 1968, **73,** 595–604.

Moser, A. J. Covert punishment of hallucinatory behavior in a psychotic male. *Journal of Behavior Therapy and Experimental Psychiatry*, 1974, **5,** 297–299.

Mosher, L. R., & Feinsilver, D. Current studies on schizophrenia. *International Journal of Psychoanalytic Psychotherapy*, 1973, **2,** 7–52.

Nydegger, R. V. The elimination of hallucinatory and delusional behavior by verbal conditioning and assertive training: A case study. *Behavior Therapy*, 1972, **3,** 225–227.

O'Brien, F., & Azrin, N. H. Symptom reduction by functional displacement in a token economy: A case study. *Journal of Behavior Therapy and Experimental Psychiatry*, 1972, **3,** 205–207.

O'Brien F., Azrin, H. H., & Henson, K. Increased communication of chronic mental patients by reinforcement and by response priming. *Journal of Applied Behavior Analysis*, 1969, **2,** 23–30.

Olson, R. P., & Greenberg, D. J. Effects of contingency-contracting and decision-making groups with chronic mental patients. *Journal of Consulting and Clinical* Psychology, 1972, **38,** 376–383.

Page, S., & Copeland, E. V. Reinforcement of conversation operants in psychiatric patients. *Canadian Journal of Behavioral Science*, 1972, **4,** 348–357.

Palmer, J., & McGuire, F. L. The use of unobtrusive measures in mental health research. *Journal of Consulting and Clinical Psychology*, 1973, **40,** 431–436.

Patterson, G. R., Cobb, J. A., & Ray, R. S. A social engineering technology for retraining the families of aggressive boys. In H. E. Adams & L. Unikel (Eds.), *Issues and trends in behavior therapy*. Springfield, Ill.: Thomas, 1973.

Patterson, R. L., & Teigen, J. R. Conditioning and post-hospital generalization of nondelusional responses in a chronic psychotic patient. *Journal of Applied Behavior Analysis*, 1973, **6,** 65–70.

Paul, G. L. The chronic mental patient: Current status—future directions. *Psychological Bulletin*, 1969, **71,** 81–94.

Paul, G. L., McInnis, T. L., & Mariotto, M. J. Objective performance outcomes associated with two approaches to training mental health technicians in milieu and social-learning programs. *Journal of Abnormal Psychology*, 1973, **82,** 523–532.

Paul, G. L., Tobias, L. L., & Hally, B. L. Maintenance psychotropic drugs in the presence of active treatment programs: A "triple-blind" withdrawal study with long-term mental pateints. *Archives of General Psychiatry*, 1972, **27,** 106–115.

Pomerleau, O. F., Bobrove, P. H., & Harris, L. C. Some observations of a controlled social environment for psychiatric patients. *Journal of Behavior Therapy and Experimental Psychiatry*, 1972, **3,** 15–21.

Rappaport, J., & Chinsky, J. M. Behavior ratings of chronic hospitalized patients: Cross-situational and cross-rater agreement. *Journal of Consulting and Clinical Psychology*, 1970, **34,** 394–397.

Rappaport, J., Chinsky, J. M., & Mace, D. L., Matching of chronic hospitalized patient groups: Empirical failure of a methodologically "sound" procedure. *Journal of Consulting and Clinical Psychology*, 1972, **38,** 462.

Reisinger, J. J. The treatment of "anxiety-depression" via positive reinforcement and response cost. *Journal of Applied Behavior Analysis*, 1972, **5,** 125–130.

Rickard, H. C., Dignam, P. J., & Horner, R. F. Verbal manipulation in a psychotherapeutic relationship. *Journal of Clinical Psychology*, 1960, **16,** 364–367.

Rosenhan, D. L. On being sane in insane places. *Science*, 1973, **179,** 250–258.

Royer, F. L., Flynn, W. F., & Osadea, B. S. Case history: Aversion therapy for fire setting by a deteriorated schizophrenic. *Behavior Therapy*, 1971, **2,** 229–232.

Rutner, I. T., & Bugle, C. An experimental procedure for the modification of psychotic behavior. *Journal of Consulting and Clinical Psychology*, 1969, **33,** 651–653.

Sabatasso, A. P., & Jacobson, L. J. Use of behavior therapy in the reinstatement of verbal behavior in a mute psychotic with chronic brain syndrome: A case study. *Journal of Abnormal Psychology*, 1970, **76,** 322–324.

Salzinger, K., & Portnoy, S. Verbal conditioning in interviews: Application to chronic schizophrenics and relationship to prognosis for acute schizophrenics. *Journal of Psychiatric Research*, 1964, **2,** 1–9.

Schaefer, H., & Martin, P. L. Behavioral therapy for apathy of hospitalized schizophrenics. *Psychological Reports*, 1966, **19,** 1147–1158.

Schaefer, H., & Martin, P. L. *Behavior therapy*. New York: McGraw-Hill, 1969.

Schulman, J. L., & Reisman, J. M. An objective measure of hyperactivity. *American Journal of Mental Deficiency*, 1959, **64,** 455–456.

Sherman, J. A. Reinforcement of verbal behavior in a psychotic by reinforcement methods. *Journal of Speech and Hearing Disorders*, 1963, **28,** 398–401.

Sherman, J. A. Use of reinforcement and imitation to reinstate verbal behavior in mute psychotics. *Journal of Abnormal Psychology*, 1965, **70,** 155–164.

Slade, P. D. The effects of systematic desensitization on auditory hallucinations. *Behaviour Research and Therapy*, 1972, **10,** 85–91.

Sommer, R., Witney, G., & Osmond, H. Teaching common associations to schizophrenics. *Journal of Abnormal and Social Psychology*, 1962, **65,** 58–61.

Stahl, J. R., Thompson, L. E., Leitenberg, H., & Hasazi, J. Establishment of praise as a conditioned reinforcer in socially unresponsive psychiatric patients. *Journal of Abnormal Psychology*, 1974, **83,** 488–496.

Strauss, J. A., & Carpenter, W. T. The prediction of outcome in schizophrenia: I. Characteristics of outcome. *Archives of General Psychiatry*, 1972, **27,** 739–746.

Tarlow, G., Alevizos, P. N., & Callahan, E. G. Assessing the conversational behavior of psychiatric patients: Reliability and validity of the verbal report form (VRF). *Canadian Journal of Behavioural Science*, in press.

Tracey, D., Briddell, D. W., & Wilson, G. T. Generalization of verbal conditioning to verbal and nonverbal behaviors: Group therapy with chronic psychiatric patients. *Journal of Applied Behavior Analysis*, 1974, **1,** 391–402.

Ullmann, L. P., Forsman, R. G., Kenny, J. W., McInnis, T. L., Jr., Unikel, I. P., & Zeisset, R. M. Selective reinforcement of schizophrenic interview responses. *Behaviour Research and Therapy*, 1965, **2,** 205–212.

Ullmann, L. P., & Krasner, L. *A psychological approach to abnormal behavior*. Englewood Cliffs, N.J.: Prentice-Hall, 1969.

Ullmann, L. P., Krasner, L., & Edinger, R. L. Verbal conditioning of common associations in long-term schizophrenic patients. *Behaviour Research and Therapy*, 1964, **2,** 15–18.

Wagner, B. R., & Paul, G. L. Reduction of incontinence in chronic mental patients: A pilot project. *Journal of Behavior Therapy and Experimental Psychiatry*, 1970, **1,** 29–38.

Wahler, R. G., & Leske, G. Accurate and inaccurate observer summary reports. *Journal of Nervous and Mental Disease*, 1973, **156,** 386–394.

Wallace, C. J., & Davis, J. R. Effects of information and reinforcement on the conversational behavior of chronic psychiatric patient dyads. *Journal of Consulting and Clinical Psychology*, 1974, **42,** 656–662.

Wiggins, J. S. *Personality and prediction*. Reading, Mass.: Addison-Wesley, 1973.

Willems, E. P. Behavioral technology and behavioral ecology. *Journal of Applied Behavior Analysis*, 1974, **7,** 151–165.

Wilson, F. S., & Walters, R. H. Modification of speech output of near mute schizophrenics through social-learning procedures. *Behaviour Research and Therapy*, 1966, **4,** 59–67.

Wincze, J. P., Leitenberg, H., & Agras, W. S. The effects of token reinforcement and feedback on the delusional verbal behavior of chronic paranoid schizophrenics. *Journal of Applied Behavior Analysis*, 1972, **5**, 247–262.

Wing, J. P., Monck, E., Brown, G. W., & Carstairs, G. M. Morbidity in the community of schizophrenic patients discharged from London mental hospitals in 1959. *British Journal of Psychiatry*, 1964, **110**, 10–21.

Winkler, R. C. The relevance of economic theory and technology of token reinforcement systems. *Behaviour Research and Therapy*, 1971, **9**, 81–88. (a)

Winkler, R. C. Reinforcement schedules for individual patients in a token economy. *Behavior Therapy*, 1971, **2**, 534–537. (b)

Winkler, R. C. A theory of equilibrium in token economies. *Journal of Abnormal Psychology*, 1972, **79**, 169–173.

Wittenborn, J. R. *Psychiatric rating scales*. New York: Psychological Corp., 1955.

Author Index

Subject Index